Economic Report of the President

Economic Report of the President

To the Congress of the United States:

Over the past three years, my Administration has championed policies to restore the United States' economic strength, propelling growth to levels far exceeding preelection expectations. These results did not come about by accident. Instead, they were supported by our foundational pillars for economic growth that put Americans first, including tax cuts, deregulation, energy independence, and trade renegotiation. Our success has created a historically strong labor market and greater economic security for millions of American families.

The Transformative Power of Work

My Administration's focus on economic growth comes from a deep appreciation of the power of work to drive the economy and transform lives. The truth is, jobs do not just provide paychecks; they give people meaning, allow them to engage with their communities, and help them reach their true potential. As we have shown, the right policies offer Americans paths to self-reliance rather than trapping them in reliance on government programs.

The unemployment rate is 3.5 percent, the lowest it has been in 50 years. Since I came into office, labor force participation is up and wages are growing fastest for historically disadvantaged workers, reversing the trends seen under the previous administration. Under my Administration, and for the first time on record, job openings exceeded people looking for work, with 1 million more open jobs than job seekers at the end of 2019. Because of record-low unemployment rates across demographic categories and continued job creation, people from all backgrounds can more easily find work, build their skills, and grow their incomes.

In today's tight labor market, employers realize the vast potential of many individuals whom they may have previously overlooked. This includes those facing long-term unemployment, balancing family responsibilities, thinking they lack necessary job skills, overcoming substance abuse, returning from the justice system, or living in poverty. It is also encouraging those individuals to put themselves back in the workforce. My Administration has placed a special focus on these forgotten Americans because every individual deserves to experience the dignity that comes through work.

In the fourth quarter of 2019, three quarters of workers entering employment came from outside the labor force rather than from unemployment, the highest share in the series' history. As paid parental leave spreads across the country, including the expansion to Federal workers that I signed in December, parents will have more freedom to choose a balance between working outside the home and caring for their children. And in another encouraging sign that people previously on the sidelines will continue entering the workforce, more than 420 companies have signed the Pledge to America's Workers. These companies have pledged to create upward of 14 million new job and training opportunities for current and future employees over the next five years.

Apprenticeships are one way for these companies to deliver on their pledges, and expanding apprenticeships has been a top priority since I took office. During my presidency, more than 680,000 new apprenticeships have been created. To have a labor market that works for everyone, the Federal Government must encourage a variety of paths for people to get the skills they need to build family-sustaining careers.

Although all sectors benefit from more apprenticeships, my Administration knows that manufacturing is a pillar of the American economy. Manufacturing spurs innovation and fuels economic growth, which is why I am so pleased that more than 500,000 manufacturing jobs have been created since my election. Rather than still shrinking, American manufacturing is now growing again. Critically, wages for nonsupervisory and production workers are rising at an even higher rate than managers' wages.

Renegotiated or new trade deals with Canada and Mexico, China, South Korea, and Japan will modernize international trade and create freer, fairer, and more reciprocal trade between the United States and our largest trading partners, allowing the manufacturing renaissance to continue. Trade deals are in development with the United Kingdom and the European Union, among other countries that need access to the coveted United States market. These deals will both expand United States markets abroad and keep businesses here in America, which means keeping jobs here in America.

I have the deepest respect for America's workers and job creators who have made this economic boom possible. That is why we are fighting back against other nations that have exploited the pioneering spirit of our country's entrepreneurs. Through combating intellectual property theft and unfair trade deals, along with leading the way on 5G development and deployment, my Administration is standing up to countries around the world to give American job creators the freedom to innovate and make life better for their fellow citizens. These proactive steps will benefit everyone, from large companies that employ hundreds or thousands of Americans to budding entrepreneurs trying to turn their ideas into reality.

The labor market experiences that people are gaining today will change the trajectories of their lives—and those of their children—for years to come. No matter their pasts, people deserve agency over their own lives, and my Administration will never tell Americans that they cannot or do not deserve the ability to work and earn a living for themselves and their families.

Previously Forgotten Americans Are Forgotten No More

America's labor market successes are also helping us defeat the opioid crisis. While the causes of the crisis are multifaceted, work must play an integral role in any solution. Research shows that holding a job is a key factor in helping people overcome drug addiction. Over the rest of my presidency, I will continue to promote policies that beat back this deadly crisis and encourage work for Americans who are rebuilding their lives after struggling with addiction.

Because of my Administration's aggressive efforts to end the overprescription of opioids, promote effective treatment, and secure the border, the tide is finally turning on the opioid crisis. Overdose deaths and first-time users are down, but that does not mean the crisis is over. Failure is not an option when it comes to helping people avoid the pain and suffering caused by addiction.

Unfortunately, the largest drug crisis in our history has left many people with criminal records. After someone leaves the justice system, they face two options: find honest work and successfully reenter society, or stay out of work and face the increased likelihood of committing another crime. Finding work is one of the top indicators of whether someone who commits a crime will turn his or her life around and live crime-free. This is why work is not just essential for reforming individuals; it is also necessary for promoting public safety. Beyond signing the landmark First Step Act to promote public safety and make America's justice system fairer, my Administration is also putting substantial resources behind programs that improve employment outcomes for the formerly incarcerated. Likewise, criminal justice reform that emphasizes work helps break the cycle of generational poverty.

In 2018 alone, 1.4 million Americans were lifted out of poverty, and the poverty rate fell to its lowest level since 2001. For African Americans and Hispanic Americans, poverty rates are at historic lows, and the poverty rate for single mothers and children is falling much faster than the average. Since I took office, food insecurity has fallen and nearly 7 million people have been lifted off food stamps. Beneficiaries entering the labor market or increasing their incomes through work is likely driving falling enrollment in Medicaid, TANF, and disability insurance.

These Americans are not simply rising out of poverty; they are building careers of which they and their families can be proud. Wages are rising fastest for people with the lowest incomes, meaning people currently working in lower-paying jobs will not have low incomes for long. Getting that first job is critical, because it serves as a foundation for progressively better jobs over a worker's career.

A commitment to the transformative power of work is why I signed an Executive Order instructing agencies to reduce dependence on welfare programs by encouraging work. Less than 3 percent of people who work full time live in poverty. Individuals will not be able to build the lives they want through welfare alone: Work is a necessary condition for upward mobility.

While strengthening and expanding work requirements for public assistance programs lead people to reenter the workforce and increase their household incomes, work requirements are most effective when employers are hiring. This is one reason why my Administration emphasizes policies that lead to job creation.

Pro-Growth Policies Are Pro-Worker Policies

One foundational policy that continues to drive job creation is tax reform. Since the Tax Cuts and Jobs Act—the biggest package of tax cuts and tax reforms in our country's history—took effect, more than 4 million jobs have been created and economic growth has beaten previous projections. America's outdated tax code drove away businesses and investment, but tax reform has brought rates down and made the United States globally competitive again.

Many workers saw bonuses and raises immediately after tax reform, and nearly 40 million American families received an average benefit of $2,200 in 2019 from doubling the child tax credit. Yet the biggest payoff is still to come. Tax reform put an end to America's counterproductive policy of punishing business investments, which means that workers will see even greater benefits once these investments pay off.

My Administration has also prioritized healthcare reforms that make the system more competitive and, therefore, more affordable. We are giving patients increased choice and control, and protecting the high-quality care that Americans expect and deserve. Healthcare is a top priority because healthcare costs are among the top annual expenses for American families. Under my Administration, the Food and Drug Administration has approved more generic drugs than ever before in United States history and enhanced its approval process for new, lifesaving drugs. This past year, prescription drug prices experienced the largest year-over-year decline in more than 50 years.

Whether it is through reforms that bring choice to Veterans Administration care, promote Health Reimbursement Arrangements, or give terminally ill patients access to potentially lifesaving drugs, among many other successes, every healthcare reform that lowers costs and increases quality allows American workers to live longer, healthier lives and keep more of their paychecks.

Tax cuts and healthcare reforms put more money in the hands of working families and job creators, creating a virtuous cycle of even more jobs and even higher paychecks. On the other hand, when regulations limit individuals' ability to experience the dignity that comes through work, those regulations deserve additional scrutiny. Over the previous decades, the Federal Government has disproportionately regulated sectors of the economy—like energy and manufacturing—that offer fulfilling, blue collar jobs for the majority of Americans who do not have a college degree. These misguided policy decisions imposed real-world costs that created barriers to success and prosperity for hardworking Americans. Those days are over.

American energy powers our cities and towns, empowers innovators, and ultimately drives our economy. Energy companies across the world are ready to build in our Nation, and permitting reform that cuts red tape shows that we welcome their investments. My Administration continues to support the energy industry's growth by removing unnecessary regulations and unleashing America's vast natural and human resources. Through these actions, the United States is now on track to be a net exporter of crude oil and natural gas for all of 2020, a major milestone not achieved in at least 70 years. In addition to being the world's largest natural gas producer, we also became the world's top crude oil producer in 2018.

The positive records of our energy boom are widespread. Energy production has created jobs in areas of the United States where job opportunities were scarce. It also provides enormous benefits to families across the Nation by lowering energy prices. And it further distances us from geopolitical foes who wish to cause us harm. More jobs, lower costs, and American dominance—these are the predictable results of our pro-growth policies.

Many pundits and Washington insiders laughed when I promised to cut two regulations for every new regulation. They were correct that two-for-one was the wrong goal. Instead, the Federal Government has cut more than seven regulations for every significant new regulation. After only three years, my Administration has already cut more regulations than any other in United States history, and we have put the brakes on an endless assault of new, costly actions by Federal agencies.

Our commitment to regulatory reform stems from the simple truth that the vast majority of business owners want to do the right thing, comply with the law, and treat their workers fairly. The Federal Government ignored this reality for far too long and abused its authority to go after businesses, especially small businesses and entrepreneurs, in ways that can only be described as arbitrary and abusive.

To promote regulatory fairness, I signed two Executive Orders that will improve Federal agencies' transparency and fairness while holding them accountable for their actions. Agencies will now need to give people fair notice and a chance to respond to any Federal complaint filed against them. Furthermore, the rules agencies enforce will no longer be secret, because all agencies' interpretations of rules will need to be made publicly accessible. Additionally, significant interpretations of rules will need to go through the public review process that is central to a flourishing democracy. Deregulation and increased transparency will save job creators money, leading to more hiring and higher paychecks.

Every American, no matter his or her background, can share in the dignity of work. The era of putting American workers second and doubling down on the failed Federal policies of the past is over. While job creation during my Presidency has surpassed expectations, the credit belongs to the job creators and workers who risk everything and devote themselves to building a better future for themselves, their families, and their Nation. The Federal Government does not create jobs; hardworking Americans create jobs. My Administration's role is to follow our foundational policy pillars and allow our job creators and workers to do what they do best.

As the following *Report* shows, because of the strength, resiliency, and determination of the United States workforce, which is the envy of the world, my pro-growth policies continue producing unquestionably positive results for the economy. The *Report* also makes it clear that, though the American economy is stronger than ever, my Administration's work is not yet done. With a continued focus on policies that increase economic growth, promote opportunity, and uplift our workers, there is no limit on how great America can be.

The White House
February 2020

The Annual Report

of the

Council of Economic Advisers

Letter of Transmittal

Council of Economic Advisers

Washington, February 20, 2020

Mr. President:

The Council of Economic Advisers herewith submits its 2020 *Annual Report* in accordance with the Employment Act of 1946, as amended by the Full Employment and Balanced Growth Act of 1978.

Sincerely yours,

Tomas J. Philipson
Acting Chairman

Tyler B. Goodspeed
Member

Introduction

Three years into the Trump Administration, the U.S. economy continues to outperform expectations across numerous metrics, with growth in output, employment, and employee compensation all exceeding pre-2017 forecasts. The evident success of the Administration's economic policy agenda demonstrates that its foundational policy pillars are enabling the U.S. economy to overcome structural trends that were previously suppressing growth.

During the four quarters of 2019, real gross domestic product grew 0.7 percentage point faster than had been projected by the independent Congressional Budget Office's (CBO) August 2016 projections. As shown in figures I-1 and I-2, the U.S. labor market added 2.1 million new jobs—2.0 million more than projected in 2016—bringing the civilian unemployment rate down to 3.5 percent, which is its lowest level since 1969 (and 1.4 percentage points below 2016 CBO projections).[1] Higher pay accompanied abundant job vacancies, as employee compensation rose to 1.4 percent above the 2016 forecast, implying an additional $1,800 in compensation per household.

In July 2019, the current expansion of the U.S. economy became the longest on record. Contrary to expectations that the expansion would slow as it matured, economic output has accelerated over the past 3 years relative to the preceding 7½ years, with output growth rising from 2.2 to 2.5 percent at a compound annual rate. In the first three quarters of 2019, U.S. economic growth was the highest among the Group of Seven countries.

Reflecting this outperformance of expectations, in the first five chapters of this *Report* we present evidence that the Trump Administration's foundational policy pillars are continuing to deliver economic results. In particular, we highlight the role of the Administration's prioritization of economic efficiency and pro-market reforms in the realms of tax, labor, regulation, energy, and healthcare in elevating the growth potential of the U.S. economy and increasing the well-being of those previously left behind during the current expansion.

In the subsequent three chapters, we then identify several challenges to continued growth. Efforts to address these obstacles include ensuring that U.S. markets remain economically fair and competitive, combating the ongoing threat of widespread opioid addiction, and addressing the overregulation of housing markets. We conclude by setting forth the Administration's long-run, policy-inclusive economic projections, and highlighting potential risks to the outlook.

We begin in chapter 1 by documenting that, despite strong headwinds from the global economy and several idiosyncratic adverse shocks, Administration policies have helped to keep the U.S. economy resilient. As a result, output has grown at the fastest rate among the Group of Seven

---

[1] In preparing this *Economic Report of the President*, data available as of January 30, 2020, were incorporated as publicly reported and are reflected in the chapters that follow.

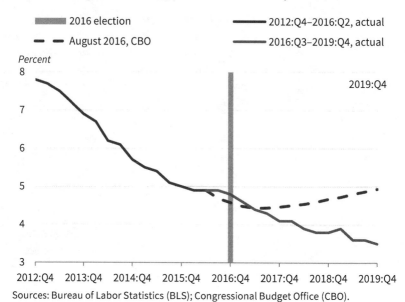

Figure I-1. The Actual Unemployment Rate in Various Quarters versus the August 2016 Rate, per the BLS and CBO, 2012–19

2016 election		2012:Q4–2016:Q2, actual
August 2016, CBO		2016:Q3–2019:Q4, actual

Percent

2019:Q4

Sources: Bureau of Labor Statistics (BLS); Congressional Budget Office (CBO).

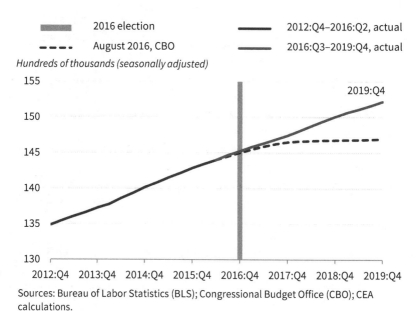

Figure I-2. Actual Nonfarm Payrolls versus the August 2016 Payroll, per the CBO, 2012–19

2016 election		2012:Q4–2016:Q2, actual
August 2016, CBO		2016:Q3–2019:Q4, actual

Hundreds of thousands (seasonally adjusted)

2019:Q4

Sources: Bureau of Labor Statistics (BLS); Congressional Budget Office (CBO); CEA calculations.

economies in the past year. During 2019, several macroeconomic indicators—including consumer spending, productivity, and labor share of income—grew at faster rates than preelection projections. The labor market also tightened further, even after strong gains during the previous two years. During this Administration, the unemployment rate hit a 50-year low, and the number of job openings exceeded job seekers for the first time in recorded U.S. history, which has helped to pull potential workers into the labor force and boost real wages. The stabilization of labor force participation after years of decline, particularly among prime-age workers, has also boosted long-term potential output.

We continue to evaluate the performance of the U.S. labor market in chapter 2, paying particular attention to how the Administration's pro-growth agenda has disproportionately benefited those previously left behind during the current expansion. We document how, in stark contrast to the expansion through 2016, policies that both raised labor demand and incentivized employers to invest more in their workers have resulted in wage gains for historically disadvantaged Americans. Average wage growth for workers now outpaces wage growth for supervisors; wage growth for individuals at the 10th percentile of the income distribution now outpaces wage growth for individuals at the 90th percentile; wage growth for those without a college degree now outpaces wage growth for those with a college degree; and wage growth for African Americans now outpaces wage growth for white Americans. With monthly payroll employment growth outpacing that required to maintain a stable employment-to-population ratio, we also document the extent to which the U.S. economy is pulling millions back into the labor force and out of poverty.

Looking ahead, we outline the Administration's continued prioritization of initiatives aimed at promoting alternative paths to work, supporting on-the-job training and reskilling, reducing recidivism, combating opioid abuse, expanding access to affordable childcare, and enabling economic growth that provides expanded employment opportunities for every American who seeks work.

In chapter 3, we analyze the effects of the Administration's regulatory reform agenda. We estimate that after 5 to 10 years, the Administration's approach to Federal regulation will have raised real incomes by $3,100 per household per year, with 20 notable Federal deregulatory actions alone saving American consumers and businesses about $220 billion per year once they go into full effect, which will raise real incomes by about 1.3 percent. We further calculate that the ongoing introduction of costly regulations had previously been subtracting 0.2 percent a year from real incomes. By increasing competition, productivity, and wages, and reducing the prices of consumer goods, the Administration's approach to regulation is raising real incomes while maintaining regulatory protections for workers, public health, safety, and the environment.

Continuing the focus on regulation, in chapter 4 we focus specifically on U.S. energy markets. By lowering prices, the CEA estimates that the shale revolution saves the average family of four $2,500 annually. Because low-income households spend a larger share of their income on energy bills, they benefit disproportionately from lower energy prices: shale-driven savings represent a much larger percentage of income for the poorest fifth of households than for the richest fifth. At the same time, shale-driven production growth has affected U.S. energy independence. This goal, initiated by President Nixon and pursued by every subsequent Administration, was finally achieved under the Trump Administration. In September 2019, the United States became a net exporter of petroleum, and the United States is projected to remain a net exporter for all of 2020, for the first time since at least 1949. We estimate that from 2005 to 2018, the shale revolution in particular was responsible for reducing carbon dioxide emissions in the electric power sector by 21 percent. Finally, we demonstrate how, by limiting unnecessary constraints on private innovation and investment, the Administration's approach to eliminating excessive regulation of energy markets supports further unleashing of the country's abundant human and energy resources.

In chapter 5, we identify government barriers to market competition in healthcare that increase prices, reduce innovation, and hinder improvements in quality. We also summarize the achievements and expected effects of the Administration's health policy initiatives to reduce these impediments and facilitate greater competition in healthcare markets. The Administration's reforms aim to foster a healthcare system that delivers high-quality services at affordable prices through greater choice, competition, and consumer-directed spending, in contrast to government mandates that too often reduce consumer choice in healthcare markets and increase premiums. The Administration has addressed many of these problems through a series of Executive Orders, regulatory reforms, and legislation.

Turning to potential obstacles, in chapter 6, we analyze concerns about possible trends in market competition, recognizing the vital role that competition plays in economic growth, promoting innovation and entrepreneurship, and serving consumers. We find that the best available evidence suggests there is no need to rewrite the Federal Government's antitrust rules. Because Federal enforcement agencies are already empowered with a flexible legal framework, they possess the necessary tools to promote economic dynamism. Ongoing investigations and resolved cases show that these agencies are well equipped to handle the competition challenges posed by the changing U.S. economy. We conclude that in addition to vigorously combating anticompetitive behavior from companies using existing tools, the Administration will focus on changing government policies that create an unfair playing field. As the recent historic regulatory reform across American industries has shown, eliminating government-imposed barriers to innovation leads to increased competition, stronger economic growth, and a revitalized private sector.

In chapter 7, we analyze the ongoing threat of widespread opioid addiction that, since 2000, has been responsible for more than 400,000 deaths. We find that actions taken by the Administration to lower the supply of opioids, reduce new demand for opioids, and treat those with current opioid use disorder may have contributed to a flattening in overdose deaths involving opioids. Recognizing that understanding the origins of the crisis is essential to effectively combating it, we find that a first wave of the crisis, from 2001 to 2010, was driven in large part by steep declines in out-of-pocket prescription opioid prices. Prices fell due to expanded government healthcare coverage, as well as to the increased availability of prescription opioids due to pain management practices that encouraged liberalized dispensing practices by doctors. We then find that a second wave of the opioid crisis, starting in 2010, likely began because of efforts to limit the supply of the powerful prescription opioid OxyContin, an unintended consequence of which was the creation of a large illicit market for the development and sale of cheaper illegal substitutes.

In chapter 8, we study the challenges posed by rising housing unaffordability in some U.S. real estate markets. We find that a key driver of the housing unaffordability problem is the overregulation of housing markets by State and local governments, which limits supply. By driving up home prices, overregulation adversely affects low-income Americans in particular, who spend the largest share of their income on housing. Among 11 particularly supply-constrained metropolitan areas, we estimate that regulatory reform would increase the housing supply and decrease rents enough to reduce homelessness by 31 percent on average. In addition, we find that overregulation of housing markets has broader negative effects on all Americans by reducing labor mobility and thus productivity growth, amplifying inequality across regions and workers, and harming the environment by forcing longer commutes. We conclude by documenting the Administration's actions to address the housing unaffordability challenge by incentivizing State and local governments to increase housing supply in supply-constrained areas and by establishing the White House Council on Eliminating Regulatory Barriers to Affordable Housing.

Finally, in chapter 9, we present the Trump Administration's full, policy-inclusive economic forecast for the next 11 years, including risks to the economic outlook. Overall, assuming full implementation of the Administration's economic policy agenda, we project that real U.S. economic output will grow at an average annual rate of 2.9 percent between 2019 and 2030. We expect growth to moderate, from 3.0 percent in 2020 to 2.8 percent in the latter half of the budget window, as the capital-to-output ratio asymptotically approaches its new, postcorporate tax reform steady state and as the near-term effects of the Tax Cuts and Jobs Act's individual provisions on the rate of growth dissipate into a permanent-level effect. Partially offsetting this moderation are the expected positive contributions to growth from enacting the Administration's infrastructure plan, making permanent the individual provisions of the Tax Cuts and Jobs Act, reforming the U.S. immigration system, continuing deregulatory actions, improving trade deals with international trading partners, and incentivizing higher labor force participation through additional labor market reforms.

Contents

Appendixes

Figures

Tables

Boxes

Part I

The Longest Expansion on Record

Chapter 1

The Great Expansion

Two years since the Tax Cuts and Jobs Act (TCJA) was signed into law, and buttressed by the Administration's probusiness deregulation policy and support for innovative energy infrastructure, the U.S. economy continues expanding at a healthy pace, as predicted by the 2018 and 2019 volumes of the *Economic Report of the President*. As of December 2019, the U.S. economic expansion reached its 127th month, the longest in the Nation's history.

This chapter shows that, despite headwinds from the global economy and the maturing length of the expansion, the U.S. economy remains resilient. As a result, it grew at the fastest rate among the Group of Seven countries in the first three quarters of 2019. During 2019, several macroeconomic indicators—including consumer spending, productivity, and labor shares of income—continued to grow at faster rates than pre-TCJA projections. The labor market also tightened further, even after strong gains in the previous two years. During 2019, the unemployment rate hit a 50-year low and, for the first time on record, job openings exceeded job seekers, which have helped pull potential workers from the sidelines and into the labor force. Wages rose faster than inflation, which ultimately boosted real middle-class incomes. After years of decline, the labor force participation rate stabilized because of increased prime-age participation, which also boosts long-term potential output.

The tepid recovery from the Great Recession prompted economic forecasters in 2016 to project historically modest growth into the future. Many observers concluded that low growth would persist indefinitely. However, the experience of the first three years of the current Administration proves that a prolonged period of low growth was in fact far from inevitable. This increased growth has coincided with Administration policies favoring lower taxes, substantial deregulation, and pro-innovation energy policy. The CEA forecasts that there is substantial additional room to grow—given the historically strong labor market, the potential for further deregulation, and the supply-side impact of TCJA on long-term growth.

After growing briskly in 2017 and 2018, the U.S. economy continued to expand at a healthy pace in 2019. During the year's four quarters, real gross domestic product (GDP) moderated to 2.3 percent at an annual rate, from its 2.5 percent pace in 2018. This growth rate is notable considering the maturing length of the current expansion and that it was achieved despite headwinds from a slowing global economy. As of December, the U.S. economy marked the 127th month and the 42nd consecutive quarter of expansion (figure 1-1), surpassing the longest U.S. expansion, which ended in March 2001 after 120 months or 40 quarters.

The U.S. economy is currently operating with a strong labor market and subdued inflationary pressure. Evidence of the strength of the labor market can be observed across many indicators. The U.S. unemployment rate was 3.5 percent as of December 2019, a 50-year low previously hit in September and November 2019. Nominal average hourly earnings increased 2.9 percent during the 12 months of 2019, but had been at or above 3 percent for the prior 16 consecutive months. The tightness of the labor market and rising demand for workers have continued to pull people from outside of the labor force into the labor market, increasing the labor force participation rate to 63.1 percent for the year as a whole, up 0.2 percentage point from a year earlier. Specifically, the prime-age adult (25–54 years) participation rate increased to 82.5 percent during these 12 months, the fourth year of increases after years of decline since 2008. During the 12 months of 2019, the U.S. economy added 2.1 million nonfarm jobs, averaging 176,000 jobs per month.

Despite the strong labor market, core consumer price inflation was subdued, at 1.6 percent in 2019 (as measured by the price index for core personal consumption expenditures, PCE). Because nominal disposable personal income grew faster than inflation, real disposable personal income grew at a 2.6 percent annual rate during the four quarters of 2019. For the median household, real income rose by $1,834 in the first 10 months of 2019, reaching the highest level on record, at about $66,500 in 2019 dollars (Green and Coder 2019). In addition to rising real income, household wealth surged as stock market valuations rose to new heights in 2019.

An increase in real household income and wealth has supported consumer spending, which constitutes 70 percent of GDP. In the four quarters of

Figure 1-1. Real GDP per Working-Age Population by Expansion Period, 1960–2019

Index (100 = real GDP per working-age population at the quarterly business-cycle trough)

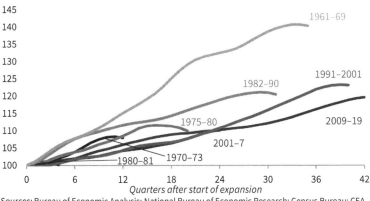

Sources: Bureau of Economic Analysis; National Bureau of Economic Research; Census Bureau; CEA calculations.

Note: The working-age population refers to those age 25–64 years. Series are smoothed using a four-quarter, centered moving average. Quarterly population estimates are interpolated from annual data.

2019, real consumer spending maintained the 2.6 percent pace of 2018, and accounted for nearly 80 percent of real GDP growth. Government purchases have also supported aggregate demand, rising 3.0 percent during 2019, compared with 1.5 percent in 2018.

Although American consumers have sustained the U.S. expansion, a general slowdown in the global economy has restrained U.S. growth. The Group of Seven (G7) countries' economies slowed sharply in the past year; in particular, real GDP growth in Germany and the United Kingdom contracted in 2019:Q2. Major emerging market economies such as China and India also experienced slowdowns. These countries' slowdowns reduced global aggregate demand, which dampened U.S. economic growth.

Despite the headwinds from abroad, the U.S. economy was the fastest-growing in the G7 in the first three quarters of 2019. The United States was one of only two G7 countries (the other being Japan, where projected growth was a moribund 0.9 percent) that did not require the International Monetary Fund to make large downward revisions to its one-year-ahead growth projections for 2019 (IMF 2018, 2019c), whereas the other advanced countries saw large downward revisions.

Moreover, growth in the U.S. economy, for the third consecutive year, exceeded the consensus real GDP growth projection made before the 2016 election, as well as projections made before the 2017 TCJA. Three years ago, a widespread belief among economic forecasters was that subpar growth in the

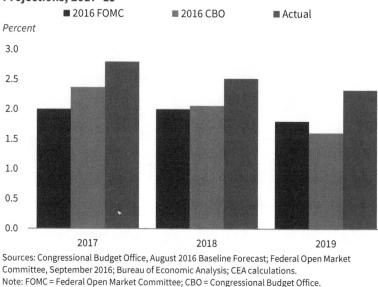

Figure 1-2. Real GDP Growth Relative to Pre–November 2016 Projections, 2017–19

■ 2016 FOMC   ■ 2016 CBO   ■ Actual

Percent

Sources: Congressional Budget Office, August 2016 Baseline Forecast; Federal Open Market Committee, September 2016; Bureau of Economic Analysis; CEA calculations.
Note: FOMC = Federal Open Market Committee; CBO = Congressional Budget Office.
Q4-over-Q4 growth rates are used.

U.S. economy will be permanent, with one of the more prominent explanations being secular stagnation.[1] This pessimism was reflected in the modest growth projections by outside forecasters at the time. In 2016, the Federal Open Market Committee (FOMC) forecast real GDP over the four quarters of 2019 to be 1.8 percent, while the Congressional Budget Office (CBO) forecast real GDP growth of just 1.6 percent over the same period (see figure 1-2). The 2.3 percent real GDP growth during 2019 surpassed these forecasts. Similarly, actual real GDP growth in 2017 and 2018 surpassed preelection projections from the FOMC and the CBO. Relative to the 2016 real GDP projections by the Blue Chip panel of private professional forecasters, the annual level of U.S. real GDP in 2019 was 1.2 percent higher (figure 1-3).

Although the strong growth was a surprise relative to pre-2017 forecasts by the FOMC, the CBO, and the Blue Chip consensus panel, it was largely anticipated by the current Administration. In May 2017, the Administration forecasted average annualized growth over the three years 2017–19 to be 2.5 percent; subsequently the Administration revised 2018 and 2019 forecasts up to 3.1 percent, which was deemed optimistic and unrealistic compared with external forecasts. The optimism of the CEA's forecasts was grounded

---

[1] Hansen (1939) was the first to put forward this concept, which was popularized by Summers (2013, 2014, 2016) and more recently by Rachel and Summers (2019). Specifically, Summers argued that when neutral real interest rates fall to an abnormally low level because of decreasing propensity to invest but increasing propensity to save, and are below nominal interest rates, the resultant excessive savings would act as a persistent drag on demand and growth.

Figure 1-3. Actual versus Consensus Projections of Real Gross Domestic Product, 2014–19

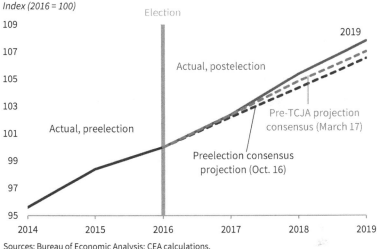

Sources: Bureau of Economic Analysis; CEA calculations.
Note: Consensus forecasts from the October 2016 and March 2017 issues of *Blue Chip Economic Indicators* begin with 2017 growth for levels implied by year-over-year forecasts.

in the expectation that the Administration's tax policies and deregulatory policies would have a more positive effect than projected by others. In the 2018 *Economic Report of the President*, the CEA drew on an extensive body of academic literature to predict that tax reform would raise real capital investment and the growth rate of output. In the 2019 *Report*, we reviewed data through 2018:Q3 showing that the U.S. economy's responses along multiple margins were consistent with predictions from that academic literature. Over the 12 quarters through 2019:Q4, the actual average annual growth rate of real GDP was 2.5 percent, slightly outpacing the May 2017 forecast, and an increase compared with the 2.2 percent average annual growth rate over the 26-quarter expansion period from 2009:Q3 through 2016:Q4 (see figure 1-4). As figure 1-5 shows, the average absolute errors of the ex-ante Administration forecasts under the current Administration were the lowest among those of the last five administrations.

The Trump Administration adopted structural reforms and policies that were designed to support continued U.S. economic growth. The TCJA, which was enacted on December 22, 2017, permanently reduced the statutory corporate tax rate from 35 to 21 percent, sharply lowering the user cost of capital. It also enabled 100 percent expensing of new equipment investment, retroactive to September 27, 2017 (the date of the first draft of the proposed tax legislation that included the 100 percent expensing provision from the House Ways and Means Committee). The international provisions of the TCJA, specifically

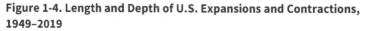

Figure 1-4. Length and Depth of U.S. Expansions and Contractions, 1949–2019

Annual growth rate (percent)

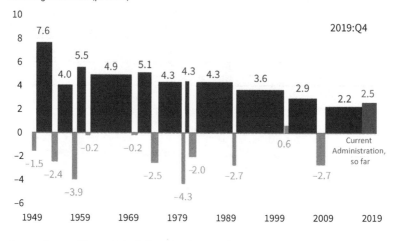

Sources: Bureau of Economic Analysis; National Bureau of Economic Research; CEA calculations.
Note: Values represent the change in real GDP as an annual growth rate for each quarterly expansion and contraction period, as defined by the National Bureau of Economic Research.

Figure 1-5. Average of Absolute Troika Forecasting Errors, by Horizon and Administration

■ Current-year error   ■ One-year-ahead error
■ Two-year-ahead error   ➤ Average error across horizons

Forecasting errors (percentage points)

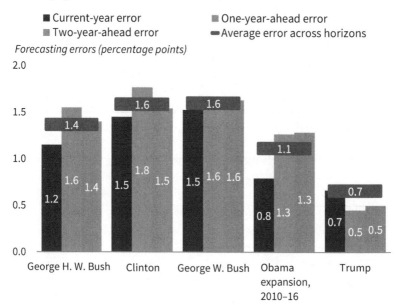

Sources: Federal Reserve Bank of Saint Louis (FRED); CEA calculations.
Note: Budget forecasts and Q4-over-Q4 growth rates were used to evaluate errors.

the change in the tax treatment of earnings from foreign affiliates (CEA 2019b), led to repatriation of past overseas earnings of U.S. multinationals in low-tax jurisdictions, as evidenced by the $1.04 trillion capital inflows from direct investment income on equity from dividends and withdrawals since 2017:Q4. The alterations in the tax treatment of foreign affiliates came in two parts: one for past earnings (a one-time transition tax at a low rate on past earnings held overseas), and one for future foreign-subsidiary earnings (eliminating the tax on normal repatriated dividends).

Businesses responded to the lower user cost of capital and geographical incentives under the TCJA with an increase in domestic investment. This investment led to capital deepening, increasing capital services per unit of labor input, which raised labor productivity, real wages, and U.S. real output. In addition, as discussed in more detail in chapter 3 of this *Report*, the Administration's deregulatory agenda also helped lower prices, from Internet prices to drug prices, and increased real income for American households. The 2018 Bipartisan Budget Act also increased government spending, raising aggregate demand. The combination of these factors lays the foundation for continued prosperity in the future.

As the current record expansion matures beyond the 42nd quarter, some worry that the expansion will "die of old age." But evidence suggests that expansions do not end simply because of their length. A study by Diebold and Rudebusch (1990) was among the first to find that in the postwar period, the probability of an expansion coming to an end was not increasing in the age of the expansion. In a follow-up study, Rudebusch (2016) provided empirical evidence that long expansions during the past 70 years are "no more likely to end than short ones." Australia's economy, which has experienced the longest expansion of any advanced economy in modern history, at 28 years, exemplifies how expansions can continue for decades. Old age does not kill expansions, though bad policies and adverse shocks can lead to recessions.

The remainder of this chapter provides evidence on the strength of different areas of the U.S. economy in the recent past, including: productivity, wages and income, consumer spending, employment, investment, and subdued inflation. The chapter also discusses the impact of the global economic downturn, monetary policy, and domestic factors slowing U.S. growth.

Productivity

Productivity growth is a key driver of long-term real output growth. Labor productivity in the post-TCJA period, 2018:Q1–2019:Q3, increased at an average annual pace of 1.4 percent—in particular, it picked up to 1.9 percent in the three quarters through 2019:Q3, a faster pace than the average growth rate

Figure 1-6. Nonfarm Business Sector Labor Productivity Growth, 2009–19

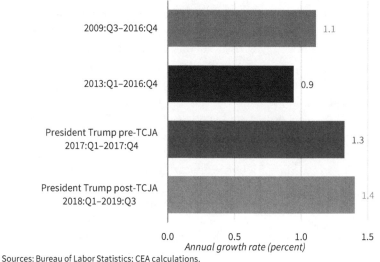

Sources: Bureau of Labor Statistics; CEA calculations.
Note: The annual growth rate is calculated for real output per hour of all persons in the nonfarm business sector.

of 1.1 percent in the pre-TCJA economic expansion period 2009:Q3–2016:Q4 (figure 1-6).[2]

Academic research suggests at least two channels through which the current Administration's policies can increase labor productivity. The first is through deregulatory actions pursued since the end of 2016 that have increased competition and productivity (CEA 2019a). The second channel is through capital deepening in response to a lower cost of capital under the TCJA. By raising investment, capital services per worker rises and, as a result, so does labor productivity (CEA 2019b). Since the passage of the TCJA, capital services have grown faster than projected by outside forecasters.[3]

Comparing the performance of the U.S. economy with other advanced economies provides another instructive benchmark. Since the start of the current Administration and through 2019:Q3 (the latest quarter available for all G7 countries as of the date of writing), U.S. productivity growth, as measured by output per worker, notably outperformed that of other countries (figure 1-7).

---

[2] Comparisons can be made with other subperiods in the past. Excluding the contractionary periods during the Great Recession, labor productivity grew at just a 1.1 percent compound annual rate during the period 2009:Q3–2016:Q4.

[3] Actual capital services grew at an annual rate of 3.2 percent over the two years after passage of the TCJA, compared with 2.9 percent as projected by Macroeconomic Advisers in October 2017, and 3.1 percent projected by Blue Chip Econometric Detail in February 2018. With a slightly different accounting method, the CBO also expected overall capital services to grow at 2.3 percent, compared with the actual annual growth rate of 2.7 percent.

Figure 1-7. Growth in Real GDP per Employed Person among the Advanced Economies, 2009–19

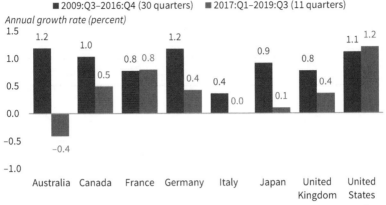

Sources: Australian Bureau of Statistics; Statistics Canada; Institut national de la statistique et des études économiques; Deutsche Bundesbank; Istituto Nazionale di Statistica; Japan Cabinet Office; U.K. Office for National Statistics; Bureau of Economic Analysis; Bureau of Labor Statistics; Haver Analytics; CEA calculations.

Note: Values represent an annual growth rate calculated over the given quarters. Growth rates are based on real GDP divided by seasonally adjusted employment. Employment includes goverment employees.

While U.S. labor productivity, as measured by output per employed person for cross-country consistency, grew at a compound annual rate of 1.2 percent during this period, the average growth rate among non-U.S. G7 member countries and Australia was just 0.3 percent.

Another striking observation is that the United States is the only economy among this group of advanced economies to experience an acceleration in labor productivity. As noted in the 2017 *Economic Report of the President*, from 2005 to 2015 all G7 countries experienced a sharp decline in labor productivity growth from the 10 earlier years, due to slowdowns in both capital deepening and total factor productivity (CEA 2017). Figure 1-7 shows the later of these periods, with the inclusion of 2016, when labor productivity growth in the United States was similar to that in the other G7 countries (plus Australia). In the 11 quarters since that period, productivity growth has been flat or falling in all these advanced economies, while productivity growth has risen in the United States.

Wages and Income

In traditional economic models, equilibrium in the labor market requires that nominal hourly compensation equals the marginal product of labor. Although real output per unit of labor is a measure of the average instead of the marginal product, the measure is a convenient proxy for the marginal product.

Figure 1-8. Actual versus Consensus Projections for Real Disposable Personal Income, 2014–19

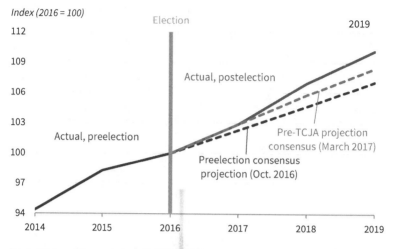

Index (2016 = 100)

Sources: Bureau of Economic Analysis; CEA calculations.
Note: Consensus forecasts from the October 2016 and March 2017 issues of *Blue Chip Economic Indicators* and begin with 2017 growth for levels implied by year-over-year forecasts.

Figure 1-9. Growth of Real Disposable Personal Income per Household, 2009–19

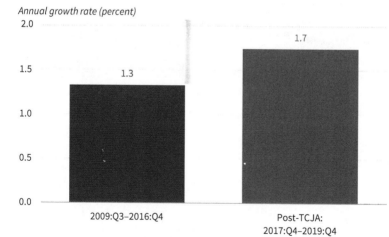

Annual growth rate (percent)

Sources: Bureau of Economic Analysis; Census Bureau; CEA calculations.
Note: Values represent growth at an annual rate over the given quarters. Households are measured from the Census Bureau's housing database as the break-adjusted total number of households.

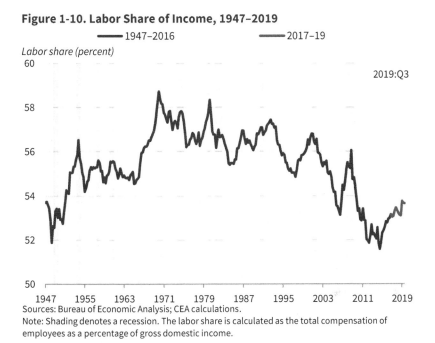

Figure 1-10. Labor Share of Income, 1947–2019

━━━ 1947–2016   ━━━ 2017–19

Labor share (percent)

Sources: Bureau of Economic Analysis; CEA calculations.
Note: Shading denotes a recession. The labor share is calculated as the total compensation of employees as a percentage of gross domestic income.

Coincident with the increase in labor productivity growth has been an increase in real average hourly earnings growth, particularly for many disadvantaged groups (see chapter 2 of this *Report*). Real average hourly earnings grew at an annual rate of 1.1 percent during the post-TCJA period and 1.3 percent for non-supervisory workers, compared with 0.4 percent and 0.5 percent, respectively, in the first seven and a half years of the expansion through 2016:Q4. Real wage growth further picked up for nonsupervisory workers, to 1.4 percent in the four quarters of 2019, as the labor market continued to heat up.

The net tax savings from the TCJA—from a combination of increasing standard deductions, lowering marginal rates, and doubling the child tax credit—is also expected to boost real disposable income. In its pre-TCJA projections (March 2017), the Blue Chip consensus panel forecasted that real disposable personal income would grow at an average of 2.65 percent during 2018 and 2019; in actuality, it grew at a 3.5 percent rate (figure 1-8), well above the consensus forecast and well above the 2.1 percent average annual growth rate over the period 2009:Q3–2016:Q4. A similar pattern is observed on a per-household basis, where real disposable personal income per household grew in the post-TCJA period at an annual average rate of 1.7 percent, outpacing the 1.3 percent of the earlier period (figure 1-9).

As income accelerates, labor's share of gross domestic income (GDI) also continues on an upward trajectory. Measuring labor's share as total employee

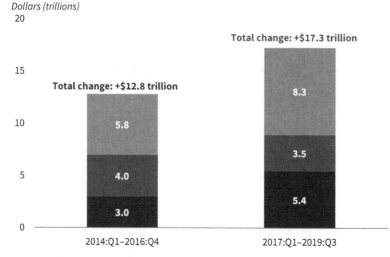

Figure 1-11. Cumulative Change in Nominal Household and Nonprofit Wealth, 2014–19

■ Stock market wealth   ■ Net housing wealth   ■ Other wealth

Dollars (trillions)

Total change: +$17.3 trillion

Total change: +$12.8 trillion

	2014:Q1–2016:Q4	2017:Q1–2019:Q3
Other wealth	5.8	8.3
Net housing wealth	4.0	3.5
Stock market wealth	3.0	5.4

Sources: Federal Reserve Board (Financial Accounts of the United States); CEA calculations.

compensation as a percentage of GDI, the series partially retraced a multide-cade trend decline through 2014. During the 11 quarters through 2019:Q3, it rose a further 0.5 percentage point, to 53.6 percent (figure 1-10).

While labor's share of GDI and real disposable income growth has increased, total household wealth has also increased. The cumulative change in nominal household and nonprofit-sector wealth, as reported by the Federal Reserve's Financial Accounts of the United States, in the first 11 quarters through 2019:Q3 exceeds the cumulative change in the preceding 11 quarters by over $4 trillion (figure 1-11).

Consumer Spending

A more productive workforce with greater disposable income has bolstered overall economic growth. Consumer spending as a share of nominal gross domestic product averaged 67.9 percent during the 10 years through 2018. Given this sizable share of GDP, changes in consumer spending carry substantial contributions to overall real GDP growth. In 2019, real consumer spending grew by 2.6 percent, maintaining the same pace as in 2018. Since the TCJA's passage, real consumer spending has grown 2.6 percent at an annual rate, higher than the 2.3 percent pace during the 7½ years from 2009:Q3 through 2016:Q4, when real consumer spending contributed 1.6 percentage points to real GDP growth. In the 12 quarters through 2019:Q4, real consumer spending

Figure 1-12. Main Contributors to Real GDP Growth, 2017–19

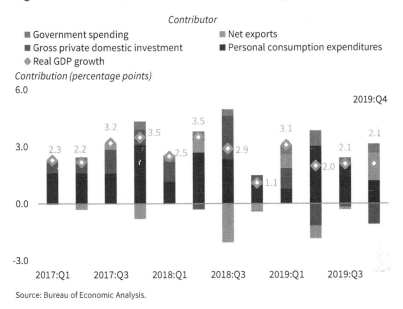

Source: Bureau of Economic Analysis.

Figure 1-13. Consumption and Wealth Relative to Disposable Personal Income, 1952–2019

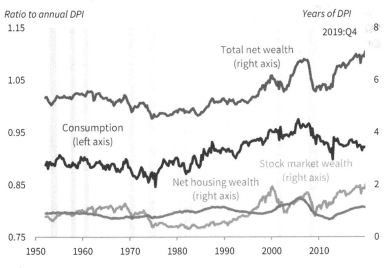

Sources: Federal Reserve; Bureau of Economic Analysis; CEA calculations.
Note: DPI = disposable personal income. Data for 2019:Q4 values are estimated from the latest daily or monthly data. Shading denotes a recession.

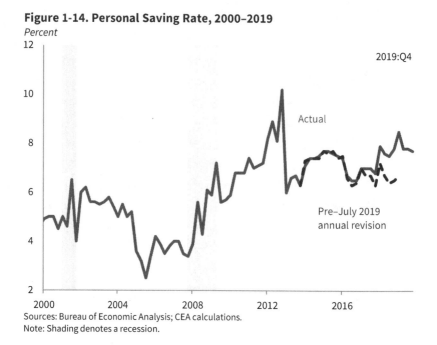

Figure 1-14. Personal Saving Rate, 2000–2019

Percent

2019:Q4

Actual

Pre–July 2019
annual revision

Sources: Bureau of Economic Analysis; CEA calculations.
Note: Shading denotes a recession.

contributed on average 1.9 percentage points to the quarterly real GDP growth rate (figure 1-12).

Gains in household wealth (also known as net worth) have supported the solid growth of real consumer spending during the past three years (figure 1-13), with gains in stock-market wealth and other housing wealth accounting for the increase. Over long-periods, gains in the wealth-to-income ratio are correlated with consumer spending (Poterba 2000; Lettau and Ludvigson 2004). From that point of view, the gains in the wealth-to-income ratio could have supported an even larger increase in consumer spending.

The prospect of future consumer spending supporting overall output growth is strong, given the elevated levels of consumer confidence. The University of Michigan's Index of Consumer Sentiment rose to 97.2 in 2019:Q4—in the middle of the range in which it has fluctuated in the past three years—and is currently 5.4 points above its 2016 level. The Conference Board's version of consumer sentiment fell to 126.5 in 2019:Q4, toward the lower end of the range in which it has fluctuated in the past three years, but is still 26.7 points above 2016. These persistently strong readings for both measures indicate resilient consumer demand, which represents a sizable portion of the U.S. economy, and thus point to its continued support of growth.

Further, personal saving as a share of disposable personal income remains elevated. After notable upward revisions by the Bureau of Economic Analysis in July 2018, as reported in chapter 10 of the 2019 *Economic Report of the President*, the saving rate was further revised upward in the Bureau's July 2019 annual revision. The personal saving rate during 2019 of 8.0 percent far exceeds the average of the last two decades (figure 1-14). The saving rate has been increasing in the past three years due to the faster increase in personal disposable income relative to the already robust growth in personal outlays. The high saving rate together with elevated levels of household wealth, leave some room for saving to buffer consumer spending against temporary adverse developments in income.

Investment

In the past volumes of the *Economic Report of the President*, the CEA projected that the Tax Cuts and Jobs Act would raise real capital investment on the basis that lowering the user cost of capital would increase the target steady-state flow of capital services; and this projection was based on a substantial body of academic research. Chapter 1 of the 2019 *Economic Report of the President* confirmed these anticipated positive effects with the then–available data up through 2018:Q3. The positive effect of the TCJA on investment was also corroborated by outside studies (Kopp et al. 2019).

During the 9-quarter post-TCJA period, the annual rate of real private nonresidential fixed investment growth averaged 3.4 percent, with growth being faster in the first 4 quarters (6.8 percent) than in the next 5 quarters (0.8 percent).[4] Some moderation of the investment growth rate was anticipated by most models, which predicted that the positive effects on investment and overall economic activity would be front-loaded in 2018 (CEA 2019b; Mertens 2018). In particular, standard neoclassical growth models suggest that during the transition to the new steady state, the rate of growth in fixed investment would initially spike, and would subsequently return to its pre-TCJA trend. Absent other, exogenous shocks, the level would then remain at a higher, post-TCJA level, with the capital-to-output ratio thereby asymptotically approaching its new, higher steady-state level (CEA 2019b).

Figure 1-15 shows that the *level* of investment has been higher throughout the post-TCJA period than the consensus pre-TCJA projections (the March 2017 Blue Chip consensus). In 2018 as a whole, investment was 2.3 percent higher than the consensus projection. In 2019, even with the recent investment slowdown, private nonresidential fixed investment was still 0.8 percent higher than the pre-TCJA consensus projection. Also, compared with other G7 countries, the cumulative increase in investment, or the cumulative addition

---

[4] Nine quarters are included in the post-TCJA period because the TCJA's allowance for full expensing of new equipment investment was retroactive to September 27, 2017 (the date of the first draft of the proposed tax legislation that included the full expensing provision from the House Ways and Means Committee).

Figure 1-15. Actual versus Preelection Projections for Nonresidential Private Fixed Investment, 2014–19

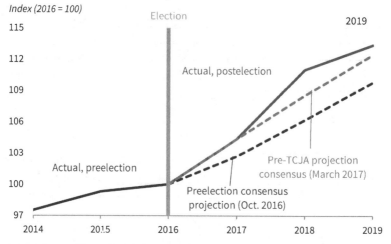

Sources: Bureau of Economic Analysis; CEA calculations.
Note: Consensus forecasts from the October 2016 and March 2017 issues of *Blue Chip Economic Indicators* begin with 2017 growth for levels implied by year-over-year forecasts.

Figure 1-16. Cumulative Change in Gross Fixed Private Capital Formation among the Group of Seven Member Countries, 2017:Q4–2019:Q3

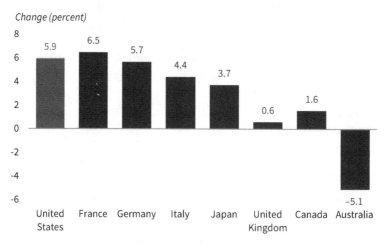

Sources: Australian Bureau of Statistics; Statistics Canada; Institut national de la statistique et des études économiques; Deutsche Bundesbank; Istituto Nazionale di Statistica; Cabinet Office of Japan; U.K. Office for National Statistics; Bureau of Economic Analysis; CEA calculations.

Figure 1-17. The User Cost of Capital, 2011–19

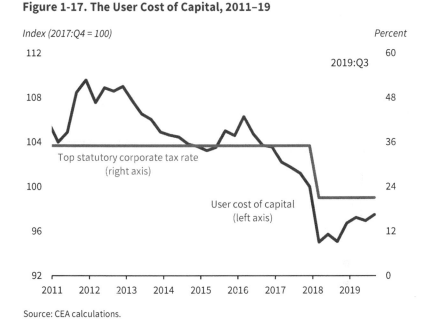

Index (2017:Q4 = 100) · *Percent*

Source: CEA calculations.

to the capital stock, since the TCJA's enactment has been one of the highest (figure 1-16).

Outside the expected slowdown in investment growth, other forces suppressed investment in 2019. One is the increase in the user cost of capital since 2018:Q3. From the CEA's calculations, the user cost of capital is measured by the Shiller cyclically adjusted Standard & Poor's price/earnings ratio, in addition to a function of corporate tax rates and depreciation allowances. As seen in figure 1-17, the user cost of capital fell sharply in 2018:Q1, when the TCJA lowered the top statutory corporate tax rate from 35 percent to 21 percent, but increased over the period 2018:Q4–2019:Q3. A confluence of factors—tighter domestic monetary policy and lower stock market valuations, possibly due to a global growth slowdown—all ultimately led to a tightening of financial conditions in 2018:Q4 and thereafter raised the user cost of capital.

The imprints of weaker global factors on investment can be seen in a decomposition of nonresidential investment growth (figure 1-18). The slowdown in nonresidential investment in 2019 was mainly accounted for by business structures, which shrank 7.0 percent in 2019, and by equipment, which decreased 1.5 percent. Intellectual property products investment, which is less exposed to fluctuations in global conditions, grew at a robust pace of 6.2 percent in 2019.

The decline in structures investment was primarily because of a pullback in energy investment. Mining and wells investment fell 16.7 percent in 2019, and were a factor in about 45 percent of the slowdown in structures

Figure 1-18. Average Annual Growth in Real Business Fixed Investment and Component Contributions, 2010–19

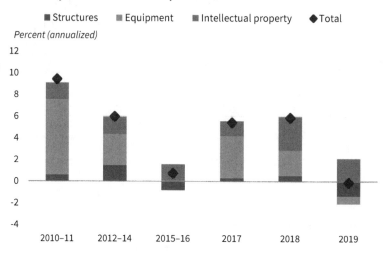

■ Structures ■ Equipment ■ Intellectual property ◆ Total

Sources: Bureau of Economic Analysis; CEA calculations.
Note: Average annual growth is measured on a Q4-over-Q4 basis for each year or multiyear period.

Figure 1-19. Real Mining and Drilling Structures Investment versus Oil Rigs Operating in the United States, 2007–19

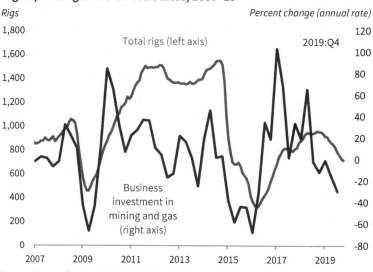

Sources: Bureau of Economic Analysis; Baker-Hughes; CEA calculations.

Figure 1-20. Brent Crude Oil Prices versus Oil Rigs Operating in the United States, 2007–19

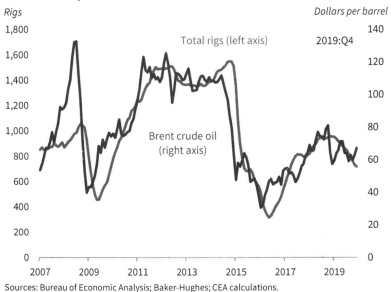

Sources: Bureau of Economic Analysis; Baker-Hughes; CEA calculations.

investment. As seen in figure 1-19, investment in mining and wells started contracting in 2018:Q3, when market concerns about global growth escalated and as oil prices fell to near the breakeven price for shale producers, which is about $50 a barrel. As oil prices approached or fell below the breakeven price for some producers, they responded by slowing drilling or deciding to reduce the large inventory of drilled but not completed wells (figure 1-20). Indeed, the U.S. rig count fell by 236 in December compared with a year earlier.

Equipment investment also contracted by 1.5 percent in 2019, compared with 5.0 percent growth in 2018. Investment in equipment turned negative in the first quarter, briefly bounced back in the second quarter, and returned to negative in the third quarter. The two main equipment categories that most exacerbated the slowdown are information processing and transportation. As is discussed in more detail in the "Global Macroeconomic Situation" section of this chapter, the transportation sector experienced a series of negative supply and demand shocks from economies abroad, but by far the largest drag was the decrease in domestic sales at the aircraft supplier Boeing. Confirming the importance of global factors, the CEA finds that an investment accelerator model augmented with foreign growth (proxied by a weighted average of non-U.S. G7 growth) can explain a sizable portion of the recent slowdown in equipment investment (see figure 1-21), compared with a fundamental version of the neoclassical model.

Figure 1-21. Predictions of an Investment Accelerator Model, 2014–19

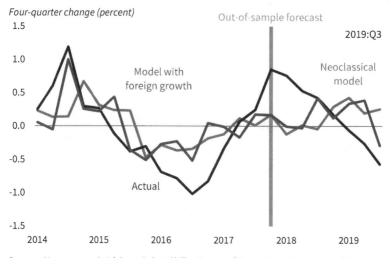

Sources: Macroeconomic Advisers; Robert Shiller; Bureau of Economic Analysis; Internal Revenue Service; various national statistical offices; CEA calculations.
Note: Foreign growth is a weighted average of Group of Seven country growth, excluding the United States.

Figure 1-22. The Growth in Number of Private Establishments versus Small Business Optimism, 2000–2019

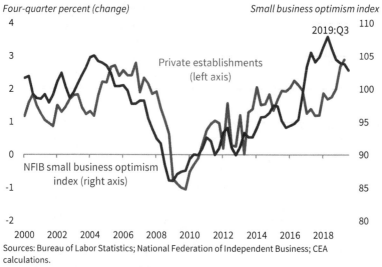

Sources: Bureau of Labor Statistics; National Federation of Independent Business; CEA calculations.
Note: A three-month moving average is used for the index from the National Federation of Independent Business (NFIB). Data for private establishments are only available through 2019:Q2.

The decreases in both structures and equipment investment suggest that the slowdown in growth in the rest of world has constituted a strong headwind to U.S. investment. Indeed, as figure 1-18 shows, the current slowdown in investment is similar to the slowdown in 2015–16, a period that also experienced an investment slowdown precipitated by weakening conditions abroad. A later section of this chapter further explores the international economic developments that are weighing on U.S. growth.

To the extent that changes in business fixed investment predominantly reflect actions of large multinational firms that were responding to fluctuations in global demand conditions, this situation could conceal the developments among smaller firms that are more domestically oriented.[5] One of the TCJA's aims is lowering the business costs of small firms, which tend to be more credit-constrained than large multinational firms. As figure 1-22 shows, this predicted effect of the TCJA is supported by survey data, with 2018 level small business optimism rising to the highest level in almost two decades, and the number of private establishments surging in 2019.

Inflation

Despite a tight labor market, price inflation remains low and stable. Measures of inflation expectations have also been stable. The stability of price inflation and of inflation expectations indicate the economy is not facing supply constraints and has been a key factor in extending the duration of the current expansion.

What is different about the structure of the recent economy that accounts for the coexistence of a tight labor market and low and stable inflation—that is, the flattening of the Phillips curve? Partial explanations include the falling relative price of imports, a different monetary policy regime, and recent deregulatory actions.

Price Inflation

Key measures of price inflation are essentially flat, and are all roughly in the range of 2 percent at an annual rate. The price index for GDP, the aggregate price for everything that is produced in the United States, rose 1.7 percent during the four quarters of 2019, down from 2.0 and 2.3 percent in 2017 and 2018, respectively. Consumer price inflation—as measured by the price of personal consumption expenditures in the National Income and Product Accounts (known as the PCE Price Index)—was only 1.5 percent during the four quarters of 2019. With the exception of the third quarter in 2016, consumer price inflation has generally been below (or equal to) GDP price inflation for each of the past eight years, as shown in figure 1-23.

---

[5] A well-documented stylized fact in the international economics literature is that larger firms have a higher propensity to export and import (WTO 2016).

Figure 1-23. Inflation: The GDP Price Index versus PCE Price Index, 2009–19

Four-quarter change (percent)

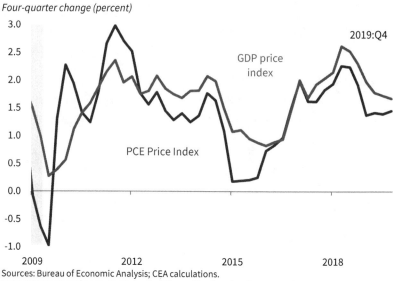

Sources: Bureau of Economic Analysis; CEA calculations.
Note: PCE = personal consumption expenditures. Shading denotes a recession.

Figure 1-24. Import Prices versus GDP Price Index, 1955–2019

Log levels

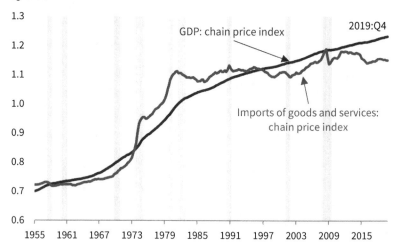

Sources: Bureau of Economic Analysis; CEA calculations.
Note: Import prices are measured by the prices for goods and services from the National Income and Product Accounts. The indices are logged and renormalized. Shading denotes a recession.

One reason that consumer price inflation has been below the pace of GDP price inflation has been the persistent decline in the relative price of imports. During the eight quarters through 2019:Q4, import prices did not increase, while GDP prices (i.e., goods and services produced in the United States) increased at a much faster rate of 2.0 percent, so that the *relative* price of imports fell at a 2.0 percent annual rate. The declining *relative* price of imports has held down consumer price inflation (1.7 percent over eight quarters) by more than it has held down GDP price inflation because imported goods and services are included directly in consumer prices, but influence GDP prices only indirectly through competition.

A situation of declining relative prices of imports has not always been the case, as can be seen in figure 1-24, which shows the log levels of GDP prices and the log levels of import prices. In particular, import prices increased 1.6 percentage points per year faster than GDP prices from 1955 to 1981, increased 1.7 percentage points more slowly from 1981 through 2011, and increased 3.1 percentage points more slowly during the eight years since 2011. As can be seen in figure 1-24, the separation between the log levels of GDP and import prices is currently the largest recorded in the 1955–2019 period.

Different Measures of Inflation: The CPI, Chained CPI, and PCE Price Index and Their Cores

The Consumer Price Index (CPI) tends to increase slightly faster—by about 0.29 percentage point a year, on average—than the PCE Price Index.[6] These two commonly used measures of consumer prices are both important. The CPI tends to overstate a cost-of-living price index, however, largely because it uses a fixed market basket updated every two years, which means that it does not capture real-time substitution by consumers toward goods and services with declining relative prices. Another version of the CPI, known as the chained CPI, corrects for this substitution bias, and as a result also rises about 0.28 percentage point per year less than the official CPI. The chained CPI is now used to index the notches in the new TCJA tax schedules. The PCE Price Index also begins with most of the same CPI components and aggregates with a formula that allows for substitution.

Price indices that exclude the volatile components of food and energy provide a smoother signal of inflation trends than the overall index. The core CPI (which excludes food and energy) increased 2.3 percent during the 12 months of 2019, up only slightly from the 2.2 percent year-earlier pace. The PCE Price Index version of core inflation rose 1.6 percent in 2019, down from the year-earlier pace of 1.9 percent. The 2019 rate of core PCE inflation was below the Federal Reserve's target of 2.0 percent, as was the rate of overall PCE inflation, as shown in figure 1-25.

---

[6] Computed from 2002:Q4 to 2018:Q4.

Figure 1-25. Consumer Price Inflation, 2012–19

Percent change (12-month)

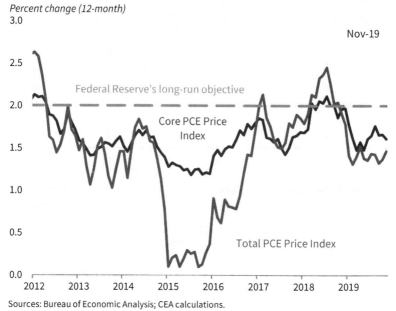

Sources: Bureau of Economic Analysis; CEA calculations.
Note: PCE = personal consumption expenditures.

Figure 1-26. Core CPI Inflation and Inflation Expectations, 1960–2019

Percent

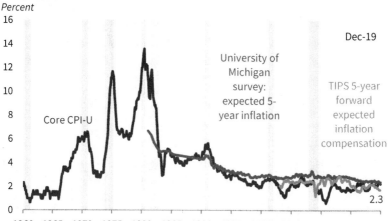

Sources: University of Michigan; Federal Reserve Board; Bureau of Economic Analysis; Haver Analytics.
Note: The 12-month percent change is taken for Core CPI-U. A 3-month centered moving average is taken for the University of Michigan survey and Treasury Inflation Protected Securities (TIPS). Shading denotes a recession.

Measures of inflation *expectations* have also been stable at a rate close to the 2.0 percent Federal Reserve target, as shown in figure 1-26, which graphs two measures: one from the University of Michigan's Survey of Consumers, and one extracted from the market for the Treasury's Inflation Protected Securities.

Buttressed by the stability of core inflation, and of expectations of core inflation, the Administration forecasts rates of increase in the CPI at 2.3 percent and the GDP price index at 2.0 percent during the 11-year Budget forecasting interval.

Hourly Compensation Inflation, Productivity Growth, and Stable Inflation

Nominal hourly compensation inflation—as measured by the Employment Cost Index for the private sector—increased by 2.7 percent at an annual rate during the 12 months of 2019, down slightly from the 3.0 percent 2018 pace. This 2.7 percent pace edged up from the annual pace of 2.1 percent during the four years through 2016.

Over long periods, wage inflation can exceed price inflation by the rate of labor productivity growth. And over the seven quarters through 2019:Q3, nonfarm labor productivity grew at a 1.4 percent annual rate. As a result, the roughly 3.0 percent rate of annual hourly compensation growth (which suggests unit labor costs rising at 1.6 percent) is compatible with price inflation of 2 percent (or slightly less), without putting upward pressure on the price structure.

The sensitivity of inflation to fluctuations in the unemployment rate has decreased during the past two decades, as shown in the scatter diagram given in figure 1-27, which illustrates a version of the Phillips curve. The vertical axis shows the difference in core PCE inflation relative to a year-earlier survey of inflation expectations. The horizontal axis shows a version of the unemployment rate, one that is demographically adjusted to control for the major fluctuations in the share of young people in the labor force during these past 60 years. (The share of young people in the labor force was exceptionally high in the 1970s, when the baby boom cohorts entered the labor market.)

As can be seen in figure 1-27 by the blue regression line fitted through the early years 1960–2000, an extra percentage point of unemployment lowered the rate of inflation by 0.36 percentage point a year. In contrast, the red regression line fitted on the last 19 years (2000–2018) indicates that an extra percentage point of unemployment lowered the rate of inflation by only 0.08 percentage point. One could argue that this shallow slope estimated during the past 20 years provides the best guide to the future. Or one might argue that the best estimate of the slope is the one covering the entire 60-year sample (0.27 percentage point of inflation per 1 percentage point of unemployment; not shown).

Figure 1-27. Price-Price Phillips Curve Scatter Diagram, 1960-2018

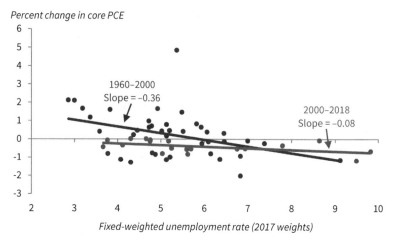

Percent change in core PCE

1960-2000
Slope = -0.36

2000-2018
Slope = -0.08

Fixed-weighted unemployment rate (2017 weights)

Sources: Federal Reserve Bank of Philadelphia; Bureau of Economic Analysis; Bureau of Labor Statistics; CEA calculations.
Note: PCE = Personal consumption expenditures. Inflation expectations are measured by the Livingston Survey for 1960-70; by the Survey of Professional Forecasters' (SPF) 10-year Consumer Price Index for 1970-90; and by the SPF expectation for 10-year PCE inflation for 1990-2018.

Table 1-1. Effects of Deregulation on Relative Price Increases on the Core CPI, 2006-19

Priced good/service	Ten-year % change in relative prices, Dec. 2006-Dec. 2016, AR	34-month % change since Dec. 2016, AR	Change in trend, p.p.	Relative importance weight in Core CPI	Effect on Core CPI inflation
	(1)	(2)	(3) = (2) − (1)	(4)	(5) = (3) * (4)
Prescription drugs	1.62	-0.96	-2.58	1.711	-0.044
Internet services	-1.83	-2.28	-0.44	0.952	-0.004

Sources: Bureau of Labor Statistics; CEA calculations.
Note: AR = annualized rate; p.p. = percentage point; CPI = Consumer Price Index.

Explanations for the declining slope of the Phillips curve include the influence of import prices in holding down the rate of inflation in recent years (as argued above), the wage and price rigidity that kept inflation from falling below zero during the early years of this recovery (2009-13), the diminishment of the Phillips curve coefficient in a monetary policy regime that effectively targets inflation (Hooper, Mishkin, and Sufi 2019), and the evolution of the input-output structure of the economy toward increasing intermediate inputs (Rubbo 2020). Another possible explanation is the deregulation efforts of the current Administration.

Deregulation and Inflation

As discussed in chapter 3 of this *Report*, estimates suggest that deregulation has lowered the relative price of prescription drugs and Internet services. We calculate that these effects lower total inflation by about 0.05 percentage point a year. The relative price of prescription drugs, in particular, is increasing by 2.6 percentage points a year less that during the 10 years through 2016; see table 1-1. To summarize this analysis, inflation remains low and stable, inflation expectations are well anchored at this low level, and recent estimates of the Phillips curve suggest a diminishing sensitivity of inflation to unemployment rates.

The Global Macroeconomic Situation

As alluded to in previous sections, a major headwind to growth in 2019 was a synchronized slowdown in global growth. In its latest semiannual economic outlook, the International Monetary Fund (IMF 2019c) revised down global growth sharply, by 0.7 percentage point, to what would be the lowest growth rate since the Global Recession, 3 percent—one of the largest one-year downward-revisions in recent years (figure 1-28). Among advanced econo- mies, growth was revised down by 0.4 percentage point, with growth disap- pointments concentrated in Europe, especially Germany. Emerging market economies also saw a downward revision, of 0.8 percentage point. Amid this global slowdown, the U.S. economy has performed largely as projected by the IMF in October 2018, growing faster than any other G7 country in the first three quarters of 2019 (figure 1-29).

At the heart of the current global slowdown has been a manufacturing downturn. Uncertainty about trade policy is one often-cited culprit in the manu- facturing slowdown, particularly uncertainty surrounding the Administration's negotiations toward a bilateral trade agreement with the People's Republic of China on enforceable commitments to remove or lower structural barriers in China (BIS 2019a, 2019b; IMF 2019a, 2019b; OECD 2019a; World Bank 2019a, 2019b). However, other reasons for the global manufacturing slowdown also preceded, or were contemporaneous with, trade policy developments. These reasons make it difficult to isolate the effects of trade policy uncertainty, and possibly result in an upward bias of its effects on the global economy. Other factors weighing on manufacturing include a change in European automobile emission standards in September 2018 that caused a production bottleneck in Europe, especially Germany, and a growth slowdown in China caused by the government's efforts to deleverage the financial system beginning in 2017. The manufacturing sectors of these two countries—two of the world's preeminent manufacturing powerhouses—had begun slowing down before or around the time of the imposition of tariffs on Chinese goods by the current Administration (figure 1-30).

Figure 1-28. IMF Five-Year Real GDP Growth Forecasts for the World, 2012–24

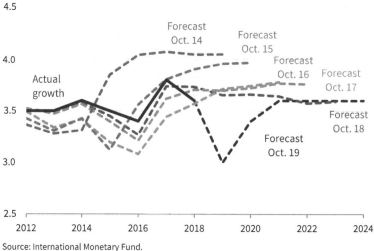

Year-over-year percent change

Source: International Monetary Fund.
Note: Each forecast is taken from *World Economic Outlook*, which is published by the IMF in October of each year.

Figure 1-29. Forecast of 2019 Real GDP Growth

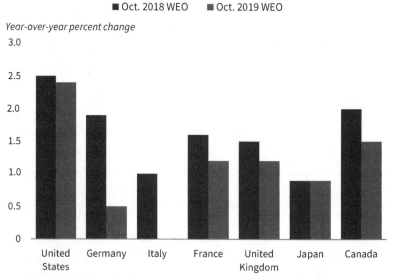

Year-over-year percent change

Source: International Monetary Fund.
Note: WEO = *World Economic Outlook*, published annually by the IMF.

Figure 1-30. Composite Output Purchasing Manager's Index (PMI), 2015–19

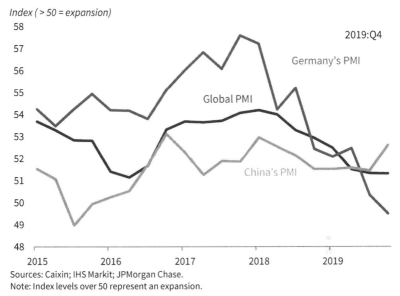

Index (> 50 = expansion)

Sources: Caixin; IHS Markit; JPMorgan Chase.
Note: Index levels over 50 represent an expansion.

The Administration's efforts to create a more reciprocal environment and rebalance the trading relationship between the United States and China required negotiation over how this new relationship should be shaped. Negotiations have covered a wide range of critical issues, including the ways that U.S. companies are required to transfer proprietary technology as a condition of market access; the numerous tariff and nontariff barriers faced by U.S. businesses in China; and China's other market-distorting practices and policies that have weighed on U.S. and global economic growth, such as industrial subsidies and support for state-owned enterprises.

China's weak protection and enforcement of intellectual property rights is symptomatic of a broader challenge. Chinese firms engage in systematic theft of U.S. intellectual property because the costs are insufficient to incentivize them to do otherwise.[7] Instead of pursuing an enforceable bilateral trade agreement through targeted tariffs, prior Administrations took a multilateral approach that imposed no costs on the offenders and failed to resolve these issues. The Administration first imposed tariffs on imports from China based on

---

[7] There is a common misconception that the grievances against China relate exclusively to intellectual property. Although Chinese forced technology transfer and intellectual property theft (discussed at length in the Section 301 investigation) are important, the actions are also designed to address a number of other long-standing trade issues with China: expanding the Chinese market access for services and agriculture, implementing an agreement like the United States–Mexico–Canada Agreement's provision on currency, addressing the many nontariff barriers on U.S. exports to China, and increasing Chinese purchases of U.S. products (White House 2018).

the findings of the Section 301 investigation of China's acts, policies, and practices related to technology transfer, intellectual property, and innovation. The Administration then took supplemental action in 2018 and 2019 in response to China's imposition of retaliatory tariffs and failure to eliminate these unfair acts, policies, and practices.

These Administration actions have prompted a renegotiation of the trading relationship between the two countries. Studies that examined the effect of the tariffs point out that tariffs impose near-term costs on the United States (Amiti, Redding, and Weinstein 2019a, 2019b; Caldara et al. 2019; Fajgelbaum et al. 2019).[8] Negotiations over a new agreement necessitate a degree of uncertainty over how that agreement will be shaped, exacerbating near-term costs. However, achieving a new trade relationship with China that is balanced and reciprocal will deliver long-term economic benefits for the United States, including a reduction in near-term costs.

In January 2020, the Administration finalized a historic and enforceable agreement on phase one of the trade deal. The trade deal requires structural reforms and other changes to China's economic and trade policies in the areas of intellectual property, technology transfer, agriculture, financial services, and currency and foreign exchange. The ultimate goal is that, with lower market barriers and further market orientation in China, the global trading system will operate in a more balanced, reciprocal environment. Global growth, as a result, would benefit from the increase in trade liberalization.

While trade policy uncertainty has held the spotlight, another underappreciated reason for the global manufacturing slump was both supply and demand problems in the global motor vehicle industry. Supply problems in the European motor vehicle industry were precipitated by a change in the European Union's emissions regulations in September 2018, which led to bottlenecks at testing agencies and production cuts from automobile manufacturers to avoid unwanted inventory accumulation. Germany, a global hub for automobile production, particularly felt the impact of the supply disruption (Deutsche Bundesbank 2019; IMF 2019b). German automobile production fell 10 percent in 2018 as a whole, and shrank another 9 percent in 2019. Given its long global value chains and sizable share in global output and global exports, weaknesses in the automobile sector extend well beyond the industry in Europe, propagating the shock through upstream industries around the world like steel, metal, and automobile parts, as well as downstream industries like services (OECD 2019b).[9]

---

[8] Caldara et al. (2019) look at the costs imposed by this trade policy uncertainty and find cumulative costs of up to 1 percent of GDP after two years. Amiti, Redding, and Weinstein (2019b) examine the direct impact of implemented tariffs in 2018 and 2019 and find that they impose a net deadweight loss of 0.4 percent of GDP per year. Fajgelbaum et al. (2019) find that the additional tariffs in 2018 imposed a cost of 0.04 percent on GDP after accounting for tariff revenues and gains to domestic producers.

[9] The automobile sector accounts for 5 percent of global output and 8 percent of global exports.

Figure 1-31. China's Change in Automobile Sales, 2014–19

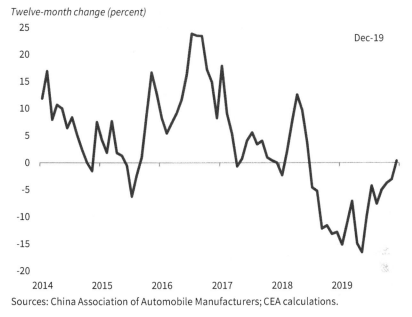

Twelve-month change (percent)

Sources: China Association of Automobile Manufacturers; CEA calculations.

These adverse shocks to the motor vehicle industry were further compounded by a cyclical downturn in automobile demand in China. Efforts by China's authorities to deleverage the shadow-banking sector since 2017 have led to a protracted slowdown in credit growth, including consumer credit. Increasing difficulty in accessing credit, heightened risk aversion among households in a slowing economy, and the termination—in 2019—of consumer tax breaks for automobile purchases in 2017–18 all led to a substantial pullback in Chinese automobile consumption. As a result, China's automobile consumption has contracted in consecutive quarters since mid-2018 (figure 1-31), and has accounted for over half the global contraction of automobile sales. Accordingly, the quantity of German automobile exports, for which China is an important market, have plunged since early 2018, and were 14 percent below the mid-2018 level, as of November 2019 (figure 1-32).

Beyond the problems in the automobile industry and the slowdown in China, country-specific shocks have also exacerbated the global slowdown. In the United Kingdom, uncertainty over Brexit has continued to weigh on growth. After the U.K. Parliament failed to ratify a deal negotiated between Prime Minister Boris Johnson's government and the EU, his government secured an extension of the Brexit deadline to January 2020. With the December 2019 elections in the U.K. securing a large majority for Johnson's party in Parliament, Parliament passed legislation for Britain to leave the European Union with a

Figure 1-32. German Vehicle and Car Engines Exported, 2016–19

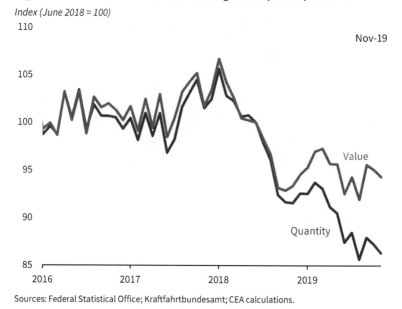

Index (June 2018 = 100)

Sources: Federal Statistical Office; Kraftfahrtbundesamt; CEA calculations.

withdrawal agreement on January 31, 2020, after which the U.K. will enter a transitional period and adhere to EU rules until end of 2020.

Japan, after experiencing surprisingly positive growth of 2.3 percent at annual rate in the first half of 2019, saw its growth edge down to a 1.8 percent annual rate in the third quarter, as exports slumped amid weakening global demand, mainly due to a drop in demand from China and a boycott of Japanese goods in South Korea. The long-planned sales tax increase from 8 to 10 percent also came into effect in October, causing consumer spending to plummet.

Emerging market economies, which until 2018 had been an engine of global growth, became a drag in 2019. After months of antigovernment protests, Hong Kong entered its first recession since the global financial crisis.[10] In India, increasing defaults in the shadow-banking sector have resulted in a large pullback of domestic credit growth, causing GDP growth to slow sharply. In Mexico, uncertainty over domestic policies, reinforced by the sudden resignation of Mexico's financial minister, and the slowdown in global trade have impeded growth. Meanwhile, growth remains weak in Brazil, as high public debt levels have constrained the government from using fiscal stimulus to further support the economy in the face of subdued domestic and external demand.

---

[10] Hong Kong's real GDP contracted by 1.9 percent at an annual rate in 2019:Q2 and by 12.1 percent in 2019:Q3.

Figure 1-33. Central Bank Policy Rates, 2010–19

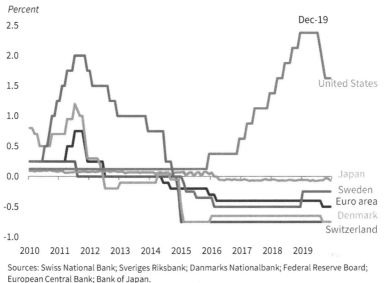

Sources: Swiss National Bank; Sveriges Riksbank; Danmarks Nationalbank; Federal Reserve Board; European Central Bank; Bank of Japan.
Note: For Japan, the effective uncollateralized overnight call rate was used.

The U.S. Dollar and Monetary Policy

Because of the weak international economic outlook, several non-U.S. major economies eased monetary policies throughout 2019. In particular, the European Central Bank announced in September that it would resume its asset purchase program at a pace of €20 billion a month, and it lowered its policy rate by 10 basis points to –0.5 percent. The National Bank of Denmark (a non-euro country) also followed the European Central Bank in lowering its policy rate further into negative territory. Global negative-yielding sovereign debt—mostly issued by European countries—has recently reached a record amount of about $15 trillion.

In contrast, in response to an improved outlook for the U.S. economy, the Federal Reserve began to normalize its balance sheet in December 2015. During the years 2016–18, the Federal Reserve raised its policy rate eight times, while several central banks across Europe (Denmark, the European Central Bank, Sweden, and Switzerland) kept their policy rates negative (figure 1-33). Though the Federal Reserve subsequently reduced rates on three occasions in 2019, U.S. policy rates continued to exceed those of other advanced economies, which induced capital inflows into the United States, and in turn contributed to an appreciation of the dollar through September 2019, before it edging lower during the final three months of the year.

Looking through the fluctuations of 2019, the real and nominal trade-weighted broad dollar was little changed from December to December.

Figure 1-34. Federal Reserve Trade-Weighted Broad Nominal versus Real Dollar, 1973–2019

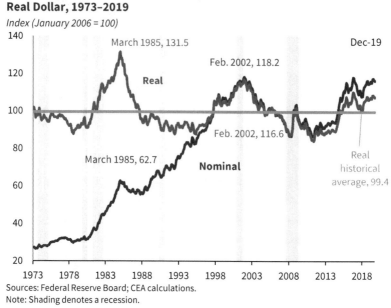

Index (January 2006 = 100)

Sources: Federal Reserve Board; CEA calculations.
Note: Shading denotes a recession.

Relative to other major advanced country currencies, the dollar edged up 0.6 percent over the same period in real terms. Curcuru (2017) finds that for every divergence of 1 percentage point in interest rates between the United States and other advanced economies, the real advanced dollar index appreciates 3.4 percent. Applying this elasticity, one finds that the interest rate differential between the United States and the other G7 countries would have predicted a *depreciation* of 2.6 percent in the advanced dollar.[11] As of December, the real level of the broad dollar is 7.8 percent higher than its historical average calculated from 1973 January to the present, though most of the appreciation occurred from the summer of 2014 to 2015 (figure 1-34). The real broad dollar is, however, still below the record highs of 1985 and 2002.

Although higher U.S. interest rates than in other advanced countries would, ceteris paribus, cause some dollar appreciation and reduce U.S. exports, monetary spillovers from abroad also have an offsetting positive economic effect by lowering the longer end of the Treasury yield curve. This effect could be observed in August 2019, when data in Germany and China that were weaker than expected triggered global growth concerns that caused an immediate influx of safe haven flows to the U.S. Treasury market. Market expectations of future easing actions by the European Central Bank then caused an immediate decrease in U.S. 10-year Treasury yields, contributing to the

---

[11] Collins and Truman (2019) employed the same methodology for the period July 2014–September 2019, and found that 4.1 percentage points of the 21 percent appreciation in the major dollar over this period was due to the United States / G7 interest rate differential.

inversion of the yield curve at that time. As a result, U.S. mortgage rates came down, which on the whole supported the U.S. housing market and allowed U.S. households to refinance their mortgages, unlocking more disposable income for consumption.

Domestic Headwinds

In addition to international headwinds, four other idiosyncratic domestic factors impeded U.S. growth by almost 0.3 percentage point in 2019: (1) the partial government shutdown for 25 days in January, (2) the grounding of Boeing 737 MAX jets, (3) industrial action at General Motors, and (4) the Midwest's spring flooding.[12]

Boeing. After two fatal accidents of the Boeing 737 MAX in 2018 and 2019, civil aviation authorities around the world (including the United States) grounded the aircraft. The accidents and eventual grounding caused Boeing 737 deliveries to collapse to nearly zero, and production to fall. This drop in production and deliveries lowered GDP because fewer planes were produced, and those produced were placed into inventory instead of being delivered. The CEA estimates that these effects depressed real GDP growth during the four quarters of 2019 by 0.14 percentage point.

GM strikes. In mid-September, the United Auto Workers began a work stoppage that halted production at General Motors for six weeks. The CEA estimates that the strike subtracted at most 0.08 percentage point from GDP growth in the four quarters of 2019; but the effects will be reversed by an equal amount in 2020.

Midwest flooding. Production of corn and soybeans (the Nation's most valuable crops, at about $51 billion and $39 billion in 2018, respectively) fell in 2019 by 4.4 percent and 19.8 percent. Spring flooding—due to excessive rain and snowmelt, which damaged production in the Upper Midwest—may be partly responsible for the decline in production. We estimate that these declines reduced the value of corn and soybean crops (the major crops throughout the Midwest) by $10 billion in 2019, or 0.04 percent of GDP.

Conclusion

This chapter has shown that despite strong headwinds from the global economy and expectations of growth moderating as the current expansion matures, the U.S. economy continued expanding at a healthy pace in the past year. During 2019, consumer spending continued to grow strongly, while the labor share of income continued to increase. The labor market tightened further, even after strong gains in the previous two years. Wages rose faster

---

[12] The partial government shutdown affected the 2019 level of real GDP, as well as the 2019 annual average-to-annual average growth rate, but not the 2019 fourth quarter–to–fourth quarter growth rate.

than inflation, which ultimately boosted real middle-class incomes. After years of decline, the stabilization of labor force participation, due to increased prime-age participation, combined with capital deepening to boost potential long-term output.

The tepid recovery from the Great Recession in the years before the Trump Administration prompted economic forecasters to project pessimistic growth into the future, reflecting a widespread belief that the U.S. economy is in the midst of a period of secular stagnation. But the first three years of the current Administration have demonstrated that stagnation is not inevitable. And the Administration's structural reforms—including lower taxes, deregulation, and pro-innovation energy policies—can overcome secular stagnation and have set the stage for continued economic strength.

As the current record expansion matures beyond the 42nd quarter, some worry that the expansion will "die of old age." But academic evidence indicates that expansions do not end simply because of their length. Old age does not kill expansions, though bad policies and exogenous shocks can and do lead to recessions. The United States' historically strong labor market, the potential for further deregulation, and the capital deepening that is having a positive impact on productivity suggest that there is still substantial room to grow in the present U.S. expansion.

Chapter 2

Economic Growth Benefits Historically Disadvantaged Americans

The U.S. labor market is the strongest it has been in the last half century, as President Trump's pro-growth economic policies continue boosting labor demand and lowering structural barriers to entering the labor market. Economic data show that recent labor market gains disproportionately benefit Americans who were previously left behind. These groups are becoming more and more self-reliant through their economic activity, rather than remaining inactive in the labor market to qualify for means-tested government programs.

Under the Trump Administration, and for the first time on record, there are more job openings than unemployed people. In 2019, the U.S. unemployment rate has reached 3.5 percent, the lowest rate in five decades. Falling unemployment has reduced the share of the population on unemployment insurance to the lowest level since recording started in 1967. Importantly, the African American unemployment rate has hit the lowest level on record, and series lows have also been achieved for Asians, Hispanics, American Indians or Alaskan Natives, veterans, those without a high school degree, and persons with disabilities, among others.

Since the 2016 election, the economy has added more than 7 million jobs, far exceeding the 1.9 million predicted by the Congressional Budget Office in its final preelection forecast. These gains have brought people from the sidelines into employment. In parts of 2019, nearly three quarters of people entering employment came from out of the labor force—the highest rate on record. And the prime-age labor force is growing, reversing losses under the prior administration's expansion period. This evidence suggests that the labor market's revival over the past three years is not a continuation of past trends but instead is the result of President Trump's pro-growth policies.

The Trump Administration's policies are not only leading to more jobs but also to higher pay. While nominal wage growth for all private-sector workers has been at or above 3 percent for all but one month in 2019, wage growth for many historically disadvantaged groups is now higher than wage growth for more advantaged groups, as is the case for lower-income workers compared with higher-income ones, for workers compared with managers, and for African Americans compared with whites. These income gains mark a fundamental change relative to those opposite trends observed over the expansion before President Trump's inauguration, contributing to reduced income inequality.

Employment and earnings gains continue pulling people out of poverty and off of means-tested welfare programs. The number of people living in poverty decreased by 1.4 million from 2017 to 2018, and the poverty rates for blacks and Hispanics reached record lows. Food insecurity has fallen, and there are nearly 7 million fewer people participating in the Supplemental Nutrition Assistance Program (SNAP, formerly known as the Food Stamp Program) than at the time of the 2016 election. The caseload for Temporary Assistance for Needy Families (TANF) has fallen by almost 700,000 individuals, and the number of individuals on Social Security Disability Insurance has fallen by almost 380,000 since the 2016 election. Similarly, due primarily to rising incomes, Medicaid rolls are decreasing.

Today's strong labor market helps all Americans, but the largest benefits are going to people who were previously left behind during the economic recovery. Additional deregulatory actions targeted at remaining barriers in the labor market will allow the economy to add to its record-length expansion and lead to further employment and income gains, particularly for these historically disadvantaged groups.

T
he U.S. labor market is the strongest it has been in the last half century, as shown by economic data across various metrics. President Trump's pro-growth economic policies are contributing to this strength. While the economic gains realized over the past three years are widespread, this chapter shows that they are disproportionately benefiting Americans who were previously left behind during the recovery. The Administration's policies increase labor demand and decrease structural barriers to entering labor markets. This approach has contributed to reduced inequality through an economic boom that is greatly benefiting historically disadvantaged groups. These groups are becoming more and more self-reliant through economic activity rather than by remaining economically inactive to qualify for means-tested government programs.

Today's tighter labor market and the resulting wage growth are predictable outcomes of the Administration's historic tax cuts and deregulatory actions, which have delivered continued economic expansion. Eliminating unnecessary regulatory burdens and lowering taxes spur labor demand and incentivize firms to make productivity-enhancing investments (see chapter 3). As a result, worker productivity, wages, and employment all increase.

Ultimately, these policies help boost the job market's continued expansion, as increased demand with unchanged supply raises quantity (employment) and prices (wages) in labor markets.[1] The United States has experienced 111 consecutive months of positive job growth, continuing the longest positive job growth streak on record. The civilian unemployment rate, which in December 2019 remained at its 50-year low of 3.5 percent, has been at or below 4 percent for 22 consecutive months. Today's historically low level of unemployment makes rapid job creation more difficult as it becomes harder for companies to find available workers. Since the Bureau of Labor Statistics (BLS) started collecting data on job openings in 2000, the number of unemployed people exceeded the number of recorded available jobs until March 2018. Since then, there have been more job openings than unemployed people for a remarkable 20 consecutive months.

In total, since the 2016 election, the economy has added 7 million jobs, more than the population of Massachusetts.[2] These job gains are impressive, given that the economic recovery since the Great Recession became the longest in United States history during the summer of 2019. Figure 2-1 shows the total number of jobs by quarter. Before the 2016 election, the Congressional Budget Office (CBO) expected job growth to slow and the total number of jobs to level off, as workers who were out of the labor force were largely expected to remain on the sidelines (CBO 2016). Instead, job growth under President Trump

---

[1] Tax cuts also increase the supply of labor, as after-tax wages increase for a given pretax wage. Because supply and demand both increase, quantity will increase and the effect on price (wage) will depend on the relative magnitude of the increases.

[2] The most recent jobs data are preliminary and are subject to revision.

Figure 2-1. Total Jobs versus Preelection Forecast, 2012–19

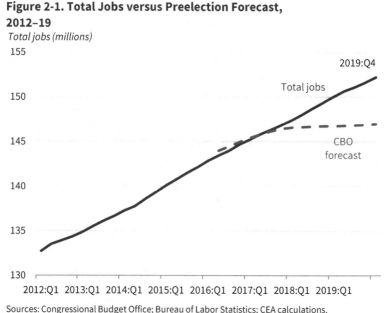

Total jobs (millions)

Sources: Congressional Budget Office; Bureau of Labor Statistics; CEA calculations.
Note: CBO = Congressional Budget Office. CBO forecast is from August 2016.

has far exceeded the 1.9 million predicted by this point in the recovery by the CBO in its final preelection forecast. Americans coming from the sidelines to get jobs have led to employment growth at a similar rate as before the election, even as the unemployment rate has fallen to historic lows. Similarly, before the election, the CBO and the Federal Reserve forecasted that the unemployment rate, which had been declining steadily for many years, would level off at about 4.5 percent, as seen in figure 2-2 (FOMC 2016).

As it becomes more difficult for employers to find available workers, employers will offer higher pay or expand the pool of workers whom they consider. Annual nominal wage growth reached 3 percent in 2019 for the first time since the Great Recession, and nominal wage growth has been at or above 3 percent for all but one month in 2019. Importantly, wage growth for many disadvantaged groups is now higher than wage growth for more advantaged groups. And the lowest wage earners have seen the fastest nominal wage growth (10.6 percent) of any income group since the Tax Cuts and Jobs Act was signed into law. Beyond this pay increase for low-income workers, from the start of the current expansion to December 2016, average wage growth for workers lagged that for managers, and that for African Americans lagged that for white Americans. Since President Trump took office, each of these trends has been reversed, contributing to reduced income inequality. When measured as the share of income held by the top 20 percent, income inequality fell in 2018 by the largest amount in over a decade. The Gini coefficient, an overall measure of inequality in the population, also fell in 2018 (U.S. Census 2019).

Figure 2-2. Unemployment Rate versus Preelection Forecasts, 2011–19

Unemployment rate (percent)

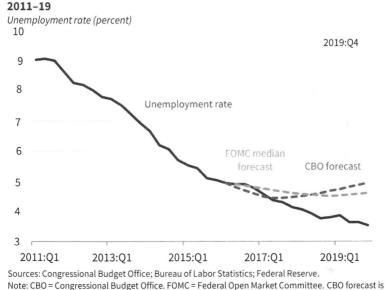

Sources: Congressional Budget Office; Bureau of Labor Statistics; Federal Reserve.
Note: CBO = Congressional Budget Office. FOMC = Federal Open Market Committee. CBO forecast is from August 2016. FOMC forecast is from September 2016.

These employment and income gains have brought people from the sidelines into employment. In the fourth quarter of 2019, 74.2 percent of workers entering employment came from out of the labor force rather than from unemployment, which is the highest share since the series began in 1990.[3] Additionally, the prime-age labor force is growing, reversing losses under the prior administration's expansion period until the 2016 election. Under the prior administration's expansion period, the prime-age labor force shrank by roughly 1.6 million; in contrast, under the current Administration it has expanded by 2.3 million people so far. Importantly, a strong market for jobs creates work opportunities for those with less education or training, prior criminal convictions, or a disability.

This movement from the sidelines into the labor market also pulls people out of poverty and off of means-tested welfare programs, increasing their self-reliance through economic activity while decreasing their reliance on government programs that incentivize people to limit their hours or stop working to qualify. The number of people living in poverty decreased by 1.4 million from 2017 to 2018, and the poverty rates for blacks and Hispanics reached record lows. Furthermore, the number of working-age adults without health insurance who are below the Federal poverty line fell by 359,000 between 2016 and 2018. Because of the strong job market and sustained wage gains, food insecurity has fallen and, as of August 2019, there are nearly 7 million fewer

---

[3] This CEA calculation is from labor force transition data reported by the BLS.

people participating in the Supplemental Nutrition Assistance Program (SNAP, formerly known as the Food Stamp Program) than at the time of the 2016 election. The caseload for Temporary Assistance for Needy Families (TANF) has fallen by almost 700,000 individuals, and the number of individuals on Social Security Disability Insurance has fallen by almost 380,000 since the 2016 election. Similarly, Medicaid rolls are decreasing even as the U.S. population increases. Our analysis shows that this decrease is predominantly due to a reduction in the number of Medicaid-eligible individuals because of income growth, not eligibility restrictions.

In addition to having encouraged these unprecedented gains for disadvantaged groups, the Trump Administration is launching several new initiatives to increase economic opportunity by removing barriers to work. One of the most significant barriers is that available workers do not always have the skills and training required to fill available jobs. Additionally, available workers may not be located near available jobs. The increase in prevalence in occupational licensing has made it more difficult for individuals to find and take jobs in different States. Individuals' labor market participation can also be limited by a struggling local economy, childcare responsibilities, opioid addiction, and prior criminal convictions. The Administration is addressing these barriers with initiatives like the National Council for the American Worker, the Pledge to America's Workers, the Initiative to Stop Opioid Abuse, and the Second Chance Hiring Initiative.

The Trump Administration continues its relentless focus on reducing poverty by expanding self-sufficiency. The CEA (2019a) accounted for the value of government subsidies for goods (in-kind transfers) like healthcare, food, and housing, and we found that—contrary to claims from the policy community and the media—poverty has decreased dramatically since the War on Poverty began in the 1960s. However, the war was largely "won" through increasing government dependency (demand side) rather than through promoting self-sufficiency (supply side), meaning that there is still more progress to be made. This is where Opportunity Zones come in.

Opportunity Zones, which were created by the 2017 Tax Cuts and Jobs Act, are best understood as supply-side economic policies. These zones entail tax cuts, analogous to the corporate tax cut, designed to spur investment and drive up labor demand, and thus directly help the disadvantaged achieve self-sufficiency through increased economic activity. Supply-side tax cuts are the opposite of the traditional, failed approach to fighting poverty, which entails higher taxes to fund demand-side subsidies for healthcare, food, and other goods or services that incentivize people to limit their hours or stop working to qualify.

Although the economic benefits of the Trump Administration's policies are widespread, this chapter's main finding is that a stronger U.S. economy over the past three years has especially helped racial and ethnic minorities, less-educated individuals, people living in poverty, and those who had been out of the labor force. As the Administration continues to implement a pro-growth agenda, the benefits to these historically disadvantaged groups are likely to persist and intensify.

This chapter is organized in two main sections. In the first, we outline how today's strong labor market is benefiting lower-income individuals and individuals in historically disadvantaged groups. In the second section, we discuss barriers that continue keeping some individuals from benefiting from a strong national economy, along with the actions the Administration is taking to address these barriers and add to historically disadvantaged groups' employment and income gains.[4]

Shared Prosperity from Strong Economic Growth

The Trump Administration's tax and deregulatory policies increase labor demand of firms. The continued economic expansion enabled by these policies has predictably been accompanied by a very strong labor market. As additional workers became more difficult to find, firms started considering a broader pool of potential workers. Low unemployment and strong wage growth have drawn workers into the labor force from the sidelines, increasing the quantity of labor supplied.

The Current State of the Labor Market

In December 2019, the national unemployment rate was 3.5 percent—matching the lowest rate in 50 years.[5] The unemployment rate has been at or below 4 percent for 22 consecutive months. This consistently low unemployment rate is an indication of a relatively tight labor market.

Just as a low unemployment rate signals a strong labor market, a high number of job openings—as measured by the BLS's Job Opening and Labor Turnover Survey (JOLTS)—indicates strong labor demand. Compared with the time of the 2016 election, there were over 1.4 million more job openings in October 2019. In total, there were 7.3 million job openings in October—1.4 million more than the number of unemployed persons. October was the 20th consecutive month in which there were more job openings than unemployed. Figure 2-3 shows the number of unemployed workers and job openings over time. Since the JOLTS data began being collected by the BLS in 2000, the current period beginning under the Trump Administration is the first time when there have been more job openings than unemployed people.

---

[4] A version of this chapter was previously released as "The Impact of the Trump Labor Market on Historically Disadvantaged Americans" (CEA 2019b).

[5] Unemployment statistics are produced by the BLS and are calculated from data collected in the monthly Current Population Survey (CPS). Unless otherwise stated, the data are seasonally adjusted.

Figure 2-3. Number of Unemployed People versus Number of Job Openings, 2001–19

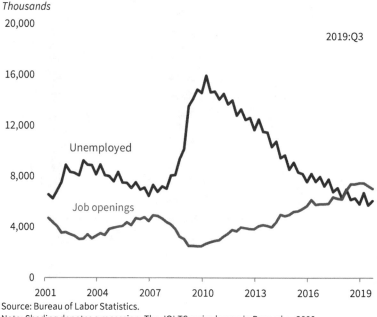

Thousands

Source: Bureau of Labor Statistics.
Note: Shading denotes a recession. The JOLTS series began in December 2000.

As a result of a more robust U.S. economy, many groups that historically have had a tougher time getting ahead are now gaining ground. Under the Trump Administration, many of these groups have reached notable lows in their unemployment rates (see table 2-1). In August 2019, the unemployment rate for African Americans fell to 5.4 percent—the lowest rate on record since the series began in 1972. Meanwhile, the unemployment rate for African American women also reached its series low in August 2019. For Hispanics, the September 2019 unemployment rate achieved its series low of 3.9 percent (the series began in 1973). In 2019 the unemployment rate for American Indians or Alaska Natives fell to 6.1 percent—the lowest rate since the series began in 2000. Figure 2-4 shows the unemployment rates for different racial and ethnic groups compared with their prerecession lows. The decline in unemployment after the recession and before the start of the Trump Administration was largely the result of a recovery from the losses during the recession. During the last two years, the black and Hispanic unemployment rates have fallen below their prerecession lows and Asian unemployment has fallen to its prerecession low.

Among various levels of educational attainment, those with less education typically face tougher labor market prospects. The Administration's tax and regulatory policies, however, are stimulating labor demand and are helping to provide labor market opportunities for those with less education and

Table 2-1. Unemployment Rates by Demographic Group

Characteristic	December 2019 (percent)	Series low (percent)	Low of the Trump Administration (date)	The Trump low is lowest since
Education				
Less than high school	5.2	4.8 (Sept. 2019)	4.8 (Sept. 2019)	Series began (Jan. 1992)
High school diploma	3.7	3.2 (Nov. 1999)	3.4 (April 2019)	April 2000
Some college	2.7	2.4 (Oct. 2000)	2.7 (Dec. 2019)	Nov. 2000
Bachelor's or higher	1.9	1.5 (Dec. 2000)	1.9 (Dec. 2019)	Mar. 2007
Race and ethnicity				
African American	5.9	5.4 (Aug. 2019)	5.4 (Aug. 2019)	Series began (Jan. 1972)
Hispanic	4.2	3.9 (Sept. 2019)	3.9 (Sept. 2019)	Series began (Mar. 1973)
White	3.2	3.0 (May 1969)	3.1 (April 2019)	May 1969
Asian	2.5	2.1 (June 2019)	2.1 (June 2019)	Series began (Jan. 2003)
Age and gender				
Adult women (age 20+)	3.2	2.4 (May 1953)	3.1 (Sept. 2019)	Aug. 1953
Adult men (age 20+)	3.1	1.9 (Mar. 1969)	3.1 (Dec. 2019)	Oct. 1973
Teenagers (age 16–19)	12.6	6.4 (May 1953)	12.0 (Nov. 2019)	Dec. 1969

Sources: Bureau of Labor Statistics, Current Population Survey; CEA calculations.
Note: The series for "high school diploma," "some college," and "bachelor's or higher" began in 1992. The series for "white" began in 1954. The series for "adult women," "adult men," and "teenagers" began in 1948.

Figure 2-4. Unemployment Rate by Race, 2003–19

Unemployment rate (percent)

Source: Bureau of Labor Statistics.
Note: Dotted lines denote the previous low achieved over the prior expansion. Shading denotes a recession.

Figure 2-5. Multiple Jobholders as a Percentage of All Employed, 1994–2019

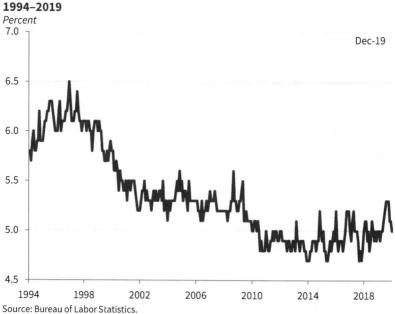

Source: Bureau of Labor Statistics.

training. In September 2019, the unemployment rate for individuals without a high school degree fell to 4.8 percent, achieving a series low (the series began in 1992). Since the President's election, the unemployment rate for those without a high school degree has fallen at a faster rate than the rate for those with a bachelor's degree or higher. The gap between the two rates reached a series low under the Trump Administration. For people with a high school degree but not a college education, the unemployment rate fell to 3.4 percent in April 2019, the lowest it has been in over 18 years. And for individuals with some college experience but no bachelor's degree, the rate fell to 2.7 percent in December 2019, the lowest since 2001.

Persons with disabilities can have a harder time finding work, as can veterans. However, President Trump's policies are translating into economic gains for these populations as well. In September 2019, the unemployment rate for persons with a disability dropped to 6.1 percent, the lowest it has been since the series began in 2008.[6] In April 2019, the unemployment rate for American veterans fell to 2.3 percent, matching the series low previously achieved in 2000.[7]

---

[6] The unemployment rate by disability status is not seasonally adjusted.
[7] The unemployment rate for veterans is not seasonally adjusted.

Working multiple jobs can be a negative labor market indicator if individuals must work multiple part time jobs due to the lack of available full time work. However, having multiple jobs is not necessarily a negative economic indicator as the opportunities to supplement one's main source of income may be greater during expansions. The share of people with multiple jobs has been around 5 percent since the end of the Great Recession (figure 2-5). It reached a high of 6.5 percent in 1996 and has been decreasing since that year. The data does not exhibit a strong cyclical trend, as the share of people working multiple jobs has declined during the last two recessions. It has declined by 0.2 percentage point since the election; but the average under the Trump Administration has been 5 percent, and the annual average has been between 4.9 and 5.1 percent since 2010.

Demographic Change and Labor Force Statistics

In this subsection, we construct labor force participation rates that control for changing demographics over time. The demographically adjusted participation rates are near prerecession levels for Hispanics and have exceeded prerecession levels for blacks. The adjusted participation rates show that due to the strong labor market in recent years, many workers are coming from the sidelines and are reentering the labor force.

Various measures of the labor market such as job growth and the unemployment rate indicate a strong labor market, but the labor force participation rate has not recovered to its prerecession level. Before the recession, in December 2007, the participation rate was 66.0 percent. The participation rate fell during the recession and continued to fall during the recovery, reaching a low of 62.4 percent in September 2015, before rebounding slightly to its current level of 63.2 percent (in December 2019). In past recoveries, workers reentering the labor force due to the stronger economy caused the participation rate to increase. However, comparing participation rates over time can be complicated by demographic changes. To get a clearer picture of the labor market, we construct demographically adjusted participation rates by race and ethnicity, using 2007 as the reference period.[8]

Adjusting the labor force participation rate for changing demographics is necessary because participation varies predictably over a person's lifetime. The overall participation rate will depend on participation at each age and on the share of people in each age group. For example, as the overall population ages, a larger share of people are in the older age groups, where participation is lower due to retirement. The aging of the population therefore will likely cause a decrease in the participation rate, even if participation at each age is unchanged. The baby boom generation, which is currently leaving the labor force through retirement, is a relatively large generation. Even though workers

---

[8] The choice of reference year is arbitrary; 2007 is chosen to facilitate comparison between current rates and precrisis rates.

Figure 2-6. Demographically Adjusted Labor Force Participation for African Americans, 1973–2018

Labor force participation rate (percent)

Sources: Bureau of Labor Statistics; CEA calculations.

are coming from the sidelines and reentering the labor force due to the strong labor market, the positive effect on the participation rate is largely offset by retiring baby boomers, even as some boomers are working longer.

Narrower measures such as the prime-age labor force participation rate (i.e., those age 25–54 years) offer one alternative to mitigate the effects of demographic changes on labor market measures across time. But this is only a partial solution, because there is still heterogeneity among groups of prime-age individuals, so prime-age participation is still subject to demographic shifts among the different age groups within the larger prime-age category. There can also be important participation trends among both older and younger workers that will affect the overall participation rate. Demographically adjusted participation rates are a single measure of participation that separates changes in participation from changes in demographics by holding demographics constant (Szafran 2002). To find this adjusted rate, the age and sex distribution of the population is first held fixed at a given reference period. The demographically adjusted participation rate for each period is constructed by using that period's age- and gender-specific participation rates and the population of the reference period.[9]

Keeping in mind that the demographically adjusted labor force participation rate holds the age, race, and sex population distribution constant at 2007 levels, figure 2-6 presents the demographically adjusted labor force

---

[9] We use the following age groups: 16–19, 20–24, 25–34, 35–44, 45–54, 55–64, and 65 and over.

Figure 2-7. Demographically Adjusted Labor Force Participation Rate for Hispanics, 1994–2018

Labor force participation rate (percent)

Demographically adjusted labor force participation rate

Unadjusted labor force participation rate

Sources: Bureau of Labor Statistics; CEA calculations.

participation rate for blacks. The data are aggregated to the annual level due to the relatively small sample size at the level of race by gender by age group.[10] The overall participation rate for blacks has fallen since the global financial crisis of 2007–8, although the decline during the recession was the continuation of a longer-term, downward trend starting in the late 1990s. The adjusted participation rate shows that much of this decline can be explained by demographic changes. The participation rate for blacks was higher in 2018 than it was before the Great Recession, and it is slightly below the peak in 2000 once the effects of an aging population are removed. For comparison, the adjusted participation rate for the entire population age 16 and above fell from 66 percent in 2007 to a low of 64.5 percent in 2015, before recovering to 65.9 percent in 2019.

Adjusting for demographic change has a large impact on the labor force participation rate for Hispanics in recent years. Figure 2-7 shows the demographically adjusted participation rate for Hispanics. From 1994 to the start of the Great Recession, demographic changes had a minimal effect on the overall participation rate for this group, as there tends to be little difference between the adjusted and unadjusted rates. However, the adjusted and unadjusted participation rates have diverged since the Great Recession. The unadjusted rate

---

[10] The BLS does not produce seasonally adjusted monthly or quarterly labor force participation data by race for the finer-grained age groups needed to produce the demographically adjusted participation rate.

Figure 2-8. Nominal Weekly Wage Growth among All Adult Full-Time Wage and Salary Workers, 2010–19

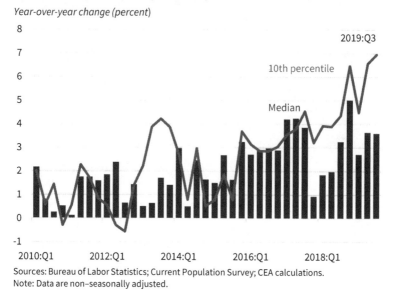

Year-over-year change (percent)

Sources: Bureau of Labor Statistics; Current Population Survey; CEA calculations.
Note: Data are non–seasonally adjusted.

initially fell by a relatively large amount and has only increased slightly during the recovery. The demographically adjusted rate has fully recovered and now exceeds its preelection level.

Wage and Income Growth

Over the past three years, the higher demand for labor and the tighter job market have been leading to larger wage gains, especially for the lowest-income workers. In the third quarter of 2019, the 12-month change in nominal weekly wages for the 10th percentile of full-time workers was up 7.0 percent (see figure 2-8).[11] This is higher than the year-over-year change in the nominal weekly wage for the median worker (3.6 percent), and well above inflation. Furthermore, in 2019:Q3, median weekly wages for full-time workers without a high school degree were up 9.0 percent over the year.

Figure 2-9 shows that, as of November 2019, nominal average hourly earnings of production and nonsupervisory workers grew at 3.4 percent year over year.[12] Inflation, as measured by the Personal Consumption Expenditures (PCE) Price Index, remains modest, at 1.5 percent year over year in November.[13] Therefore, the real wages of private sector production and nonsupervisory workers increased by 1.9 percent during the year ending in November 2019.

---

[11] Weekly earnings data are released by the BLS and are from the CPS.

[12] Average hourly earnings are measured by the BLS in the Current Employment Statistics.

[13] December inflation data are not yet available at the time of writing.

Figure 2-9. Average Hourly Earnings for Production and Nonsupervisory Workers and the Personal Consumption Expenditures Price Index, 2007–19

Year-over-year change (percent)

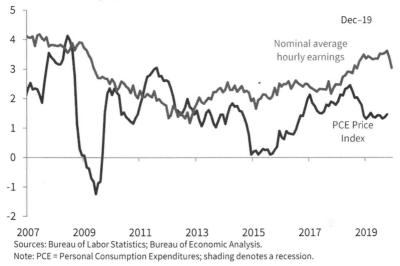

Sources: Bureau of Labor Statistics; Bureau of Economic Analysis.
Note: PCE = Personal Consumption Expenditures; shading denotes a recession.

Minorities are experiencing some of the fastest increases in pay. In 2019:Q3, African Americans saw their weekly earnings grow by 6.0 percent over the year, while Hispanics' weekly earnings grew by 4.2 percent. For comparison, the 12-month change in weekly earnings for all Americans rose by 3.6 percent. In addition to faster earnings growth, lower-income households are seeing the largest benefits from deregulatory actions that lower the costs of goods and services. Box 2-1 shows an example of the beneficial impact of the Administration's deregulatory agenda on lower-income households.

Poverty and Inequality

The gains in employment and wages for those who had previously been left behind are lifting many out of poverty. In September 2019, the Census Bureau released its official measures of the economic well-being of Americans for 2018 using data from the Annual Social and Economic Supplement (ASEC) to the Current Population Survey (CPS). While Americans across the board generally saw improvements, the data show that there were larger gains among historically disadvantaged groups.

In 2018, the official poverty rate fell by 0.5 percentage point, to 11.8 percent, the lowest level since 2001, lifting 1.4 million Americans out of poverty. This decline follows a decline of 0.4 percentage point in 2017, meaning that the U.S. poverty rate fell almost a full percentage point over the first two years of the Trump Administration. In the CPS-ASEC, income is defined as

Box 2-1. Who Bears the Burden of Regulatory Costs?

Well-designed regulations promote important social purposes, but at a cost. The question of who bears the burden of regulatory costs is like the question of who bears the burden of the taxes needed to fund government spending programs. The Federal income tax has a progressive structure; thus, compared with lower-income households, higher-income households bear a greater share of the burden of taxation. Unfortunately, however, lower-income households can bear a disproportionate share of the burden of regulatory costs. We estimate that the cost savings from deregulatory actions in two sectors—Internet access and prescription drugs (see figure 2-i)—especially helped lower-income households. These are two of the regulations whose benefits were estimated by the CEA (2019c). The lower burden of regulatory costs reinforces the gains in employment and wages from today's strong labor market.

Figure 2-i. Consumer Savings on Prescription Drugs and Internet Access by Household Income Quintile

Share of income (percent)

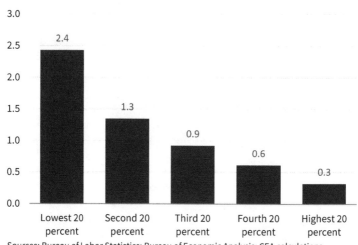

Sources: Bureau of Labor Statistics; Bureau of Economic Analysis; CEA calculations.
Note: Values represent the CEA's estimates of consumers' savings as a share of their income, which applied the Consumer Expenditure Survey's quintile and expenditure data to national income data.

Costly regulations hurt lower-income households because they spend a larger share of their budgets on goods and services produced by regulated sectors of the economy. For example, in data from the 2018 Consumer Expenditure Survey, the poorest fifth of households spend 2.7 percent of their incomes out-of-pocket on prescription drugs, while the richest fifth of households spend only 0.3 percent. The poorest fifth of households also spend a higher percentage of their incomes on Internet access. As a result, the costs savings from deregulatory actions in these two sectors represent 2.4 percent of the income for the poorest fifth of households, compared with 0.3 percent for the richest fifth.

Many regulations also hurt lower-income households because they impose standards that tend to increase the price of those goods that are disproportionately purchased by lower-income households. For example, after controlling for other differences, Levinson (2019) finds that higher-income households purchase more fuel-efficient cars. As a result, he estimates that the corporate average fuel economy (CAFE) standards are regressive and disproportionately burden lower-income households. The CAFE standards matter less to higher-income households because they prefer to purchase more fuel-efficient cars anyway. The 20 notable actions analyzed by the CEA (2019c) include other deregulations of standards that restricted the ability of lower-income households to choose the products that best suited their preferences and budgets.

money income before taxes. It includes cash assistance but not the value of in-kind benefits for government assistance programs or refundable tax credits targeted at low-income working families. Including the value of these benefits raises the total resources available to households at the bottom of the income distribution. We conduct an analysis later in this chapter that examines the effect of using after-tax and after-transfer income (including the value of in-kind transfers) on the changes in poverty during the Administration.

Disadvantaged groups experienced the largest poverty reductions in 2018. The poverty rate fell by 0.9 percentage point for black Americans and by 0.8 percentage point for Hispanic Americans, with both groups reaching historic lows (see figure 2-10). The poverty rates for black and Hispanic Americans in 2018 were never closer to the overall poverty rate in the United States. Children fared especially well in 2018, with a decrease in poverty of 1.2 percentage points for those under 18. Poverty among single mothers with children fell by 2.5 percentage points.

Although real income at the bottom of the income distribution increased and the percentage of people in poverty fell, it can also be informative to examine how these gains compare with gains elsewhere in the income distribution, which will be reflected in the changes in various measures of income inequality. Inequality fell in 2018, as the share of income held by the top 20 percent fell by the largest amount in over a decade, as did the Gini index (an overall measure of inequality in the population). In fact, households between the 20th and

Figure 2-10. Poverty Rates by Race and Ethnicity, 1966–2018

Poverty rate (percent)

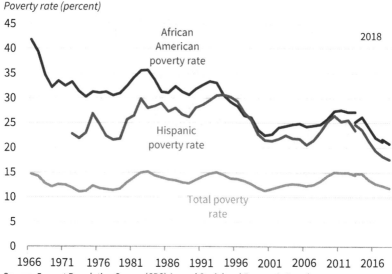

Source: Current Population Survey (CPS) Annual Social and Economic Supplement.
Note: The data for 2013 and beyond reflect the implementation of the redesigned income questions. The data for 2017 and beyond reflect the implementation of an updated CPS Annual Social and Economic Supplement processing system.

40th percentiles of the distribution experienced the largest increase in average household income among all quintiles in 2018, with a gain of 2.5 percent.[14]

Low unemployment, rising incomes, and declining poverty mean that more Americans are becoming self-sufficient. The caseload for Temporary Assistance for Needy Families (TANF) is on the decline, falling by almost 700,000 individuals since the election, as of March 2019. Meanwhile, the number of individuals on Social Security Disability Insurance (SSDI) has fallen by almost 380,000 since the 2016 election. The decline in the official poverty rate mirrors a decline of 0.7 percentage point in food insecurity in 2018.[15] Since the 2016 election, nearly 7 million Americans have moved off the SNAP rolls. These substantial declines in enrollment suggest that a growing economy may lead to positive outcomes in moving families toward self-sufficiency. While some of the enrollment decline in welfare programs could be due to administrative or policy changes designed to prevent ineligible individuals from receiving

---

[14] Data from the American Community Survey (ACS), which is a separate data source also released by the Census Bureau, showed that inequality increased from 2017 to 2018. The ACS has a much larger sample size than the CPS-ASEC, but it measures income less accurately. For this reason, the Census recommends using the CPS-ASEC for national income statistics, like inequality.

[15] U.S. Department of Agriculture, Economic Research Service, using data from the December 2018 Current Population Survey Food Security Supplement (https://www.ers.usda.gov/topics/food-nutrition-assistance/food-security-in-the-us/key-statistics-graphics.aspx).

benefits, it is possible that some otherwise-eligible individuals would be affected.[16] However, the decline in food insecurity combined with the decline in poverty suggests that the net effect of any administrative changes and the strong economy has been to reduce hardship, in turn reducing reliance on public benefits.

Health Insurance and Medicaid

Strong job growth is the key to expanding and improving access to health insurance. Employer-sponsored health insurance is by far the largest source of health insurance coverage in the United States. The employment and earnings gains that are reducing poverty are also driving a decrease in the number of people on Medicaid. Medicaid rolls are decreasing in both expansion and nonexpansion States, even though the U.S. population is increasing (see figure 2-11). Our analysis of the data indicates that the reduction in the number of people on Medicaid is due predominantly to a reduction in the number of Medicaid-eligible individuals because of income growth as opposed to eligibility restrictions.

The Census Bureau asks about health insurance coverage during the previous year in the CPS-ASEC. Individuals are classified as being uninsured if they lack coverage for the entire year. For each of the insurance types, individuals are asked if they were covered by that type of insurance at any point during the year. Comparisons of insurance coverage in recent years have been complicated by changes in the CPS-ASEC data. In 2014, the CPS-ASEC revised its questionnaire to better measure health insurance coverage. Starting with the release of the 2019 data, the Census Bureau implemented improvements in data processing to fully take advantage of the revised questionnaire. Data for 2017 and 2018 have been released with the updated data processing, so consistent comparisons can be made for health insurance coverage in 2016, 2017, and 2018 using CPS-ASEC data.[17]

Table 2-2 shows the change from 2016 to 2018 in the number of people between age 18 and 64 with different types of health insurance coverage at different levels of income in the CPS-ASEC. For all individuals, the number of uninsured increased by about 2 million and the number covered by employer provided coverage increased by about 1.4 million. Directly purchased individual coverage fell by 2.35 million people and Medicaid fell by 1.6 million people. The distribution of income relative to the Federal poverty line for the overall population of those age 18–64 shows that income relative to the poverty level

---

[16] Administrative costs of program participation can prevent eligible individuals from enrolling in public programs (Aizer 2007). Administrative changes that increase the nonmonetary cost of enrollment could lead to an increase in the number of eligible individuals choosing not to enroll.

[17] The updated files are the 2018 ASEC bridge files and the 2017 ASEC research files. Note that the updated data processing will cause the health insurance estimates for these years to differ from the results using the production files that were published by the Census Bureau in the works by Barnett and Berchick (2017) and Berchick, Hood, and Barnett (2018).

Figure 2-11. Number of Medicaid and CHIP Enrollees by Month in Expansion and Nonexpansion States, 2014–19

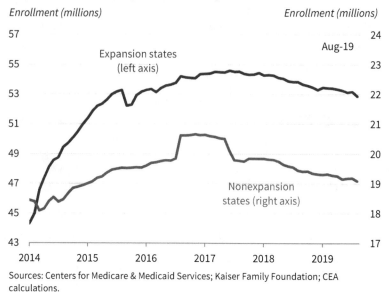

Sources: Centers for Medicare & Medicaid Services; Kaiser Family Foundation; CEA calculations.
Note: "Expansion" refers to states that have expanded Medicaid coverage following the Affordable Care Act.

increased, and the number of people living below the Federal poverty line fell by 1.6 million. Of the 2 million increase in the number of uninsured, 1.35 million have a family income 300 percent or more of the Federal poverty line. The number of people without insurance who are below the Federal poverty line fell by 359,000 between 2016 and 2018. These results indicate that from 2016 to 2018, the income gains for working age adults led to reduced participation in Medicaid.

A particularly vulnerable population is children living in poverty. Table 2-3 presents the change in the number of people under the age of 18 years with different types of insurance by family income level. The number of uninsured children increased by 340,000 between 2016 and 2018, even as the total number of children fell. Almost half the increase in the number of uninsured children is due to children in families that earn at least 300 percent of the Federal poverty line. The number of children on Medicaid (includes the Children's Health Insurance Program, CHIP) fell by 1.45 million, which is largely due to a decline in the number of children living in poverty. Some have argued that the decrease in the number of children enrolled in Medicaid and the increase in the number of uninsured is due to administrative changes that exclude eligible children and discourage otherwise-eligible children from being enrolled.[18] The small increase in the number of children below the poverty line who are

---

[18] For example, see Goodnough and Sanger-Katz (2019).

Table 2-2. Change in the Number of People Age 18–64 Years Old with Different Types of Insurance by Family Income Level, 2016–18

Income level	Population (thousands)	Uninsured (thousands)	Employer provided (thousands)	Direct purchase (thousands)	Medicaid (thousands)
All	736	1,961	1,369	–2,347	–1,613
Below FPL	–1,576	–359	–283	–182	–1,042
100–199 percent of FPL	12	608	–121	–494	–507
200–299 percent of FPL	–608	362	–460	–667	26
300 percent of FPL and over	2,066	1,350	2,233	–1,004	–91

Sources: Current Population Survey, Annual Social and Economic Supplement; CEA calculations.
Note: FPL = federal poverty line.

Table 2-3. Change in the Number of Children with Different Types of Insurance by Family Income Level, 2016–18

Income level	Population (thousands)	Uninsured (thousands)	Employer provided (thousands)	Direct purchase (thousands)	Medicaid
All	–423	340	231	–389	–1,445
Below FPL	–1,351	25	–270	–131	–1,223
100–199 percent of FPL	231	68	73	–113	–28
200–299 percent of FPL	202	85	120	–53	–154
300 percent of FPL and over	495	162	309	–94	–40

Sources: Current Population Survey, Annual Social and Economic Supplement; CEA calculations.
Note: FPL = federal poverty line.

uninsured suggests that administrative changes may be playing a small role. However, the data indicate that income gains and the reduction in the number of children living in poverty are primarily responsible for the large decline in the number of children on Medicaid.

The number of people without health insurance can increase for a number of reasons. Two factors behind the increase in the number of uninsured over the past couple of years are the elimination of the Affordable Care Act's (ACA) individual mandate penalty and a decline in the number of people who qualify for Medicaid and ACA exchange subsidies. One consequence of higher household incomes is that households will lose eligibility for public assistance programs. Because households have a choice to remain eligible by working less, revealed preference shows that the higher income more than offsets the loss of Medicaid or ACA subsidies in terms of their overall level of utility. The other reason why a lack of insurance is increasing is that some individuals thought the elimination of the mandate penalty applied to 2018, while the Tax Cuts and Jobs Act set the mandate penalty to $0 starting in 2019. The CBO estimates that about 1 million people opted out of insurance coverage in 2018 due to the mistaken belief about the timing of the elimination of the mandate penalty (CBO 2019). For individuals who were only buying insurance to avoid the mandate penalty, the elimination of the penalty makes them better off (CEA 2018b).

Full-Income Measures of Poverty

Income at the bottom of the distribution is rising, and poverty, based on the Official Poverty Measure (OPM), is falling. As people move out of poverty, their benefits under various public assistance programs are phased out. The potential to lose government benefits acts as a disincentive to participate at all in the labor market for those who are out of the labor market or to increase participation for those who are in the labor market, as the loss of benefits acts as a tax on increasing engagement with the labor market. Because of the level of wages and the available jobs, the labor market gains that are pulling people out of poverty on average more than offset the loss in government benefits in terms of total available resources.

The OPM, which is based on pretax money income, has many limitations as a measure of the total resources available to a family, which leads it to understate resources for low-income families. The Full-Income Poverty Measure (FPM) overcomes these limitations by considering a broader resource-sharing unit—the household instead of the family—and by including a comprehensive set of income sources.

The FPM estimates the share of people living in poverty using a posttax, posttransfer definition of income. It subtracts Federal income and payroll taxes and adds tax credits (e.g., the Earned Income Tax Credit and Child Tax Credit) and cash transfers. It also includes the market value of SNAP, subsidized school lunches, rental housing assistance, employer-provided health insurance, and public health insurance (Medicare and Medicaid).[19] It is important to note, however, that despite using a comprehensive set of income sources, the FPM may still understate income due to the underreporting of income sources and especially transfers in survey data (Meyer, Mok, and Sullivan 2015). For more details on the FPM, see Burkhauser and others (2019) and chapter 9 of the CEA's 2019 *Economic Report of the President*.

The OPM and FPM differ in how they define the unit that shares resources. Because there are economies of scale in consumption, the cost per person of achieving a given standard of living falls as the number of people in the unit increases. The FPM treats the household as the resource-sharing unit and adjusts the thresholds proportionally based on the square root of the number of people in the household. In contrast, the OPM restricts the sharing unit to those in the same household who have family ties. By using the household as the resource-sharing unit (which is standard in studies of income distribution), the FPM reflects the increasing rates of cohabitation among non–family members in the United States.

Figure 2-12 shows the change in the poverty rate under the OPM from 2016 to 2018 compared with poverty measures that incorporate progressively broader measures of income. All measures are anchored to equal the official

---

[19] We calculate the market value of public health insurance based on the cost of its provision, and it is adjusted for risk based on age, disability status, and State of residence (for additional details, see Elwell, Corinth, and Burkhauser 2019). The market value of employer-provided health insurance is included as well, and is imputed for 2018 because employer contributions are no longer reported in the CPS-ASEC. The CBO has used a similar method for valuing health insurance since 2013 in its reports on the distribution of income.

Figure 2-12. Change in the Official Poverty Measure versus Other Poverty Measures, 2016 and 2018

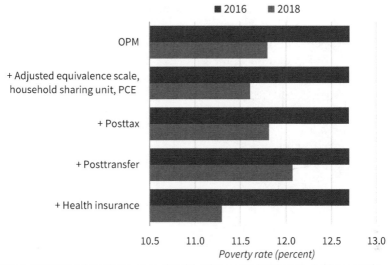

Sources: Current Population Survey, Annual Social and Economic Supplement; Burkhauser et al. (2019); CEA calculations.
Note: OPM = Official Poverty Measure. PCE = Personal Consumption Expenditures.

poverty rate in 2016 of 12.7 percent. The official poverty rate fell by 0.9 percentage point from 2016 to 2018. Using the adjusted equivalence scale, making the sharing unit the household, and using the PCE as the preferred measure of inflation instead of the Consumer Price Index for All Urban Consumers (called the CPI-U) caused the poverty rate to fall by 1.1 percentage points from 2016 to 2018. Moving to posttax and posttransfer income causes the reduction in poverty to be smaller. This reflects the fact that as individuals gain labor income (which is included in the OPM poverty measure), they receive less in tax credits and transfer income (including the value of in-kind transfers).The effective tax rate of individuals on public assistance can be very high, which can be a disincentive to increasing labor market participation. Given that the posttax and posttransfer poverty rate still fell by 0.6 percentage point, we can conclude that, overall, the increase in labor income more than offset the decrease in tax credits and transfers. Finally, including the value of employer-provided and publicly provided health insurance leads to an even larger decline in poverty, of 1.4 percentage points. This occurred even as enrollment in Medicaid fell, because the individuals losing coverage tended to be living above the poverty threshold. The decline is partially due to the value of public health insurance increasing over this period, which raised the full incomes of those who remain enrolled.

The choice of income measure also affects the measurement of income inequality. When taxes and transfers are progressive, using pretax income will tend to overstate the level of inequality. The United Nations' handbook on income statistics notes that the preferred measure of income is posttax and posttransfer (including in-kind transfers), as that allows for an evaluation of the effectiveness of redistributive policies as well as for meaningful comparisons between countries with different degrees of redistribution (Canberra Group 2011). Elwell, Corinth, and Burkhauser (2019) calculate income growth by decile from 1959 to 2016. Using a posttax and posttransfer measure of income that includes government health insurance and the value of employer-sponsored health insurance, they calculate that the Gini coefficient was 0.341 in 2016, but it was 0.502 for the same year using pretax and pretransfer market income adjusted for household size.[20] Furthermore, the posttax and posttransfer income Gini coefficient was lower in 2016 than it was in 1959.

Supporting Further Economic Gains

The strong U.S. labor market has led to historic labor market successes, including higher incomes, lower poverty, and a reduced reliance on government programs for many groups of people who had been previously left behind during the economic recovery. In this section, we discuss some of the remaining barriers that are preventing people from fully benefiting from the strong labor market. The skills of the available workers may not match those needed by employers. There can also be a geographic mismatch between workers and jobs. Childcare costs, a criminal record, or drug addiction can also prevent certain individuals from fully participating in the labor market. Continuing the current rate of job growth, with the unemployment rate at a historically low level, will likely require drawing even more workers from the sidelines. This will require targeted policies, which the Trump Administration is pursuing, to address the barriers that have prevented these individuals from entering the labor force despite a very strong labor market.

Making Sure That Workers Have the Skills to Succeed

In a previous report, "Addressing America's Reskilling Challenge" (CEA 2018a), we outlined the emerging issue of the skills gap in the ever-changing U.S. economy. The skills gap refers to the situation whereby the skills of available workers are not matching the skills needed by employers. Even in a booming economy, the lack of necessary skills can prevent some individuals from enjoying the benefits of a robust labor market. Our previous report highlighted the importance of addressing this issue, as well as the challenges facing workers and firms that seek to do so.

The CEA also examined the existing infrastructure of Federal worker training programs and reviewed the evidence regarding their effectiveness

---

[20] The Gini coefficient measures inequality on a scale from 0 to 1, where values closer to 0 indicate greater equality.

(CEA 2019d). Overall, we found mixed evidence that these programs improve labor market outcomes. The programs may have small positive effects overall, but they may be more effective for particular groups of people and at certain times in the business cycle. The large number of these programs and their heterogeneity make it difficult to reach a single, general conclusion, but rather suggest that some programs are effective whereas others are failing to live up to their hoped-for potential.

To help close the skills gap, the Trump Administration has taken action to address the limitations of these existing Federal worker training/reskilling programs. The United States needs innovative solutions for worker training given the mixed effectiveness of the existing Federal programs. Addressing this problem is necessary in response to employers' struggles to find skilled workers and to enable more people on the sidelines to benefit from the booming economy.

In this context, to develop a national strategy for workforce development, the Administration has created the National Council for the American Worker (NCAW). The NCAW is addressing issues related to improving skills-training programs, focusing on private-sector-led approaches and promoting multiple education and training pathways for individuals to enable them to achieve family-sustaining careers. The NCAW is also focusing on enhancing transparency in the outcomes of Federal and State workforce programs to allow job seekers, policymakers, and program administrators to better understand which programs are effective. Additionally, with better data, there are opportunities to learn from the successes and failures across public programs and to shift resources to the types of programs that show the greatest returns.

In the previous CEA (2019d) report, we did not determine an optimal level of government spending on employment and training programs, but we did argue that Federal efforts should shift their spending, depending on what the evidence says is the most effective. Among the current Federal worker training programs, Registered Apprenticeships have shown strong improvements in labor market outcomes, and the Administration has already increased spending on these types of "learn while you earn" models. Additionally, job search assistance provided through the Workforce Innovation and Opportunity Act is more effective in improving job outcomes than is access to training funded by this act. Job search assistance aims to reduce the time an individual is unemployed and helps individuals assess their skill sets and address other barriers that may be preventing them from entering the workforce.

Along with existing dedicated Federal programs, industry-led and non-profit-led sectoral training programs have shown significant promise in randomized studies. Sectoral training programs are industry-specific programs that seek to provide training for skilled, entry-level positions within a given industry. Currently, these programs tend to be small, focusing on a particular industry in a particular city, and are run by nonprofit groups in cooperation with State and local governments. A randomized study of three sectoral training

Box 2-2. The Federation of Advanced Manufacturing Education

Industry collaboration is one solution to the shortage of skilled workers in a given area. An example of a program built on this model is the Federation for Advanced Manufacturing Education (FAME), which is a cooperative organization of employers that seeks to build advanced manufacturing career pathways. Businesses form partnerships with local community colleges to provide a specialized degree program whereby students can work at the businesses while completing their associate degrees. FAME began as a successful partnership between Toyota and Bluegrass Community and Technical College in Lexington, Kentucky. A company sponsors a student in the Advanced Manufacturing Technician (AMT) program. The student goes to classes two days a week, and works at the sponsoring company three days a week. Once the student completes the associate degree, they have the option to continue full time at the company or to continue on to pursue a four-year engineering degree.

The first class completed the AMT program in 2010, and FAME has expanded rapidly to additional sites. There are currently FAME operations in eight States, with multiple operations in the original state, Kentucky, where FAME now coordinates directly with and receives support from the State government.

programs found that they were effective at increasing participants' earnings (Maguire et al. 2010). A follow-up study of one of these programs found that the gains persisted and may have grown over time (Roder and Elliot 2019). Other randomized studies of sectoral training programs have also shown evidence of effectiveness (Hendra et al. 2016; Fein and Hamadyk 2018).

The sector-based approach guides the Administration's proposed Industry Recognized Apprenticeship Program, which seeks to expand the apprenticeship model into sectors that have not traditionally used it. The private sector has taken note of the success of the sector-based approach and has launched similar programs to address industry-level worker shortages (see box 2-2). One option is to further scale up these existing industry-led sectoral training programs through Federal support.

Finally, it could be beneficial to incentivize the private sector to invest in training. Private firms generally have a disincentive to provide training in general human capital because trained workers can be poached by other firms before the firm has recovered the cost of training. Yet even with this risk of employee poaching, firms will provide training in general skills when the labor market is tight and new workers are difficult to find. Firms also provide general training as a fringe benefit in order to improve employee retention. Financial incentives, in the form of subsidies for private sector training, are less likely to be effective if they end up subsidizing training that the firms would have provided even in the absence of the subsidy. The difficulty is to design incentives to encourage more private sector training without subsidizing training that would otherwise occur in any case.

The Administration is working to better highlight the efforts of the private sector and to show the return on those investments to a company's bottom line as well as to a worker's increased wages and career opportunities. Through the Administration's Pledge to America's Workers, companies commit to provide a given number of training or reskilling opportunities for their current and future workforces over a five-year period. To date, more than 350 companies have pledged to provide over 14 million new opportunities for American students and workers.

Limiting Geographic Frictions in the Labor Market

Although labor market data are often presented for the Nation as a whole, the national labor market is a collection of local labor markets. Available jobs and available workers do not always match geographically. Economic theory predicts that wages will rise in areas with worker shortages and fall in areas with surpluses of workers, causing workers to move to the areas with worker shortages. Yet moving itself can be very costly, which limits the degree to which migration can alleviate local labor market imbalances; but government policies and regulations can impose additional barriers and costs to moving to a different labor market.

For over a year, monthly JOLTS data have illustrated the strong job market for people looking for work. The JOLTS data show that at a national level, there are more job openings than unemployed workers. For the first time, the BLS is producing experimental State JOLTS estimates that also allow for an analysis of job openings at the State level. These new data demonstrate that not only are there more job openings than unemployed workers nationwide, but this is true in most States as well (see figure 2-13). Comparing the number of unemployed people in each state from BLS data on State-level employment and unemployment to the number of job openings shows that, as of the second quarter of 2019, there were more job openings than people looking for work in 43 States and the District of Columbia.[21] Although State-level labor markets appear to generally be strong, some are in greater need of additional workers than others. The very best States in which to be looking for work, where there were fewer than 60 unemployed workers per 100 job openings, include many States in the Midwest and the Great Plains. The States where there are as many or more unemployed workers as job openings are Alaska, Arizona, Connecticut, Kentucky, Louisiana, Mississippi, and New Mexico.

---

[21] The experimental JOLTS data are monthly. However, due to the limited sample size, they are calculated as three-month moving averages. The analysis here uses the June 2019 experimental State JOLTS data, which correspond to the average of the months in the second quarter.

Figure 2-13. Number of Unemployed Workers per 100 Job Openings, Q2:2019

(U.S. total = 79)

59 or fewer
60 to 69
70 to 79
80 to 89
90 to 99
100 or higher

Sources: Bureau of Labor Statistics; CEA calculations.

Figure 2-14. Share of U.S. Residents Who Moved, 1948–2018

Percentage share

2018

Source: Current Population Survey.
Note: The one-year geographic mobility question was not asked between 1972 and 1975 or between 1977 and 1980, so the value is interpolated, as shown by the dotted line.

In addition to booming job markets in many States, geographic mobility has reached the lowest rate in at least 70 years, declining by 0.8 percentage point over the year, to 9.8 percent in 2018 (see figure 2-14). This decline in mobility, which could be exacerbated by government policies that limit worker mobility, is one reason for the persistence of geographic disparities in the labor market. Although not discussed in this chapter, unnecessary regulations that drive up housing costs can also limit mobility into certain metropolitan areas with strong labor markets (see chapter 8).

Reforming Occupational Licensing

Occupational licensing requirements impose an additional cost on entering a given occupation. There is a wide range of licensed occupations, including plumbers, electricians, florists, and barbers (Meyer 2017). Some occupational licensing restrictions can be justified to protect the public, but the existing requirements for many occupations in many States include jobs that pose no physical or financial risk to the public. Instead, licensing is being used as a barrier to entry into a profession to artificially inflate wages for those already in the profession. A 2018 report from the Federal Trade Commission found that the share of American workers holding an occupational license has increased five-fold, from less than 5 percent in the 1950s to 25–30 percent in 2018 (FTC 2018).

Obtaining the needed license and paying the necessary fees is a barrier that can be particularly prohibitive for those with low incomes, negatively affecting these workers by preventing them from entering professions where they would earn more even if they have the skill set to do the job. A 2015 report from the Obama Administration supports this claim, finding that the licensing landscape in the United States generates substantial costs for workers (White House 2015).

One such cost is how licensing adversely affects worker mobility. Workers in licensed occupations see the largest reductions in interstate migration rates (Johnson and Kleiner 2017). Absent State agreements to recognize outside licenses, State-by-State occupational licensing laws prevent workers from being able to provide their services across State lines, or move to another State to work in a licensed profession.

Johnson and Kleiner (2017) find that the relative interstate migration rate of workers in occupations with State-specific licensing requirements is 36 percent lower than that of workers in other occupations. There are substantial differences in relative interstate migration rates across occupations, particularly for jobs frequently held by middle- to low-income people. Teachers have one of the lowest relative interstate migration rates (about –39 percent). Electricians have a reduced relative interstate migration rate of –13 percent, while barbers and cosmetologists have such a rate of –7.5 percent. Occupational licensing can also serve as a barrier to upward economic mobility for low- to middle-income workers because it is associated with hefty administrative charges, test fees, tuition payments, and education and time requirements.

Occupational licensing also affects the employment of military spouses. Military spouses had an unemployment rate of 18 percent in 2015, more than four times greater than the U.S. overall employment rate at that time (Meyer 2017). This is partially because military spouses regularly move across State lines, and those in licensed occupations are required to renew or reissue their licenses after moving to a new State. Additionally, military spouses are more likely to be licensed than the civilian population, and they are 10 times more likely to move across State lines in a given year. (For more details, see chapter 3 of the 2018 *Economic Report to the President*.) Overall, the evidence indicates that occupational licensing limits workers' ability to enter professions or move to new areas with greater opportunity.

The regulation of occupational licenses is primarily at the State level, so there are limited options at the Federal level to reform occupational licensing, other than recognizing and supporting best practices at the State level. The Administration is currently evaluating these options. States can enter reciprocal agreements to recognize out-of-State licenses, work to standardize the licensing requirements for a given occupation across States, and expedite license applications for military spouses and others who hold an out-of-State license (FTC 2018).

Opportunity Zones: Matching People, Communities, and Capital

Historically, areas with less income grew faster than areas with more income, leading to convergence in income per capita. Since the late 20th century, however, this convergence has stopped or has possibly been reversed (Nunn, Parsons, and Shambaugh 2016). There are many explanations for this change, such as a slowdown in individuals with lower incomes moving to higher-income areas for better-paying jobs or businesses moving to lower-wage regions that have lower input costs (Ganong and Shoag 2017).

The Opportunity Zone provision of the 2017 Tax Cuts and Jobs Act seeks to counter the solidification of geographic economic inequality by bringing capital to low-income communities through tax cuts on capital gains. It contrasts with antipoverty policies that increase taxes to fund transfers to low-income households, giving them income but not necessarily spurring opportunity in their communities. Under the Opportunity Zone provision, an investor who realizes a capital gain can defer and lower taxes on the gain if he or she invests it in an Opportunity Zone Fund. The fund, in turn, invests in businesses or properties in census tracts that have been selected as Opportunity Zones. If the investor keeps his or her money in the fund for at least 10 years, they receive the additional benefit of paying no taxes on the gains earned while invested in the fund. In doing so, the provision acts like a means-tested reduction in the cost of capital, where the cost reduction only occurs in selected communities that meet the provision's eligibility requirements.

The design of the Opportunity Zone provision improves upon that of the Federal New Markets Tax Credit (New Markets), which has arguably been the most significant Federal place-based incentive in recent years. Investors must complete an extensive application to the Department of the Treasury for approval before receiving these tax credits. In the 2018 allocation round, only 34 percent of applicants received credits (CRS 2019). This highlights another limitation of New Markets—it has a cap. In 2018, the Treasury only awarded $3.5 billion in credits. In addition, recipients of credits must adhere to substantial compliance and reporting requirements (CDFI Fund 2017, 2019). The complexity of participating in New Markets and the limit on total allocations have led some to conclude that New Markets is unable to induce large-scale investment that can revitalize entire communities (Bernstein and Hassett 2015).

The Opportunity Zone incentive, in contrast, has no application process or limitation on scale (CRS 2019). Within broad guidelines, the incentive lets investors act upon their insights about where to invest, in what to invest, and how much to invest. The Opportunity Zone statute also carves out roles for State and local governments and communities. States nominated tracts to become Opportunity Zones, and the Department of the Treasury made the final designation and ensured that the tracts met the income or poverty criteria in the statute. Many areas have incorporated the incentive into their broader development initiatives. Alabama, for example, adopted a new law to align its development incentives with the Opportunity Zone incentive.

Today, there are 8,764 Opportunity Zones across all 50 States, the District of Columbia, and five U.S. possessions (CDFI Fund 2018). The zones are home to nearly 35 million Americans, and on average they have a poverty rate nearly twice as high as the average census tract.

Opportunity Zones: Evidence of Investor Interest and Activity

Early evidence indicates considerable investor interest in Opportunity Zones. The National Council of State Housing Agencies maintains an Opportunity Zone Fund Directory. As of July 2019, the directory listed 163 funds seeking to a raise a total of $43 billion (NCSHA 2019). The funds are diverse, with two-thirds having a regional focus and the rest a national focus. Most funds plan to invest in commercial development, such as multifamily residential or in hospitality, but more than half also plan to invest in economic or small business development.

Evidence from real estate markets also suggests that the Opportunity Zone incentive is getting attention from investors. Data from Real Capital Analytics, which tracks commercial real estate properties and portfolios valued at $2.5 million or more, show that year-over-year growth in development site acquisitions in zones surged by more than 25 percent late in 2018 after the Department of the Treasury had designated the zones, greatly exceeding growth in the rest of the United States. Similarly, Sage, Langen, and Van de Minne (2019), using the same data, find that a zone designation led to a 14 percent increase in the price of redevelopment properties and a 20 percent increase in the price of vacant development sites.

Sage, Langen, and Van de Minne (2019) only find appreciation effects for particular property types, and they conclude that the Opportunity Zone incentive is having limited economic spillovers in communities. Their data, however, only include very particular types of properties—commercial properties valued at less than $2.5 million. An analysis by Zillow, which uses many more properties and transactions, suggests that the zone incentive is bringing a broader economic stimulus. The year-over-year change in the average sales price for properties in zones reached over 20 percent in late 2018, compared with about 10 percent in tracts that met the zone eligibility criteria but that were not selected (Casey 2019). The greater appreciation in zones suggests that buyers expect zone tracts to become more economically-vibrant in years to come.

Expanding Opportunities for Ex-Offenders

Another barrier to employment is a prior criminal conviction, and not only because incarceration lowers the available labor force. Having a job can help someone just released from prison reenter society, and it reduces the likelihood of recidivism. There is evidence that strong job growth, particularly in manufacturing and construction, can reduce recidivism (Schnepel 2016). Guo, Seshadri, and Taber (2019) estimate that an increase of 0.01 percent in county-level construction employment decreases the county's working age population's recidivism rate by 1 percent.

In December 2018, President Trump signed into law the historic First Step Act, which is aimed at establishing a fairer justice system for all, reducing recidivism, and making communities across America safer. Since this reform was signed into law, 90 percent of the individuals who have had their sentences reduced have been African American.

Also since then, the Trump Administration has taken steps to provide individuals leaving prison with the opportunities and resources needed to obtain employment. This Second Chance hiring initiative is an effort coordinated across the Federal government, States, the private sector, and the nonprofit sector. Nonprofits serve a crucial role in assisting former prisoners to obtain transitional housing, counseling, and education. Across the Federal government, the Department of Justice and Bureau of Prisons have launched the Ready to Work Initiative, which links employers to former prisoners; the Department of Education is expanding an initiative that will help people in prison receive Pell Grants; the Department of Labor has issued grants to support comprehensive reentry programs that promote work as well as grants to expand fidelity bonds to employers to assist formerly incarcerated individuals with job placement; and the Office of Personnel Management has made the

Federal government's job posting website accessible to people serving in and released from Federal prisons.

Americans are reaping the benefits of the First Step Act. Data in this area are scarce, but a number of positive anecdotes have been reported in the news. For instance, Troy Powell, a former prisoner and guest at the White House, had served 16 years in prison. When he was released in February 2019 under the First Step Act, he found a job at a lumber company in less than 10 days. A Cleveland native, Andre Badley, was released from a Federal prison in February 2019, and within three months was hired as a driver for Amazon. The number of such success stories will continue to grow as more inmates who have served their time and pose no danger to society are released and as more is done to prepare them for employment and a second chance.

The Administration's initiatives in this area, like the First Step Act and Second Chance hiring, can help assist former prisoners seeking to reenter society as productive members of the community, meet the needs of businesses that may be struggling to find workers, and reduce crime across American communities.

Supporting Working Families

Since the start of the Trump Administration, supporting working families has been a top priority. In December 2017, the President signed into law the Tax Cuts and Jobs Act, which increased the reward for working by doubling the Child Tax Credit and increasing its refundability. The President signed into law the largest-ever increase in funding for the Child Care and Development Block Grants—expanding access to high-quality childcare for nearly 800,000 families across the country. In addition, President Trump was the first president to include nationwide paid parental leave in his annual budget.

The President has continued to support pro-growth, pro-family policies, including those that address obstacles that mothers of young children may face in entering the labor force. Figure 2-15 shows the labor force participation rate of mothers and fathers with young children. For fathers with a youngest child age 5 or under, the participation rate fell from 98 percent in 1968 to 94 percent in 2018. A similar decline occurred among fathers of older children. Though participation rates have fallen, the vast majority of fathers continue to either work or look for work. This high level of participation contrasts with participation among mothers with young children. For mothers with a child under age 6, participation increased from 30 percent to 66 percent between 1968 and 2000. This increase was driven largely by shifting cultural norms, as well as welfare reforms that rewarded and required work for those receiving welfare benefits and tax credits. However, participation rates stopped growing in 2000. Today, the participation rate of mothers with a child under 6 is 67 percent—just 1 percentage point higher than their rate 19 years earlier. Moreover, the gender

Figure 2-15. Labor Force Participation Rate among Parents by Age of Youngest Child in Household and Sex of Adult, 1968–2019

Labor force participation rate (percent)

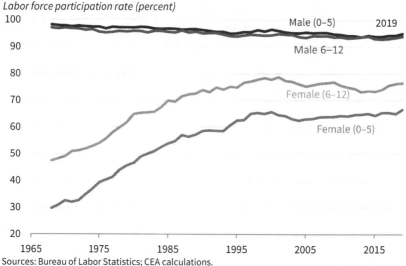

Sources: Bureau of Labor Statistics; CEA calculations.
Note: The age of the youngest child is shown in parentheses. Only biological children, adopted children, or stepchildren living in the same household as the adult are counted. Only adults between the ages of 18 and 64 are included.

gap in participation rates stands at 29 percentage points for parents of children under age 6 and at 17 percentage points for parents of children age 6 to 12.

Some parents opt out of the labor force on the basis of personal preference. For others—especially mothers with young children—the inefficiently high cost of childcare may play a role in their decision to remain out of the labor force. Thus, addressing this barrier to work by reducing inefficiently high childcare costs could potentially bring more parents into the formal labor force and increase economic efficiency.

As documented in a recent CEA report (2019e), regulations that do not improve the health and safety of the children increase childcare costs, and these inefficiently high costs can weaken incentives to work. For the average State, as of 2017, the average hourly price of center-based childcare for a child age 4 represented 24 percent of the hourly median wage. Evidence on the responsiveness of work status and hours to childcare costs suggests that some of these parents would enter the labor force or increase their work hours in response to a reduction in the cost of childcare. The Administration is focused on ensuring that more parents have safe options for their children while simultaneously giving parents more opportunities to work.

Globally, the Administration is working to expand female labor opportunities as discussed in box 2-3.

Box 2-3. The Women's Global Development and Prosperity Initiative and Female Labor Force Participation Globally

A wide range of circumstances can have an effect on a woman's decision about whether to participate in the labor force. For example, some women desire to partake in productive activities outside the formal labor market, such as taking care of children or family members. At the same time, increasing female labor force participation by offering opportunities to women not in the labor force who might otherwise elect to participate could have a substantial effect on a country's economy.

Among the developed countries that belong to the Organization for Economic Cooperation and Development (OECD), in 2018, the United States had a female labor force participation rate higher than 22 of 36 OECD countries (the most recently available data for OECD-wide comparisons are from 2018). The lowest rate within the OECD was 34.2 percent (Turkey)—a full 22.9 percentage points below the United States. Iceland had the highest female participation rate of all OECD countries—about 21 percentage points higher than the United States. Although the United States has a relatively high female participation rate compared with other OECD nations, there may yet be opportunities for additional growth, given the higher rates in some peer countries (figure 2-ii).

A number of factors can likely explain the differences in female labor force participation rates among developed countries in the OECD, including policy differences, cultural factors, and demographics. For example, Blau and Kahn (2013) estimate that almost 30 percent of the decrease in women's prime-age participation in the United States relative to other OECD countries between 1990 and 2010 can be attributed to differences in family-related policies such as those relating to childcare.

For developing countries, too, there could be a range of reasons that women may opt against, or be prevented from, pursuing formal employment opportunities, including but not limited to discriminatory laws and practices, a failure to enforce relevant laws, and social and cultural practices that limit female employment opportunities or in other instances, a desire to participate in other productive activities that are outside the formal labor market. Nevertheless, research has found that increasing opportunities for women to participate in the workforce has several potential positive outcomes. For example, the World Bank has suggested that increasing opportunities for women's workforce participation increases political stability and reduces the likelihood of violent conflict (Crespo-Sancho 2018).

For low-income countries, increasing female labor force participation rates also creates an opportunity for countries to increase the size of their workforce and achieve additional economic growth. When women are empowered economically, they reinvest back into their families and communities, producing a multiplier effect that spurs economic growth and can potentially create societies that are more peaceful.

Economic Growth Benefits Historically Disadvantaged Americans | 101

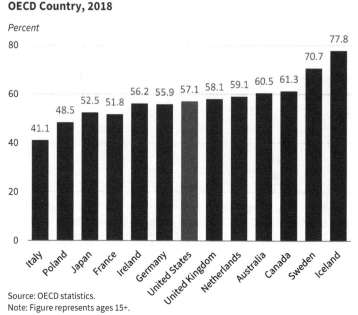

Figure 2-ii. Female Labor Force Participation Rate, by Selected OECD Country, 2018

Percent

Italy 41.1, Poland 48.5, Japan 52.5, France 51.8, Ireland 56.2, Germany 55.9, United States 57.1, United Kingdom 58.1, Netherlands 59.1, Australia 60.5, Canada 61.3, Sweden 70.7, Iceland 77.8

Source: OECD statistics.
Note: Figure represents ages 15+.

Accelerating women's economic empowerment is critical to ensuring that developing countries can achieve economic self-reliance, and transition from being aid partners to trade partners. To this end, the Trump Administration established the Women's Global Development and Prosperity (W-GDP) initiative, which seeks to spur growth in developing countries by promoting economic empowerment among women. W-GDP aims to economically empower 50 million women in the developing world by 2025 through U.S. government activities, private-public partnerships, and a new, innovative fund.

W-GDP focuses on three pillars: vocational education for women, empowering women to succeed as entrepreneurs, and eliminating barriers that prevent women from fully participating in the economy. W-GDP's third pillar addresses legal and cultural, employer practices, and social and cultural barriers that preclude women's economic empowerment in developing countries. On legal barriers specifically, W-GDP focuses on five foundational factors: economic empowerment on the basis of five principles: (1) accessing institutions, (2) building credit, (3) owning and managing property, (4) traveling freely, and (5) working in the same jobs and sectors as males. There is much evidence showing that amending or passing laws in these categories results in measurable economic benefits—both on an individual level and also on a global scale.

One estimate shows that eliminating discriminatory laws and practices (both formal and informal) could have added $12 trillion to the global
economy, 16 percent of global gross domestic product (GDP)in 2011 (Ferrant
and Thim 2019). In terms of gender parity in the workforce, a McKinsey &
Company report estimates that if barriers to participation in the workforce
were removed and women chose to participate in the economy identically to
men, up to $28 trillion would be added to global GDP (or 26 percent) in 2025
(Woetzel et al. 2015). This includes adding $2.9 trillion to India, $2.7 trillion
to the Middle East and North Africa, $2.6 trillion to Latin America, and $721
billion to Sub-Saharan Africa.

Additionally, a World Bank (2014) report found that strengthening land
rights has a positive impact on female farmer productivity. Evidence using
data on women's property rights spanning 100 countries over a period of 50
years shows that legal reforms was correlated with higher female labor force
participation and higher rates of women in formal (wage-earning) labor, in
addition to higher educational enrollment.

Overall, the W-GDP initiative is backed by economic research and
evidence-based policy recommendations that would help empower women
around the globe and boost global GDP.

Combating the Opioid Crisis

Another barrier to labor market success for many are the high rates of drug
addiction and overdoses. Beyond deaths from opioids, research suggest that
the abuse of prescription opioids decreases labor force participation (Krueger
2017). The CEA estimates that the full cost of the opioid crisis was $2.5 trillion
over the four-year period from 2015 to 2018 (CEA 2019f). This cost estimate
includes the value of lives lost and also higher criminal justice costs, lost labor
productivity, and higher healthcare and treatment costs. See chapter 7 for a
discussion of the trends in opioid overdose deaths and steps the Administration
has taken to address the opioid crisis.

Conclusion

The U.S. labor market is strong, even as the economy continues its record
expansion. The Trump Administration's agenda of tax cuts and deregulation
has contributed to a strong demand for labor and an increasing labor supply.
We would expect to find the largest increases in labor demand in the industries that benefit the most from deregulatory actions, but further research is
required to confirm this. As unemployment falls to record low rates, groups
that were previously left behind in the economy's recovery are beginning to
see substantial benefits in job opportunities and income growth. The increase
in labor market earnings is pulling millions of families out of poverty and off

public assistance, showing how economic growth likely benefits historically disadvantaged Americans more than expanded government programs.

However, there are still barriers that prevent lower-income workers from realizing the full benefits of the strong labor market—such as skill mismatches, geographic mismatches, occupational licensing, distressed communities, prior criminal convictions, childcare affordability, and drug addiction. These barriers prevent many from finding jobs. The Administration is seeking to reduce these barriers to both labor demand and supply by focusing on improving worker training, reforming occupational licensing, incentivizing private investment in disadvantaged areas, facilitating the successful reentry of ex-offenders, assisting working families with access to high-quality and affordable childcare, and reducing the impact of the opioid crisis. Successful reforms in these areas will help to grow the economy by increasing the number and productivity of workers. The Administration's current and future economic agenda will focus on ensuring that all American households can benefit from strong, sustained economic growth.

Chapter 3

Regulatory Reform
Unleashes the Economy

The Trump Administration's focus on deregulation has led to historic reductions in costly regulation. The Administration has cut more than two significant regulations for each new significant regulation it has finalized, while maintaining critical protections for workers, public health, safety, and the environment. This fundamental shift in how the Federal government views regulation breaks with the decades-long accumulation of regulatory mandates that place high costs on the U.S. economy.

The Council of Economic Advisers estimates that after 5 to 10 years, this new approach to Federal regulation will have raised real incomes by $3,100 per household per year by increasing choice, productivity, and competition. Twenty notable Federal deregulatory actions alone will be saving American consumers and businesses about $1,900 per household per year after they go into full effect. These results show that the Trump Administration's deregulatory actions across a vast array of American industries are among the most significant in U.S. history.

Beyond eliminating outdated or costly regulations established by prior administrations, the Trump Administration has also sharply reduced the rate at which new Federal regulations are introduced. The ongoing introduction of these costly regulations had previously been subtracting an additional 0.2 percent per year from real incomes, thereby giving the false impression that the American economy was fundamentally incapable of anything better than slow growth in real incomes and gross domestic product. Now, consumers and small businesses no longer need to dread the steadily accumulating costs of new Federal regulations.

Concurrently with the 2017 Presidential inauguration, real growth in gross domestic product began outperforming experts' forecasts where it was previously underperforming them. This should not come as a surprise, because studies that evaluate regulation across countries show that, all else being equal, countries that deregulated experienced more economic growth.

The new regulatory approach also significantly reduces consumer prices in many markets—such as those for prescription drugs, health insurance, and telecommunications—while it prevents price increases in other markets. Furthermore, deregulation removes mandates from employers, which especially benefits smaller businesses that, unlike their large companies, do not typically have a team of in-house lawyers and regulatory compliance staff to help them understand and comply with onerous regulations.

By increasing choice, productivity, and competition, the Trump Administration's regulatory reforms have cut red tape for American businesses and have extended them greater freedom to create jobs. Given the Administration's ambitious plans for this year, deregulatory benefits for consumers, job creators, and the economy are bound to grow further in 2020.

The Trump Administration's focus on deregulation has led to historic reductions in costly regulation, while protecting workers, public health, safety, and the environment. In January 2017, President Trump signed Executive Order 13771, "Reducing Regulations and Controlling Regulatory Costs," which is the cornerstone of the Administration's regulatory reform success. Executive Order 13771 requires Federal agencies to eliminate two regulations for every new regulation issued (2-for-1), and has created incremental regulatory cost caps. After Executive Order 13771 was issued in fiscal year (FY) 2017, there were 13 significant deregulatory actions and only 3 significant regulatory actions (4-for-1). In FY 2018, there were 57 significant deregulatory actions and only 14 significant regulatory actions (4-for-1). In FY 2019, there were 61 significant deregulatory actions and only 35 significant regulatory actions (2-for-1). In total, the Trump Administration has exceeded its 2-for-1 goal, though many critics thought that even 2-for-1 would not happen.

The Council of Economic Advisers (CEA) previously looked at regulation across countries, finding that, all else being equal, countries that deregulated experienced more economic growth (CEA 2018a). We then related cross-country regulatory indices to potential regulatory developments in the United States and estimated that regulatory reform had the potential to increase U.S. gross domestic product (GDP) by at least 1.0 to 2.2 percent over a decade.

This chapter reexamines the impact of the Administration's regulatory reform agenda now that it has been more completely implemented. It also takes an alternative approach to the CEA's earlier analysis and estimates the aggregate economic effects of deregulation by examining specific Federal rules and by accounting for the unique circumstances of the industries targeted by the rules, in addition to the rules and industries similarly analyzed in previous CEA reports.[1] Our analysis utilizes an economic framework that situates each industry in a larger economy that includes market distortions from taxes, imperfect competition, and other sources. To date, we have conducted industry-specific analyses for 20 deregulatory actions.

The primary subject of this chapter is the impact of regulation and deregulation on nationwide real income. In contrast, guided by the Office of Management and Budget (OMB 2003), Federal agencies and OMB's Office of Information and Regulatory Affairs (OIRA) prepare and discuss related calculations of the benefits and costs of Federal regulations that do not typically calculate effects on GDP or nationwide real incomes. GDP and real income are of independent interest because they are important aspects of national accounting, and they are included in the budget forecasts made by OMB, the Social Security and Medicare Trustees, and the Congressional Budget Office, to name a few.[2] Moreover, economists and journalists routinely use GDP and real income as familiar metrics of the performance of the economy (Brynjolfsson, Eggers, and Gannamaneni 2018).

The CEA estimates that after 5 to 10 years, regulatory reform will have raised real incomes by $3,100 per household per year.[3] Twenty notable Federal deregulatory actions alone will be saving American consumers and businesses about $220 billion per year after they go into full effect. They will increase real (after-inflation) incomes by about 1.3 percent. Many of the most notable deregulatory efforts in American history, such as the deregulation of airlines

---

[1] The CEA previously released research on some of the topics covered in this chapter; the text that follows builds on these reports (CEA 2019a, 2019b, 2019c).

[2] Estimates of the welfare effects of deregulation are therefore not enough by themselves to know, among other things, how GDP forecasts should be revised to account for the economic impact of deregulation.

[3] Throughout this chapter, all dollar amounts are in 2018 dollars unless noted otherwise.

and trucking that began during the Carter Administration, did not have such large aggregate effects.

Regulatory reform not only reduces or eliminates costly regulations established by prior Administrations, but also sharply reduces the rate at which costly new Federal regulations are introduced. The ongoing introduction of costly regulations had previously been subtracting an additional 0.2 percent a year from real incomes, thereby giving the false impression that the American economy was fundamentally incapable of anything better than slow growth. Now, new regulations are budgeted and kept to a minimum.

In the first section of this chapter, we review the trends in Federal regulation before and after regulatory reform. We next turn to describing our general analytical approach and how we selected 20 deregulatory actions for analysis. The subsequent sections discuss the industry-specific deregulatory actions with the largest aggregate effects. We estimate large reductions in regulatory costs in the market for Internet access, healthcare markets, labor markets, and financial markets. Next, we estimate the additional cost-savings from reversing the trend of adding new regulations and regulatory costs each year. We also explain why some pre-2017 regulations carried disproportionate costs, and we offer a brief conclusion.

Reversing the Regulatory Trend

Before turning to industry-specific analyses, we provide an overview of the recent history of Federal regulation. This history is one of rapid growth until 2017, when the growth was halted by regulatory reform. Between 2000 and 2016, Federal agencies added an average of 53 economically significant regulatory actions each year (figure 3-1). In 2017 and 2018, the average dropped to less than 30. Figure 3-1 excludes rules that were deregulatory actions. As in previous years, in 2017 and 2018 a subset of the economically significant rules included in figure 3-1 are considered "transfer rules" and are not considered by OMB/OIRA to be either regulatory or deregulatory actions. When the transfer rules are excluded, in 2017 and 2018 the average number of economically significant regulatory actions falls to 10. The economically significant rules shown in figure 3-1 are those the Federal agencies and OMB/OIRA expected to have an aggregate impact on the economy of at least $100 million or to adversely affect the economy in a material way (Executive Order 12866). Figure 3-1 also shows the total numbers of "significant" rules, which include economically significant rules and "other significant" rules that meet part of the definition for economic significance or are important for other reasons described in Executive Order 12866. Including economically significant and other significant rules, Federal agencies added an average of 279 significant regulatory actions per year between 2000 and 2016; the average fell to 61 in 2017 and 2018 after regulatory reform.

Figure 3-1. Significant Final Rules by Presidential Year, Excluding Deregulatory Actions, 2000–2018

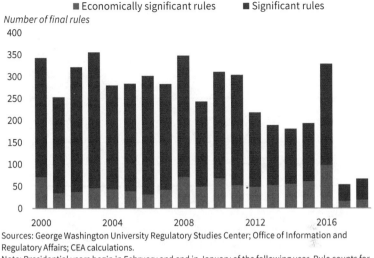

Sources: George Washington University Regulatory Studies Center; Office of Information and Regulatory Affairs; CEA calculations.

Note: Presidential years begin in February and end in January of the following year. Rule counts for 2017 and 2018 exclude rules considered economically significant deregulatory actions. Before 2017, we estimate one economically significant deregulatory action per year.

Last year, the CEA discussed in depth the cumulative economic impact of regulatory actions on the U.S. economy and explained why the regulatory whole is greater than the sum of its parts (CEA 2019b). Based on the annual accounting of rules published in OMB's annual *Reports to Congress*, we found that regulatory costs grew by an average of $8.2 billion each year from 2000 through 2016. However, OMB's annual *Reports* for 2000–2016 only included 200 rules with fully quantified cost-benefit analyses. Over this same period, there were just over 900 economically significant rules; including other significant rules increases the count to almost 5,000. By definition, the regulatory actions expected to have the largest effects on the economy are included in the count of economically significant rules. However, this focus misses the sheer bulk of Federal regulation.

This year, we use textual analysis of the *Code of Federal Regulations* (*CFR*) to provide a broader and longer perspective on the cumulative regulatory burden. The *CFR* lists all regulations issued by Federal agencies and departments that are currently in force at the time of its publication; it is updated annually. RegData is a database applying textual analysis to the *CFR* that measures the restrictions imposed by the regulations based on the number of times words such as "shall" and "must" appear (Al-Ubaydli and McLaughlin 2014). Figure 3-2 shows the RegData index of regulatory restrictions from 1970 through 2019.

The total number of regulatory restrictions in the *CFR* nearly tripled between 1970 (the earliest available data) and 2016, increasing from 400,000

Figure 3-2. Regulatory Restrictions by All Agencies, 1970–2019

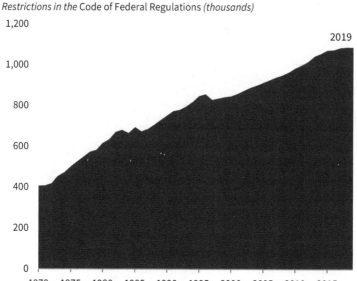

Restrictions in the Code of Federal Regulations *(thousands)*

Sources: *Code of Federal Regulations*; Mercatus Center RegData.

to almost 1.1 million. Aside from a few isolated year-to-year declines, the trend was steadily upward through 2016. From 2017 through 2019 the trend flattened and began to reverse, showing the first declines in regulatory restrictions that have been sustained for more than a single year. The turnaround in the growth of regulatory restrictions parallels the turnaround in the growth of regulatory costs that the CEA documented last year (CEA 2019b). Last year we reviewed estimates of the total regulatory costs in the United States that ranged from almost half a trillion to over a trillion dollars. Putting those estimates together with the total number of regulatory restrictions implies that each restriction is on average associated with somewhere between $380,000 and $1 million of regulatory costs.

Because deregulatory actions might involve words like "shall" and "must," the RegData index of restrictions shown in figure 3-2 cannot distinguish between the impact of regulatory and deregulatory actions. To explore this, we searched the text of two Final Rules published in the *Federal Register*—the 2016 regulatory action and the 2018 deregulatory action on short-term health insurance (discussed in more detail below and in CEA 2019a). The *Federal Register* text of the 2018 deregulatory action was longer and included 97 restrictions, compared to only 30 regulatory restrictions in the text of the 2016 regulatory action. It is not known to what extent this pattern generalizes to the RegData index of restrictions in the *CFR*. It seems likely that if it were possible to adjust for restrictions included in the deregulatory actions taken since 2017, the index in figure 3-2 would show an even steeper decline beginning in 2017.

Figure 3-2 includes restrictions due to Federal agencies covered by Executive Order 13771 as well as restrictions due to independent Federal agencies that are not subject to Executive Order 13771 accounting. In recent years restrictions due to independent agencies account for about 15 percent of all restrictions. Since 1990, the number of restrictions due to independent agencies has grown by about 75 percent. Even though the independent agencies were not subject to Executive Order 13771 accounting, starting in 2017 the growth in their regulatory restrictions began to decline.

In addition to regulations, Federal agencies also issue guidance documents that advise the public about the agency's approach to adjudication or enforcement. Figure 3-2 does not include regulatory restrictions stemming from guidance documents because they are not part of the *CFR*. Moreover, guidance documents are non-binding, so in principle they cannot impose binding restrictions. However, a common concern is that agencies can treat guidance documents as binding in practice. Estimates suggest that some agencies issue anywhere from twenty to two-hundred pages of guidance documents for every page of regulations they issue (Parrillo 2019). To the extent those guidance documents impose regulatory restrictions that are binding in practice, the restrictions should ideally be added to the count of regulatory restrictions in figure 3-2. Although not reflected in figure 3-2, Federal agencies' guidance documents are subject to Executive Order 13771 accounting of the 2-for-1 requirement and regulatory cost caps. Significant guidance documents that increase costs are defined to be regulatory actions; guidance documents that yield cost savings are defined to be deregulatory actions.

Figure 3-3 shows how *CFR* regulatory restrictions on the manufacturing industry has grown over time, until regulatory reform. RegData uses further text analysis to determine the applicability of the regulatory restrictions to specific industries. The method uses search strings to identify phrases related to each industry (Al-Ubaydli and McLaughlin 2014). The resulting measure shows that regulatory restrictions on manufacturing remained roughly constant from the late 1970s until 1986. From 1986 through 2016, the number of regulatory restrictions almost quadrupled, from a little over 50,000 to more than 200,000. Again, starting in 2017, the upward trend reverses; the index shows sustained declines in regulatory restrictions on manufacturing from 2017 and 2018.

The regulatory reform results to date are notable accomplishments, given that it is difficult and time-consuming to identify opportunities for appropriate deregulatory actions. In a follow-up to Executive Order 13771, in February 2017 President Trump signed Executive Order 13777, "Enforcing the Regulatory Reform Agenda," which requires each Federal agency to designate a regulatory reform officer to oversee deregulatory initiatives and policies. In an innovative response to meet this challenge, the Department of Health and

Figure 3-3. Regulatory Restrictions on Manufacturing, 1970–2018

Restrictions in the Code of Federal Regulations *(thousands)*

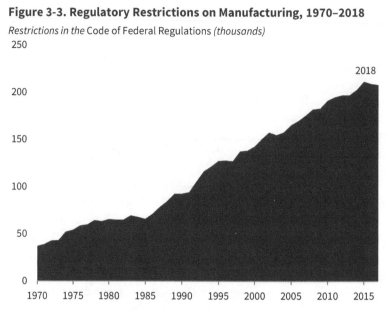

Sources: *Code of Federal Regulations*; Mercatus Center RegData.

Human Services began exploring the use of artificial intelligence and machine-learning algorithms to identify opportunities for regulatory reform. As an example of the project's potential, the department discovered that 85 percent of its regulations created before 1990 have never been updated.

Because regulatory reform takes time, Federal agencies' efforts that began in 2017 are continuing to unfold. As a result, important pending and in-progress deregulatory actions cannot be included in this chapter. For example, our analysis does not include the deregulatory actions related to emission and fuel economy standards for automobiles; once finalized, the SAFE rule might be the largest deregulatory effort to date. Other important deregulatory efforts include the Department of Energy's reforms of regulatory restrictions on residential dishwashers and lightbulbs.

Analyzing Regulatory Reform

The Trump Administration uses regulatory cost caps to reduce the cumulative burden of Federal regulation. In addition to regulation-specific cost-benefit tests, the cost caps induce agencies to view all their regulations as a portfolio, which is more congruent with the experiences of the households and businesses subject to them. While pursuing their agency-specific missions, the regulatory cost caps provide the framework for agencies to evaluate regulatory costs, to consider deregulatory actions, and to set priorities among new regulatory actions.

The CEA uses a pragmatic, streamlined approach to analyze the costs that regulatory actions impose on consumers, small businesses, and other economic actors. This approach requires making estimates of a small set of key parameters that describe the market that is primarily affected by the regulatory action in question. We follow a standard approach in cost-benefit analysis and rely on revealed preferences in markets (OMB 2003). For example, the price-elasticity of demand—which shows how consumers change their consumption in response to a price change—reflects the value consumers place on the good or service, relative to their next-best alternatives. For this reason, the price-elasticity of demand serves as one of the "sufficient statistics" to analyze the impact of a policy change on consumer welfare within the regulated industry (Chetty 2009).[4] Detailed applications, and a sensitivity analysis, of our approach are given in our earlier reports (CEA 2019a, 2019b, 2019c).

To account for effects outside the regulated industry, the analysis again takes a streamlined approach that does not require a fully detailed model of the economy (known as a structural general equilibrium model), but instead relies on an implementable formula that provides a good approximation of the excess burden that a regulatory action imposes on the markets for labor and capital (Goulder, Parry, and Williams 1999; Parry, Williams, and Goulder 1999; Goulder and Williams 2003; Dahlby 2008; CEA 2019b). For example, anticompetitive regulation reduces the demand for labor and capital in the regulated industry and thereby reduces the aggregate quantities of those production factors. Marginal excess burdens in labor and capital markets are translated into an additional increment to aggregate output by dividing them by our 48 percent estimate of the marginal tax wedge, which is broadly interpreted

---

[4] Our analysis is not as detailed as the regulatory impact analyses that Federal agencies conduct to comply with Executive Order 12866 (OMB 2003).This chapter is independent of the rulemaking process. Instead, this chapter contributes to the CEA's mission, as established by Congress in the Employment Act of 1946, to offer objective economic advice based on economic research and empirical evidence. Our analysis is consistent with the economic principles that guide cost-benefit analysis, including our focus on the key concepts of willingness to pay and opportunity cost. Another report (CEA 2019b) provides an additional discussion of our approach; and still another report (CEA 2019a) provides a detailed discussion of the methods used to conduct prospective cost-benefit analyses of three of the deregulatory actions considered in this chapter. Our approach complements agencies' completed analyses and fills in gaps, for example, when a regulatory impact analysis was not able to quantify costs or benefits, or when a regulatory impact analysis was not required. Note that, consistent with standard practice, shifts of resources between industries are not counted as a cost or a benefit or a real income effect, except to the extent that market prices indicate that the industries put different values on those resources.

to include implicit taxes and imperfect competition.[5] This formula captures general equilibrium interactions that would be left out of an analysis that only considered the impact of the regulatory action in the primary market. OMB's guidance on cost-benefit analysis of federal programs (Circular A-94) recommends analysis of the marginal excess tax burden. To date, however, for practical reasons the guidelines for regulatory cost accounting for the Executive Order 13771 regulatory budget have not required agencies to include the costs imposed on the private sector by excess tax burdens induced by regulatory actions. The analysis in this chapter demonstrates the feasibility and importance of a more complete accounting of regulatory costs, including marginal excess tax burdens.

The economic effects of regulation can be summarized in several ways, such as the costs to businesses, nationwide costs, nationwide benefits, or national incomes. The CEA employs three nationwide outcome concepts in this chapter: costs savings, net benefits, and real income. The distinction between the first two arises because a single regulation can create costs for one segment of the population while it creates a benefit for other segments. We refer to the aggregate of these as the "net cost" of the regulation, which (aside from sunk startup costs) is equal to the "net benefit" of overturning the regulation. We refer to the "cost savings" of overturning the regulation as the costs imposed on the segment of the population that was harmed by the regulation.[6] Real income is similar to GDP, except that real income subtracts depreciation and reflects the effects of international terms of trade on the purchasing power of U.S. residents, which is an important result of one of the larger deregulatory actions. GDP and real income, which can differ from welfare or "utility," subtract the opportunity costs of the Nation's labor and capital as well as environmental and other nonpecuniary costs. As used in this chapter, all these concepts refer only to domestic benefits, costs, and incomes.

The primary subject of this chapter is the impact of regulation and deregulation on nationwide real income; we estimate that over time, the impact of regulatory reform will be worth $3,100 per household each year. This chapter also estimates the net benefits of deregulatory actions. Some regulatory actions trade private goods for public goods, such as environmental quality. With public goods, and in other situations where private markets may fail, it is necessary to carefully consider the benefits and costs of regulatory actions. Even if the original regulatory action addressed a private market

---

[5] An aggregate increase in a factor of production by 1 unit increases output by its marginal product (MP), but the entire output exceeds the net benefit (i.e., marginal excess burden) because the production factor has a marginal opportunity cost of supply. The net aggregate benefit of that 1 unit is 0.48*MP, where 0.48 is the marginal tax wedge. The additional output is therefore the net aggregate benefit divided by 0.48.

[6] The CEA's concept of cost savings is analogous to the revenue savings from eliminating a Federal program, whereas the net benefit would be the difference between revenue savings and the forgone benefits of the program's expenditures.

Box 3-1. Looking Forward and Backward to Study Regulatory Reform

Federal agencies conduct forward-looking, or prospective, cost-benefit analyses of proposed regulatory and deregulatory actions. In contrast, academic policy analysts typically conduct backward-looking, or retrospective, analyses of past public policies. For example, the definitive academic studies of the Airline Deregulation Act of 1978 were conducted in the 1980s and early 1990s (Winston 1993). The retrospective studies took advantage of data that reflected what actually happened in the deregulated airline market.

However, analysts conducting either prospective or retrospective studies face the challenging task of predicting market outcomes in a world that they cannot observe. Analysts in Federal agencies observe current market outcomes that, in many cases, reasonably approximate the "no action" baseline of "what the world will be like [in the future] if the proposed rule is not adopted" (OMB 2003, 2). But the agency analysts cannot look into the future and observe how the proposed rule would change market outcomes. In their prospective studies, the agency analysts use economic reasoning and empirical evidence to predict what an unobserved, counterfactual world would be like if the proposed rule were adopted. Academics who conduct retrospective analyses of past policies face the opposite challenge. They observe market outcomes in the real world, where the policy was implemented, but they cannot observe the counterfactual world without the policy. The academic policy analysts must also rely on economic reasoning and empirical evidence to predict outcomes in a counterfactual world.

Academic studies of airline deregulation illustrate the difficulty of doing an accurate retrospective analysis. Although the analysts observed airline market outcomes both before and after deregulation, they had to disentangle the effects of deregulation from other changes that affected the airline industry. In particular, airline deregulation in 1978 happened to coincide with an energy crisis that increased fuel prices and led to higher air fares and lower airline profits. Analysts took a counterfactual approach to isolate the effects of the energy crisis and to estimate the causal effects of deregulation—lower air fares and higher profits (Winston 1993).

When done well, prospective and retrospective analyses contribute valuable evidence about regulatory reform. Federal agencies, by necessity, must conduct prospective analysis of proposed actions. Likewise, in this chapter we mainly rely on prospective analysis in order to predict outcomes of the Trump Administration's regulatory reform agenda. Future academic research will undoubtedly conduct retrospective analysis and provide more evidence and new insights about the effects of the regulatory reforms that began in 2017. Research on the deregulations of the 1970s and 1980s provides reasons to be both optimistic and cautious about prospective analysis. When Winston compared predictions that deregulation would lead to lower prices to retrospective assessments, he described them as "surprisingly close,"

> even though they were "often made more than a decade apart by different researchers" (Winston 1993, 1272). At the same time, he noted that the economics profession's predictions failed to quantify the value of reducing the inconvenience costs of airline travel restrictions and "grossly underestimated the benefits from deregulation" (Winston 1993, 1276).

failure, a deregulatory action is still warranted when the regulatory cost savings outweigh the forgone regulatory benefits.[7] GDP and real income capture the value of private goods production, but these measures do not capture the value of public goods or other important nonpecuniary effects. However, when including nonpecuniary costs and benefits that are not part of real income, we estimate that the deregulatory actions have a net benefit of more than $2,500 per household each year, compared with the previous trend of growing regulatory costs. This gain stems from the implementation of the regulatory reform agenda and from achieving a better balance between the cost of regulations and their societal benefits.

Because the preparation of this chapter occurred long enough after some of the regulatory or deregulatory actions to enable us to adequately measure relevant market outcomes, the CEA could also deviate from the regulatory impact analyses that accompany economically significant rulemaking by relying more heavily on retrospective analysis (see box 3-1).

Deregulatory Actions Considered

We sampled deregulatory actions for industry-specific analyses. When applicable, we also examined the corresponding regulatory action taken by the previous Administration. The actions were sampled from four broad categories.[8] The first category consists of the statutes passed by Congress and signed by President Trump. The second category consists of the 16 Federal rules or guidance overturned under the Congressional Review Act (CRA) since January 2017.[9] The third category consists of the rules in FY 2018 Regulatory Budget (i.e., the rules covered by Executive Order 13771 and finalized during that fiscal year, of which there are 261), as well as the rules in the FY 2019 Regulatory Budget

---

[7] The concept of market failure plays a central role in cost-benefit analysis, but the existence of a market failure does not guarantee that the original regulatory action's benefits outweighed its costs. Market failure is a necessary but not sufficient condition for this conclusion. In practice, it is not clear that many of the 20 deregulatory actions we consider overturned regulations that addressed market failures.

[8] In statistical terms, the categories are strata, and the overall population of interest consists of all economically important Federal regulatory actions taken since January 2017. Also see CEA (2019b, appendix I).

[9] For each rule, Congress passed a resolution of disapproval that was signed by President Trump, thereby overturning the rule.

(OMB 2018).[10] The fourth category consists of agency guidance documents and rulemaking by independent agencies.

Because the purpose of this chapter is to estimate the aggregate economic effect of all new regulatory and deregulatory actions, as opposed to the effect of an "average" deregulatory action, we designed a sampling procedure to identify the likely largest actions in terms of economic impact. The average effect of the sampled actions is not necessarily a good estimate of the effect of the average unsampled action, but that is not our purpose. Rather, if the unsampled actions have an average effect that is in the same direction (but not necessarily magnitude) as the sampled actions, then the total effect of the sampled actions is a conservative estimate of the total effect of all the actions. Moreover, sampling the potentially larger effects yields a more accurate estimate of the total effect than sampling randomly. The omitted regulatory actions are those with few (most often, zero) comments from the public and little attention from Congress. These are the regulations where we have more confidence that the effects are comparatively small, so that excluding them from the total is less likely to have a large effect on our estimate of the total.[11]

Our sampling procedure is not perfect. Some regulations attract attention from the public or Congress for various reasons unrelated to their regulatory costs. Our sample includes a few actions that we estimate have comparatively small aggregate effects, even though they received many comments from the public. At the same time, there might be regulatory actions that will have large aggregate effects but are excluded from our sample because they did not receive many public comments.

From the first category/stratum, we selected sections of two important new Federal laws enacted during the Trump Administration: the 2017 Tax Cuts and Jobs Act; and the 2018 Economic Growth, Regulatory Relief, and Consumer Protection Act. From the second category, we selected three employment rules that affect a large number of workers as well as the top four economic regulatory actions, in terms of number of comments received from the public. From the third category, we selected the top six regulatory actions from FY 2018, in terms of the number of comments received from the public.

We selected four regulatory actions from the FY 2019 Regulatory Budget that we expected to be among the comment leaders. Three of these contribute to both our estimate of the cost savings from deregulation since 2017 and to

---

[10] A number of the 16 rules disapproved under the CRA were part of the FY 2017 Regulatory Budget.

[11] To analogize, suppose that you wanted to measure the number of automobiles in a house. It would be unnecessarily inaccurate to take a random sample of rooms, because most of the time the garage would not be sampled and therefore most of the time the conclusion would be zero automobiles. Looking exclusively in the garage is the obviously superior alternative to a random sample. That is what the CEA has done with regulations: we looked exclusively at those with a significant chance of having a large economic effect. The formal statistical proof of this conclusion is provided above.

our estimate of the costs of the growing regulatory state before that.[12] A fourth regulatory area with heavy commenting, and potentially large costs imposed by the previous Administration, relates to emission and fuel economy standards for automobiles. To be conservative, we do not include any cost savings from deregulatory actions in this area.[13]

Finally, our sample of regulatory actions includes important guidance at the Food and Drug Administration (FDA) regarding the approval of generic drugs, as well as a rule from the Federal Communications Commission (FCC) that received millions of comments from the public. All the comment leaders for FY 2017 and FY 2018 were deregulations rather than regulations, and most of them have had an economically significant nationwide impact.[14] And though we have not measured the economic impact of hundreds of other FY 2017 and FY 2018 Federal rules, the aggregate cost savings for the other rules reported in the *Federal Register* are in the direction of additional cost savings.[15]

Table 3-1 lists the regulations and our estimates, with 2 of the 18 rows ("Savings arrangements" and "Joint Employer") each showing the combined effect of a pair of deregulatory actions, so the table represents a total of 20 deregulatory actions.[16]

Although numbers of pages of regulations are not part of our quantitative analysis, it is interesting to note that the regulatory actions and their deregulatory companions in our sample were promulgated with more than 6,000 pages of Federal statutes, the *Federal Register*, or separate agency impact analyses.

---

[12] These are the Joint-Employer proposed rule (RIN 3142-AA13) from the National Labor Relations Board (NLRB), and the Joint Employer proposed rule (RIN 1235-AA26) from the Department of Labor (DOL). Because our analysis does not separate the effects of the DOL guidance and the NLRB proposed rule on joint employers, technically we have also selected the NLRB rule, even though it is not part of any year's Regulatory Budget. The Fiduciary Rule (RIN 1210-AB82) is in the FY 2019 budget, but its temporary predecessor rule (82 *FR* 31278) also appears in the FY 2018 Regulatory Budget, with many comments.

[13] The Trump Administration has not yet finalized a rule establishing fuel economy or emissions standards for automobiles. The CEA plans to estimate its economic effects after such a rule is finalized.

[14] The top 10 commented rules from each of the FY 2017 and FY 2018 budgets were all deregulatory actions. Most rules in the Regulatory Budget receive no comments.

[15] Some analysts have concluded that many regulatory impact analyses reported in the *Federal Register* omit important resource and opportunity costs of regulation (Harrington, Morgenstern, and Nelson 2000; Belfield, Bowden, and Rodriguez 2018), which holds on average in our sample. An example is the 2016 rule restricting short-term, limited duration health insurance while asserting that "this regulatory action is not likely to have economic impacts of $100 million or more in any one year" (81 *FR* 75322), whereas the CEA (2019a) found the annual costs to exceed $10 billion (100 times the upper bound cited by the rule). This suggests that estimates of the costs savings from deregulation based on the *Federal Register* would be understated, although not necessarily relative to the cost additions of regulations.

[16] As is explained in more detail below, the pre-2017 regulatory actions that made table 3-1's deregulatory actions necessary are used to estimate the economic effects of a regulatory freeze.

Table 3-1. Regulatory and Statutory Actions' Annual Impact on Real Income Relative to a Regulatory Freeze, by Sampling Strata

Sampling Strata	Name/Description	Impact on Real Income (in $ Billions per Year)
CRA Nullification: Economic Regulation with High Comment Volume	Protecting the Privacy of Customers of Broadband and Other Telecommunications Services (Opt-In)	$22
	Disclosure of Payments by Resource Extraction Issuers	$3
	Stream Protection Rule	$2
	Arbitration Agreements	$1
CRA Nullification: Broad Employment Regulation	Savings Arrangements Established by States for Non-Governmental Employees & Qualified State Political Subdivisions for Non-Governmental Employees	$13
	Federal Acquisition Regulation; Fair Pay and Safe Workplaces	$0
FY 2018 or FY 2019 Regulatory Budget: Economic Regulation with High Comment Volume	DOL Guidance/Rule and NLRB Rule regarding the Standard for Determining Joint-Employer Status	$17[a]
	Definition of "Employer" Under Section 3(5) of ERISA-Association Health Plans (AHP Rule)	$17[b]
	Rescission of Rule Interpreting "Advice" Exemption in Section 203(c) of the LMRDA* (Persuader Rule)	$15
	Short-Term, Limited-Duration Insurance* (STLDI)	$13
	Payday, Vehicle Title, and Certain High-Cost Installment Loans	$7
	18-Month Extension of Transition Period and Delay of Applicability Dates* (Fiduciary Rule)	$5
	Scope of Sections 202(a) and (b) of Packers and Stockyards Act	$0
	Waste Prevention, Production Subject to Royalties, and Resource Conservation; Rescission or Revision*	$0
Independent Agency and Guidance Documents	Repeal of Protecting and Promoting the Open Internet and Issuance of Restoring Internet Freedom	$54
	FDA and HHS Modernization Efforts	$32
Notable Statutes	The Tax Cuts and Jobs Act- Reduced the Individual Mandate Penalty to Zero	$28
	Economic Growth, Regulatory Relief, and Consumer Protection Act	$6
Sum = total impact relative to a regulatory freeze		**$235**
Total impact relative to 2001–16 regulatory trend		$377

Sources: Office of Information and Regulatory Affairs; Government Accountability Office; eRulemaking Program Management Office; Library of Congress; CEA calculations.

Note: FDA = Food and Drug Administration; HHS = Department of Health and Human Services. An asterisk (*) signifies the use of a shortened name for the regulation. All annual effects on real income are rounded to the nearest billion. The estimate for joint employer rules includes anticompetitive effects of other DOL and NLRB regulations.

a. The estimate for joint employer rules includes anticompetitive effects of other DOL and NLRB regulations.

b. The calculation for AHPs assumes that the expansions of the definition of an employer for AHPs will be found lawful when adjudication is complete.

Consumer Savings on Internet Access

Deregulation frequently reduces consumer prices by enhancing competition and productivity. To show how this happens, we begin our analysis of specific Federal rules with two examples from the broadband or Internet service provider (ISP) industry, which includes wireless smartphone service as well as home Internet service over cables, telephone lines, fiber-optics, and satellites.

Before 2016, ISPs were permitted to, and often did, use and share customer personal data, such as Internet browsing history, unless the consumer "opted out" of data sharing. With so many consumers staying with the default sharing option, ISPs could earn revenue both from subscriber fees, which are tracked by the industry's consumer price index (CPI), and from using or sharing customer data. Equivalently, the receipt of customer data allowed ISPs to earn the same profits with a lower subscriber fee. In effect, consumers paid for their subscription part with money and part by providing personal data.

In 2016 the FCC proposed and finalized a broadband privacy rule requiring ISPs to have consumers to pay by default with only money, thus prohibiting the opt-out system and instead requiring the opt-in system. This rule, which was likely anticipated well before 2016 as the FCC was moving ISPs under the stricter "Title II" regulation (see below), was to go into effect on January 3, 2017. However, in 2017, Congress passed and President Trump signed a resolution of disapproval under the Congressional Review Act to overturn the 2016 FCC rule and prevent future Administrations from adopting similar rules. This 2017 deregulatory action assured market participants that the ISP market would proceed with low subscriber fees. By overturning the 2016 rule, the 2017 action restored the FCC's pre-2016 regulatory approach to protecting customer privacy. Consumers with privacy concerns may opt out and request that their ISP not share their data.[17]

Overturning the FCC's opt-in rule resulted in lower prices for wired and wireless Internet service, as shown by the CPIs graphed in figure 3-4. Wireless service prices fell at the same time that Congress was considering the resolution of disapproval, and wired Internet prices fell a couple of months later. Both these declines are about $40 per subscriber over the life of the subscription, which is similar to independent estimates of the per-subscriber cost of

---

[17] In 2013, AT&T introduced its Internet Preferences Program, which gave consumers the choice to opt out of data sharing. If consumers opted in and allowed data sharing, they received the lowest available subscription rate, which was at least $29 per month lower. Media reports suggest that the vast majority of consumers opted in; i.e., they were willing to allow data sharing in order to qualify for the lower subscription rate.

Figure 3-4. Wireless and Wired Internet Service Provider Price Cuts Close to Congressional Review Act Nullification of Federal Communications Commission Rule, 2016–17

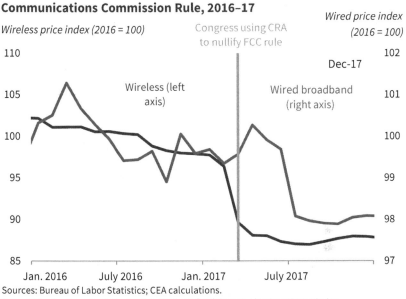

Sources: Bureau of Labor Statistics; CEA calculations.
Note: CRA = Congressional Review Act; FCC = Federal Communications Commission.

obtaining personal data consent from retail customers that are the basis for our quantitative analysis.[18]

At the aggregate level, we estimate the effect of overturning the opt-in rule to be a net savings (including a subtraction for the cost to consumers of providing personal data and an addition for producer surplus) of about $11 billion per year.[19] Overturning the rule also encourages the aggregate supplies of capital and labor (CEA 2019b), as well as competition in online advertising and other markets where consumer data are valuable. We estimate that these effects would create additional net benefits of $5 billion per year and

---

[18] Staten and Cate (2003) report results from a credit card issuer that tried an opt-in program for personal customer information, and found that it cost an average of about $37 (converted to 2018 prices) per customer in terms of mailings and phone calls to obtain opt-in from their customers. Amortized over a 24-month wireless contract and over a wired Internet contract lasting 60 months—i.e., about 4.0 percent and 1.0 percent of the retail price, respectively. Assuming that costs are passed through retail price according to the 60 percent markup rate measured by Goolsbee (2006) for the broadband industry, we predict retail price effects of 6.5 percent and 1.6 percent, respectively. The actual price drops shown in figure 3-4 are 7.0 percent and 1.6 percent, respectively.

[19] We estimate that broadband industry revenue (wired and wireless combined) would be $202 billion per year under the FCC rule. We estimate that the consumers providing personal data as a result of the overturning of the FCC rule do so at an aggregate annual cost of $1.5 billion, offsetting an aggregate annual savings in subscription fees of $11 billion as well as an addition to producer surplus.

corresponding additional real income of about $11 billion per year, which is small compared with total activity in those other markets but significant compared with the regulated market.[20] After 5 to 10 years when these effects are fully realized, the total impact on real incomes is estimated to be $22 billion (see table 3-1).

Before the Trump Administration, another FCC rule adopted in 2015 restricted the vertical pricing arrangements of ISPs—that is, monetary transactions between ISPs and the providers of Internet content such as Netflix and Yahoo.[21] The 2015 rule also imposed government oversight on communication services, making it difficult for these companies to quickly respond to competition and provide new goods and services on the market. These vertical pricing and other restrictions are being removed by the FCC through its "Restoring Internet Freedom" order, returning to regulating ISPs under Title I of the Communications Act.

Previous research shows that vertical pricing restrictions in broadband significantly reduce the quantity and quality of services received by broadband consumers.[22] Hazlett and Caliskan (2008), for example, looked at "open access" restrictions that were applied to U.S. Digital Subscriber Line service (DSL) but not Cable Modem (CM) access. They found that three years after restrictions on DSL services were relaxed, in 2003 and 2005, U.S. DSL subscriptions grew by about 31 percent relative to the trend, while U.S. CM subscriptions increased slightly relative to the trend. Average revenue per DSL subscriber fell, while average revenue per CM subscriber was constant (although quality increased). At the same time, DSL and CM subscriptions in Canada, which was not experiencing the regulatory changes, did not increase relative to the trend. Applying these findings to ISPs in the years 2017–27, we find that, by removing vertical pricing regulations, the Trump Administration's "Restoring Internet Freedom"

---

[20] See also Goulder and Williams (2003) and Dahlby (2008). Throughout this chapter, as in our other reports (CEA 2019a, 2019b), we use a 0.5 marginal cost of public funds to approximate the extra-industry net costs of an industry's regulation, except when we estimate those costs to be primarily outside the United States (see especially figure 3-4 and the associated discussion).

[21] Both the vertical pricing restrictions and the opt-in requirement are linked to the alternative regulatory frameworks that the FCC has variously proposed for ISPs—Title I versus Title II of the Communications Act. However, vertical pricing restrictions and the opt-in requirement are economically distinct and were also implemented by separate rulemaking (see, respectively, 81 *FR* 8067 and 81 *FR* 87274).

[22] See also Becker, Carlton, and Sider (2010, 499), who conclude that regulating vertical pricing in broadband "interfere[s] with the development of business models and network management practices that may be efficient responses to the large, ongoing, and unpredictable changes in Internet demand and technology, . . .[which] is likely to harm investment, innovation, and consumer welfare." Flexible contracting between customer and supplier is generally expected to increase productivity because of the complementary relationship between the two, in contrast to contracts between two suppliers of the same good that have the potential to increase market power.

order will increase real incomes by more than $50 billion per year and consumer welfare by almost $40 billion per year.

Consumer and Small Business Savings on Healthcare

Deregulation is also reducing prices for healthcare. Figure 3-5 shows an inflation-adjusted index of retail prescription drug prices compared with its previous trend growth. Prescription drug prices outpaced general inflation for decades; but in the past two years, they have fallen more than 11 percent below the previous trend as of May 2019, and below general inflation. In 2018, prescription drug prices even declined in nominal terms over the calendar year for the first time since 1972. Much of this is the result of the Trump Administration's efforts at the FDA, such as its 2017 Drug Competition Action Plan and 2018 Strategic Policy Roadmap, to enhance choice and price competition in the biopharmaceutical markets. Under these policies, the FDA has approved a record number of generic and new brand name drugs to compete against existing drugs (CEA 2018b).[23] We estimate that the results of these actions will save consumers almost 10 percent on retail prescription drugs, which results in an increase of $32 billion per year in the purchasing power of the incomes of Americans (including both consumers and producers).[24]

The Trump Administration has also taken deregulatory actions in other healthcare markets, such as insurance. Previous CEA reports provided analyses of four healthcare deregulatory actions: the process improvements at the FDA reflected in figure 3-5, and three actions deregulating health insurance for individuals and small groups (CEA 2019a, 2019b).[25] These four actions, which remove restrictions and alleviate some of the costs of Federal policies introduced during the years 2010–16, are by themselves expected to increase average real incomes by about 0.5 percent, or an average of about $700 per

---

[23] Another indicator of the quantitative importance of new FDA procedures is the July 2017 crash of the stock price of at least one foreign generic drug maker, which analysts attributed to "greater competition as a result of an increase in generic drug approvals by the U.S. FDA." See Sheetz (2017).

[24] The 10 percent assumes that 1 standard deviation below the pre-2017 trend is due to factors other than deregulation. Retail prescription drug expenditures of $326 billion per year were measured by Roehrig (2018). Note that prices may have fallen even more than shown in figure 3-5, because in 2016 the Bureau of Labor Statistics changed its formula from geometric to Laspeyres, which increases the measured rate of inflation (CEA 2018b).

[25] The three health insurance actions are (1) reducing, through the Tax Cuts and Jobs Act of 2017, the individual mandate penalty to zero owed by consumers who did not have federally approved coverage or an exemption; (2) permitting, via a June 2018 rule, more small businesses to form Association Health Plans (AHPs) to provide lower-cost group health insurance to their employees; and (3) expanding, through an August 2018 rule, short-term, limited-duration insurance plans.

Figure 3-5. Inflation-Adjusted CPI for Prescription Drugs, 2009–19

Prescription drug CPI / all items CPI (ratio)

Sources: Bureau of Labor Statistics; CEA calculations.
Note: The Consumer Price Index (CPI) covers retail transactions, which are about three-fourths of all prescription drug sales. Inflation adjustments are calculated using the ratio of the CPI of prescription drugs relative to the CPI-U for all items. The preinauguration expansion trend in annual growth rates is estimated over a sample period July 2009–December 2016, with 2017–19 projected levels then reconstructed from projected growth rates.

household each year.[26] Among those who benefit from these deregulatory actions are an estimated 1 million consumers who will save on their individual health insurance policy premiums by switching to less-regulated short-term plans, with savings that may exceed 50 percent.[27] Also included are small businesses, which may see substantial premium savings from obtaining access to cheaper large-group health insurance coverage.

Employment Regulations

Unlike large companies, small businesses do not typically have a team of in-house lawyers and regulatory compliance staff, making understanding

---

[26] This average includes zeros for households not affected by the four deregulatory actions. For the purposes of calculating real income effects, we do not count parts of the net benefit that are consumer hassle costs because those costs are traditionally excluded from GDP, even though they are genuine costs from a consumer's point of view. Similarly, we treat the revealed preference value of public health insurance as part of "net benefits" but not GDP or real income, which traditionally are assigned those values according to cost rather than revealed preference value. As a result, the GDP effect of the health insurance deregulations is less than the net benefit, while the opposite tends to occur for other deregulations.

[27] Part of the premium savings comes from the fact that the short-term plans restricted by the Obama Administration have different characteristics than the individual plans regulated by the Affordable Care Act. The CEA's (2019a) analysis shows how the Trump Administration's deregulatory actions reduced health insurance prices significantly, even after adjusting for differences in plan characteristics. See also our report (CEA 2019a) for sources on short-term plan premiums.

and complying with regulations particularly onerous. Of the small businesses surveyed monthly by the National Federation of Independent Business (NFIB) between 2012 and the election of President Trump, a plurality of surveyed businesses selected "government requirements and red tape"—that is, regulations—as their single most important problem 45 percent of the time they were asked. Though a plurality of small businesses have never selected regulations as their single most important problem since President Trump's election, regulations remain an important issue.

During President Trump's Administration, the Department of Labor (DOL) and National Labor Relations Board (NLRB) have been working to eliminate a number of regulations that disproportionately burden small businesses, reduce worker productivity and real wages, and distort competition in the labor market. The NLRB, under the Obama Administration, expanded the definitions of both joint employer and independent contractor, which, among other things, would have categorized some franchisers as joint employers of their franchisee employees. DOL had also changed its guidance under certain statutes regarding joint employers and independent contractors.

Without the Trump Administration's proposed deregulatory actions, thousands of small businesses, including franchisees and subcontractors, would no longer be able to compete against larger corporations, and millions of workers' wages would have fallen due to the effect of these labor regulations. The CEA (2019b) estimates that, together, the Obama Administration's DOL guidance and the NLRB standard related to joint employers would have created more than $5 billion in annual net costs and reduced real incomes by about $11 billion.

Federal rulemaking also plays a role in maintaining a level playing field for small businesses that are subject to State regulations. In 2015, DOL determined that Federal rulemaking was likely required in order to permit States to mandate private employers to administer payroll deductions, with proceeds to be invested in State-managed individual retirement accounts (IRAs), and automatically enroll their employees in those accounts. In the revealed preference framework, the fact that a number of small businesses did not voluntarily offer these plans strongly suggests that the costs of administering these plans exceeded the value they create for employees.[28] Nevertheless, a number of States are requiring all employers to automatically enroll employees, and legislation is pending before other State legislatures to require the same.[29] If employers are forced to comply, the administrative costs, or the penalty for noncompliance, reduce what can be paid out in employee compensa-

---

[28] Between 39 million and 72 million people work for an employer that does not offer a retirement plan (AARP 2014; Panis and Brien 2015; and the final rule). Following the standard approach in labor economics (Lazear 1979, 1981; Mortensen 2010), we assume that the composition of employee compensation maximizes the joint surplus of employer and employee.

[29] See State of Oregon (2015).

tion, which is why Congress and President Trump overturned previous DOL rulemaking designed to facilitate the State-level employer mandates.

The CEA uses the same economic framework for analyzing the IRA mandate that it used for health insurance mandates (CEA 2019a).[30] We assume that Federal rulemaking is relevant and will be affecting 10 million workers with an average annual IRA contribution of $1,571 per year.[31] We estimate that each $1,571 deposited in an IRA is, in present value terms, a transfer from the Federal Treasury to the worker of $526. Because employers need to be forced to provide the accounts, we infer that there is some combination of marginal employer and employee costs of providing a retirement plan that equals or exceeds $526 per worker each year. Conversely, this cost is bounded above by $526, plus the annual per-worker fine for noncompliance, which we take to be $250 per employee each year.[32] Following Harberger (1964), this makes the aggregate of the employer and employee costs $6.5 billion per year.[33] Adding in the deadweight cost of taxes, that is a net cost of $10 billion per year, most of which is borne outside the State implementing the program. As a real income loss (i.e., ignoring factor-supply costs in the net cost calculation), it is $13 billion per year.

In 2011, DOL proposed costly "Persuader Rule" amendments to the Labor-Management Reporting and Disclosure Act that would potentially have generated reporting requirements for consultants (including attorneys) when the employer posed labor law questions, even if the attorney or consultant did not communicate directly with employees.[34] These amendments were

---

[30] One difference is that the IRA mandates allow individuals to opt out without penalty. Our analysis assumes that some, but not all, workers affected by the rule will opt out. Research has found that automatic enrollment in retirement plans generates substantial inertia, so workers remain in plans that they would not have voluntarily chosen (Madrian and Shea 2001; Bernheim, Fradkin, and Popov 2015).

[31] "Since 2012, 40 States have studied proposals for State-facilitated savings programs or considered or adopted legislation to create them. At least 10 States enacted legislation to expand access to retirement savings for nongovernmental workers. California, Connecticut, Illinois, Maryland, and Oregon have all adopted auto IRA models" (NCSL 2018). As to the average contribution, the CEA notes that the Illinois pilot had 196 employees investing an average of $392.86 per employee per quarter (about $1,571 a year) (Hayden 2018).

[32] The Illinois fine is $250 per employee a year (Hopkins 2015). California has a $250 penalty 90 days after receiving a noncompliance notice and a $500 penalty after 180 days (UC Berkeley Labor Center 2017). It is unclear whether and how often the State will send notices. It does not appear that Oregon has yet established its penalty.

[33] It is often the case in cost-benefit analysis that a reduction in subsidy payments is merely a transfer that leaves social benefits unchanged; the benefits to taxpayers are exactly offset by the costs to the recipients who lose the subsidy. The tax subsidy to IRA deposits is properly treated as a transfer when the task is evaluating the effects of the subsidy—i.e., when comparing current policy with a hypothetical policy that has no tax subsidy for IRAs. But the purpose of this chapter is to evaluate the effect of relaxing restrictions on choices by employers and employees, not changing the tax subsidy rules for IRAs. See also CEA (2019a).

[34] Cummings (2016) and 81 FR 15924.

finalized and set to take effect in 2016, but were delayed due to ongoing litigation.[35] The Persuader Rule amendments were rescinded by DOL in 2018.[36]

Under the Persuader Rule, consultants (including attorneys) would have needed to file with DOL a Form LM-20, which becomes publicly available, reporting the amount of their fee and the type of advice provided.[37] As another example, persons attending an invited talk at their local Chamber of Commerce related to employment law would have had their names "likely disclosed to DOL and made [publicly] available." In order to comply with the Persuader Rule, a practitioner of labor law might have had to "identify and segregate every increment of time billed to each of [their] clients for 'labor relations advice or services' even if the firm was not doing any 'persuader' consulting under the New Rule for that client currently." The American Bar Association understood the Persuader Rule to require labor lawyers to violate their ethical duties to their clients (Brown 2016, 8–10), while some labor law firms refused to take on any work that would fall under the Persuader Rule's new reporting requirements.[38]

Due to the large number of employers subject to the rule, the midpoint of Furchtgott-Roth's (2016) estimates shows the rule to have ongoing compliance costs of $5.4 billion per year combined for employers, attorneys, and consultants. Initial costs of the rule were estimated as $3.6 billion. The CEA determined that 1 of the 18 components of the estimates may be overstated, and therefore we adjusted the ongoing costs downward to $4.9 billion per year in 2018 prices. The compliance costs come out of productivity and thereby have additional net annual costs of $2.4 billion, as they reduce aggregate supplies of capital and labor.

These and other rules introduced by DOL and the NLRB during the Obama Administration had anticompetitive effects on the labor market.[39] We do not attempt to parse the combined effects among the various rules and guidance, but instead allocate it entirely to the rules regarding joint employers, and we then avoid double-counting by omitting any competition costs of other NLRB and/or DOL regulations. The combination of regulations cited in this section would have reduced real incomes by about $45 billion per year, or an average of almost $400 per household each year.

---

[35] See *NFIB v. Perez* (2016). Also see Eilperin (2017).

[36] See DOL (2017).

[37] This paragraph quotes or paraphrases Cummings (2016).

[38] See page 79 of the June 20, 2016, testimony in *NFIB v. Perez* (Federal case number 5:16-cv-66).

[39] See the CEA's (2019b) analysis (as well as 81 *FR* 15929) of how a broader definition of "joint employer" would reduce competition among employers in some industries.

Financial Regulations

In the wake of the 2007–9 global financial crisis, banking reforms attempted to address the systemic risk created by large financial institutions. Congress and regulators raised banks' capital standards, imposed new stress tests, and bestowed new regulatory powers on bank regulators. Though these reforms were intended to reduce the risks created by large financial institutions, the Dodd-Frank Act's regulations imposed costly new regulatory requirements on small and mid-sized banks that did not pose a systemic risk.

Ultimately, Dodd-Frank's overly broad regulations hurt lending to small businesses by unnecessarily burdening community and regional banks, which play an outsized role in supporting small businesses and local economies across the Nation. Per the Federal Deposit Insurance Corporation's definition, community banks make up 92 percent of federally insured banks and thrifts, and they are responsible for 16 percent of total loans and leases. Community banks also hold 42 percent of small loans to farms and businesses. Also, in 2014 there were 646 United States counties in which the only banking offices belonged to community banks, and another 598 counties where community banks held at least 75 percent of deposits. Together, these counties made up almost 40 percent of all U.S. counties.

The 2018 Economic Growth, Regulatory Relief, and Consumer Protection Act, also known as the "Crapo Bill," signed by President Trump, removes the restrictions from smaller banks that were misapplied to them as part of earlier efforts to alleviate the "too big to fail" banking problem. The CEA (2019b) posits that this act "recognizes the vital importance of small and midsized banks, as well as the high costs and negligible benefits of subjecting them to regulatory requirements better suited for the largest financial institutions. [It] is expected to reduce regulatory burdens and help to expand the credit made available to small businesses that are the lifeblood of local communities across the nation."

Heightened consolidation among small banks (those with assets less than $1 billion) followed the enactment of Dodd-Frank, with the number of institutions declining by more than 2,000 (–31.0 percent) since 2011. Bank consolidation is not inherently uncompetitive, but consolidation that is driven by regulations reflects the distortionary burden of regulatory costs. After Dodd-Frank, the total loans by small banks has declined from $889 billion to $815 billion (–8.3 percent) since 2011. If these small banks had instead grown their loan portfolios by 1.55 percent—the average of the past three expansions—during this period, there would have been about 20 percent more small bank loans now than there actually are. These missing loans are associated with about $6.3 billion in additional annual value added in small banking, which we estimate to produce about $3 billion in annual surplus for lenders and borrowers.[40] Including effects on the entire economy due to additional employment and investment, the Crapo Bill has annual net benefits of almost $5 billion and raises real annual incomes by about $6 billion by removing regulatory burdens from small bank lenders.

The CEA has also conducted industry-specific analyses of the effects of several other regulations that were introduced during the years 2010–16 and have been removed (or are in the process of being removed) during the Trump Administration. One of these was the attempt by the Consumer Financial Protection Bureau (CFPB) to largely eliminate the small dollar lending industry, which had revenues of about $7 billion per year in 2015 (82 *FR* 54479). Small dollar lending is a valuable service that provides consumers with important resources and flexibility to better manage their finances. The CFPB's analysis acknowledged that consumers found the loans helpful for paying "rent, childcare, food, vacation, school supplies, car payments, power/utility bills, cell phone bills, credit card bills, groceries, medical bills, insurance premiums, student educational costs, daily living costs," and other pressing expenses (82 *FR* 54515). The CFPB predicted that its rule would reduce activity in the small dollar lending industry by 91 percent. The lost flexibility to use small dollar lending to help pay for pressing expenses is indicative of the opportunity costs of sharply contracting the industry. Using revealed preference methods, the CEA estimates a corresponding loss of consumer and producer surplus of $3 billion, and a reduction of real incomes by about $7 billion.[41]

Additional Regulations

Among our sample of 20 rules, we find that 6 have comparatively small aggregate effects: DOL's Fiduciary Rule, the Security and Exchange Commission's Disclosure of Foreign Payments by Resource Extraction Issuers, the Department of the Interior's Stream Protection Rule, the CFPB's prohibition of arbitration agreements in financial contracts, the Waste Prevention Rule, and a U.S. Department of Agriculture (USDA) rule implementing the Packers and

---

[40] Our estimate of lender surplus uses the Lerner-index estimates from Koetter, Kolari, and Spierdijk (2012) and assumes a unit price-elasticity of loan demand with respect to net interest margin.

[41] Assuming that the industry demand for small dollar lending is linear in the fees charged and has a point elasticity of −1, the lost consumer surplus alone is $2.7 billion. The lost consumer surplus is even more if the demand for small dollar lending has a constant elasticity, even if this elasticity were as far from zero, as is the firm-level elasticity of −4.28 estimated by McDevitt and Sojourner (2016).

Stockyards Act.[42] We estimated that eliminating these 6 rules, as the Trump Administration has done, increases real incomes by about 0.06 percent in total, which is about $11 billion per year. A 7th rule that has also been eliminated, the Fair Pay and Safe Workplaces Rule, may technically have zero effect on GDP and real incomes because it raises the costs of Federal contractors whose contribution to GDP is by definition its costs.[43] Although the effects of these 7 rules are likely large compared with many of the rules not in our sample, $11 billion per year is a small fraction of the combined effects of the other 13 rules in our sample.

We have not measured the economic impact of hundreds of FY 2017 and FY 2018 Federal rules, including a few regulations. However, the aggregate cost savings reported for the other rules as recorded in the *Federal Register* are in the direction of additional cost savings, suggesting that the cost savings from our sample of 20 deregulatory actions may be a conservative estimate of the cost savings from all regulatory and deregulatory actions since January 2017.

The Doubling Effect of Shifting from a Growing Regulatory State to a Deregulatory One

Before 2017, the Federal regulatory norm was the perennial addition of new regulations. As shown above, in figure 3-1, between 2000 and 2016, the Federal government added an average of 53 economically significant regulations each year. During the Trump Administration, the average has been only 10 (not counting deregulatory actions or transfer rules).

Even if no old regulations were removed, freezing costly regulation would allow real incomes to grow more than they did in the past, when regulations were perennially added (shown by the dark blue line in figure 3-6), as with the

---

[42] The Fiduciary Rule added to the costs of saving for retirement by further expanding the circumstances under which a financial adviser is considered to be fiduciary. DOL estimated at the time the rule was published in 2016 that it would benefit investors on net. The rule was vacated in toto by the Fifth Circuit Court of Appeals in *Chamber of Commerce v. Department of Labor*, 885 F.3d 360 (5th Cir. 2018). The Disclosure of Foreign Payments by Resource Extraction Issuers Rule raised costs for U.S. extraction companies. "Hydrological balance" provisions of the Stream Protection Rule would shut down much of the U.S. longwall mining industry (*Murray Energy Corporation v. U.S. Department of the Interior*, 2016). The CFPB "prohibit[ed] consumers and providers of financial products and services from agreeing to resolve future disputes through arbitration rather than class-action litigation," which would have raised the prices of consumer financial products (U.S. Department of the Treasury 2017). The Waste Prevention Rule added additional restrictions on "oil and gas drilling and extraction operations on Federal and tribal lands" (CEA 2019b, 287). The USDA rule interfered with vertical contracts in the production of poultry and pork, raising costs throughout the supply chains (8th circuit 2018).

[43] In contrast, raising the costs of private enterprises typically does reduce GDP and real incomes because their contribution to GDP depends on the value those enterprises create for their customers, as measured by what customers pay. The CEA notes that the production of some of the Federal contractors may be measured like those of private enterprises, in which case zero is a conservative estimate of the real income effect of overturning the rule.

Figure 3-6. Deregulation Creates More Growth Than a Regulatory Freeze, 2001–21

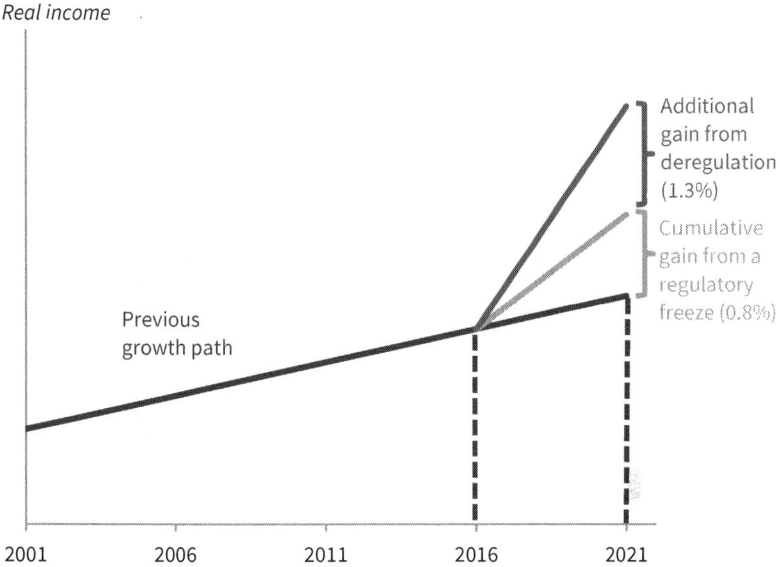

Real income

Additional gain from deregulation (1.3%)

Cumulative gain from a regulatory freeze (0.8%)

Previous growth path

2001   2006   2011   2016   2021

Source: CEA calculations.

yellow line in figure 3-6. The amount of extra income from a regulatory freeze depends on (1) the length of time that the freeze lasts and (2) the average annual cost of the new regulations that would have been added along the previous growth path. For the sake of illustration, figure 3-6 shows a freeze through 2021. We also have a conservative estimate of the average annual cost of regulatory additions during the years 2010–16, namely, the cost of 20 of the rules created during those years and identified in our sampling. At 1.3 percent of real income spread over those 7 years, that is an annual cost addition of about 0.19 percent a year (i.e., about $1,900 per household after 7 years). Those years are somewhat unusual in terms of numbers of new economically significant regulations, so we take the previous trend (for 2001–16) to be 0.16 percent a year. In other words, by the fifth year of a regulatory freeze, real incomes would be 0.8 percent (about $1,200 per household in the fifth year) above the previous growth path.

As well as restraining the addition of new regulations, the Trump Administration has removed previous ones. As shown by the red line in figure 3-6, removing costly regulations allows for even more growth than freezing them. As explained above, the effect, relative to a regulatory freeze, of removing 20 costly Federal regulations has been to increase real incomes by 1.3 percent. In total, this is 2.1 percent more income—about $3,100 per household

Box 3-2. How Old Are Midnight Regulations?

A number of the regulations reversed by the Trump Administration have been called "midnight regulations," which are final rules published between Election Day and the inauguration of a new President. (Thus, midnight regulations refer to regulations finalized at the end of a Presidential term and before the change to a President of the other political party.)

A new President can reverse the midnight regulations by using the standard rulemaking process to refuse to defend the regulations in court, or by (together with Congress) overturning them with procedures established by the 1996 Congressional Review Act (CRA). In theory, the publishing of a costly midnight regulation, along with its reversal soon afterward, could have little or no effect on industry or the wider economy if market participants recognize that the midnight rules would not last long enough to constrain economic activity. (If market participants anticipate use of the Congressional Review Act, a costly midnight regulation could have the opposite effect, because the CRA would prohibit all future administrations from promulgating the same or a similar rule imposing those costs, until a future Congress expressly approved that type of regulation.) However, the most costly of the 2016 midnight regulations cannot be characterized this way because (1) they had been in the rulemaking process for years before the 2017 inauguration, (2) most of the 2016 polls and media predicted a different election outcome, and (3) the CRA had been used only once before 2017.

Sixteen Obama-era regulations were ultimately nullified by the CRA. The more economically important of these are the Federal rule allowing States to mandate employers to provide retirement accounts (the "IRA-mandate rule"), the FCC rule regarding broadband privacy, and the Securities and Exchange Commission's rule requiring public disclosure of foreign payments (RIN 1210-AB71; see also 1210-AB76, document FCC-2016-0376-0001, and RIN 3235-AL53, respectively). They date back as far as 2010 but became eligible for CRA nullification in the 115th Congress because challenges from courts and the public extended the rulemaking process until late 2016, or later. (See also Public Citizen 2016, which found that midnight regulations "of Presidents Bill Clinton and George W. Bush took longer [3.6 years], and underwent more days of OIRA review than the average rule over the past 17 years.") The IRA-mandate rule dates back to at least 2015. The proposed FCC privacy rule was released April 1, 2016, although arguably it was anticipated by the FCC's actions on "net neutrality" dating back to 2010.

The CEA therefore sees the Obama-era economic regulations as part of a normal rulemaking process rather than an economically irrelevant signaling of a political platform. Although final rules follow their notices of proposed rulemakings with a time lag, and a new Administration may decline to finalize notices of proposed rulemaking from a previous Administration, the length of the time lag should not affect estimation of the medium- to long-term economic effects of deregulation or of a regulatory freeze. The length of the time lag does affect the timing of the economic effects.

each year—relative to the previous growth path.[44] (Also see box 3-2 on so-called midnight regulations.)

Regulations Before 2017 with Disproportionate Costs

The analysis thus far has primarily considered the effects of regulation on income, but regulation—or the lack of it—can affect well-being in nonpecuniary ways not captured by income. However, even when including nonpecuniary costs and benefits, we estimate that deregulatory actions have a net benefit of more than $2,500 per household each year, compared with the previous trend of growing regulatory costs. The gain stems from the fact that the new level of regulation strikes a better balance between the costs of regulations and their societal benefits, where benefits include things valued by people but not necessarily bought or sold in the marketplace (and that thus are not included in the National Income and Product Accounts or in the usual income measures). The Trump Administration requires Federal agencies to conduct cost-benefit analyses of significant regulatory actions, including deregulatory actions, and that they only be issued "upon a reasoned determination that benefits justify costs" (OMB 2017).

An example from health policy illustrates how regulations before 2017 created disproportionate incremental costs and benefits. The Affordable Care Act created an individual mandate in order to reduce the costs of uncompensated care.[45] But the average annual costs of uncompensated care are about $1,000 per uninsured person (including zeros in the average for those who are uninsured who do not use uncompensated care during the year), whereas the annual economic costs of the individual mandate are over $3,000 per uninsured person induced to purchase coverage (CEA 2019a).

One economic reason that regulations before 2017 were so costly is that some of them were implemented with only a little "safety valve" in terms of an option for regulated businesses to pay a moderate fine in instances when compliance is especially costly. For example, whereas automobile manufacturers had the option of paying a penalty to the National Highway Traffic Safety Administration (NHTSA) for falling short of Federal fuel economy standards, the EPA is prohibited by the Clean Air Act from adopting the NHTSA's penalty structure to enforce the greenhouse gas standard that began with model year 2012 (75 *FR* 25482). As another example, a consultant incorrectly filling out DOL Form LM-21 (one of the requirements under the rescinded Persuader Rule) would be exposed to criminal penalties. Another reason is that the labor

---

[44] The red line's path in figure 3-6 is drawn as linear for illustration purposes only. The 1.3 percent effect (relative to a freeze) of deregulation is likely nonlinear over time, and it may take more than five years to be fully realized.

[45] Section 1501(a)(2)(F) of the Patient Protection and Affordable Care Act.

market is arguably the largest market of all, with annual revenues of more than $10 trillion, and it was the object of active rulemaking by DOL during the Obama Administration.

Conclusion

Coincidentally with the 2017 Presidential inauguration, real GDP growth changed from underperforming experts' forecasts to outperforming them (Tankersley 2019). The CEA's findings on the aggregate effects of regulations and deregulations may help explain this turnaround. Regulatory actions and their aggregate effects may be easily overlooked and underestimated because the actions are numerous and, if not seen through the lens of economic analysis, may appear cryptic to the general public. This chapter helps to narrow this information gap by showing the importance of the deregulatory agenda for everyday Americans as well as the national economy.

Since 2017, consumers and small businesses have been able to live and work with more choice and less Federal government interference. They can purchase health insurance in groups or as individuals without paying for categories of coverage that they do not want or need. Small businesses can design compensation packages that meet the needs of their employees, enter into a genuine franchise relationship with a larger corporation, or seek confidential professional advice on how to organize their workplaces. Consumers have a variety of choices for less expensive wireless and wired Internet access. Small banks are no longer treated as "too big to fail" (which they never actually were) and as subject to the costly regulatory scrutiny that goes with this designation.

In addition to regaining freedoms that they once had, consumers and small businesses no longer need to dread the steady accumulation of costly new Federal regulations. In a time frame of 5 to 10 years, these landmark changes to regulatory policy are anticipated to increase annual incomes by about $3,100 per household ($380 billion in the aggregate), by increasing choice, productivity, and competition. This chapter arrives at its aggregate total by building estimates from the industry level. In doing so, it closely examines specific Federal rules, accounts for the unique circumstances of the industries targeted by these rules, and quantifies benefits of regulation—such as consumer data privacy, environmental protection, fuel savings, and reductions in uncompensated healthcare. The analysis employs an economic framework that situates each industry in a larger economy that includes market distortions caused by taxes, imperfect competition, and other factors.

The benefits of the newest wave of deregulation compare favorably with those during the most significant deregulatory waves of American history. Take the deregulation of airlines and trucking that occurred four decades ago, as the major parts of a deregulation wave described as "one of the most important experiments in economic policy of our time" (Winston 1993). Combined, the

Carter Administration's deregulation of these two industries provided net aggregate benefits of about 0.5 percent of national income. Although no 2 of the 20 deregulatory actions analyzed in this chapter have had (according to our estimates) such a large net benefit, their combined net aggregate benefits exceed 0.6 percent of national income.[46]

Other notable historical deregulations were of natural gas markets between 1985 and 1993, which had benefits estimated at about 0.2 percent of national income (Davis and Kilian 2011). This is hardly more than the combined net benefit of the three health insurance rules analyzed in this chapter. Moreover, the totals reported in this chapter reflect only deregulatory actions occurring during less than three years, whereas the full effects of the deregulation of airlines, trucking, and natural gas each reflect actions taken over almost a decade.[47].

There is room for additional deregulation to further grow the economy, increasing benefits to American consumers, workers, and businesses. According to the accounting for Executive Order 13771, the projected cost savings from planned deregulatory actions in FY 2020 exceed the combined cost savings achieved in 2017, 2018, and 2019. The Administration has also taken further steps to promote regulatory reform. On October 9, 2019, President Trump signed two regulatory reform Executive Orders. The first is titled "Promoting the Rule of Law Through Improved Agency Guidance Documents." Many discussions of Federal regulatory and deregulatory actions, including most of this chapter, focus on rules adopted through the Administrative Procedure Act's notice-and-comment rulemaking process. In addition to such rules, Federal agencies issue nonbinding guidance documents. Although guidance documents are not subject to the notice-and-comment requirements, some impose substantial regulatory costs. The new Executive Order's improvements to guidance documents include requirements that clarify their nonbinding status. Significant guidance documents are also now subject to cost-benefit analysis. The second Executive Order, signed on October 9, is titled "Promoting the Rule of Law Through Transparency and Fairness in Civil Administrative Enforcement and Adjudication." In an economic framework, agencies' enforcement strategies can have important implications for regulatory costs (Fenn and Veljanovski 1988). Perhaps more important, the enforcement of regulations should be fair to the public. The new Executive Order "prohibits agencies from enforcing rules they have not made publicly known in advance." Finally, in parallel with the

---

[46] Winston (1993, table 6) reports net benefits accruing in the airline and trucking industries that hold aggregate factor supplies constant. In calculating the 0.6 percent for comparison, we also held aggregate factor supplies constant.

[47] Murphy (2018, 76) cites "U.S. Federal intervention into the petroleum industry in the 1970s [as] arguably the largest peacetime government interference with the economy in the nation's history." Arrow and Kalt (1979) estimate the cost of this intervention to be 0.2 percent of national income. Moreover, the 1979–81 deregulation did not realize this full amount in cost savings because price controls were replaced with a windfall profits tax.

reforms of Federal regulations, the Administration has created the Governors' Initiative on Regulatory Innovation to encourage States to adopt regulatory reforms. The initiative will help governors and the White House work with leaders in local and tribal governments to cut regulatory costs, advance reforms to occupational licensing, and align regulations across levels of government.

Chapter 4

Energy: Innovation and Independence

U.S. energy innovation has continued to flourish under the Trump Administration. Innovation—and the policies that support it—lowers costs and prices, and increases production. This is illustrated by the American shale revolution and its dramatic rise in oil and gas drilling productivity in shale and similar geologic formations. Gains in shale drilling productivity have led to lower prices for natural gas, electricity, and oil, saving the average family of four $2,500 annually. Shale-driven savings represent a much larger percentage of income for the lowest fifth of households than for the highest fifth.

Production growth due to shale innovation has also brought energy independence to the United States, a goal first set by President Richard M. Nixon, and pursued by subsequent Administrations, but accomplished under the Trump Administration. In 2017, the United States became a net exporter of natural gas for the first time since 1958; and in September 2019, the United States became a net exporter of crude oil and petroleum products and is projected to remain a net exporter for all of 2020 for the first time since at least 1949. Historically, a rise in energy prices increased the trade deficit and costs for firms and households, sometimes pushing the U.S. economy into a recession. The innovation-driven surge in production and exports has made the U.S. economy more resilient to global oil price spikes. It has also improved the country's geopolitical flexibility and influence, as evidenced by concurrent sanctions on two major oil-producing countries, Iran and Venezuela.

In addition to consumer savings and energy independence benefits, the shale revolution has reduced carbon dioxide and particulate emissions through changes in the composition of electricity generation sources. We estimate that from 2005 to 2018, the shale revolution in particular lowered carbon dioxide emissions in the electric power sector by 21 percent. This contributed to a greater decline in carbon dioxide and particulate emissions (relative to the size of the economy) in the United States than in the European Union, according to the most recent data.

The Trump Administration's deregulatory energy policy follows earlier Federal deregulatory policies that helped to spur the shale revolution. By limiting unnecessary constraints on private innovation and investment, the Administration supports further unleashing of the country's abundant human and energy resources. In contrast, the State of New York has banned shale production and stymied new pipeline construction, leading to falling natural gas production in the State, greater reliance on energy produced elsewhere, and higher energy prices. Similarly, evidence on renewable energy mandates at the State and Federal levels shows their costs and limitations. More broadly, predicting the evolution of energy markets and technologies remains difficult—few anticipated the shale revolution's effect on lower prices for natural gas, electricity, and oil or the current economic challenges in the nuclear power sector. This difficulty highlights the value of policies that avoid picking winners and losers and instead provides a broad platform upon which innovation will flourish.

The classic effects of innovation are improvements in productivity, which lower costs and prices and increase production.[1] Energy sector innovations—and the policies that support them—have similar effects and ultimately reduce prices for American households and businesses. This chapter describes the causes and consequences of growth in oil and natural gas production from shale and similar geologic formations, while also highlighting broader energy sector innovations and policy questions. We first discuss the dramatic rise in productivity and its effects on cost, production, and price. Second, we estimate the consumer savings brought by shale-driven declines in energy prices. Third, we document how the surge in shale production has led to

---

[1] The CEA previously released research on topics covered in this chapter. The text that follows builds on the report "The Value of U.S. Energy Innovation and Policies Supporting the Shale Revolution" (CEA 2019).

U.S. energy independence, as measured by positive net exports of both oil and natural gas. Fourth, we assess total and shale-related changes in emissions in the United States. Finally, we consider the implications of deregulatory versus government-directed energy policies.

From 2007 to 2019, innovation in shale production brought an 8-fold increase in extraction productivity (new well production per rig) for natural gas and a 19-fold increase for oil. These productivity gains have reduced costs and spurred production to record-breaking levels. As a result, the United States has become the world's largest producer of both commodities, surpassing Russia in 2011 (for natural gas) and Saudi Arabia and Russia in 2018 (for oil). The Council of Economic Advisers (CEA) estimates that greater productivity reduced the domestic price of natural gas by 63 percent as of 2018 and led to a 45 percent decrease in the wholesale price of electricity. The increase in U.S. oil production linked to shale oil development helped not only moderate but also reduce the global price of oil over the same period in the face of "peak oil" forecasts. By lowering energy prices, we estimate that the shale revolution saves U.S. consumers $203 billion annually, or $2,500 for a family of four. Nearly 80 percent of the total savings stem from a substantially lower price for natural gas, of which more than half comes from lower electricity prices. Because low-income households spend a larger share of their income on energy bills, lower energy prices disproportionately benefit them; shale-driven savings represent 6.8 percent of income for the lowest fifth of households, compared with 1.3 percent for the highest fifth. These consumer savings are in addition to economic benefits linked to greater employment in the sector.

At the same time, shale-driven production growth has fulfilled the nearly 50-year goal of U.S. energy independence. In 2017, the United States became a net exporter of natural gas for the first time since 1958; and in September 2019, the United States became a net exporter of crude oil and petroleum products and is projected to remain a net exporter for all of 2020 for the first time since at least 1949. The long-standing goal of energy independence was motivated by the historic vulnerability of the U.S. economy to oil price spikes. Historically, a rise in energy prices increased the trade deficit and costs for firms and households, potentially pushing the U.S. economy into a recession. In fact, a sudden rise in the price of oil preceded 10 of the 11 postwar recessions in the United States (Hamilton 2011). With energy independence, spikes in global energy prices continue to affect U.S. households and businesses, but they now have a more muted effect on gross domestic product (GDP) because they do not inflate the trade deficit as they did when net imports were high. From 2000 to 2010, a $1 increase in oil prices reduced the U.S. trade balance in goods by $0.83 billion; from 2011 to 2019, it reduced it by only $0.17 billion. Higher prices could even increase GDP if they cause a large enough increase in investment by U.S. energy producers. Greater exports and resilience to price shocks have also improved the country's geopolitical flexibility and influence, as evidenced by concurrent sanctions on two major oil producers.

In addition to consumer savings and energy independence benefits, the shale revolution has reduced carbon dioxide and particulate emissions through changes in the composition of electricity generation sources. The CEA estimates that from 2005 to 2018, the shale revolution in particular was responsible for reducing electric power sector carbon dioxide emissions by 21 percent. This contributed to a greater decline in carbon dioxide emissions and particulate emissions (relative to the size of the economy) in the United States than in the European Union from 2005 to 2017, the most recent year for data in both areas.

The Trump Administration's deregulatory energy policy follows earlier Federal deregulatory policies that helped to spur the shale revolution. By limiting unnecessary constraints on private innovation and investment, the Administration's deregulatory policy supports further unleashing of the country's abundant human and energy resources. In contrast, the State of New York has banned shale production and stymied new pipeline construction, leading to falling natural gas production in the State, greater reliance on energy produced elsewhere, and higher energy prices. Similarly, evidence on renewable energy mandates at the State and Federal levels shows their costs and limitations. More broadly, predicting the evolution of energy markets and technologies remains difficult—few anticipated the shale revolution's effect on lower prices for natural gas, electricity, and oil or the current economic challenges in the nuclear power sector. This highlights the value of policies that avoid picking winners and losers and instead provides a broad platform upon which innovation will flourish.

Market Pricing, Resource Access, and Freedom to Innovate

Growth in the extraction of oil and natural gas from shale and similar geologic formations—often referred to as the shale revolution—is arguably the most consequential energy development in the last half century. Its far-reaching consequences are in part because fossil fuels account for 80 percent of U.S. energy consumption (EIA 2019b). Most oil goes to fuel the planes, trains, and automobiles of the transportation sector, while most natural gas generates electric power or heat for industry and households.

Since at least the late 1970s, geologists knew that shale and other low-permeability formations contained prodigious amounts of natural gas. For decades, methods to profitably extract the gas eluded the industry, much of which pursued easier-to-access resources in the United States and abroad. Although various countries have abundant shale resources, entrepreneurs and engineers working in the United States' innovation-friendly context first unlocked the potential of shale, which would eventually bring large savings to consumers and environmental benefits relative to a scenario without shale development.

The shale revolution came after major deregulatory changes in the governance of natural gas pricing and distribution. Three major deregulatory actions—the 1978 Natural Gas Policy Act, the Federal Energy Regulatory Commission's 1985 Open Access Order, and the 1989 Natural Gas Wellhead Decontrol Act—liberalized access to pipelines and increased the role of market forces in determining prices paid to natural gas producers. Earlier price controls discouraged production and exploration, leading to supply shortages. Once freed to move with supply and demand, wellhead prices increased, encouraging more innovation, which eventually lowered prices (MacAvoy 2008). Prices, however, would begin to increase again in the late 1990s and early 2000s.

Higher wellhead prices justified taking innovative risks on new methods and geologic formations, and private ownership of underground resources made it easy for firms to access these resources and experiment in diverse locations. The United States is unique in that the private sector—homeowners, farmers, and businesses—owns the majority of subsurface mineral rights. This system allows private owners to grant access to energy firms through lease contracts, which can be for one-tenth of an acre or 10,000 acres (Fitzgerald 2014). As a result, energy firms do not need to navigate a cumbersome central government bureaucracy to begin accessing subsurface resources. Although firms must still abide by Federal and State regulations, gaining the right to access resources is straightforward—they just need to adequately compensate the owner of the relevant acreage.

The role of the Federal government in unlocking the shale revolution is often overstated. Certainly, the U.S. Department of Energy's (DOE) investment of about $130 million from 1978 to 1992 in Federal funding for research on drill bit technology, directional drilling, modeling for shale basin reservoirs, and microseismic monitoring of multistage hydraulic fracturing treatment helped spur sector innovation. A more detailed analysis shows that primary credit belongs to the private sector. Federally subsidized research to aid the development of shale gas in the East carried limited transferability to the early breakthroughs in Barnett shale formation. Moreover, an early tax credit aimed at stimulating the production of natural gas from unconventional sources expired in 1992, well before important breakthroughs in the early 2000s.[2]

Among firms pioneering in shale extraction, the most important is arguably Mitchell Energy. In the 1980s and 1990s, Mitchell Energy, which had long-term contracts to sell its natural gas, experimented with methods to coax natural gas from a Texas geologic formation known as the Barnett Shale.

---

[2] Wang and Krupnick (2015) discuss Federal government policies that may have aided Mitchell Energy as it experimented in the Barnett and generally conclude that subsidies, tax credits, tax-preferred business structure, and research and development played a secondary role.

Consistent commercial success emerged in the early 2000s, when Devon Energy acquired Mitchell Energy. This acquisition accelerated the merger of two complementary technologies. Devon had considerable experience with horizontal drilling, which involves drilling a conventional vertical well, and at the bottom of the vertical leg, transitioning to a horizontal leg, which can extend for several miles. Mitchell Energy had more experience pumping liquids and sand under high pressure into wells to fracture low-permeability formations, thereby releasing gas and/or oil trapped in the rock. This stimulation technique is known as hydraulic fracturing (Wang and Krupnick 2015). Promising results from Devon's wells, coupled with rising natural gas prices, spurred a drilling boom in the Barnett Shale. Thus, the number of well permits issued in the Barnett grew from less than 300 in 2000 to more than 4,000 in 2008. The revolution had begun.

The shale revolution may not have been sustained if it had not been for continued innovation by scores of engineers, geologists, and entrepreneurs, who refined and adapted methods to draw oil from western North Dakota and southern Texas as well as natural gas from Appalachia in the Eastern United States. Persistent innovation and opportunity for its diffusion has transformed energy markets, with considerable implications for consumers and the environment.

Important innovations have also occurred elsewhere in the energy sector. Advances in the design of combined-cycle turbines in natural gas plants have allowed the plants to generate more electricity from each unit of heat. From 2008 to 2017, the amount of heat needed to generate a kilowatt-hour of electricity declined by 10 percent. In addition, the cost of turbines, measured in dollars per unit of capacity, has fallen by 11 percent since 2014. Alongside more efficient and less costly natural gas turbines, the cost of wind power projects has also fallen recently, causing wind power prices to fall by more than 50 percent from 2010 to 2017. These gains stem from various factors, including larger turbines and lower manufacturing costs. Solar power generation has made similar gains.

Innovations in these sectors proved complementary. Electricity from wind and solar technologies remain variable and present challenges for grid management because generation may not align with the demands of the electric grid in any given hour. Relative to most other sources of electricity, natural-gas-fired generators can quickly ramp up and ramp down generation to assist with grid integration and systems balancing requirements. Gains from innovation, however, have not occurred everywhere. Cellulosic biofuel production has grown slowly and is well below levels prescribed by a Federal mandate (see box 4-1).

Box 4-1. The Limits of Energy Mandates to Induce Innovation

The directness of government mandates can have great appeal. Commands that the market conform to government targets, however, have limits in what they can achieve, as illustrated by the Federal Renewable Fuel Standard. Even when targets are met, they can come at a much higher cost than projected.

Figure 4-i. U.S. Cellulosic Biofuel Statute and Final Volumes, 2010–19

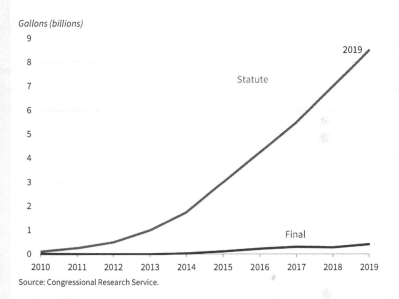

Source: Congressional Research Service.

To further U.S. energy independence and provide additional revenue sources to U.S. farmers, the Federal Renewable Fuel Standard, which was set in 2005 and expanded in 2007, mandated increases in the domestic production and consumption of renewable fuels. The standard mandated the use of different categories of renewable fuels, with type-specific targets increasing over time for most categories. Technology to produce ethanol from corn was well established by the mid-2000s, and corn-based ethanol production and consumption quickly increased and have generally kept in line with the targets set in the 2007 statute. In contrast, technology to convert cellulosic plant material, such as corn fodder, into renewable fuels was not well established when the standard went into effect, and progress has been slow despite the mandate. As a result, the EPA has utilized its waiver authority, authorized in the 2007 statute, when setting targets for cellulosic biofuel (figure 4-i). The cellulosic mandate has been waived every year since its establishment in 2010, resulting in no significant production of cellulosic biofuel. By 2019, the industry was to have produced 8.5 billion gallons of cellulosic biofuel.

The Effects of Innovation on Productivity, Prices, and Production

Innovation raises productivity and lowers production costs, allowing firms to offer lower prices. This dynamic corresponds to the textbook case of an outward shift in the domestic supply curve, as shown in figure 4-1, for the case of natural gas. The shift means that firms produce more at every price level than they did before innovation, which lowers the market equilibrium price, which is shown on the vertical axis in figure 4-1 as a change in P, while increasing the quantity produced, as shown on the horizontal axis as the change in Qp. The lower price stimulates an increase in consumption, as shown on the horizontal axis as the change in Qc.

Because of imports and exports of natural gas, the market price is affected by the global price and does not occur at the intersection of domestic supply and domestic demand. Before shale gas development, domestic consumption exceeded domestic production, leading to imports, as shown in figure 4-1 as the difference between domestic production and consumption before shale. After shale, domestic production exceeds domestic consumption, leading to exports.

The Impact on Productivity

Horizontal drilling and hydraulic fracturing made the development of shale and other low-permeability formations economical. In the last decade, all growth in onshore oil and gas production has come from the development of these formations. One measure of innovation and productivity gains by energy producers is the quantity that new wells are producing relative to the number of rigs in use, which the DOE's Energy Information Administration (EIA) tracks for all major shale formations. This measure, known as new-well production per drilling rig, is defined as the total production of wells recently brought into production divided by the number of drilling rigs recently in operation.

New–well production per rig increased by more than 8-fold between 2007 and 2019 for key shale gas regions and by more than 19-fold for key shale oil regions. Particularly strong growth has occurred in the last five years for both oil and gas (figure 4-2).[3] The recent growth highlights how energy firms have continued to improve upon the earlier breakthroughs of shale pioneers.

The productivity gains in production per rig stem from several factors that allow firms to generate more production from each rig per unit time. For example, across regions and over time, the number of days needed to drill a

---

[3] The sharp rise in productivity in 2016 largely reflects firms deciding to operate fewer drilling rigs (because of very low prices) and focus on bringing wells already drilled into production. This can be seen by a sharp decline in drilled but uncompleted wells in 2016. Similarly, a rise in drilled but uncompleted wells in 2017 helps explain the apparent slowdown in productivity in that year. See EIA (2019) for estimates of drilled but uncompleted wells.

Figure 4-1. Innovation in Natural Gas Production

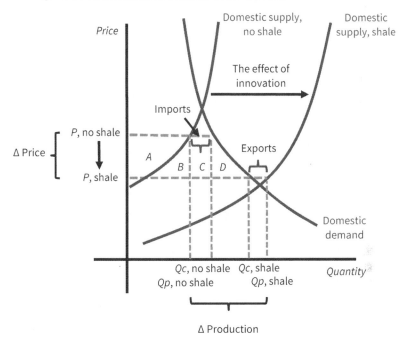

Figure 4-2. Productivity Gains: New-Well Production per Rig, Oil and Natural Gas, 2007–19

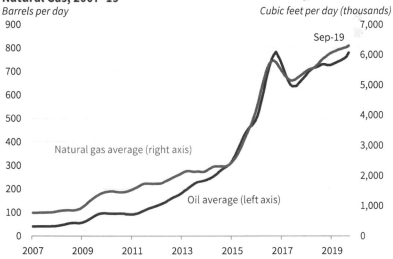

Sources: Energy Information Administration; CEA calculations.
Note: New-well production is the number of oil (or gas) wells, and their output, that are in their first month of production. The rig count is the number of active oil (or gas) drilling rigs two months prior.

Figure 4-3. Gains in Productivity Lower Breakeven Prices Across Key Shale Formations, 2014–19

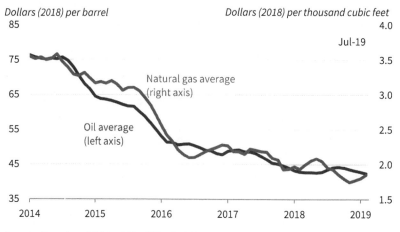

Dollars (2018) per barrel

Dollars (2018) per thousand cubic feet

Sources: Bloomberg; BTU Analytics; CEA calculations.
Note: Breakeven prices include the cost of drilling and operating a well and bringing the resource to market, including royalties, taxes, and gathering and compression costs. The oil average is the average price between Bakken Formation, Denver Basin, Eagle Ford, and Permian Basin. The natural gas average is the average price between Marcellus-Utica and Haynesville. Data, adjusted to 2018 dollars using the Consumer Price Index (CPI-U), are a six-month moving average.

well has fallen (EIA 2016), and the average production from a well's first month has grown (EIA 2018b). The improvements come partly from firms drilling wells with longer horizontal portions, and from placing more wells per pad—both of which allow each well and pad to access more oil and gas.

Greater productivity reduces the cost of producing each barrel of oil or cubic foot of natural gas. Lower unit costs lead to a lower breakeven price, which is the price needed to cover the costs of drilling and operating an oil or gas well. Figure 4-3 shows an estimated breakeven price based on modeling of production costs in different regions.[4] From 2014 to 2019, the breakeven price for natural gas (averaged across key shale formations) fell by 45 percent; for oil, it fell by 38 percent. The link between productivity—as measured by new-well production per rig in operation—and breakeven prices is direct. Well operators typically lease drilling rigs, paying as much as $26,000 per day, so finishing a well in half the time yields considerable savings. Similarly, higher volumes of initial production return cash more quickly to the firm and can mean greater lifetime production from the well.

---

[4] The breakeven price, calculated by BTU Analytics, is best interpreted as the price needed to justify drilling another well, assuming that the energy firm already holds the necessary acreage. The price for a given period is calculated based on historical production data and projections of future production to model revenue and costs for every well brought into production in the period. This analysis assumes a discount rate of 10 percent and a well life of 240 months. It is not based on energy firm calculations of their own breakeven costs and excludes potential costs that energy firms may incur, such as interest payments on debt and costs to acquire their acreage.

The Impact on Prices and Production

In its *Annual Energy Outlook*, the EIA projects energy-related outcomes for the coming decades. The projections incorporate detailed information and assumptions on resource reserves, emerging technologies, new policies, and numerous other relevant trends. The difference between projected and actual outcomes provides one measure of the surprise and disruption brought by the shale revolution. This difference does not necessarily isolate the shale revolution's contribution because markets may have evolved differently than expected for reasons other than shale.

The 2006 *Annual Energy Outlook*, which made projections for 2005 and later, projected that natural gas production in the lower 48 States would rise gradually and reach 19 trillion cubic feet by 2018. Actual dry gas production for the lower 48 states reached more than 30 trillion cubic feet in 2018, 58 percent higher than projected, and now greatly exceeds that of any other country (figure 4-4). The production growth was not because of higher-than-expected prices. To the contrary, prices in 2018 were 46 percent lower than projected (figure 4-5).

Figure 4-4. Natural Gas Actual Production versus Projected Production, 2005–18

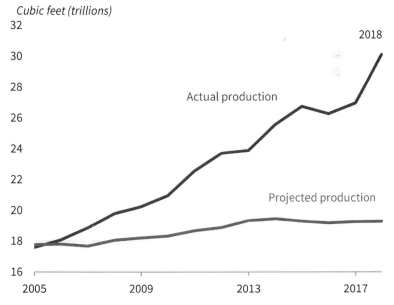

Cubic feet (trillions)

Sources: Energy Information Administration (EIA); CEA calculations.
Note: Projections are from the EIA *2006 Annual Energy Outlook*. Production is for the lower 48 States, which exclude Alaska and Hawaii. Dry gas refers to gas that is primarily methane, rather than hydrocarbon compounds.

Figure 4-5. Natural Gas Actual Prices versus Projected Prices, 2005–18

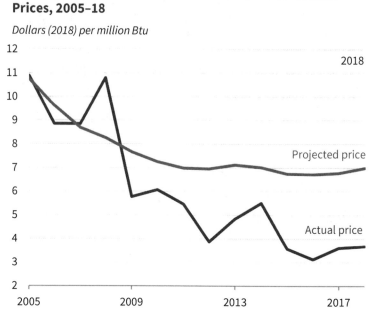

Dollars (2018) per million Btu

Sources: Energy Information Administration (EIA); CEA calculations.
Note: Btu = British thermal unit. Projections are from the EIA *2006 Annual Energy Outlook*. Prices are adjusted to 2018 dollars using the Consumer Price Index (CPI-U). Dry gas refers to gas that is primarily methane, rather than hydrocarbon compounds.

Figure 4-6. U.S. Monthly Wholesale Electricity Price and Natural Gas

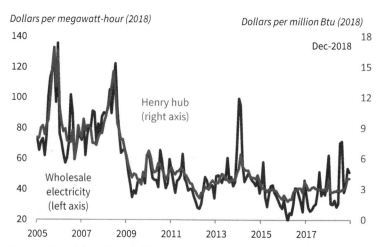

Dollars per megawatt-hour (2018)   *Dollars per million Btu (2018)*

Sources: Energy Information Administration; Intercontinental Exchange; CEA calculations.
Note: Btu = British thermal unit. Wholesale electricity prices were weighted by volume across weeks and eight wholesale electricity hubs. Wholesale natural gas prices are the Henry Hub spot price. Prices are adjusted to 2018 dollars using the Consumer Price Index (CPI-U).

Figure 4-7. U.S. Crude Oil Production, 2005-18

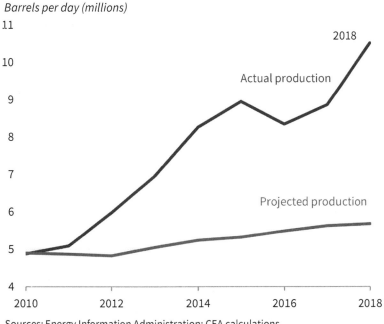

Barrels per day (millions)

2018

Actual production

Projected production

Sources: Energy Information Administration; CEA calculations.
Note: Projections are from the *EIA 2011 Annual Energy Outlook*. Production is for the lower 48 states, which excludes Alaska and Hawaii. Production includes both onshore and offshore production.

The unexpected production growth and price decline of natural gas spilled over to electricity markets. Wholesale electricity prices oscillated around $80 per megawatt–hour from 2005 to 2008, but then dropped markedly as the price of natural gas fell. Although natural gas-fired generators have accounted for less than one-third of electricity generating in recent years, they play an outsized role in influencing prices in competitive wholesale electricity markets. This is because such generators are often the marginal generator of electricity, and their operators can adjust output quickly in response to the market with relative ease, making their costs and bid prices an important determinant of the market price of electricity. Figure 4-6 shows the close tracking of wholesale natural gas and electricity prices, and several studies have documented a strong causal effect of natural gas prices on wholesale electricity prices (Linn, Muehlenbachs, and Wang 2014; Borenstein and Bushnell 2015).

Turning to oil, the difference between projected and actual oil production is even starker than the case of natural gas. Actual production in the lower 48 States in 2018 exceeded the production projected by the EIA in 2011 by 85 percent, leading the United States to surpass Russia and Saudi Arabia to become the top global oil producer. Some of the difference between actual

Figure 4-8. Imported Oil Prices, 2005–18

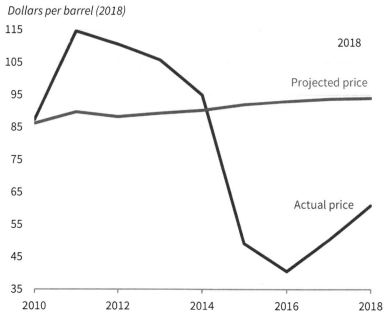

Dollars per barrel (2018)

Sources: Energy Information Administration; CEA calculations.
Note: Projections are from the *EIA 2011 Annual Energy Outlook*. Prices are adjusted to 2018 dollars using the Consumer Price Index (CPI-U). Imported crude prices are the refiners' average acquisition cost for imported crude oil.

and projected production stems from greater-than-expected oil prices in the first half of the 2010–18 period. The benefit of oil sector innovation, however, is still evident; since 2015, actual prices have been below projected prices, while production has greatly exceeded projections (figures 4-7 and 4-8).

The Impact of the Shale–Induced Decline in Energy Prices

A simple supply-and-demand framework permits estimating how much energy prices have fallen because of the shale revolution as opposed to other factors that have changed over time. For natural gas, we draw from Hausman and Kellogg (2015), who look at the market effects of shale gas from 2007 to 2013. Their analysis focuses on estimating the price of natural gas in a world without the shale revolution, noting that the actual change in price before and after the emergence of shale is not necessarily the causal effect of shale because the demand curve could have shifted. As a result, they estimate supply and demand curves for natural gas for 2007 and for 2013. The price of natural gas in the no-shale scenario is then estimated as the price at the intersection of the 2007 supply (pre-shale) curve and the 2013 demand curve.[5] (For details on estimating the shale-driven price effect, see Hausman and Kellogg 2015). Our primary modifications to their price analysis are to use 2018, the most recent year for annual data, as the end year, not 2013; and to use more recent estimates of the supply elasticity of natural gas from Newell, Prest, and Vissing (2019).

We also estimate the effect of lower natural gas prices on wholesale electricity prices. Natural gas plays a unique role in the electricity sector. In many parts of the United States that have competitive wholesale electricity markets, natural-gas-fired plants generated the marginal unit of electricity sold. As a result, a decline in their costs lowers the market price of electricity, meaning that all electricity generators, regardless of their fuel source, receive a lower price. Likewise, all buyers, regardless of who provides their electricity, pay a lower price. Linn, Muehlenbachs, and Wang (2014) studied the effect of the shale-driven decline in natural gas prices on electricity prices and found that across wholesale market hubs, a 1 percent decrease in the price of natural gas lowers the price of electricity by 0.72 percent. To estimate the shale-driven change in the wholesale price of electricity, we therefore multiply the shale-driven percentage change in the price of natural gas (described in the prior paragraph) by 0.72.

For estimating the effect of shale oil on prices, we consider two surges in shale oil production, with the second surge associated with production cuts by the Organization of the Petroleum Exporting Countries (OPEC). The first wave is defined by Kilian (November 2008–August 2015), and the second we define as January 2017–May 2019. For the first wave, we draw from Kilian (2017), who estimates the monthly Brent crude oil price absent U.S. shale oil development. For the second wave, we take the Killian effect from the end of the first wave and apply it to the change in U.S. shale oil production in the second wave, after taking into account the production cuts among OPEC countries since 2016.

Kilian (2017) estimates the first shale oil wave reduced the global oil price by roughly $5.00 per barrel by August 2015. Extending his analysis to the second wave of production growth from shale, we estimate that the additional production further cut $1.29 per barrel by May 2019, resulting in a total price drop of $6.29 per barrel. This represents a 10 percent decline in the 2018 price of oil relative to what it would have been if the shale revolution had never occurred.

Turning to natural gas, we estimate that in a no-shale scenario, the price of natural gas would be $7.79 per thousand cubic feet, which is given by the

---

[5] Both prices are estimated by finding the price that solves a similar basic equation: Quantity Supplied (P) + Net Imports (P) = Residential Demand (P) + Commercial Demand (P) + Industrial Demand (P) + Electric Power Demand (P), where P is the price of natural gas. The demand and supply curves are assumed to take the form $Q = A \cdot (P + markup)^{\eta}$, where η is an elasticity. The net import function is assumed to be linear in price and is estimated using data from 2000 to 2018.

intersection of the 2007 natural gas supply curve and the 2018 demand curve. With the shale-driven outward shift in the supply curve, the price falls to $2.87 per thousand cubic feet, a 63 percent decrease. Put differently, natural gas prices in 2018 were 63 percent lower than they would have been if the shale revolution had never occurred, and they were far less variable. This is roughly the same percentage change in the Henry Hub price of natural gas over the 2007–18 period.

Based on the estimates by Linn, Muehlenbachs, and Wang (2014), the lower price of natural gas implies that shale gas led to a 45 percent decrease in the wholesale price of electricity as of 2018. This estimated decline is also consistent with the wholesale futures price data listed by the EIA from the Intercontinental Exchange. In real terms, the weighted-average wholesale price across market hubs fell by 44 percent from 2007 to 2018.

We note that retail electricity prices did not decline during the same period, in part because of State renewable portfolio standards mandating that a certain percentage of a State's electricity must come from renewable sources like wind or solar. At least 29 States have adopted such standards, with the first being Iowa in 1983. The most recent study of these standards finds that even modest renewable electricity targets bring considerable retail price increases (Greenstone and Nath 2019). They find that 12 years after a State adopted a renewable portfolio standard, retail electricity prices increased by an average of 17 percent. Over the same period, the standards raised the proportion of renewable electricity generation by at most 7 percentage points.[6]

Innovation-Driven Consumer Savings, Energy Independence, and Environmental Benefits

This section first explores methods of estimating consumer savings from lower energy prices. Then it examines the salient findings related to these consumer savings. Next, it delineates the United States' path toward energy independence. And finally, it discusses the environmental benefits of the shale revolution.

Consumer Savings—Methods

Lower energy prices can benefit consumers in diverse ways—through lower bills for heating or lighting, less spending at the gas pump, and lower prices for goods or services that require considerable energy inputs such as airline travel or building materials. The standard approach to estimating the total consumer

---

[6] This assumes that the state started with zero renewable electricity generation, which is why it is a generous estimate of the increase in renewable generation caused by the standard. The 7 percent is based on the finding by Greenstone and Nath (2019) that the gross renewable requirement increased to roughly 11 percent 12 years after adopting a standard and that the actual level of renewable generation was about 4 percentage points below the grow requirement.

benefit from a price decline is to calculate the savings for those consuming before the price decline, whose value is represented in figure 4-1 above by the rectangle formed by areas A, B, and C, and the savings on additional consumption spurred by the price decline, represented by area D.[7] We take this approach for oil, multiplying the shale-induced change in the price of oil ($6.29 per barrel) with the pre-shale quantity consumed (about 7.0 billion barrels annually), and adding it to one-half the product of the price change and the price-induced change in consumption (0.1 billion barrels).

We modify this approach for natural gas to account for the spillover effects in the electricity market. First, we estimate savings using the standard approach described above and following Hausman and Kellogg (2015), who break total demand into its sectoral components, including the electricity sector. We first estimate savings for the electric power sector in the same manner as Hausman and Kellogg (2015); call this S^{HK}. Their approach assumes that each $1 saved because of cheaper natural gas translates into $1 saved for electricity consumers. This is a reasonable approach for the share of the power sector with cost-of-service regulation, in which case regulators would only reduce compensation to natural-gas-fired generators, not to other generators, and only by as much as such generators had cost reductions.

For the share of the sector without cost-of-service regulation, however, we translate the lower natural gas prices into lower wholesale electricity prices, following Linn, Muehlenbachs, and Wang (2014). The price-setting effect of natural-gas-fired electricity generators magnifies the effect of lower natural gas prices because the gas-driven decline in wholesale electricity prices applies to all electricity consumed in deregulated markets, not just the electricity generated by natural gas. We then assume that wholesale market savings pass through to retail savings, dollar for dollar, which is consistent with the research of Borenstein and Bushnell (2015), who find high rates of pass-through in deregulated markets.

One-third of the electricity generated in the United States in 2018 was generated in States without cost-of-service regulation of generators.[8] Based on this share, we estimate total electric power sector savings to be the sum of the savings in regulated markets (= 0.67 x S^{HK}) and the savings from unregulated markets (= 0.33 x $S^{Wholesale}$).

---

[7] The supply shift and price change will also affect producer surplus (not shown in figure 4-1), which is the difference between revenue and cost across all units produced and all producers. Whether producers benefit from innovation (as measured by producer surplus) depends in large part on how much prices fall and quantities increase. It is likely that there is a net loss in producer surplus for natural gas producers (Hausman and Kellogg 2015) but a gain for oil producers, whose production has increased greatly with only a modest price decline.

[8] The EIA provided the CEA with an analysis of data from EIA Form 923, which collects detailed information from the electric power sector. The analysis showed that in 2018, 33 percent of electric power supply occurred in regional transmission organizations in unregulated states.

The approach to estimating natural gas savings, which involves sector-specific consumption amounts and demand curves, permits calculating savings for the residential, commercial, industrial, and electric sectors, which we collapse into two sectors: the nonelectric sector and the electric sector. For oil, we break savings into transportation and nontransportation sector savings, allocating savings to the transportation sector based on its share of total petroleum consumption in the United States (70 percent) as reported by the EIA for 2018.

Regarding the pass-through of energy savings to household income groups, we first allocate residential natural gas and residential electricity savings based on each income group's share of spending on natural gas and electricity, as reported in the 2018 Consumer Expenditure Survey of the Bureau of Labor Statistics. We then estimate the oil-related transportation sector savings associated with direct household consumption by multiplying the total oil savings by the share of transportation sector energy use accounted for by light-duty vehicles such as cars and sport utility vehicles. These direct household savings are then distributed to household income groups based on each group's spending on "gasoline, other fuels, and motor oil," as reported in the 2018 Consumer Expenditure Survey.

Finally, we allocate the natural gas, electricity, and oil-related savings that initially occur in the commercial and industrial sectors. We assume that the savings are eventually passed through to households in the form of lower product prices, with savings allocated to each household income group according to its share of total household expenditures, as reported in the 2018 Consumer Expenditure Survey. This is a common approach in the literature on the incidence of carbon taxes, which increase energy prices (Mathur and Morris 2014). It also has empirical support in important product markets (e.g., Muehlegger and Sweeney 2017). The exporting of some of the industrial sectors' output to global markets would suggest that the approach overstates savings to U.S. consumers. The shale revolution, however, has also reduced global energy prices, which would lower the costs of foreign producers, some of whom serve the U.S. market. We assume that these competing effects offset each other.

Consumer Savings—Findings

By lowering energy prices, the shale revolution is saving U.S. consumers $203 billion annually, or an average of $2,500 for a family of four. Nearly 80 percent of the savings stem from a substantially lower price for natural gas, of which more than half comes through lower electricity prices (figure 4-9). The large decline in the price of natural gas, and therefore large savings, is because domestic supply has overwhelmed domestic demand, and the capacity to liquefy and export natural gas to global markets has expanded too slowly to absorb the supply growth. Oil, in contrast, is economical to transport and is traded on a

Figure 4-9. Shale Oil and Gas Consumer Savings per Year by Sector

Dollars (billions)

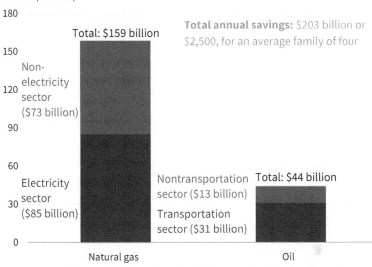

Total: $159 billion

Total annual savings: $203 billion or $2,500, for an average family of four

Non-electricity sector ($73 billion)

Electricity sector ($85 billion)

Nontransportation sector ($13 billion)

Total: $44 billion

Transportation sector ($31 billion)

Natural gas   Oil

Sources: Energy Information Administration; Kilian (2016); Caldara et al. (2019); CEA calculations.

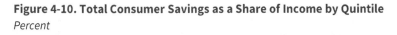

Figure 4-10. Total Consumer Savings as a Share of Income by Quintile

Percent

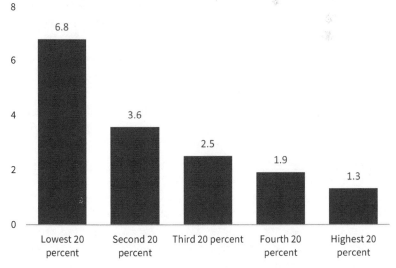

Sources: Bureau of Labor Statistics; CEA calculations.
Note: Values represent the CEA's estimates of consumer savings as a share of pretax income in 2018.

Box 4-2. Economic Effects Linked to Drilling and Production

Although much of this chapter focuses on the shale revolution's effect on consumers, growth in drilling and production has also brought employment, income, and public revenues to producing regions and beyond. Relative to the State of New York's border counties, which have not had shale development, Komarek (2016) found that counties in the Marcellus region that were developed had a 6.6 percent increase in earnings. Across the United States, Feyrer, Mansur, and Sacerdote (2017) estimate that new extraction increased aggregate employment by as much as 640,000 jobs. In addition to creating wage-earning opportunities, expanded drilling in places like North Dakota and Pennsylvania has also brought large payments to landowners holding rights to subsurface resources. Energy firms typically compensate resource owners by paying them a share of the value of production from their land. In 2014, production from major shale formations generated nearly $40 billion in payments to resource owners (Brown, Fitzgerald, and Weber 2016).

Drilling and production can also generate revenue for some State and local governments and local school districts. Between 2004 and 2013, State revenues from taxes on oil and gas production in the lower 48 states nearly doubled, reaching $10.3 billion in real terms (Weber, Wang, and Chomas 2016). At the local level, increases in revenues have largely outweighed costs for local governments in most producing states (Newell and Raimi 2018). In certain states, such as Texas, oil and gas wells are also taxed as property and can therefore provide revenues to local school districts. For example, shale development in Texas's oil formations increased the property tax base by over $1 million per student in the average shale district, leading to 20 percent more spending per student (Marchand and Weber 2019).

massive global market, which domestic oil production has influenced but not overwhelmed. As a result, oil accounts for the other 20 percent of the savings, most of which are transportation sector savings on fuel.

Because lower-income households spend a larger share of their income on energy bills, the savings have greater relative importance for them. Energy savings represent 6.8 percent of income for the lowest fifth of households, compared with 1.3 percent for the highest fifth (figure 4-10). In other words, lower energy prices are like a progressive tax cut that helps the lowest households the most. The variation in savings stems heavily from differences in spending on electricity; according to the 2018 Consumer Expenditure Survey, the bottom 20 percent of households account for 8.6 percent of expenditures in general but for 14.1 percent of electricity expenditures. We also considered the economic benefits of increased drilling and production on employment, income, and public revenues in differing regions as well (box 4-2).

Energy Independence

Historically, a rise in energy prices increases the trade deficit and costs for firms and households, sometimes pushing the U.S. economy into a recession. For example, a sudden rise in the price of oil preceded 10 of the 11 postwar recessions in the United States (Hamilton 2011). The vulnerability of the U.S. economy to price shocks motivated a long-standing goal of U.S. Presidents: U.S. energy independence.

President Richard M. Nixon began the push for energy independence, announcing Project Independence in 1973 when the Organization of Arab Petroleum Exporting Countries halted oil shipments to the United States. In the ensuing years, Congress and the executive branch directed much attention and resources to pursue energy independence, including the Energy Policy and Conservation Act (1975), the establishment of the Department of Energy (1977), the Energy Policy Act (2005), and the Energy Independence and Security Act (2007).

By a common measure of independence—net exports (Greene 2010)—the United States essentially achieved independence in both natural gas and oil at the end of 2019, and net exports are projected to grow in 2020 and beyond. Today's achievement, however, does not stem primarily from these government efforts but rather from private sector innovation that few expected. The shale-driven growth in domestic production documented earlier in this chapter reduced imports and, most recently, led to a surge in exports of both oil and gas. Fewer imports and more exports caused U.S. net imports of natural gas to fall below zero in 2017, making the United States a net exporter of natural gas for the first time since 1957 (figure 4-11). And, in September 2019, net imports of crude oil and petroleum products fell below zero on a monthly basis (figure 4-12). The United States is projected to remain a net exporter of crude oil and petroleum products for all of 2020 for the first time since at least 1949.

Energy independence—as measured by positive net exports, and by increased sectoral diversification of the U.S. economy, especially in places like Texas—means that higher global energy prices have a negligible or perhaps positive effect on the U.S. economy in the aggregate. With a large domestic energy sector, increases in investment by the domestic energy sector offset the effect of higher prices on consumers (Baumeister and Kilian 2016). If, for example, higher oil prices induce substantial new investment in drilling wells, with its associated demands for steel and equipment, GDP would likely increase as long as the reduced disposable income of consumers has a small effect on their overall spending (see box 4-2 for an in-depth explanation of the economic impact of increased drilling and production). This does not mean that the typical U.S. consumer is unaffected by higher oil prices or benefits from them. Rather, it means that the country's total output may expand as prices rise.

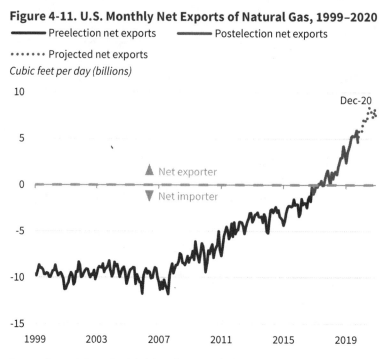

Figure 4-11. U.S. Monthly Net Exports of Natural Gas, 1999–2020

Preelection net exports   Postelection net exports

•••••• Projected net exports

Cubic feet per day (billions)

Sources: Energy Information Administration; CEA calculations.

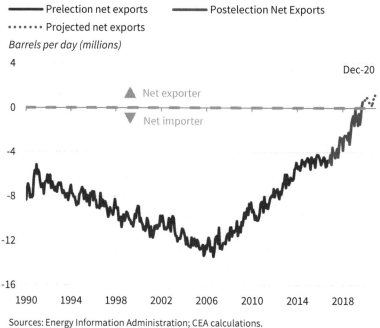

Figure 4-12. U.S. Monthly Net Exports of Crude Oil and Petroleum Products, 1990–2020

Prelection net exports   Postelection Net Exports

•••••• Projected net exports

Barrels per day (millions)

Sources: Energy Information Administration; CEA calculations.

Figure 4-13. Changes in Price of Oil (Prior Month) and Changes in the Goods Trade Balance, 2000–2010 and 2011–19

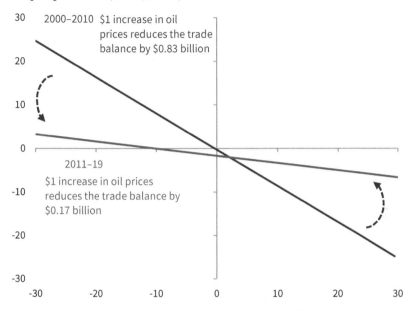

Change in goods deficit (dollars, billions)

Sources: Energy Information Administration; *Wall Street Journal*; Census Bureau; CEA calculations.

In addition, if net imports are near zero, large changes in the global price of oil will have negligible effects on the U.S. trade balance, which directly affects the country's GDP (Cavallo 2006). Figure 4-13 shows that over the 2000–10 period, when the United States imported record amounts of oil and petroleum products, a $1 per barrel increase in the price of oil reduced the trade balance in goods by $0.83 billion. In the 2011–19 period, which saw falling net imports, the same price increase reduced the trade balance by only $0.17 billion. As U.S. net exports increase, higher prices should eventually increase the trade balance, reflecting greater transfers from foreign consumers to domestic producers.

Energy independence also brings geopolitical benefits, such as more influence abroad and fewer constraints on foreign policy. The rise of the United States as a net contributor to the global oil market has reduced oil prices (Kilian 2016), and has also reduced the dependence of the global market on particular producers. Currently, the United States has sanctions on two major oil-producing countries, Iran and Venezuela. These sanctions, combined with internal factors in the case of Venezuela, have taken millions of barrels of oil per day off the market. Since the United States announced sanctions in November 2018, Iranian exports have declined by 1.4 million barrels per day, an 89 percent decrease from their pre-sanction level; since sanctions on Venezuela took effect in January 2019, exports have fallen by 0.7 million barrels per day, a 60 percent decrease. Energy independence increases the feasibility of such sanctions. In addition, it reduces the incentive to expend foreign policy resources on efforts to lower global energy prices.

Geopolitical gains also stem from net exports of U.S. natural gas. For example, exports of U.S. LNG to Europe have and will continue to provide a diversified source of competitively priced natural gas to reduce the continent's dependence on Russian gas supplies. The U.S. share of Europe's total natural gas imports increased from 0.1 percent in the first five months of 2018 to 1.3 percent in the first five months of 2019. The potential for greater exports of U.S. natural gas to Europe gives U.S. leaders greater influence when discouraging them from supporting the controversial new Nord Stream 2 pipeline project from Russia to Germany. Poland's and Lithuania's leaders are the most recent heads of state to denounce the project as a threat to energy security that would increase European dependence on Russian natural gas supplies.

Environmental Benefits

In addition to bringing energy independence and saving the average family of four $2,500, the shale revolution has brought several environmental benefits. The shift to generating more electricity from natural gas and renewable energy sources reduced energy-related carbon dioxide emissions at the national level to a degree that was not predicted before these innovations. In its 2006 *Annual Energy Outlook*, the EIA projected a 16.5 percent *increase* in carbon dioxide emissions from 2005 to 2018 (figure 4-14). Actual emissions *decreased* by about 12 percent.

Actual energy-related carbon emissions for 2018 were 24 percent lower than projected in 2006. Some of the decline is because projections assumed greater GDP growth and therefore greater electricity demand than what actually occurred, in part because of the Great Recession and slow recovery. An important part of the decline, however, stems from lower natural gas prices reducing reliance on electricity generated from coal. Over the period, the proportion of generation from coal-fired power plants fell from 50 percent to 28 percent, while the share from natural gas increased from 19 percent to 35 percent.

Low natural gas prices also aided growth in the generation of wind power, which expanded from less than 1 percent of generation to 7 percent. Although Federal and State policies, such as renewable portfolio standards and tax credits, contributed to the increase in wind power generation, Fell and Kaffine (2018) document the important role of lower natural gas prices in spurring greater market penetration by wind generation. The complementarity stems from the ability of natural gas generators to quickly ramp up or slow down in response to the intermittent wind generation from gusts or lulls in wind.

Figure 4-14. Actual versus Projected Carbon Dioxide Emissions, 2005–18

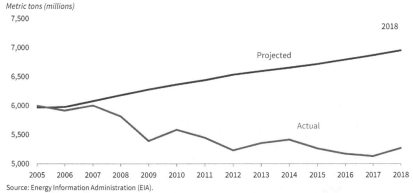

Metric tons (millions)

Source: Energy Information Administration (EIA).
Note: Carbon dioxide emissions represent total emissions from the consumption of energy as reported by the EIA. Projections are from the EIA 2006 *Annual Energy Outlook.*

We estimate that from 2005 to 2018, the shale revolution lowered annual electric power carbon dioxide emissions by 506 million metric tons, a 21 percent decline relative to electric power sector emissions in 2005 (figure 4-15). For the estimate, we assume that coal emissions in the electricity sector would have otherwise remained constant, and we calculate the observed decline in coal emissions, which is 833 million metric tons. We assume that 92 percent of the decline is from shale-driven decreases in natural gas prices. This percentage is from Coglianese, Gerarden, and Stock (2019), who estimate the share of the decline in coal use attributable to the decline in the price of natural gas relative to the price of coal apart from other factors such as environmental regulations, which accounted for another 6 percent of the decline.[9] Finally, we subtract the increase in emissions from greater use of natural gas in electricity generation (506 million metric tons = 833 x 0.92 – 260).[10]

The shale-driven reduction in electric power emissions is larger than what the U.S. Environmental Protection Agency (EPA) projected its 2012

[9] Note that the decline in coal use and coal emissions is linked to the decline in the price of natural gas relative to the price of coal, not to the number of coal plants that are replaced with natural gas plants. Natural-gas-driven changes in electricity prices have caused coal plants to close, and the retired generation capacity has been replaced with a mix of natural gas plants and renewable sources. Also, we note that Coglianese, Gerarden, and Stock (2018) look explicitly at coal production, not consumption, but the two are similar. Over most of their study period, more than 90 percent of production was consumed domestically.

[10] A more detailed analysis could be done to estimate the net greenhouse gas (GHG) effects from shale gas. For example, the CEA estimate does not include leaks from natural gas wells or pipelines. According the EPA's emissions inventory, total GHG emissions from natural gas systems declined from 2005 to 2017. Alvarez et al. (2018) estimate that emissions are 60 percent greater than what the EPA reports. Even if this were true for the 2005 and 2017 EPA measurements, emissions from natural gas systems would have still declined over the period. If emissions were understated in 2017 but not in 2005, the shale-driven declines in emissions would still be larger than those from the policies mentioned in figure 4-15. In general, innovation in leak detection has lowered leak rates over time (see box 4-3).

Figure 4-15. Annual GHG Emission Reductions from Shale Innovation and Major Environmental Policies

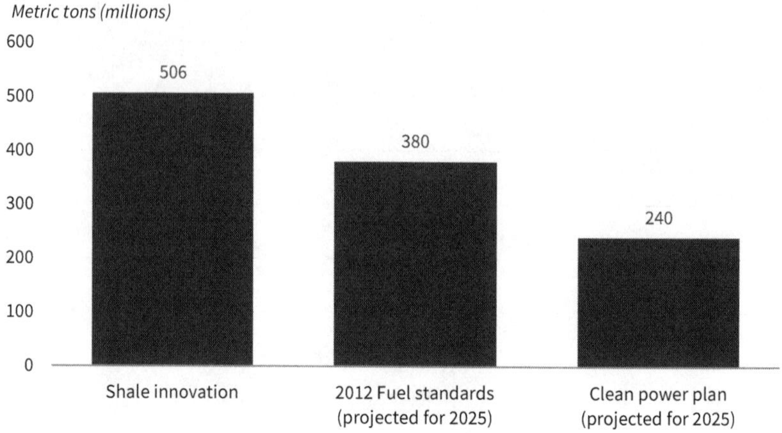

Metric tons (millions)

Sources: Environmental Protection Agency; Stock (2017); CEA calculations.
Note: The Fuel Standards refer to the 2012 Light-Duty Vehicle Greenhouse Gas Emissions and Corporate Average Fuel Economy Standards, which applied to the 2017–25 period.

Light-Duty Vehicle Greenhouse Gas Emissions and Corporate Average Fuel Economy Standards would achieve in 2025 (380 million metric tons) following a considerable increase in stringency. The shale reduction is also more than double what the EPA initially projected that the now-rescinded Clean Power Plan would achieve by 2025 (240 million metric tons).

The shale-driven decline in emissions allowed the United States to have a greater rate of decline in total greenhouse gas (GHG) emissions than the European Union, holding constant the size of the two economies (figure 4-16). From 2005 to 2019, the European Union has developed and expanded an increasingly stringent cap-and-trade system for GHG emissions across its member countries. Although it substantially raised electricity prices for consumers (Martin, Muuls, and Wagner 2015), the system helped the European Union achieve a 20 percent decline in GDP-adjusted emissions from 2005 to 2017, the most recent year of data. Over the same period, emissions fell by 28 percent in the United States, which did not implement a national cap-and-trade system, although various States have pursued policies to cap emissions.

If policymakers had averted the shale revolution through a ban on hydraulic fracturing or other integral components of shale development, energy sector GHG emissions would most likely be higher today. Absent low natural gas prices, renewable electricity sources are unlikely to have enabled similar emissions reductions. A megawatt-hour of coal-fired electricity generates about 1 metric ton of GHG emissions. Achieving the 506 million metric ton decline in GHG emissions is roughly equivalent to reducing coal-fired electricity generation by about 506 million megawatt-hours and replacing it with renewable power generation. This amounts to a 150 percent increase in wind and

Figure 4-16. U.S. versus EU GDP-Adjusted Carbon Dioxide Emissions, 2005–17

Metric tons of CO_2 per billion dollars of GDP (2005 = 100)

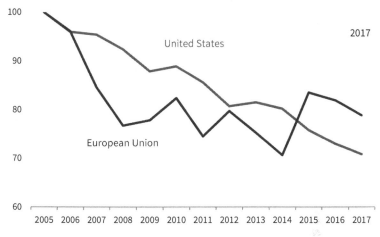

Sources: Environmental Protection Agency; Bureau of Economic Analysis; European Environment Agency; Statistical Office of the European Communities; CEA calculations.
Note: Data are total CO_2 emissions per $1 billion (2017) of each region's GDP.

solar generation above their 2018 level, an increase that is not projected to happen until the 2040s.[11]

During the shale era, the percentage decline in coal-fired generation has roughly equaled the percentage decline in the wholesale price of electricity, suggesting that prices would need to fall 25 percent below their pre-shale level to reduce coal generation by 506 million megawatt-hours (25 percent). This decline would leave wholesale electricity prices about one-third above their 2018 level. This higher price is unlikely to have supported a 150 percent increase in wind and solar generation over their 2018 level (and an even larger percentage increase over their pre-shale level). It implies an elasticity of supply close to 5, roughly twice as large as the empirical estimate by Johnson (2014).

Shale-driven declines in emissions have been large as well as economical. Many policies seek to reduce emissions. Most of them, however, impose a cost on the economy. Gillingham and Stock (2018) summarize research on the cost of reducing a ton of carbon emissions by various methods. They report that renewable fuel subsidies cost $100 per ton of carbon abated, Renewable Portfolio Standards cost up to $190 per ton, and vehicle fuel economy standards cost up to $310 per ton. By comparison, shale innovation brings emissions savings without requiring greater public spending (e.g. subsidies) or costly regulations or mandates.

---

[11] The year 2046 is estimated using the EIA's 2019 *Annual Energy Outlook* forecast of wind and solar generation in the electric power sector through 2050 (EIA 2019c).

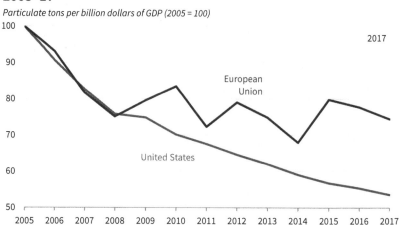

Figure 4-17. U.S. versus EU GDP Adjusted Particulate Emissions, 2005–17

Particulate tons per billion dollars of GDP (2005 = 100)

Sources: Environmental Protection Agency; Bureau of Economic Analysis; European Environment Agency; Statistical Office of the European Communities; CEA calculations.
Note: Values are total particulate matter emissions that are 2.5 microns or less in size per billion 2017 U.S. dollars of each respective region's GDP. Values are normalized such that 2005 is equal to 100. U.S. emissions exclude miscellaneous sources.

Lower natural gas prices have also affected emissions of particulates such as soot, which can affect heart and lung health, especially for those with asthma or heart or lung disease. As with GHG emissions, GDP-adjusted particulate emissions have declined faster in the United States than in the European Union over the 2005–17 period (figure 4-17). The difference in the rate of reduction is considerable, with U.S. particulate emissions per $1 of GDP declining by 57 percent and EU emissions declining by 41 percent. The decline has brought health benefits. Johnsen, LaRiviere, and Wolff (2019) estimate that, as of 2013, the shale-driven decline in particulate and related emissions had $17 billion in annual health benefits (see box 4-3).

The Value of Deregulatory Energy Policy

This section explores the value of deregulatory energy policy. First, it shows how deregulation allows innovation to flourish. Then it explains the private sector's part in the critical responsibilities of building and maintaining energy infrastructure.

Allowing Innovation to Flourish

Government deregulation of natural gas markets—including the 1978 Natural Gas Policy Act, the Federal Energy Regulatory Commission's 1985 Open Access Order, and the 1989 Natural Gas Wellhead Decontrol Act—helped encourage

Box 4-3. Innovation in Pipeline Leak Detection

Pipelines are one of the most effective methods of transporting oil and gas, but they require monitoring and maintenance. Traditionally, monitoring has required that people travel along pipelines by foot, automobile, plane, or all-terrain vehicle. Innovation in technologies such as drones and advanced acoustics has allowed the industry to prevent leaks and more quickly find and stop them when they occur. For example, a Shell pilot drone program illustrates how well-equipped drones can identify pipeline corrosion, abnormal heat signatures, and any effects on wildlife. This helps the company identify leaks, but also reveals areas where preventive maintenance is most needed. With improvements to technology for monitoring pipeline leaks and other improvements across the supply chain, the leak rate for natural gas and petroleum systems fell 31 percent from 2005 to 2017 (figure 4-ii).

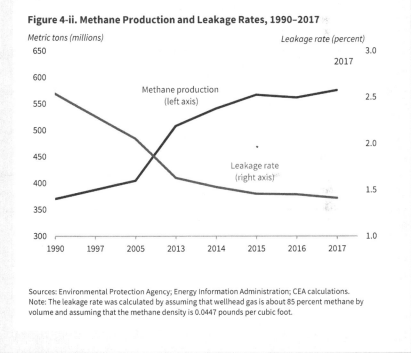

Figure 4-ii. Methane Production and Leakage Rates, 1990–2017

Sources: Environmental Protection Agency; Energy Information Administration; CEA calculations.
Note: The leakage rate was calculated by assuming that wellhead gas is about 85 percent methane by volume and assuming that the methane density is 0.0447 pounds per cubic foot.

the innovation that brought the shale revolution. In the same vein, the Trump Administration has sought to identify and remove regulations that unduly stifle energy development. This is seen in the Presidential Executive Order on Promoting Energy Independence and Economic Growth and the Executive Order on Promoting Energy Infrastructure and Economic Growth. It is also seen in actions such as permitting for the Keystone XL Pipeline and the DOE's approval of a record amount of Liquefied Natural Gas export capacity to non-free trade agreement countries.

The laboratory of State policy experiments provides examples of contrasting policy approaches and their effects. State governments have the primary responsibility to regulate oil and gas development on non-Federal lands, specifying where wells can be drilled, how they must be drilled and monitored, and how they are to be reclaimed at the end of their useful life. Subject to such regulations, most States allow shale development. Maryland, Vermont, and New York, however, have banned hydraulic fracturing, a practice integral to shale development. Of the three States, the New York ban is most consequential because the Marcellus Shale formation, which is the most prolific shale gas formation in the United States, extends into much of Southern New York. Since New York's initial 2010 moratorium on fracking, which morphed into a ban in 2014, energy firms have drilled more than 2,500 wells in Pennsylvania counties adjacent to the New York border (see box 4-4 for further discussion on the risks and benefits of shale development).

The difference in energy-related outcomes in the two States is stark. Development of the Marcellus and Utica Shale in Pennsylvania caused natural gas production to increase 10-fold from 2010 to 2017. Over the same period, New York's production fell by nearly 70 percent. Pennsylvania leads the country in net exports of electricity to other States and produces more than twice the amount of energy it consumes. New York, in contrast, has grown more dependent on electricity generated elsewhere; and in 2017, the State consumed four times as much energy as it produced.

Despite the growth in energy production in Pennsylvania, total energy-related carbon dioxide emissions fell 15 percent from 2010 to 2016, the most recent year of data, twice as much as in New York (7 percent). The greater decline in Pennsylvania stems from larger reductions in the electric power sector.

Innovation, however, can create challenges for particular sectors. Despite substantial and sustained Federal support, including a mid-2000s expectation of a nuclear renaissance, low wholesale electricity prices have reduced the profitability of the nuclear power sector. As a result, a wave of early retirements from existing nuclear power plants has occurred, with more closures planned in coming years (CRS 2018). Given that changes in the market are impossible to predict, a diversified research-and-development portfolio for new energy technologies will best prepare the economy for tomorrow's market realities.

The Critical Role of Energy Infrastructure

Pipelines, electric transmission lines, and export facilities allow energy resources to flow from resource-rich places to resource-scarce ones. The growth in oil and gas supply documented above increases demand for pipelines. For example, with a dramatic rise in production over the last decade,

Box 4-4. Shale Development and Local Communities

Many academic studies have explored the effects of shale oil and gas development on nearby communities. Two studies estimate measures of local net benefits across all major shale regions and reach a similar conclusion: on average, local wage and income effects from development exceed increases in living costs or deterioration in local amenities (Bartik et al. 2019; Jacobsen 2019). Jacobsen (2019) finds that wages across all occupations increased in response to the growth in drilling, regardless of whether they had direct links to the oil and gas industry. Similarly, Bartik and others (2019) estimate that shale development generated $2,500 in net benefits to households in surrounding communities.

It is also evident that local effects can vary greatly, which is illustrated in the diverse effects of development on housing values. Housing values reflect an area's standard of living, including earnings opportunities and amenities, such as good roads. Shale development affects both, creating jobs but also truck traffic and associated disamenities, particularly during times of drilling (Litovitz et al. 2013; Graham et al. 2015). In addition, development, when poorly managed, can pose a risk to groundwater and health, and improper disposal of wastewater can induce earthquakes when best management practices are not followed (Darrah et al. 2014; Keranen et al. 2014; Wrenn, Klaiber, and Jaenicke 2016; Hill and Ma 2017; Currie, Greenstone, and Meckel 2017). Development has had large, positive effects on average housing values over time in many places (Boslett, Guilfoos, and Lang 2016; Weber, Burnett, and Xiarchos 2016; Bartik et al. 2019; Jacobsen 2019). Drilling itself, however, has depressed property values, at least temporarily, for groundwater-dependent homes in Pennsylvania or properties without mineral rights in Colorado (Muehlenbachs, Spiller, and Timmins 2015; Boslett, Guilfoos, and Lang 2016). Welfare effects can also vary across households in shale areas based on the value that households place on greater earning opportunities relative to disamenities, such as noise and congestion.

The nuisances and risks that can come with drilling and fracturing wells highlight the value of prudent State and local policies that match local realities, safeguard the environment and human health, and allow private landowners to contract with energy firms to bring valuable energy resources to market. Almost all major producing States have revised oil and gas laws to address hydraulic fracturing and shale development more generally. North Dakota, for example, adopted rules limiting the flaring of natural gas in 2014, a practice that is especially common in the State because oil producers there have limited infrastructure to deliver to market the natural gas that accompanies oil production. Similarly, as shale development grew in Pennsylvania, the State adopted a policy that effectively ended the treatment of fracking wastewater at publicly owned treatment plants, which were shown to be poorly equipped to properly treat the water.

Pennsylvania has switched from being a major importer of natural gas to being a major exporter. Acquiring regulatory approval and building the necessary pipelines has taken time, progressing to completion in some places but not others.

In 2017 and 2018, private firms finished two major pipeline projects, the Rover and Nexus pipelines, to take Appalachian gas into Michigan and beyond, with the projects adding nearly 1,000 miles of pipeline and 3.2 billion cubic feet of gas per day of capacity. The first phase of the Rover pipeline was finished in August 2017 and ran from Southeastern Ohio (near the Pennsylvania border) to Northwestern Ohio (near the Michigan border). The second phase was finished in May 2018 and extended the pipeline through Michigan and into Canada. The Nexus pipeline was also completed in 2018 and follows a similar route, eventually connecting with existing pipelines near Detroit.

No new interstate pipelines were built from Pennsylvania into New York (and therefore into New England) over the same period. Total expansions or extensions of existing pipelines that transit New York totaled 21 miles in length and 0.46 billion cubic feet per day in additional capacity. The 125-mile Constitution Pipeline, which would take Pennsylvania gas to New York and beyond, has been repeatedly delayed since the project's inception in 2012, with a major source of delay being the refusal of the New York Department of Environmental Conservation to grant a necessary certification.

Natural gas price differences across States and over time illustrate the implications of new investments in pipelines. As natural gas production grew in Pennsylvania, Ohio, and West Virginia, citygate prices in Michigan fell relative to the national average price, plausibly reflecting the benefit of being closer to a place of burgeoning supply growth. (The citygate price measures local wholesale natural gas prices). From 2016 to 2018, when two main pipeline projects were being completed, the Michigan price relative to the national average price fell 14 percent. The New York price went in the opposite direction, increasing by 16 percent, potentially reflecting the interaction between high demand (from an above-average number of cooling-degree days in 2018) and pipeline constraints (figure 4-18).

The 14 percent decline in the Michigan citygate price relative to the national price provides a credible estimate of the price effect of expanded pipeline capacity. It is similar to estimates of the effect of major capacity expansions (Oliver, Mason, and Finnoff 2014) or the price premium associated with insufficient capacity (Avalos, Fitzgerald, and Rucker 2016).

A 14 percent decline in the New York and New England citygate price would save consumers in the region an estimated $2.0 billion annually, or $233 for a family of four. Some of the savings would be from residential, commercial, and industrial consumers paying less for the natural gas that they consume, but the bulk of savings would be from lower electricity prices. New York and most of New England have deregulated electricity markets, where

Figure 4-18. Citygate Natural Gas Prices in Michigan and New York Relative to National Average Prices, 2005–18

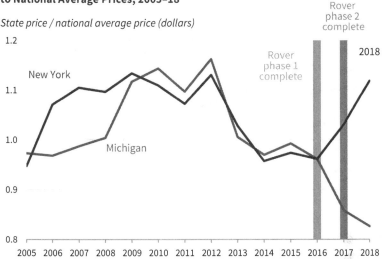

State price / national average price (dollars)

Sources: Energy Information Administration; CEA calculations.
Note: The Rover Pipeline phase 1 was completed in August 2017, and phase 2 was completed in May 2018. Vertical bars represent the beginning of the year when the pipeline was completed, given annual data.

electricity-generating firms sell into competitive markets. Linn, Muehlenbachs, and Wang (2014) find that for New York and New England, a 1 percent decrease in the price of natural gas lowers the price of electricity by 0.8 percent. Applying this gas-driven decline in wholesale prices to the region's consumption of electricity in 2018 provides $1.2 billion of the total $2.0 billion in savings.

Other infrastructure investments could provide similar value. The Atlantic Coast Pipeline, for example, would take natural gas from West Virginia to North Carolina, where citygate prices have been about 10 percent higher than in West Virginia in 2019. We also note that pipelines are not the only means of transporting natural gas domestically. The Pipeline and Hazardous Materials Safety Administration recently approved a permit request to transport LNG by rail.

Just as pipelines allow producers to reach high-price markets in other states, facilities for exporting LNG allow U.S. producers–whose production now exceeds domestic consumption–to reach high-price markets abroad. In response, export volumes have surged, averaging 4.7 billion cubic feet per day (Bcf/d) in the first 10 months of 2019, compared with less than 2 Bcf/d in the first 10 months of 2017. Under the Natural Gas Act, exports of LNG must be approved by the DOE on the basis of whether the exports are consistent with the public interest. Under the Trump Administration, the DOE has doubled the volume of LNG approved for export, increasing capacity from 17 Bcf/d to more than 34 Bcf/d as of October 2019.

Conclusion

The shale revolution provides a striking example of the potential of private sector energy innovation and the resulting implications for consumers and the environment. In less than a decade, productivity in oil and gas extraction has increased several-fold. As a result, production costs have fallen, making energy goods and services more affordable for consumers, especially lower-income households. By several measures, the shale revolution has led to greater environmental progress in the United States than in the European Union, which exercises more government control and has more stringent emissions policies.

The Trump Administration's deregulatory policies aim to support private sector innovation and initiative by reducing excessively prescriptive government regulation. In doing so, the Administration seeks to further unleash the country's abundant human and energy resources. This policy stance is consistent with the approach taken by most States, which have allowed shale production to flourish as long as companies meet updated State policies that limit risks to human health and the environment. However, some States have taken a more command-and-control approach, which has had predictable effects. In particular, New York State has taken an alternative, unsafe-at-any-speed approach to shale development. As it has done so, its natural gas production has fallen, its imports of electricity have increased, and its rate of GHG emissions reduction has been less than that of neighboring Pennsylvania.

State and Federal policy questions related to shale will persist in debates about environmental and energy policy. The shale revolution will continue to influence energy prices because the private sector has shown that large amounts of oil and gas can be extracted from shale and similar formations at moderate prices. The knowledge and capability gained from innovation will remain through periods of low energy prices that drive overleveraged firms into bankruptcy. In addition, policies that would severely constrain use of this capability come with large, forgone benefits—in large part the consumer savings and environmental gains documented in this chapter. The Trump Administration's deregulatory energy agenda, in contrast, seeks to overcome government barriers to private sector innovation that lowers energy prices and benefits the environment.

Chapter 5

Free-Market Healthcare Promotes Choice and Competition

Driven by unparalleled medical innovation, the American healthcare system remains the envy of the world. However, its past success does not mean that healthcare in the United States always delivers the value that it should. Costs for many procedures and medications are too high, access to the healthcare that patients demand is limited, and competition is lacking. But these challenges do not mean that the only solution is increased government intervention. These improvements can be accomplished by enhancing healthcare choice and competition in ways that embrace the value of the market while focusing on patients' needs.

The Trump Administration has already made major progress in delivering high-quality, lower-cost healthcare by creating more choice in health insurance markets and more competition among healthcare providers. In other words, it is possible to keep what works and fix what is broken. For example, the Administration has sought to make healthcare more affordable by lowering out-of-control prescription drug prices and expanding access to more affordable healthcare options. Additional policy changes put patients in control of their healthcare by ensuring price transparency and allowing Americans to pick the care that fits their needs. At the same time, accelerating medical innovation has provided new treatment options for patients living with disease.

Under the Trump Administration, the Food and Drug Administration approved more generic drugs than ever before in U.S. history and updated its approval process for new, lifesaving drugs. This past year, prescription drug prices experienced the largest year-over-year decline in more than 50 years. Whether it is through reforms that seek to expand association health plans, promote health reimbursement arrangements, or give terminally-ill patients access to potentially lifesaving drugs, among many other successes, every healthcare reform that lowers costs and increases quality allows American workers to live longer, healthier lives and keep more of their paychecks.

The Administration's focus on consumer-centric health policies will make the healthcare marketplace more competitive and protect as well as enable consumers to obtain life-enhancing technologies. For example, the Administration's recent policy change to permit insurers to offer policies with additional benefits covered before a deductible is met and allow enrollees to maintain health savings accounts are real changes already helping those with preexisting conditions. And with future changes under way to enable patients using the real price for major medical services, the effect of the free market to lower health care costs for all consumers has just begun.

Healthcare regulations at all levels of government can increase price, limit choice, and stifle competition—which, in combination, lead U.S. healthcare to fail to provide its full value. These regulations can also harm the broader economy. For example, the Affordable Care Act has impeded economic recovery by introducing disincentives to work. The Trump Administration's successes in addressing these policies over the past three years show the value of empowering the market to deliver the affordable healthcare options that Americans rightly expect. Further patient-centered reforms will provide Americans with improved healthcare through enhanced choice and competition.

The United States' healthcare system relies more on private markets to provide health insurance and medical care than do those of other countries. And the U.S. system is supplemented by public sector programs to finance the care of vulnerable populations, which include low-income and senior populations. Most Americans are in employer-sponsored group health plans and are often satisfied with the insurance coverage and medical care they receive. However, the U.S. system does not always deliver the value it should. Market competition leads to an efficient allocation of resources that should lower prices and increase quality. But every market has features that deviate from optimal conditions, and healthcare is no exception. Last year (CEA 2019), we discussed obstacles in healthcare markets and concluded that they are not insurmountable problems that mandate the government's intervention.

This chapter identifies government barriers on the Federal and State levels to healthcare market competition that lead to higher prices, reduce innovation, and hinder quality improvements. The chapter proceeds with a review of barriers to competition and choice, and then it provides a summary of the accomplishments and expected effects of Administration health policy in reducing these impediments and creating competitive innovation in the healthcare markets for all Americans. The Administration's reforms aim to foster healthcare markets that create value for consumers through the financing and delivery of high-quality and affordable care. Government mandates can reduce competitive insurance choices and raise premiums.

By focusing on choice and competition, the Administration is encouraging States to provide flexibility to develop policies that accommodate numerous consumer preferences for healthcare financing and delivery. The Administration has addressed these problems through a series of Executive Orders, deregulatory measures, and signed legislation. By 2023, we estimate that 13 million Americans will have new insurance coverage that was previously unavailable due to high prices and overregulation.[1]

Building a High-Quality Healthcare System

A key goal for the healthcare marketplace is to provide effective, high-value care to all Americans. Achieving this goal requires careful consideration and revision of specific Federal and State regulations and policies that inhibit choice and competition. This section identifies two ways to increase choice and competition: creating more choice in health insurance markets, and creating more competition among healthcare providers.

Creating More Choice in Health Insurance Markets

The majority of Americans obtain health insurance coverage through private sector, employer-sponsored group plans and other private (individual or nongroup) plans (see figure 5-1). The public sector Medicaid program provides coverage to people with low incomes, while Medicare provides coverage to older Americans. Figure 5-1 shows the percentages of Americans that have various

---

[1] The CEA previously released research on topics covered in this chapter. The text of this chapter builds on the 2019 *Economic Report of the President*; the CEA report "Measuring Prescription Drug Prices: A Primer on the CPI Prescription Drug Index" (CEA 2019c); the CEA report *Mitigating the Impact of Pandemic Influenza through Vaccine Innovation* (CEA 2019d); the report "Reforming America's Healthcare System through Choice and Competition," from the Department of Health and Human Services (HHS 2018); and policy announcements from the Executive Office of the President.

Figure 5-1. Health Insurance Coverage by Type of Insurance, 2018

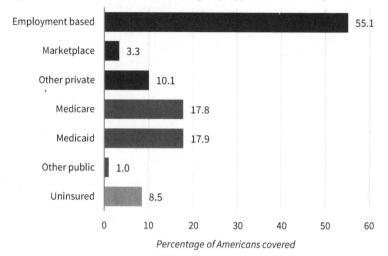

Percentage of Americans covered

Sources: Census Bureau; CEA calculations.
Note: Numbers do not sum to 100 percent due to overlap for individuals with multiple health insurance plans. Other private plans include nongroup, direct-purchase plans, and TRICARE. Other public plans include veterans health insurance. Blue indicates private health insurance plan types, and red indicates public health insurance plan types.

types of health insurance coverage, but many people have multiple coverage sources; for instance, many older adults on Medicare purchase private supplemental insurance plans. In 2018, more than 67 percent of all Americans were covered by private health insurance plans, while just over 34 percent were covered by public plans. Among the insured population, 12.2 percent had more than one type for all of 2018 (Census Bureau 2019). Employer-sponsored insurance dominates most of the private health insurance market. The individual insurance market accounts for a smaller share of the insured population. In the individual market, consumers buy their insurance through the insurance exchanges established by the Affordable Care Act (ACA) or through ACA-compliant individual policies.

Since earlier in the 2000s, when private health insurance premiums grew rapidly, growth rates have moderated, especially since 2017 (Claxton et al. 2019). Figure 5-2 shows the inflation-adjusted growth in the average premium for family coverage through employer-sponsored group plans. The total premium is paid partly through the employer contribution and partly through the employee contribution. We focus on the total premium because health economists agree that, ultimately, employees also pay the employer-contribution in the form of reduced wages. In the individual insurance market, after the Affordable Care Act established health insurance exchanges, the premiums almost doubled in the first few years. From 2018 to 2019, the benchmark ACA premiums dropped by 1.5 percent. From 2019 to 2020, the benchmark ACA premiums dropped by an additional 4 percent (CMS 2018, 2019).

Figure 5-2. Annual Change in Average Family Premium Including Employee and Employer Contributions, 2000–2018

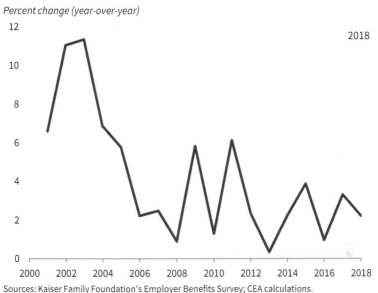

Percent change (year-over-year)

Sources: Kaiser Family Foundation's Employer Benefits Survey; CEA calculations.

Recent health policy changes at the Federal and State levels have sought to give consumers more control over their medical expenditures so they can seek greater value for their health investment. Two of the best illustrations of these consumer-focused policies are health saving accounts (HSAs) and health reimbursement arrangements (HRAs). As described in the Department of Health and Human Services' (HHS) report "Reforming America's Healthcare System through Choice and Competition," the promotion and expansion of these policies, combined with price and quality transparency initiatives, will encourage consumers to make better and more informed care choices to enhance their health (HHS 2018).

"Consumer-directed health plans" (CDHPs) is an all-encompassing term for HRAs, HSAs, and similar medical accounts that allow patients to have greater control over their health budgets and spending. The growth of CDHPs has been substantial, especially by large employers that offer these high-deductible plans, HRAs, and HSAs in a larger strategy to introduce consumerism in employer-sponsored health insurance. HRAs allow employees to shop in the individual market for their preferred plans. Expanding consumer choice in health plans decreases the deadweight loss associated with poor plan matching and leads to gains in consumer surplus (Dafny, Ho, and Varela 2013). HSAs may be especially attractive to consumers because they may be used for nonmedical healthcare expenses and are portable (Greene et al. 2006). In an analysis of firms that completely replaced traditional managed care plans with

Figure 5-3. Percentage of Covered Workers Enrolled in a Plan with a General Annual Deductible of $2,000 or More for Single Coverage, 2009–19

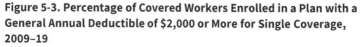

Percentage of covered workers

Source: Kaiser Family Foundation's Employer Benefits Survey.
Note: Small firms have 3 to 199 workers, and large firms have 200 or more workers.

CDHPs for their employees, Parente, Feldman, and Yu (2010) saw significant decreases in total healthcare costs, though they were inconsistent among firms that offered different mixes of HRAs and HSAs. CDHPs may also be beneficial for low-income families and high-risk families, where total health spending significantly decreased for vulnerable (low-income or high-risk) families with CDHPs (Haviland et al. 2011). Healthcare costs are also lower for employers offering CDHPs, whose costs in the first three years after a CDHP is offered are significantly lower relative to firms that do not offer a CDHP (Haviland et al. 2016).

As seen in figure 5-3, the share of individuals enrolled in high-deductible health plans in the employer-sponsored health insurance market has risen substantially. This has led consumers to have greater incentives to shop for medical services that are not reimbursed before their deductible is met.

Although the growth of CDHPs has increased out-of-pocket medical expenses on average, the plans are available with significantly lower premiums than other health insurance choices, as seen in figures 5-4 and 5-5. Furthermore, with the Administration's new options to cover predeductible care for the chronically ill with little to no out-of-pocket expense, as discussed later is this chapter, more choices are available for more vulnerable populations than before 2016.

Figure 5-4. Average Annual Worker and Employer Premium Contributions for Single Coverage, 2019

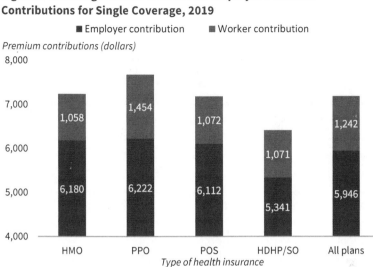

Source: Kaiser Family Foundation's Employer Health Benefits Survey.
Note: HMO = health maintenance organization; PPO = preferred provider organization; POS = point-of-service plan; HDHP/SO = high-deductible health plan with savings option.

Figure 5-5. Average Annual Worker and Employer Premium Contributions for Family Coverage, 2019

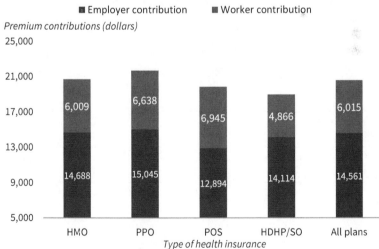

Source: Kaiser Family Foundation's Employer Health Benefits Survey.
Note: HMO = health maintenance organization; PPO = preferred provider organization; POS = point-of-service plan; HDHP/SO = high-deductible health plan with savings option.

Creating More Competition among Healthcare Providers

Recent studies of variation in health service pricing suggest that the market lacks needed competition. If competition is reduced among providers (e.g., physicians or hospitals), and in addition there is no change in patient demand, then higher prices and fewer choices are likely to result. These can also lower overall healthcare quality and limit the efficient allocation of resources. Government policies can diminish competition by adversely limiting the supply of providers and the scope of services they offer.

Choice and competition can be limited by State policies that restrict entry into provider markets. This, in turn, can stifle innovation that could lead to more cost-effective care provision. Higher healthcare prices and fewer incentives for quality improvement by providers can be the results of these market-stifling State policies. In particular, state-specific certificate-of-need laws could reduce provider access and create unnecessary monopoly pricing where there is limited competition. In chapter 6 of this *Report*, we discuss advocacy efforts by the Trump Administration to limit the harmful effects of certificate-of-need regulation.

Since the 1990s, markets for a variety of healthcare services have become more consolidated (NCCI 2018). Some consolidation involves cross-market mergers—as, for example, when hospitals operating in different regions form a system—but there is also evidence of increasing concentration in local markets. As discussed in chapter 6, the Federal Trade Commission (FTC) and the Department of Justice's (DOJ) Antitrust Division classify markets using the Herfindahl-Hirschman Index (HHI). Between 1990 and 2006, the proportion of metropolitan statistical areas (MSAs) with hospital market HHIs classified as "highly concentrated" (i.e., with an HHI above 2,500) rose from 65 percent to more than 77 percent (Gaynor, Ho, and Town 2015). Concentration has also risen significantly in health insurance markets. Even when consolidation occurs between close competitors, consumers can benefit from substantial efficiency gains.

However, the trends of rising concentration have properly drawn attention to the question of how consumers are affected. A recent but growing body of literature has linked increasing concentration in hospital markets to rising prices, markups, and falling quality. A number of studies have found that mergers between hospitals that are close competitors leads to significantly higher prices without improving quality (Vogt and Town 2006; Gaynor and Town 2012), or in settings with regulated prices, to lower quality (Kessler and McClellan 2000; Cooper et al. 2011). This literature is still young, and more needs to be done, particularly to assess what is driving the consolidations. Fuchs (1997) argued that the rise of health maintenance organizations is a contributing factor, as hospitals seek to offset the bargaining power of large insurers by becoming large themselves; but as discussed by Gaynor, Ho, and Town (2015), the empirical evidence for this is mixed.

More generally, it is important to understand if rising concentration is associated with factors, such as rising fixed-cost investments or economies of scale, that may benefit consumers. This causality issue is discussed in chapter 6. At a minimum, however, these results suggest that market structure is an important aspect of healthcare markets.

Consolidation is also seen in the prescription drug market. The growth in importance of pharmacy benefit managers (PBMs) to serve as intermediaries between drug manufacturers and health insurers also increased the size of the largest PBMs, their purchasing power, and their ability to obtain rebates and discounts from manufacturers (Aitken et al. 2016). PBMs are resistant to list drug price increases, as their profits are usually a percentage of drug list prices—thus, there is little incentive to reduce the amount charged to insurers. As discussed later in this chapter, the three largest PBMs hold 85 percent of market share.

One way to gauge the uneven competition among healthcare providers is to examine the degree of competition (or lack thereof) in major metropolitan markets. Data made available by the Health Care Cost Institute (HCCI 2016) used negotiated provider price data to illustrate the degree of lack of competition present in the market at the national and regional levels. Using data from HCCI, Newman and others (2016) examined variations in the negotiated rates of providers from 242 possible medical services. They calculated the ratio of the average price paid in each State to the average national price for a given medical service by ratio categories for each of the 242 services. Figure 5-6 presents a map depicting variation in cataract surgery prices by state.

The map illuminates both regional patterns and variations among State-level average cataract removal prices. For example, Iowa, Illinois, and Indiana all have prices between 125 and 150 percent of the national average price. Alternatively, across four States in the Southeast, the ratio of State average price to national average price decreases from 150 through 175 percent in the Carolinas to a ratio of less than 75 percent in Florida.

Kansas and New York have prices close to the national average price for cataract surgery, at $3,382 and $3,678, respectively, compared with $3,541 (HCCI 2016). However, the average prices in the neighboring States of Nebraska and Connecticut are $957 and $1,181 more. With respect to knee replacements, New Jersey and Kansas have the lowest average prices; and Washington, Oregon, and South Carolina have the highest average prices. Prices in Connecticut and Iowa are about the same as the national average price of roughly $36,000. The data show that Arizona, Texas, Rhode Island, and West Virginia have the lowest average prices for a pregnancy ultrasound, while Oregon, Wisconsin, and Alaska have some of the highest average prices.

Figure 5-6. Ratio of State Average Price to National Average Price of Cataract Removal, 2015

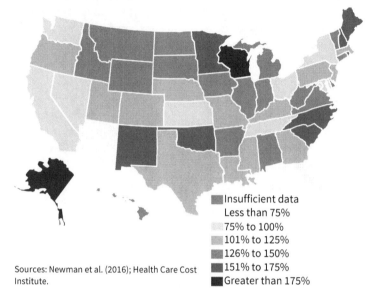

Insufficient data
Less than 75%
75% to 100%
101% to 125%
126% to 150%
151% to 175%
Greater than 175%

Sources: Newman et al. (2016); Health Care Cost Institute.

Although the national average price for a knee replacement is more than 100 times larger than a pregnancy ultrasound, there is greater variation in average prices for ultrasounds. For example, in South Carolina, the average knee replacement price is more than 30 percent higher than the national average, while in Wisconsin the average pregnancy ultrasound is more than 220 percent greater than the national average. This suggests that relative to the average price, there are higher high prices and lower low prices among the pregnancy ultrasound prices. Much of this variation could be due to the lack of transparency in shoppable services to create a truly competitive market.

There is also variation within regions or States in price trends. HCCI (2016) also calculated the ratio of each State's average price relative to the national average price for each medical service. The percentages of services within eight ranges of ratios were then graphed for each state (Newman et al. 2016). Figure 5-7 provides a visual representation of the distribution of all care medical services and can be compared across States.

Figure 5-7 shows the distribution of prices for four States: Florida, Ohio, Connecticut, and Minnesota. Of the 241 care bundles calculated for Florida, the prices for 95 percent of them were at or below the national averages. Ohio, with 240 care bundles, had higher prices on average than Florida; but roughly 75 percent of all prices were at or below the national averages. Connecticut, with 232 care bundles estimated, on average had higher prices than Florida and Ohio, with 30 percent of its care bundle prices being at least 20 percent

Figure 5-7. Distribution of Average State Price Relative to Average National Price of Care Bundles in Four States, 2015

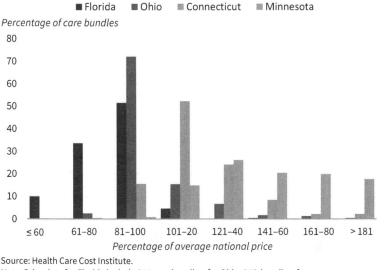

■ Florida   ■ Ohio   ■ Connecticut   ■ Minnesota

Percentage of care bundles

Percentage of average national price

Source: Health Care Cost Institute.
Note: Price data for Florida include 241 care bundles; for Ohio, 240 bundles; for Connecticut, 232 bundles; and for Minnesota, 221 bundles.

higher than the respective national averages. Minnesota, with 221 estimated care bundles, had the highest prices on average, with more than 45 percent of the care bundles having prices 50 percent or more above the national average.

Table 5-1 presents the highest average and lowest average price for a knee replacement reported for a metropolitan statistical areas in 12 States.[2] Sacramento has the highest average price ($57,504)—more than twice as high as Tucson, Miami, Saint Louis, Syracuse, Toledo, Allentown, Knoxville, and Lubbock. California also has the largest within-State difference in average price ($27,243) across any paired set of MSAs in the State. Though the two California markets are 440 miles apart, it is worth noting that a three-hour drive from Palm Bay, Florida, to Miami could potentially save $17,122 on knee replacement surgery—a difference of roughly $100 per mile driven—assuming one's insurance plan design covered the individual in both locations. Absolute dollar differences across MSAs were small in Connecticut, South Carolina, and Virginia for the MSAs for which we had sufficient data to calculate prices.

These findings demonstrate that there is wide geographic variation in prices within the privately insured population. Although some of the variation may be a result of the differences in the costs of doing business (e.g., supplies,

---

[2] These are indicative differences because prices could not be calculated for every MSA in a State. There could have been higher or lower prices in an unreported MSA in a State. These reported prices should drive inquiries into why these differences exist and whether any differences are justified by local differences or other evidence.

Table 5-1. Variation in Knee Replacement Prices across MSAs within States, 2015

State	Number of MSAs	Highest MSA-level average price (dollars)	Lowest MSA-level average price (dollars)	Difference between highest and lowest MSA-level average price (dollars)	Distance between MSA cities (miles)
Arizona	2	28,264	21,976	6,288	116
California	6	57,504	30,261	27,243	440
Connecticut	3	37,417	33,594	3,823	39
Florida	8	44,237	27,115	17,122	173
Missouri	2	26,601	23,114	3,487	248
New York	4	36,584	24,131	12,453	247
Ohio	7	34,573	24,491	10,082	203
Pennsylvania	3	33,338	27,188	6,150	62
South Carolina	2	46,591	43,635	2,956	103
Tennessee	2	34,895	26,291	8,604	180
Texas	5	45,275	28,456	16,819	345
Virginia	2	39,298	39,292	6	107

Source: Health Care Cost Institute.
Note: MSA = metropolitan statistical area.

wages, and rent), the remaining variation could be attributable to other factors, such as a lack of transparency, market power, or alternative treatments.

A patient-centered healthcare policy's goal would be the least unjustified price difference as possible and a low average price for a service. For example, Arizona has the sixth-largest price difference ($123) in the pregnancy ultrasound prices—a service that should be similar in scope and quality across providers, care settings, cities, and States. The average of the average prices paid in Tucson and Phoenix is the lowest ([$320 + $197] / 2 = $258.5).

To address how competition can lower prices more broadly, the Administration's report "Reforming America's Healthcare System through Choice and Competition" outlined many other important measures to increase competition for the entire healthcare sector, including hospitals and doctors, which make up the bulk of total spending. For example, a recent Executive Order set the way for increasing price transparency in healthcare, which allows competition to more effectively operate.

Healthcare Accomplishments under the Trump Administration

Since the beginning of his Administration, President Trump has sought to make healthcare more affordable by lowering prescription drug prices and making new, affordable healthcare options available. Policies have been advanced to provide transparency and choice so patients can choose the care that fits their needs. In addition, pathways have been sought to unleashing American innovation that will provide new treatment options for patients living with disease. To increase choice, the Administration has increased insurance options and reduced the regulatory burden. To increase competition, the Administration has focused on three major areas: (1) accelerating innovation, (2) increasing access to valuable therapies, and (3) making the health market stronger with greater transparency. Efforts in each of these areas are discussed in this section, with the goal of setting out how to keep what works and fix what is broken.

Increasing Choice

This subsection addresses a number of key aspects of how to increase choice. These include reducing regulatory burdens, stabilizing health insurance exchanges, lowering the individual mandate penalty to zero, encouraging State innovation in insurance design, expanding association health plans and short-term limited-duration insurance, strengthening Medicare, expanding health reimbursement arrangements, and modernizing high-deductible health plans.

Reducing regulatory burdens. In our 2019 *Report*, we estimated the impact of deregulated health insurance markets to provide more plan competition and choice for small businesses and American consumers through expanding association health plans and short-term, limited duration plans. These deregulations, in addition to eliminating the individual mandate, were estimated to generate $450 billion in benefits over the next decade. We estimated that the reforms will benefit lower- and middle-income consumers and all taxpayers but will impose costs on some middle- and higher-income consumers, who will pay higher insurance premiums. The benefits of giving a large set of consumers more insurance options will far outweigh the projected costs imposed on the smaller set who will pay higher premiums. In 2019, we provided estimates supporting the claim that these reforms do not "sabotage" the ACA but rather provide a more efficient focus of tax-funded care for those in need.

Stabilizing health insurance exchanges. In April 2017, HHS issued a final rule aimed at stabilizing the exchanges. Among other provisions, this rule made it more difficult for consumers to wait until they needed medical services to enter the exchanges. This limits gaming of the program and the driving up of premiums for those who maintain continuous coverage.

The 2019 HRA rule is expected to cause a significant increase in individual market enrollment in the early 2020s. The rule is projected to do so through additional choice and market competition and without any new government mandates. Younger and healthier employees may be more likely to prefer the typical individual market coverage of relatively high deductibles and more limited provider networks due to their lower premiums, so it is possible that the HRA rule could lead to an improved individual market risk pool (Effros 2009). This would occur if the HRA rule generates greater demand in the individual market and from younger and older workers, given the relative attractiveness of lower premium cost generated by the HRA contribution to the employee when they purchase insurance.

Lowering the individual mandate penalty to zero. In December 2017, President Trump signed the Tax Cuts and Jobs Act, which set the ACA's individual mandate penalty to zero. This benefits society by allowing people to choose not to have ACA-compliant health coverage without facing a tax penalty, and by saving taxpayers money if fewer consumers purchase subsidized ACA coverage. As we discussed last year, the CEA estimates that from 2019 through 2029, setting the mandate penalty to zero will yield $204 billion in net benefits for consumers (CEA 2019).

Encouraging State innovation in insurance design. As of 2019, seven States operated State Innovation waivers under Section 1332 of the ACA that utilized a reinsurance component. As a way to lower risk, the State establishes a fund to subsidize insurers for a certain amount of the expenses from people with costly claims. These waivers lead to lower ACA plan premiums and thus lower associated premium tax credit costs. These seven States had a median premium decline of 7.5 percent, compared with an increase in nonwaiver states of 3.0 percent (Badger 2019). Compared with what would have occurred if the States had not passed waivers, the decrease in premiums has likely caused increased enrollment in these States. By the end of 2019, States received back roughly 60 percent of savings of their initial contribution in Federal pass-through funding (Blase 2019a).

Expanding association health plans and short-term limited-duration insurance. In June 2018, the Department of Labor (DOL) finalized a rule to expand the ability of employers, including sole proprietors, to join together and purchase health coverage through association health plans (AHPs).[3] For many employers, employees, and their families, AHPs offer more affordable premiums by reducing the administrative costs of coverage through economies of scale. The AHP rule also gave small businesses more flexibility to offer their employees health coverage that is more tailored to their needs.

In August 2018, HHS, the Department of the Treasury, and DOL finalized a rule to expand Americans' ability to purchase short-term, limited-duration

---

[3] The revised definition of an employer for bona fide AHPs established under this rule is being adjudicated.

insurance (STLDI). STDLI premiums generally cost less than premiums for individual insurance on the ACA exchanges. Because of lower costs, additional choice, and increased competition, millions of Americans, including middle-class families that cannot afford ACA plans, stand to benefit from this reform. Recently, the Congressional Budget Office (CBO 2019) stated that is will count some short-term plans as health coverage, just as it did with pre-ACA plans with benefit exclusions or annual and lifetime limits (Aron-Dine 2019). Though these plans are more limited in coverage than the ACA-compliant insurance plans, they are priced at up to 60 percent less than the unsubsidized premium cost of ACA exchange plans and give consumers more insurance protection than being uninsured.

As a result of STLDI and AHP rules, the CBO and the U.S. Congress's Joint Committee on Taxation estimates that over the next decade, roughly 5 million more people are projected to be enrolled in AHPs or short-term plans. Of this increase, almost 80 percent constitute individuals who would otherwise have purchased coverage in the small-group or nongroup markets. The remaining 20 percent (roughly 1 million people) are made up of individuals who are projected to be newly insured as a result of the rules (CBO 2019).

Strengthening Medicare. The Administration's reforms to Medicare include payment policies that align with patients' clinical needs rather than the site of care, simplified processes for physicians' documentation of evaluation and management visits, new consumer-transparency measures, and increased flexibility for insurers so that they can offer more options and benefits through Medicare Advantage.

In 2019, President Trump signed an Executive Order to improve seniors' healthcare outcomes by providing patients with more plan options, additional time with providers, greater access to telehealth and new therapies, and greater alignment between payment models and efficient healthcare delivery (White House 2019b). In addition, a priority will be streamlining the approval, coverage, and payment of new therapies while reducing obstacles to improved patient care. Finally, the effort improves the fiscal sustainability of Medicare by eliminating waste, fraud, and abuse.

Expanding health reimbursement arrangements. In June 2019, HHS, the Treasury Department, and DOL issued a final rule expanding the flexibility and use of health reimbursement arrangements to employers (84 *FR* 28888). The rule issued two new types of tax-advantaged HRA plans—excepted benefit HRAs (EBHRAs) and individual coverage HRAs (ICHRAs)—to be offered as early as January 2020. EBHRAs may be offered to employees with traditional group plans to receive an excepted benefit HRA of up to $1,800 a year in 2020 (indexed to inflation afterward) for the purchase of certain qualified medical expenses, such as short-term, limited duration, vision, and dental plans. ICHRAs allow employers to reimburse employees who purchase their own health plans and equalizes the tax treatment of a traditional employer-sponsored insurance plan and an individual market plan paid by employer contributions.

The Treasury Department performed microsimulation modeling to evaluate the coverage changes and transfers that are likely to be induced by the final rules. The Treasury's model of health insurance coverage assumes that workers are paid the marginal product of their labor. Employers are assumed to be indifferent between paying wages and payroll taxes and paying compensation in the form of benefits. The Treasury model therefore assumes that total compensation paid by a given firm is fixed, and the employer allocates this compensation between wages and benefits based on the aggregated preferences of their employees. As a result, employees bear the full cost of employer-sponsored health coverage (net of the value of any tax exclusion) in the form of reduced wages and the employee share of premiums.

The Treasury Department's model assumes that employees' preferences regarding the type of health coverage (or no coverage) are determined by their expected healthcare expenses and the after-tax cost of employer-sponsored insurance, exchange coverage with the premium tax credit (PTC), or exchange or other individual health insurance coverage integrated with an individual coverage HRA, and the quality of different types of coverage (including actuarial value).

When evaluating the choice between an individual coverage HRA and the PTC for exchange coverage, the available coverage is assumed to be the same, but the tax preferences are different. Hence, an employee will prefer the individual coverage HRA if the value of the income and payroll tax exclusion (including both the employee and employer portion of payroll tax) is greater than the value of the PTC. In modeling this decision, the Federal departments assume that premiums paid by the employee are tax-preferred through the reimbursement of premiums from the individual coverage HRA, with any additional premiums (up to the amount that would have been paid under a traditional group health plan) paid through a salary reduction arrangement.

In the Treasury Department's model, employees are aggregated into firms, based on tax data. The expected health expenses of employees in the firm determine the cost of employer-sponsored insurance for the firm. Employees effectively vote for their preferred coverage, and each employer's offered benefit is determined by the preferences of the majority of employees. Employees then decide whether to accept any offered coverage, and the resulting enrollment in traditional or individual health insurance coverage determines the risk pools and therefore premiums for both employer coverage and individual health insurance coverage.

Based on microsimulation modeling, the Federal departments expect that the final rules will cause some participants (and their dependents) to move from traditional group health plans to individual coverage HRAs. As noted above, the estimates assume that for this group of firms and employees, employer contributions to individual coverage HRAs are the same as contributions to traditional group health plans would have been, and the estimates assume that tax-preferred salary reductions for individual health insurance coverage are the same as salary reductions for traditional group health plan coverage. Thus, by modeling construction, there is no change in income or payroll tax revenues for this group of firms and employees (other than the changes in the PTC discussed below).

Although the tax preference is assumed to be unchanged for this group, after-tax, out-of-pocket costs could increase for some employees (whose premiums or cost sharing are higher in the individual market than in a traditional group health plan) and could decrease for others. A small number of employees who are currently offered a traditional group health plan nonetheless obtain individual health insurance coverage and the PTC, because they cannot afford a traditional group health plan or such a plan does not provide minimum value. Some of these employees would no longer be eligible for the PTC for their exchange coverage when the employer switches from a traditional group health plan to an individual coverage HRA because the HRA is determined to be affordable under the final PTC rules.

The regulatory impact analysis conducted by the Treasury Department concluded that the benefits of the HRA rule substantially outweigh its costs. The Treasury Department estimated that 800,000 employers are expected to provide HRAs after being fully ramped up. In addition, it is estimated that there will be a reduction in the number of uninsured by 800,000 by 2029. From these employers' HRA contributions, it is expected that firms will cover more than 11 million employees with individual health insurance by 2029.

Modernizing high-deductible health plans. A major component of the Trump Administration's health policy has been a focus on consumer-directed health plans, in particular modernizing high-deductible health plans (HDHPs) and their accompanying HSAs. As directed by the President, the Treasury released a new Internal Revenue Service (IRS) guidance (Notice 2019-45) on July 17, 2019, that allows high-deductible health plan issuers to permit coverage of prevention therapies for those with certain chronic conditions, including diabetes, asthma, heart disease, and major depression. The impact could be profound. For example, these plans could now cover all or nearly all the cost of insulin for diabetic patients before the deductible being met.

HSA-eligible plans are a growing proportion of the overall HDHP market. In 2018, about 21.8 million Americans were enrolled in HSA-eligible HDHPs, up from an estimated 15.5 million in 2013 (AHIP 2017). In 2018, nearly 29 percent of all firms offered an HDHP with a savings option, such as an HSA (KFF 2018). Among companies studied in 2018 by a survey of the National Business Group on Health, 30 percent offered a full replacement HSA-type plan to employees in 2019 (NBGH 2018). HSA market growth is expected to continue.

According to the Centers for Disease Control and Prevention (CDC 2019), about 60 percent of Americans have a chronic disease such as heart disease or diabetes. The economic burden of chronic diseases in the United States is estimated to be about $1 trillion per year (Waters and Graf 2018). Decreasing financial barriers to evidence-based care for chronic conditions provides opportunities to enhance clinical outcomes and reduce the long-term growth rate of healthcare spending. Because about 75 percent of total U.S. health spending is due to chronic diseases, appropriate chronic disease management is key to lowering long-term healthcare cost growth (NACDD n.d.). The IRS guidance allows for the creation of an enhanced HSA-eligible plan to provide predeductible coverage for targeted, evidence-based, secondary preventive services that prevent chronic disease progression and related complications. This can improve patient outcomes, enhance HDHP attractiveness, and add efficiency to medical spending.

The creation of these new high-deductible health plans plus secondary prevention coverage (HDHP+) will give patients with certain conditions better access. VBID Health (2019) estimated that it could increase tax revenue in a variety of scenarios dependent on the updating of the new plan. Note that VBID Health's analysis was performed before Congress repealed the Cadillac tax in December 2019.

The authors of this report (VBID Health 2019) used the ARCOLA microsimulation model to gauge the Federal tax revenue and insurance take-up impact of an HDHP+ among those under 65 and not in the Medicare market. The model assumes bronze plans in health insurance exchanges migrate into the new HDHP+ design. That said, it is challenging for HSA-eligible plans in the exchanges to meet bronze level actuarial value given their lower out-of-pocket maximum required in statute compared with the out-of-pocket maximum limits for the individual market. Providing more predeductible coverage will make this more challenging. The model also assumes that everyone in the individual market has the option of an out-of-exchange HSA-eligible plan that does not switch to the HDHP+ design. The results are split into four scenarios for firms that offer an HSA-HDHP: all firms additionally offer HDHP+, half of all firms additionally offer HDHP+, all firms replacing current plans with HDHP+, and half of all firms replacing current plans with HDHP+. Differences across employer scenarios illustrate a range of possibilities that may play out.

Across all employer scenarios, the initial uptake and forecasted growth of the novel HDHP+ are positive as people switch plan types. What varies by employer scenario, however, are the magnitude and growth of uptake over time. The HDHP+ generally has high initial uptake across employer scenarios. The lowest uptake is in the scenario where half of employers additionally offer the HDHP+ with other HDHP options. Because of the higher HDHP+ premiums, due to selection, this result is expected (figure 5-8).

Figure 5-8. Health Insurance Enrollment across Employer Scenarios, 2019–29

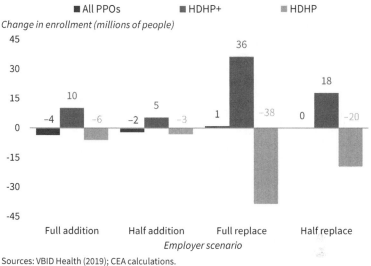

Sources: VBID Health (2019); CEA calculations.
Note: PPOs = preferred provider organizations; HDHP+ = enhanced high-deductible health plan; HDHP = high-deductible health plan.

Figure 5-9. The Net Revenue Impact of Expanding High-Deductible Health Plans, 2019–29

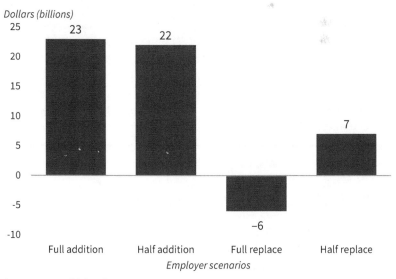

Source: VBID Health (2019).
Note: Scenarios apply to the 7 percent premium for enhanced high-deductible health plans.

Net revenue effects can be seen in three of the four scenarios modeled after introducing HDHP+ to employer and individual markets and the migration of people across plan types (figure 5-9).

Different employer decisions regarding plan offerings, as seen in the scenarios modeled, may lead one scenario to have a larger effect than another one (VBID Health 2019). More than the magnitudes of the different budget effects is the clustering of each scenario around budget neutrality. The one scenario that shows a small net reduction in tax revenue (full replacement) was modeled as an extreme case. The net effects of each scenario are small relative to the net impact of tax subsidy of the entire employer-sponsored insurance market. Thus, the net impact of expanding the secondary prevention safe harbor is likely close to zero, if not modestly positive.

Increasing Competition

This subsection explores how to increase competition in providing healthcare. The topics it covers include enforcing antitrust laws, accelerating generic drug approvals, creating price and quality transparency, promoting new vaccine manufacturing, and clarifying the Physician Self-Referral Law and the Federal Anti-Kickback Statute.

Enforcing antitrust laws. Chapter 6 discusses the importance of sound antitrust policy, which protects consumers from anticompetitive mergers. As discussed there, the Antitrust Division of the DOJ and the FTC—collectively, the Agencies—share responsibility for enforcing the Nation's antitrust laws. Although the vast majority of mergers do not raise competitive concerns, the Agencies use their investigative powers to identify those that do by obtaining and analyzing the detailed evidence that is needed to make this distinction.

Challenging a merger is often risky, as evidenced by the fact that between 1994 and 2000, the Agencies lost all seven lawsuits that they filed to block hospital mergers (Moriya et al. 2010). In response to this, the FTC engaged in a retrospective study of hospital mergers that advocated against the outdated methodology that the courts had been using to evaluate these mergers. Joseph Simons, the FTC chairman, recently reported to Congress that the FTC has successfully defended in blocking a merger between healthcare providers (*FTC v. Sanford Health*). This was the FTC's fifth straight appellate victory involving health provider mergers.

The DOJ has worked to stop anticompetitive mergers among health insurers. In 2016, the DOJ successfully blocked two proposed mergers that would have combined four of the largest health insurers (Anthem, Cigna, Aetna, and Humana) into two companies. More recently, the DOJ reached a settlement with CVS in its bid to acquire Aetna. The DOJ raised concerns relating to the sale of individual prescription drug plans (PDPs) under Medicare's Part D program. CVS and Aetna competed head-to-head in U.S. regions covering 9.3 million PDPs, of which 3.5 million had coverage from CVS or Aetna.

The DOJ alleged that this competition had led to lower premiums and lower out-of-pocket-expenses, and had improved formularies and service in many regional markets. To preserve competition, the DOJ required Aetna to divest its individual prescription drug plan. As discussed in an earlier report (CEA 2018), CVS, Express Scripts, and OptumRx are the three largest pharmacy benefit managers in the United States. The American Medical Association (2018) expressed concern to the DOJ that but for the CVS-Aetna merger, Aetna might become a disruptive competitor in PBM markets. At the time, Aetna engaged in some PBM activities while outsourcing other activities to CVS. The DOJ did not raise concerns along these lines.

The DOJ also recently reached a settlement in a conduct case against Atrium Health (formerly the Carolinas HealthCare System). The DOJ was concerned about provisions in Atrium's contracts with health insurers that were preventing insurers from offering financial incentives to their customers to choose providers that offer better value than Atrium, in terms of lower prices, better service, or both. The restrictions undercut the efforts of health insurers to induce competition between providers by creating health plans that provide incentives for consumers to use providers that qualify for preferred tiers or in-network status. As discussed by Gee, Peters, and Wilder (2019), the DOJ's economic analysis was consistent with academic research suggesting that these plans help to reduce premiums.

Accelerating generic drug approvals. HHS has taken a number of actions to empower consumers and promote competition, building on accomplishments such as the Food and Drug Administration's (FDA's) record pace of generic drug approvals (CEA 2018). Initiatives to clarify regulatory expectations for drug developers, coupled with internal review process enhancements, improved the speed and predictability of the generic drug review process at the FDA, resulting in a record number of generic drug approvals in the first three years of the Trump Administration. In fiscal year 2019, the FDA approved a record 1,171 generic drugs, after record approvals from the previous two years (HHS 2019c). These actions contributed to the recent decrease (see box 5-1) in prescription drug prices; in June 2019, these prices saw their largest year-over-year decrease in 51 years (see chapter 2 for more discussion of the Administration's deregulatory actions).

Creating price and quality transparency. On June 24, 2019, the President signed an Executive Order to promote price and quality transparency through a set of new initiatives (White House 2019b). A major problem in the healthcare market is that patients often do not know the price or quality of healthcare services. This lack of transparency denies patients the vital information they need to make informed choices and exacerbates increased costs, suppressed competition, and lower quality. As a result, there are wide variations in prices across healthcare markets, even for the same services, as was described earlier in this chapter. Accurate, accessible price and quality information will allow

Box 5-1. The Consumer Price Index for Prescription Drugs

Despite arguments that prescription drug prices have increased in 2019, drug prices according to the Consumer Price Index for prescription drugs (CPI-Rx) have declined (year-over-year) in 9 of the past 11 months, as of the October 2019 release of CPI. The CPI is designed to provide an empirical measure of the impact of price changes on the cost of living. As a component of the general CPI, the CPI-Rx measures how prices are changing in the prescription drug market by indexing the weighted average of the price changes in a random sample of prescription drugs (see figure 3-5).

The CPI-Rx has several strengths (CEA 2019c). First, it includes a random sample of prescription drugs and provides a summary measure that is representative of the entire market of prescription drugs. Even if prices are increasing for a large number of rarely prescribed drugs, the CPI-Rx can show an average decrease if the prices of the most commonly prescribed drugs are decreasing. A second strength of the CPI-Rx is that it accounts for generic drugs. Lower-cost generic bioequivalents of many prescription drugs are widely available and are often purchased over name brands, and the CPI-Rx captures price decreases from new generic entries. The CPI-Rx also measures transaction prices instead of list prices. The transaction price includes all payments received by the pharmacy, including out-of-pocket payments and payments from insurance companies, and it corresponds to the negotiated price and reflects discounts—though not rebates. The list price does not include discounts and rebates and is less representative of what the customer pays.

Though the CPI-Rx is the best measure of overall prescription drug inflation, it is not a perfect measure. One of its main limitations is that it does not account for the improvement in consumer value that occurs with the entry of new goods, particularly when they are of a higher quality than existing goods. This bias is believed to cause the CPI-Rx to overstate the true level of prescription drug inflation and has been estimated to be as high as 2 percentage points a year (Boskin et al. 1996). A comparison between the CPI-Rx and a separately constructed large alternative data set of drug prices from the research firm IQVIA showed larger price increases in the IQVIA index, indicating that the CPI-Rx may not be fully representative of a larger sample (Bosworth et al. 2018). Additionally, even though the CPI-Rx for drug prices indicates reasonable increases or declines, there may be some drug products for which price changes can appear extreme.

patients to identify savings by "shopping" for healthcare services and make choices that fit their healthcare needs and financial situations. Additionally, transparency in healthcare prices and quality will lead to better value and more innovations by facilitating increased competition among healthcare providers. One of the first results of this initiative is a rule requiring hospitals to publish their negotiated hospital charges (84 *FR* 61142). The new Executive Order directs providers as well as insurers to reveal negotiated prices on a routine basis to aid consumers in their purchase of competitively priced medical care and treatments.

The Executive Order also includes the development of the Health Quality Roadmap (HHS 2019a). The Roadmap will align and improve reporting on data and quality measures across Medicare, Medicaid, the Children's Health Insurance Program, the Health Insurance Marketplace, the Military Health System, and the Veterans Affairs Health System. To accomplish this goal, the Roadmap will provide a strategy for advancing common quality measures, aligning inpatient and outpatient measures; and eliminating low-value or counterproductive measures.

The Executive Order also calls for increased access to de-identified claims data from taxpayer-funded healthcare programs and group health plans. Healthcare researchers, innovators, providers, and entrepreneurs can use these de-identified claims, which will still ensure patient privacy and security, to develop tools that enable patients to access information that helps with decisions about healthcare goods and services. Increased data access can reveal inefficiencies and opportunities for improvement, including performance patterns for medical procedures that are outside the recommended standards of care.

The 2019 Price and Quality Transparency Executive Order seeks to make all healthcare prices negotiated between payers and providers non-opaque and to help those shopping for healthcare to get the best value and lowest price, as they do in other markets outside healthcare. The policy execution of revealing negotiated prices between payers is currently under way, and the impact will be able to be assessed in future analyses. One estimate places the potential savings from common medical procedures to be nearly 40 percent on a nationwide basis (Blase 2019b).

Promoting new vaccine manufacturing. In September 2019, the President signed an Executive Order promoting new influenza vaccine manufacturing technologies to reduce production times and increase vaccine effectiveness. Millions of Americans suffer from seasonal influenza every year, and new vaccines are formulated each year to decrease infections from the most prevalent influenza viruses. Vaccines are incredibly effective against influenza, with one study finding that vaccines prevented over 40,000 influenza-related deaths between 2005 and 2014 (Foppa et al. 2015). Despite their effectiveness, current methods of vaccine production are often very slow and can diminish vaccines' efficacy in protecting against seasonal influenza infection. Production delays could be even more important in the event of a pandemic influenza outbreak. The CEA (2019d) found that the cost of delay in vaccine availability in the case of a pandemic is $41 billion per week for the first 12 weeks and $20 billion per week for the next 12 weeks.

The new Executive Order identifies the weaknesses in current methods of vaccine production and promotes new technologies, such as cell-based and recombinant vaccine manufacturing, to speed vaccines' development and improve their efficacy. Additionally, the new initiative establishes a task force to increase Americans' access to vaccines. If sufficient doses of vaccines are delivered at the outset of an influenza pandemic, the CEA (2019c) estimates that $730 billion in economic benefits could be gained by Americans, primarily due to the prevention of loss of life and health.

Clarifying the Physician Self-Referral Law and the Federal Anti-Kickback Statute. The Administration proposed two rules in 2019 to provide coordinated care for patients (84 *FR* 55766) and to ensure that there are safeguards and flexibility for healthcare providers in value-based arrangements (84 *FR* 55694). The first rule proposed by CMS is part of the Administration's efforts to promote value-based care by lifting Federal restrictions on healthcare providers so that they have greater ability to work together on delivering coordinated patient care.

The second proposed rule issued by the HHS Office of the Inspector General focuses on the Federal Anti-Kickback Statute and the Civil Monetary Penalties Law. This proposal addresses the concern that these laws needlessly limit how healthcare providers can coordinate patient care. Expanding flexibility could, for example, encourage outcome-based payment arrangements that reward improved health outcomes. The changes would also offer specific safe harbors to make it easier for healthcare providers to ensure they are complying with the law (HHS 2019b).

Increasing Access to Valuable Therapies

This section covers a number of key topics on how to increase access to valuable therapies. These include ending the HIV epidemic, expanding kidney disease treatment options, combating the opioid crisis, and expanding the right to try clinical trials.

Ending the HIV epidemic. For the last four decades, the Human Immunodeficiency Virus (HIV) has been one of the most prominent health risks confronting people in our country and around the world. In 2019, President Trump announced a plan to end the HIV epidemic within 10 years. This epidemic has claimed the lives of about 700,000 Americans since 1981. The new initiative is designed to reduce the number of new HIV infections in the United States by 75 percent over the next five years, and by at least 90 percent over the next decade. Through efforts across HHS, an estimated 250,000 HIV infections could be averted over the next 10 years. The Administration also facilitated a large private donation of pre-exposure prophylaxis (PrEP) medication, which will help reduce the risk of HIV infection for up to 200,000 patients per year for up to 11 years to provide critical PrEP medication to uninsured individuals who might otherwise be unable to access or afford it.

Expanding kidney disease treatment options. In July 2019, the President signed an Executive Order to enable better diagnosis, treatment, and preventive care for Americans suffering from chronic kidney disease. In line with the Administration's broader deregulatory agenda, a key focus of the Executive Order is an effort to remove regulatory barriers to the supply of kidneys. Currently, the Federal Government bears most of the cost paying for chronic kidney disease and end-stage renal disease care, which affect more than 37 million Americans (White House 2019d). More than 100,000 Americans begin dialysis each year to treat end-stage renal disease, half of whom die within five years. The Executive Order seeks to modernize and increase patient choice through affordable treatment options that are too expensive and fail to provide a high quality of life.

As directed by the Executive Order, the Centers for Medicare and Medicaid Services issued a proposed rule to hold organ procurement organizations more accountable for their performance (84 *FR* 70628). More than 113,000 Americans are currently on the waiting list for an organ transplants, a number that far exceeds the number of organs available. The rule raises performance standards for organ procurement organizations to reduce discarding viable organs, encourage higher donation rates, and shorten transplant waiting lists (CMS 2019a). Additionally, the Health Resources and Services Administration issued a proposed rule to alleviate financial barriers of organ donations (84 *FR* 70139). This rule would allow for reimbursement of lost wages and childcare and eldercare expenses for living donors lacking other means of financial support, potentially increasing the number of transplant recipients over a shorter time period.

Combating the opioid crisis. The Trump Administration is using Federal resources to fight against the opioid crisis in U.S. communities. Actions are focused on supporting those with substance use disorders and involving the criminal justice system to crack down on illicit opioid suppliers, both foreign and domestic. Over $6 billion in funding was secured in fiscal years 2018 and 2019 for preventing drug abuse, treating use disorders, and disrupting the supply of illicit drugs (OMB 2019). Investments include funding for programs supporting treatment and recovery, drug diversion, and State and local assistance. Chapter 7 outlines in more detail many of the Administration's accomplishments in combating the opioid crisis.

Expanding the right to try. The Administration has *made* increased access to new and critical therapies a priority. One of the new bold programs in 2018 was the passage of "Right-to-Try" legislation for patients with terminal illnesses, such as cancer. The National Cancer Institute (n.d.) estimates that 1.76 million new Americans will be diagnosed with cancer and 606,880 will die from cancer in 2019. Currently, only 2 to 3 percent of adult cancer patients are enrolled in clinical trials—an indication of the limited options for patients with life-threatening diseases (Unger et al. 2019). For these patients who are ineligible to participate in clinical trials and have exhausted all approved treatment options, this bill amended Federal law to provide a new option, in addition to the FDA's long-standing expanded access program, for unapproved, experimental drugs (including biologics) to potentially extend their lives. To ensure safety and transparency, manufacturers or sponsors of an eligible drug that has undergone the FDA Phase I (safety) testing are required to provide annual summary reports to the FDA on any use of the drug under Right-to-Try provisions.

Conclusion

This chapter has identified Federal and State barriers to healthcare that increase prices, reduce innovation, and hinder improvements in quality. It also provided a summary of the accomplishments and expected effects of the Trump Administration's policies to address these barriers and deliver a healthcare system that offers high-quality care at affordable prices. By 2023, we estimate that 13 million Americans will have new insurance coverage that was previously unavailable due to high prices and overregulation.

In contrast to the Administration's focus on improving consumer-directed healthcare spending, government mandates often reduce consumer choice. At all levels of government, healthcare regulations that limit choice, stifle competition, and increase prices should be updated so that the U.S. healthcare system can provide greater value. These regulations can also harm the broader economy. For example, the Affordable Care Act has impeded economic recovery by introducing disincentives to work (Mulligan 2015). Though market competition leads to an efficient allocation of resources that should lower prices and increase quality, every market has features that deviate from optimal conditions, and healthcare is no exception. Although the U.S. healthcare system has challenges, they are not insurmountable problems that mandate greater government intervention. The healthcare policy successes over the past three years show the value of empowering the market to deliver the affordable healthcare options that Americans rightly expect, and further reform will provide Americans with improved healthcare through enhanced choice and competition.

Part II

Evaluating and Addressing Threats to the Expansion

Chapter 6

Evaluating the Risk of Declining Competition

America's economic strength has always been driven by private sector competition. When large corporations, small businesses, and entrepreneurs all must innovate to compete for market share on a level playing field, American consumers win and the economy grows stronger.

Yet even with the economic expansion becoming the longest in U.S. history, wage growth consistently meeting or exceeding 3 percent, unemployment falling to a 50-year low, and small business optimism within the top 20 percent of historical results, there is growing concern that the playing field is no longer level, harming innovation and thus the American economy. The increasing size of many of the Nation's largest companies and the growing importance of economies of scale has led some to hold the mistaken, simplistic view that "Big Is Bad." Though anticompetitive behavior by companies of any size should lead to investigations and specific enforcement actions against offenders, an across-the-board backlash against large companies simply because of their size is unwarranted. Antitrust enforcers should continue to be particularly vigilant where firms have significant market power, given the harm they can cause if they engage in anticompetitive conduct. Moreover, under U.S. antitrust law, conduct that may be procompetitive for a small firm can become problematic if undertaken by a monopolist. However, the focus must be on the conduct and not on size alone. Successful companies benefit the economy and consumers, and they are not necessarily the threat to competition and economic growth that they are sometimes perceived to be. Instead, companies that achieve scale and large market share by innovating and providing their customers with value are a welcome result of healthy competition.

As this chapter explains, the Trump Administration understands the vital role competition plays in growing the economy, promoting new business, and serving consumers. This understanding is underpinned by a deep appreciation of economic evidence, and the best available evidence shows that there is no need to hastily rewrite the Federal Government's antitrust rules. Federal enforcement agencies, which are already empowered with a flexible legal framework, have the tools they need to promote economic dynamism; as ongoing investigations and resolved cases show, they are well equipped to handle the competition challenges posed by the changing U.S. economy.

This does not mean that the Trump Administration's work promoting competition is finished. In addition to vigorously combating anticompetitive behavior from companies, the Administration is especially focusing on government policies that distort and limit competition. As historic regulatory reform across American industries has shown, cutting government-imposed barriers to innovation leads to increased competition, strong economic growth, and a revitalized private sector.

Vigorous competition is essential for well-functioning markets and a dynamic economy. Therefore, the Trump Administration has championed policies that promote competition, such as reforming the tax code and removing costly and burdensome regulations. The Administration also promotes competition through sound antitrust policy, which protects consumers from anticompetitive mergers and business practices. Effective antitrust enforcement supports the Administration's deregulatory agenda by fostering self-regulating, competitive free markets. The Antitrust Division of the Department of Justice (DOJ) and the Federal Trade Commission (FTC)—collectively, the Agencies—share responsibility for enforcing the Nation's antitrust laws. This chapter evaluates antitrust policy and the Agencies' roles in light of recent trends in the U.S. economy and pressing debates about competition.

In recent years, new technologies and business models have revolutionized the relationships between firms and consumers. Some of these changes, such as rapidly improving information technology, have enabled firms to grow, expanding their offerings from local markets to national ones, and from national markets to international ones.

These changes have exacerbated concerns about rising concentration. That is, in some parts of the economy, the largest firms appear to account for an increasing share of revenues. An influential Obama-era CEA report, "Benefits of Competition and Indicators of Market Power" (CEA 2016), argued that competition may be decreasing. This report is part of a broader debate—currently taking place in government, academia, and policy circles—about the state of competition in the economy. Proponents of the view that competition is declining (e.g., Faccio and Zingales 2018; Gutiérrez and Philippon 2019; Philippon 2019) argue that big businesses face little competition and are earning profits at the expense of consumers and suppliers. Advocates such as Furman (2018) and the Stigler Committee on Digital Platforms (2019) have called for changes to competition policy that would broaden the scope of antitrust enforcement. Others have cautioned that these proposals are not supported by the economic evidence (Syverson 2019), or that current antitrust rules are adequate to address legitimate concerns about anticompetitive behavior (Yun 2019).

Calls for changing the goals of the antitrust laws are based on empirical research that misinterprets high concentration as necessarily harmful to consumers and reflective of underenforcement. That argument was discredited long ago, when economists such as Demsetz (1973) and Bresnahan (1989) articulated the fundamental reasons why high concentration is not in and of itself an indicator of a lack of competition. The main point is that concentration may result from market features that are benign or even benefit consumers. For example, concentration may be driven by economies of scale and scope that can lower costs for consumers. Also, successful firms tend to grow, and it is important that antitrust enforcement and competition policy not be used to punish firms for their competitive success. Finally, antitrust remedies may not be required, even when firms exercise market power, because monopoly profits create incentives for new competitors to enter the market—unless substantive entry barriers or anticompetitive behavior stand in their way.

Moreover, recent empirical arguments that competition is in decline have been based on broad, cross-industry studies. The findings from these studies are both problematic and incomplete, and their implications for competition remain speculative. In contrast, the methods that the Agencies use to analyze competition are rooted in microeconomic, empirical evidence and involve detailed analyses of competitive conditions in specific industries. Any conclusions about the state of competition should be made on the basis of this type of careful research.

In addition, criticisms about the capabilities of antitrust enforcement to address novel enforcement challenges in dynamic markets fail to account for the flexibility of antitrust rules to accommodate a range of market conditions. Effective antitrust enforcement takes account of the evidence and economics appropriate to particular markets, and in turn adapts to innovation and development in the markets over time.

In short, we argue that major policy initiatives to completely rewrite antitrust rules and to create a new regulator for the digital economy are premature. In this chapter, we discuss and critique proposals for such initiatives advanced by proponents in the debate. As we explain, because these proposals are likely to impose significant costs, they should not be undertaken on the basis of current evidence.

Finally, we discuss competition policy beyond antitrust law and the Administration's efforts to combat the negative impact of overly burdensome regulation on competition. We highlight the Trump Administration's successful efforts to streamline the process by which new drugs are brought to market, particularly generic drugs. We also discuss the Agencies' efforts to advocate for the removal of unnecessary occupational licensing requirements that limit entry into professions, certificate-of-need laws that limit entry by new hospitals, and automobile franchising laws that limit the ability of car manufacturers to sell cars directly to consumers. Here, we also discuss the Agencies' work at the intersection of intellectual property law and antitrust law.

The structure of the chapter is as follows. We first provide an overview of antitrust policy and the economic analyses that the Agencies do to evaluate whether there is a need for the Federal Government to be involved to prevent anticompetitive mergers or other similar conduct. We then discuss the claims of rising concentration and the evidence on which they are based, contrasting this to the type of analysis that the Agencies do. Next, we discuss the proposals for regulation, with a focus on the digital economy. In the last section, we discuss the Trump Administration's policies to spur competition outside the context of antitrust rules.

The Origin and Principles of Antitrust Policy

The Agencies follow the guiding principle that the role of antitrust law is to protect the competitive environment and the process of competition. The Agencies use their given authority for robust enforcement of antitrust law to prevent anticompetitive behavior by firms. They also seek to avoid undue interference by the Federal Government in the competitive process.

The main antitrust statutes are the Sherman Antitrust Act of 1890, the Clayton Act of 1914, and the Federal Trade Commission Act of 1914. Together, these laws address three categories of conduct: mergers, monopolization, and anticompetitive agreements. First, under the Clayton Act, both Agencies challenge mergers that have a reasonable likelihood of reducing competition. They also challenge acts of monopolization under Section 2 of the Sherman Act or the equivalent provision of the Federal Trade Commission Act. Finally, both Agencies challenge agreements among separate economic actors that place unreasonable restraints on trade under Section 1 of the Sherman Act or the Federal Trade Commission Act (FTC 2019d).

Certain types of conduct, such as collusion among competitors to fix prices or rig bids, are considered so harmful to competition that they are categorized as criminal violations of the Sherman Act. The DOJ has long prioritized criminal enforcement of the antitrust laws, and violations carry significant financial fines and, for culpable individuals, jail time.

For noncriminal conduct, whether for mergers or monopolization, a central challenge facing the Agencies is determining when conduct is procompetitive and when it is anticompetitive. It can be difficult to distinguish between the two, and optimal enforcement is often a balancing act. The Agencies and the Courts want to avoid mistakenly prohibiting conduct that is procompetitive, and they also want to avoid allowing conduct that is anticompetitive.

To understand these challenges, consider a merger between direct competitors (i.e., a horizontal merger). The reduction in competition could encourage the merged firm—and also, perhaps, its competitors—to raise prices. If higher prices or other competitive types of harm to consumers are the likely outcome of a merger, then the Agencies may file a lawsuit to seek to block the transaction. Conversely, a merger, even one between close competitors, can enhance competition by creating a stronger competitor. Mergers often allow firms to combine complementary assets to realize a variety of efficiencies. For example, they may realize cost reductions, improve the quality of their products, or develop new products. Cost reductions, in particular, create an incentive to reduce prices that can offset or even reverse any incentives to raise prices. As a result, horizontal mergers may in some cases lead to lower prices, not higher ones. As we discuss in the next section, when the Agencies review mergers, they conduct a detailed economic analysis to assess these complex issues.

Most mergers do not raise competition issues. For example, the merging firms may not operate in the same or even related markets. Antitrust concerns are usually greatest when the merging parties are direct competitors. In rarer cases, antitrust concerns can arise when the merging firms are vertically related, such as when one firm sells inputs to the other. This was the case in the DOJ's challenge of the merger between AT&T and Time Warner, as is discussed by Gee, Peters, and Wilder (2019).

When mergers are large enough, the merging parties must notify the Agencies in advance of merging. In 2018, the most recent year for which data are available, the Agencies received notice of 2,028 mergers that were potentially subject to review (DOJ and FTC 2019a). Most deals were allowed to proceed after an initial review that takes place within 30 days of the notification. In 45 matters, the reviewing agency identified competition issues and sought additional discovery from the parties to allow an in-depth investigation, in what is referred to as a "Second Request." As figure 6-1 shows, the number

Figure 6-1. Summary of Transactions by Fiscal Year, 2009–18

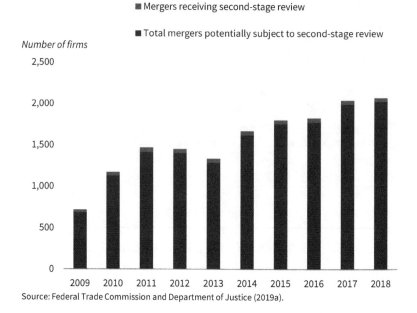

■ Mergers receiving second-stage review

■ Total mergers potentially subject to second-stage review

Source: Federal Trade Commission and Department of Justice (2019a).

of second requests conducted by the Agencies has remained relatively stable over time.

Economic Analysis at the Agencies

To aid in distinguishing between procompetitive and anticompetitive conduct, the Agencies employ Ph.D. economists who specialize in the analysis of competition. The Agencies also hire outside economic experts to examine evidence in particular cases. Here, we provide an overview of how economic analysis is used in merger enforcement. Similar methods are used in other areas of antitrust enforcement.

The central question in any merger review is whether the merger may substantially lessen competition. As explained in the "Horizontal Merger Guidelines" (DOJ and FTC 2010), this means that one or more firms affected by the merger are reasonably likely to raise prices, reduce output, decrease quality, reduce consumer choice, diminish innovation, or otherwise harm consumers. This is sometimes referred to as a consumer welfare standard, because the focus is on economic harm to consumers. Usually, this means harm to downstream customers of the merging firms, but the Agencies may also evaluate harm to upstream suppliers if there is a concern that the merger will enhance monopsony power, leading to lower prices or other types of economic harm for the suppliers deprived of competition for the sale of their goods or services; see box 6-1. Importantly for the digital age, the consumer welfare

Box 6-1. Antitrust and Monopsony:
George's Foods and Tyson Foods

Although most merger reviews focus on types of harm to downstream consumers, the Agencies may also investigate antitrust concerns relating to monopsony. In 2011, the DOJ challenged George's Foods' acquisition of a chicken-processing complex in Harrisonburg, Virginia, that was owned by Tyson Foods. Both companies provide chicken-processing services for birds that are raised by the surrounding area's farmers. The processors own the birds, provide the chicks and feed, and transport the birds between the farm and processing plants. The farmers ("growers") work under contract with the processors, providing chicken houses, equipment, and labor for raising the chickens.

Before the merger, George's Foods and Tyson Foods competed directly with each other for purchasing the services of growers in the Shenandoah Valley. The merger reduced the number of competitors from three to two, leaving George's Foods with about 40 percent of local processing capacity. The DOJ raised concerns that the merger would allow George's Foods to decrease prices or degrade contract terms to growers in the region. The other competing processor lacked the capacity to take on significant numbers of growers if George's were to depress prices. To remedy these concerns, George's agreed to invest in improvements in Tyson's chicken processing facilities, giving it an incentive to operate at a greater scale than before the merger. With an increased demand for chickens, George's also had an increased demand for the local growers (DOJ 2011a, 2011b).

standard considers harm beyond price effects, including harm to innovation, quality, and choice. The consumer welfare standard is also different from a total welfare standard, which would focus on overall efficiency, or outcomes that maximize the joint surplus of consumers and firms.[1]

To evaluate the likelihood of consumer harm, the Agencies analyze a variety of evidence. They may seek documents, testimony, and data from the merging parties. They may also seek information from other affected parties including customers, suppliers, and rival firms.

An important part of the analysis is to determine the nature of competition. Competition takes a variety of forms, and the effect of a merger depends on how competition works in the affected markets. For example, firms set prices in a variety of ways. They may be posted, as is common in the retail sector, or they may be negotiated, as is common in business-to-business services. In some cases, negotiations between buyers and sellers are structured with a formal auction process. These and other differences shape the nature of competition. In some markets, competition is so fierce that two competing firms

---

[1] Wilson (2019) has a discussion of the pros and cons of alternative antitrust standards.

are enough to drive prices down to the marginal cost. In other markets, many firms can profitably set prices significantly above the marginal cost.

The strength of competition between any firms depends on the extent to which consumers view their products as substitutes. Firms often sell differentiated products. This means that their products are similar, but not identical, and consumers may have strong (or weak) preferences between them. An important part of the economic analysis is assessing how close the merging firms' products are to each other in the view of consumers. Concerns about a lessening of competition will usually be greatest if many consumers view the firms' products as each other's closest substitutes. For example, some brands of breakfast cereal are so different in flavor, nutrition, and other attributes that few consumers regard them as substitutes, and competition between them is weak. Other brands of breakfast cereal probably compete head-to-head. To assess the closeness of products, economists at the Agencies review evidence such as win/loss reports, discount approval processes, customer switching patterns, and consumer surveys.

Based on such evidence, the Agencies identify relevant markets where competition is likely to be harmed. This analysis is based on demand substitution, or how consumers would respond to the increase in the price of a product. For example, if the evidence were to show that few people would switch to eating sugary breakfast cereals if the price of "heart-healthy" breakfast cereals were to rise, the Agencies might define a market for "heart-healthy" breakfast cereals that excludes the sugary alternatives. How broadly or narrowly to define markets can be a source of contention, as the shares of the merging firms will appear lower in broader markets. If markets are defined too broadly, they will contain products that do not significantly constrain the prices of the merging firms. The lower shares of the merging firms may then wrongly suggest that there is more competition than actually exists.

The Agencies also identify the relevant geography for a market. Markets may have a limited geography based either on consumers' preferences or on sellers' ability to serve them. For example, for most people, restaurants in Los Angeles and New York are probably not close substitutes. Nor would a flight from Los Angeles to New York be a good substitute for a flight from New York to Washington. In mergers of airlines, the DOJ often defines markets consisting of origin and destination pairs. A relevant market might include nonstop flights from San Francisco to Los Angeles if the merging parties both offer such flights.

The Agencies use a methodological tool, known as the hypothetical monopolist test, to delineate relevant markets. The test imagines that a single profit-maximizing firm monopolizes the candidate market and then analyzes whether the monopolist would "impose at least a small but significant and non-transitory increase in price" (DOJ and FTC 2010, 9). The Agencies usually define markets to be the smallest ones that satisfy the test. When a market is defined this way, products in the market significantly constrain each other's prices, but products outside the market do not.

After defining a relevant market, the Agencies calculate shares for all firms in the market and assess the level of concentration. Markets are classified as unconcentrated, moderately concentrated, or highly concentrated, based on thresholds of the HHI; see box 6-2. Markets with HHIs above 2,500 are considered highly concentrated. In such markets, the Agencies presume that mergers that increase the HHI by more than 200 points are likely to be anticompetitive. However, the merging parties can rebut this presumption with persuasive evidence.

To illustrate the role of market definition, consider the recent merger of the Walt Disney Company and Twentieth-Century Fox. The DOJ was concerned about competition between ESPN, which was owned by Disney, and the Fox Regional Sports networks. A key question was how much competition these cable sports networks faced from the sports programming shown on the major broadcast networks. The DOJ alleged that the licensing of cable sports programming to multichannel video programming distributors, such as Comcast and FIOS, was a relevant market, and one in which the merging parties had high shares. In excluding broadcast programming from the market, the DOJ alleged that the broadcast networks did not provide sufficiently close competition to prevent competitive harm. As stated in the complaint, multichannel video programming distributors do not typically consider broadcast network programming as a replacement for cable sports programming because broadcast networks offer limited airtime to sports programming and are focused on marquee events with broad appeal. The DOJ approved the merger only after the parties agreed to divest Fox's interests in its regional sports networks (DOJ 2018a, 2018b).

The inquiry into market share is a starting point for economic analysis, but the ultimate goal is to assess whether the merger is likely to have adverse competitive effects. A merger may harm competition because there are fewer competitors competing (unilateral effects), or it could harm competition by encouraging explicit or tacit coordination between rivals (coordinated effects). As noted above, mergers may harm competition in prices, or they may harm competition in nonprice dimensions, such as quality or innovation.

To evaluate competitive effects, the Agencies use a variety of evidence. Market shares are one type of evidence, but other evidence is also considered. For example, the Agencies may analyze how a recent merger in the same market affected competition. Or, if the merging firms compete in some local markets, but not others, the Agencies may compare prices across regions where the firms do and do not compete. In markets with differentiated products, such as breakfast cereal, the Agencies may estimate diversion ratios. A diversion ratio is a measure of how closely two products compete. For a first product sold by one of the merging firms and a second product sold by the other merging

Box 6-2. Measuring Concentration and the HHI

Concentration is a measure of the number and size of firms competing in a market. When markets are delineated around competition, concentration can be a useful reflection of competitive conditions. In highly concentrated markets—those markets with a small number of large firms—mergers between large firms are relatively likely to enhance market power, leading the merged firm to raise prices, reduce quality, reduce innovation, or otherwise harm consumers.

The Agencies usually measure concentration in terms of a firm's share of market revenues, but concentration can be defined around other measures, such as unit sales. The Agencies use the measure that best reflects the competitive significance of firms in the market. For example, if physical capacity limits the ability of firms to expand their production, market shares may be measured in terms of physical capacity. A firm that is poised to enter a market, but is not yet selling anything, may be assigned a market share based on projected revenues.

The Agencies measure concentration using the Herfindahl-Hirschman Index (HHI), which is calculated as the sum of the squares of the individual firms' market shares in a relevant market. In a monopolized market with only one firm, the firm's share is 100 percent, and the HHI is 100^2, or 10,000. In a market with 100 firms each with 1 percent share, the HHI is much lower, at 100. A higher HHI corresponds to a more concentrated market. A merger between two firms combines their shares, so the HHI increases. For example, if a market has four equal-sized firms and two of the firms merge, the HHI increases from 2,500 to 3,750.

firm, the diversion ratio is the percentage of sales that the first product would lose to the second product, if the price of the first product increases. The higher the diversion ratio, the closer the competition. The Agencies sometimes use diversion ratios in the context of economic models that simulate how firms would change their prices after a merger. The Agencies also consider whether efficiencies or entry are likely to offset or reverse adverse competitive effects.

The analysis of competitive effects has become more important over time. As discussed by Shapiro (2010), the Agencies revised the Horizontal Merger Guidelines in 1982 to downplay the emphasis on market shares and to increase the emphasis on competitive effects.[2] With this change in emphasis, antitrust enforcement also became less interventionist. Shapiro (2010) observes that the 1968 Horizontal Merger Guidelines stated that the Agencies "ordinarily challenge" mergers between an acquiring firm with at least 15 percent market share and an acquired firm with at least 1 percent market share.

---

[2] Shapiro (2010, 51–52). See also Lamoreaux (2019); Berry, Gaynor, and Morton (2019); and Peltzman (2014).

Mergers of this sort would be unlikely to be challenged today, because the analysis of competitive effects is rarely supportive of antitrust enforcement in such cases.

However, many people argue that the Agencies intervène too rarely in the modern era. Opponents of this view argue that antitrust overenforcement is more harmful than antitrust underenforcement. This is because if markets become overly concentrated to the point that profits are excessive, new firms are likely to enter to take up the slack. Proponents of more aggressive enforcement argue that new firm entry is often not guaranteed. In markets where entry is difficult (i.e., there are high barriers to entry), established firms may reap excessive profits for long periods of time (Baker 2015). In the next section, we turn to this debate.

A Renewed Interest in Concentration and the State of Competition

Some observers of the U.S. economy have raised concerns that it is becoming less competitive. As noted above, in 2016, an influential CEA policy brief (CEA 2016) argued that competition may be decreasing in many sectors, and President Obama issued an executive order directing Federal Government agencies to promote competition (White House 2016). Similar diagnoses and calls to regulatory action have been sounded by pundits and economists alike.[3]

In this section, we first discuss problems with the evidence presented in the 2016 CEA report, and then we explain how similar issues are manifested in other research on this topic. We explain why drawing inferences about the state of competition or antitrust enforcement from this weak evidence is problematic. Finally, we discuss alternative approaches to assessing if there is in fact a competition problem in the United States.

Problems with the CEA's 2016 Report

A central argument made in the 2016 CEA report, "Benefits of Competition and Indicators of Market Power," is that the rising market shares of the largest firms in many industries constitute evidence of declining competition. This argument is flawed both in terms of the evidence on market shares and the inference about competition.

Table 6-1, which is taken from the 2016 CEA report, examines trends in the revenue share of the 50 largest firms—known as the CR50—in different industry segments. For background, the U.S. Census Bureau classifies firms using the North American Industry Classification System (NAICS), which divides the entire economy into 24 sectors classified with two-digit numerical codes, or

---

[3] Examples include Furman (2018); Grullon, Larkin, and Michaely (2019); Krugman (2016); Kwoka (2015); Lamoreoux (2019); Wessel (2018); Wu (2018); and the *Economist* (2016).

Table 6-1. Change in Market Concentration by Sector, 1997–2012

Industry	Revenue earned by 50 largest firms in 2012 (dollars, billions)	Revenue share earned by 50 largest firms in 2012 (percent)	Change in revenue share earned by 50 largest firms from 1997 to 2012 (percentage points)
Transportation and warehousing	307.9	42.1	11.4
Retail trade	1555.8	36.9	11.2
Finance and insurance	1762.7	48.5	9.9
Wholesale trade	2183.1	27.6	7.3
Real estate rental and leasing	121.6	24.9	5.4
Utilities	367.7	69.1	4.6
Educational services	12.1	22.7	3.1
Professional, scientific, and technical services	278.2	18.8	2.6
Administrative and support	159.2	23.7	1.6
Accommodation and food services	149.8	21.2	0.1
Other services	46.7	10.9	-1.9
Arts, entertainment and recreation	39.5	19.6	-2.2
Healthcare and assistance	350.2	17.2	-1.6

Source: Census Bureau.
Note: Data represent all North American Industry Classification System sectors for which data were available from 1997 to 2012.

two-digit sectors. These sectors are further divided into three-, four-, five-, and six-digit subsectors. The CEA (2016) and Furman (2018) examine concentration in 13 of the two-digit NAICS sectors. Table 6-1 shows that 10 sectors became concentrated by this measure over the 15-year period from 1997 to 2012.

A key problem with table 6-1 is that the two-digit sectors are aggregations of overly broad geographic and product markets that shed little light on the state of competition. For example, retail trade includes all grocery stores, hardware stores, and gasoline stations, among many others, across the Nation. But grocery stores in Florida and Wisconsin do not compete for the same customers, and hardware stores and gas stations, even those in the same local area, largely sell products that are unrelated in demand. Concentration measures defined by national segments also miss the dimension of local competition. Rossi-Hansberg, Sarte, and Trachter (2019) find that the expansion of national firms into local markets has been a factor both in increasing concentration at the national level *and* in decreasing concentration at the local level.

This approach contrasts with how the Agencies define relevant markets for antitrust analysis. As discussed above, the Agencies, and antitrust economists more generally, analyze data on demand that reveal the extent to which consumers regard products as substitutes. In this way, markets are defined to include products that are in competition with each other in the local product markets where they compete. Even the finest six-digit NAICS sectors are far broader than typical antitrust markets. Werden and Froeb (2018) calculate the volume of commerce of the relevant markets alleged in DOJ merger complaints between 2013 and 2015 as a share of industry shipments in the six-digit NAICS sector. They find that in most cases, the antitrust markets accounted for less than 0.5 percent of the six-digit NAICS sector. In many cases, this is because the antitrust markets where the DOJ identified a competition problem involved single localities such as a city, State, or region, whereas the NAICS sectors are national. Although studies of broad swaths of the economy, such as the 2016 CEA report, are necessarily limited by the data that are publicly available, the coarseness of the data limits what they can say about competition.

A second problem with table 6-1 is the use of the CR50. The Agencies and other economists often find evidence of robust competition in markets with only a few firms engaged in head-to-head competition. Either the HHI (discussed above) or a four-firm concentration ratio (known as the CR4) would be more appropriate for a competition study. Note that in table 6-1, the CR50 are also usually much less than 100, meaning that there are more than 50 firms operating in the segment.

Because of the overly broad market definition and the use of the CR50, the data presented in table 6-1 tell us nothing about competition in specific markets, let alone across the entire economy. Carl Shapiro, a former CEA member and Deputy Assistant Attorney General for Economics under the Obama Administration, concluded that table 6-1 "is not informative regarding overall trends in concentration in well-defined relevant markets that are used by antitrust economists to assess market power, much less trends in competition in the U.S. economy" (Shapiro 2018, 722).

Problems with Related Research

The CEA's 2016 report, "Benefits of Competition and Indicators of Market Power," is part of a larger body of recent research arguing that competition may be in decline. Much of this literature tries to infer the state of competition from correlations between flawed concentration measures, such as those presented in table 6-1, and market outcomes, such as prices, profits, and markups. This methodology rests on a problematic assumption that increases in concentration create conditions of softer competition. That is, if undesirable outcomes—such as higher prices, profits, and markups—are correlated with concentration, then the cause of these outcomes is assumed to be weaker competition. Recent papers in this vein include the 2016 CEA report; and those by Furman (2018); Furman and Orszag (2018); Gutiérrez and Philippon (2017a, 2017b); and Grullon, Larkin, and Michaely (2019).

Problems with this assumption have been understood since at least the 1970s (Demsetz 1973; Bresnahan 1989).[4] The most fundamental problem is that there are alternative explanations for why a market might demonstrate both high concentration and high markups that are consistent with

---

[4] For a recent, in-depth discussion, see Berry, Gaynor, and Morton (2019); and Syverson (2019).

procompetitive behavior by firms. These include fixed costs, scale economies, and globalization.

To see that this is true, consider the issue of fixed costs. In many markets, firms make upfront investments in assets such as physical plant, equipment, research and product development, and information technology. Firms will make these investments only if they anticipate earning sufficient profit margins to recoup them. In terms of basic economics, if a firm has substantial fixed costs, then its average cost may be substantially higher than its marginal cost. A firm may earn a profit close to zero when fixed costs are accounted for, but still maintain a positive margin between price and marginal cost. The Agencies do not regard this as inherently problematic. As the Horizontal Merger Guidelines state, "High margins commonly arise for products that are significantly differentiated. Products involving substantial fixed costs typically will be developed only if suppliers expect there to be enough differentiation to support margins sufficient to cover those fixed costs. High margins can be consistent with incumbent [established] firms earning competitive returns" (DOJ and FTC 2010, 4); see box 6-3.

Even if high concentration and high markups are not inherently problematic, what about rising concentration and rising markups? This depends on why the markups and concentration are rising. Suppose that fixed costs are rising. If they are rising for anticompetitive reasons, such as if new and unnecessary government regulations are raising the cost of entry, then the trend may be associated with higher prices and consumer harm. But fixed costs could also be rising because firms are making increasingly expensive investments to become more competitive. Information technology in particular can involve upfront investments in business systems that help to reduce a firm's marginal cost of production or improve product quality. A firm that makes such investments may outcompete less efficient firms and grow its market share. Through such a process, information technology could transform a market to one with fewer, more efficient firms. Because the surviving firms have lower marginal costs, their prices may fall even as their markups rise. This scenario is procompetitive because consumers derive benefits from the lower prices or improved quality.

Berry, Gaynor, and Morton (2019) review recent research, providing evidence that investments in intangible assets such as software and business processes are becoming more important. Crouzet and Eberly (2019), in particular, find a positive correlation between firms' market shares (in broad industry segments) and their investments in intangible assets. In the view of Berry, Gaynor, and Morton (2019), the broad category of "increasing investments in fixed and sunk costs" may be the most important source of rising global markups. Autor and others (2019) find evidence that increases in concentration reflect a reallocation of output toward large, productive firms. They argue that this could be the result of globalization and technological change, and further observe that their explanation for rising concentration has "starkly different

Box 6-3. Concentration, Innovation, and Competition

Industries that rely on innovation often provide dramatic examples of high fixed costs. Consistent with this situation, concentration is often high. The relationship between concentration, competition, efficiency, and consumer welfare is complex. Competition can spur firms to innovate, but it can also weaken their incentives to innovate by making it difficult for them to recoup their investments. In research spanning decades, economists have found that different models give different answers about whether higher concentration increases or decreases innovation, and results about the optimal level of concentration are often sensitive to market conditions (Marshall and Parra 2019).

To illustrate, Igami and Uetake (2019) study these trade-offs in the hard disk drive industry. As shown in figures 6-i and 6-ii, the period had waves of entry and exit as the industry matured and consolidated. Innovation was of central importance, as the industry followed Kryder's law, that the storage capacity of hard disk drives doubles roughly every 12 months. After estimating a model of dynamic oligopoly, Igami and Uetake (2019) simulate the effect of alternative merger policies on expected social welfare. They conclude that a policy to block mergers if there are three or fewer firms would have found "approximately the right balance between pro-competitive effects and value-destruction side effects." Although such a policy might not be optimal in

Figure 6-i. New Entry of Hard Disk Drive Firms, 1976–2012

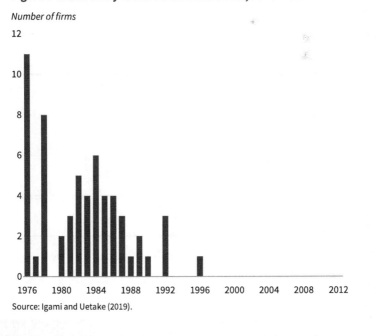

Number of firms

Source: Igami and Uetake (2019).

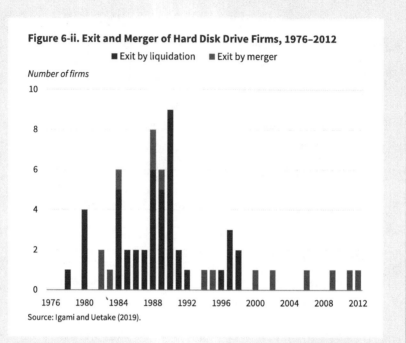

Figure 6-ii. Exit and Merger of Hard Disk Drive Firms, 1976–2012

■ Exit by liquidation   ■ Exit by merger

Number of firms

Source: Igami and Uetake (2019).

other industries or for any particular merger, this study helps to illustrate why competition can be robust in markets with relatively few firms.

The proposed acquisition of Baker Hughes by Halliburton provides an example of when innovation was central to a merger review (DOJ 2016). Halliburton, Baker-Hughes, and Schlumberger were the three leading firms in the oilfield services industry, providing sophisticated drilling technology and related services for drilling oil wells. Each invested hundreds of millions of dollars annually in research and development; for products where innovation was most important, there were few other competitors. The DOJ sued to block Halliburton's proposed acquisition of Baker-Hughes, delineating 23 relevant products and services where the proposed merger would result in markets dominated by the merged firm and Schlumberger. The DOJ was not satisfied that Halliburton's proposed divestitures would remedy the potential harm, and the parties ultimately abandoned their plans (Chugh et al. 2016).

implications" for welfare than explanations based on weakened competition or antitrust enforcement. That is, if rising concentration and markups are driven by conduct that benefits consumers, such as can be the case for investments in intangible assets, then there may be no competition problem and no antitrust implications.

In addition to the fundamental error of equating concentration with a lack of competition, there are also other problems with the recent literature on concentration. Similar to the CEA's 2016 report, these studies' use of Census and other macroeconomic data limits them to examining concentration in NAICS industry segments that are too broad to shed light on competitive conditions in properly defined antitrust markets. Many of the studies use data for three-digit or four-digit NAICS segments (e.g., Gutiérrez and Philippon 2017a, 2017b, 2019; Grullon, Larkin, and Michaely 2019); but as discussed above, even the finest six-digit NAICS segments are far broader than antitrust markets.

Another problem is that many of the studies explore links between concentration and financial measures, such as markups and profits, that are difficult to measure—especially across broad industry segments. Price-cost markups, in particular, are a basic measure of market power, but firm-level data on markups are rarely available. Accounting data are sometimes informative about the markup of price over average variable cost, but they do not accurately measure the economic profit margins that are relevant to economic analysis. Basu (2019) reviews different approaches to estimating markups used in the recent research discussed above. He discusses problems with the methods, including that most of the estimates of markups are implausibly large.

Connecting Concentration and Markups with Antitrust Law

The assessment of the competitive health of the economy should be based on studies of properly defined markets, together with conceptual and empirical methods and data that are sufficient to distinguish between alternative explanations for rising concentration and markups. This continues to be the approach of the Agencies.

In line with this, Berry, Gaynor, and Morton (2019, 63) call for a wave of "industry-level econometric studies . . . to help us understand shifts in markups, the underlying causes, and more broadly how markets in our modern economy are functioning and evolving." In their view, regressions of market outcomes on measures of concentration should carry little weight in policy debates because they do not and cannot illuminate causal relationships. Syverson (2019) is more optimistic that economy-wide studies can be helpful to identify patterns of increasing concentration for further research, but he concludes that the evidence does not yet support conclusions that rising aggregate market power exists and is causing problematic trends in the economy. Like Berry, Gaynor, and Morton (2019), Syverson (2019) calls for more careful research.

The airline industry provides an example where detailed, publicly available data have enabled insightful research. Werden and Froeb (2018) review this literature to conclude that since deregulation in the late 1970s, studies have not found systematic increases in concentration at the route level. Berry, Carnall, and Spiller (2006) note that investments in hub-and-spokes networks enabled airlines to earn high markups, but also benefited consumers. Moreover, Berry, Gaynor, and Morton (2019) cite Borenstein (2011) to observe that for many years, the large fixed costs associated with hub-and-spokes networks were just offset by high markups, leaving the major airlines with near-zero profits.

Other useful studies focus on how consummated mergers have affected market outcomes. In these studies, the increase in concentration is explicitly caused by a merging of competitors, so there is no question about why concentration has increased. For example, Ashenfelter, Hosken, and Weinberg (2015) study the 2008 joint venture between the beer giants Miller and Coors. The DOJ approved the deal, in part because it was expected to significantly reduce the costs of shipping and distribution (Heyer, Shapiro, and Wilder, 2009). Ashenfelter, Hosken, and Weinberg (2015) find little effect on prices, because the efficiencies created by the merger nearly exactly offset the realized price increases in the average market. However, in an analysis of the same market, Miller and Weinberg (2017) find evidence that the joint venture may have facilitated price coordination between competitors. These conflicting results illustrate some of the important nuances related to competition that broad industry studies cannot assess.

At this point, the evidence that the United States has a broad competition problem is inconclusive. However, the CEA's 2016 report and the related literature discussed above have spurred debate in government, academia, and policy circles about ways to strengthen antitrust enforcement to deal with the perceived competition problem. We now turn to this debate.

Calls for a Broader Interpretation of Antitrust Policy

The 2016 CEA report, "Benefits of Competition and Indicators of Market Power," and the related literature discussed above are part of a broader movement that is concerned with the growth of large firms across the U.S. economy. Lamoreaux (2019) provides a useful overview. Some of these observers want to amend or rewrite the antitrust laws to expand the Federal Government's involvement beyond its traditional scope to consider outcomes unrelated to market competition, including the political influence of large corporations, control of advertising and news media, and rising income inequality. For example, Furman and Orszag (2018) raise the question of whether a rising share of firms earning "supernormal returns on capital" might increase wage inequality due to workers at these firms sharing in the supernormal returns. Also, as we discuss in the next section, some observers are calling for regulations specifically for the digital economy.

Other observers are focused on traditional antitrust law, but would like enforcement to be expanded by lowering the threshold for an act to be considered anticompetitive. For example, one Senate bill would change the language of the Clayton Act, which prohibits mergers where the effect "may be substantially to lessen competition." The bill would change the standard of "substantially" to a standard of "materially." This would mean that the Federal Government could block a merger that has a smaller effect on competition (U.S. Congress 2019a).

As we have discussed, the argument that the U.S. economy is suffering from insufficient competition is built on a weak empirical foundation and questionable assumptions. Antitrust law has evolved through careful development of its case law, based on the legal system's accumulated experience with enforcement actions and the effects of specific types of acts on industries characterized by specific competitive dynamics. Throughout its development, antitrust law has consistently proven flexible to the evolving market conditions presented by new industries and business models in the ever-changing American economy. Before making radical changes to the law, the case for such change should be better grounded.

Moreover, the antitrust laws are a poor tool for addressing issues that go beyond questions of anticompetitive market conduct. Using antitrust law to regulate markets in the absence of competition problems will exact costs on the economy by preventing efficient market organization. If society wants to pursue goals such as rising income inequality or the political power of large firms, there are better policy tools to deal with these issues (Shapiro 2018).

We next turn to the related debate about whether more expansive antitrust enforcement is needed for the digital economy.

Antitrust Enforcement for the Digital Economy

In this section, we focus on the rapidly evolving issue of antitrust enforcement and competition in the digital economy. In recent years, digital platforms have come under increasing scrutiny. In the United Kingdom, the government commissioned an expert panel to review competition policy for the digital economy (Digital Competition Expert Panel 2019c). Since the panel made its recommendations, the U.K. has been working to create its Digital Markets Unit. The European Union has also commissioned an expert report (Crémer, Montjoye, and Schweitzer 2019), and has introduced several regulations for digital platforms.[5]

In the United States, the FTC has conducted hearings to examine whether new technologies and business practices, including those associated with digital platforms, require adjustments to competition policy (FTC 2019b).The House and Senate Judiciary Committees have also held hearings related to competition policy for digital platforms (U.S. House 2019a, 2019b, 2019c; U.S.

---

[5] The U.K. Digital Markets Unit would develop and enforce regulations related to data interoperability, data mobility, and data openness. It would have the authority to designate certain platforms as having "strategic market status." Such platforms would be subject to stronger regulations. In July 2019, the European Union issued new regulations governing how platforms interact with businesses (European Commission 2019). Rules on data portability and privacy, known as the General Data Protection Regulation (GDPR), went into effect in 2018.

Senate 2019). Independently, the Stigler Center at the University of Chicago has organized a committee on digital platforms that has developed recommendations for stronger antitrust enforcement and a digital regulator (Stigler Committee on Digital Platforms 2019). The Agencies have also opened reviews into market-leading online platforms, focusing on antitrust and related issues (Bloomberg 2019; DOJ 2019).

Although this chapter focuses on competition concerns, we note that some of these reviews also consider whether consumer protection regulations are warranted for issues such as data privacy and the moderation of media content.

Background

Digital platforms are intermediaries that enable interactions between users. They include search engines, online market places, social networks, communication and media platforms, and home-sharing and ride-sharing services, among other examples. Many of these platforms have been enormously successful and have reshaped the economy over the last 20 years.

Some concerns about digital platforms rest on the idea that they often operate in markets with economic features that naturally tend toward high concentration. One such feature is network effects, which arise when consumers place more value in a platform because many other people use it. For example, the more people one can reach with a messaging service, the more valuable that service is to users. When network effects are important, the largest platforms enjoy an advantage over their rivals simply because they have more users, regardless of the quality of their services. In some cases, the advantage may be so great that other firms are unable to compete. For example, in the videocassette recording industry, the Betamax technology essentially disappeared after VHS technology pulled ahead (Werden 2001).

In markets with network effects or other types of economies of scale, firms may compete for the entire market, rather than for shares in the market. The resulting monopolies may not be permanent. Bourne (2019) gives many examples of firms that achieved dominance through network effects or production economies of scale, only to eventually lose out to competition from innovative rivals. His examples range from the Great Atlantic & Pacific Tea Company in the 1920s to MySpace and Nokia in the early part of this century.

One of the current debates is about the extent to which digital platform industries are characterized by high barriers to entry. A barrier to entry is an obstacle that puts new firms at a disadvantage relative to firms already in the market.[6] Network effects can be a barrier to entry, particularly if an entrant must simultaneously attract two groups of users. For example, in the payments

---

[6] The formal definition of a barrier to entry has a long history of debate among economists. For a discussion, see Werden (2001).

industry, a new payment system might need to sign up thousands of merchants before consumers see it as valuable, and vice versa. However, network effects are not always sufficient to deter entry. If an entrant has an offsetting advantage, it may be able to overcome the advantage enjoyed by the established platform. For example, when Microsoft introduced the Xbox platform for video gaming, it was able to overcome the network effects enjoyed by the Sony PlayStation 2 by focusing on a few blockbuster games (Lee 2013).

There is also a debate about the extent to which access to data can be a barrier to entry. Mahnke (2015) discusses the issue in the context of the DOJ's 2008 investigation of the merger of the media firms Thomson and Reuters. The DOJ alleged that the merger would lead to higher prices for data sets related to company fundamentals, earnings, and aftermarket research, and that entrants would not be able to replicate the high quality of these data sets. The DOJ approved the merger, but only after the parties agreed to divest copies of the data sets along with supporting assets (DOJ 2008).

Data can also be a barrier to entry in the digital economy. Because dominant platforms have more users, they often have access to much more data than new entrants, and this can give them an insurmountable advantage (Rubinfeld and Gal 2017). For example, dominant platforms may be better able to target advertising at their users and so earn more revenues from advertising. However, a lack of access to data does not always deter entry. Lambrecht and Tucker (2015) observe that Airbnb, Uber, and Tinder entered markets where established firms (e.g., Expedia) had better data. They were able to succeed because of their innovative products. Lambrecht and Tucker (2015) also observe that data are nonrivalrous, in the sense that data can be shared and consumed by many users, in contrast to rivalrous goods such as food, which are consumed only once. Because of this, entrants can sometimes buy data as a substitute for collecting them internally from their users. However, this is not always the case, and the role of data as a barrier to entry depends on the facts and context of each market.

Finally, another debate asks whether dominant platforms are harming competition by buying too many smaller firms, such as start-ups funded with venture capital. It is common for large platforms to acquire smaller firms. The digital economy relies heavily on innovation, and being acquired by an established firm can be an important exit path for initial investors. Acquisition can also be important for a start-up's success. The acquiring firm may bring marketing, financing, and other business assets that enable the start-up to grow. However, if a start-up is not acquired, it might instead grow into an independent, full-fledged competitor. Some acquisitions may occur precisely to prevent such competition, as Cunningham, Ederer, and Ma (2019) find to be the case in the pharmaceutical industry.[7] However, as we discuss further below, it can be challenging for the Agencies to assess whether acquisitions of nascent competitors are procompetitive or anticompetitive in light of the benefits associated with them.

In summary, many digital platform markets have demand and supply features, suggesting that high concentration is efficient. The concentration has led to concerns about market dominance, anticompetitive behavior, and a lack of competition. But concentration can also be efficient, and there may be robust competition for the market, even in the face of high concentration.

Proposals for Intervention

Advocates of stronger regulation for digital platforms recommend a range of measures encompassing both antitrust reform and regulation—see, for example, the Stigler Committee on Digital Platforms (2019); the Digital Competition Expert Panel (2019c); and Crémer, Montjoye, and Schweitzer (2019). Here, we consider proposals related to data portability and interoperability, acquisitions of nascent competitors, and the creation of a digital regulatory authority.

Data portability and interoperability. Proposals to increase data portability and interoperability involve new regulations and legislation. Portability regulations would require digital platforms to enable customers to access their data from different platforms on request. Interoperability legislation would require digital platforms to enable their customers to switch their data from one platform to another. For example, a bill recently proposed in the Senate would require large communication platforms that generate income from their users' data to enable data portability and interoperability with other communication platforms. The goal is to reduce entry barriers for competitors to these platforms by making it less costly for customers to switch from one platform to another, and also by allowing customers of dominant platforms to communicate easily with customers of rival platforms (U.S. Congress 2019b).

As with any regulation, however, this would impose costs on the regulated platforms. Jia, Jin, and Wagman (2019) study the effect of the recent rollout of rules on data privacy and portability in Europe, known as the General Data Protection Regulation (GDPR), on venture capital funding. They find negative effects on European firms relative to their U.S. counterparts in terms of total funding, the number of deals and the amount raised per deal, with more pronounced effects for newer and data-related firms.

Acquisitions of nascent competitors. As discussed above, proponents of stronger antitrust enforcement raise concerns that dominant platforms are protecting themselves by acquiring small firms that would otherwise develop

---

[7] In a study of the pharmaceutical industry, Cunningham, Ederer, and Ma (2019) conclude that about 6 percent of acquisitions in their sample were "killer acquisitions" that forestalled the development of new drugs that would otherwise have competed with the acquirer's existing products.

into future competitors. Antitrust law has an existing framework to challenge such mergers under theories of potential competition and disruptive entrants (DOJ and FTC 2010). In 2018, the FTC challenged a merger between CDK Global and Auto/Mate. The acquiring firm, CDK, was a market leader in specialized business software for franchise automotive dealers. Auto/Mate was a much smaller competitor with an innovative business model that was an emergent threat. Although Auto/Mate was already competing, the FTC was largely concerned about the competition it would likely provide in the future (FTC 2018b; Ohlhausen 2019).

Predicting future competition can be difficult in the digital economy because products and services evolve rapidly. Dominant platforms may acquire start-ups that offer no competing products, but that could compete with them in the future through expansion into adjacent markets. To address this issue, some proposals for revising the antitrust laws would weaken the evidentiary standards when a dominant firm seeks to acquire a firm in a separate but adjacent market. For example, the Agencies might meet their initial burden of proof by showing that there is a reasonable likelihood that the target firm would compete with the acquiring firm in the future, even if the target firm has no specific plans to do so (Shapiro 2019).

Such policies could have important downsides. More aggressive standards for blocking mergers of nascent competitors would raise the likelihood that procompetitive mergers would be blocked. As discussed above, the digital economy relies heavily on innovation. If dominant platforms were routinely deterred from acquiring start-ups, such a policy could reduce venture capital funding in this segment. During the U.K. panel review, a variety of organizations and individuals raised these concerns (Digital Competition Expert Panel 2019a, 2019b). At a minimum, the potential effect of any new policy on venture capital deserves study. More research, including merger retrospectives focused on acquisitions in the digital economy, would also be helpful.

Creation of a digital regulatory authority. The Stigler Committee on Digital Platforms (2019) found that "the strongest indication emerging from the four reports is the importance of having a single powerful regulator capable of overseeing all aspects of [digital platforms]." In terms of competition goals, the digital regulator would have a mandate to design and enforce regulations aimed to enhance competition, such as standards for data portability and interoperability. The authority would be able to designate dominant platforms as "bottlenecks" and subject them to stronger regulations. For example, such platforms might need to obtain approval from the authority for any acquisition, no matter how small, and the digital authority would be able to challenge these acquisitions under a legal standard that imposes a lower burden of proof on the Agencies than does current antitrust law.

The Stigler Committee on Digital Platforms (2019) also makes recommendations that fall outside antitrust and competition policy. A subcommittee on politics, in particular, recommends that a digital authority have the power to take actions to limit concentration, not due to concerns about economic harm to consumers, but due to concerns about the political power of large platforms. A subcommittee on data privacy and security recommends that a digital authority oversee consumer protection regulation that would develop, among other regulations, rules similar to the GDPR in Europe.

Proposals to establish a new digital authority raise a host of issues. A basic concern is that the breadth of the mandate is far from obvious. As noted above, digital platforms provide a wide-ranging set of goods and services, from search engines, to operating systems, to ride-sharing services. The Stigler Committee on Digital Platforms (2019) points to the Federal Communications Commission (FCC) as a model for a digital regulator, but the scope of the FCC's authority is the telecommunications sector. The scope of a digital authority would likely be harder to delineate, and firms in some of the most innovative sectors of the economy would face uncertainty as to whether they fall under its regulations.

Perhaps the most serious concern is for the possibility of regulatory capture. In a speech, FCC chair Ajit Pai (2013) relays a cautionary tale of FCC regulatory capture, describing how AT&T made commitments to the FCC in 1913 that effectively allowed it to divide up territories with independent local telephone companies. These commitments tamed competition that had emerged after the patents of Alexander Graham Bell began to expire. The Stigler Committee on Digital Platforms (2019) discusses the need to deter regulatory capture and cites Pai's speech. It also cites the foundational work on regulatory capture by the Nobel laureate economist George Stigler, for whom the Stigler Center is named. Though there is some irony here, the point is that the downsides of new, far-reaching regulation need to be taken seriously.

Although today's digital economy warrants further study—and, where necessary, vigilant antitrust enforcement—a cautious approach to regulation is clearly warranted. As we have discussed, there is a fundamental problem in inferring that high concentration is indicative of a lack of competition. The nature of competition also varies across markets, so one-size-fits-all policies may not work well. Instead, fact-specific investigations along the lines of what the Agencies already do are more sensible.

Competition Policy to Reduce Entry Barriers

In the preceding sections, we have argued for caution in responding to calls for Federal Government intervention to address increasing concentration in the U.S. economy. However, it is true that entry barriers can protect firms from competition. Sometimes, these entry barriers are structural, in that they are associated with the nature of the market itself, such as products that require large investments in research and development. In other cases, entry barriers

Box 6-4. The Effects of Deregulation within the Pharmaceutical Drug Market

As noted, some barriers to entry are purposefully constructed. To illustrate, consider the pharmaceutical drug industry, where the Food and Drug Administration (FDA) plays a crucial role in supplying drugs through the management of drug application reviews. The FDA ultimately determines if and when a drug will be available on the market. Although the stringent evaluations conducted by the FDA are necessary to ensure the safety and efficacy of drugs, they are also partly responsible for raising entry barriers for many generic and new drugs. This has led to a higher concentration of brand name drugs in some markets, along with higher prices that reduce consumer welfare.

The Trump Administration realizes the significance of improving competition in markets for pharmaceutical drugs, and it has implemented a series of deregulatory reforms with the hope of reducing costs for consumers. One of its proposals highlights the need for the transparency of negotiated discount rates with insurers, requiring hospitals to disclose this information to their patients (CEA 2018a). The Administration also signed the Food and Drug Administration Reauthorization Act in 2017, which reauthorized the FDA to collect user fees from generic drug applications and to process applications efficiently for another five years. Since the start of the Trump Administration, aspects of the FDA's drug application process, most prominently that for generic drugs, have been streamlined to encourage quick market entry. In the first 20 months of the Administration, an average of 17 percent more generic drugs were approved each month than were approved during the previous 20-month period (CEA 2018b).

In 2018, the FDA expanded its Strategic Policy Roadmap in efforts to not only increase efficiencies in the drug review process but also reduce anti-competitive behavior from brand name drug makers that try to inhibit generic market entry. The FDA is also taking steps to address scientific and regulatory barriers that are obstacles to entry of some complex generic medicines. The FDA's efforts to lower barriers and have a more predictable and efficient development process may enable new and innovative drug makers to enter the market. Consumers would benefit both from the development of new classes of drugs and from new therapies for conditions treated by existing drugs. Such new therapies could discipline the prices of existing drugs. This was the case for drugs such as simvastatin, which held a large portion of the market for lowering cholesterol in the 1990s. However, starting in 1996, after the introduction of the therapy drug atorvastatin, competition flourished, and cholesterol-lowering drugs are now affordable (CEA 2018b).

are purposefully constructed by governments in situations where private markets may fail; see box 6-4. However, as discussed in chapter 3 of this *Report,* even if a regulatory action addresses a private market failure, a deregulatory action is still warranted if the costs of the regulation outweigh the regulatory benefits. This section describes the Agencies' efforts to call attention to regulations that harm consumers by creating entry barriers that limit competition. It also discusses how the Agencies apply the antitrust laws to intellectual property rights to promote sound competition.

Other Government–Created Barriers to Entry

As we discuss in chapter 2 of this *Report*, occupational licensing requirements impose an additional cost on a person entering a given occupation. Some licensing requirements may be justified on public safety grounds; but in many professions, they also function as barriers to entry that artificially inflate wages by protecting those already in the profession from competition. To support the claim that the majority of State occupational licensing requirements are unnecessary to protect public safety, the FTC points out that 1,100 occupations require a license in at least one State but only 60 occupations are licensed by every State. If an occupation poses a substantiated threat to public safety, the argument goes, then that occupation would be universally licensed (FTC 2018a, 2019c).

The Agencies have long advocated measures to limit the competitive harm associated with occupational licensing. In 2017, the FTC established a task force on the issues, and in 2018, it released a report outlining options to mitigate the harm. These options include interstate pacts that allow groups of States to recognize a common license, as well as other portability and mutual recognition measures (FTC 2018a).

Certificate-of-need (CON) laws were originally designed in the 1970s to discourage overinvestment in healthcare markets (e.g., building too many hospitals) in an attempt to limit costs. A CON law requires a firm to convince a State regulator that there is an unmet need for the new services. Over years of review, the Agencies have found that these laws often harm competition, and they regularly advocate for their removal. In 2019, for example, staff at the Agencies sent letters to legislatures in Alaska and Tennessee in support of their plans to revise these laws (DOJ and FTC 2019b, 2019d). The Agencies' analysis of evidence, accumulated over decades, finds that instead of reducing healthcare costs, CON laws tend to create inefficiencies by suppressing healthcare supply to the benefit of established suppliers, preventing investment that would stimulate competition and lower consumer prices.

Many States require car manufacturers to distribute vehicles through independent, franchised dealerships. The Agencies have long advocated against such automobile franchising laws. They argue that when manufacturers are free to choose their method of distribution, the competitive process aligns their interests with those of consumers, so the products and services are brought to market as efficiently as possible. In 2019, Nebraska took up a bill that would remove restrictions on direct vehicle sales to consumers, but only for vehicle manufacturers that had not used independent, franchised dealers in the State before. The Agencies sent a joint letter to the Nebraska Legislature encouraging it to remove the restrictions for all vehicle manufacturers (DOJ and FTC 2019c).

Promoting Innovation through Sound Enforcement of Competition Law

As we have discussed, consumers often benefit most from dynamic competition, as driven by investment and innovation in new products, inventions, and technologies. Intellectual property rights—such as patents, trademarks, and copyrights—limit competition from infringing products in order to encourage this dynamic competition. However, in certain circumstances, intellectual property rights, like any asset, may be used in a manner that unlawfully limits competition. To prevent this, the Agencies apply the same antitrust principles to conduct involving intellectual property as they do to conduct involving other forms of property (DOJ and FTC 2017). They apply an effects-based economic analysis to conduct involving intellectual property that considers its efficiencies and weighs procompetitive benefits of the conduct against any competitive harm. The Agencies also engage in advocacy for the correct application of antitrust law to intellectual property rights.

The DOJ has emphasized the need to avoid rigid presumptions in the intellectual property area that could deter innovation. In particular, it has cautioned against the misapplication of antitrust laws, which carry the specter of treble damages, to commercial disputes involving the exercise of patent rights. In December 2017, the DOJ withdrew its support from its 2013 joint policy statement with the Patent and Trademark Office on remedies associated with standard essential patents, because the statement had been construed to suggest that the antitrust laws should limit patent holders from seeking injunctions or exclusionary remedies to defend their intellectual property rights. The DOJ's work in this area ensures that there are strong incentives to invest in developing technologies, and thus fostering dynamic competition.

A top priority of the FTC is to oppose "pay-for-delay" patent settlements, whereby branded drug manufacturers pay generic drug producers to stay out of the market. In 2013, in *FTC v. Actavis, Inc.*, the Supreme Court held that, in certain circumstances, the FTC can challenge such settlements under the antitrust law, provided that courts weigh anticompetitive effects against the procompetitive benefits of such conduct. Since that year, the FTC has regularly reported on these settlements. In its most recent report, the FTC found that the number of pay-for-delay payments of the type that are likely to be anticompetitive has been decreasing (FTC 2019a).

Conclusion

The Trump Administration understands the vital role that competition plays in the economy, promoting new businesses and serving consumers. Timely antitrust enforcement is an important tool for protecting the competitive process. By contrast, confusion surrounding the effects of rising concentration appears to be driven by questionable evidence and an overly simple narrative that "Big Is Bad." When companies achieve scale and large market share by innovating and providing their customers with value, this is a welcome result of healthy competition.

This chapter has explained why recent calls for changing the goals of the antitrust laws and expanding the scope of regulations are based on inconclusive evidence that competition is in decline. These calls also ignore the flexibility of the existing legal system to accommodate changing market circumstances. Research purporting to document a pattern of increasing concentration and increasing markups uses data on segments of the economy that are far too broad to offer any insights about competition, either in specific markets or in the economy at large. Where data do accurately identify issues of concentration or supercompetitive profits, additional analysis is needed to distinguish between alternative explanations, rather than equating these market indicators with harmful market power.

Antitrust actions and any major changes to competition policy should be based on sound economic evidence, including evidence on consumer harm. Research based on broad industry studies may be helpful for indicating trends in concentration, but is unable to diagnose the underlying causes or determine whether consumers in relevant antitrust markets have been harmed. Ultimately, today's detailed, evidence-based approach to antitrust remains the most powerful lens available to protect consumers and suppliers by accurately diagnosing and responding to anticompetitive behavior.

For these reasons, this chapter argues that the DOJ's Antitrust Division and the FTC are well-equipped to protect consumers from anticompetitive behavior. The Agencies have maintained their focus on illegal or anticompetitive actions by businesses, while expanding their scope to advocate against government policies that harm competition. Vigorous competition is essential for building upon the economy's record expansion, and the Trump Administration will continue following the economic evidence and using the Federal Government's authority to promote competition in ways that lead to greater consumer benefits.

Chapter 7

Understanding the Opioid Crisis

The opioid crisis poses a major threat to the U.S. economy and America's public health. Since 2000, more than 400,000 people have lost their lives because of opioids. This staggering number of deaths has pushed drug overdoses to the top of the list of leading causes of death for Americans under the age of 50 years, and has cut 2.5 months from U.S. life expectancy. The Council of Economic Advisers (CEA) has previously estimated that the annual economic cost of the opioid crisis is substantially higher than previously thought, at over half a trillion dollars in 2015. Using a similar methodology, the CEA estimates that the crisis cost $665 billion in 2018, or 3.2 percent of gross domestic product.

There are signs that the opioid crisis is past its peak because the growth in opioid overdose deaths has stopped during the Trump Administration, stopping the upward trend that has persisted since at least 1999. From January 2017 through May 2019, the CEA estimates that there were 37,750 fewer opioid overdose deaths—representing an economic cost savings of over $397 billion—relative to the number of deaths expected based on previous trends. Actions taken by the Trump Administration to reduce the supply of opioids, reduce new demand for opioids, and treat those with current opioid use disorder may have contributed to the flattening in overdose deaths involving opioids.

The Trump Administration understands that the crisis is ongoing and that there is much more work to do to combat this threat to American lives and the American economy. In order to continue mitigating the cost of the opioid crisis, it is crucial to understand all its underlying factors. We describe and analyze two separate waves of the crisis—the first wave, from 2001 to 2010, which was characterized by growing overdose deaths involving the misuse of prescription opioids; and the second wave, from 2010 to 2016, which was characterized by growing overdose deaths involving illicitly manufactured opioids (heroin and fentanyl).

We find that in the first wave, between 2001 and 2010, out-of-pocket prices for prescription opioids declined by an estimated 81 percent. This dramatic drop in prices was a consequence of the expansion of government healthcare coverage, which increased access to all prescription drugs—including opioids. We argue that these falling out-of-pocket prices effectively reduced the price of opioid use in the primary market and in the secondary (black) market for diverted opioids, from which most people who misuse prescription opioids obtain their drugs. We estimate that the decline in observed out-of-pocket prices is capable of explaining between 31 and 83 percent of the growth in the death rate involving prescription opioids from 2001 to 2010.

However, falling out-of-pocket prices could not have led to a major rise in opioid misuse and overdose deaths without the increased availability of prescription opioids resulting from the new specialty of pain management, the creation of pain management practices that encouraged liberalized dispensing practices by doctors, illicit "pill mills," increased marketing and promotion efforts from industry, and inadequate monitoring or controls against drug diversion. The subsidization of opioids is in stark contrast to the taxation of other addictive substances such as tobacco and alcohol. The dilemma this poses is how to make available the appropriate medical use of opioids for pain relief while preventing nonmedical use of subsidized products.

We find that the second wave of the opioid crisis likely started in 2010 because of efforts to limit the misuse of prescription OxyContin, enabling a large market for the sale and innovation of illegal opioids. Although these efforts eventually successfully reduced prescription opioid-involved overdose deaths, they had the unintended consequence of raising demand for cheaper substitutes in the illicit market among misusers of prescription drugs. An expansion in foreign-sourced supply was also important for the growth of illicitly manufactured opioids, as evidenced by falling quality-adjusted prices, largely due to expanded heroin trafficking from Mexico and relatively inexpensive synthetic opioids from both Mexico and China, specifically fentanyl and its analogues, which can be many times more potent than heroin.[1]

The Trump Administration has undertaken serious efforts to tackle the ongoing opioid crisis that continues to threaten the American economy and American lives. This is demonstrated by the declaration of the opioid epidemic as a public health emergency, the establishment of the President's Commission on Combating Drug Addiction and the Opioid Crisis, the highest expenditures in history directed toward the opioid epidemic, and ongoing efforts throughout the Federal government to address the crisis. The damage resulting from the opioid crisis is dramatic in its proportions compared with other health crises. For example, in 2017, the number of people who died of an opioid-involved drug overdose (47,600) exceeded the number of deaths from the HIV/AIDS epidemic at its peak in 1995 (CDC 2019).[2] Additionally, since 2000, the United States has lost as much of its population to the opioid crisis as it lost to World War II—with both causing more than 400,000 fatalities (DeBruyne 2017). This staggering number of deaths has pushed drug overdoses to the top of the list of leading causes of death for Americans under the age of 50 years, and has cut 2.5 months from U.S. life expectancy (Dowell et al. 2017).

To assess the full damage caused by this crisis, the CEA has previously assessed its full economic cost. In 2015 alone, the CEA estimated that the total cost of the opioid crisis was $504 billion, several times larger than previous cost estimates (CEA 2017). The CEA's approach constituted a more complete assessment of the costs because it incorporated the full cost of increased morbidity and mortality from the crisis. We also adjusted opioid-involved deaths—which had been underreported—upward and incorporated nonfatal costs. Using similar methods as in the earlier CEA assessment, the annual cost of the opioid crisis has only risen since 2015, amounting to $665 billion in 2018. The annual number of reported opioid-involved overdose deaths increased from 33,091 in 2015 to 47,600 in 2017, a 44 percent increase. According to preliminary data, deaths have since decreased slightly in 2018, an indication of a flattening in

---

[1] The CEA previously released research on topics covered in this chapter. The text that follows builds on this research paper produced by the CEA: "The Role of Opioid Prices in the Evolving Opioid Crisis" (CEA 2019b).

[2] We identify overdose deaths throughout the report using the 10th revision of the International Statistical Classification of Diseases and Related Health Problems (ICD-10) underlying cause-of-death classification codes: X40–X44 (unintentional), X60–X64 (suicide), X85 (assault), and Y10–Y14 (undetermined). Deaths involving opioids are identified using ICD–10 multiple cause-of-death classification codes: T40.0–T40.4 and T40.6.

the trend of increasing annual deaths that has persisted since 1999 (see figure 7-1).[3]

When President Trump took office in January 2017, monthly overdose deaths involving opioids had reached an all-time record high, a 41 percent increase from the number of deaths 12 months earlier, in January 2016. Since then, the growth in opioid deaths may have finally stopped. Monthly overdose deaths fell by 9.6 percent between January 2017 and May 2019, the latest month for which provisional data are available (see figure 7-1). If the growth rate in opioid overdose deaths from 1999 through 2016 had continued, 37,750 additional lives would have been lost due to opioid overdoses between January 2017 and May 2019, a 33 percent increase over the actual number of deaths that occurred over this period. The economic cost savings since January 2017 from reduced mortality compared with the preexisting trend was over $397 billion.[4]

In order to continue mitigating the large costs imposed by the opioid crisis through appropriate policy measures, it is crucial to understand the forces that underlie it. We separate our analysis into two sections: The first one analyzes the first wave of the crisis, lasting through 2010, which was characterized by growth in prescription opioid-involved overdose deaths; and the second analyzes the period since 2010, which has been characterized by growth in illicit opioid-involved overdose deaths.[5]

During the first wave, between 2001 and 2010, the annual population-based rate of overdose deaths involving prescription opioids increased by 182 percent (CDC WONDER n.d.). Throughout this period, opioid manufacturers aggressively promoted the safety and effectiveness of opioids, and guidelines for the treatment of pain were liberalized to encourage physicians to prescribe

---

[3] Official estimates of opioid-involved overdose deaths are extracted from the CDC's WONDER Multiple Cause of Death Database (https://wonder.cdc.gov/mcd.html). As of December 31, 2019, official data were available through December 2017. Preliminary estimates of opioid-involved overdose deaths are extracted from Ahmad et al. (2019). The provisional data include deaths of foreign residents and include approximately 500 additional drug overdose records compared with data from CDC WONDER that is limited to residents of the United States.

[4] The number of lives saved is calculated from the difference between the projected trend in deaths from January 2017 to May 2019, the most recent month of preliminary data as of December 31, 2019 (see figure 7-1). The calculated number of lives saved is sensitive to the assumption that the projected trend is nonlinear. We use the value of a statistical life to estimate the value of lives saved, adjusting the Department of Transportation's value of a statistical life to about $10.5 million in 2018 dollars (DOT 2016).

[5] We use "illicit opioids" throughout the chapter to refer to illicitly produced opioids such as heroin and fentanyl, which excludes the misuse of prescription opioids such as OxyContin. It is important to note that data on overdose deaths do not distinguish between illicitly manufactured synthetic opioids, such as illicitly manufactured fentanyl, and synthetic prescription opioids, such as prescription fentanyl. This analysis includes this broader category of synthetic opioids other than methadone in the illicit opioid category, given that illicitly manufactured fentanyl is commonly believed to have dominated this category in recent years, and that the category was much less important in the earlier years of the crisis.

Figure 7-1. Opioid-Involved Overdose Deaths, 1999–2019

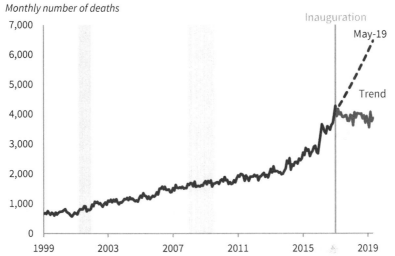

Monthly number of deaths

Sources: Centers for Disease Control and Prevention (CDC); CEA calculations.
Note: Data from before January 2018 are compiled from the CDC WONDER database, and monthly data beginning in January 2018 are calculated using the provisional reported number of deaths from the CDC. The preinauguration trend is calculated for January 1999 to January 2017. Shading denotes a recession.

more opioids (Van Zee 2009). Over the same period, we estimate that the out-of-pocket price of prescription opioids fell by 81 percent (see also Zhou, Florence, and Dowell 2016). We argue that the falling out-of-pocket price translated into a lower price of misuse not only for those who obtain prescriptions in the primary market but also for the majority of misusers who obtain prescription opioids from the secondary (black) market.

The decline in out-of-pocket prices between 2001 and 2010 occurred in conjunction with a rising share of generic opioids in the market as well as increased public subsidies. Though we do not attempt to apportion their respective roles, these two factors may have contributed significantly to the out-of-pocket price decline. With regard to a rising generic share in the prescription opioid market, we note that supply prices paid to pharmacies fell by 45 percent between 2001 and 2010, fueled by an increase in the cheaper generic opioid share, from 53 percent to 81 percent.

In addition, we document a large increase in the share of prescription opioids funded by public programs. As shown in figure 7-2, the share of prescribed opioids purchased with public subsidies increased from 17 percent in 2001 to 60 percent in 2010, rising further to 63 percent in 2015. Public programs accounted for three-fourths of the growth in total prescription opioids between 2001 and 2010 (data from the Medical Expenditure Panel Survey, MEPS). The introduction of the Medicare Part D prescription drug benefit in January 2006

Figure 7-2. Share of Potency-Adjusted Prescription Opioids, by Primary Payer, 2001–15

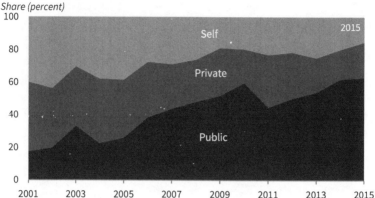

Share (percent)

Sources: Medical Expendtiure Panel Survey; National Drug Code Database; CEA calculations.
Note: The primary payer is the third-party payer with the highest payment for a given prescription. In addition to Medicare, Medicaid, and private insurers, the other possible primary payers include veterans' benefits, workers' compensation, other Federal government insurance, other State or local goverment insurance, or other public insurance. All prescriptions are converted into morphine gram equivalents based on the quantity of pills prescribed and their potency.

coincided with a growing share of prescriptions reimbursed by the program, including for many opioids. Additionally, Social Security Disability Insurance (SSDI) enrollment has rapidly increased since the late 1990s (see figure 7-16). More than half of SSDI recipients received drug coverage before the 2006 start of Medicare Part D through Medicaid and other programs. After 2006, SSDI recipients, along with the general Medicare population, were for the most part eligible for prescription drug coverage through Medicare Part D.

Expansions in insurance coverage that reduce out-of-pocket prices make misused prescription opioids more affordable for patients with prescriptions and users who purchase the drugs on the secondary market. Before generics were as widely available, it was very costly for the average American with opioid use disorder to afford prescription opioids, if not subsidized through insurance. In 2007, Americans could buy 1 gram of OxyContin—one of the most common brand name opioids prescribed—for an average of $144 without health insurance. Some individuals on opioids may require up to a gram or more per day of OxyContin for pain relief (Schneider, Anderson, and Tennant 2009). Without insurance, a person with an opioid use disorder consuming between 0.5 gram and 1 gram of OxyContin every day for a year would have spent between $26,280 and $52,560 in 2007—which could be more than the median household income of about $50,000 in 2007 (in 2007 dollars) (Fontenot,

Semega, and Kollar 2018).[6] To put this in perspective, a person on Medicare would only pay $9.78 per gram, or between $1,785 and $3,570 per year (in 2007 dollars), to support an opioid use disorder in the same year.

The subsidization of opioids is in stark contrast to the taxation of other addictive substances such as tobacco and alcohol. The challenge this poses is how to ensure access to opioids for legitimate medical needs, such as for pain relief, when other substances are contraindicated or insufficient, while not subsidizing nonmedical uses.

Given the role the government played in subsidizing the purchase of prescription opioids through the expansion of health insurance, we examine the possible roles of specific public programs. We find that the number of potency-adjusted opioids per capita subsidized by Medicare increased by 2,400 percent between 2001 and 2010, the largest increase among all third-party payers. SSDI rolls also expanded over this period. We estimate that SSDI recipients, who are generally eligible for Medicare (including prescription coverage in Part D, starting in 2006), were prescribed a disproportionate share of 26 to 30 percent of total potency-adjusted opioids in 2011 across all payer types (while representing under 3 percent of the U.S. population). Of course, any role of SSDI expansion in the opioid crisis would be attributable to the design of the program rather than program recipients. SSDI recipients generally have debilitating conditions that prevent them from working, and these conditions are often associated with high levels of pain. These conditions are the primary reason SSDI recipients are prescribed a disproportionate share of opioids; indeed, SSDI benefits, in conjunction with Medicare coverage, provide vital protection for these disabled workers. Additionally, the majority of SSDI recipients prescribed opioids use them appropriately and do not contribute to opioid misuse directly or indirectly.

As a calibration exercise, we take published estimates of the price elasticity of prescription opioid sales to estimate the increase in sales resulting from an 81 percent price decline. This exercise suggests that, without the price decline, per capita opioid sales would have increased by half as much or less than the actual increase between 2001 and 2010. In order to estimate the size of the price decline as a factor in the increase in the number of deaths involving prescription opioids, we assume that (1) secondary market prices are proportional to out-of-pocket prices in the primary market, and (2) the price elasticity of opioid use ranges from the elasticity of prescriptions at the low end to the own-price elasticity of heroin use at the high end. This second calibration

---

[6] Due to heightened risk to patients, the CDC recommends that physicians avoid prescriptions at or above 90 morphine milligram equivalents per day, equivalent to 60 milligrams of oxycodone or 0.06 gram, or carefully justify a decision to titrate dosage to 90 or more milligram equivalents per day (CDC n.d.). Schneider, Anderson, and Tennant (2009) observe that some chronic pain patients require doses that may range from 1,000 to 2,000 or more milligram equivalents per day. These doses would be equivalent to 667 to 1,333 milligrams (0.7 to 1.3 grams) of oxycodone per day.

exercise suggests that the observed decline in out-of-pocket prices for pre-scription opioids, which makes physicians' prescriptions more affordable for beneficiaries to fill, was a factor in between 31 and 83 percent of the increase in overdose deaths involving prescription opioids between 2001 and 2010.

However, falling out-of-pocket prices could not have led to a major rise in opioid misuse and deaths without the increased availability of prescription opioids resulting from changes in pain management practice guidelines that encouraged liberalized dispensing practices by doctors, illicit "pill mills," increased marketing and promotion efforts from industry, and inadequate monitoring or controls against diversion. Without these factors, patients would have been unable to respond to lower prices by obtaining prescription opioids and diverting them to the secondary market. In other words, the change in the environment for obtaining prescription opioids was a precondition for the effect of falling out-of-pocket prices on opioid misuse. In addition, it is impor-tant to emphasize that the falling price of the *medical* use of opioids—due to expanded insurance coverage and generic entry—benefited patients because they could access needed drugs at a lower out-of-pocket cost. By contrast, the falling price of the *nonmedical* use of opioids, enabled by a lax prescribing environment in conjunction with lower out-of-pocket prices, may have played an important role in fueling the opioid crisis.

More generally, these findings of increased opioid misuse associated with the growth of public programs do not imply that these programs lack social value, but rather show the importance of instituting safeguards to ensure the appropriate prescribing and use of opioids, and measures to reduce the misuse of opioids.[7] Government policy for other addictive products, such as cigarettes, deliberately discourages consumption by raising prices through sales taxes and placing restrictions on purchase and sales; most analysts agree that such policies successfully reduced cigarette use and made new addiction cases less likely (HHS 2014). Unlike cigarettes, which are not safe or beneficial for anyone in any quantity, opioids have legitimate medical uses. The challenge of prescription opioids is balancing the goal of subsidizing opioids when they are prescribed for appropriate use with the need to discourage overprescription and misuse.

Next, we analyze the second wave of the opioid crisis, which was char-acterized by the growth of illicit, opioid-involved overdose deaths between 2010 and 2016. In this case, demand-side expansions due to efforts to curtail prescription opioid use disorder along with supply-side expansions appear to have been important. Most notably on the demand side, an abuse-deterrent formulation of the widely abused prescription opioid OxyContin was released in 2010, and the original formulation was no longer made available from the manufacturer. Research has found that although the reformulation stemmed

---

[7] See HHS (2016) for further discussion.

Figure 7-3. Opioid-Involved Overdose Death Rate by the Presence of Prescription Opioids, 2001–16

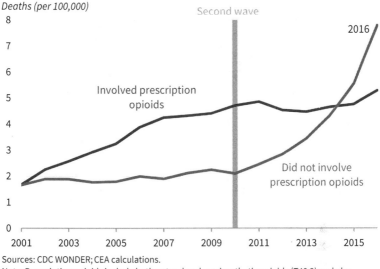

Sources: CDC WONDER; CEA calculations.
Note: Prescription opioids include both natural and semisynthetic opioids (T40.2) and also methadone (T40.3).

the rise of overdose deaths involving prescription opioids, it led opioid misusers to substitute toward cheaper, more available heroin, resulting in increased heroin-involved deaths (Alpert, Powell, and Pacula 2018; Evans, Lieber, and Power 2019). Thus, the buildup of a pool of people with addictions to prescription opioids during the first wave ultimately facilitated the increase in demand for illicit opioids in the second wave. This large pool of new demand created additional profit opportunities for illegal sellers entering the market. Supply increased as Mexican heroin traffickers increased shipments to the United States in response to shrinking markets for cocaine, and other foreign manufacturers—especially in China—introduced cheaper and more potent synthetic opioids like fentanyl. Figure 7-3 illustrates how overdose deaths involving prescription opioids leveled off after 2010, while other opioid deaths (those only involving illicit opioids and possibly nonopioid drugs) escalated rapidly.

In an attempt to assess the relative importance of demand and supply expansions in driving the second wave of the opioid crisis, we estimate the price of illicit opioids over time. Though these estimates are subject to a number of highly imperfect assumptions, we find that the price of illicit opioids was roughly constant between 2010 and 2013, before falling by about half by 2016, due to the increased supply of illicit fentanyl (see figure 7-17) starting in about 2013 (increasingly available via shipment from China and from other foreign sources). Given the extreme potency and low cost of fentanyl, it dramatically reduced the "cost of a high" for users. It is notable that even though demand for illicit opioids increased beginning in 2010, the price of illicit opioids remained constant until about 2013, implying that in these first years of the illicit wave, the heroin supply must have also expanded to keep prices steady; if supply had remained constant, prices would have risen. Falling prices between 2013 and 2016 imply that supply expansions of illicit opioids were more important drivers of the crisis in these later years.

Due to constraints on data availability for prices of both prescription and illicit opioids, this analysis focuses on the period ending in 2016. However, provisional mortality data are available through part of 2019.

The rest of the chapter proceeds as follows. The next section presents our basic methodology in assessing how demand, supply, and government policies can affect quantities and prices of opioids. The subsequent section analyzes the first wave of the crisis based on prescription opioids, and the section after that analyzes the substantial growth in public subsidies for opioids during this period. The last section turns to the second wave, which spawned the rise of illicit opioids.

The Supply-and-Demand Framework

Although we cannot quantify the extent to which government-subsidized drugs are diverted and resold for nonmedical use, a simple supply-and-demand framework can provide powerful insights into how changing prices and quantities reflect the underlying forces driving the opioid crisis. Figures 7-4 and 7-5 consider the case of prescription opioids, showing how market dynamics and government subsidies in the primary market ultimately affect market prices and quantities in the secondary market. First, a supply expansion (e.g., due to generic entry) in the primary market for patients obtaining opioids via prescription reduces the price of prescription opioids (from P_0 to P_1) and increases the quantity prescribed (from Q_0 to Q_1)—assuming, of course, that prescribers are willing to provide additional pills to patients as their demand rises. This expansion has the effect of reducing the price of prescription opioids in the secondary market because individuals purchasing prescription opioids in the primary market now face a lower acquisition cost if pills are diverted to family members, friends, and others. On top of a supply expansion, the introduction of a government subsidy for prescription opioids in the primary market drives a wedge between the price consumers pay (the demand price, $P_{2,D}$) and the price prescription drug suppliers receive (the supply price, $P_{2,S}$), with the difference made up by the amount of the subsidy. The demand price is lower than the price paid by patients before the introduction of the subsidy (P_1), which further reduces the price of prescription opioids in the secondary market. Thus, both supply expansions and government subsidies in the primary market for prescription opioids decrease the price and increase the quantity of opioid misuse in the secondary market, especially in an environment where there is overprescribing. As noted above, however, whether secondary market prices

Figure 7-4. Effect of Supply Expansions and Government Subsidies on the Price and Quantity of Prescription Opioid Misuse, Primary Market

Prescription opioid price

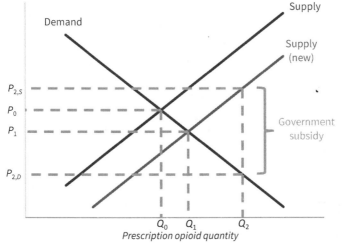

Prescription opioid quantity

Note: This figure shows the impact on prices and quantities of an outward supply shift and government subsidy in the primary market for prescription opioids.

Figure 7-5. Effect of Supply Expansions and Government Subsidies on the Price and Quantity of Prescription Opioid Misuse, Secondary Market

Prescription opioid price

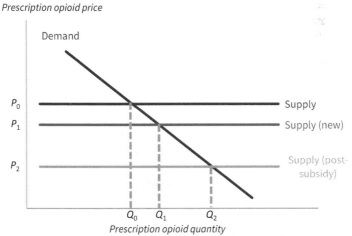

Prescription opioid quantity

Note: This figure shows the corresponding impact of an outward supply shift and government subsidy in the primary market (shown in figure 7-4) on prices and quantities in the secondary market.

can actually respond to changes in the primary market depends on an environment in which obtaining prescriptions is relatively easy.

Figures 7-6 and 7-7 consider the case of illicit opioids (i.e., heroin and illicitly manufactured fentanyl), for which a legal market does not exist. Because the quantity of illicit opioid use increased substantially between 2010 and 2016, it stands to reason that demand or supply expanded, or both did. However, whether it was demand or supply that drove the increase in illicit opioid misuse has a testable implication. If demand expansions dominate, then the price of illicit opioids must rise, whereas if supply expansions dominate, then the price must fall.[8] In fact, we find that illicit opioid prices were relatively stable between 2010 and 2013, suggesting that both demand—itself fueled in part by efforts to curtail the prescription opioid wave of the crisis—and supply expansions were important during this period. Then, between 2013 and 2016, the price of illicit opioids fell markedly with the influx of illicitly manufactured fentanyl, suggesting that supply expansions were most important during this later period.

Our findings suggest that subsidies and supply expansions, in combination with changes in prescribing behavior, can account for much of the rise in opioid overdose deaths. Some have argued that demand-side factors, such as economic stagnation in past years, was an important driver of increasing mortality from drug use and other causes (Stiglitz 2015). However, there is direct evidence that demand growth due to worsening economic conditions was not the primary factor driving the growth of the opioid crisis.

First, the hypothesis that lower incomes raise demand does not explain the aggregate time series within the United States. If worsening economic conditions increase demand, then one would expect that the Great Recession would have fueled a substantial increase in opioid-involved overdose fatalities. However, figure 7-8 suggests that the growth rate of opioid-involved overdose deaths was unaffected by the Great Recession. The crisis grew at roughly the same pace straight through one of the greatest recessions experienced in the last century, and in fact picked up growth well after the recession ended. More important, two of the four lowest growth rates in opioid deaths occurred between 2008 and 2010, in the midst of the Great Recession. It was not until 2014, 2015, and 2016 that growth rates again rose significantly—but that was in a period of lower unemployment, the opposite prediction of demand growth of opioids being fueled by lower incomes unless effects are lagged by several years.

Despite this lack of association between aggregate economic conditions and opioid deaths, Hollingsworth, Ruhm, and Simon (2017) do report a positive association between county-level unemployment and opioid-involved overdose deaths—a 1-percentage-point increase in a county's unemployment

---

[8] The relative price elasticities of demand and supply also affect which expansion dominates.

Figure 7-6. Effect of Demand Expansions on the Quantity and Price of Illicit Opioids

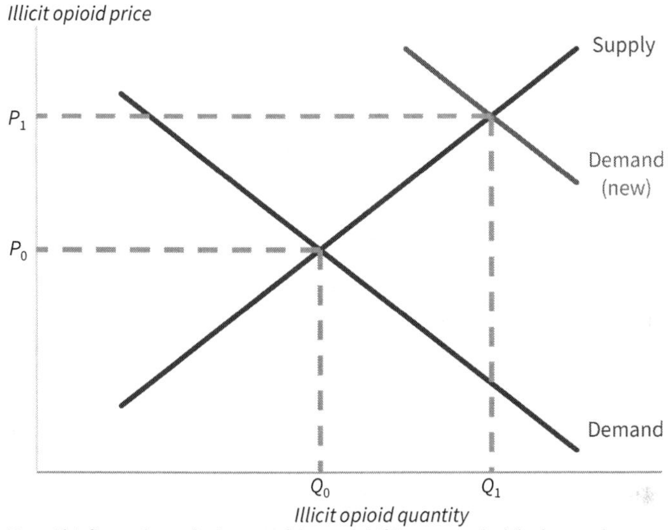

Illicit opioid price

Supply

Demand (new)

Demand

P_1

P_0

Q_0 Q_1

Illicit opioid quantity

Note: This figure shows the impact of demand shifting outward while the supply curve remains in place; in this case, the price must rise.

Figure 7-7. Effect of Supply Expansions on the Quantity and Price of Illicit Opioids

Illicit opioid price

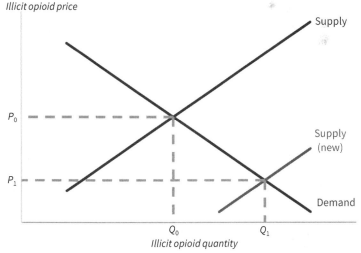

Supply

Supply (new)

Demand

P_0

P_1

Q_0 Q_1

Illicit opioid quantity

Note: This figure shows the impact of supply shifting outward while the demand curve remains in place; in this case, the price must fall. If the price falls while the quantity increases, then the supply must have expanded.

Figure 7-8. Opioid Overdose Death and Unemployment Rate, 1999–2016

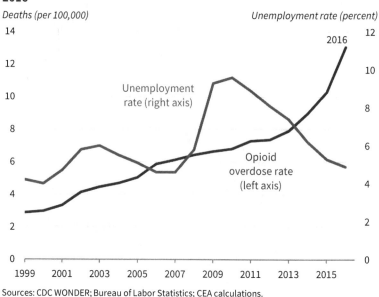

Sources: CDC WONDER; Bureau of Labor Statistics; CEA calculations.

rate is associated with a 0.19-person increase in the rate of opioid-involved overdose deaths per 100,000. However, this association does not appear quantitatively large enough to be a primary driver of the massive growth in opioid deaths. It would take a 54-percentage-point increase in the unemployment rate between 1999 and 2016 to explain the 10.2-person increase in the rate of opioid-involved overdose deaths during this period. However, the unemployment rate increased by a net 0.7 percentage point (from 4.2 to 4.9 percent) between 1999 and 2016.

In addition, Ruhm (2019) formally tests whether a number of demand-side factors that reflect changing economic conditions can explain the growing crisis during this period. He finds that very little of the rise in opioid overdose deaths during this period can be explained by economic conditions. Instead, he points to changes in the drug environment, reflective of supply conditions, as being central. Consistent with Ruhm's findings, Currie, Yin, and Schnell (2018) find no clear evidence of a substantial overall effect of the employment-to-population ratio on the amount of opioids prescribed in a county.

The First Wave of the Crisis: Prescription Opioids

The opioid crisis unfolded in two waves. The first wave, beginning in about 2001 and lasting until about 2010, was characterized by a rising misuse of prescription opioids.[9] The second wave began in about 2010, when, prescription opioids were made more difficult to abuse and illicit opioids—including heroin and, more recently, illicitly manufactured fentanyl—grew in the market. This and the next sections focus on the first wave, and the subsequent section focuses on the second wave.

Between 2001 and 2010, the rate of overdose deaths involving prescription opioids (which we define as natural and semisynthetic opioids and methadone) increased by 182 percent, while other opioid-involved deaths grew much more slowly (figure 7-3).[10] In order to analyze the potential roles of expanded supply of prescription opioids, we first estimate the out-of-pocket price of prescription opioids. We then conduct a calibration exercise, in which we assume that secondary market prices for prescription opioids are proportional to out-of-pocket prices, and that prescription opioid misusers respond to these prices of misuse in the same way that heroin users respond to heroin prices. We also assume that prescription opioid deaths are proportional to prescription opioid misuse. If falling prices suggest a large quantity response relative to the magnitude of the observed increase in prescription opioid-involved overdose deaths, then this would suggest that these price declines, when combined with other factors, may have played a role in the first wave of the opioid crisis.

An environment in which opioid prescriptions were promoted and easier to obtain and fill is a necessary precondition for falling out-of-pocket prices to have played a substantial role—otherwise, it is unlikely that secondary market prices could have responded to falling out-of-pocket prices. This environment was created by a campaign to persuade doctors that pain was being undertreated and that opioids were the solution. Pain-alleviation societies, patient advocacy groups, and professional medical organizations urged physicians to treat pain more aggressively (Max et al. 1995). Pain was labeled "the 5th Vital Sign," which should be regularly assessed and treated (VA 2000). Starting in 2001, the Joint Commission, an accrediting body for hospitals and other health facilities, instituted new standards requiring facilities to establish procedures to assess the existence and intensity of pain and to treat it with "effective pain medicines." At the same time, multiple medical organizations promoted opioids as a safe and effective treatment for chronic, noncancer pain (DuPont, Bezaitis, and Ross 2015). This coincided with aggressive marketing efforts by opioid manufacturers starting in the late 1990s to assure physicians that their products were safe with little abuse potential (Van Zee 2009; President's

---

[9] We focus on the 2001–10 period throughout the chapter, due to the unavailability of consistent overdose data before 1999, the unavailability of illicit drug seizure data before 2001 used for estimating the illicit opioid price series, and the substantial volatility in the out-of-pocket price series before 2001.

[10] Some opioid-involved deaths include both prescription and other opioids. Figure 7-3 distinguishes between opioid-involved overdose deaths with prescription opioids present versus those without prescription opioids present. Similarly, figure 7-18 distinguishes between opioid-involved overdose deaths with illicit opioids present versus those without illicit opioids present.

Commission 2017). Because of space limitations, this chapter does not provide a comprehensive review of either the change in medical guidance regarding the appropriate use of opioids or the marketing and promotion efforts by opioid manufacturers.

We use the Medical Expenditure Panel Survey to construct a time series of the out-of-pocket price per potency-adjusted unit of prescription opioids. The MEPS asks respondents to report all prescription drugs they obtain and how much they pay out of pocket for each drug. Opioid prescriptions are converted into morphine gram equivalents (MGEs), and then prices are estimated by dividing expenditures by the total number of MGEs. We use the terms MGEs and potency-adjusted units interchangeably throughout. Prices are converted into real dollars, and then a real price index is shown. Figure 7-9 shows the real supply and out-of-pocket price index for prescription opioids. The supply price is calculated as the ratio of total expenditures to total MGEs, and the out-of-pocket price is calculated as the ratio of self (out-of-pocket) expenditures to total MGEs. Note that out-of-pocket expenditures include individual payments made for prescriptions without third-party coverage as well as individual copayments made for prescriptions that are only partially covered by third parties.

Between 2001 and 2010, the out-of-pocket price fell by 81 percent before stabilizing. One potential factor in this decline, which is analyzed in depth in the next section, was the inception of Medicare Part D in 2006, which introduced subsidies for prescription drugs, including opioids, and lowered the out-of-pocket price for enrolled consumers. Another potential factor was the rapid expansion of disability (SSDI) enrollment, which before 2006 provided drug coverage for many enrollees through Medicaid or other programs, and after 2006 provided coverage through Medicare Part D. Finally, between 2001 and 2010, supply prices fell by 45 percent in conjunction with the expansion of generic opioids. A recent analysis by the Food and Drug Administration (FDA) similarly finds that potency-adjusted opioid acquisition prices for pharmacies fell by about 28 percent during this same period, although it also finds that prices substantially increased during the 1990s before the crisis took off (FDA 2018a). Figure 7-10 shows the decline in the brand market share of potency-adjusted opioids as the generic market share rose from about 55 to 81 percent between 2001 and 2010 (FDA 2018a).

The law of demand says that, all else remaining the same, consumers engage in more of an activity when the activity becomes cheaper. However, the law by itself does not tell us the magnitude of the effect of an 81 percent reduction in the potency-adjusted price of prescription opioids on either the quantity of prescriptions or the number of deaths involving prescription opioids. Previous econometric studies that have related opioid prescriptions and other prescriptions to out-of-pocket prices suggest a range of likely quantitative effects of the price changes shown in figure 7-9 on the number of opioid

Figure 7-9. Real Supply Price and Real Out-of-Pocket Price Index of Potency-Adjusted Prescription Opioids, 2001–15

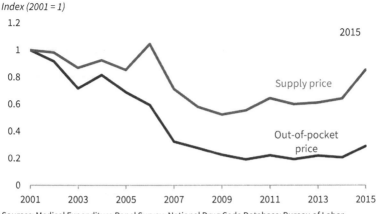

Index (2001 = 1)

Sources: Medical Expenditure Panel Survey; National Drug Code Database; Bureau of Labor Statistics; CEA calculations.
Note: Prices are calculated by dividing real total spending in a given year by the total number of morphine gram equivalents prescribed in that year. All prescriptions are converted into morphine gram equivalents based on the quantity of pills prescribed and their potency, using the National Drug Code database.

Figure 7-10. Brand Share of Potency-Adjusted Prescription Opioids and Supply Price, 2001–16

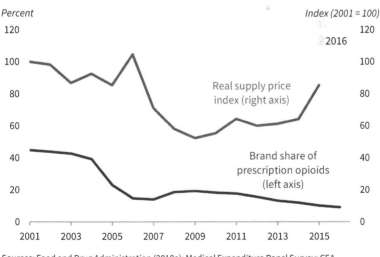

Percent   *Index (2001 = 100)*

Sources: Food and Drug Administration (2018a); Medical Expenditure Panel Survey; CEA calculations.
Note: Price data are available up to 2015. Brand share data are provided up to 2016.

prescriptions. Predicting the effect on the number of deaths requires additional information because the deaths derive from misuse. Only a fraction of opioid prescriptions is given to people with opioid use disorder, and their price sensitivity of demand may differ from the sensitivity of average consumers.

We begin with the effect of reduced prescription opioid prices on the number of opioid prescriptions. A number of studies look at the effects of drug prices and insurance coverage on the sales of all prescription drugs as well as the sales of opioid prescriptions specifically. The more responsive drug users are to prices, the more they consume as prices decline. This price responsiveness is typically measured by the price elasticity of demand—the percentage change in quantity demanded when the price increases by 1 percent.[11] Because elasticity studies typically make cross-sectional comparisons, they are holding constant physician prescribing norms and marketing efforts by sellers that are changing over time. In other words, the effects of changing prescribing norms and marketing efforts need to be added to the price effects measured by the cross-sectional studies of the price elasticity of demand. Box 7-1 offers an overview of the ongoing opioid settlements between governments and opioid manufacturers over misleading marketing efforts by the manufacturers.

Soni (2018) found that the introduction of Medicare Part D increased opioid prescriptions for the population age 65 to 74 (relative to the population age 55 to 64 and not on Medicare) over a four-year period by a factor of 1.5. At the same time and for the same population, Soni (2018) found that the out-of-pocket price was reduced by a factor of 0.44 from the introduction of Part D, which is less than the price change for the entire U.S. population from 2001 to 2010, as shown in figure 7-9. These estimated effects of Part D are economically significant and do not support the hypothesis that the changes shown in figure 7-9 have a minimal effect on the number of prescriptions. Indeed, they show an arc elasticity (calculated with the natural logarithm) of –0.49 which suggests that the price change shown in figure 7-9 would increase potency-adjusted prescriptions per capita by a factor of 2.3 between 2001 and 2010. A factor of 2.3 is close to the actual change as estimated with data from the Automation of Reports and Consolidated Orders System (ARCOS) and shown in figure 7-11 (DOJ n.d.).

Insurance plans should have coinsurance rates varying across drugs to the extent that the sensitivity of consumer demand to the out-of-pocket price varies across drugs (Feldstein 1973; Besley 1988). Health insurance plans behave that way in practice (Einav, Finkelstein, and Polyakova 2018). Coinsurance rates for opioids (43 percent) are higher than for other common therapeutic classes (39 percent). Similarly, coinsurance rates for hydrocodone

---

[11] When sales effects are estimated from small price changes, the result is sometimes called "point elasticity." "Arc elasticity" refers to an estimate from large price changes and typically uses midpoints for calculating percentage changes or uses logarithm changes so that the same elasticity can be applied to price increases as to price decreases.

Box 7-1. Opioid Crisis Lawsuits

Thousands of municipal governments nationwide and nearly two dozen states have sued the pharmaceutical industry in an effort to hold opioid manufacturers and distributers accountable for the opioid crisis. These lawsuits argue that opioid manufacturers launched misleading marketing campaigns underplaying the risks and exaggerating the benefits of opioids. Additionally, these lawsuits allege that opioid distributors unlawfully allowed the drugs to proliferate.

These civil litigation cases have resulted in the conclusion of multiple settlement agreements, at least one large trial, and the promise of more settlements to come. OxyContin maker Purdue Pharma, as well as its owners, the Sackler family, announced a tentative settlement expected to be worth more than $10 billion in September 2019. Under the proposed agreement, the company will be restructured into a public corporation, with profits from drug sales going toward the plaintiffs. The settlement would be the largest payout from any company involved in the opioid crisis. Purdue Pharma previously agreed to pay a total of $270 million to Oklahoma to settle a lawsuit in March 2019. Purdue's Oklahoma settlement set the stage for subsequent settlements with the State, including Teva Pharmaceutical's $85 million settlement in May 2019. Johnson & Johnson refused to settle, and the landmark trial resulted in an order to pay $572 million to Oklahoma in August 2019. Both the State and Johnson & Johnson are contesting this verdict—alleging, respectively, that the award is too small or too large.

The three largest drug distributors—McKesson, Cardinal Health, and AmerisourceBergen—and the generic opioid manufacturer Teva Pharmaceuticals reached a settlement worth about $260 million in October 2019. These settlements are the early conclusions to nearly two years of legal battles and may serve as a benchmark for resolution in other opioid cases. The first of a new series of Federal trials began on October 21, 2019, after talks dissolved of a deal worth $48 billion to resolve all opioid lawsuits filed against the three drug distributors, Teva, and Johnson & Johnson.

The settlements include a combination of donations to substance use disorder treatment program research, and cash payouts and will likely provide a benchmark for thousands of similar cases brought before the courts in an attempt to hold pharmaceutical companies accountable for an opioid crisis that has killed hundreds of thousands and cost trillions.

(50 percent) are higher than for other common nonopioid drugs (40 percent). The observed coinsurance rates thus suggest that opioid prescriptions are not less price sensitive than the average prescription drug over the annual time frame (or longer) that is of interest to the sponsors of insurance plans.[12] If

---

[12] The coinsurance rates are inferred from the estimates by Einav, Finkelstein, and Polyakova (2018) and are for Part D participants who have not yet reached the "donut hole."

Figure 7-11. Potency-Adjusted Quantity (MGEs) of Prescription Opioids per Capita in the United States, 2001–15

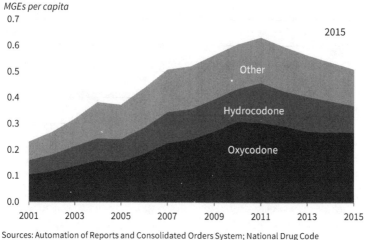

MGEs per capita

Sources: Automation of Reports and Consolidated Orders System; National Drug Code database; CEA calculations.
Note: MGEs = morphine gram equivalents. Quantities are converted into MGEs and divided by the total U.S. population in a given year to calculate MGEs per capita.

Einav, Finkelstein, and Polyakova (2018)'s one-month arc elasticity of –0.27 for therapeutic drug classes were applied to the price change from 2001 to 2010 shown in figure 7-9, it suggests that opioid prescriptions would have increased by a factor of 1.6 due to price changes alone.[13]

A factor of 1.6 is economically significant, but is still only a minority of the actual change in opioid prescriptions between 2001 and 2010. The discrepancy between the findings of Soni (2018) and Einav, Finkelstein, and Polyakova (2018) could be that behavior is more sensitive to a price change that lasts more than one month, or that applies to a larger population of people.[14] But this discrepancy may also reflect the imprecision of estimating price effects, which is why our data are consistent with the view that the increase in prescriptions cannot be explained by price reductions alone but also reflect changes in physicians' prescribing norms and marketing efforts by opioid sellers.

---

[13] Einav, Finkelstein, and Polyakova (2018) report a point elasticity for a linear demand curve, but their reports of price and quantity changes are sufficient for their readers to calculate the corresponding arc elasticity. We also note that the authors' elasticity is estimated for a selected group of Part D participants who have high drug costs.

[14] The demand for habit-forming products responds more to price changes that last longer (Pollak 1970; Becker and Murphy 1988; Gallet 2014), which is why it would be especially problematic to apply the approach of Einav, Finkelstein, and Polyakova (2018) specifically to opioids because it refers to price changes lasting only a month. The estimates by Einav, Finkelstein, and Polyakova (2018) also exclude "social multiplier" price effects that may occur when the entire population experiences a price change, rather than a selected few who are at a special spot in their prescription-benefit formula (Glaeser, Sacerdote, and Scheinkman 2003).

Figure 7-12. Proportion of Users Obtaining Misused Prescription Opioids by Most Recent Source, 2013–14

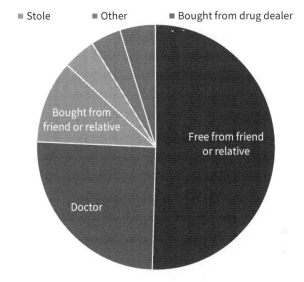

Source: Lipari and Hughes (2017).

One reason that falling opioid prices may increase opioid deaths at a different rate than they increase opioid prescriptions is that opioid prices for medical purposes might follow a different trend than the prices paid by opioid misusers. In fact, only 25 percent of people who misuse prescription opioids most recently obtained the drugs from a doctor, while the remaining 75 percent obtained them from friends or relatives, via theft, from a drug dealer, or from some other source (figure 7-12). But even when the drugs are obtained on the secondary market, the price is likely positively correlated with the out-of-pocket price. A lower out-of-pocket price decreases the acquisition cost for those selling the drugs in the secondary market. It also should decrease the implicit price for those giving the drugs away with no expected reciprocal gifts, and it should reduce the precautions taken by individuals to safeguard their drugs against theft.[15] Of course, the out-of-pocket price is only one component of the total price of obtaining prescription opioids for misuse. The ease of finding a doctor to prescribe the opioids and a pharmacy that receives a supply and is willing to fill the prescription is also important.

As a calibration exercise for contextualizing whether falling out-of-pocket prices could have played a role in the first wave of the opioid crisis, we assume that the price of prescription opioid misuse is proportional to the out-of-pocket price. For example, a 10 percent decline in the out-of-pocket price of

---

[15] This does not mean that the amount of theft varies with the price because thieves can be expected to put more effort toward stealing more valuable items. We only assume that thieves experience greater cost of theft for high-priced items, due to owners' precautions.

prescription opioids is assumed to reduce the price of pills in the secondary market (and for misusers obtaining pills in the primary market) by 10 percent. This assumption is clearly reasonable for the 25 percent of prescription opioid misusers who obtain their pills directly from drugs prescribed by medical providers in the primary market because they only face the out-of-pocket price.

We may also expect the secondary market price to be proportional to the out-of-pocket price. Consider, first, the misusers who purchase their pills in the secondary market (as opposed to receiving them complimentarily). The sellers of these pills seek to maximize their profits, which are equal to the price of each pill P minus the cost of obtaining each pill in the primary market C (the out-of-pocket price), multiplied by the number of pills sold, Q:

$$\pi = (P - C)Q$$

In a competitive market, profits are competed down to zero for all sellers, so that the price charged on the secondary market is equal to the out-of-pocket price. In a noncompetitive market, each seller has the power to influence the secondary market price based on how many pills it sells. In terms of the equation above, this means that the price is a function of quantity. It can be shown that a necessary condition for maximizing profits is

$$P = \frac{1}{1+r}C$$

where r is the responsiveness, in percentage terms, of the market price to the quantity of pills provided by a particular seller. Thus, an increase in the cost (or the out-of-pocket price) C leads to a proportional increase in the secondary market price P, assuming that r remains constant.

Assuming that the share of prescription opioids obtained via various segments of the secondary market with different markups remains constant over time, the average secondary market price across all segments would change proportionally with changes in the out-of-pocket price. It is important to emphasize that this assumption would be plausible only if suppliers to the secondary market face relatively low transaction costs for obtaining prescriptions from doctors and filling prescriptions from pharmacies. For this reason, changes in prescribing guidelines and practices, a greater emphasis on pain management, and the expansion of "pill mills" and supplies to pharmacies are preconditions for falling prices to have a potentially significant effect on opioid misuse.

Another reason that falling opioid prices can increase opioid deaths at a different rate than they increase opioid prescriptions is that most opioid prescriptions are likely used for medical purposes, and those who misuse opioids may have a different sensitivity to prices. One point of view is that medical users are less price sensitive because they are just following their providers' orders, whereas misusers are necessarily price sensitive to the extent that most

Table 7-1. Estimates of the Price Elasticity of Demand for Heroin

Studies	Study type and outcomes	Elasticity estimates
Silverman and Spruill (1977); Caulkins (1995); Dave (2008); Olmstead et al. (2015)	Outcomes related to heroin use (crime, emergency room visits, etc.)	−0.27; −1.50; −0.10; −0.80
Saffer and Chaloupka (1999)	National household surveys	−0.94
van Ours (1995); Liu et al. (1999)	Government historical records	−0.7 to −1.0; −0.48 to −1.38
Bretteville-Jensen and Biorn (2003); Bretteville-Jensen (2006); Roddy and Greenwald (2009)	Interviews with heroin users	−0.71 to −0.91; −0.33 to −0.77; −0.64
Petry and Bickel (1998); Jofre-Bonet and Petry (2008); Chalmers et al. (2010)	Laboratory studies	−0.87 to −1.3; −0.82 to −0.92; −1.54 to −1.73

Source: Olmstead et al. (2015).

of their income is exhausted by purchasing opioids.[16] Another perspective is that those who misuse opioids are less price sensitive because they are less interested in saving money on their drug acquisitions.

Unfortunately, we are not aware of studies estimating price elasticities for the misuse of prescription opioids distinctly from price elasticities for the overall number of prescription opioids (regardless of their use). Thus, we use estimates of the price elasticity of heroin, a substitute for prescription opioids, for which a large body of academic literature is available. Olmstead and others (2015) provide an extensive review of the literature and categorize studies based on the methods used—table 7-1 summarizes their work. Although the literature contains a broad range of estimates, studies generally find that higher prices reduce demand. For our calibration exercise, we rely on a meta-analysis of the literature on illicit drug price elasticities by Gallet (2014), who synthesizes 462 price elasticities from 42 studies, mostly based on U.S. data. He finds that the price elasticity of heroin falls in the range of −0.47 to −0.56, which coincides with the arc elasticity of −0.49 calculated from Soni's (2018) results for

---

[16] People who misuse opioids—who, for example, spend all disposable income on opioids—have a price elasticity of −1 because the quantity purchased is the ratio of disposable income to price. See Becker (1962) for a more general analysis.

prescription opioids but is further from zero than the short-run estimates for all prescription drugs reported by Einav, Finkelstein, and Polyakova (2018).[17]

Because previous studies show a range of price elasticities, we can only provide a range of estimates of the role of price changes as a factor in the growth of opioid misuse and the number of deaths involving prescription opioids. As a low value, we take one interpretation of the short-run findings of Einav, Finkelstein, and Polyakova (2018) for all prescription drugs, namely, that the price elasticity of demand is constant and equal to –0.27. As a middle value, we take the other interpretation of their results: that the demand curve is linear in price.[18] As a high value, we take Gallet's high-end elasticity of –0.56. The corresponding results for predicted deaths are shown in figure 7-13 as "low constant elasticity," "low linear demand," and "high constant elasticity," respectively.[19] For reference, figure 7-13 also shows the actual rate of overdose deaths involving prescription opioids. Price changes would be capable of explaining between 31 and 83 percent of the growth between 2001 and 2010 in the death rate involving prescription opioids, assuming that the rise in overdose deaths is proportional to the rise in misuse. In other words, without the price changes, the estimates suggest that there would have been between 11,500 and 22,800 fewer deaths involving prescription opioids during those years.[20]

Figure 7-13 suggests that a greater fraction of the increase in actual overdose deaths is explained with constant elasticity models (the red and gold lines in the figure) in 2010 than in earlier years, such as 2005. This pattern occurs because our price measure shows proportionally fewer price declines in the early years than in the later ones and likely reflects the substantial influences of nonprice factors (e.g., prescribing norms and marketing efforts) in addition to price factors. However, the linear demand specification shows a time pattern of predicted deaths (as opposed to a total increase) that is closer to actual deaths,

---

[17] Gallet (2014) finds that demand for drugs (1) is more responsive to price at the extensive margin (in decisions about whether to use drugs) than at the intensive margin (how much of the drug to use), and (2) is more responsive in the long run than in the short run.

[18] Einav, Finkelstein, and Polyakova (2018) calculate an elasticity of –0.15 based on percentage changes from the low price to the high price, which is a valid point elasticity only if the demand curve is linear in price, with a point elasticity of –0.15 at the average out-of-pocket price paid by low-cost Medicare Part D recipients between 2007 and 2011. It is a valid arc elasticity only if converted to –0.27 so that it can be applied to price increases as well as decreases.

[19] For the constant elasticity predictions, we use a demand function of the form $Q_D = AP^\epsilon$, where A is a parameter and determined based on the initial quantity and price as of 2001, Q_D is the quantity demanded, P is the price, and $\epsilon < 0$ is the constant elasticity of demand with respect to the price.

[20] Powell, Pacula, and Taylor (2017, 1) directly link the introduction of Medicare Part D—a source of some of the price reduction between 2001 and 2010—to deaths involving prescription opioids, including "deaths among the Medicare-ineligible population, suggesting substantial diversion from medical markets."

Figure 7-13. Actual and Predicted Rates of Overdose Deaths Involving Prescription Opioids, by the Price Elasticity of Demand for Misuse, 2001–15

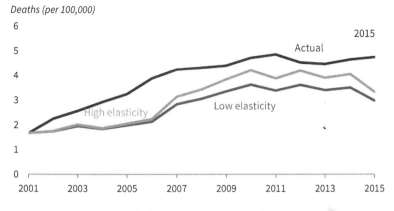

Sources: CDC WONDER; Bureau of Labor Statistics; Medical Expenditure Panel Survey; National Drug Code database; CEA calculations.
Note: Predicted deaths are calculated by holding the demand curve constant and moving down the demand curve based on the amount of the price decrease. The functional form of the demand function is provided in the text. The low elasticity is 0.47; the high elasticity is 0.56.

which suggests that constant elasticity might not be the correct model of the effects of price changes.[21]

Again, it is important to emphasize that the potential role of prices in explaining the rise of overdose deaths depends on the ability of consumers in the primary market to obtain more pills as prices decline. This was facilitated by an environment in which prescribers were encouraged and even required to aggressively treat pain with opioids (President's Commission 2017).[22] As a result, physicians wrote more opioid prescriptions for more patients, lowering the amount of time and effort needed to acquire the drugs. In some places, the rise of pill mills further increased the convenience of acquiring these drugs by combining prescription writing with dispensing.

We further note that the death rate involving prescription opioids increased by a factor of 2.8 between 2001 and 2010 (figure 7-13), at the same time that the per capita quantity of prescription opioids increased by a factor of 2.6 (figure 7-11). This suggests that whatever factor was increasing prescriptions over this period was also increasing opioid use, with only somewhat

---

[21] Given that the research of price effects on drug sales finds most of them to be on the "extensive margin," the market demand curve largely reflects the inverse distribution of consumer heterogeneity. Distribution functions can generate convex demand functions like the constant-elasticity function, concave demand functions, or a combination of both, such as with the normal distribution.

[22] In technical terms, prescribing norms affect both the number of prescriptions at a given price and the sensitivity of that number to price changes.

greater proportional effects on misuse. One possible explanation for this result is that the price elasticity of misuse is similar to—but somewhat further from zero than—the price elasticity of medical use, so price declines increase both types of use but proportionally somewhat more for misuse.

Public Subsidies for Opioids

A potentially relevant factor for the 81 percent decline in out-of-pocket prices for prescription opioids between 2001 and 2010 is the expansion of public health insurance programs that subsidize access to and the purchasing of prescription drugs, including opioids. These subsidies lower out-of-pocket prices in the legal market, thereby lowering prices directly for the 25 percent of prescription opioid misusers who obtain their drugs from a physician and indirectly for the 75 percent of misusers (see figure 7-12) who receive them on the secondary market from friends, family, and dealers who first obtained the drugs in the primary market.[23]

The share of potency-adjusted prescription opioids funded by government programs grew from 17 percent in 2001 to 60 percent in 2010 (figure 7-14). However, this may understate the share of diverted opioids that were obtained with the assistance of funding from public programs. The diversion of opioids to the secondary market is more profitable when out-of-pocket prices are lower, and drugs purchased with government subsidies cost less on average than drugs purchased out of pocket or with private insurance (MEPS). Thus, government subsidies that cut out-of-pocket prices the most may lead to opioids obtained with the assistance of funding from these programs to be the most likely to be diverted. In fact, government programs funded 74 percent of all opioids that were covered at least in part by a third-party payer in 2010 (MEPS).

Figure 7-14 shows the shares of potency-adjusted opioids covered by public programs, private insurers, and no third-party payer. Public programs have become much more important sources for funding opioids over time, and Medicare coverage expansions appear to have largely driven this growth. The share of opioids covered by Medicare spiked in 2006, coinciding with the implementation that year of Medicare Part D, which offers prescription drug benefits to Medicare beneficiaries.[24] It is important to note that the vast majority of Medicare Part D enrollees dispensed opioids do not misuse them. Carey, Jena,

---

[23] See Schnell (2017), who analyzes the linkages between the primary and secondary markets.

[24] In a similar calculation, Zhou, Florence, and Dowell (2016) find that the share of expenditures on prescription opioids accounted for by Medicare increased from 3 percent in 2001 to 26 percent in 2012. As shown in figure 7-14, we find that the number of prescriptions for which Medicare was the primary payer increased from 5 percent in 2001 to 29 percent in 2012. The slight differences may be because the Medicare share of expenditures (as reported by Zhou, Florence, and Dowell 2016) does not include out-of-pocket copayments made by Medicare enrollees for prescriptions where Medicare was the primary payer (figure 7-14).

Figure 7-14. Share of Potency-Adjusted Prescription Opioids, by Primary Payer, 2001–15

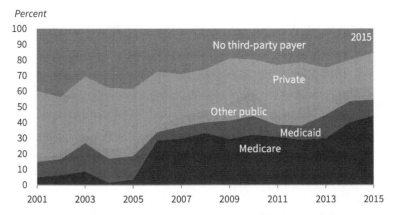

Sources: Medical Expenditure Panel Survey; National Drug Code Database; CEA calculations.
Note: The primary payer is defined as the third-party payer with the highest payment for a given prescription. In addition to Medicare, Medicaid, and private insurers, the other possible primary payers include veterans' benefits, workers' compensation, other Federal government insurance, other State or local government insurance, or other public insurance. All prescriptions are converted into morphine gram equivalents based on the quantity of pills prescribed and their potency, using the National Drug Code database.

and Barnett (2018) studied a sample of more than 600,000 Medicare beneficiaries who had an opioid prescription. Using several different measures, only 0.6 to 8.5 percent of the beneficiaries fulfilled a misuse measure.

The implementation of Medicare Part D and the resulting growth in the share of opioids funded by Medicare do not appear to have simply displaced opioids covered by other sources. Figure 7-15 shows the quantity of opioids per capita funded by each source. Though the number of potency-adjusted opioids covered by Medicaid fell between 2005 and 2006, the increase in the number of opioids covered by Medicare was over three times larger than this decline.[25] The number of potency-adjusted opioids covered by private insurance also increased between 2005 and 2006. Furthermore, between 2005 and 2008, the MEPS data suggest that the total quantity of potency-adjusted opioids that

---

[25] An estimated 6.2 million Medicaid beneficiaries became eligible for Medicare Part D prescription drug coverage on January 1, 2006 (KFF 2006). These "full dual eligibles" included low-income seniors and low-income disabled individuals under age 65. Nonelderly disabled dual eligibles, including both full and partial, made up about one-third of all duals (2.5 million out of almost 7.5 million—per Holahan and Ghosh 2005, 3). Applying this one-third ratio to 6.2 million means that about 2.0 to 2.1 million nonelderly disabled Medicaid participants transitioned from Medicaid to Medicare prescription drug coverage in 2006. For comparison, the SSDI rolls grew from 6.5 million to 6.8 million individuals between 2005 and 2006.

Figure 7-15. Potency-Adjusted Prescription Opioids per Capita, by Primary Payer, 2001–15

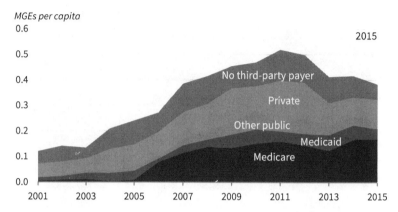

MGEs per capita

Sources: Medical Expenditure Panel Survey; National Drug Code Database; CEA calculations.
Note: MGEs = morphine gram equivalents. The primary payer is the third-party payer with the highest payment for a given prescription. In addition to Medicare, Medicaid, and private insurers, the other possible primary payers include veterans' benefits, workers' compensation, other Federal government insurance, other State or local government insurance, or other public insurance. All prescriptions are converted into MGEs based on the quantity of pills prescribed and their potency, using the National Drug Code Database.

were dispensed increased by 73 percent, with almost three-fourths of this growth coming from opioids paid for by Medicare.[26]

Between 2001 and 2010, Medicare-covered opioids increased by over 2,400 percent, Medicaid-covered opioids increased by over 360 percent, and total publicly covered opioids increased by over 1,200 percent (MEPS). Given that Medicare covers the elderly and SSDI recipients who tend to have greater needs related to pain relief, it is not surprising that Medicare is the largest payer of prescription drugs as well as the largest public payer of prescription opioids.

Previous research has studied the implications of the rise in public funding for opioids fueling the opioid crisis and, in particular, the diversion of pills to the secondary market. Powell, Pacula, and Taylor (2017) found that a Medicare Part D–driven 10 percent increase in opioid prescriptions results in 7.4 percent more opioid-involved overdose deaths among the Medicare-ineligible population. The authors use the fact that Medicare Part D was plausibly more important in driving prescription drug benefits in States with a greater share of the population over age 65 to estimate the impact of drug benefits on opioid-involved overdose deaths.

---

[26] As shown in a comparison of figures 7-11 and 7-15, the MEPS data undercount the total number of prescription opioids. See also Hill, Zuvekas, and Zodet (2011, 242), which looks more systematically at the propensity of MEPS respondents "to underreport the number of different drugs taken." MEPS underreporting presents greater challenges for measuring total quantities rather than average prices, which is why the CEA measures the former from ARCOS and the latter from MEPS.

Moreover, because the elderly—the major population that is eligible for Medicare benefits—are a disproportionately small fraction of those reported to die of drug overdoses, these results suggest that the impact of Medicare expansion on opioid-involved death rates may have been due to an increased supply of prescription opioids in the secondary market. Others have examined opioid prescriptions covered by Medicaid.[27] In a recent report, the U.S. Senate Committee on Homeland Security and Governmental Affairs (2018) notes numerous examples of Medicaid fraud that fuel abuse of prescription opioids—for example, with drug dealers paying Medicaid recipients to obtain taxpayer-funded pills.

Similarly, Eberstadt (2017) suggests that Medicaid has helped finance increasing nonwork by prime-age adults by subsidizing prescription opioids that could be sold on the secondary market. Goodman-Bacon and Sandoe (2017), Venkataramani and Chatterjee (2019), and Cher, Morden and Meara (2019), however, find little evidence for Medicaid expansion fueling the opioid crisis. These findings are not necessarily inconsistent with other evidence that public programs worsened the opioid crisis. It is possible that Medicaid expansion did not increase opioid misuse because the expansion population is less likely to be prescribed opioids. Before State expansions, Medicaid already covered all disabled adults receiving Supplemental Security Income (SSI), as well as elderly adults not eligible for Medicare. Medicaid expansion only covered nondisabled, nonelderly adults with low incomes, a population less likely to be prescribed opioids. In fact, figure 7-15 shows that the per capita quantity of opioids covered by Medicaid decreased between 2013 and 2015, despite the fact that Medicaid enrollment grew from 60 million to 70 million people over this same period, as the majority of States expanded Medicaid coverage. In addition, the Medicaid expansions studied by Goodman-Bacon and Sandoe (2017) occurred in 2014, after measures had been taken to reduce the ability of people to misuse prescription opioids (e.g., the reformulation of OxyContin in 2010 and the introduction of other medicines along with the rescheduling of certain opioids to higher schedules with more restrictions).

Public subsidies for prescription opioids have also been fueled by the growing number of Americans claiming disability insurance. SSDI is a Federal disability assistance program that offers a maximum possible benefit of $2,687 a month, with an average monthly benefit of $1,173. Only adults who have significant work experience are eligible to receive SSDI, and the amount of

---

[27] In 2017, 15.6 percent of the total U.S. population was age 65 or older, but only 3.6 percent of all opioid-involved overdose deaths were age 65 or older (CDC WONDER).

benefits is higher for those who had higher lifetime earnings before becoming disabled.[28]

SSDI disabled workers are generally eligible for Medicare after 24 months of enrollment in the program. SSDI rolls have increased dramatically since 1990. The growth in SSDI rolls can be attributed to several factors, including the aging of the population, the increased labor force participation of women, and more lenient disability determinations (Autor 2015). Another disability program, SSI, provides more modest benefits to Americans without sufficient work experience to qualify for SSDI, and provides automatic eligibility for Medicaid in most States. Figure 7-16 shows the rise in SSDI and SSI rolls per 100,000 people over time. Notably, SSDI rolls and opioid overdose deaths, especially those involving prescription opioids, have risen in tandem. It is also important to note SSDI growth occurred over the same period as increased treatment of pain conditions with opioids.

The 8.6 million SSDI disabled workers in 2011 represent less than 3 percent of the total U.S. population, and thus are overrepresented as a source of prescription opioids given disabilities (increasingly related to pain) that lead to a greater use of prescription opioids. The CEA estimates the total market share of SSDI recipients in two ways, each suggesting that SSDI recipients make up about 26 to 30 percent of the prescription opioid market. First, we use data from Morden and others (2014), who estimate the average potency-adjusted opioid prescriptions for SSDI recipients across the United States in 2011 (6.9 MGEs per SSDI recipient). We multiply this average rate by the total number of SSDI recipients in 2011 (8.6 million recipients). And finally, we divide the total opioids prescribed to $SDI recipients (59.2 million MGEs) by the total opioids distributed in the United States according to ARCOS data (196.9 million MGEs). The result is that 30 percent of potency-adjusted opioid prescriptions in the U.S. are filled by SSDI recipients, which is over 10 times their proportion of the U.S. population.

Second, the CEA uses MEPS data that report opioid prescriptions for a random sample of Americans each year. We identify SSDI recipients as individuals between age 18 and 64 who receive Medicare. This may slightly overstate the SSDI population, given that a small number of non-SSDI recipients under age 65 are eligible for Medicare as well, including people with end-stage renal disease and amyotrophic lateral sclerosis.[29] Nonetheless, dividing the potency-adjusted opioids prescribed to these recipients by the total in the population

---

[28] Qualification for SSDI requires a sufficient number of work credits that were earned recently enough. Up to 4 credits can be earned in one year and are accrued based on sufficient annual earnings. Applicants generally require 40 credits to qualify for SSDI, although standards are different for younger workers.

[29] There were just under 273,000 Medicare recipients under age 65 with end-stage renal disease in 2013 (HHS 2014). The prevalence of amyotrophic lateral sclerosis is just 5 per 100,000, implying that in 2013, there were just under 16,000 Americans with the disease (Stanford Medicine n.d.).

Figure 7-16. Adults Receiving Social Security Disability Insurance and Supplemental Security Income, and Opioid-Involved Drug Overdose Deaths, per 100,000 People, 1980–2016

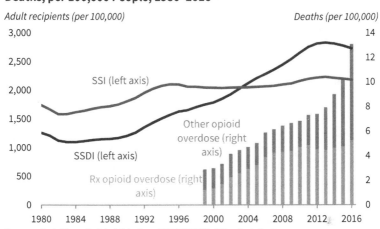

Sources: Social Security Administration; CDC WONDER; CEA calculations.
Note: SSDI = Social Security Disability Insurance. SSI = Supplemental Security Income. Prescription opioids include natural and semisynthetic opioids as well as methadone. Data for opioid overdose deaths were accessed in CDC WONDER beginning in 1999.

results in an estimated SSDI market share of 26 percent for the period 2010–12.[30] The somewhat lower share estimated using MEPS data may be due to the exclusion of SSDI recipients who have been on the program for less than two years.[31] These SSDI recipients would not yet be eligible for Medicare and may instead receive coverage via Medicaid or other programs.[32]

It is important to emphasize that the disproportionate market share of SSDI recipients receiving prescription opioids is a result of their higher levels of conditions that prevent them from working and that may also cause pain. SSDI benefit payments, in conjunction with Medicare coverage, provide a vital means of support for disabled workers with major healthcare needs. Thus, reforms that seek to reduce nonmedical use of opioids should be careful to preserve access to needed pain relief through the medical use of opioids for SSDI recipients.

---

[30] Based on a five-year average centered on 2011, we similarly estimate a market share of 26 percent.

[31] MEPS excludes the institutionalized population, so if SSDI recipients are overrepresented in this population, this could further affect our estimate.

[32] We note that Finkelstein, Gentzkow, and Williams (2018) estimate that SSDI recipients account for about 13 percent of opioid prescriptions. However, they do not appear to analyze potency-adjusted opioids, as we do. Indeed, when we use the MEPS data to estimate the market share of non-potency-adjusted opioid prescriptions for the same 2006–14 period that Finkelstein, Gentzkow, and Williams (2018) appear to consider, we estimate a similar 15.5 percent market share.

The Second Wave of the Crisis: Illicit Opioids

The second wave of the opioid crisis began in about 2010, when prescription opioids became more difficult to access due to efforts to rein in abuse. However, the buildup of a pool of people misusing prescription opioids that they could no longer access provided a large pool of new demand and a profit opportunity for sellers entering the illicit opioid market. Because, for people suffering from addiction, legal and illicit opioids can function as substitutes, raising the price (in terms of both money and time) of legal opioids raises the demand for illicit ones.

The reformulation of OxyContin in 2010 made it more physically difficult to use. States have implemented prescription drug monitoring programs that require doctors to consult patient prescription histories before prescribing opioids (Dowell et al. 2016; Buchmueller and Carey 2018; Dave, Grecu, and Saffer 2018). Professional societies and accrediting organizations have reconsidered their pain treatment guidelines. These changes have reduced the overall quantity of prescription opioids distributed, with potency-adjusted quantities of opioids peaking in 2011 (DOJ n.d.). Unfortunately, recent research has shown that overdose deaths averted from prescription opioid overdoses, at least those resulting from the reformulation of OxyContin, have been replaced by overdose deaths from heroin (Alpert, Powell, and Pacula 2018; Evans, Lieber, and Power 2019).

As users have substituted toward heroin, it has increasingly been made even more potent—suppliers and drug dealers now frequently lace heroin with illicitly manufactured fentanyl. Fentanyl is 30 to 50 times more potent in its analgesic properties than heroin, so even small amounts can vastly increase the potency of the drugs with which it is mixed. Illicitly manufactured fentanyl can also be obtained independently of heroin. Figure 7-17 documents the rise of fentanyl, showing both the rate of overdose deaths involving synthetic opioids other than methadone (a category dominated by fentanyl, although whether the product is illicit or by prescription is not determinable), and the rate of fentanyl reports in forensic labs acquired by law enforcement during drug seizures.

Figure 7-18 shows the rise in overdose deaths involving heroin and fully synthetic opioids (mostly fentanyl), along with opioid deaths not involving heroin and synthetic opioids. As a reminder, we refer to overdose-related opioid deaths from heroin and fentanyl as "illicit deaths," even though fentanyl can also be prescribed.[33] From 2010 through 2016, the rate of illicit opioid deaths has increased by 364 percent, while the rate of opioid deaths not involving illicit opioids has fallen by 17 percent. Importantly, fentanyl also tends to be combined with nonopioids, and deaths in which fentanyl and nonopioids are factors are included in the illicit opioid series shown in figure 7-18.

---

[33] We use ICD-10 codes T40.1 and T40.4 to identify deaths involving heroin and fentanyl.

Figure 7-17. Rate of Overdose Deaths Involving Synthetic Opioids Other Than Methadone, and Fentanyl Reports in Forensic Labs per 100,000 Population, 2001–16

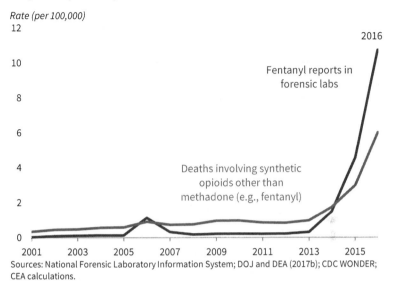

Sources: National Forensic Laboratory Information System; DOJ and DEA (2017b); CDC WONDER; CEA calculations.

Figure 7-18. The Opioid-Involved Overdose Death Rate by the Presence of Illicit Opioids, 2001–16

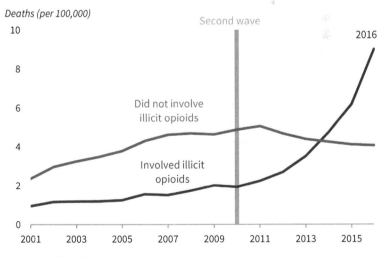

Sources: CDC WONDER; CEA calculations.
Note: Illicit opioids include both heroin (T40.1) and the category "synthetic opioids other than methadone" (T40.4) in the CDC data, which is primarily composed of illicitly produced fentanyl.

Given their illegal nature, the price of illicit opioids is more difficult to measure than the price of prescription opioids. Accurate data cannot be reliably obtained from dealers or users, who may fear criminal sanctions for truthful reporting. In recent years, the influx from Mexico and China of cheap but highly potent fentanyl, which can vastly increase the potency of drugs with which it is mixed, has complicated matters (U.S. Department of State n.d.). Market quantities of heroin and fentanyl also cannot be directly observed, so the extent to which added fentanyl reduces the price per potency-adjusted unit of opioids is difficult to determine. Subject to these limitations, the CEA has assembled data from several sources to create a time series for the price of illicit opioids.

The Drug Enforcement Administration's (DEA's) System to Retrieve Information from Drug Evidence (STRIDE) and STARLIMS databases collect heroin price data. Heroin prices in these data sets are obtained by government agents, who pay informants to purchase heroin on the street. The price is recorded, and the heroin sample is analyzed in a laboratory to determine its potency so that prices can be adjusted for quality. Between 2010 and 2016, the potency-adjusted real price of heroin increased by 10 percent.

However, any fentanyl contained within heroin is not considered when determining the price per pure gram of heroin in the DEA data. Thus, the true price per potency-adjusted unit of heroin purchases has likely increased by less than 10 percent or has even declined. In addition, fentanyl can be consumed on its own outside heroin, which, if cheaper on a potency-adjusted basis, would lead overall illicit opioid prices to fall even more. Moreover, increased heroin purity and product modifications have increasingly allowed for heroin use by means other than injection. These changes lower the nonmonetary costs of using heroin, and although nonmonetary costs are not estimated here, these changes would have further reduced the cost of illicit opioid use.

The CEA uses data from several sources to estimate the quantity of fentanyl mixed with heroin and available on its own, along with the potency-adjusted price of heroin (including the fentanyl with which it is mixed) and the potency-adjusted price of fentanyl when consumed alone or with other drugs. Quantity data are based on seizures of heroin and fentanyl recorded in the National Seizure System, along with exhibits of each drug recorded in the National Forensic Laboratory Information System. Price data are based on the DEA heroin price series and on DEA reports on the cost of fentanyl relative to heroin, along with the quantity data in order to adjust heroin prices based on fentanyl with which it is mixed. A detailed methodology for estimating illicit opioid prices is provided in the appendix of a previously published CEA report (CEA 2019b). We acknowledge that seizure data are a highly imperfect proxy of the relative presence of heroin and fentanyl. Seized products reflect a combination of market shares and law enforcement priorities rather than market shares

Figure 7-19. Real Price Index of Potency-Adjusted Illicit Opioids, 2001–16

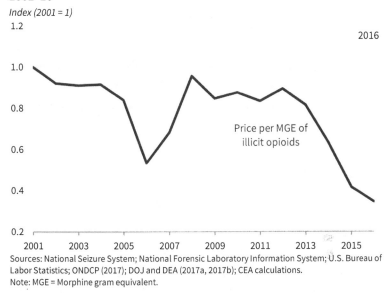

Index (2001 = 1)

Sources: National Seizure System; National Forensic Laboratory Information System; U.S. Bureau of Labor Statistics; ONDCP (2017); DOJ and DEA (2017a, 2017b); CEA calculations.
Note: MGE = Morphine gram equivalent.

alone. Still, absent an alternative data source, and without a clear direction for the bias in this proxy for market shares, we use the seizure data as reported.

Figure 7-19 shows a real price index for illicit opioids between 2001 and 2016, which, given the data limitations involved, should be used only to draw qualitative conclusions. The price of illicit opioids is relatively stable before falling temporarily in 2006, and then quickly recovering, and then falls by over half (58 percent) between 2013 and 2016. Each of these declines is due to surges in fentanyl that is either mixed with heroin or sold on its own or with other drugs. The 2006 price decline was due to a laboratory in Mexico that dramatically increased the supply of fentanyl to the United States but was quickly shut down through cooperative action between the United States and Mexico. The price decline between 2013 and 2016 is attributed to the widely documented influx of fentanyl into the United States, including from China and Mexico (NIDA 2017). The price series shown in figure 7-19 is the outcome of a series of assumptions documented more completely in the appendix of the CEA's previously published report and is necessarily only a highly imperfect estimate of the real price from which only qualitative conclusions should be drawn (CEA 2019b). If data on the illicit opioid market in this period improve, revisions to this series may be possible.

It is clear from figure 7-19 that supply expansions were important for driving the growth in overdose deaths involving illicit opioids. Between 2010 and 2013, the price of illicit opioids was relatively stable. This implies that both supply and demand expansions were important during the first three years of the illicit wave of the opioid crisis. If only demand had expanded, then prices would have increased; and if only supply had expanded, then prices would have decreased. Demand expansions can likely be traced at least in part to efforts to clamp down on abuse that grew during the first wave of the crisis without providing additional access to quality treatment services. Expanded supply is likely due to increased supply from source countries, including Mexico and Colombia, and it may reflect a substitution of drug production from marijuana (which has been legalized or decriminalized in some U.S. States) to heroin (ONDCP 2019). Meanwhile, supply expansions are likely more important than demand expansions for the 2013–16 period, given that the price of illicit opioids fell by more than half during these three years. The shift toward fentanyl produced in China and distributed through the mail has increased the potency of drugs without significantly increasing their prices, and may have increased competition in the illicit opioid market, thereby also putting downward pressure on the price of heroin.

To the extent that monetary price declines have been accompanied by an increased ease of obtaining illicit opioids (given the proliferation of drug dealers in more locations and the increased availability of online markets), supply expansions may have been even more important than the falling illicit price series suggests. For instance, Quinones (2015) notes that Mexican heroin dealers who illegally cross the border have become much more efficient in delivering heroin to users rather than forcing users to find them. These drug dealers communicate with users via cell phones to establish a place to meet, at which point the user enters the dealer's car to receive their heroin.

Conclusion

The opioid crisis poses a major threat to the U.S. economy and American lives, and many factors have exacerbated this threat. In addition to taking more than 400,000 lives since 2000, the opioid crisis cost $665 billion in 2018, or 3.2 percent of U.S. gros domestic product. In this chapter, the CEA presents evidence that falling prices may have played a role in increasing opioid misuse and opioid-involved overdose deaths.

During the first wave of the opioid crisis, which was characterized by growing overdose deaths involving prescription opioids between 2001 and 2010, the out-of-pocket price of prescription opioids fell by 81 percent. This likely reduced the price of prescription opioids in the secondary market, from which most people who misuse prescription opioids obtain their drugs. Using the proportional price assumption and given elasticities from the academic literature, we find that the decline in observed out-of-pocket prices is capable of explaining between 31 and 83 percent of the growth in the number of overdose deaths involving prescription opioids between 2001 and 2010. At the same time that out-of-pocket prices were falling, government subsidies and the market share of generic opioids were expanding. We estimate that the share of prescribed opioids funded by government programs increased from 17 percent in 2001 to 60 percent in 2010 (and to 63 percent in 2015). The share of publicly funded opioids diverted to the secondary market may be even higher, given the relatively low acquisition cost for suppliers of diverted opioids.

Falling prices could not elicit a change in the quantity of opioids misused and the resulting opioid deaths unless providers were encouraged to prescribe the opioids, health plans were paying for the prescriptions, and pharmacies were filling these prescriptions. We describe the change in the environment resulting from changing pain management guidelines and aggressive marketing tactics that reduced barriers to obtaining larger quantities of opioids.

The CEA finds that the second wave of the opioid crisis—characterized by growing deaths from illicit opioids between 2010 and 2016—was driven by a combination of supply and demand expansions. Efforts to restrict the supply and misuse of prescription opioids led an increased number of users from the first wave to substitute illicit opioids in place of prescription opioids. At the same time, the supply of illicit opioids expanded, and this substitution decreased quality-adjusted prices to reduce the "cost of a high." Despite the importance of demand through a substitution effect in the initial years of the second wave, the CEA finds that the evidence supports the idea that supply expansions have been more important causes of the crisis's growth than demand increases.

The Trump Administration has taken significant steps to stem the tide of the opioid crisis. In October 2017, the Administration declared a nationwide Public Health Emergency. President Trump later established his Initiative to Stop Opioid Abuse and Reduce Drug Supply and Demand in March 2018 (White House 2018). These and other measures taken by the government include securing more than $6 billion in new funding in 2018 and 2019 to address the opioid crisis by reducing the supply of opioids, reducing new demand for opioids, and treating those with opioid use disorder.

To restrict the supply of illicitly produced opioids, there have been increased efforts to prevent the flow of illicit drugs into the U.S. through ports of entry and international shipments. The President also signed into law the International Narcotics Trafficking Emergency Response by Detecting Incoming Contraband with Technology (INTERDICT) Act, which funds U.S. Customs and Border Protection (CBP) to expand technologies to help interdict illicit substances including opioids. The CBP is also training all narcotic detector dogs at ports of entry to detect fentanyl. These efforts have seen success—during fiscal year 2019, the CBP seized almost 2,800 pounds of fentanyl and over 6,200 pounds of heroin (CBP 2019). The Administration has also increased enforcement against illicit drug producers and traffickers. In 2018, the Department of Justice (DOJ) indicted two Chinese nationals accused of manufacturing and shipping fentanyl analogues, synthetic opioids, and 250 other drugs to at least 37 U.S. States and 25 other countries (DOJ 2018). In addition, the Department of the Treasury has levied kingpin designations against fentanyl traffickers that operate in China, India, the United Arab Emirates, and Mexico, and also throughout Southeast Asia, including Vietnam, Thailand, and Singapore. To stop the flow of this deadly drug before it reaches Americans, the Administration is working with more than 130 nations that signed onto President Trump's Call to Action on this issue. The Federal government is also engaging private sector partners to help secure U.S. supply chains against traffickers attempting to exploit those platforms (ONDCP 2019). One example is the promotion of increased private sector self-policing of products entering the U.S. via third-party marketplaces, and other intermediaries to an e-commerce transaction (via the Department of Homeland Security).

Immigrations and Customs Enforcement's Homeland Security Investigations (HSI) organization has also increased its efforts targeting transnational criminal organizations (TCO) involved with the opioid epidemic. HSI has increased its partnerships—such as the Border Enforcement Security Taskforce (BEST) platforms—with other Federal, international, tribal, State, and local law enforcement agencies to increase information and resource sharing within U.S. communities. BESTs eliminate the barriers between Federal and local investigations (access to both Federal and State prosecutors), close the gap with international partners in multinational criminal investigations, and create an environment that minimizes the vulnerabilities in our operations that TCOs have traditionally capitalized on to exploit the Nation's land and sea borders.

To better combat 21st-century crime exploiting ecommerce, HSI has increased its presence at international mail facilities and express consignment centers by establishing BESTs at John F. Kennedy International Airport in New York, Los Angeles International Airport, Memphis International Airport, Cincinnati–Northern Kentucky International Airport, and Louisville International Airport as part of HSI's comprehensive and multilayered strategy to combat TCOs and their smuggling activities. This strategy facilitates the immediate application of investigative techniques on seized parcels, which aid in establishing probable cause needed to effect enforcement actions on individuals associated with narcotics laden parcels. Consequently, these seizures and arrests disrupt the movement of narcotics transiting through the mail and express consignment shipments, and aid in the dismantling of distribution networks. BEST partners with the CBP, the United States Postal Inspection Service, and DEA at these facilities. As of September 2019, BESTs are located at 69 locations throughout the nation, including Puerto Rico.

Along with reducing the supply of opioids, Federal and State governments are also playing a key role in curtailing the demand for prescription and illicit opioids. Prescription drug monitoring programs that track controlled substance prescriptions are operational in 49 states, the District of Columbia, and Guam, and they can provide timely information about prescribing and patient behaviors that exacerbate the crisis and enable response (CRS 2018). In 2017, the number of high-dose opioid prescriptions dispensed monthly declined by over 16 percent, and the prescribing rate of opioids fell to its lowest rate in more than 10 years. The Administration has also invested over $1 billion in innovative research to develop effective nonopioid options for pain management. In addition to reducing opioid prescriptions to decrease new initiates to opioid misuse, the Administration has launched information campaigns to create awareness and inform the public about opioid use disorder to prevent new drug users. In June 2018, the White House's Office of National Drug Control Policy, the Ad Council, and the Truth Initiative announced a public education campaign over digital platforms, social media, and television targeting youth and young adults. Importantly, nearly 60 percent fewer young adults between the age of 18 and 25 began using heroin in 2018 than in 2016.

Improved guidelines are also being established to target the vulnerable veteran population, who are twice as likely as the average American to die from an opioid drug overdose (Wilkie 2018). The Department of Veterans Affairs (VA) and the Department of Defense updated their Opioid Safety Initiative in 2017 to provide prescribers with a framework to evaluate, treat, and manage patients with chronic pain, including ways to better aggregate electronic medical records and track opioid prescriptions. In the first six years of the program, from 2012 to 2018, the number of veteran patients receiving opioids was reduced by 45 percent. Over the same period, the number of veterans on long-term opioid therapies declined by 51 percent and the number of veterans on high-dose opioid therapies declined by 66 percent (Wilkie 2018).

Finally, the Administration is also focusing on treating and saving the lives of those currently struggling with opioid addictions by expanding access to the life-saving drug naloxone and other evidence-based interventions, such as medication-assisted treatment and other recovery support services. Prevention of drug use is important, but in addition, the Trump Administration has invested in increased treatment and recovery support for people who suffer from opioid use disorder. The Surgeon General has promoted access and carrying naloxone, the lifesaving reversal agent of an opioid overdose. In October 2018, President Trump signed into law the bipartisan Substance Use Disorder Prevention That Promotes Opioid Recovery and Treatment (SUPPORT) for Patients and Communities Act, which includes provisions to improve substance use disorder treatments for Medicaid patients and to expand Medicare coverage of opioid use disorder treatment services. In fiscal years 2018 and 2019, a total of $3 billion was appropriated for State grants to fund opioid use disorder prevention and treatment. Many States—including West Virginia, Indiana, Wyoming, Tennessee, Florida, and Virginia—have implemented legislation to expand the availability of naloxone, and inpatient and outpatient use of the life-saving treatment is increasing (ASTHO 2018).

Many of the measures taken by the Trump Administration to cut the supply of opioids, prevent new demand, and save the lives of those currently struggling with opioid use disorders may have contributed to the flattening growth of overdose deaths involving opioids. Between January 2017 and May 2019, monthly overdose deaths fell by 9.6 percent. If the growth rate in opioid overdose deaths from January 1999 through December 2016 had continued, the CEA estimates that 37,750 additional lives would have been lost due to opioid overdoses between January 2017 and May 2019. The CEA estimates the economic cost savings since January 2017 from reduced mortality compared with the preexisting trend was over $397 billion. The opioid crisis remains at an emergency level, but its dramatic growth has been halted. Despite successful efforts to curb the opioid crisis and stop the increase in overdose deaths, there has been an increase in psychostimulant-related overdose deaths, primarily driven by methamphetamine use, that is a cause of concern. Psychostimulant-related deaths now outnumber fentanyl deaths in 12 States (Wilner 2019).

The economic and human costs of drug misuse continue to pose a threat to the United States. The Trump Administration is working to determine the underlying causes of the opioid crisis so that it can implement effective solutions. Lower drug prices clearly played a role in the opioid crisis's growth, and understanding this dynamic will help policymakers successfully respond to this threat and avoid mistakes that could lead to another costly, deadly crisis.

Chapter 8

Expanding Affordable Housing

Incomes in the United States are rising, but home prices are rising much faster in some highly regulated markets. While overall homeownership rates have increased since 2016, some disadvantaged groups lag behind. As households turn to the rental market, moderate-income households are dedicating a large share of their incomes to rent. The housing affordability problem shows no signs of subsiding in certain markets, as housing construction fails to keep up with demand, putting upward pressure on home prices and rents.

Fortunately, the majority of areas in the United States have relatively well-functioning housing markets in which regulations do not significantly drive up prices. Indeed, smart regulations that balance the need to build enough housing to meet growing demand while reflecting the reasonable concerns of neighborhood residents are achieved by many growing areas in the country. While areas with relatively moderate home prices may still suffer from some issues, such as delays for building permits, regulations do not necessarily make homes substantially less affordable.

However, research has shown that there are 11 metropolitan areas where the inability to build enough housing to meet demand has driven home prices far higher than the cost to produce a home. These 11 metropolitan areas include San Francisco, Honolulu, Oxnard, Los Angeles, San Diego, Washington, Boston, Denver, New York City, Seattle, and Baltimore.

Housing is particularly difficult to build in these 11 metropolitan areas due to excessive regulatory barriers imposed by State and local governments. Such overly restrictive regulations include zoning and growth management controls, rent controls, building and rehabilitation codes, energy and water efficiency mandates, maximum-density allowances, historic preservation requirements, wetland or environmental regulations, manufactured-housing regulations and restrictions, parking requirements, permitting and review procedures, investment or reinvestment tax policies, labor requirements, and impact or developer fees. Research has linked higher home prices and lower housing supply to many of these regulations.

Resulting higher housing prices in these 11 metropolitan areas make homeownership less attainable for otherwise-qualified borrowers, thereby constraining their ability to achieve sustainable homeownership and putting additional pressure on rental markets for lower- and middle-income households. The lowest-income households are especially burdened. Among these 11 metropolitan areas, homelessness would fall by an estimated 31 percent on average if overly burdensome regulations were relaxed. Higher rents resulting from these regulations also deprive families of Federal rental housing assistance, because higher government expenditures on households in high-rent areas, through higher Fair Market Rents, reduce the amount of funds available to serve other needy families. For example, housing a family in a three-bedroom apartment can cost the Federal Government more than $4,000 per month in San Francisco County, California, compared with about $1,500 per month in Harris County, Texas.

Excessive regulatory barriers to building more housing in these specific areas also have broader negative effects beyond those imposed on lower-income Americans. State and local housing regulations reduce labor mobility by pricing workers out of several of the Nation's most productive cities, which stunts aggregate economic growth and increases inequality across regions and workers. Excessive regulatory barriers also reduce parents' ability to access neighborhoods that best advance their children's economic opportunity. And by incentivizing families to venture further from their places of work to find affordable housing, overregulation can increase commuting times to work, thus harming the environment, straining local budgets, and decreasing worker productivity.

Removing government-imposed barriers to more affordable housing is a priority for the Trump Administration. Beyond establishing the White House Council on Eliminating Regulatory Barriers to Affordable Housing, the Department of Housing and Urban Development is encouraging State and local governments to focus on increasing housing supply in areas where supply is constrained. Increasing housing choice for all Americans requires taking on regulatory barriers that place housing in large swaths of specific areas out of reach for lower-income families.

Since 2000, real median (posttax/posttransfer) household income has grown by 20 percent, while real home prices have grown by almost 50 percent, according to the Standard & Poor's / Case-Shiller Index (CBO 2019). With rising home prices outpacing income gains in some areas, households are spending larger portions of their incomes on housing, and fewer people can afford to purchase their own homes.

Although the overall homeownership rate has increased since 2016, some groups lag behind. Based on the four-quarter moving average, the black homeownership rate remains 31.5 percentage points below that of non-Hispanic white households (see figure 8-1). The Hispanic homeownership rate remains 26.2 percentage points lower than that of non-Hispanic white households, despite increasing by 1.3 percentage points since the fourth quarter of 2016, when President Trump was elected. Differences in homeownership between races exacerbate the wealth gap. In 2016, white families had a median wealth of $171,000, while black families had a median wealth of $17,600, resulting in part from their lower homeownership rate (Dettling et al. 2017).

Many American households, particularly low-income households, spend a large portion of their income on rent. According to the American Community Survey, out of 43 million renter households in the United States in 2017, 46 percent paid more than 30 percent of their income on housing, 31 percent paid more than 40 percent, and 23 percent paid more than 50 percent. Among renters with incomes of less than $20,000 in 2017, about 74 percent paid more than 30 percent of their income in rent. For those renters with income between $20,000 and $50,000, about 61 percent paid more than 30 percent of their income in rent.

Meanwhile, a significant number of Americans go without housing altogether, sleeping instead on the streets or in homeless shelters. Just over

Figure 8-1. Homeownership Rates by Race and Ethnicity, 2000–2019

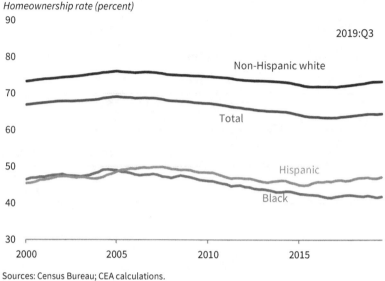

Sources: Census Bureau; CEA calculations.
Note: Data represent a four-quarter moving average.

half a million people were homeless on a single night in January 2018, with 35 percent of those found in unsheltered locations not intended for human habitation, such as sidewalks and public parks (HUD 2018). Research has linked higher rents to higher rates of homelessness (e.g., Quigley, Raphael, and Smolensky 2001; Corinth 2017; Hanratty 2017; Nisar et al. 2019).

The housing affordability problem shows no signs of subsiding, given that home construction fails to keep up with demand in some places, putting upward pressure on home prices and rents. Indeed, from 2010 to 2016, housing construction failed to keep pace with household formation, according to the Census Bureau. Home construction per capita has declined every decade since the 1970s. While an average of 8.2 homes were built for every 1,000 residents between 1970 and 1979, annual average construction fell to 3.0 homes per 1,000 residents between 2010 and 2018. Across States, there is large variation in housing construction, according to State-level data from the Bank of Tokyo–Mitsubishi. For example, from 2010 to 2018, Texas built 5.3 homes and Florida built 4.3 homes per 1,000 residents, on average. Meanwhile, over the same period, California built 2.0 homes and New York built 1.7 homes per 1,000 residents.

A key driver of the housing affordability problem is excessive regulatory barriers to building (single and multifamily) housing in a selected number of areas in the United States. In a competitive market, developers will build homes until (economic) profits fall to zero or, in other words, until the price the developer receives for the home equals the cost to produce the home.

However, overly burdensome regulations in some areas restrict housing supply and drive the price of a home above its minimum profitable production cost: the cost of construction plus the price of land to build on in a free market and a normal profit margin. In terms of the standard model of supply and demand, regulations make supply less elastic, causing prices to increase and quantity to decrease. In this way, Glaeser and Gyourko (2018) note that regulation that drives home prices above production costs acts as a "regulatory tax" on housing. Regulations that can potentially drive up home prices include, for example, overly burdensome permitting and review procedures, overly restrictive zoning and growth management controls, unreasonable maximum-density allowances, historic preservation requirements, overly burdensome environmental regulations, and undue parking requirements.

It is important to emphasize that an adequate amount of smart regulation is important to address market failures and reflect the reasonable concerns of current neighborhood residents regarding new housing development. In chapter 1 of this *Report*, we review evidence that gains in housing wealth contributed to the growth of total household wealth from 2016 through 2019. Many growing areas are highly successful in balancing neighborhood concerns with the need to expand housing supply to meet growing demand. In fact, housing prices are near or below the cost to produce a home in most areas of the United States, suggesting that low income levels (despite incomes rising in recent years) rather than high home prices are the reason some households struggle to cover housing costs in those areas. However, research has shown that as a result of excessive local regulatory barriers to building housing, there are 11 metropolitan areas where the inability to build enough housing to meet demand has driven home prices far higher than the cost to produce a home (Glaeser and Gyourko 2018). These 11 metropolitan areas include San Francisco, Honolulu, Oxnard, Los Angeles, San Diego, Washington, Boston, Denver, New York City, Seattle, and Baltimore. Even in these areas, it is not necessary to build high-rise apartments throughout neighborhoods currently zoned for single-family homes or to eliminate all regulations. Rather, steps to remove excessive regulatory barriers must be taken so that housing supply can expand to meet demand and alleviate extreme housing cost burdens placed on low- and middle-income families.

The excessive regulatory barriers placed on building housing in these 11 metropolitan areas cause economic distress to their current and potential residents. In addition to restricting the ability of property owners to use their property in reasonable ways, these regulations increase costs for both renters and those trying to buy a home. Based on estimates from Glaeser and Gyourko (2018), excessive regulatory barriers (defined as regulations that drive up home prices at least 25 percent above home production costs) drive up home prices by between 36 and 184 percent in each of these 11 metropolitan areas, which also leads to higher rents. These cost burdens are especially problematic for low-income Americans, who pay the largest share of their income on housing.

By increasing rents, overly burdensome regulatory barriers to building housing increase homelessness. As estimated by the CEA (2019), relaxing excessive regulatory barriers in these 11 metropolitan areas where housing supply is significantly constrained would reduce homelessness by an average of 31 percent in these areas. For example, homelessness would fall by 54 percent in San Francisco, 40 percent in Los Angeles, and 23 percent in New York. Because these areas contain 42 percent of the U.S. homeless population, homelessness would fall by 13 percent in the United States overall if each area adequately addressed its regulatory barriers.

Overregulation of these selected housing markets also reduces the efficiency of government housing assistance because fewer American families receive assistance for a given budget outlay. In 2019, the Department of Housing and Urban Development (HUD) was provided $42 billion for its largest rental housing assistance programs: Section 8 Housing Choice Vouchers ($23 billion), Section 8 Project-Based Rental Assistance ($12 billion), and Public Housing ($7 billion). Because HUD rental assistance is tied to market rents in an area, regulations that drive up rents also increase the costs of serving a fixed number of families. Deregulation that reduces rents in supply-constrained areas could produce savings for HUD that could be used to serve more families. For example, Federal taxpayers can pay more than $4,000 per month in rental assistance toward a three-bedroom unit in San Francisco County, California, compared with about $1,500 per month in Harris County, Texas.

In addition to specific harmful effects on low-income Americans, excessive regulatory barriers in selected markets have other negative consequences for all Americans. First, they reduce labor mobility across areas, which stunts aggregate economic growth and increases inequality across regions and workers. When it is more expensive for workers to live in areas where they are most productive, they are less likely to do so and their productivity falls. Hsieh and Moretti (2019), for example, estimate that gross domestic product would have been 3.7 percent higher by 2009 if housing supply restrictions in the New York, San Jose, and San Francisco areas were relaxed beginning in 1964.

Second, excessive regulatory barriers to building housing in selected markets reduces parents' ability to access neighborhoods that advance their children's economic opportunity. A series of papers by Raj Chetty and his colleagues have identified neighborhoods that are most likely to improve long-term outcomes of children (Chetty et al. 2018). High home prices are a common characteristic of such neighborhoods, suggesting that excessive regulation that artificially increases home prices may reduce in-migration and diminish opportunity for children. A report from the U.S. Senate Joint Economic Committee similarly found that the average U.S. zip code with the highest-quality public elementary schools has a median home price that is four times as high as those zip codes with the lowest-quality public schools (JEC 2019). This is partly due to the willingness of some parents to pay more for homes located in high-quality school districts. Many of these areas have excessive regulatory barriers, however.

Third, excessive regulatory barriers to building housing increase commuting times because housing cannot be built near where people work, increasing driving time and traffic congestion, which harm the environment. The average commuter spent 54 hours in traffic congestion in 2017, up from 20 hours in 1982 (Schrank, Eisele, and Lomax 2019). The aggregate travel delay increased from 1.8 billion hours to 8.8 billion hours over this period, and the total cost associated with congestion rose from $15 billion to $179 billion. As a result of this rise in average commuting times, an extra 3.3 billion gallons of fuel were consumed.

Fortunately, growing evidence of the importance of addressing excessive regulatory barriers to building housing has led to increased bipartisan focus on the issue. The CEA under the previous Administration released a "Housing Development Toolkit" in 2016 for State and local regulators. While some of the proposed reforms could be problematic, the toolkit called for a number of productive steps to reduce local government barriers to housing development. These reforms include establishing by-right development to streamline the process for approving projects, permitting multifamily zoning to boost urban density, and shortening the process for obtaining building permits (CEA 2016). Some counterproductive reforms were also suggested, including requirements that developers build certain types of units with regulated rents in exchange for building more market-rate units, a policy that can potentially hinder overall supply expansions and increase prices in some areas (Schuetz, Meltzer, and Been 2011). The CEA (2016) connected regulatory barriers to a number of problems, including stunted economic growth, increased inequality, harm to the environment, and increased homelessness.

To more successfully address the overregulation of housing markets, President Trump signed an Executive Order on June 25, 2019, establishing the White House Council on Eliminating Regulatory Barriers to Affordable Housing. Recognizing the harmful impact of these regulations on economic growth, opportunities for children, homelessness, and the cost of government programs, the council is tasked with identifying the most burdensome Federal, State, and local regulatory barriers to housing supply as well as actions that can best counter them. The Executive Order requires the council to determine how each Federal agency can curtail impediments to housing development, including in ways that "align, support, and encourage" State and local authorities to address local regulatory barriers.

HUD has also taken action under the Trump Administration to counter regulatory barriers to building affordable housing. The Affirmatively Furthering Fair Housing rule, which was finalized during the previous Administration, is being revised to focus more clearly on increasing housing supply in areas where supply is constrained, rather than encouraging localities to subsidize housing in more affluent areas. This rule recognizes that increasing housing choice for disadvantaged groups requires taking on regulatory barriers that place housing in large swaths of specific areas out of reach for lower-income families.

This chapter proceeds by first documenting the housing affordability problem in the United States. It then identifies the key role that excessive regulatory barriers play in the problem in a selected number of metropolitan areas. Next, it provides evidence of the many harmful consequences of these barriers, especially harm to low-income Americans. Finally, it concludes by discussing actions the Administration has taken to encourage the relaxation of excessive regulatory barriers in local housing markets.[1]

The Housing Affordability Problem

When home prices rise faster than incomes, fewer households can afford to purchase a home. Those still able to qualify for a loan and purchase a home may do so in neighborhoods or regions with fewer opportunities, and they may commit larger shares of their income to mortgage payments and savings to a down payment. Renter households may pay a greater portion of their income in rent, leaving less income available for other needs. The burden is especially severe for lower-income households. By these definitions, the "housing affordability" problem in America is worsening, a result of home prices that have outpaced income gains and home construction that has not kept up with demand in certain areas.

Based on a four-quarter moving average, as of the third quarter of 2019, 64.5 percent of households owned their own homes (figure 8-1). This represents an increase of 1.1 percentage points since reaching its low point in 2016:Q3. However, the current homeownership rate is still 4.6 percentage points below its 69.1 percent peak in 2005:Q1.

Some groups have particularly low homeownership rates. The black homeownership rate was 41.8 percent in 2019:Q3, 31.5 percentage points below the non-Hispanic white homeownership rate (figure 8-1). While the Hispanic homeownership rate increased by 1.3 percentage points since 2016:Q4, when President Trump was elected, it was still at 47.2 percent in 2019:Q3, 26.2 percentage points lower than that of non-Hispanic white households (figure 8-1).

For those who are homeowners, owned homes are an important source of wealth. Thus, gaps in homeownership rates have direct implications for

---

[1] The CEA previously released research on topics covered in this chapter. The text that follows builds on the research paper produced by the CEA titled "The State of Homelessness in America" (CEA 2019).

wealth gaps. According to the Federal Reserve Board's Survey of Consumer Finances, in 2016, white families had a median wealth of $171,000, while black families had a median wealth of $17,600 and Hispanic families had a median wealth of $20,700, partly as a result of their much lower homeownership rates (Dettling et al. 2017).

Among those who own a home, mortgages can take up a large share of income, especially for lower-income families. In 2017, housing costs represented 67.5 percent of household income for homeowners with less than $20,000 in annual income, and 40.6 percent of income for homeowners with between $20,000 and $50,000 in annual income (Dumont 2019). Thus, housing affordability can be a problem even for those able to purchase their own home. In chapter 1 of this *Report*, we discuss how current low mortgage rates on the whole should support the housing market. However, other factors, such as high mortgage underwriting costs, hurt mortgage affordability.

As homeownership rates have fallen, the number of renter households has grown. The Federal Reserve Board estimates that of the 6.2 million households formed between 2009 and 2017, 5.7 million (92 percent) were new renter households (Dumont 2019). Renter households pay large shares of their income on rent—without building equity—which can make it difficult for low- and moderate-income households to address other needs. From 1970 to 2010, the share of renter households spending more than half of their income on housing increased from 16 percent to 28 percent; over the same period, the share spending at least 30 percent on housing increased from 31 percent to 52 percent (Albouy, Ehrlich, and Liu 2016). According to the 2017 American Community Survey, out of 43 million renter households in the United States, 46 percent pay more than 30 percent of their income on housing, 31 percent pay more than 40 percent, and 23 percent pay more than 50 percent. As shown in table 8-1, among renters with incomes of less than $20,000 in 2017, about 74 percent paid more than 30 percent of their income in rent, a smaller share than in 2009. For those renters with incomes between $20,000 and $50,000, 61 percent paid more than 30 percent of their income in rent, rising from about 50 percent in 2009.

Meanwhile, a significant number of Americans go without housing altogether, sleeping instead on the streets or in homeless shelters. Just over half a million people were homeless on a given night in January 2018, with 35 percent of those found in unsheltered locations not intended for human habitation, such as sidewalks and public parks (HUD 2018). Research has linked higher rents to higher rates of homelessness (e.g., Quigley 2001; Corinth 2017; Hanratty 2017; Nisar et al. 2019).

The growing housing affordability problem is not driven by falling incomes (with the exception of the Great Recession, which led to severe housing problems, including widespread foreclosures; see Steffen et al. 2013). Since 2000, real median (posttax, posttransfer) household income increased by 20

Table 8-1. Percentage of Renter Households Paying More Than 30 Percent of Income on Housing by Income, 2009 versus 2017

Household income	2009 (percent)	2017 (percent)	Percentage point change	Percent change
Less than $20,000	76.6	74.3	-2.3	-3.0
$20,000 to $49,999	50.2	61.0	10.8	21.5
$50,000 to $74,999	15.2	23.5	8.3	54.4
$75,000 to $99,999	6.8	10.3	3.5	51.3
$100,000 or more	2.1	3.5	1.3	61.8
All renter households	47.7	46.0	-1.7	-3.6

Sources: American Community Survey; CEA calculations.

percent (CBO 2019). Real income gains were even larger for the bottom fifth of households (CBO 2019). The driver of growing unaffordability is rising home prices. According to the Standard & Poor's / Case-Shiller U.S. National Home Price Index, real home prices have increased by 49 percent since 2000, outpacing real median income gains. Home prices have increased the fastest for entry-level homes—according to the American Enterprise Institute National Home Price Appreciation Index, home prices in the lowest price tier have increased more than 50 percent more than home prices in the highest price tier since 2012 (Pinto and Peter 2019). As shown in box 8-1, the housing affordability problem is concentrated in a selected number of areas in the United States, where the people who build houses are unable to afford them.

Although home prices are rising, home construction has been slow to respond, implying that supply is not keeping up with the demand for homes in certain places. Home construction per capita has declined every decade since the 1970s, according to the Census Bureau. While an average of 8.2 homes were built for every 1,000 residents between 1970 and 1979, annual average construction fell to 3.0 homes per 1,000 residents between 2010 and 2018. Across States, there is large variation in housing construction. For example, from 2010 to 2018, Texas built 5.2 homes and Florida built 4.3 homes per 1,000 residents, on average. Meanwhile, over the same period, California built 2.0 homes and New York built 1.7 homes per 1,000 residents. This represents a large decline for California, which built more than 7.0 homes per 1,000 residents in the 1970s and 1980s before falling to less than 4.0 per 1,000 residents in every decade since then. Meanwhile, New York is one of only two States in the country (along

Box 8-1. Measuring the Housing Affordability Problem with the Carpenter Index

One way to assess the affordability of housing is to ask whether the people who build homes can afford to buy them. The American Enterprise Institute's Carpenter Index compares the average income of households headed by carpenters to home prices in a given area. If the price of a home is less than three times the carpenter's household income, then that home is deemed "affordable." For each metropolitan area, the index calculates the share of entry-level homes that are affordable to the carpenter.

Figure 8-i shows the share of the entry-level housing stock that is affordable for the 100 largest CBSAs, with the darker shades illustrating areas where housing is less affordable to the average carpenter. The average carpenter can afford only 6.5 percent of entry-level homes built in the San Diego–Carlsbad, California, CBSA; 8.2 percent in the Oxnard–Thousand Oaks–Ventura, California, CBSA; 10.3 percent in the Los Angeles–Long Beach–Anaheim, California, CBSA; 10.7 percent in the San Jose–Sunnyvale–Santa Clara, California, CBSA; and 11.8 percent in the San Francisco–Oakland–Hayward, California, CBSA—the five least affordable areas in the country. By contrast, the average carpenter can afford 100 percent of entry-level homes in the Chicago–Naperville–Elgin, Illinois–Indiana–Wisconsin, CBSA; the Pittsburgh, Pennsylvania, CBSA; the Saint Louis, Missouri–Illinois, CBSA;

Figure 8-i. The Carpenter Index by CBSA, 2018

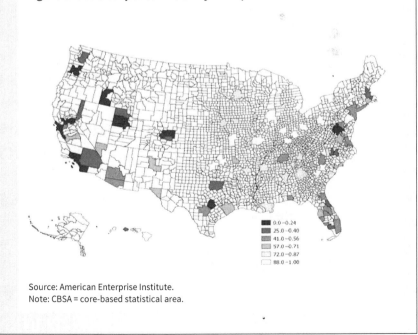

Source: American Enterprise Institute.
Note: CBSA = core-based statistical area.

and a number of other areas in the Midwest. The index signals that the most expensive metropolitan areas are located in California and to a lesser extent the rest of the West Coast and the Northeast, while most of the affordable metropolitan areas are located in the Midwest.

with West Virginia) that has never built more than 3.0 homes per 1,000 residents in an average year across every decade since the 1970s.

The Role of Overregulation in the Housing Affordability Problem

When the housing affordability problem is defined as housing expenditures that constitute a sufficiently large share of income, there are three potential causes: (1) rising home prices, (2) falling household incomes, and (3) choices among households to consume higher-quality homes (with either high physical quality or in closer proximity to desirable amenities). As reported in the previous section, real home prices have risen 49 percent since 2000. Meanwhile, household incomes are rising rather than falling, and consumer decisions to choose higher-quality homes should not be considered an affordability problem. Thus, the fundamental problem with housing affordability in the United States today is excessively high home prices in certain areas.

Overly stringent housing regulations play a key role in driving up home prices in the face of growing demand. Figure 8-2 shows how excessive regulatory barriers to building housing in some areas constrain supply and thus increase home prices. In a market unconstrained by excessive regulation, developers can build new homes at a constant cost when demand shifts outward (for example, because higher wages increase the desirability of living in an area), and thus, price remains constant at P_1 while quantity increases to Q_2. By contrast, new home construction cannot keep up with growing demand in a market constrained by excessive regulations, such as lengthy permitting processes and unreasonable land use regulations. Excessive regulations lead to an upward sloping, relatively more inelastic housing supply curve, which drives home prices above the cost to produce a home in a market without excessive regulatory barriers. Prices rise to P_2 and quantity falls to Q_1. In this way, Glaeser and Gyourko (2018) note that excessive regulation that drives home prices above production costs acts as a "regulatory tax" on housing. This regulatory tax is represented in figure 8-2 as the gap between P_1 and P_2.

Some regulations add additional costs to the development process, driving up the total cost of housing development and reducing supply. For example, environmental reviews can delay construction, imposing additional costs on developers. An unintended consequence of these regulations is that housing is

Figure 8-2. The Effect of Regulation on Supply and Demand for Housing

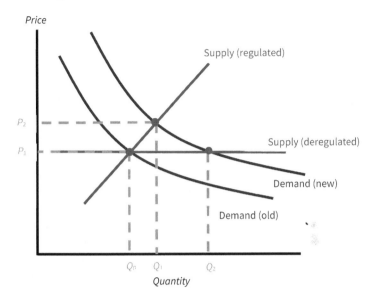

Sources: Glaeser and Gyourko (2018); CEA calculations.

instead built in less central areas where regulations do less to drive up home prices, which can increase commuting times and ultimately cause even greater environmental harm. More generally, approval processes for new development can be lengthy and uncertain, thus increasing the price and reducing the supply of housing by, for example, forcing developers to carry high-cost construction loans for a longer period of time, or having to spend additional money on extending options to purchase land. Gyourko, Hartley, and Krimmel (2019) formulate an Approval Delay Index and find that the review time for housing construction projects is more than twice as long in highly regulated areas compared with relatively lightly regulated areas, with an average review time of 8.4 months. Environmental reviews alone can add substantial costs to a housing project. For example, the California Environmental Quality Act, which requires certain construction in California to undergo an environmental impact assessment, can add an estimated $1 million in costs to completing a housing development (Jackson 2018).

Other regulations that can potentially constrain supply are focused explicitly on reducing density. Building permit caps, population caps, and density restrictions limit the amount of new housing that can be built in an area. Similarly, urban growth boundaries prevent urban expansion beyond designated areas. Other kinds of regulations reduce density by regulating the type and size of housing that can be constructed in a locality. Minimum lot size requirements prevent homebuilders from subdividing a lot in order to build more homes. Height restrictions prevent taller buildings with more floors and more housing units. Maximum floor area ratios (which are calculated by dividing floor area by lot area) limit the amount of living space, potentially across multiple units, that can be built on a given lot. Zoning regulations also may prevent certain types of housing, such as multifamily buildings, from being constructed.

Of course, when these types of regulations are not excessive, they can be beneficial—for example, by maintaining standards that promote safety, or by providing information about housing characteristics—without significantly constraining supply. In addition, certain types of land use may generate pollution or congestion externalities, and some amount of regulation, such as impact fees, can help developers internalize these costs of construction. Local citizens may also wish to preserve certain land for public use or conservation purposes, such as parks. However, in a selected number of places, excessive regulations prevent supply from expanding to meet housing demand, substantially driving up home prices.

It is generally believed among economists that the overall effect of excessive regulatory barriers that constrain housing supply is to reduce overall well-being. For example, Albouy and Ehrlich (2018, 117) not only find that stringent housing regulation increases home prices, but also that any benefits of these regulations for improving quality of life are outweighed by their cost. They note: "On net, the typical land-use regulation in the United States reduces well-being by making housing production less efficient and housing consumption less affordable." Glaeser and Gyourko (2018, 14) summarize the literature and state: "Empirical investigations of the local costs and benefits of restricting building generally conclude that the negative externalities are not nearly large enough to justify the costs of regulation."

The stringency of housing regulations and their impact on housing supply vary across the country. One way to measure the stringency of regulations is to analyze the regulations themselves. One measure that is heavily relied upon is the Wharton Residential Land Use Regulatory Index. Gyourko, Saiz, and Summers (2008) constructed the index from a national survey of municipalities regarding their regulatory process and land use regulations. The resulting index is shown by metropolitan statistical area in figure 8-3, with a darker shade of blue indicating cities that have more stringent land use regulations. The South and the Midwest have the least restrictive regulations, while California and the Northeast have the most.

Areas with higher regulatory burdens tend to have higher home prices. Figure 8-4 shows metropolitan areas by the ratio of their median home prices to the cost to produce a home, as constructed by Glaeser and Gyourko (2018). Where regulations are lax, the ratio of home prices to production costs should be near or below 1. Where regulations are more stringent and demand is strong,

Figure 8-3. Wharton Land Use Index by Metropolitan Statistical Area, 2008

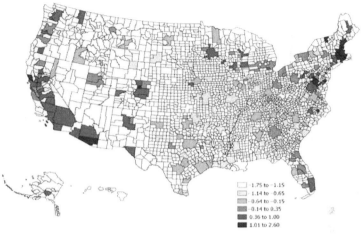

Source: Gyourko, Saiz, and Summers (2008).

Figure 8-4. Ratio of Home Prices to Production Costs by CBSA, 2013

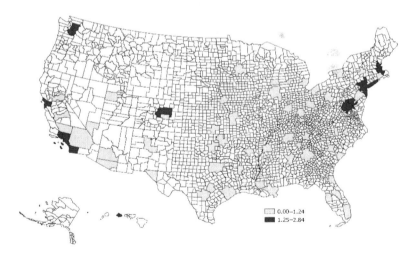

Sources: Glaeser and Gyourko (2018); CEA calculations.
Note: CBSA = core-based statistical area.

ratios may exceed 1. It is important to note that production costs include not only the construction cost of the home but also a normal profit margin and a small cost of land on which to build the home that would be achieved in a market without overly stringent regulations.

It is certainly the case that, even in an unconstrained market, land prices for a fixed size plot (i.e., an acre) of land will be higher in more desirable locations. Davis and others (2019) document large variation in land prices per acre across the United States—much of this variation would remain even if all areas relaxed overly stringent housing regulations. However, the price of a parcel of land used for each housing unit may be similar across areas absent excessive regulation. In dense areas, each housing unit would require a smaller plot of land, and so, though the price of an acre of land is likely to be higher in denser areas, the cost of the smaller piece of land used for each two-bedroom housing unit may be similar to the cost of the larger piece of land used for a two-bedroom unit in less dense areas. Of course, this will only roughly be true, and other factors, such as differences in property taxes, may drive some remaining differences. Partly for this reason, Glaeser and Gyourko (2018) focus on areas where home prices significantly exceed production costs.

Figure 8-4 shows that the places where ratios of home price to production cost significantly exceed 1 (i.e., where home prices are at least 25 percent higher than home production costs) are largely the same places with high regulatory indices. Though correlational, this provides suggestive evidence that housing regulations help determine home prices. Figure 8-4 also indicates that excessive regulation is currently a major problem in a selected number of places, indicated by the darker shade of blue. As noted earlier in this chapter, these 11 metropolitan areas include San Francisco, Honolulu, Oxnard, Los Angeles, San Diego, Washington, Boston, Denver, New York City, Seattle, and Baltimore.

Examples of overly burdensome regulations abound in these 11 CBSAs. Four of the 11 are located in California, where multifamily homes may be built on less than a quarter of the land in Los Angeles, Long Beach, Anaheim, and San Diego and less than half of the land in San Francisco and Oakland (Mawhorter and Reid 2018). In the cities of Los Angeles and San Diego, two parking spaces are required for every typical two-bedroom apartment, one and a half parking spaces are required for every typical one-bedroom apartment, and one parking space is required for every studio apartment, increasing costs for multifamily housing developers and, ultimately, renters (San Francisco eliminated its parking requirements in early 2019). Across Hawaii, only 4 percent of land may be developed due to its network of local and State zoning regulations.

Although overly burdensome permitting processes and other barriers may still be a problem and put some degree of upward pressure on home prices in the rest of the country, the major problem with excessive regulation is currently limited to these 11 areas. Nonetheless, future demand growth in additional areas with excessive regulatory barriers could increase the number of areas with artificially inflated home prices.

Consistent with figures 8-3 and 8-4, a number of academic studies find that stringent regulation increases housing prices. In a review of much of the earlier literature, Ihlanfeldt (2004) concludes that growth controls and minimum lot size restrictions reduce the supply of housing and increase its price. Quigley and Raphael (2005) find that cities in California with more stringent regulations have higher levels and growth in home prices and rents, and that housing supply is much less responsive to price increases in more regulated areas. Glaeser, Gyourko, and Saks (2005) argue that land-use restrictions explain why prices for high-rise apartments in Manhattan far exceed the cost to construct them. Ihlanfeldt (2007) finds that more stringent land-use regulation increases home prices in Florida. Glaeser and Ward (2009) find that more stringent regulations, especially minimum lot sizes, are associated with higher home prices and less construction in Massachusetts. Saiz (2010) finds that land-use regulations, in addition to geographical constraints, are important determinants of the responsiveness of housing supply to price increases. Summarizing the literature, Glaeser and Gyourko (2018, 8) state: "The general conclusion of existing research is that local land use regulation reduces the elasticity of housing supply, and that this results in a smaller stock of housing, higher house prices, greater volatility of house prices, and less volatility of new construction."

Some might argue that there are reasons other than regulation that might be driving higher home prices. One reason could be that construction costs are rising. However, Gyourko and Molloy (2015) find that real construction costs (including the cost of labor and materials) remained relatively constant from 1980 to 2013. Another potential cause is geographical constraints on building. For example, Saiz (2010) argues that many areas with supply constraints have steep-sloped terrain that prevents the development of new housing. Nonetheless, even in areas that appear to have land constraints, developers could build more densely and with fewer permitting delays, which would exert downward pressure on housing prices. Finally, though we focus on supply, housing regulations may also increase prices through increased demand for housing if land use restrictions increase the appeal of living in a certain community. Empirically, however, Albouy and Ehrlich (2018) find that supply effects dominate demand effects.

Consequences of Overregulation of Housing

The overregulation of housing markets in selected metropolitan areas has several negative consequences. By increasing home prices well above home production costs, it increases the cost of attaining homeownership and increases the rent for renter households. It hurts low-income Americans in particular by increasing homelessness and by reducing the number of people government housing assistance programs can serve. More generally, it reduces labor mobility across areas and thus weakens economic growth, reduces the ability of children to access high-opportunity neighborhoods, and harms the environment.

The Increased Cost of Attaining Homeownership and Higher Rents

In most areas in the United States, reasonable regulations do not substantially drive up home prices. But in a selected number of metropolitan areas, excessive regulatory barriers to building housing substantially increase the price of purchasing a home above the cost to produce it.

Figure 8-5 shows the extent to which excessive regulations drive up home prices in these 11 metropolitan areas, according to data published by Glaeser and Gyourko (2018) and shown above in figure 8-4. Home prices are more than 150 percent higher in the San Francisco–Oakland–Hayward, California, CBSA, and the Urban Honolulu, Hawaii, CBSA; are about 100 percent higher in the Oxnard–Thousand Oaks–Ventura, California, CBSA; the Los Angeles–Long Beach–Anaheim, California, CBSA; and the San Diego–Carlsbad, California, CBSA—and are 36 percent higher in the Baltimore–Columbia–Towson, Maryland, CBSA, the smallest price premium of the 11 supply-constrained metropolitan areas.

The higher home prices resulting from excessive regulations make it more difficult for households to purchase their own homes and build wealth. As HUD Secretary Ben Carson recently stated, "As a result [of the shortage in the housing supply], Americans have fewer housing opportunities, including the opportunity to achieve sustainable homeownership, which is the No. 1 builder of wealth for most U.S. families" (Carson 2019). Excessive regulation also increases rents in these 11 metropolitan areas, because higher home prices increase the amount property owners need to receive in revenue each year to maintain a normal profit margin. Higher rents are especially burdensome for lower- and moderate-income Americans—and, for some, may make it prohibitively expensive to live in these excessively regulated areas.

Increased Homelessness

Another harmful effect of overregulation of housing markets is its impact on homelessness. Several studies that rely on data on homelessness over time in various communities find that a 1 percent increase in rent is associated with about a 1 percent increase in homelessness. Because housing regulations generally drive up rents, they should thus be expected to also increase homelessness.

The CEA (2019) estimates the extent to which removing excessive regulatory barriers that reduced home prices to their production costs would reduce

Figure 8-5. Home Price Premium Resulting from Excessive Housing Regulation

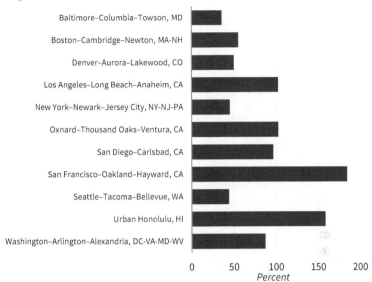

Sources: Glaeser and Gyourko (2018); CEA calculations.

Figure 8-6. Percentage Reduction in Homelessness by CBSA from Deregulating Housing Markets

Sources: Department of Housing and Urban Development, Point-in-Time Counts, 2018; Census Bureau; Corinth (2017); Glaeser and Gyourko (2018); Goodman (2004); CEA calculations.
Note: CBSA = core-based statistical area. Each continuum of care is merged into the metropolitan area where the majority of its overall population lives. This simulation assumes that deregulation reduces the ratio of home value to production cost to 1 for all metropolitan areas with a ratio of at least 1.25; see the text for further details about the simulation.

Expanding Affordable Housing | 285

homelessness. The results are summarized in figure 8-6. Homelessness would fall by 54 percent in the San Francisco–Oakland–Hayward, California, CBSA; by 50 percent in the Urban Honolulu, Hawaii, CBSA; by 40 percent in the Los Angeles–Long Beach–Anaheim, California, CBSA; by 38 percent in the San Diego–Carlsbad, California, CBSA; by 36 percent in the Washington–Arlington–Alexandria, D.C.–Virginia–Maryland–West Virginia, CBSA; and by between 19 and 26 percent in the Boston–Cambridge–Newton, Massachusetts–New Hampshire, CBSA; the Denver–Aurora–Lakewood, Colorado, CBSA; the New York–Newark–Jersey City, New York–New Jersey–Pennsylvania, CBSA; the Seattle–Tacoma–Bellevue, Washington, CBSA; and the Baltimore–Columbia–Towson, Maryland, CBSA.

The aggregate reduction in homelessness in these 11 metropolitan areas, which contain 42 percent of the U.S. homeless population, would have important effects for the United States as a whole, with total U.S. homelessness falling by just under 72,000 people, or 13 percent. These findings are also broadly consistent with results from Raphael (2010), who uses a different methodology to assess how housing market regulation drives up homelessness rates. Using an index of housing market regulation by metropolitan area, he finds that deregulation could reduce overall United States homelessness by 7 to 22 percent. He does not show how homelessness reductions would vary across specific areas. It is important to note that the housing supply responses resulting from deregulation would take many years to translate into the types of price reductions, and thus homelessness reductions, shown here. Still, these results suggest that the severe homelessness problems in a selected number of metropolitan areas are substantially driven by city-created regulations on housing.

Fewer People Are Served by Housing Assistance Programs

By driving up rents, overly stringent housing regulations in selected metropolitan areas increase the government's cost of providing rental housing assistance, resulting in fewer assisted families. The Federal Government provides rental housing assistance across a number of programs that are administered by different agencies. Three major programs are administered by HUD—these include (1) Section 8 Housing Choice Vouchers, (2) Section 8 Project-Based Rental Assistance, and (3) public housing. The largest of these three HUD programs is the Housing Choice Voucher program, which served 2.3 million families at a cost of $23 billion in fiscal year (FY) 2019 (42 percent of the overall HUD budget). Under the voucher program, qualified tenants receive Federal subsidies that cover a portion of their rent in private rental apartments of their choosing. The second-largest HUD program is Section 8 Project-Based Rental Assistance, which served 1.2 million families at a cost of $12 billion in FY 2019. Under Project-Based Rental Assistance, apartment owners receive government subsidies to lease units to low-income families. The third-largest

HUD program is public housing, which served 1.0 million families in FY 2019, at a Federal operating cost of $7 billion (excluding the opportunity cost of holding the property). Public housing is built and managed by government authorities. Unlike with Housing Choice Vouchers, tenants living in units covered by Project-Based Rental Assistance and in public housing do not maintain their subsidy if they move.

Eligibility for these programs is based on a family's income relative to median income in their area. However, only about one in four eligible families actually receives assistance, because housing costs are too high to serve every family that meets the income requirements for the programs, especially in high-cost areas. For example, the maximum payment standard for a three-bedroom unit is more than $4,500 per month in San Francisco County, California, compared with about $1,500 per month in Harris County, Texas. Many areas have waiting lists for assistance that extend multiple years, and in some cases, waiting lists are not reopened for long periods of time.

Housing deregulation that removes excessive barriers and reduces market rents could extend assistance to many eligible families not currently being served in expensive markets. Under each of the three major HUD programs, the government generally covers the difference between 30 percent of a household's adjusted income and the allowable rent or operating cost for housing units. For the voucher program, if market rents decrease, Public Housing Authorities would pay less for contract rent, assuming the tenants' payments remain mostly constant at 30 percent of adjusted income. HUD would also need to pay private property owners less to house people under Project-Based Rental Assistance. These savings from deregulation could be used to serve additional families under current funding amounts.

Removing excessive regulatory barriers could also improve the effectiveness of the Low-Income Housing Tax Credit (LIHTC), a program that subsidizes the developers of affordable housing units. The Federal Government is estimated to spend about $9 billion per year on LIHTC (JCT 2017). Given the budgetary restrictions on how much can be spent on this program, excessive housing regulation increases the costs of building subsidized housing and reduces the amount of it that can built.

Weakened Labor Mobility and Economic Growth

Aside from its specific harm to low-income Americans, excessive regulation in selected housing markets also has negative consequences for the general population. One important example is the reduction in labor mobility across areas because higher home prices in certain areas reduce the incentive to move to places where wages may be higher. This reduces the productivity of workers and shrinks aggregate economic output. Hsieh and Moretti (2019) estimate that reducing housing regulations in New York City, San Jose, and San Francisco to that of the median U.S. city would have substantially increased growth from

1964 to 2009, leading to 3.7 percent higher gross domestic product in 2009. Hsieh and Moretti argue that this missing growth is the result of spatial misallocation of workers, as high-productivity cities construct barriers to increasing housing supply to meet demand from workers. Glaeser and Gyourko (2018) find that restrictive land use regulations reduce national output by a smaller but still important 2 percent. Herkenhoff and others (2018) similarly find significant economic growth effects from relaxing land use restrictions.

Reducing labor mobility has important regional effects in addition to aggregate ones. When home prices are higher due to overregulation, workers are less able to migrate to areas with higher wages. This results in a persistent gap in wages between high-productivity and low-productivity areas that cannot be reduced through migration that would expand the supply of workers in high-wage areas. Zabel (2012) finds that housing prices increase more in response to an increase in labor demand in cities with an inelastic housing supply than in those with a more elastic housing supply, thus reducing the incentive for in-migration to areas with an inelastic housing supply. Saks (2008) similarly finds that more heavily regulated housing markets are less responsive to changes in demand for housing, lowering employment growth in areas with relatively more extensive land use regulations. Saks estimated that the employment response to an increase in labor demand in an area in the 75th percentile of her State regulatory index is 11 percentage points smaller than the response in an area in the 25th percentile.

Ganong and Shoag (2017) find that higher home prices resulting from stringent land use regulation can help explain why disparities between economic regions have grown since 1980, breaking from the previous pattern of regional economic convergence. Hämäläinen and Böckerman (2004) examine migration in Finland and come to a similar conclusion as Ganong and Shoag: high housing prices discourage in-migration.

Even within cities, high levels of land use regulations can increase socioeconomic segregation. Owens (2019) examines segregation between neighborhoods, between places (municipalities, cities, and towns), and between cities and their suburbs and finds that most housing segregation occurs between neighborhoods, rather than between places or between cities and their suburbs, which suggests that zoning regulations could play an important role. Rothwell and Massey (2010) find that restrictive zoning laws lead to greater socioeconomic segregation and reduce interaction between the poor and the affluent. Lens and Monkkonen (2016) find that land-use regulation and income segregation are positively related, with density restrictions leading to a concentration of more affluent households, although not necessarily a concentration of poor households.

Reduced Opportunity for Children

Overregulation of housing markets can also potentially reduce the ability of children to access neighborhoods that advance opportunity. A series of papers by Raj Chetty and his colleagues have identified neighborhoods that are most likely to improve long-term outcomes of children. A child that moves from a neighborhood at the 25th percentile to the 75th percentile of the opportunity index increases his or her lifetime earnings by $206,000. Chetty and others (2018) calculate the "cost of opportunity," and find that an additional $1,000 in children's future annual income costs $190 each year for rent for every year of childhood. The cost of opportunity varies considerably across the United States, however, and much of the variance is due to differences in land use regulatory regimes. An additional $1,000 in future annual income for a child costs only $47 in Wichita but $260 in Boston or Baltimore. Thus, relaxing excessive regulatory barriers to building housing could reduce the cost for families of accessing higher-opportunity neighborhoods for their children and potentially improve their long-term prospects.

Similarly, a report from the U.S. Senate Joint Economic Committee finds that U.S. zip codes with the highest-quality public elementary schools have a median home price that is four times as large as those zip codes with the lowest-quality public schools (JEC 2019). Many of these areas have highly restrictive zoning. Although expanded school choice weakens the association between home prices and the quality of public schools, housing deregulation could potentially promote greater access to high-quality schools for students (JEC 2019).

Increased Traffic Congestion and Harm to the Environment

Finally, excessive regulatory barriers to building housing in certain areas increases commuting times and traffic congestion because sufficient housing cannot be built near where people work. The average commuter spent 54 hours sitting in traffic in 2017, up from 20 hours in 1982 (Schrank, Eisele, and Lomax 2019). The aggregate travel delay increased from 1.8 billion hours to 8.8 billion hours during this period, and the total cost associated with congestion rose from $15 billion to $179 billion.

As a result of this rise in average commuting times, an extra 3.3 billion gallons of fuel were consumed, increasing carbon emissions and harming the environment. Moreover, as Glaeser notes, "when environmentalists resist new construction in their dense but environmentally friendly cities, they inadvertently ensure that it will take place somewhere else—somewhere with higher carbon emissions" (Glaeser 2009). Indeed, Glaeser (2009) finds that households in urban areas emit less carbon than those in the suburbs, even after adjusting for differences in climate and environmental regulation across these areas. Factors contributing to fewer emissions in cities include smaller housing units and that people are less likely to drive or would drive shorter distances than

Box 8-2. Poor Substitutes for Regulatory Reform

Policymakers have proposed a litany of policies aside from regulatory reform to lower rents or incentivize affordable housing construction in high-cost areas. However, these proposals alone—such as rent control, increases in rental housing assistance, and so-called inclusionary zoning—are unlikely to have their intended effects on rents or construction, and in some cases may be counterproductive.

Rent controls, or policies that limit rent increases for certain rental units, are sometimes offered as a means of addressing high housing costs. Though existing tenants in rent-controlled units may benefit from smaller rent increases, supply is reduced for new potential tenants and the incentive for developers to build more units is diminished. There are few issues where economists are in as much as agreement as they are regarding the outcomes of rent control. In a 2012 University of Chicago Booth poll of economists across the political spectrum, 95 percent disagreed that rent control ordinances, such as those imposed in New York and San Francisco, had boosted affordable housing or improved the quality of rental units (IGM 2012).

The economists' consensus is supported not only by economic theory but also by the empirical literature. In a recent paper examining the effect of a 1994 rent control law on housing supply and prices in San Francisco, Diamond, McQuade, and Qian (2019) find that the law had the opposite of its intended effect on rents. While those living in rent-controlled units benefit from lower rents, and remain in these units longer than they would without rent control, those who do not have access to these units are substantially harmed in the long run. Landlords responded to the law by converting existing buildings into condominiums and by taking other steps to avoid being subject to rent control laws. This *lowered* the supply of rental housing by 15 percent and incentivized the creation of housing that served the preferences of high-income households. As a result, this rent control law likely raised rents in the long run rather than lowering them. Moreover, even existing tenants who benefit from rent control may suffer from unintended consequences. Jiang (2019) finds that rent control increases unemployment among tenants in New York City, potentially because they can sustain longer bouts of joblessness given their lower housing costs, or because tenants are tied to a particular housing unit and restrict their job search to opportunities nearby.

Expansions of government housing programs to combat rising rents are also unlikely to provide much relief to the general population of residents in supply-constrained areas. When the supply of housing is inelastic, expanding demand by increasing government subsidies increases prices rather than quantities. As a result, government rental subsidies to low income-renters will likely increase rents in markets with overly restrictive housing regulations. Eriksen and Ross (2015) find that housing vouchers increased rents for housing within 20 percent of the Fair Market Rent threshold in supply-constrained communities. They estimate that a 10 percent increase in the number of vouchers increased rents by 0.39 percent for these units. LIHTC, a program that subsidizes developers of below market-rate rental housing units, may also be ineffective at addressing the underlying supply problem according to some evidence. Eriksen and Rosenthal (2010) find that new LIHTC development largely crowds out private development, leaving total housing supply unchanged. Glaeser and Gyourko (2008) note that the credit tends to increase the profits of subsidized builders, while pushing unsubsidized builders out of the housing market.

Regulations that require a certain share of housing units to be set aside for low-income residents, often referred to as "inclusionary zoning," also fail to solve the affordable housing problem. For example, Schuetz, Meltzer, and Been (2011) find that inclusionary zoning can increase home prices and in some cases reduce housing development. Hamilton (2019), in a study of Washington and Baltimore, similarly finds that inclusionary zoning increases prices.

they would if they lived in the suburbs. As discussed in box 8-2, regulatory reform—rather than rent control, expansion of government programs, or inclusionary zoning—offers the most effective solution to the problems posed by high housing costs and overregulation.

Conclusion

How to increase housing affordability through regulatory reform is an issue that has garnered bipartisan attention in recent years. In this chapter, we have focused on excessive regulations that substantially drive up home prices in a selected number of metropolitan areas. Relaxing these regulations would greatly benefit Americans, especially those with lower incomes, by reducing the cost of attaining homeownership and reducing rents in supply-constrained areas. Falling rents resulting from relaxing excessive regulations would reduce homelessness by 31 percent on average in these areas, and more families could be served by Federal rental housing assistance programs. Broader benefits would include increased economic growth, reduced regional disparities, expanded opportunities for children, and a cleaner environment.

We have also emphasized that addressing the problem of overregulation with more regulation would be counterproductive. Rent control can increase housing prices by reducing the incentive for developers to build new housing. Similarly, expanded government subsidies for housing do not solve the problem of overregulation. When housing supply is constrained, housing subsidies for tenants may increase market rents without increasing the quantity of housing, counteracting the goals of these programs.

The Trump Administration has taken steps to address onerous housing regulations. President Trump issued an Executive Order in 2019 to establish the White House Council on Eliminating Regulatory Barriers to Affordable Housing, which is tasked with reviewing housing regulations at all levels of government and submitting a report to the President in 2020 with recommendations on how to ameliorate these excessive regulatory burdens.

HUD has also taken action under the Trump Administration to counter regulatory barriers to building affordable housing. The Affirmatively Furthering Fair Housing rule, which was finalized during the previous Administration, is being revised to focus more clearly on increasing housing supply in areas where supply is constrained. This rule recognizes that increasing housing choice for disadvantaged groups requires taking on regulatory barriers that place housing in large swaths of specific areas out of reach for lower-income families.

Part III

The Economic Outlook

Chapter 9

The Outlook for a Continued Expansion

As this *Report* has shown, under the Trump Administration, economic growth and the labor market gains it enables have exceeded pre-2017 expectations. The U.S. economy's performance has withstood strong headwinds from a weak global economy and several idiosyncratic domestic shocks, as pro-growth policies have kept the U.S. economy resilient.

By increasing competition, productivity, and wages, and reducing the prices of consumer goods and services, the Administration's approach to regulation is raising real incomes while maintaining regulatory protections for workers, public health, safety, and the environment. Specifically, the Administration's approach to eliminating excessive regulation of energy markets supports further unleashing of the country's abundant human and energy resources. Furthermore, the Administration's healthcare reforms are building a system that delivers high-quality care at affordable prices through greater choice and competition. Across the board, this pro-growth agenda has disproportionately benefited those previously left behind during the current expansion.

To further expand the economy and extend the longest expansion in U.S. history, additional policy issues may need to be addressed. This challenge is why the Trump Administration remains focused on promoting competitive markets, combating the opioid crisis, promoting affordable housing, enacting a comprehensive infrastructure plan, rendering the individual provisions of the 2017 Tax Cuts and Jobs Act permanent, updating the U.S. immigration system, continuing deregulatory actions, improving trade agreements and international trade practices, and incentivizing higher labor force participation through additional labor market reforms.

Overall, assuming full implementation of the Trump Administration's economic policy agenda, we project real U.S. economic output to grow at an average annual rate of 2.9 percent over the budget window from 2019 to 2030. During that time, inflation is expected to settle at a 2.0 percent fourth-quarter-over-fourth-quarter rate, and the unemployment rate is expected to remain at or below an annual average rate of 4.0 percent. Relative to the current-law baseline projection, we estimate that full policy implementation of the Administration's economic agenda would cumulatively raise output by 4.3 percent over this budget window.

The first three years of the Trump Administration show that long-lamented structural trends that were constraining potential growth in the United States are not policy-invariant. The right pro-growth policies attract greater investment, encourage more people to enter the labor market, and lead to higher wages from businesses investing in and competing for workers. Even with recent success, there is ample room for the U.S. economy to expand, especially if the Administration's approach to international trade produces results that are greater than expected.

Since 1975, the Council of Economic Advisers, in collaboration with the Office of Management and Budget and the U.S. Department of the Treasury, has published a long-run forecast for the U.S. economy that assumes full enactment and implementation of the Administration's economic policy agenda. This reflects the Council's mandate, as stipulated in the Employment Act of 1946, to set forth in the *Economic Report of the President* "current and foreseeable trends in the levels of employment, production, and purchasing power," and a program for carrying out the objective of "creating and maintaining . . . conditions under which there will be afforded useful employment opportunities, including self-employment, for those able, willing, and seeking to work, and to promote maximum employment, production, and purchasing power." Since 1996, execution of this mandate has involved providing an 11-year, policy-inclusive economic forecast.

Because of this charge, the Administration's forecast is historically unique from other long-run economic forecasts, both official and private. The Congressional Budget Office, for example, publishes a current-law forecast, which assumes no change in economic policy (CBO 2019). The Blue Chip panel of professional private sector forecasters often reveals substantial heterogeneity in expectations, reflecting both different estimates of economic potential under current law, as well as objective and subjective estimations of the probability of policy implementation. Although the assumptions underlying projections of the Federal Open Market Committee are ambiguous, those forecasts presumably also reflect committee members' differing views both on potential growth under current law, as well as potential growth under possible future law.

To better distinguish the estimated effects of the Administration's economic policy objectives—the results of which may be contingent on legislative support and other factors—from current-law projections, beginning with the 2018 *Economic Report of the President* and continuing through this *Report*, we have decomposed this forecast into a current-law baseline and intermediate and top lines that reflect estimated growth effects discussed in this *Report*, as well as in the 2018 and 2019 *Reports* and the President's Fiscal Year 2021 Budget. We then build up to our top-line, policy-inclusive forecast by successively adding to the current-law baseline the estimated effects of future deregulatory actions, immigration reform, additional labor market reforms to incentivize higher labor force participation, rendering the individual provisions of the Tax Cuts and Jobs Act (TCJA) permanent, additional fiscal policy proposals, including the Administration's infrastructure plan, and improved trade deals with international trading partners. The top-line forecast constitutes the Administration's official "Troika" forecast of the Council of Economic Advisers, Office of Management and Budget, and Department of Treasury. For comparison, we also report a pre-policy baseline consisting of the Congressional Budget Office's 2019–27 projection made in August 2016, extended by its August 2019 current-law projection.

GDP Growth during the Next Three Years

As illustrated in figure 9-1 and reported in the third column ("real GDP") of table 9-1, the Administration anticipates economic growth to rise in 2020 from its projected 2019 pace of 2.5 percent, and to remain at or above 3.0 percent through 2022, assuming full implementation of the economic agenda detailed in this *Report*, its two predecessors, and the President's Fiscal Year 2021 Budget. We expect near-term growth to be supported by the continuing effects of the TCJA, as well as new measures to promote increased labor force participation, deregulatory actions, immigration reform, reciprocal trade deals,

Figure 9-1. Forecast of Growth Rate in Real GDP, 2019–30

- Aug. 2016 CBO forecast, 2019–26
- Aug. 2019 CBO forecast, 2027–29
- Current-law forecast
- + Labor market and deregulation policies
- + Fiscal and trade policies

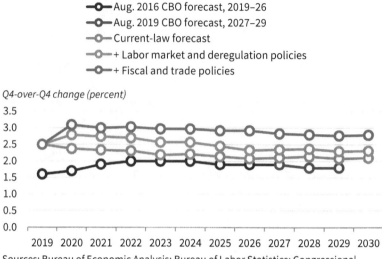

Q4-over-Q4 change (percent)

Sources: Bureau of Economic Analysis; Bureau of Labor Statistics; Congressional Budget Office; Department of the Treasury; Office of Management and Budget; CEA calculations.

Note: The current-law forecast is based on data available as of October 31, 2019.

and an infrastructure program, which we assume will commence in 2020 with observable effects on output beginning in 2021.

The Administration also expects the labor market to continue to exhibit strength in the near term, with the civilian unemployment rate remaining below 4.0 percent through 2022, as reported in the sixth column, "unemployment rate," of table 9-1. Despite low unemployment, inflation is expected to remain low and close to the Federal Reserve Board's 2.0 percent target for the Personal Consumption Expenditures Price Index. The Administration expects broad inflation beyond 2019 to remain stable at 2.0 percent through 2022, as shown in the fourth column ("GDP price index") of table 9-1.

GDP Growth over the Longer Term

As discussed in the 2018 and 2019 volumes of the *Economic Report of the President*, over the longer term, the Administration's current-law baseline forecast is for output growth to moderate as the capital-to-output ratio asymptotically approaches a higher steady state level in response to corporate tax reform, and as the near-term effects of the TCJA's individual provisions on the rate of growth dissipate into a permanent level effect. As reflected by our intermediate forecast, we expect the latter moderation would be partially offset in

Table 9-1. The Administration's Economic Forecast, 2018–30

Year	Percent change (Q4-to-Q4)				Level (calendar year average)		
	Nominal GDP	Real GDP (chain-type)	GDP price index (chain-type)	Consumer price index	Unemployment rate (percent)	Interest rate, 91-day Treasury bills (percent)	Interest rate, 10-year Treasury notes (percent)
2018 (Actual)	4.9	2.5	2.3	2.2	3.9	1.9	2.9
2019	4.2	2.5	1.8	1.9	3.7	2.1	2.2
2020	5.2	3.1	2.0	2.3	3.5	1.4	2.0
2021	5.1	3.0	2.0	2.3	3.6	1.5	2.2
2022	5.1	3.0	2.0	2.3	3.8	1.5	2.5
2023	5.1	3.0	2.0	2.3	4.0	1.6	2.7
2024	5.1	3.0	2.0	2.3	4.0	1.7	3.0
2025	5.0	2.9	2.0	2.3	4.0	2.0	3.1
2026	4.9	2.8	2.0	2.3	4.0	2.2	3.1
2027	4.9	2.8	2.0	2.3	4.0	2.4	3.1
2028	4.9	2.8	2.0	2.3	4.0	2.5	3.1
2029	4.9	2.8	2.0	2.3	4.0	2.5	3.2
2030	4.9	2.8	2.0	2.3	4.0	2.5	3.2

Sources: Bureau of Economic Analysis; Bureau of Labor Statistics; Department of the Treasury; Office of Management and Budget; CEA calculations.
Note: This forecast was based on data available as of October 31, 2019. The interest rate on 91-day T-bills is measured on a secondary-market discount basis. Nominal GDP and the sum of real GDP and the GDP price index may differ slightly due to rounding.

2026 and 2027 if the individual provisions of the TCJA—currently legislated to expire on December 31, 2025—were instead made permanent.

The Administration's full policy-inclusive forecast is reported as the green line in figure 9-1. In addition to successful implementation of the President's infrastructure plan and extension of the individual provisions of the TCJA, this forecast assumes full achievement of the Administration's agenda with respect to deregulation, immigration, improved trade agreements, fiscal consolidation, and labor market policies designed to incentivize higher labor force participation. The latter includes expanding work requirements for nondisabled, working-age welfare recipients in noncash welfare programs; increasing child-care assistance for low-income families; and enhancing assistance for reskilling programs through the National Council for the American Worker.

Though we anticipate growth moderating toward the end of the budget window, to 2.8 percent on average between 2019 and 2030, the policy-inclusive forecast is for output to grow at an average annual rate of 2.9 percent. Relative to the current-law baseline, we estimate that full policy implementation would cumulatively raise the level of output by 4.3 percent over the budget window. Reflecting moderating growth in the latter half of the budget window, the Administration expects unemployment to converge to 4.0 percent, consistent

Table 9-2. Supply-Side Components of Actual and Potential Real Output Growth, 1953–2030

	Component	Growth rate (percentage points)	
		1953:Q2 to 2019:Q3	2019 to 2030
1	Civilian noninstitutional population age 16+	1.4	0.9
2	Labor force participation rate	0.1	−0.2
3	Employed share of the labor force	0.0	0.0
4	Ratio of nonfarm business employment to household employment	0.0	0.0
5	Average weekly hours (nonfarm business)	−0.2	0.1
6	Output per hour (productivity, nonfarm business)	2.0	2.6
7	Ratio of real GDO to nonfarm business output	−0.3	−0.5
8	Sum: Actual real GDO[a]	3.0	3.0
	Memo:		
9	Potential real GDO	3.0	3.0
10	Output per worker differential: GDO vs. nonfarm	−0.3	−0.4

[a] Real GDO and real nonfarm business output are measured as the average of income- and product-side measures.
Sources: Bureau of Labor Statistics; Bureau of Economic Analysis; Department of the Treasury; Office of Management and Budget; CEA calculations.
Note: All contributions are in percentage points at an annual rate, forecast finalized November 1, 2019. Total may not add up due to rounding. The quarter 1953:Q2 was a business-cycle peak; 2019:Q3 is the latest quarter with available data. Gross domestic output (GDO) is the average of GDP and gross domestic income. Population, labor force, and household employment have been adjusted for discontinuities in the population series.

with the Federal Open Market Committee's December 2019 "Summary of Economic Projections," which reports a range of participant estimates from 3.9 to 4.3 percent (Federal Reserve 2019). The unemployment rate rising to 4.0 percent is also expected to maintain a rate of inflation of 2.0 percent, as measured by the GDP chained price index (see the fourth column of table 9-1).

As shown in table 9-2, the Administration anticipates that the primary contributor to increased growth through 2029 will be higher output per hour worked. During much of the current expansion, U.S. labor productivity growth was disappointing by historical standards, partly due to low contributions of capital deepening. By substantially raising the capital stock and consequent flows of capital services, attracting increased net capital inflows—including investment both by foreign firms and overseas affiliates of U.S. multinational enterprises—and facilitating efficient capital reallocation from mature firms to more dynamic enterprises, we expect enactment of corporate tax reform to considerably increase capital per worker, and thus labor productivity. Already, during the first seven quarters since the TCJA was enacted, labor productivity growth in the nonfarm business sector rose substantially relative to its pre-TCJA, postrecession average, as reported in chapter 1 of this *Report*. If fully implemented, we also expect the Administration's labor market reforms to partially offset the effects of demographic-related trends in labor force participation, as reflected in line 2 of table 9-2.

Upside and Downside Forecast Risks

Since the Administration's forecast is a policy-inclusive one, a key downside risk is the political contingency of full implementation of the President's economic agenda, particularly in light of the inherent unpredictability of the legislative process. In addition, by definition the policy-inclusive forecast assumes that the Administration's policies will be implemented and remain in place throughout the forecast window. In scenarios where future Administrations or Congress partially or fully reverse the TCJA, otherwise raise taxes, or significantly expand the Federal regulatory state, economic growth would be lower or even negative. For example, the 2019 *Economic Report of the President* estimated that "Medicare for All" bills then discussed in Congress would reduce real GDP by about 9 percent in the long run if financed by taxes on labor income, while recent proposals to introduce a top marginal income tax rate of 70 percent on personal income over $10 million would lower the long-run level of GDP by 0.2 percent.

As observed in the 2019 *Report* and discussed in chapter 1 of this *Report*, a sharp slowdown in the global economy also poses a significant downside risk to the outlook, through both direct and indirect channels. In particular, continued or worsening weakness in other advanced economies—particularly Germany and Italy, but also Europe more broadly, in the event of Brexit-related disruptions—would have an adverse impact on U.S. growth through both a direct export channel and indirect exchange rate, financial market, and supply chain channels. A significant growth slowdown in the People's Republic of China, similar to that observed in the years 2015–16, would also introduce substantial risks to the outlooks for advanced economies, including the United States. High public debt levels in several advanced and emerging economies may generate economic headwinds, while high corporate debt levels in the United States could act as an accelerant to potential adverse financial shocks.

Idiosyncratic shocks also pose risks to the outlook. In 2019, these included but were not limited to production cuts at Boeing—whose production accounts for 0.23 percent of U.S. GDP—a partial government shutdown in the first quarter, and industrial action at General Motors. As this *Report* was being finalized, Boeing announced plans to halt production of the 737 MAX, a development that could subtract 0.5 percent from annualized real GDP growth in the first quarter of 2020.

Perhaps the single biggest upside risk to the outlook is that the Administration's more robust approach to international trade achieves greater-than-expected success in its pursuit of freer, fairer trade, with zero tariffs, zero nontariff barriers, and zero subsidies. Recent research by the Organization for Economic Cooperation and Development (Cadot, Gourdon, and van Tongeren 2018; Lamprecht and Miroudot 2018; OECD 2018) finds that lowering international tariff and nontariff barriers to trade, as well as reducing international restrictiveness on trade in services, would substantially raise U.S. and global trade and output. With investment in intellectual property products now accounting for about one-third of U.S. private nonresidential fixed investment, trade agreements that enhance international protection of intellectual property—such as the United States–Mexico–Canada Agreement and Phase I of U.S.-China negotiations—could also elevate the level of innovation and productivity growth.

Additional upside risks to the forecast include, first, higher net capital inflows due to international capital mobility exceeding estimates, which would attenuate the potential crowding out of private fixed investment in response to individual tax reform and public infrastructure investment. Second, academic studies demonstrating that individual marginal income tax rates may have differential effects across the age distribution suggest that estimated trends in labor force participation may overstate the growth-detracting effect of demography. Third, insofar as the growth estimates presented in this *Report* and its predecessor have been derived from standard neoclassical growth models, they may omit the positive externalities and spillover effects captured by endogenous growth models, such as that of Ehrlich, Li, and Liu (2017). Tax reform that incentivizes investment in human capital, regulatory reform that eliminates prohibitive barriers to entry for more innovative and entrepreneurial firms, and health investments and labor market policies that facilitate human capital accumulation may, therefore, yield higher-growth dividends than those estimated here.

References

Chapter 1

Amiti, M., S. Redding, and D. Weinstein. 2019a. "The Impact of the 2018 Trade War on U.S. Prices and Welfare." CEP Discussion Paper dp1603.

———. 2019b. "New China Tariffs Increase Cost to U.S. Households." Liberty Street Economics. https://libertystreeteconomics.newyorkfed.org/2019/05/new-china-tariffs-increase-costs-to-us-households.html.

BIS (Bank for International Settlements). 2019a. "Annual Economic Report." https://www.bis.org/publ/arpdf/ar2019e.htm.

———. 2019b. "BIS Quarterly Review: International Banking and Financial Market Developments." https://www.bis.org/publ/qtrpdf/r_qt1909.htm.

Caldara, D., M. Iacoviello, P. Molligo, A. Prestipino, and A. Raffo. 2019. "Does Trade Policy Uncertainty Affect Global Economic Activity?" *FEDS Notes*. Washington: Board of Governors of the Federal Reserve System.

CEA (Council of Economic Advisers). 2017. *Economic Report of the President*. Washington: U.S. Government Publishing Office.

———. 2018. *Economic Report of the President*. Washington: U.S. Government Publishing Office.

———. 2019a. "The Economic Effects of Federal Deregulation since January 2017: An Interim Report." https://www.whitehouse.gov/wp-content/uploads/2019/06/The-Economic-Effects-of-Federal-Deregulation-Interim-Report.pdf.

———. 2019b. *Economic Report of the President*. Washington: U.S. Government Publishing Office.

Collins, C., and E. Truman. 2019. "The U.S. Dollar's Strength Is Not at Historical Highs." Peterson Institute for International Economics. https://www.piie.com/research/piie-charts/us-dollars-strength-not-historical-highs.

Curcuru, S. 2017. "The Sensitivity of the U.S. Dollar Exchange Rate to Changes in Monetary Policy Expectations." *IFDP Notes*. Washington: Board of Governors of the Federal Reserve System. https://doi.org/10.17016/2573-2129.36.

Deutsche Bundesbank. 2019. "Monthly Report: October 2019." https://www.bundesbank.de/resource/blob/811960/a0bf7575c07b3754dda37ec6739d4b13/mL/2019-10-monatsbericht-data.pdf.

Diebold, F., and G. Rudebusch. 1990. "A Nonparametric Investigation of Duration Dependence in the American Business Cycle." *Journal of Political Economy* 98, no. 3.

Fajgelbaum, P., P. Goldberg, P. Kennedy, and A. Khandelwal. 2019. *The Return to Protectionism*. NBER Working Paper 25638. Cambridge, MA: National Bureau of Economic Research.

Green, G., and J. Coder. 2019. "Household Income Trends." Sentier Research LLC.

Hansen, A. 1939. "Economic Progress and Declining Population Growth." *American Economic Review* 29, no. 1: 1–15.

Hooper, P., F. Mishkin, and A. Sufi, 2019. *Prospect for Inflation in a High Pressure Economy: Is the Phillips Curve Dead or Is It Just Hibernating?* NBER Working Paper 25792. Cambridge, MA: National Bureau of Economic Research.

IMF (International Monetary Fund). 2018. *World Economic Outlook: Challenges to Steady Growth*. Washington: IMF.

———. 2019a. "People's Republic of China. 2019 Article IV Consultation—Press Release; Staff Report; Staff Statement; and Statement by the Executive Director for China." IMF Country Report 19/266. Washington: IMF.

———. 2019b. "Germany: 2019 Article IV Consultation—Press Release; Staff Report; and Statement by the Executive Director for Germany." IMF Country Report 19/213. Washington: IMF.

———. 2019c. *World Economic Outlook: Global Manufacturing Downturn, Rising Trade Barriers*. Washington: IMF.

———. 2019d. "United States: 2019 Article IV Consultation—Press Release; Staff Report; and Statement by the Executive Director for the United States." IMF Country Report 19/174. Washington: IMF.

Kopp, E., D. Leigh, S. Mursula, and S. Tambunlertchai. 2019. *U.S. Investment since the Tax Cuts and Jobs Act of 2017*. IMF Working Paper 19/120. Washington: IMF.

Lettau, M., and S. Ludvigson. 2003. *Understanding Trend and Cycle in Asset Values: Reevaluating the Wealth Effect on Consumption*. NBER Working Paper 9848. Cambridge, MA: National Bureau of Economic Research.

Londono, J., S. Ma, and B. Wilson. 2019. "Quantifying the Impact of Foreign Economic Uncertainty on the U.S. Economy." *FEDS Notes*. Washington: Board of Governors of the Federal Reserve System. https://doi.org/10.17016/2380-7172.2463.

Mertens, K. 2018. "The Near Term Growth Impact of the Tax Cuts and Jobs Act." Federal Reserve Bank of Dallas Working Paper 1803. https://doi.org/10.24149/wp1803.

OECD (Organization for Economic Cooperation and Development). 2019a. *OECD Economic Outlook, Volume 2019, Issue 2*. Paris: OECD Publishing.

———. 2019b. "Trade Simulations in the Car Sector." Presentation given at STEP Meeting, October 22.

Poterba, J. 2000. "Stock Market Wealth and Consumption." *Journal of Economic Perspectives* 14, no. 2.

Rachel, L., and L. Summers. 2019. "On Falling Neutral Real Rates, Fiscal Policy, and the Risk of Secular Stagnation." *Brookings Papers on Economic Activity*, conference draft, spring.

Rubbo, E. 2020. "Networks, Phillips Curves, and Monetary Policy." Working paper. https://scholar.harvard.edu/files/elisarubbo/files/rubbo_jmp.pdf.

Rudebusch, G. 2016. "Will the Economic Recovery Die of Old Age?" Economic Letter. San Francisco: Federal Reserve Bank of San Francisco.

Summers, L. 2013. "IMF Fourteenth Annual Research Conference in Honor of Stanley Fischer." http://larrysummers.com/ imf-fourteenth-annual-research-conference-in-honor-of-stanley-fischer/.

———. 2014. "U.S. Economic Prospects: Secular Stagnation, Hysteresis, and the Zero Lower Bound." *Business Economics* 49, no. 2: 65–73.

———. 2016. "The Age of Secular Stagnation." *Foreign Affairs*, February 17. http://larrysummers.com/2016/02/17/the-age-of-secular-stagnation/.

White House. 2018. "Statement from the Press Secretary Regarding the President's Working Dinner with China" https://www.whitehouse.gov/briefings-statements/ statement-press-secretary-regarding-presidents-working-dinner-china/.

World Bank. 2019a. *Global Economic Prospects: Heightened Tensions, Subdued Investment*. Washington: World Bank. https://elibrary.worldbank.org/doi/abs/10.1596/978-1-4648-1398-6.

———. 2019b. *Global Monthly: October 2019*. Washington: World Bank.

WTO (World Trade Organization). 2016. *World Trade Report 2016: Levelling the Trading Field for SMEs*. Geneva: WTO Publishing.

Chapter 2

Aizer, A. 2007. "Public Health Insurance, Program Take-Up, and Child Health." *Review of Economics and Statistics* 89, no. 3: 400–415.

Barnett, J., and E. Berchick. 2017. "Health Insurance Coverage in the United States: 2016." U.S. Census Bureau. https://www.census.gov/library/ publications/2017/demo/p60-260.html.

Berchick, E., E. Hood, and J. Barnett. 2018. "Health Insurance Coverage in the United States: 2017." U.S. Census Bureau. https://www.census.gov/library/ publications/2018/demo/p60-264.html.

Bernstein, J., and K. Hassett. 2015. *Unlocking Private Capital to Facilitate Economic Growth in Distressed Areas*. Washington: Economic Innovation Group.

Blau, F., and L. Kahn. 2013. *Female Labor Supply: Why is the U.S. Falling Behind?* NBER Working Paper 18702. Cambridge, MA: National Bureau of Economic Research.

Burkhauser, R., K. Corinth, J. Elwell, and J. Larrimore. 2019. "Evaluating the Success of President Johnson's War on Poverty: Revisiting the Historical Record Using a Full-Income Poverty Measure." Working paper. https://papers.ssrn.com/sol3/papers.cfm?abstract_id=3353906.

Canberra Group. 2011. *Handbook on Household on Household Income Statistics*, 2nd ed. Geneva: United Nations Economic Commission for Europe.

Casey, A. 2019. "Sale Prices Surge in Neighborhoods with New Tax Break." Zillow. https://www.zillow.com/research/prices-surge-opportunity-zones-23393/.

CBO (U.S. Congressional Budget Office). 2016. *An Update to the Budget and Economic Outlook: 2016 to 2026.* https://www.cbo.gov/sites/default/files/recurringdata/51135-2016-08-economicprojections-2.xlsx.

———. 2019. "Federal Subsidies for Health Insurance Coverage for People Under Age 65: 2019 to 2029." https://www.cbo.gov/system/files/2019-05/55085-HealthCoverageSubsidies_0.pdf.

CDFI Fund (U.S. Department of the Treasury, Community Development Financial Institutions Fund). 2017. "Compliance Review of New Markets Tax Credit Program." https://www.cdfifund.gov/Documents/Summit%20-%20Compliance%20Review%20of%20New%20Markets%20Tax%20Credit%20Program%20-%20August%20Date%20-%20508%20Compliant.pdf.

———. 2018. "Opportunity Zones Resources." https://www.cdfifund.gov/Pages/Opportunity-Zones.aspx.

———. 2019. "New Markets Tax Credit Program Compliance Monitoring: Frequently Asked Questions." https://www.cdfifund.gov/programs-training/Programs/new-markets-tax-credit/Pages/compliance-step.aspx#step5.

CEA (Council of Economic Advisers). 2018a. "Addressing America's Reskilling Challenge." https://www.whitehouse.gov/wp-content/uploads/2018/07/Addressing-Americas-Reskilling-Challenge.pdf.

———. 2018b. "Deregulating Health Insurance Markets: Value to Market Participants." https://www.whitehouse.gov/wp-content/uploads/2019/02/Deregulating-Health-Insurance-Markets-FINAL.pdf.

———. 2018c. *Economic Report of the President.* Washington: U.S. Government Publishing Office.

———. 2019a. *Economic Report of the President.* Washington, U.S. Government Publishing Office.

———. 2019b. "President Trump's Policies Continue to Benefit All Americans, Especially the Disadvantaged." https://www.whitehouse.gov/articles/president-trumps-policies-continue-benefit-americans-especially-disadvantaged/.

———. 2019c. "Economic Effects of Deregulation." https://www.whitehouse.gov/wp-content/uploads/2019/06/The-Economic-Effects-of-Federal-Deregulation-Interim-Report.pdf.

———. 2019d. "Government Employment and Training Programs: Assessing the Evidence on Their Performance." https://www.whitehouse.gov/wp-content/uploads/2019/06/Government-Employment-and-Training-Programs.pdf.

———. 2019e. "The Role of Affordable Child Care in Promoting Work Outside the Home." https://www.whitehouse.gov/wp-content/uploads/2019/12/The-Role-of-Affordable-Child-Care-in-Promoting-Work-Outside-the-Home-1.pdf.

———. 2019f. "The Full Cost of the Opioid Crisis: $2.5 Trillion Over Four Years." https://www.whitehouse.gov/articles/full-cost-opioid-crisis-2-5-trillion-four-years/.

Crespo-Sancho, C. 2018. "Can Gender Equality Prevent Violent Conflict?" The World Bank Blogs, March 28. http://blogs.worldbank.org/dev4peace/can-gender-equality-prevent-violent-conflict.

CRS (Congressional Research Service). 2019. "New Market Tax Credit: An Introduction." https://fas.org/sgp/crs/misc/RL34402.pdf.

Dev Bhardwaj, R. 1992. "China's Economic Reform: The Role and Significance of SEZs." *Indian Journal of Political Science* 53, no. 3: 332–73.

Elwell, J., K. Corinth, and R. Burkhauser. 2019. *Income Growth and Its Distribution from Eisenhower to Obama: The Growing Importance of In-Kind Transfers (1959–2016)*. NBER Working Paper 26439. Cambridge, MA: National Bureau of Economic Research.

Fein, D., and J. Hamadyk. 2018. *Bridging the Opportunity Divide for Low-Income Youth: Implementation and Early Impacts of the Year Up Program*. OPRE Report 2018-65. Washington: Office of Planning, Research, and Evaluation, Administration for Children and Families, U.S. Department of Health and Human Services. https://www.yearup.org/wp-content/uploads/2018/06/Year-Up-PACE-Full-Report-2018.pdf.

Ferrant, G., and A. Thim. 2019. *Measuring Women's Economic Empowerment: Time Use Data and Gender Inequality*. OECD Development Policy Paper 16. Paris: OECD Publishing. http://www.oecd.org/dev/development-gender/MEASURING-WOMENS-ECONOMIC-EMPOWERMENT-Gender-Policy-Paper-No-16.pdf.

FOMC (Federal Open Market Committee). 2016. "Chair FOMC's Press Conference Projections Materials, September 21, 2016." Press release, September 21. https://www.federalreserve.gov/monetarypolicy/files/fomcprojtabl20160921.pdf.

Food and Nutrition Service. 2019a. "Food Security in the U.S.: Key Statistics & Graphics." U.S. Department of Agriculture. https://www.ers.usda.gov/topics/food-nutrition-assistance/food-security-in-the-us/key-statistics-graphics/.

———. 2019b. "SNAP Data Tables." U.S. Department of Agriculture. https://www.fns.usda.gov/pd/supplemental-nutrition-assistance-program-snap.

Fry, R. 2018. "Millennials Projected to Overtake Baby Boomers as America's Largest Generation." Pew Research Service. https://www.pewresearch.org/fact-tank/2018/03/01/millennials-overtake-baby-boomers/.

FTC (Federal Trade Commission). 2018. "Policy Perspectives: Options to Enhance Occupational License Portability." https://www.ftc.gov/reports/options-enhance-occupational-license-portability.

Ganong, P., and D. Shoag. 2017. "Why Has Regional Income Convergence in the U.S. Declined?" *Journal of Urban Economics* 102: 76–90.

Goodnough, A., and M. Sanger-Katz. 2019. "Medicaid Covers a Million Fewer Children. Baby Elijah Was One of Them." *New York Times,* Upshot Blog, October 22. https://www.nytimes.com/2019/10/22/upshot/medicaid-uninsured-children.html.

Guo, J., A. Seshadri, and C. Taber. 2019. *Jobs, Skills, and the Prison-to-Work Transition.* Madison: Center for Research on the Wisconsin Economy.

Hendra, R., D. Greenberg, G. Hamilton, A. Oppenheim, A. Pennington, K. Schaberg, and B. Tessler. 2016. "Encouraging Evidence on a Sector-Focused Advancement Strategy." MDRC. https://www.mdrc.org/sites/default/files/2016_Workadvance_Final_Web.pdf.

Johnson, J., and M. Kleiner. 2017. *Is Occupational Licensing a Barrier to Interstate Migration?* NBER Working Paper 24107. Cambridge, MA: National Bureau of Economic Research.

Krueger, A. 2017. "Where Have All the Workers Gone? An Inquiry into the Decline of the U.S. Labor Force Participation Rate." Washington: Brookings Institution. https://www.brookings.edu/wp-content/uploads/2017/09/1_krueger.pdf.

Levinson, A. 2019. "Energy Efficiency Standards Are More Regressive Than Energy Taxes: Theory and Evidence." *Journal of the Association of Environmental and Resource Economists* 6, no. S1: S7–S36.

Maguire S., J. Freely, C. Clymer, M. Conway, and D. Schwartz. 2010. "Tuning In to Local Labor Markets: Findings from the Sectoral Employment Impact Study." Public/Private Ventures.

Meyer, B., W. Mok, and J. Sullivan. 2015. "Household Surveys in Crisis." *Journal of Economic Perspectives* 29, no. 4: 199–226.

Meyer, J. 2017. *How Occupational Licensing Inhibits Economic Opportunity.* Naples, FL: Foundation for Government Accountability. https://thefga.org/wp-content/uploads/2017/10/How-Occupational-Licensing-Inhibits-Economic-Opportunity-10-23-17.pdf.

NCSHA (National Council of State Housing Agencies). 2019. "Opportunity Zone Target Investment Surges to Nearly $43 Billion Nationwide." https://www.cdfifund.gov/Documents/Summit%20-%20Compliance%20Review%20of%20New%20Markets%20Tax%20Credit%20Program%20-%20August%20Date%20-%20508%20Compliant.pdf.

Nunn, R., J. Parsons, and J. Shambaugh. 2018. "The Geography of Prosperity." In *Place-Based Policies for Shared Economic Growth*, edited by J. Shambaugh and R. Nunn. Washington: Brookings Institution. Office of Family Assistance. 2019. "TANF Caseload Data 2018." U.S. Department of Health and Human Services. https://www.acf.hhs.gov/ofa/resource/tanf-caseload-data-2018.

Real Capital Analytics. "U.S. Opportunity Zones: A Baseline." https://www.rcanalytics.com/opportunity-zones-baseline/

Roder, A., and M. Elliot. 2019. "Nine Year Gains: Project QUEST's Continuing Impact." Economic Mobility Corporation. https://economicmobilitycorp.org/wp-content/uploads/2019/04/NineYearGains_web.pdf.

Sage, A., M. Langen, and A. Van de Minne. 2019. "Where Is the Opportunity in Opportunity Zones? Early Indicators of the Opportunity Zone Program's Impact on Commercial Property Prices." https://papers.ssrn.com/sol3/papers.cfm?abstract_id=3385502.

Schnepel, K. 2016. "Good Jobs and Recidivism." *Economic Journal* 128: 447–69.

Szafran, R. 2002. "Age-Adjusted Labor Force Participation Rates, 1960–2045." *Monthly Labor Review* 125: 25–38.

U.S. Census Bureau. 2019. "Income and Poverty in the United States: 2018." https://www.census.gov/library/publications/2019/demo/p60-266.html.

White House. 2015. "Occupational Licensing: A Framework for Policymakers." https://obamawhitehouse.archives.gov/sites/default/files/docs/licensing_report_final_nonembargo.pdf.

Woetzel, J., A. Madgavkar, K. Ellingrud, E. Labaye, S. Devillard, E. Kutcher, J. Manyika, R. Dobbs, and M. Krishnan. 2015. "The Power of Parity: How Advancing Women's Equality Can Add $12 Trillion to Global Growth." McKinsey Global Institute.

World Bank. 2014. "Levelling the Field: Improving Opportunities for Women Farmers in Africa." https://www.one.org/international/policy/levelling-the-field-improving-opportunities-for-women-farmers-in-africa/.

Chapter 3

AARP (American Association of Retired Persons). 2014. "Workplace Retirement Plans Will Help Workers Build Economic Security." https://www.aarp.org/content/dam/aarp/ppi/2014-10/aarp-workplace-retirement-plans-build-economic-security.pdf.

Al-Ubaydli, O., and P. McLaughlin. 2014. *RegData: A Numerical Database on Industry-Specific Regulations for All U.S. Industries and Federal Regulations, 1997–2012.* Working paper. Arlington, VA: Mercatus Center at George Mason University.

Arrow, K., and J. Kalt. 1979. *Petroleum Price Regulation: Should We Decontrol?* Studies in Energy Policy. Washington: American Enterprise Institute.

Becker, G., D. Carlton, and H. Sider. 2010. "Net Neutrality and Consumer Welfare." *Journal of Competition Law and Economics* 497.

Belfield, C., A. Bowden, and V. Rodriguez. 2018. "Evaluating Regulatory Impact Assessments in Education Policy." *American Journal of Evaluation*, 1–19.

Bento, A., K. Gilingham, M. Jacobsen, C. Knittel, B. Leard, and J. Linn. 2018. "Flawed Analyses of U.S. Auto Fuel Economy Standards." *Science* 362, no. 6419: 1119–21.

Berry, S., J. Levinsohn, and A. Pakes. 2004. "Differentiated Products Demand Systems from a Combination of Micro and Macro Data: The New Car Market." *Journal of Political Economy* 112, no. 1: 68–105.

Bernheim, B., A. Fradkin, and I. Popov. 2015. "The Welfare Economics of Default Options in 401(k) Plans." *American Economic Review* 105, no. 9: 2798–2837.

Brown, P. 2016. "Statement Submitted to the House Committee on Education and the Workforce." April 27.

Brynjolfsson, E., F. Eggers, and A. Gannamaneni. 2018. *Using Massive Online Choice Experiments to Measure Changes in Well-Being*. NBER Working Paper 24514. Cambridge, MA: National Bureau of Economic Research.

Busse, M., C. Knittel, and F. Zettelmeyer. 2013. "Are Consumers Myopic? Evidence from New and Used Car Purchases." *American Economic Review* 103, no. 1: 220–56.

CEA (Council of Economic Advisers). 2018a. *Economic Report of the President*. Washington: U.S. Government Publishing Office.

———. 2018b. "The Administration's FDA Reforms and Reduced Biopharmaceutical Drug Prices." https://www.whitehouse.gov/wp-content/uploads/2018/10/The-Administrations-FDA-Reforms-and-Reduced-Biopharmaceutical-Drug-Prices.pdf.

———. 2019a. "Deregulating Health Insurance Markets: Value to Market Participants." https://www.whitehouse.gov/wp-content/uploads/2019/02/Deregulating-Health-Insurance-Markets-FINAL.pdf.

———. 2019b. *Economic Report of the President*. Washington: U.S. Government Publishing Office.

———. 2019c. "The Economic Effects of Federal Deregulation since January 2017: An Interim Report." https://www.whitehouse.gov/wp-content/uploads/2019/06/The-Economic-Effects-of-Federal-Deregulation-Interim-Report.pdf.

Chetty, R. 2009. "Sufficient Statistics for Welfare Analysis: A Bridge Between Structural and Reduced-Form Methods." *Annual Review of Economics* 1: 451–88.

Congressional Budget Office. 2003. "The Economic Costs of Fuel Economy Standards versus a Gasoline Tax."

Covert, T., and R. Kellogg. 2017. *Crude by Rail, Option Value, and Pipeline Investment*. NBER Working Paper 23855. Cambridge, MA: National Bureau of Economic Research.

Cummings, S. 2016. "Preliminary Injunction Order in *NFIB vs. Perez*."

Dahlby, B. 2008. The Marginal Cost of Public Funds: Theory and Applications. Cambridge, MA: MIT Press.

Davis, L., and L. Kilian. 2011. "The Allocative Cost of Price Ceilings in the U.S. Residential Market for Natural Gas." *Journal of Political Economy* 119, no. 2: 212–41.

DOL (U.S. Department of Labor). 2017. "U.S. Department of Labor Rescinds 2016 Persuader Rule." News release, July 17. https://www.dol.gov/newsroom/releases/olms/olms20180717.

Eilperin, J. 2017. "In a Setback for Unions, Labor Department Moves to Revoke Obama-Era 'Persuader Rule.'" June 9. https://www.washingtonpost.com/news/wonk/wp/2017/06/09/in-a-setback-for-unions-labor-department-moves-to-revoke-obama-era-persuader-rule/.

Feldman, R., J. Schmidt, and K. Heinecke. 2013. *Quantifying the Costs of Additional Regulation on Community Banks*. Economic Policy Paper 13-3. Minneapolis: Federal Reserve Bank of Minneapolis.

Fenn, P., and C. Veljanovski. 1988. "A Positive Economic Theory of Regulatory Enforcement." *Economic Journal*, no. 393: 1055–70.

Furchtgott-Roth, D. 2016. "The High Costs of Proposed New Labor-Law Regulations." Manhattan Institute Issue Brief, updated.

Furth, S., and D. Kreutzer. 2016. *Fuel Economy Standards Are a Costly Mistake*. Washington: Heritage Foundation.

Goolsbee, A. 2006. "The Value of Broadband and the Deadweight Loss of Taxing New Technology." *Contributions to Economic Analysis and Policy* 5, no. 1: article 8.

Goulder, L., I. Parry, and R. Williams III. 1999. "The Cost-Effectiveness of Alternative Instruments for Environmental Protection in a Second-Best Setting." *Journal of Public Economics* 72, no 3: 329–60.

Goulder, L., and R. Williams III. 2003. "The Substantial Bias from Ignoring General Equilibrium Effects in Estimating Excess Burden, and a Practical Solution." *Journal of Political Economy* 111, no. 4: 898–927.

Harberger, A. 1964. "The Measurement of Waste." *American Economic Review* 54, no. 3: 58–76.

Harrington, W., R. Morgenstern, and P. Nelson. 2000. "On the Accuracy of Regulatory Cost Estimates." *Journal of Policy Analysis and Management* 19, no. 2: 297–322.

Haveman, R., and B. Weisbrod. 1975. "Defining Benefits of Public Programs: Some Guidance for Policy Analysts." *Policy Analysis* 1, no. 1: 169–96.

Hayden, K. 2018. "Illinois First State in U.S. to Pass Mandatory Secure Choice Retirement Savings." HR Source. https://www.hrsource.org/maimis/Members/Articles/2018/11/November_27/Illinois_First_State_in_U.S._to_Pass_Mandatory_Secure_Choice_Retirement_Savings_Via_AARP_Illinois.aspx.

Hazlett, T., and A. Caliskan. 2008. "Natural Experiments in U.S. Broadband Regulation." *Review of Network Economics* 7, no. 4: 460–80.

Hopkins, J. 2015. "Illinois Enacts Automatic IRAs; Is Federal Mandate Coming?" *Forbes*, January 7. https://www.forbes.com/sites/jamiehopkins/2015/01/07/automatic-enrollment-iras-first-government-mandated-automatic-ira-is-enacted-in-illinois/#4f37805e290c.

Koetter, M., J. Kolari, and L. Spierdijk. 2012. "Enjoying the Quiet Life Under Deregulation? Evidence from Adjusted Lerner Indices for U.S. Banks." *Review of Economics and Statistics* 94, no. 2: 462–80.

Lazaer, E. 1979. "Why Is there Mandatory Retirement?" *Journal of Political Economy* 87, no. 6: 1261–84.

———. 1981. "Agency, Earnings Profiles, Productivity, and Hours Restrictions." *American Economic Review* 71, no. 4: 606–20.

Madrian, B., and D. Shea. 2001. "The Power of Suggestion: Inertia in 401(k) Participation and Savings Behavior." *Quarterly Journal of Economics* 116, no. 4: 1149–87.

McDevitt, R., and A. Sojourner. 2016. "Demand, Regulation, and Welfare on the Margin of Alternative Financial Services." Working paper, Duke University.

Mortensen, D. 2010. "Nobel Lecture: Markets with Search Friction and the DMP Model." https://www.nobelprize.org/uploads/2018/06/mortensen-lecture.pdf.

Murphy, R. 2018. "Removing the 1970s Crude Oil Price Controls: Lessons for Free-Market Reform." *Journal of Private Enterprise* 33, no. 1: 63–78.

Murray Energy Corporation v. U.S. Department of the Interior. 2016. https://www.courthousenews.com/wp-content/uploads/2016/12/murraysuit.pdf.

NCSL (National Conference of State Legislatures). 2018. "State-Facilitated Retirement Savings Programs for Private Sector Workers." http://www.ncsl.org/research/fiscal-policy/state-facilitated-retirement-savings-programs-for-private-sector-workers.aspx.

NFIB v. Perez (National Federation of Independent Business v. Perez). 2016. http://www.constangy.net/nr_images/nfib-v-perez-pl-order.pdf.

OMB (Office of Management and Budget). 1992. "Circular A-94: Guidelines and Discount Rates for Benefit-Cost Analysis of Federal Programs." https://www.whitehouse.gov/sites/whitehouse.gov/files/omb/circulars/A94/a094.pdf.

———. 2003. "Circular A-4: Regulatory Impact Analysis—A Primer." https://obamawhitehouse.archives.gov/omb/circulars_a004_a-4/.

———. 2017. "Guidance Implementing Executive Order 13771, Titled 'Reducing Regulation and Controlling Regulatory Costs.'" https://www.whitehouse.gov/sites/whitehouse.gov/files/omb/memoranda/2017/M-17-21-OMB.pdf.

———. 2018. "Regulatory Reform: Regulatory Budget for Fiscal Year 2019." https://www.reginfo.gov/public/pdf/eo13771/EO_13771_Regulatory_Budget_for_Fiscal_Year_2019.pdf.

Panis, C., and M. Brien. 2015. "Target Populations of State-Level Automatic IRA Initiatives." Department of Labor. https://www.dol.gov/sites/default/files/ebsa/researchers/analysis/retirement/target-populations-of-state-level-automatic-ira-initiatives.pdf.

Parrillo, N. 2019. "Should the Public Get to Participate Before Federal Agencies Issue Guidance? An Empirical Study." *Administrative Law Review* 71, no. 1: 57–125.

Parry, I., R. Williams III, and L. Goulder. 1999. "When Can Carbon Abatement Policies Increase Welfare? The Fundamental Role of Distorted Factor Markets." *Journal of Environmental Economics and Management* 37, no. 1: 52–84.

Public Citizen. 2016. "Shining a Light of the 'Midnight Rule' Boogeyman: An Analysis of Economically Significant Final Rules Reviewed by OIRA." Washington: Public Citizen.

Roehrig, C. 2018. The Impact of Prescription Drug Rebates on Health Plans and Consumers. Ann Arbor, MI: Altarum Institute.

Sheetz, M. 2017. "Teva Stock Plummets 18% After Rough Quarter in U.S. Generic Drug Market." CNBC, August 3. https://finance.yahoo.com/news/teva-stock-plummets-18-rough-135334052.html.

Staten, M., and F. Cate. 2003. "The Impact of Opt-In Privacy Rules on Retail Credit Markets: A Case Study of MBNA." *Duke Law Journal* 52: 745–86.

State of Oregon. 2015. "78th Oregon Legislative Assembly: 2015 Regular Session— Enrolled House Bill 2960." https://olis.leg.state.or.us/liz/2015R1/Downloads/MeasureDocument/HB2960/Enrolled.

Tankersley, J. 2019. "Fed, Dimming Its Economic Outlook, Predicts No Rate Increases This Year." *New York Times*, March 20. https://www.nytimes.com/2019/03/20/us/politics/fed-rates.html.

UC Berkeley Labor Center. 2017. "California Secure Choice Retirement Savings Program (SB 1234): FAQ for Unions and Union Members." http://laborcenter.berkeley.edu/pdf/2017/SB-1234-Fact-Sheet.pdf.

U.S. Court of Appeals for the Eighth Circuit. 2018. "Decision in *Organization for Competitive Markets, et al. v. U.S.D.A.*"

U.S. Department of the Treasury. 2017. Limiting Consumer Choice, Expanding Costly Litigation: An Analysis of the CFPB Arbitration Rule.

Winston, C. 1993. "Economic Deregulation: Days of Reckoning for Microeconomists." *Journal of Economic Literature* 31: 1263–89.

Chapter 4

Alvarez, R., D. Zavala-Araiza, D. Lyon, D. Allen, Z. Barkley, A. Brandt, K. Davis, S. Herndon, D. Jacob, A. Karion, and E. Kort. 2018. "Assessment of Methane Emissions from the U.S. Oil and Gas Supply Chain." *Science* 361, no. 6398: 186–88.

Avalos, R., T. Fitzgerald, and R. Rucker. 2016. "Measuring the Effects of Natural Gas Pipeline Constraints on Regional Pricing and Market Integration." *Energy Economics* 60: 217–31.

Barteczko, A. 2019. "Poland and Lithuania see Nord Stream 2 as Threat to Energy Security." Reuters. Edited by Jason Neely. https://www.reuters.com/article/us-poland-lithuania-nordstream2/poland-and-lithuania-see-nord-stream-2-as-threat-to-energy-security-idUSKBN1W20TQ.

Bartik, A., J. Currie, M. Greenstone, and C. Knittel. 2019. "The Local Economic and Welfare Consequences of Hydraulic Fracturing." *American Economic Journal: Applied Economics* 11, no. 4: 105–55.

Baumeister, C., and L. Kilian. 2016. "Lower Oil Prices and the U.S. Economy: Is this Time Different?" *Brookings Papers on Economic Activity*, no. 2: 287–357.

Borenstein, S., and J. Bushnell. 2015. "The U.S. Electricity Industry After 20 Years of Restructuring." *Annual Review of Economics* 7, no. 1: 437–63.

Boslett, A., T. Guilfoos, and C. Lang. 2016. "Valuation of Expectations: A Hedonic Study of Shale Gas Development and New York's Moratorium." *Journal of Environmental Economics and Management* 77: 14–30.

Brown, J., T. Fitzgerald, and J. Weber. 2016. "Capturing Rents from Natural Resource Abundance: Private Royalties from U.S. Onshore Oil & Gas Production." *Resource and Energy Economics* 46: 23–38.

Caldara, D., M. Iacoviello, P. Molligo, A. Prestipino, and A. Raffo. 2019. "Does Trade Policy Uncertainty Affect Global Economic Activity?" *FEDS Notes*. Washington: Board of Governors of the Federal Reserve System.

Cavallo, M. 2006. "Oil Prices and the U.S. Trade Deficit." *Federal Reserve Bank of San Francisco Economic Letter*. http://www.frbsf.org/economic-research/ publications/economic-letter/2006/september/ oil-prices-and-the-us-trade-deficit/.

CEA (Council of Economic Advisers). 2019. "The Value of U.S. Energy Innovation and Policies Supporting the Shale Revolution." https://www.whitehouse.gov/ wp-content/uploads/2019/10/The-Value-of-U.S.-Energy-Innovation-and-Policies-Supporting-the-Shale-Revolution.pdf.

Coglianese, J., T. Gerarden, and J. Stock. 2019. "The Effects of Fuel Prices, Regulations, and Other Factors on U.S. 2008–2016." *Energy Journal* 41, no. 1, forthcoming. https://scholar.harvard.edu/files/stock/files/coglianese_gerarden_stock.pdf.

CRS (Congressional Research Service). 2018. "Nuclear Energy: Overview of Congressional Issues." https://fas.org/sgp/crs/row/IF10715.pdf.

———. 2019. "Venezuela: Overview of U.S. Sanctions." https://fas.org/sgp/crs/row/ IF10715.pdf.

Currie, J., M. Greenstone, and K. Meckel. 2017. "Hydraulic Fracturing and Infant Health: New Evidence from Pennsylvania." *Science Advances* 3, no. 12: 1–9.

Darrah, T., A. Vengosh, R. Jackson, N. Warner, and R. Poreda, 2014. "Noble Gases Identify the Mechanisms of Fugitive Gas Contamination in Drinking-Water Wells Overlying the Marcellus and Barnett Shales." *Proceedings of the National Academy of Sciences* 111, no. 39: 14076–81.

DOT (Department of the Treasury). 2019. "Iran Sanctions." https://www.treasury.gov/ resource-center/sanctions/programs/pages/iran.aspx.

EIA (U.S. Energy Information Administration). 2016. "Trends in U.S. Oil and Natural Gas Upstream Costs." https://www.eia.gov/analysis/studies/drilling/pdf/ upstream.pdf.

———. 2019a. "EIA Estimates of Drilled but Uncompleted Wells (DUCs)." https://www. eia.gov/petroleum/drilling/pdf/duc_supplement.pdf.

———. 2019b. "Fossil Fuels Continue to Account for the Largest Share of U.S. Energy." *Today in Energy*. https://www.eia.gov/todayinenergy/detail.php?id=41353.

———. 2019c. *Annual Energy Outlook 2019 with Projections to 2050*. https://www.eia.gov/outlooks/aeo/pdf/aeo2019.pdf.

———. 2019d. "The United States Is Expected to Export More Energy Than It Imports by 2020." *Today in Energy*. https://www.eia.gov/todayinenergy/detail.php?id=38152.

———. 2018a. "The United States Exported More Natural Gas Than It Imported in 2017." *Today in Energy*. https://www.eia.gov/todayinenergy/detail.php?id=35392.

———. 2018b. "U.S. Crude Oil Production Efficiency Continues to Improve." *Today in Energy*. https://www.eia.gov/todayinenergy/detail.php?id=36012.

Fell, H., and D. Kaffine. 2018. "The Fall of Coal: Joint Impacts of Fuel Prices and Renewables on Generation and Emissions." *American Economic Journal: Economic Policy* 10, no. 2: 90–116.

Feyrer, J., E. Mansur, and B. Sacerdote. 2017. "Geographic Dispersion of Economic Shocks: Evidence from the Fracking Revolution." *American Economic Review* 107 no. 4: 1313–34.

Financial Times. 2017. "In Charts: Has the U.S. Shale Drilling Revolution Peaked?" https://www.ft.com/content/e17930dc-b288-11e7-a398-73d59db9e399.

Fitzgerald, T. 2014. "Importance of Mineral Rights and Royalty Interests for Rural Residents and Landowners." *Choices* 29, no. 4: 1–7.

Gillingham, K., and J. Stock. 2018. "The Cost of Reducing Greenhouse Gas Emissions." *Journal of Economic Perspectives* 32, no. 4: 53–72.

Gopalakrishnan, S., and H. Klaiber. 2013. "Is the Shale Energy Boom a Bust for Nearby Residents? Evidence from Housing Values in Pennsylvania." *American Journal of Agricultural Economics* 96, no. 1: 43–66.

Gordon, D. 2012. *The Carbon Contained in Global Oils*, vol. 18. Washington: Carnegie Endowment for International Peace.

Graham, J., J. Irving, X. Tang, S. Sellers, J. Crisp, D. Horwitz, L. Muehlenbachs, A. Krupnick, and D. Carey. 2015. "Increased Traffic Accident Rates Associated with Shale Gas Drilling in Pennsylvania." *Accident Analysis & Prevention* 74: 203–9.

Greene, D. 2010. "Measuring Energy Security: Can the United States Achieve Oil Independence?" *Energy Policy* 38, no. 4: 1614–21

Greenstone, M., and I. Nath. 2019. "Do Renewable Portfolio Standards Deliver?" Energy Policy Institute at the University of Chicago Working Paper 2019-62.

Hamilton, J. 2011. *Historical Oil Shocks*. NBER Working Paper 16790. Cambridge, MA: National Bureau of Economic Research. https://www.nber.org/papers/w16790.pdf.

Hausman, C., and R. Kellogg. 2015. "Welfare and Distributional Implications of Shale Gas." *Brookings Papers on Economic Activity*, Spring, 71–125.

Homans, C. 2012. "Energy Independence: A Short History." *Foreign Policy*, January 3. https://foreignpolicy.com/2012/01/03/energy-independence-a-short-history/.

Hill, E., and L. Ma. 2017. "Shale Gas Development and Drinking Water Quality." *American Economic Review* 107, no. 5: 522–25.

IEA (International Energy Agency). 2019. "United States 2019 Review." https://webstore. iea.org/energy-policies-of-iea-countries-united-states-2019-review.

Jacobsen, G. 2019. "Who Wins in an Energy Boom? Evidence from Wage Rates and Housing." *Economic Inquiry* 57, no 1: 9–32.

Johnsen, R., J. LaRiviere, and H. Wolff. 2019. "Fracking, Coal, and Air Quality." *Journal of the Association of Environmental and Resource Economists* 6, no. 5: 1001–37.

Johnson, E. 2014. "The Cost of Carbon Dioxide Abatement from State Renewable Portfolio Standards." *Resource and Energy Economics* 36, no. 2: 332–50.

Keranen, K., M. Weingarten, G. Abers, B. Bekins, and S. Ge. 2014. "Sharp Increase in Central Oklahoma Seismicity since 2008 Induced by Massive Wastewater Injection." *Science* 345, no. 6195: 448–51.

Kilian, L. 2017. "The Impact of the Fracking Boom on Arab Oil Producers." *The Energy Journal, International Association of Energy Economics*, no. 8.

———. 2016. *The Impact of the Shale Oil Revolution on U.S. Oil and Gasoline Prices*. Working Paper 5723. Munich: CESifo.

Komarek, T. 2016. "Labor Market Dynamics and the Unconventional Natural Gas Boom: Evidence from the Marcellus Region." *Resource and Energy Economics* 45: 1–17.

Linn, J., L. Muehlenbachs, and Y. Wang. 2014. *How Do Natural Gas Prices Affect Electricity Consumers and the Environment?* RFF Discussion Paper 14-19. Washington: Resources for the Future.

Litovitz, A., A. Curtright, S. Abramzon, N. Burger, and C. Samaras. 2013. "Estimation of Regional Air-quality Damages from Marcellus Shale Natural Gas Extraction in Pennsylvania." *Environmental Research Letters* 8, no. 1: 14–17.

MacAvoy, P. 2008. *The Natural Gas Market: Sixty Years of Regulation and Deregulation*. New Haven, CT: Yale University Press.

Marchand, J., and J. Weber. 2019. "How Local Economic Conditions Affect School Finances, Teacher Quality, and Student Achievement: Evidence from the Texas Shale Boom." *Journal of Policy Analysis and Management*, forthcoming.

Martin, R., M. Muûls, and U. Wagner. 2015. "The Impact of the European Union Emissions Trading Scheme on Regulated Firms: What Is the Evidence after Ten Years?" *Review of Environmental Economics and Policy* 10, no. 1: 129–48.

Mathur, A., and A. Morris. 2014. "Distributional Effects of a Carbon Tax in Broader U.S. Fiscal Reform." *Energy Policy* 66. 326–34.

Muehlegger, E., and R. Sweeney. 2017. *Pass-Through of Input Cost Shocks Under Imperfect Competition: Evidence from the U.S. Fracking Boom*. NBER Working Paper 24025. Cambridge, MA: National Bureau of Economic Research.

Muehlenbachs, L., E. Spiller, and C. Timmins. 2015. "The Housing Market Impacts of Shale Gas Development." *American Economic Review* 105, no. 12: 3633–59.

Newell, R., and D. Raimi. 2018. "The Fiscal Impacts of Increased U.S. Oil and Gas Development on Local Governments." *Energy Policy* 117: 14–24.

Newell, R., B. Prest, and A. Vissing. 2019. "Trophy Hunting versus Manufacturing Energy: The Price-Responsiveness of Shale Gas." *Journal of the Association of Environmental and Resource Economists* 6, no. 2: 391–431.

Oliver, M., C. Mason, and D. Finnoff. 2014. "Pipeline Congestion and Basis Differentials." *Journal of Regulatory Economics* 46, no. 3: 261–91.

Wang, Z., and A. Krupnick. 2015. "A Retrospective Review of Shale Gas Development in the United States: What Led to the Boom?" *Economics of Energy & Environmental Policy* 4, no. 1: 5–18.

Weber, J., J. Burnett, and I. Xiarchos. 2016. "Broadening Benefits from Natural Resource Extraction: Housing Values and Taxation of Natural Gas Wells as Property." *Journal of Policy Analysis and Management* 35, no. 3: 587–614.

Weber, J., Y. Wang, and M. Chomas. 2016. "A Quantitative Description of State-Level Taxation of Oil and Gas Production in the Continental U.S." *Energy Policy* 96: 289–301.

Wrenn, D., H. Klaiber, and E. Jaenicke. 2016. "Unconventional Shale Gas Development, Risk Perceptions, and Averting Behavior: Evidence From Bottled Water Purchases." *Journal of the Association of Environmental and Resource Economists* 3, no. 4: 779–817.

Chapter 5

AHIP (America's Health Insurance Plans). 2017. "Health Savings Accounts and Consumer-Directed Health Plans Grow as Valuable Financial Planning Tools." https://www.ahip.org/2017-survey-of-health-savings-accounts/.

Aitken, M., E. Berndt, D. Cutler, M. Kleinrock, and L. Maini. 2016. "Has the Era of Slow Growth for Prescription Drug Spending Ended?" *Health Affairs* 35, no. 9: 1595–1603.

American Medical Association. 2018. "U.S. Justice Department Should Block CVS-Aetna Merger." https://www.ama-assn.org/delivering-care/patient-support-advocacy/us-justice-department-should-block-cvs-aetna-merger.

Armour, S. 2019. "Premiums for ACA Health Plans Are Set to Drop in 2020." *Wall Street Journal*, October 22. https://www.wsj.com/articles/premiums-for-aca-health-plans-are-set-to-drop-in-2020-11571749200.

Aron-Dine, A. 2019. "CBO: Administration's Short-Term Plans Rule Means a Return to Pre-ACA Practices." Center on Budget and Policy Priorities. https://www.cbpp.org/blog/cbo-administrations-short-term-plans-rule-means-a-return-to-pre-aca-practices.

Azar, A. 2019. "Ending the HIV Epidemic: A Plan for America." Department of Health & Human Services. https://www.hhs.gov/blog/2019/02/05/ending-the-hiv-epidemic-a-plan-for-america.html.

Badger, D. 2019. "Obamacare Caused Premiums to Spike; Here's How States Are Lowering Them Again." Heritage Foundation. https://www.heritage.org/health-care-reform/commentary/obamacare-caused-premiums-spike-heres-how-states-are-lowering-them.

Berchick, E., J. Barnett, and R. Upton. 2019. *Health Insurance Coverage in the United States: 2018.* U.S. Census Bureau Report P60-267. Washington: U.S. Government Publishing Office.

Berry, S., M. Gaynor, and F. Morton. 2019. "Do Increasing Markups Matter? Lessons from Empirical Industrial Organization." *Journal of Economic Perspectives* 33, no. 3: 44–68.

Blase, B. 2019a. *Health Reform Progress: Beyond Repeal and Replace.* Paeonian Springs, VA: Galen Institute.

———. 2019b. "How Price Transparency Would Revolutionize Healthcare." *New York Post*, October 12. https://nypost.com/2019/10/12/how-price-transparency-would-revolutionize-healthcare/.

Bosworth, B., J. Bieler, M. Kleinrock, E. Koepcke, and E. Berndt. 2018. *An Evaluation of the CPI Indexes for Prescription Drugs.* NBER Working Paper 24210. Cambridge, MA: National Bureau of Economic Research.

Boskin, M., J. Dulberger, R. Gordon, Z. Griliches, and D. Jorgenson. 1996. "Toward a More Accurate Measure of the Cost of Living." Final Report to the Senate Finance Committee, December 4.

Burns, L., and M. Pauly. 2018. "Transformation of the Health Care Industry: Curb Your Enthusiasm?" *Milbank Quarterly* 96, no. 1: 57–109.

Carpenter, E., and C. Sloan. 2018. "Health Plans with More Restrictive Provider Networks Continue to Dominate the Exchange Market." Press release, Avalere. https://avalere.com/press-releases/health-plans-with-more-restrictive-provider-networks-continue-to-dominate-the-exchange-market.

CBO (Congressional Budget Office). 2019. "How CBO and JCT Analyzed Coverage Effects of New Rules for Association Health Plans and Short-Term Plans." https://www.cbo.gov/system/files/2019-01/54915-New_Rules_for_AHPs_STPs.pdf.

CDC (Centers for Disease Control and Prevention). 2019. "About Chronic Diseases." National Center for Chronic Disease Prevention and Health Promotion. https://www.cdc.gov/chronicdisease/index.htm.

CEA (Council of Economic Advisers). 2019a. *Economic Report of the President.* Washington: U.S. Government Publishing Office.

———. 2019b. *Deregulating Health Insurance Markets: Value to Market Participants.* Washington: White House. https://www.whitehouse.gov/wp-content/uploads/2019/02/Deregulating-Health-Insurance-Markets-FINAL.pdf.

———. 2019c. "Measuring Prescription Drug Prices: A Primer on the CPI Prescription Drug Index." https://www.whitehouse.gov/wp-content/uploads/2019/10/Measuring-Prescription-Drug-Prices-A-Primer-on-the-CPI-Prescription-Drug-Index.pdf.

———. 2019d. *Mitigating the Impact of Pandemic Influenza through Vaccine Innovation.* Washington: White House. https://www.whitehouse.gov/wp-content/uploads/2019/09/Mitigating-the-Impact-of-Pandemic-Influenza-through-Vaccine-Innovation.pdf.

———. 2018. *Reforming Biopharmaceutical Pricing at Home and Abroad.* Washington: White House. https://www.whitehouse.gov/wp-content/uploads/2017/11/CEA-Rx-White-Paper-Final2.pdf.

Census Bureau. 2019. "Health Insurance Coverage in the United States: 2018." https://www.census.gov/content/dam/Census/library/publications/2019/demo/p60-267.pdf.

Chernew, M., A. Rosen, and A. Fendrick. 2007. "Value-Based Insurance Design." *Health Affairs* 26, no. 2: 195-203.

Claxton, G., M. Rae, A. Damico, G. Young, D. McDermott, and H. Whitmore. 2019. "Health Benefits in 2019: Premiums Inch Higher, Employers Respond to Federal Policy." *Health Affairs* 38, no 10.

CMS (Centers for Medicare and Medicaid Services). 2018. "Premiums on the Federally-facilitated Exchanges drop in 2019." https://www.cms.gov/newsroom/press-releases/premiums-federally-facilitated-exchanges-drop-2019.

———. 2019a. "Organ Procurement Organization (OPO) Conditions for Coverage Proposed Rule: Revisions to Outcome Measures for OPOs." https://www.cms.gov/newsroom/fact-sheets/organ-procurement-organization-opo-conditions-coverage-proposed-rule-revisions-outcome-measures-opos.

———. 2019b. "Premiums for HealthCare.gov Plans are down 4 percent but remain unaffordable to non-subsidized consumers." https://www.cms.gov/newsroom/press-releases/premiums-healthcaregov-plans-are-down-4-percent-remain-unaffordable-non-subsidized-consumers.

Conrad, L. 2019. "HSAs March Ever Higher, Expected to Continue." *Entertainment Benefit News.* https://www.benefitnews.com/news/number-of-hsa-expected-to-continue.

Cooper, Z., S. Gibbons, S. Jones, and A. McGuire. 2011. "Does Hospital Competition Save Lives? Evidence from the English NHS Patient Choice Reforms." *Economic Journal* 121, no. 554: 228–60.

Dafny, L., K. Ho, and M. Varela. 2013. "Let Them Have Choice: Gains from Shifting Away from Employer-Sponsored Health Insurance and Toward an Individual Exchange." *American Economic Journal* 5, no. 1: 32–58.

eHealth Insurance. 2018. "How Much Does Obamacare Cost in 2018?" June 20. https://www.ehealthinsurance.com/resources/affordable-care-act/much-obamacare-cost-2018.

Effros, R. 2009. "Increase Cost-Participation by Employees (e.g., Through High-Deductible Health Plans)." RAND Corporation. https://www.rand.org/pubs/technical_reports/TR562z4/analysis-of-high-deductible-health-plans.html.

Fehr, R., R. Kamal, and C. Cox. 2019. "Insurer Participation on ACA Marketplaces, 2014–2020." Kaiser Family Foundation. https://www.kff.org/private-insurance/issue-brief/insurer-participation-on-aca-marketplaces-2014-2020/.

Feldman, R., S. Parente, J. Abraham, J. Christianson, and R. Taylor. 2005. "Health Savings Accounts: Early Estimations on National Take-Up." *Health Affairs* 24, no. 6.

Foppa, I., P. Cheng, S. Reynolds, D. Shay, C. Carias, et al. 2015. "Deaths Averted by Influenza Vaccination in the U.S. during the Seasons 2005/06 through 2013/14." *Vaccine* 33, no. 26: 3003–9.

Frogner, B., and J. Spetz. 2017. "Health Policy Debates and the Outlook for Health Care Jobs." *Health Affairs*, Blog, November 3. https://www.healthaffairs.org/do/10.1377/hblog20171102. 115215/full/.

Fuchs, V. 2007. "Managed Care and Merger Mania." *Journal of the American Medical Association* 277, no. 11: 920–21.

Gaynor, M., and R. Town. 2012. "The Impact of Hospital Consolidation—Update." Synthesis Project Policy Brief, no. 9.

Gaynor, M., K. Ho., and R. Town. 2015. "The Industrial Organization of Health-Care Markets." *Journal of Economic Literature* 53, no. 2: 235–84.

Gee, E., C. Peters, and J. Wilder. 2019. "The Year in Review: Economics at the Antitrust Division, 2018–2019." *Review of Industrial Organization* 55: 537–50.

Greene, J., J. Hibbard, A. Dixon, and M. Tusler. 2006. "Which Consumers Are Ready for Consumer-Driven Health Plans?" *Journal of Consumer Policy* 29, no. 3: 247–62.

Haas-Wilson, D., and C. Garmon. 2011. "Hospital Mergers and Competitive Effects: Two Retrospective Analyses." *International Journal of the Economics of Business* 18, no. 1: 17–32.

Haefner, M. 2019. "Fitch Solutions: U.S. Economic Burden of Chronic Disease 'Unparalleled.'" *Beckers Hospital Review*. https://www.beckershospitalreview.com/finance/fitch-solutions-us-economic-burden-of-chronic-disease-unparalleled.html.

Haviland, A., M. Eisenberg, A. Mehrotra, P. Huckfeldt, and N. Sood. 2016. "Do 'Consumer-Directed' Health Plans Bend the Cost Curve Over Time?" *Journal of Health Economics* 46: 33–51.

Haviland, A., N. Sood, R. McDevitt, and S. Marquis. 2011. "How Do Consumer-Directed Health Plans Affect Vulnerable Populations?" *Forum for Health Economics & Policy* 14, no. 2 article 3.

HCCI (Health Care Cost Institute). 2016. "National Chartbook of Health Care Prices—2015." https://www.healthcostinstitute.org/images/pdfs/HCCI-National-Chartbook-of-Health-Care-Prices-2015.pdf.

HHS (Department of Health and Human Services). 2018. "Reforming America's Healthcare System through Choice and Competition." https://www.hhs.gov/sites/default/files/Reforming-Americas-Healthcare-System-Through-Choice-and-Competition.pdf.

———. 2019a. "HHS Announces Quality Summit to Streamline and Improve Quality Programs across Government." https://www.hhs.gov/about/news/2019/07/09/hhs-announces-quality-summit-streamline-improve-quality-programs-government.html.

———. 2019b. "HHS Proposes Stark Law and Anti-Kickback Statute Reforms to Support Value-Based and Coordinated Care." https://www.hhs.gov/about/news/2019/10/09/hhs-proposes-stark-law-anti-kickback-statute-reforms.html.

———. 2019c. "Statement on Continued Progress Enhancing Patient Access to High-Quality, Low-Cost Generic Drugs." https://www.fda.gov/news-events/press-announcements/statement-continued-progress-enhancing-patient-access-high-quality-low-cost-generic-drugs.

IRS (Internal Revenue Service), Employee Benefits Security Administration, and HHS (Department of Health and Human Services). 2019. "Health Reimbursement Arrangements and Other Account-Based Group Health Plans." *Federal Register* 84, no. 12571: 28888–9027.

Kessler, D., and M. McClellan. 2000. "Is Hospital Competition Socially Wasteful?" *Quarterly Journal of Economics* 115, no. 2: 577–615.

KFF (Kaiser Family Foundation). 2018. "Employer Health Benefits Survey." https://www.kff.org/report-section/2018-employer-health-benefits-survey-section-8-high-deductible-health-plans-with-savings-option/.

Moriya, A., Vogt, W., and Gaynor, M. 2010. Hospital Prices and Market Structure in the Hospital and Insurance Industries. *Health Economics, Policy and Law*, 5, no. 4: 459-479.

Mulligan, C. 2015. *The Economic Consequences of Health-Care Reform.* Chicago: University of Chicago Press.

NACDD (National Association of Chronic Disease Directors). No date. "Why Public Health Is Necessary to Improve Healthcare." https://cdn.ymaws.com/www.chronicdisease.org/resource/resmgr/white_papers/cd_white_paper_hoffman.pdf.

National Cancer Institute. No date. "Cancer Stat Facts: Cancer of Any Site." https://seer.cancer.gov/statfacts/html/all.html.

NBGH (National Business Group on Health). 2018. "Large U.S. Employers Eye Changes to Health Care Delivery System as Cost to Provide Health Benefits Nears

$15,000 per Employee." Press release. https://www.businessgrouphealth.org/news/nbgh-news/press-releases/press-release-details/?ID=348.

NCCI (National Council on Compensation Insurance). 2018. "The Impact of Hospital Consolidation on Medical Costs." https://www.ncci.com/Articles/Pages/II_Insights_QEB_Impact-of-Hospital-Consolidation-on-Medical-Costs.aspx.

Newman, D., S. Parente, E. Barette, and K. Kennedy. 2016. "Prices for Common Medical Services Vary Substantially Among the Commercially Insured." *Health Affairs* 35, no. 5: 923–27.

OMB (Office of Management and Budget). 2019. "Combatting the Opioid Epidemic 2020 Budget Fact Sheet." https://www.whitehouse.gov/wp-content/uploads/2019/03/FY20-Fact-Sheet_Combatting-the-Opioid-Epidemic_FINAL.pdf.

Parente, S., and R. Feldman. 2013. "Micro-Simulation of Private Health Insurance and Medicaid Take-Up Following the U.S. Supreme Court Decision Upholding the Affordable Care Act." *Health Services Research* 48, no. 2: 826–49.

Parente, S., R. Feldman, J. Spetz, B. Dowd, and E. Baggett. 2017. "Wage Growth for the Health Care Workforce: Projecting the Affordable Care Act Impact." *Health Services Research* 52, no. 2: 741–62.

Parente, S., R. Feldman, and X. Yu. 2010. "Impact of Full Replacement with Consumer Driven Health Plan on Health Care Cost and Use of Preventive Services." *Insurance Markets and Companies: Analyses and Actuarial Computations* 1, no. 1: 56–66.

Sood, N., T. Shih, K. Van Nuys, and D. Goldman. 2017. "The Flow of Money through the Pharmaceutical Distribution System." Leonard Schaeffer Center for Health Policy and Economics, University of Southern California. https://healthpolicy.usc.edu/wp-content/uploads/2017/06/USC_Flow-of-MoneyWhitePaper_Final_Spreads.pdf.

Tenn, S. 2011. "The Price Effects of Hospital Mergers: A Case Study of the SutterSummit Transaction." *International Journal of the Economics of Business* 18, no. 1: 65–82.

Unger, J., R. Vaidya, D. Hershman, L. Minasian, and M. Fleury. 2019. "Systematic Review and Meta-Analysis of the Magnitude of Structural, Clinical, and Physician and Patient Barriers to Cancer Clinical Trial Participation." *Journal of the National Cancer Institute* 111, no. 3: 245–55.

VBID Health (Value-Based Insurance Design Health). 2019. "Uptake and Federal Budgetary Impact of Allowing Health Savings Account-Eligible High Deductible Health Plans to Cover Chronic Disease Drugs and Services Pre-Deductible." http://vbidhealth.com/docs/NPC%20HDHP+%20FINAL%2005-30-2019.pdf.

Vogt, W., and R. Town. 2006. "How Has Hospital Consolidation Affected the Price and Quality of Hospital Care?" *Research Synthesis Report*, no. 9.

Waters, H., and M. Graf. 2018. "The Cost of Chronic Diseases in the U.S." Milken Institute. https://assets1b.milkeninstitute.org/assets/Publication/Viewpoint/PDF/Chronic-Disease-Executive-Summary-r2.pdf.

White House. 2019a. "President Donald J. Trump's Healthcare Agenda Puts Seniors and American Patients First." https://www.whitehouse.gov/briefings-statements/president-donald-j-trumps-healthcare-agenda-puts-seniors-american-patients-first/.

———. 2019b. "Executive Order on Improving Price and Quality Transparency in American Healthcare to Put Patients First." https://www.whitehouse.gov/presidential-actions/executive-order-improving-price-quality-transparency-american-healthcare-put-patients-first/.

———. 2019c. "Presidential Message on National HIV Testing Day, 2019." https://www.whitehouse.gov/briefings-statements/presidential-message-national-hiv-testing-day-2019/.

———. 2019d. "President Donald J. Trump Is Taking a Bold New Approach to Advance Kidney Health." https://www.whitehouse.gov/briefings-statements/president-donald-j-trump-taking-bold-new-approach-advance-kidney-health/.

Willis Towers Watson. 2013. "NBGH Employer Survey on Value in Purchasing Health Care." https://www.towerswatson.com/en/Insights/IC-Types/Survey-Research-Results/2013/03/Towers-Watson-NBGH-Employer-Survey-on-Value-in-Purchasing-Health-Care.

Chapter 6

Ashenfelter, O., D. Hosken, and M. Weinberg. 2015. "Efficiencies Brewed: Pricing and Consolidation in the US Beer Industry." *RAND Journal of Economics* 46, no. 2: 328–61.

Autor, D., D. Dorn, L. Katz, C. Patterson, and J. Reenen. 2019. *The Fall of the Labor Share and the Rise of Superstar Firms*. NBER Working Paper 23396. Cambridge, MA: National Bureau of Economic Research. https://www.nber.org/papers/w23396.pdf; forthcoming in *Quarterly Journal of Economics*, https://economics.mit.edu/files/12979.

Baker, J. 2015. "Taking the Error Out of 'Error Cost' Analysis: What's Wrong with Antitrust's Right." *Antitrust Law Journal* 80, no. 1: 1–38.

Basu, S. 2019. "Are Price-Cost Markups Rising in the United States? A Discussion of the Evidence." *Journal of Economic Perspectives* 33, no. 3: 3–22.

Berry, S., M. Carnall, and P. Spiller. 2006. "Airline Hubs: Costs, Markups and the Implications of Customer Heterogeneity." In *Competition Policy and Antitrust,* Advances in Airline Economics 1, edited by D. Lee. Bingley, U.K.: Emerald Group.

Berry, S., M. Gaynor, and F. Morton. 2019. "Do Increasing Markups Matter? Lessons from Empirical Industrial Organization." *Journal of Economic Perspectives* 33, no. 3: 44–68. https://pubs.aeaweb.org/doi/pdfplus/10.1257/jep.33.3.44.

Bloomberg. 2019. "FTC Chief Says Willing to Break Up Companies Amid Big Tech Probe." https://www.bloomberg.com/news/articles/2019-08-13/ftc-chief-says-willing-to-break-up-companies-amid-big-tech-probe.

Borenstein, S. 2011. "Why Can't U.S. Airlines Make Money?" *American Economic Review: Papers & Proceedings* 101, no. 3: 233–57. https://pubs.aeaweb.org/doi/pdfplus/10.1257/aer.101.3.233.

Bourne, R. 2019. "Is This Time Different? Schumpeter, the Tech Giants, and Monopoly Fatalism." CATO Institute. https://www.cato.org/publications/policy-analysis/time-different-schumpeter-tech-giants-monopoly-fatalism.

Bresnahan, T. 1989. "Empirical Studies of Industries with Market Power." In *Handbook of Industrial Organization* 2, edited by R. Schmalensee and R. Willig. Amsterdam: Elsevier Science.

CEA (Council of Economic Advisers). 2016. "Benefits of Competition and Indicators of Market Power." https://obamawhitehouse.archives.gov/sites/default/files/page/files/20160414_cea_competition_issue_brief.pdf.

———. 2018a. "Reforming Biopharmaceutical Pricing at Home and Abroad." https://www.whitehouse.gov/wp-content/uploads/2017/11/CEA-Rx-White-Paper-Final2.pdf.

———. 2018b. "The Administration's FDA Reforms and Reduced Biopharmaceutical Drug Prices." https://www.whitehouse.gov/wp-content/uploads/2018/10/The-Administrations-FDA-Reforms-and-Reduced-Biopharmaceutical-Drug-Prices.pdf.

Chugh, R., N. Goldstein, E. Lewis, J. Lien, D. Minehart, and N. Rose. 2016. "Economics at the Antitrust Division 2015–2016: Household Appliances, Oil Field Services, and Airport Slots." *Review of Industrial Organization* 49, no. 4: 535–56. https://www.justice.gov/atr/public-documents/rio-annual-review-articles.

Crémer, J., Y. Montjoye, and H. Schweitzer. 2019. *Competition Policy for the Digital Era*. Brussels: European Commission. https://ec.europa.eu/competition/publications/reports/kd0419345enn.pdf.

Crouzet, N., and J. Eberly. 2019. "Understanding Weak Capital Investment: The Role of Market Concentration and Intangibles." Paper prepared for Jackson Hole Economic Policy Symposium. https://www.kellogg.northwestern.edu/faculty/crouzet/html/papers/IntangiblesInvestmentConcentration_latest.pdf.

Cunningham, C., F. Ederer, and S. Ma. 2019. "Killer Acquisitions." Working paper. https://papers.ssrn.com/sol3/papers.cfm?abstract_id=3241707.

Demsetz, H. 1973. "Industry Structure, Market Rivalry, and Public Policy." *Journal of Law and Economics* 16, no. 1: 1–9.

Digital Competition Expert Panel. 2019a. "Public Responses to Call for Evidence from Individuals." Chaired by J. Furman. https://assets.publishing.service.gov.uk/

government/uploads/system/uploads/attachment_data/file/785548/DCEP_
Public_responses_to_call_for_evidence_from_individuals.pdf.

———. 2019b. "Public Responses to Call for Evidence from Organisations." https://
assets.publishing.service.gov.uk/government/uploads/system/uploads/
attachment_data/file/785549/DCEP_Public_responses_to_call_for_
evidence_from_organisations.pdf.

——— . 2019c. "Unlocking Digital Competition." https://assets.publishing.service.gov.
uk/government/uploads/system/uploads/attachment_data/file/785547/
unlocking_digital_competition_furman_review_web.pdf.

DOJ (U.S. Department of Justice). 2008. *United States v. The Thomson Corp. and Reuters
Group PLC*. Competitive Impact Statement, case 1:08, civil action 00262.
https://www.justice.gov/atr/case-document/
competitive-impact-statement-207.

———. 2011a. *United States v. George's Foods, LLC; George's Family Farms, LLC; and
George's Inc.* Competitive Impact Statement, case 5:11, civil action 00043.
https://www.justice.gov/atr/case-document/file/497376/download.

———. 2011b. *United States v. George's Foods, LLC; George's Family Farms, LLC; and
George's Inc.* Complaint, case 5:11, civil action 00043. https://www.justice.
gov/atr/case-document/file/497411/download.

———. 2016. *United States v. Halliburton Co, LLC; and Baker Hughes Inc.* Complaint, case
1:16, civil action 00233. https://www.justice.gov/atr/file/838661/download.

———. 2018a. "The Walt Disney Company Required to Divest Twenty-Two Regional
Sports Networks in Order to Complete Acquisition of Certain Assets from
Twenty-First Century Fox." https://www.justice.gov/opa/pr/
walt-disney-company-required-divest-twenty-two-regional-sports-networks-
order-complete.

———. 2018b. *United States v. The Walt Disney Company and Twenty-First Century Fox,
Inc.* Case 1:18, civil action 5800. https://www.justice.gov/atr/case-document/
file/1075201/download.

———. 2019. "Justice Department Reviewing Practices of Market Leading Online
Platforms." https://www.justice.gov/opa/pr/
justice-department-reviewing-practices-market-leading-online-platforms.

DOJ and FTC (Department of Justice and Federal Trade Commission). 2010. "Horizontal
Merger Guidelines." https://www.justice.gov/sites/default/files/atr/
legacy/2010/08/19/hmg-2010.pdf.

———. 2017. "Antitrust Guidelines for the Licensing of Intellectual Property." https://
www.justice.gov/atr/IPguidelines/download.

———. 2019a. "Hart-Scott Rodino Annual Report: Fiscal Year 2018." Annual
Competition, 41. https://www.ftc.gov/system/files/documents/reports/
federal-trade-commission-bureau-competition-department-justice-antitrust-
division-hart-scott-rodino/fy18hsrreport.pdf.

———. 2019b. "Joint Letter from the FTC and DOJ to Alaska State Senate." https://www.
justice.gov/atr/page/file/1146346/download.

———. 2019c. "Joint Letter from the FTC and DOJ to Nebraska Legislature." https://www.justice.gov/atr/page/file/1146236/download.

———. 2019d. "Joint Letter from the FTC and DOJ to Tennessee House of Representatives." https://www.justice.gov/atr/page/file/1146241/download.

European Commission. 2019. "Platform-to-Business Trading Practices." https://ec.europa.eu/digital-single-market/en/platforms-to-business-trading-practices.

Faccio, M., and L. Zingales. 2018. *Political Determinants of Competition in the Mobile Telecommunication Industry*. Finance Working Paper 494/2016. Brussels: European Corporate Governance Institute.

FTC (Federal Trade Commission). 2018a. "Options to Enhance Occupational License Portability." Policy Perspectives. https://www.ftc.gov/system/files/documents/reports/options-enhance-occupational-license-portability/license_portability_policy_paper.pdf.

———. 2018b. "United States of America before the Federal Trade Commission." Docket 9382. https://www.ftc.gov/system/files/documents/cases/docket_no_9382_cdk_automate_part_3_complaint_redacted_public_version_0.pdf.

———. 2019a. "FTC Staff Issues FY 2016 Report on Branded Drug Firms' Patent Settlements with Generic Competitors." https://www.ftc.gov/news-events/press-releases/2019/05/ftc-staff-issues-fy-2016-report-branded-drug-firms-patent.

———. 2019b. "Hearings on Competition and Consumer Protection in the 21st Century." https://www.ftc.gov/policy/hearings-competition-consumer-protection.

———. 2019c. "State-Based Initiatives: Selected Examples." https://www.ftc.gov/policy/advocacy/economic-liberty/state-based-initiatives.

———. 2019d. "The Antitrust Laws." https://www.ftc.gov/tips-advice/competition-guidance/guide-antitrust-laws/antitrust-laws.

Furman, J. 2018. "Market Concentration: Note by Jason Furman." Hearing on Market Concentration, Prepared Testimony, Organization for Economic Cooperation and Development. https://one.oecd.org/document/DAF/COMP/WD(2018)67/en/pdf.

Furman, J., and P. Orszag. 2018. "A Firm-Level Perspective on the Role of Rents in the Rise of Inequality." In *Towards a Just Society: Joseph Stiglitz and Twenty-First Century Economics*, edited by Martin Guzman. New York: Columbia University Press.

Gee, E., C. Peters, and J. Wilder. 2019. "The Year in Review: Economics at the Antitrust Division, 2018–2019." *Review of Industrial Organization* 55, no. 4: 537-550.

Grullon, G., Y. Larkin, and R. Michaely. 2019. "Are U.S. Industries Becoming More Concentrated?" *Review of Finance* 23, no. 4: 697–743. https://academic.oup.com/rof/article/23/4/697/5477414.

Gutiérrez, G., and T. Philippon. 2017a. *Declining Competition and Investment in the U.S.* NBER Working Paper 23583. Cambridge, MA: National Bureau of Economic Research. https://www.nber.org/papers/w23583.pdf.

———. 2017b. *Investment-Less Growth: An Empirical Investigation*. NBER Working Paper 22897. Cambridge, MA: National Bureau of Economic Research. https://www.nber.org/papers/w22897.pdf.

———. 2019. *How EU Markets Became More Competitive than U.S. Markets: A Study of Institutional Drift*. NBER Working Paper 24700. Cambridge, MA: National Bureau of Economic Research. https://www.nber.org/papers/w24700.pdf.

Heyer, K., C. Shapiro, and J. Wilder. 2009. "The Year in Review: Economics at the Antitrust Division, 2008–2009." *Review of Industrial Organization* 35: 349. https://doi.org/10.1007/s11151-009-9232-1.

Igami, M., and K. Uetake. 2019. "Mergers, Innovation, and Entry-Exit Dynamics: Consolidation of the Hard Disk Drive Industry, 1996–2016." *Review of Economic Studies*, forthcoming.

Jia, J., G. Jin, and L. Wagman. 2019. "GDPR and the Localness of Venture Investment." Working paper. http://dx.doi.org/10.2139/ssrn.3436535.

Krugman, P. 2016. "Robber Baron Recessions." *New York Times*, April 18. https://www.nytimes.com/2016/04/18/opinion/robber-baron-recessions.html.

Kwoka, J. 2015. *Mergers, Merger Control, and Remedies: A Retrospective Analysis of U.S. Policy*. Cambridge, MA: MIT Press.

Lambrecht, A., and C. Tucker. 2015. "Can Big Data Protect a Firm from Competition?" http://ec.europa.eu/information_society/newsroom/image/document/2016-6/computer_and_communications_industry_association_-_can_big_data_protect_a_firm_from_competition_13846.pdf.

Lamoreaux, N. 2019. "The Problem of Bigness: From Standard Oil to Google." *Journal of Economic Perspectives* 33, no. 3: 94–117. https://pubs.aeaweb.org/doi/pdfplus/10.1257/jep.33.3.94.

Lee, R. 2013. "Vertical Integration and Exclusivity in Platform and Two-Sided Markets." *American Economic Review* 103, no. 7: 2960–3000. http://www.people.fas.harvard.edu/~robinlee/papers/VIExclusivity.pdf.

Mahnke, R. 2015. "Big Data as a Barrier to Entry." Competition Policy International. https://www.competitionpolicyinternational.com/big-data-as-a-barrier-to-entry/.

Marshall, G., and A. Parra. 2019. "Innovation and Competition: The Role of the Product Market." *International Journal of Industrial Organization* 65: 221–47.

Miller, N., and M. Weinberg. 2017. "Understanding the Pricing Effects of the MillerCoors Joint Venture." *Econometrica* 85, no. 6: 1763–91.

Ohlhausen, M. 2019. "Written Statement of Proposed Testimony to U.S. House of Representatives, Hearing on 'Online Platforms and Market Power Part 2: Innovation and Entrepreneurship.'" https://docs.house.gov/meetings/JU/JU05/20190716/109793/HHRG-116-JU05-Wstate-OhlhausenM-20190716.pdf https://docs.house.gov/meetings/JU/JU05/20190716/109793/HHRG-116-JU05-Wstate-OhlhausenM-20190716.pdf.

Pai, A. 2013. "Remarks of the FCC Commissioner Ajit Pai at TechFreedom's Forum on the 100th Anniversary of the Kingsbury Commitment." https://www.fcc.gov/document/pai-remarks-100th-anniversary-kingsbury-commitment.

Peltzman, S. 2014. "Industrial Concentration under the Rule of Reason." *Journal of Law and Economics* 57, no. S3: 101–20.

Philippon, T. 2019. *The Great Reversal: How American Gave Up on Free Markets.* Cambridge, MA: Belknap Press of Harvard University Press.

Rossi-Hansberg, E., P. Sarte, and N. Trachter. 2019. *Diverging Trends in National and Local Concentration.* NBER Working Paper 25066. https://www.princeton.edu/~erossi/DTNLC.pdf.

Rubinfeld, D., and M. Gal. 2017. "Access Barriers to Big Data." *Arizona Law Review* 59, no. 2: 339–81. http://arizonalawreview.org/pdf/59-2/59arizlrev339.pdf.

Shapiro, C. 2010. "The 2010 Horizontal Merger Guidelines: From Hedgehog to Fox in Forty Years." *Antitrust Law Journal* 77, no. 1: 49–108. https://heinonline.org/HOL/Page?handle=hein.journals/antil77&id=53&collection=journals&index=#.

———. 2018. "Antitrust in a Time of Populism." *International Journal of Industrial Organization* 61: 714–48.

———. 2019. "Protecting Competition in the American Economy: Merger Control, Tech Titans, Labor Markets." *Journal of Economic Perspectives* 33, no. 3: 69–93. https://www.aeaweb.org/articles?id=10.1257/jep.33.3.69.

Stigler Committee on Digital Platforms. 2019. *Final Report.* Chicago: Booth School of Business at University of Chicago. https://research.chicagobooth.edu/-/media/research/stigler/pdfs/digital-platforms---committee-report---stigler-center.pdf.

Syverson, C. 2019. "Macroeconomics and Market Power: Context, Implications, and Open Questions." *Journal of Economic Perspectives* 33, no. 3: 23–43. https://faculty.chicagobooth.edu/chad.syverson/research/macromarketpowerjep.pdf.

Economist. 2016. "Too Much of a Good Thing." March 26. https://www.economist.com/briefing/2016/03/26/too-much-of-a-good-thing.

U.S. Congress. 2019a. "S.307, 116th Congress (2019–2020)." https://www.congress.gov/bill/116th-congress/senate-bill/307/text.

———. 2019b. "S.2658, 116th Congress (2019–2020)." https://www.congress.gov/bill/116th-congress/senate-bill/2658/text?r=2&s=1.

U.S. House, Committee on the Judiciary. 2019a. "Online Platforms and Market Power, Part 1: The Free and Diverse Press." June 11. https://judiciary.house.gov/legislation/hearings/online-platforms-and-market-power-part-1-free-and-diverse-press.

———. 2019b. "Online Platforms and Market Power, Part 2: Innovation and Entrepreneurship." July 16. https://judiciary.house.gov/legislation/hearings/online-platforms-and-market-power-part-2-innovation-and-entrepreneurship.

———. 2019c. "Online Platforms and Market Power, Part 3: The Role of Data and Privacy in Competition." September 12. https://judiciary.house.gov/legislation/hearings/online-platforms-and-market-power-part-3-role-data-and-privacy-competition-0.

U.S. Senate, Committee on the Judiciary, Subcommittee on Antitrust, Competition Policy, and Consumer Rights. 2019. "Competition in Digital Technology Markets: Examining Acquisitions of Nascent or Potential Competitors by Digital Platforms." September 24. https://www.judiciary.senate.gov/meetings/competition-in-digital-technology-markets-examining-acquisitions-of-nascent-or-potential-competitors-by-digital-platforms.

Werden, G. 2001. "Network Effects and Conditions of Entry: Lessons from the Microsoft Case." *Antitrust Law Journal* 69, no. 1: 87–112. https://heinonline.org/HOL/Page?collection=journals&handle=hein.journals/antil69&id=95&men_tab=srchresults#.

Werden, G., and L. Froeb. 2018. "Don't Panic: A Guide to Claims of Increasing Concentration." *Antitrust Magazine* 33, no. 1: 74–79.

Wessel, D. 2018. "Is Lack of Competition Strangling the U.S. Economy?" *Harvard Business Review*, March. https://hbr.org/2018/03/is-lack-of-competition-strangling-the-u-s-economy.

White House. 2016. "Executive Order: Steps to Increase Competition and Better Inform Consumers and Workers to Support Continued Growth of the American Economy." https://obamawhitehouse.archives.gov/the-press-office/2016/04/15/executive-order-steps-increase-competition-and-better-inform-consumers.

Wilson, C. 2019. "Welfare Standards Underlying Antitrust Enforcement: What You Measure is What You Get." Luncheon keynote address at George Mason Law Review 22nd annual Antitrust Symposium. https://www.ftc.gov/es/system/files/documents/public_statements/1455663/welfare_standard_speech_-_cmr-wilson.pdf.

Wu, T. 2018. *The Curse of Bigness: Antitrust in the New Gilded Age*. New York: Columbia Global Reports.

Yun, J. 2019. "Competition in Digital Technology Markets: Examining Acquisitions of Nascent or Potential Competitors by Digital Platforms." Prepared statement for U.S. Senate. https://www.judiciary.senate.gov/imo/media/doc/Yun%20Testimony.pdf.

Chapter 7

Ahmad, F., L. Rossen, M. Spencer, M. Warner, and P. Sutton. 2019. "Provisional Drug Overdose Death Counts." Centers for Disease Control and Prevention, National Center for Health Statistics. https://www.cdc.gov/nchs/nvss/vsrr/drug-overdose-data.htm.

Alpert, A., D. Powell, and R. Pacula. 2018. "Supply-Side Drug Policy in the Presence of Substitutes: Evidence from the Introduction of Abuse-Deterrent Opioids." *American Economic Journal: Economic Policy* 10, no. 4: 1–35.

ASTHO (Association of State and Territorial Health Officials). 2018. "2018 State Legislation Addressing Naloxone." http://www.astho.org/StatePublicHealth/2018-State-Legislation-Addressing-Naloxone/04-05-18/.

Autor, D. 2015. "The Unsustainable Rise of the Disability Rolls in the United States: Causes, Consequences, and Policy Options." In *Social Policies in an Age of Austerity: A Comparative Analysis of the U.S. and Korea*, edited by J. Scholz, H. Moon, and S. Lee. Northampton, MA: Edward Elgar.

Becker, G. 1962. "Irrational Behavior and Economic Theory." *Journal of Political Economy* 70, no. 1: 1–13.

Becker, G., and K. Murphy. 1988. "A Theory of Rational Addiction." *Journal of Political Economy* 96, no. 4: 675–700.

Besley, T. 1988. "Optimal Reimbursement Health Insurance and the Theory of Ramsey Taxation." *Journal of Health Economics* 7, no. 4: 321–36.

Bretteville-Jensen, A. 2006. "Drug Demand—Initiation, Continuation and Quitting." *De Economist* 154, no. 4: 491–516.

Bretteville-Jensen, A., and E. Biorn. 2003. "Heroin Consumption, Prices and Addiction: Evidence from Self-Reported Panel Data." *Scandinavian Journal of Economics* 105, no. 4: 661–79.

Buchmueller, T., and C. Carey. 2018. "The Effect of Prescription Drug Monitoring Programs on Opioid Utilization in Medicare." *American Economic Journal: Economic Policy* 10, no. 1: 77–112.

Cardinal Health Inc. 2019. "Distributors Reach Settlement with Ohio Counties in Opioids Case." Press release, October 21. https://ir.cardinalhealth.com/news/press-release-details/2019/Distributors-Reach-Settlement-With-Ohio-Counties-in-Opioids-Case/default.aspx.

Carey, C., A. Jena, and M. Barnett. 2018. "Patterns of Potential Opioid Misuse and Subsequent Adverse Outcomes in Medicare, 2008 to 2012." *Annals of Internal Medicine* 168, no. 12: 837

Case, A., and A. Deaton, A. 2017. "Mortality and Morbidity in the 21st Century." *Brookings Papers on Economic Activity*, Spring.

Caulkins, J. 1995. "Estimating Elasticities of Demand for Cocaine and Heroin with Data from the Drug Use Forecasting System." Final Report, NCJ 173823. U.S. Department of Justice, National Institute of Justice, Washington.

CBP (U.S. Customs and Border Protection). 2019. "CBP Enforcement Statistics FY2019." https://www.cbp.gov/newsroom/stats/cbp-enforcement-statistics-fy2019.

CDC (Centers for Disease Control and Prevention). 2018. "Opioid Overdose: Understanding the Epidemic." https://www.cdc.gov/drugoverdose/epidemic/index.html.

———. 2019. "Drug and Opioid-Involved Overdose Deaths—United States, 2013–2017." https://www.cdc.gov/mmwr/volumes/67/wr/mm675152e1.htm.

———. No date. "Calculating Total Daily Dose of Opioids for Safer Dosage." U.S. Department of Health and Human Services, Washington. https://www.cdc.gov/drugoverdose/pdf/calculating_total_daily_dose-a.pdf.

CEA (Council of Economic Advisers). 2017. "The Underestimated Cost of the Opioid Crisis." Executive Office of the President, the White House.

———. 2019a. "The Full Cost of the Opioid Crisis: $2.5 Trillion Over Four Years." https://www.whitehouse.gov/articles/full-cost-opioid-crisis-2-5-trillion-four-years/.

———. 2019b. "The Role of Opioid Prices in the Evolving Opioid Crisis." https://www.whitehouse.gov/wp-content/uploads/2019/04/The-Role-of-Opioid-Prices-in-the-Evolving-Opioid-Crisis.pdf.

Chalmers J., D. Bradford, and C. Jones. 2010. "The Effect of Methamphetamine and Heroin Price on Polydrug Use: A Behavioral Economics Analysis in Sydney, Australia." *International Journal of Drug Policy* 21, no. 5: 381–89.

Cher, B., N. Morden, and E. Meara. 2019. "Medicaid Expansion and Prescription Trends: Opioids, Addiction Therapies, and Other Drugs." *Medical Care* 57, no. 3: 208–12.

Chermak, J., K. Krause, D. Brookshire, and H. Burness. 2013. "Moving Forward by Looking Back: Comparing Laboratory Results with Ex Ante Market Data." *Economic Inquiry* 51, no. 1: 1035–49.

Chicago Tribune. 2016. "Chemical Weapon for Sale: A Synthetic Opioid from China That Will Kill Heroin Users." October 7.

Ciccarone, D., G. Unick, and A. Kraus. 2009. "Impact of South American Heroin on the U.S. Heroin Market 1993–2004." *International Journal of Drug Policy* 20, no. 5: 392–401.

CRS (Congressional Research Service). 2018. "Prescription Drug Monitoring Programs." https://fas.org/sgp/crs/misc/R42593.pdf.

Currie, J., J. Yin, and M. Schnell. 2018. "*U.S. Employment and Opioids: Is There a Connection?* NBER Working Paper 24440. Cambridge, MA: National Bureau of Economic Research.

Dave, D. 2008. "Illicit Drug Use Among Arrestees, Prices and Policy." *Journal of Urban Economics* 63: 694–714.

Dave, D., A. Grecu, and H. Saffer. 2018. "Mandatory Access Prescription Drug Monitoring Programs and Prescription Drug Abuse." *Journal of Policy Analysis and Management* 38, no. 1: 181–209.

DeBruyne, N. 2017. "American War and Military Operations Casualties: Lists and Statistics." Congressional Research Service, April 26.

DOJ (U.S. Department of Justice). 2018. "Two Chinese Nationals Charged with Operating Global Opioid and Drug Manufacturing Conspiracy Resulting in Deaths." https://www.justice.gov/opa/pr/

two-chinese-nationals-charged-operating-global-opioid-and-drug-manufacturing-conspiracy.

———. No date. "Automated Reports and Consolidated Ordering System." https://www.deadiversion.usdoj.gov/arcos/retail_drug_summary/.

DOJ and DEA (U.S. Department of Justice and Drug Enforcement Administration). 2017a. "2017 National Drug Threat Assessment." https://www.dea.gov/documents/2017/10/01/2017-national-drug-threat-assessment.

———. 2017b. "NFLIS Brief: Fentanyl, 2001–2015." Diversion Control Division, National Forensic Laboratory Information System. https://www.nflis.deadiversion.usdoj.gov/DesktopModules/ReportDownloads/Reports/NFLISFentanylBrief2017.pdf.

DOT (U.S. Department of Transportation). 2016. "Guidance on Treatment of the Economic Value of a Statistical Life (VSL) in U.S. Department of Transportation Analyses – 2016 Adjustment." https://www.transportation.gov/sites/dot.gov/files/docs/2016%20Revised%20Value%20of%20a%20Statistical%20Life%20Guidance.pdf.

Dowell, D., E. Arias, K. Kochanek, R. Anderson, G. Guy, J. Losby, and G. Baldwin. 2017. "Contribution of Opioid-Involved Poisonings to the Change in Life Expectancy in the United States, 2000–2015." *Journal of the American Medical Associaton* 318, no. 11: 1065–67.

Drug Enforcement Administration. 2017. "2017 National Drug Threat Assessment." U.S. Department of Justice, Washington. https://www.dea.gov/docs/DIR-040-17_2017-NDTA.pdf.

DuPont, S., A. Bezaitis, and M. Ross. 2015. "Stemming the Tide of Prescription Opioid Overuse, Misuse, and Abuse." *Health Affairs Blog*, September 22. https://www.healthaffairs.org/do/10.1377/hblog20150922.050693/full/.

Eberstadt, N. 2017. "Our Miserable 21st Century." *Commentary*, February. https://www.commentarymagazine.com/articles/our-miserable-21st-century/.

Einav, L., A. Finkelstein, and M. Polyakova. 2018. "Private Provision of Social Insurance: Drug-Specific Price Elasticities and Cost Sharing in Medicare Part D." *American Economic Journal: Economic Policy* 10, no. 3: 122–53.

Evans, W., E. Lieber, and P. Power. 2019. "How the Reforumlation of OxyContin Ignited the Heroin Epidemic."*Review of Economics and Statistics* 101, no. 1: 1–15.

FDA (Food and Drug Administration). 2018a. "FDA Analysis of Long-Term Trends in Opioid Analgesic Products: Quantity, Sales, and Price Trends." https://www.fda.gov/downloads/aboutfda/reportsmanualsforms/reports/ucm598899.pdf.

———. 2018b. "National Drug Code Directory." https://www.fda.gov/Drugs/InformationOnDrugs/ucm142438.htm.

Feldstein, M. 1973. "The Welfare Loss of Excess Health Insurance." *Journal of Political Economy* 81, no. 2: 251–80.

Finkelstein, A., M. Gentzkow, and H. Williams. 2018. "What Drives Prescription Opioid Abuse? Evidence from Migration." Stanford Institute for Economic Policy

Research Working Paper. https://siepr.stanford.edu/sites/default/files/publications/18-028.pdf.

Fontenot, K., J. Semega, and M. Kollar. 2018. "Income and Poverty in the United States." Current Population Reports, U.S. Census Bureau, September.

Gallet, C. 2014. "Can Price Get the Monkey Off Our Back? A Meta-analysis of Illicit Drug Demand." *Health Economics* 23, no. 1: 55–68.

Glaeser, E., B. Sacerdote, and J. Scheinkman. 2003. "The Social Multiplier." *Journal of the European Economic Association* 1, nos. 2–3: 345–53.

Goodman-Bacon, A., and E. Sandoe. 2017. "Did Medicaid Expansion Cause the Opioid Epidemic? There's Little Evidence That It Did." *Health Affairs Blog*, August 23. https://www.healthaffairs.org/action/showDoPubSecure?doi=10.1377%2Fhblog20170823.061640&format=full.

Guo, J. 2014. "The Postal Service Is Losing Millions a Year to Help You Buy Cheap Stuff from China." *Washington Post*, September 12.

HHS (Department of Health and Human Services). 2014. "Current Status of Tobacco Control." https://www.surgeongeneral.gov/library/reports/50-years-of-progress/sgr50-chap-14.pdf.

———. 2016. "Testimony Before the United States Senate Special Committee on Aging: Opioid Use Among Seniors—Issues and Emerging Trends." https://oig.hhs.gov/testimony/docs/2016/maxwell0216.pdf.

Hill, S., S. Zuvekas, and M. Zodet. 2011. "Implications of the Accuracy of MEPS Prescription Drug Data for Health Services Research." *Inquiry* 48: 242-59.

Hoffman, J. 2019. "$260 Million Opioid Settlement Reached at Last Minute with Big Drug Companies." *New York Times*, October 21. https://www.nytimes.com/2019/10/21/health/opioid-settlement.html.

Holahan, J., and A. Golsh. 2005. "Dual Eligibles: Medicaid Enrollment and Spending for Medicare Beneficiaries." Kaiser Commission on Medicaid and the Uninsured, July.

Hollingsworth, A., C. Ruhm, and K. Simon. 2017. "Macroeconomic Conditions and Opioid Use Disorder." *Journal of Health Economics* 56: 222–33.

Jofre-Bonet, M., and N. Petry. 2008. "Trading Apples for Oranges? Results of an Experiment on the Effects of Heroin and Cocaine Price Changes on Addicts' Polydrug Use." *Journal of Economic Behavior & Organization* 66, no. 2: 281–311.

KFF (Kaiser Family Foundation). 2006. "Dual Eligibles and Medicare Part D." Kaiser Commission on Medicaid and the Uninsured, May. https://kaiserfamilyfoundation.files.wordpress.com/2013/01/7454.pdf.

———. 2018. "What's in the Administration's 5-Part Plan for Medicare Part D and What Would it Mean for Beneficiaries and Program Savings?" https://www.kff.org/medicare/issue-brief/whats-in-the-administrations-5-part-plan-for-medicare-part-d-and-what-would-it-mean-for-beneficiaries-and-program-savings/.

Kochanek, K., E. Arias, and B. Bastian. 2016. "The Effect of Changes in Selected Age-Specific Causes of Death in Non-Hispanic White Life Expectancy between 2000 and 2014." NCHS Data Brief, no. 250.

Lipari, R., and A. Hughes. 2017. "How People Obtain the Prescription Pain Relievers They Misuse." *CBHSQ Report*, January 12.

Liu, J., J. Liub, J. Hammittc, and S. Choud. 1999. "The Price Elasticity of Opium in Taiwan, 1914–1942." *Journal of Health Economics* 18, no. 6: 795–810.

Max, M., M. Donovan, C. Miaskowski, S. Ward, D. Gordon, M. Bookbinder, C. Cleeland, N. Coyle, M. Kiss, H. Thaler, N. Janjan, A. Anderson, S. Weinstein, and W. Edwards. 1995. "Quality Improvement Guidelines for the Treatment of Acute Pain and Cancer Pain." *Journal of the American Medical Association* 274, no. 3: 1874–80.

Miroff, N. 2015. "Losing Marijuana Business, Mexican Cartels Push Heroin and Meth." *Washington Post*, January 11.

Morden, N., J. Munson, C. Colla, J. Skinner, J. Bynum, W. Zhou, and E. Meara. 2014. "Prescription Opioid Use among Disabled Medicare Beneficiaries: Intensity, Trends and Regional Variation." *Medical Care* 52, no. 9: 852.

NIDA (National Institute on Drug Abuse). 2017. "Research on the Use and Misuse of Fentanyl and Other Synthetic Opioids." https://www.drugabuse.gov/about-nida/legislative-activities/testimony-to-congress/2017/research-use-misuse-fentanyl-other-synthetic-opioids.

Olmstead, T., S. Alessi, B. Kline, R. Pacula, and N. Petry. 2015. "The Price Elasticity of Demand for Heroin: Matched Longitudinal and Experimental Evidence." *Journal of Health Economics* 41: 59–71.

ONDCP (Office of National Drug Control Policy). 2017. "National Drug Control Strategy, Data Supplement 2016." Executive Office of the President, the White House. https://obamawhitehouse.archives.gov/sites/default/files/ondcp/policy-and-research/2016_ndcs_data_supplement_20170110.pdf.

———. 2019. "21st Century Drug Trafficking Advisories on Fentanyl and Other Synthetics." Executive Office of the President, White House. https://www.whitehouse.gov/wp-content/uploads/2019/08/White-House-Fentanyl-Advisories-Summary.pdf.

———. 2019. "National Drug Control Strategy." Executive Office of the President, White House. https://www.whitehouse.gov/wp-content/uploads/2019/01/NDCS-Final.pdf.

Pacula, R., B. Kilmer, M. Grossman, and F. Chaloupka. 2010. "Risks and Prices: The Role of User Sanctions in Marijuana Markets." *B.E. Journal of Economic Analysis and Policy* 10, no. 1.

Petry, N., and W. Bickel. 1998. "Polydrug Abuse in Heroin Addicts: A Behavioral Economic Analysis." *Addiction* 93, no. 3: 321–35.

Pollak, R. 1970. "Habit Formation and Dynamic Demand Functions." *Journal of Political Economy* 78, no. 4: 745-63.

Popper, N. 2017. "Opioid Dealers Embrace the Dark Web to Send Deadly Drugs by Mail." *New York Times*, June 10.

Powell, D., R. Pacula, and E. Taylor. 2017. "How Increasing Medical Access to Opioids Contributes to the Opioid Epidemic: Evidence from Medicare Part D." Paper presented at 2017 meeting of National Tax Association.

President's Commission on Combating Drug Addiction and the Opioid Crisis. 2017. "Final Report."

Purdue Pharma. 2019a. "Purdue Pharma Announces Agreement in Principle on Landmark Opioid Litigation Settlement." Press release, September 16. https://www.purduepharma.com/news/2019/09/16/purdue-pharma-announces-agreement-in-principle-on-landmark-opioid-litigation-settlement/.

———. 2019b. "Purdue Pharma Announces Landmark Agreement with Oklahoma to Advance the Treatment of Addiction." Press release, March 22. https://www.purduepharma.com/news/2019/03/22/purdue-pharma-announces-landmark-agreement-with-oklahoma-to-advance-the-treatment-of-addiction/.

Quinones, S. 2015. *Dreamland: The True Tale of America's Opiate Epidemic*. New York: Bloomsbury Press.

Roberts, A., and A. Skinner. 2014. "Assessing the Present State and Potential of Medicaid Controlled Substance Lock-In Programs." *Journal of Managed Care Pharmacy* 20, no. 5: 439–46.

Roddy, J., and M. Greenwald. 2009. "An Economic Analysis of Income and Expenditures by Heroin-Using Research Volunteers." *Substance Use & Misuse* 44, no. 11: 1503–18.

Rosenberg, T. "When Is a Pain Doctor a Drug Pusher?" *New York Times Magazine*, June 17. https://www.nytimes.com/2007/06/17/magazine/17pain-t.html.

Rosenblum, D., J. Unick, and D. Ciccarone. 2014. "The Entry of Columbian-Sourced Heroin into the U.S. Market: The Relationship between Competition, Price and Purity." *International Journal of Drug Policy* 25, no. 1: 88–95.

———. 2017. "An Instrumental Variables Approach to Estimating the Effects of Changes in the Heroin Market on Overdose in the U.S." Canadian Centre for Health Economics Working Paper 170011.

Ruhm, C. 2019. "Drivers of the Fatal Drug Epidemic." *Journal of Health Economics* 64: 25–42.

Saffer, H., and F. Chaloupka. 1999. "The Demand for Illicit Drugs." *Economic Inquiry* 37: 401–11.

SAMHSA (Substance Abuse and Mental Health Service Administration). 2019. "Key Substance Use and Mental Health Indicators in the United States: Results from the 2018 National Survey on Drug Use and Health." https://www.samhsa.gov/data/report/2018-nsduh-annual-national-report.

Sarpatwari, A., M. Sinha, and A. Kesselheim. 2017. "The Opioid Epidemic: Fixing a Broken Pharmaceutical Market." *Harvard Law and Policy Review*, July. http://

harvardlpr.com/wp-content/uploads/2017/07/SarpatwariSinhaKesselheim. pdf.

Schneider, J., A. Anderson, and F. Tennant. 2009. "Patients Who Require Ultra-High Opioid Doses." *Practical Pain Management* 9, no. 7.

Schnell, M. 2017. "Physician Behavior in the Presence of a Secondary Market: The Case of Prescription Opioids." Working paper, November 17.

Silverman, L., and N. Spruill. 1977. "Urban Crime and the Price of Heroin." *Journal of Urban Economics* 4: 80–103.

Social Security Administration. "SSA State Agency Monthly Workload Data." https:// www.ssa.gov/disability/data/ssa-sa-mowl.htm.

Soni, A. 2018. "Health Insurance, Price Changes, and the Demand for Pain Relief Drugs: Evidence from Medicare Part D." Unpublished paper, Indiana University.

Stanford Medicine. No date. "Descriptive Epidemiology: Epidemiology of Sporadic ALS." ALS Consortium of Epidemiologic Studies. http://aces.stanford.edu/ acesmem2/EpiDescSporadic.html.

Stiglitz, J. 2015. "When Inequality Kills." Project Syndicate, December 7.

State of Oklahoma v. Purdue Pharma et al. 2019. https://int.nyt.com/data/ documenthelper/ 1660-oklahoma-opioid-trial-johnson-and-johnson/79f3fe55f5fa1a75bd48/optimized /full.pdf#page=1.

Teva Pharmaceutical Industries. 2019a. "Company Statement: Teva Reaches Agreement with State of Oklahoma to Resolve State's Claims against the Company." Press release, May 26. https://ir.tevapharm.com/investors/press-releases/press-release-details/2019/ Teva-Settles-Track-1-Opioid-Cases-and-Reaches-Agreement-on-Framework-to-Settle-Remaining-Litigation/default.aspx.

———. 2019b. "Teva Settles Track 1 Opioid Cases and Reaches Agreement on Framework to Settle Remaining Litigation." Press Release, October 21. https://ir.tevapharm.com/investors/press-releases/press-release-details/2019/ Teva-Settles-Track-1-Opioid-Cases-and-Reaches-Agreement-on-Framework-to-Settle-Remaining-Litigation/default.aspx.

U.S. Census Bureau. Various years. "Current Population Survey." https://www.census. gov/programs-surveys/cps.html.

U.S. Department of Health and Human Services. 2019. "Pain Management Best Practices Inter-Agency Task Force Report: Updates, Gaps, Inconsistencies, and Recommendations." https://www.hhs.gov/sites/default/files/pmtf-final-report-2019-05-23.pdf.

U.S. Department of Health and Human Services. "2014 CMS Statistics." https://www. cms.gov/Research-Statistics-Data-and-Systems/Statistics-Trends-and-Reports/CMS-Statistics-Reference-Booklet/Downloads/CMS_Stats_2014_final. pdf.

U.S. Department of Health and Human Services, Agency for Healthcare Research and Quality. Various years. "Medical Expenditure Panel Survey." https://meps.ahrq.gov/mepsweb/.

U.S. Department of Health and Human Services, Centers for Disease Control and Prevention. Various years. "Multiple Cause of Death, 1999–2017, on CDC WONDER Online Database." http://wonder.cdc.gov/ucd-icd10.html.

U.S. Department of Labor, Bureau of Labor Statistics. 2018. "CPI Price Index for All Urban Consumers (CPI-U)." https://www.bls.gov/cpi/tables/supplemental-files/historical-cpi-u-201801.pdf.

U.S. Department of State. No date. "Programs to Fight Opioids." https://www.state.gov/j/inl/opioid/programs/index.htm.

U.S. Department of Transportation. 2016. "Guidance on Treatment of the Economic Value of a Statistical Life (VSL) in U.S. Department of Transportation Analyses—2016 Adjustment." https://www.transportation.gov/sites/dot.gov/files/docs/2016%20Revised%20Value%20of%20a%20Statistical%20Life%20Guidance.pdf.

U.S. General Accounting Office. 2003. "Prescription Drugs: OxyContin Abuse and Diversion and Efforts to Address the Problem." GAO-04-110.

U.S. Senate Committee on Homeland Security and Governmental Affairs. 2018. "Drugs for Dollars: How Medicaid Helps Fuel the Opioid Epidemic." Majority Staff Report.

VA (U.S. Department of Veterans Affairs). 2000. "Pain as the 5th Vital Sign Toolkit." October.

———. 2019. "Opioid Safety." August 9. https://www.va.gov/PAINMANAGEMENT/Opioid_Safety/index.asp.

Van Ours, J. 1995. "The Price Elasticity of Hard Drugs: The Case of Opium in the Dutch East Indies, 1923–1938." *Journal of Political Economy* 103, no. 2: 261–79.

Van Zee, A. 2009. "The Promotion and Marketing of OxyContin: Commercial Triumph, Public Health Tragedy." *American Journal of Public Health* 99, no. 2: 221–27.

Venkataramani, A., and P. Chaterjee. 2019. "Early Medicaid Expansions and Drug Overdose Mortality in the USA: A Quasi-Experimental Analysis." *Journal of General Internal Medicine* 34, no. 1: 23–25.

White House. 2018. "President Donald J. Trump's Initiative to Stop Opioid Abuse and Reduce Drug Supply and Demand." https://www.whitehouse.gov/briefings-statements/president-donald-j-trumps-initiative-stop-opioid-abuse-reduce-drug-supply-demand/.

Wilkie, R. 2018. "Fighting Pain and Addiction for Veterans." White House, October 26. https://www.whitehouse.gov/articles/fighting-pain-addiction-veterans/.

Wilner, M. 2019. "The 'Fourth Wave' of the Opioid Crisis: Feds Warn of a Rise in Meth Use." *McClatchy DC*, August 20. https://www.mcclatchydc.com/news/politics-government/white-house/article234149267.html.

Zhou, C., C. Florence, and D. Dowell. 2016. "Payments for Opioids Shifted Substantially to Public and Private Insurers While Consumer Spending Declined, 1999–2012." *Health Affairs* 35, no. 5: 824–31.

Chapter 8

Albouy, D., G. Ehrlich, and Y. Liu. 2016. *Housing Demand, Cost-of-Living Inequality, and the Affordability Crisis*. NBER Working Paper 22816. Cambridge, MA: National Bureau of Economic Research. https://www.nber.org/papers/w22816.pdf.

Albouy, D., and G. Ehrlich. 2018. "Housing Productivity and the Social Cost of Land-Use Restrictions." *Journal of Urban Economics* 107: 101–20.

Beyer, S. 2016. "Washington, D.C., Reformed Its Zoning Code; Now Time to Ditch the Height Limits." *Forbes*, January 29. https://www.forbes.com/sites/scottbeyer/2016/01/29/washington-dc-reformed-its-zoning-code-now-time-to-ditch-the-height-limits/#228f85814db8.

Carson, B. 2019. "Ben Carson: Trump Is Getting Our Housing Market Back on Track." *Washington Post*, June 27. https://www.washingtonpost.com/opinions/ben-carson-our-affordable-housing-policy-is-failing-we-need-a-new-approach/2019/06/27/c5641dec-98fc-11e9-8d0a-5edd7e2025b1_story.html.

CEA (Council of Economic Advisers). 2016. "Housing Development Toolkit." https://www.whitehouse.gov/sites/whitehouse.gov/files/images/Housing_Development_Toolkit%20f.2.pdf.

———. 2019. "The State of Homelessness in America." https://www.whitehouse.gov/wp-content/uploads/2019/09/The-State-of-Homelessness-in-America.pdf.

Chetty, R., J. Friedman, N. Hendren, M. Jones, and S. Porter. 2018. *The Opportunity Atlas: Mapping the Childhood Roots of Social Mobility*. NBER Working Paper 25147. Cambridge, MA: National Bureau of Economic Research. https://www.nber.org/papers/w25147.

CBO (U.S. Congressional Budget Office). 2019. "The Distribution of Household Income, 2016." https://www.cbo.gov/publication/55413.

Corinth, K. 2017. "The Impact of Permanent Supportive Housing on Homeless Populations." *Journal of Housing Economics* 35: 69–84.

Davis, M., W. Larson, S. Oliner, and J. Shui. 2019. "The Price of Residential Land for Counties, ZIP codes, and Census Tracts in the United States." Federal Housing Finance Agency Working Paper. https://www.fhfa.gov/PolicyProgramsResearch/Research/PaperDocuments/wp1901.pdf.

Dettling, L., J. Hsu, L. Jacobs, K. Moore, J. Thompson, and E. Llanes. 2017. "Recent Trends in Wealth-Holding by Race and Ethnicity: Evidence from the Survey of Consumer Finances." *FEDS Notes*. Washington: Board of Governors of the Federal Reserve System. https://www.federalreserve.gov/econres/notes/feds-notes/recent-trends-in-wealth-holding-by-race-and-ethnicity-evidence-from-the-survey-of-consumer-finances-20170927.htm.

Diamond, R., T. McQuade, and F. Qian. 2019. "The Effects of Rent Control Expansion on Tenants, Landlords, and Inequality: Evidence from San Francisco." *American Economic Review* 109, no. 9: 3365–94.

Dumont, A. 2019. "Housing Affordability in the U.S.: Trends by Geography, Tenure, and Household Income." *FEDS Notes*. Washington: Board of Governors of the Federal Reserve System. https://www.federalreserve.gov/econres/notes/feds-notes/housing-affordability-in-the-us-trends-by-geography-tenure-and-household-income-20190927.htm.

Eriksen, M., and S. Rosenthal. 2010. "Crowd Out Effects of Place-Based Subsidized Rental Housing: New Evidence from the LIHTC Program." *Journal of Public Economics* 94: 953–66.

Eriksen, M., and A. Ross. 2015. "Housing Vouchers and the Price of Rental Housing." *American Economic Journal* 7, no. 3: 154–76.

Ganong, P., and D. Shoag. 2017. "Why Has Regional Income Convergence in the U.S. Declined?" *Journal of Urban Economics* 102: 76–90.

Glaeser, E. 2009. "Green Cities, Brown Suburbs." *City Journal*, February 16. https://www.city-journal.org/html/green-cities-brown-suburbs-13143.html.

Glaeser, E., and J. Gyourko. 2008. *Rethinking Federal Housing Policy: How to Make Housing Plentiful and Affordable*. Washington: AEI Press.

———. 2018. "The Economic Implications of Housing Supply." *Journal of Economic Perspectives* 32, no. 1: 3–30.

Glaeser, E., J. Gyourko, and R. Saks. 2005. "Why Have Housing Prices Gone Up?" *American Economic Review* 95, no. 2: 329–33.

Glaeser, E., and B. Ward. 2009. "The Causes and Consequences of Land Use Regulation: Evidence from Greater Boston." *Journal of Urban Economics* 65: 265–78.

Gray, N. 2019. "Do Minimum Lot Size Rules Matter?" *Strong Towns*, June 20. https://www.strongtowns.org/journal/2019/6/19/do-minimum-lot-size-rules-matter.

Gyourko, J., and R. Molloy. 2015. "Chapter 19: Regulation and Housing Supply." In *Handbook of Regional and Urban Economics*, vol. 5, edited by G. Duranton, J. Henderson, and W. Strange. Amsterdam: Elsevier.

Gyourko, J., A. Saiz, and A. Summers. 2008. "A New Measure of the Local Regulatory Environment for Housing Markets: The Wharton Residential Land Use Regulatory Index." *Urban Studies* 45, no. 3: 693–729.

Gyourko, J., J. Hartley, and J. Krimmel. 2019. *The Local Residential Land Use Regulatory Environment across U.S. Housing Markets: Evidence from a New Wharton Index*. NBER Working Paper 26573. Cambridge, MA: National Bureau of Economic Research. https://www.nber.org/papers/w26573.pdf.

Hämäläinen, K., and P. Böckerman. 2004. "Regional Labor Market Dynamics, Housing, and Migration." *Journal of Regional Science* 44, no. 3: 543–68.

Hamilton, E. 2019. "Inclusionary Zoning and Housing Market Outcomes." Arlington, VA: Mercatus Center at George Mason University. https://www.mercatus.org/publications/urban-economics/inclusionary-zoning-and-housing-market-outcomes.

Hanratty, M. 2017. "Do Local Economic Conditions Affect Homelessness? Impact of Area Housing Market Factors, Unemployment, and Poverty on Community Homeless Rates." *Housing Policy Debate* 27, no. 4: 640–55.

Herkenhoff, K., L. Ohanian, and E. Prescott. 2018. "Tarnishing the Golden and Empire States: Land-Use Restrictions and the U.S. Economic Slowdown." *Journal of Monetary Economics* 93: 89–109.

Hsieh, C., and E. Moretti. 2019. "Housing Constraints and Spatial Misallocation." *American Economic Journal: Macroeconomics* 11, no. 2: 1–39.

HUD (U.S. Department of Housing and Urban Development). 2018. "The 2018 Annual Homeless Assessment Report (AHAR) to Congress." https://files.hudexchange. info/resources/documents/2018-AHAR-Part-1.pdf.

———. 2015. "Chapter 6: Calculating Rent and HAP Payments." https://www.hud.gov/ sites/documents/DOC_35616.PDF.

———. 2019a. "Fair Market Rents: Introductory Overview." https://www.huduser.gov/ portal/sites/default/files/pdf/fmr-overview.pdf.

———. 2019b. "Payment Standards" In *Housing Choice Voucher Program Guidebook*. https://www.hud.gov/sites/dfiles/PIH/documents/HCV_Guidebook_ Payment_Standards.pdf.

IGM (Initiative on Global Markets). 2012. "Rent Control." http://www.igmchicago.org/ surveys/rent-control.

Ihlanfeldt, K. 2004. "Exclusionary Land-Use Regulations within Suburban Communities: A Review of the Evidence and Policy Prescriptions." *Urban Studies* 41, no. 2: 261–83.

———. 2007. "The Effect of Land Use Regulation on Housing and Land Prices." *Journal of Urban Economics* 61, no. 3: 420–35.

Ikeda, S., and E. Washington. 2015. "How Land-Use Regulation Undermines Affordable Housing." Mercatus Center, George Mason University. https://www.mercatus. org/system/files/Ikeda-Land-Use-Regulation.pdf.

Jackson, K. 2018. "Why Is Liberal California the Poverty Capital of America?" Manhattan Institute, January 14. https://www.manhattan-institute.org/html/why-liberal- california-poverty-capital-america-10882.html.

JCT (Joint Committee on Taxation). 2017. "Present Law and Data Relating to Tax Incentives for Rental Housing." JCX-40-17. Washington: Joint Committee on Taxation.

JEC (Joint Economic Committee of the U.S. Congress). 2019. "Zoned Out: How School and Residential Zoning Limit Educational Opportunity." https://www.jec. senate.gov/public/_cache/files/e18ff012-908e-4521-b1ce-a8b7b7f28ee3/ jec-report-zoned-out.pdf.

Jiang, H. 2019. "Ignorance Is Bliss? Rent Regulation, Policy Awareness, and Labor Market Outcomes: Evidence from New York City." http://www.econ2.jhu.edu/ jobmarket/2019/JiangH/JobPaper/JobPaperJiangH.pdf.

Lens, M., and P. Monkkonen. 2016. "Do Strict Land Use Regulations Make Metropolitan Areas More Segregated by Income?" *Journal of the American Planning Association* 82, no. 1: 6–21.

Mawhorter, S., and C. Reid. 2018. "Local Housing Policies Across California: Presenting the Results of a New Statewide Survey." Terner Center for Housing Innovation. https://californialanduse.org/download/Terner_California_Residential_Land_Use_Survey_Report.pdf.

McCarty, M. 2018. "HUD FY2018 Appropriations: In Brief." Congressional Research Service. https://fas.org/sgp/crs/misc/R44931.pdf.

Nisar, H., M. Vachon, C. Horseman, and J. Murdoch. 2019. "Market Predictors of Homelessness: How Housing and Community Factors Shape Homelessness Rates Within Continuums of Care." U.S. Department of Housing and Urban Development. https://www.huduser.gov/portal/sites/default/files/pdf/Market-Predictors-of-Homelessness.pdf.

Owens, A. 2019. "Building Inequality: Housing Segregation and Income Segregation." *Sociological Science* 6: 497–525.

Pinto, E., and T. Peter. 2019. "Home Price Appreciation Index and Months' Remaining Inventory." AEI Housing Center, American Enterprise Institute.

Quigley, J., S. Raphael, and E. Smolensky. 2001. "Homeless in America, Homeless in California." *Review of Economics and Statistics* 83, no. 1: 37–51.

Quigley, J., and L. Rosenthal. 2005. "The Effects of Land Use Regulation on the Price of Housing: What Do We Know? What Can We Learn?" *Cityscape* 8, no. 1: 69–137. http://www.jstor.org/stable/20868572.

Quigley, J., and S. Raphael. 2005. "Regulation and the High Cost of Housing in California." *American Economic Review* 95, no. 2: 323–28. https://www.jstor.org/stable/pdf/4132841.pdf.

Raphael, S. 2010. "Housing Market Regulation and Homelessness." In *How to House the Homeless*, edited by I. Ellen and B. O'Flaherty. New York: Russell Sage Foundation.

Rossi, A. and F. D'Acunto. 2017. "How Dodd-Frank Helped the Wealthy and Left the Middle Class Behind." *The Hill*, April 16. https://thehill.com/blogs/pundits-blog/finance/328998-how-dodd-frank-hurt-the-middle-class.

Rothwell, J., and D. Massey. 2010. "Density Zoning and Class Segregation in U.S. Metropolitan Areas." *Social Science Quarterly* 91, no. 5: 1123–43. https://www.ncbi.nlm.nih.gov/pmc/articles/PMC3632084/pdf/nihms453211.pdf.

Saiz, A. 2010. "The Geographic Determinants of Housing Supply." *Quarterly Journal of Economics* 125, no. 3: 1253–96.

Saks, R. 2008. "Job Creation and Housing Construction: Constraints on Metropolitan Area Employment Growth." *Journal of Urban Economics* 64, no. 1: 178–95.

Schrank, D., B. Eisele, and T. Lomax. 2019. "2019 Urban Mobility Report." Texas A&M Transportation Institute. https://static.tti.tamu.edu/tti.tamu.edu/documents/mobility-report-2019.pdf.

Schuetz, J., R. Meltzer, and V. Been. 2011. "Silver Bullet or Trojan Horse? The Effects of Inclusionary Zoning on Local Housing Markets in the United States." *Urban Studies* 48, no. 2: 297–329.

Schwartz, M., and E. Wilson. 2007. "Who Can Afford To Live in a Home? A Look at Data from the 2006 American Community Survey." U.S. Census Bureau. https:// www.census.gov/housing/census/publications/who-can-afford.pdf.

Steffen, B., S. Bucholtz, M. Martin, D. Vandenbroucke, and Y. Yao. 2013. "Worst Case Housing Needs 2011: Report to Congress." U.S. Department of Housing and Urban Development. https://www.huduser.gov/portal//Publications/pdf/ HUD-506_WorstCase2011_reportv3.pdf.

White House. 2019. "Executive Order Establishing a White House Council on Eliminating Regulatory Barriers to Affordable Housing." https://www.whitehouse.gov/ presidential-actions/ executive-order-establishing-white-house-council-eliminating-regulatory-barriers-affordable-housing/.

Zabel, J. 2012. "Migration, Housing Market, and Labor Market Responses to Employment Shocks." *Journal of Urban Economics* 72, nos. 2–3: 267–84.

Chapter 9

Cadot, O., J. Gourdon, and F. van Tongeren. 2018. *Estimating Ad Valorem Equivalents of Non-Tariff Measures: Combining Price-Based and Quantity-Based Approaches*. OECD Trade Policy Paper 215. Paris: OECD Publishing. https://doi. org/10.1787/f3cd5bdc-en.

CBO (U.S. Congressional Budget Office). 2019. "The Budget and Economic Outlook: 2019 to 2029." https://www.cbo.gov/publication/54918.

CEA (Council of Economic Advisers). 2019. *Economic Report of the President*. Washington: U.S. Government Publishing Office.

Ehrlich, I., D. Li, and Z. Liu. 2017. *The Role of Entrepreneurial Human Capital as a Driver of Endogenous Economic Growth*. NBER Working Paper 23728. Cambridge, MA: National Bureau of Economic Research.

Federal Reserve. 2018. "Economic Projections of Federal Reserve Board Members and Federal Reserve Bank Presidents under Their Individual Assessments of Projected Appropriate Monetary Policy, December 2019." December 11. https://www.federalreserve.gov/monetarypolicy/files/fomcprojtabl20191211. pdf.

Lamprecht, P., and S. Miroudot. 2018. *The Value of Market Access and National Treatment Commitments in Services Trade Agreements*. OECD Trade Policy Paper 213. Paris: OECD Publishing. https://doi.org/10.1787/d8bfc8d8-en.

OECD (Organization for Economic Cooperation and Development). 2018. *OECD Economic Surveys: United States*. Paris: OECD Publishing. https://www.oecd. org/economy/surveys/Overview-United-States-2018-OECD.pdf.

Appendix A

Report to the President on the Activities of the Council of Economic Advisers During 2019

Letter of Transmittal

Council of Economic Advisers
Washington, December 31, 2019

Mr. President:

The Council of Economic Advisers submits this report on its activities during calendar year 2019 in accordance with the requirements of the Congress, as set forth in section 10(d) of the Employment Act of 1946, as amended by the Full Employment and Balanced Growth Act of 1978.

Sincerely yours,

Tomas J. Philipson
Acting Chairman

Tyler B. Goodspeed
Member

Council Members and Their Dates of Service

Name	Position	Oath of office date	Separation date
Edwin G. Nourse	Chairman	August 9, 1946	November 1, 1949
Leon H. Keyserling	Vice Chairman	August 9, 1946	
	Acting Chairman	November 2, 1949	
	Chairman	May 10, 1950	January 20, 1953
John D. Clark	Member	August 9, 1946	
	Vice Chairman	May 10, 1950	February 11, 1953
Roy Blough	Member	June 29, 1950	August 20, 1952
Robert C. Turner	Member	September 8, 1952	January 20, 1953
Arthur F. Burns	Chairman	March 19, 1953	December 1, 1956
Neil H. Jacoby	Member	September 15, 1953	February 9, 1955
Walter W. Stewart	Member	December 2, 1953	April 29, 1955
Raymond J. Saulnier	Member	April 4, 1955	
	Chairman	December 3, 1956	January 20, 1961
Joseph S. Davis	Member	May 2, 1955	October 31, 1958
Paul W. McCracken	Member	December 3, 1956	January 31, 1959
Karl Brandt	Member	November 1, 1958	January 20, 1961
Henry C. Wallich	Member	May 7, 1959	January 20, 1961
Walter W. Heller	Chairman	January 29, 1961	November 15, 1964
James Tobin	Member	January 29, 1961	July 31, 1962
Kermit Gordon	Member	January 29, 1961	December 27, 1962
Gardner Ackley	Member	August 3, 1962	
	Chairman	November 16, 1964	February 15, 1968
John P. Lewis	Member	May 17, 1963	August 31, 1964
Otto Eckstein	Member	September 2, 1964	February 1, 1966
Arthur M. Okun	Member	November 16, 1964	
	Chairman	February 15, 1968	January 20, 1969
James S. Duesenberry	Member	February 2, 1966	June 30, 1968
Merton J. Peck	Member	February 15, 1968	January 20, 1969
Warren L. Smith	Member	July 1, 1968	January 20, 1969
Paul W. McCracken	Chairman	February 4, 1969	December 31, 1971
Hendrik S. Houthakker	Member	February 4, 1969	July 15, 1971
Herbert Stein	Member	February 4, 1969	
	Chairman	January 1, 1972	August 31, 1974
Ezra Solomon	Member	September 9, 1971	March 26, 1973
Marina v.N. Whitman	Member	March 13, 1972	August 15, 1973
Gary L. Seevers	Member	July 23, 1973	April 15, 1975
William J. Fellner	Member	October 31, 1973	February 25, 1975
Alan Greenspan	Chairman	September 4, 1974	January 20, 1977
Paul W. MacAvoy	Member	June 13, 1975	November 15, 1976
Burton G. Malkiel	Member	July 22, 1975	January 20, 1977
Charles L. Schultze	Chairman	January 22, 1977	January 20, 1981
William D. Nordhaus	Member	March 18, 1977	February 4, 1979
Lyle E. Gramley	Member	March 18, 1977	May 27, 1980
George C. Eads	Member	June 6, 1979	January 20, 1981
Stephen M. Goldfeld	Member	August 20, 1980	January 20, 1981
Murray L. Weidenbaum	Chairman	February 27, 1981	August 25, 1982
William A. Niskanen	Member	June 12, 1981	March 30, 1985
Jerry L. Jordan	Member	July 14, 1981	July 31, 1982
Martin Feldstein	Chairman	October 14, 1982	July 10, 1984
William Poole	Member	December 10, 1982	January 20, 1985
Beryl W. Sprinkel	Chairman	April 18, 1985	January 20, 1989

Council Members and Their Dates of Service

Name	Position	Oath of office date	Separation date
Thomas Gale Moore	Member	July 1, 1985	May 1, 1989
Michael L. Mussa	Member	August 18, 1986	September 19, 1988
Michael J. Boskin	Chairman	February 2, 1989	January 12, 1993
John B. Taylor	Member	June 9, 1989	August 2, 1991
Richard L. Schmalensee	Member	October 3, 1989	June 21, 1991
David F. Bradford	Member	November 13, 1991	January 20, 1993
Paul Wonnacott	Member	November 13, 1991	January 20, 1993
Laura D'Andrea Tyson	Chair	February 5, 1993	April 22, 1995
Alan S. Blinder	Member	July 27, 1993	June 26, 1994
Joseph E. Stiglitz	Member	July 27, 1993	
	Chairman	June 28, 1995	February 10, 1997
Martin N. Baily	Member	June 30, 1995	August 30, 1996
Alicia H. Munnell	Member	January 29, 1996	August 1, 1997
Janet L. Yellen	Chair	February 18, 1997	August 3, 1999
Jeffrey A. Frankel	Member	April 23, 1997	March 2, 1999
Rebecca M. Blank	Member	October 22, 1998	July 9, 1999
Martin N. Baily	Chairman	August 12, 1999	January 19, 2001
Robert Z. Lawrence	Member	August 12, 1999	January 12, 2001
Kathryn L. Shaw	Member	May 31, 2000	January 19, 2001
R. Glenn Hubbard	Chairman	May 11, 2001	February 28, 2003
Mark B. McClellan	Member	July 25, 2001	November 13, 2002
Randall S. Kroszner	Member	November 30, 2001	July 1, 2003
N. Gregory Mankiw	Chairman	May 29, 2003	February 18, 2005
Kristin J. Forbes	Member	November 21, 2003	June 3, 2005
Harvey S. Rosen	Member	November 21, 2003	
	Chairman	February 23, 2005	June 10, 2005
Ben S. Bernanke	Chairman	June 21, 2005	January 31, 2006
Katherine Baicker	Member	November 18, 2005	July 11, 2007
Matthew J. Slaughter	Member	November 18, 2005	March 1, 2007
Edward P. Lazear	Chairman	February 27, 2006	January 20, 2009
Donald B. Marron	Member	July 17, 2008	January 20, 2009
Christina D. Romer	Chair	January 29, 2009	September 3, 2010
Austan D. Goolsbee	Member	March 11, 2009	
	Chairman	September 10, 2010	August 5, 2011
Cecilia Elena Rouse	Member	March 11, 2009	February 28, 2011
Katharine G. Abraham	Member	April 19, 2011	April 19, 2013
Carl Shapiro	Member	April 19, 2011	May 4, 2012
Alan B. Krueger	Chairman	November 7, 2011	August 2, 2013
James H. Stock	Member	February 7, 2013	May 19, 2014
Jason Furman	Chairman	August 4, 2013	January 20, 2017
Betsey Stevenson	Member	August 6, 2013	August 7, 2015
Maurice Obstfeld	Member	July 21, 2014	August 28, 2015
Sandra E. Black	Member	August 10, 2015	January 20, 2017
Jay C. Shambaugh	Member	August 31, 2015	January 20, 2017
Kevin A. Hassett	Chairman	September 13, 2017	June 30, 2019
Richard V. Burkhauser	Member	September 28, 2017	May 18, 2019
Tomas J. Philipson	Member	August 31, 2017	
	Acting Chairman	July 1, 2019	
	Vice Chairman	July 24, 2019	
Tyler B. Goodspeed	Member	May 22, 2019	

Report to the President on the Activities of the Council of Economic Advisers During 2019

The Employment Act of 1946 established the Council of Economic Advisers to provide the President with objective economic analysis on the development and implementation of policy for the full range of domestic and international economic issues that can affect the United States. Governed by a Chairman, who is appointed by the President and confirmed by the United States Senate, the Council has two additional Members who are also appointed by the President.

The Chairman of the Council

On June 28, 2019, Kevin A. Hassett resigned as Chairman of the Council of Economic Advisers. In accordance with the Employment Act of 1946, the duties and responsibilities of the Chairman have been subsequently executed by Tomas J. Philipson, who has served as a Member of the Council since 2017 and was appointed Vice Chairman on July 24, 2019.

The Members of the Council

Tomas J. Philipson is the Vice Chairman of the White House Council of Economic Advisers, and in this capacity serves as acting Chairman. He is on leave from the University of Chicago, and has been a Member of the Council of Economic Advisers since his appointment in 2017. Previously, he served in the George W. Bush Administration, among other public sector positions. He received his M.A. and Ph.D. in economics from the Wharton School at the University of Pennsylvania. He has been a visiting faculty member at Yale University and a visiting senior fellow at the World Bank. He previously served as a fellow, board member, or associate with a number of other organizations, including the University of Chicago, the National Bureau of Economic Research, the American Enterprise Institute, the Manhattan Institute, the Heartland Institute, the Milken Institute, the RAND Corporation, and the University of Southern California's Schaeffer Center for Health Policy & Economics.

Tyler Beck Goodspeed is a Member of the Council of Economic Advisers, having previously served as Chief Economist for Macroeconomic Policy and Senior Economist for Macroeconomics. Before joining the CEA, he was a member of the Faculty of Economics at the University of Oxford and was a lecturer in economics at King's College London. He has published extensively on financial regulation, banking, and monetary economics, with particular attention to the role of contingent liability and access to credit in mitigating the effects of adverse aggregate shocks in historical contexts. His research has appeared in three full-length monographs from academic publishers, as well as numerous articles in peer-reviewed and edited journals. He received his B.A., M.A., and Ph.D. from Harvard University; and he received his M.Phil from the University of Cambridge, where he was a Gates Scholar. He is a current member of the American Economic Association, and was previously a member of the Economic History Association, Economic History Society, and Royal Economic Society, as well as an adjunct scholar at the Cato Institute.

Areas of Activity

Macroeconomic Policies

Throughout 2019, fulfilling its mandate from the Employment Act of 1946, the Council continued "to gather timely and authoritative information concerning economic developments and economic trends, both current and prospective." The Council appraises the President and the White House staff of new economic data and their significance on an ongoing basis. As core products of the Council, these regular appraisals include written memoranda. The Council also prepares in-depth briefings on certain topics, as well as public reports that address macroeconomic issues.

One of the Council's public reports this year addressed the economic effects of Federal deregulation. According to the report, this historic reduction in costly Federal regulation will raise real household incomes by a large enough magnitude to have macroeconomic implications.

On employment and the labor market, the Council actively disseminated analyses to the public. One report addressed the effectiveness of public job-training programs in improving participants' labor market outcomes. Another report showed that economic growth is more effective in lifting Americans out of poverty than expanded government assistance programs. The Council also released a report on how lower market costs for childcare could affect parents' labor force participation. Reports on employment policies complement the Council's regular blog posts on new releases of labor market data.

The Council also released a report that shows U.S. energy innovation, epitomized by the shale revolution in oil and natural gas production, increases household incomes by lowering consumers' energy costs. Furthermore, the report highlighted how the shale revolution led the United States to experience a greater decline in energy-related emissions than European Union countries.

Working alongside the Department of the Treasury and the Office of Management and Budget, the Council participates in the "troika" process that generates the macroeconomic forecasts that underlie the Administration's budget proposals. The Council, under the leadership of the acting Chairman and the Members, continued to initiate and lead this forecasting process.

The acting Chairman and Members maintained the Council's tradition of meeting regularly with the Chairman and Members of the Board of Governors of the Federal Reserve System to exchange views on the economy.

Microeconomic Policies

The Council participated in discussions, internal to the Federal Government as well as external, on a range of issues in microeconomic policy. Publication topics included healthcare deregulation, vaccines, prescription drug pricing, the opioid crisis, and homelessness.

On healthcare, the Council published a paper on the Trump Administration's policies to expand healthcare choice and competition. This paper finds that these policy changes—including reducing the individual mandate penalty; permitting more association health plans; and expanding short-term, limited-duration insurance plans—will keep costs down for consumers and taxpayers. The Council also released a report that estimates the potentially large health and economic losses associated with influenza pandemics and discusses policy options to increase vaccine innovation and moderate pandemics' risk.

Additionally, the Council published a paper that shows average prescription drug prices are falling because of improved Food and Drug Administration policies that, if continued, will benefit patients by further lowering drug prices. The Council also released a report on how lower prices and easier access to opioids exacerbated the crisis's growth, which finally shows signs of leveling off.

Another Council report documents the state of homelessness in America. This report finds that the Administration's actions to reduce regulatory barriers in the housing market, combat the drug crisis, expand mental illness treatment, improve the chances of people leaving prison, promote self-sufficiency, support effective policing, and increase incomes for people at the bottom of the distribution will address the root causes of homelessness.

International Economics

The Council participated in the analysis of numerous issues in the area of international economics. The Council engages with a number of international organizations. The Council is a leading participant in the activities of the Organization for Economic Cooperation and Development, a forum for facilitating economic coordination and cooperation among the world's high-income countries. Council Members and Council staff have also engaged with the organization's working-party meetings on a range of issues and shaped its agenda.

In addition, the Council analyzed a number of proposals and scenarios in the area of international trade and investment. These included generating estimates of the benefits, as well as any trade-offs, of prospective trade agreements as well as revisions to existing agreements.

The Council continues to actively monitor the U.S. international trade and investment position and to engage with emerging issues in international economics, such as malicious cyber activity. The Council looks forward to continuing to analyze the United States' international economic position.

The Staff of the Council of Economic Advisers

Executive Office

Rachael S. Slobodien . . . . Chief of Staff
Paige E. Terryberry . . . . Deputy Chief of Staff
Robert M. Fisher . . . . General Counsel and Senior Economist
Cale A. Clingenpeel . . . . Special Adviser to the Chairman and Economist
Jared T. Meyer . . . . Special Adviser to the Chairman on Communications
David N. Grogan . . . . Staff Assistant
Emily A. Tubb . . . . Staff Assistant

Senior Research Staff

Joseph V. Balagtas . . . . Senior Economist; Agriculture, International Trade, and Infrastructure
Andre J. Barbe . . . . Senior Economist; International Trade
Steven N. Braun . . . . Director of Macroeconomic Forecasting
Kevin C. Corinth . . . . Chief Economist for Domestic Policy
Jason J. Galui . . . . Senior Advisor to the Chairman; National Security
LaVaughn M. Henry . . . . Senior Economist; Education, Banking, and Finance
Donald S. Kenkel . . . . Chief Economist
Ian A. Lange . . . . Senior Economist; Energy
Brett R. Matsumoto . . . . Senior Economist; Labor and Health
Deborah F. Minehart . . . . Senior Economist; Industrial Organization
Stephen T. Parente . . . . Senior Economist; Health
Joshua D. Rauh . . . . Principal Chief Economist
Eric C. Sun . . . . Senior Economist; Health
Jeremy G. Weber . . . . Senior Advisor to the Council and Chief Energy Economist
Anna W. Wong . . . . Chief International Economist

Junior Research Staff

Jackson H. Bailey . . . . Research Assistant; Housing and Education
Andrew M. Baxter . . . . Staff Economist; Deregulation and Macroeconomics
Adam D. Donoho . . . . Research Economist; Macroeconomics and International Trade

Alex J. Durante . . . . Staff Economist; International Trade and Public Finance

Troy M. Durie . . . . Research Economist; International Trade, Macroeconomics

William O. Ensor . . . . Staff Economist

Amelia C. Irvine . . . . Research Assistant; Labor, Macroeconomics

Gregory K. Kearney . . . . Research Economist; Tax, Deregulation, and Macroeconomics

Nicole P. Korkos . . . . Research Economist; National Security

David J. Laszcz . . . . Staff Economist

Caroline J. Liang . . . . Research Economist; Deregulation, Health, and Education

Julia A. Tavlas . . . . Economist; Education, Labor, and Poverty

Grayson R. Wiles . . . . Research Assistant; Macroeconomics, Health, and Deregulation

Statistical Office

Brian A. Amorosi . . . . Director of Statistical Office

Administrative Office

Doris L. Searles . . . . Operations Manager

Interns

Student interns provide invaluable help with research projects, day-to-day operations, and fact-checking. Interns during the year were: Justin Arenas, William Arnesen, Michelle Bai, Quinn Barry, Matthew Baumholtz, Michael Bugay, John Camara, Blythe Carvajal, Cross Di Muro, Ayelet Drazen, Soleine Fechter, Kiyanoush Forough, Jelena Goldstein, Caroline Hui, Jacob Kronman, Meg Leatherwood, Andrew Liang, Eric Menser, Hailey Ordal, Raj Ramnani, Jacqueline Sands, Cindy Shen, Matthew Style, Sharon Yen, Michael Yin, and Chris Zhao.

ERP Production

Alfred F. Imhoff . . . . Editor

Appendix B

Statistical Tables Relating to Income, Employment, and Production

Contents

National Income or Expenditure

Labor Market Indicators

Production and Business Activity

Prices

Money Stock, Credit, and Finance

Government Finance

Corporate Profits and Finance

International Statistics

General Notes

Detail in these tables may not add to totals due to rounding.

Because of the formula used for calculating real gross domestic product (GDP), the chained (2012) dollar estimates for the detailed components do not add to the chained-dollar value of GDP or to any intermediate aggregate. The Department of Commerce (Bureau of Economic Analysis) no longer publishes chained-dollar estimates prior to 2002, except for selected series.

Because of the method used for seasonal adjustment, the sum or average of seasonally adjusted monthly values generally will not equal annual totals based on unadjusted values.

Unless otherwise noted, all dollar figures are in current dollars.

Symbols used:
p Preliminary.
... Not available (also, not applicable).
NSA Not seasonally adjusted.

Data in these tables reflect revisions made by source agencies through January 31, 2020.

Excel versions of these tables are available at www.gpo.gov/erp.

National Income or Expenditure

Table B–1. Percent changes in real gross domestic product, 1969–2019

[Percent change, fourth quarter over fourth quarter; quarterly changes at seasonally adjusted annual rates]

Year or quarter	Gross domestic product	Personal consumption expenditures			Gross private domestic investment								Change in private inventories
		Total	Goods	Services	Total	Fixed investment							
						Total	Nonresidential					Residential	
							Total	Total	Structures	Equipment	Intellectual property products		
1969	2.0	3.1	2.0	4.2	2.2	2.5	5.5	6.4	5.2	4.5	-5.4		
1970	-.2	1.7	.0	3.4	-6.4	-.9	-4.4	-2.6	-5.8	-3.4	9.4		
1971	4.4	5.4	6.6	4.3	13.1	10.5	4.7	-1.1	8.5	4.8	25.2		
1972	6.9	7.3	8.5	6.2	15.0	12.0	11.5	5.1	17.0	6.2	12.9		
1973	4.0	1.8	.4	3.2	10.2	3.5	10.6	7.9	13.5	5.1	-10.5		
1974	-1.9	-1.6	-5.6	2.4	-10.4	-9.9	-3.9	-6.4	-3.7	1.6	-24.6		
1975	2.6	5.1	6.1	4.1	-9.8	-2.6	-5.9	-8.1	-6.7	2.8	7.8		
1976	4.3	5.4	6.4	4.5	15.2	12.1	7.8	3.8	9.0	11.8	23.8		
1977	5.0	4.2	4.9	3.7	14.9	12.1	11.9	5.7	17.2	4.8	12.6		
1978	6.7	4.0	3.5	4.4	14.3	13.1	16.0	21.7	14.5	10.3	6.8		
1979	1.3	1.7	.3	2.9	-3.4	1.1	5.5	8.8	2.7	9.4	-9.1		
1980	.0	.0	-2.5	2.2	-7.2	-4.8	-.9	2.7	-4.4	4.7	-15.3		
1981	1.3	.1	-.2	.3	6.7	1.5	9.0	14.1	4.6	12.1	-22.0		
1982	-1.4	3.5	3.6	3.4	-17.3	-8.0	-9.5	-13.5	-10.0	3.4	-1.7		
1983	7.9	6.6	8.3	5.3	31.3	18.3	10.4	-3.9	19.9	13.0	49.7		
1984	5.6	4.3	5.3	3.6	14.2	11.3	13.9	15.7	13.4	12.6	3.7		
1985	4.2	4.8	4.6	5.0	1.9	3.7	3.2	3.3	1.7	7.7	5.2		
1986	2.9	4.4	6.5	3.0	-4.1	.6	-3.2	-14.3	.8	5.4	11.8		
1987	4.5	2.8	.4	4.6	9.8	1.5	2.2	4.9	.1	4.2	-.5		
1988	3.8	4.6	4.5	4.7	-.5	3.7	5.1	-3.3	8.2	9.8	.1		
1989	2.7	2.4	1.8	2.7	.7	1.5	4.5	3.3	2.5	11.3	-6.5		
1990	.6	.8	-1.6	2.3	-6.5	-4.2	-.9	-3.2	-2.7	6.2	-13.6		
1991	1.2	.9	-.8	2.0	2.1	-1.9	-3.4	-12.8	-3.2	7.2	2.9		
1992	4.4	4.9	5.3	4.7	7.7	8.7	7.1	1.0	11.3	4.8	13.6		
1993	2.6	3.3	4.4	2.7	7.6	8.4	7.6	.2	13.1	2.9	10.6		
1994	4.1	3.8	5.5	2.8	11.5	6.6	8.5	1.6	12.5	5.8	1.6		
1995	2.2	2.8	2.3	3.0	.8	5.5	7.4	4.7	8.1	8.3	.1		
1996	4.4	3.4	4.8	2.7	11.2	9.9	11.3	10.9	11.1	12.1	5.6		
1997	4.5	4.5	5.3	4.0	11.4	8.3	9.7	4.4	10.7	12.4	4.0		
1998	4.9	5.6	8.1	4.3	9.7	11.5	11.6	4.3	14.8	11.5	11.3		
1999	4.8	5.1	6.6	4.3	8.5	7.2	8.4	-.1	9.5	13.3	3.5		
2000	3.0	4.4	4.0	4.7	4.3	5.9	8.5	10.8	8.5	6.6	-1.5		
2001	.2	2.5	4.9	1.2	-11.1	-4.7	-6.8	-10.6	-7.7	-2.1	2.0		
2002	2.1	2.1	1.7	2.4	4.4	-1.5	-5.1	-15.7	-3.7	.9	8.1		
2003	4.3	3.8	6.6	2.3	8.7	8.6	6.8	1.9	9.6	5.8	12.7		
2004	3.3	3.8	4.3	3.5	8.0	6.5	6.5	.3	9.8	5.7	6.6		
2005	3.1	3.0	3.0	3.0	6.1	5.8	6.1	1.5	8.7	5.1	5.2		
2006	2.6	3.2	4.6	2.5	-1.5	.0	8.1	9.0	7.1	9.3	-15.2		
2007	2.0	1.6	1.8	1.5	-1.8	-1.1	7.3	17.7	3.9	4.0	-21.2		
2008	-2.8	-1.8	-6.8	.9	-15.3	-11.1	-7.0	-.8	-15.9	.9	-24.7		
2009	.2	-.1	.6	-.4	-9.2	-10.5	-10.3	-27.1	-8.4	3.8	-11.5		
2010	2.6	2.7	4.3	1.9	12.1	6.1	8.9	-3.6	22.6	1.6	-5.7		
2011	1.6	1.2	.9	1.4	10.4	9.2	10.0	8.6	12.7	7.2	5.3		
2012	1.5	1.6	2.4	1.2	4.0	7.2	5.6	4.0	7.8	3.7	15.4		
2013	2.6	1.9	3.5	1.1	9.3	5.7	5.4	6.7	5.4	4.5	7.1		
2014	2.9	3.8	5.0	3.2	5.3	7.0	6.9	9.3	5.6	6.9	7.7		
2015	1.9	2.9	3.7	2.5	1.5	1.0	-.9	-10.9	1.9	2.9	9.1		
2016	2.0	2.8	3.6	2.4	1.5	2.8	2.4	4.3	-1.4	6.6	3.9		
2017	2.8	2.9	5.0	2.0	4.8	5.1	5.4	1.5	8.5	4.0	4.2		
2018	2.5	2.6	2.9	2.5	5.1	3.5	5.9	2.6	5.0	9.3	-4.4		
2019 p	2.3	2.6	4.1	2.0	-1.9	.2	-.1	-7.0	-1.5	6.2	1.5		
2016: I	2.0	3.2	4.2	2.7	-1.6	2.6	-.6	-11.4	-3.9	12.9	14.7		
II	1.9	2.9	4.5	2.2	-1.7	2.7	4.0	10.0	-2.3	9.3	-2.0		
III	2.2	2.6	4.0	1.9	.5	3.8	5.6	18.4	.3	4.7	-2.6		
IV	2.0	2.5	1.9	2.8	9.3	2.0	.7	2.4	.4	.0	6.4		
2017: I	2.3	2.4	3.2	2.0	3.4	7.7	6.6	7.3	6.3	6.3	11.9		
II	2.2	2.4	5.5	1.0	3.6	2.8	4.4	2.0	8.9	.3	-2.2		
III	3.2	2.4	4.1	1.6	7.4	1.4	2.4	-7.7	6.2	4.9	-2.0		
IV	3.5	4.6	7.5	3.4	4.7	8.7	8.4	5.2	12.9	4.7	9.9		
2018: I	2.5	1.7	1.3	1.9	6.2	5.5	8.8	12.1	6.6	9.7	-5.3		
II	3.5	4.0	5.4	3.4	-1.8	5.2	7.9	11.0	3.4	11.9	-3.7		
III	2.9	3.5	3.6	3.4	13.7	.7	2.1	-2.1	2.9	4.1	-4.0		
IV	1.1	1.4	1.6	1.4	3.0	2.7	4.8	-9.0	7.4	11.7	-4.7		
2019: I	3.1	1.1	1.5	1.0	6.2	3.2	4.4	4.0	-.1	10.8	-1.0		
II	2.0	4.6	8.6	2.8	-6.3	-1.4	-1.0	-11.1	.8	3.6	-3.0		
III	2.1	3.2	5.3	2.2	-1.0	-.8	-2.3	-9.9	-3.8	4.7	4.6		
IV p	2.1	1.8	1.2	2.0	-6.1	.1	-1.5	-10.1	-2.9	5.9	5.8		

See next page for continuation of table.

TABLE B-1. Percent changes in real gross domestic product, 1969–2019—*Continued*

[Percent change, fourth quarter over fourth quarter; quarterly changes at seasonally adjusted annual rates]

| Year or quarter | Net exports of goods and services | | | Government consumption expenditures and gross investment | | | | | Final sales of domestic product | Gross domestic pur-chases [1] | Final sales to private domestic pur-chasers [2] | Gross domestic income (GDI) [3] | Average of GDP and GDI |
| | Net exports | Exports | Imports | Total | Federal | | | State and local | | | | | |
					Total	National defense	Non-defense						
1969	....	8.7	5.9	-1.2	-3.6	-4.6	-0.2	1.8	2.1	1.9	2.9	2.1	2.1
1970	....	5.9	3.0	-1.2	-5.8	-8.6	3.9	4.3	.7	-.3	1.1	-.8	-.5
1971	....	-4.5	1.3	-2.4	-7.3	-11.5	5.6	2.8	4.0	4.7	6.5	4.8	4.6
1972	....	19.5	17.9	-.1	-2.6	-5.8	6.1	2.3	6.4	6.8	8.3	7.1	7.0
1973	....	18.4	-.5	-.3	-3.6	-5.0	-.3	2.9	2.8	2.9	2.2	3.8	3.9
1974	....	3.1	-1.0	3.0	3.7	1.2	9.5	2.4	-1.7	-2.3	-3.5	-2.9	-2.4
1975	....	1.5	-5.6	3.0	.8	.5	1.4	4.9	3.9	2.0	3.4	2.7	2.6
1976	....	4.3	19.2	-1.3	-1.0	-2.1	1.3	-1.6	3.8	5.4	6.7	3.8	4.1
1977	....	-1.4	5.7	1.9	2.3	.1	6.8	1.7	4.5	5.6	5.9	6.0	5.5
1978	....	18.8	9.9	4.4	3.5	2.9	4.8	5.2	6.4	6.1	6.1	5.4	6.0
1979	....	10.5	.9	.9	1.2	2.4	-1.1	.7	2.2	.5	1.5	.8	1.0
1980	....	3.9	-9.3	.3	4.0	3.7	4.6	-2.9	.5	-1.4	-1.2	1.3	.6
1981	....	.7	6.2	2.5	6.0	7.9	2.0	-.7	.3	1.8	.4	1.2	1.2
1982	....	-12.2	-3.9	2.6	4.5	7.3	-1.6	.8	.4	-.7	.8	-1.3	-1.3
1983	....	5.5	24.6	1.9	2.7	6.5	-6.6	1.1	6.0	9.5	9.1	6.6	7.3
1984	....	9.1	18.9	6.3	7.1	5.6	11.5	5.4	5.0	6.5	5.9	6.7	6.1
1985	....	1.5	5.6	6.1	6.7	8.2	2.8	5.5	4.6	4.5	4.6	3.4	3.8
1986	....	10.6	7.9	4.7	5.3	4.7	6.8	4.1	3.9	2.9	3.5	2.7	2.8
1987	....	12.8	6.3	3.0	3.6	5.3	-1.0	2.4	3.0	4.1	2.5	5.5	5.0
1988	....	14.0	3.8	1.4	-1.4	-.8	-3.0	4.1	4.6	3.0	4.4	4.7	4.2
1989	....	10.2	2.6	2.5	.5	-1.3	5.8	4.3	2.9	2.1	2.2	1.0	1.9
1990	....	7.4	-.2	2.6	1.5	.0	5.4	3.6	1.0	-.1	-.3	1.0	.8
1991	....	9.2	5.7	.0	-2.3	-4.9	4.3	1.9	.5	.9	.3	.7	.9
1992	....	4.5	6.5	1.3	1.6	-.4	6.2	1.1	4.5	4.6	5.6	3.9	4.1
1993	....	4.4	9.9	-.7	-4.5	-5.4	-2.5	2.2	2.7	3.2	4.3	3.0	2.8
1994	....	10.8	12.2	.0	-4.2	-6.7	1.1	3.1	3.3	4.3	4.4	4.3	4.2
1995	....	9.4	4.8	-.6	-4.8	-5.0	-4.3	2.2	3.0	1.8	3.3	2.9	2.6
1996	....	10.1	11.1	2.6	1.1	.3	2.6	3.6	4.2	4.6	4.8	4.8	4.6
1997	....	8.3	14.2	1.7	.2	-.8	1.9	2.7	3.9	5.2	5.3	5.5	5.0
1998	....	2.6	11.0	2.8	-.3	-2.4	3.3	4.6	5.2	5.9	6.9	4.9	4.9
1999	....	6.3	12.0	3.9	3.5	3.9	2.8	4.1	4.5	5.5	5.6	4.6	4.7
2000	....	6.0	10.9	.4	-2.0	-3.3	.1	1.8	3.3	3.7	4.7	3.3	3.1
2001	....	-12.2	-7.8	4.9	5.5	4.7	6.7	4.6	1.4	.3	.9	.1	.1
2002	....	3.9	9.5	3.9	8.1	8.1	8.2	1.6	1.0	2.8	1.4	2.8	2.4
2003	....	7.2	5.7	1.9	6.5	8.9	2.5	-.7	4.3	4.3	4.8	2.8	3.6
2004	....	7.4	11.2	.8	2.6	2.8	2.4	-.2	3.0	4.0	4.3	3.8	3.6
2005	....	7.4	6.3	.9	1.8	1.8	1.9	.3	3.0	3.2	3.6	4.3	3.7
2006	....	10.3	4.3	1.9	2.4	3.1	1.3	1.6	2.9	2.1	2.5	2.7	2.6
2007	....	9.2	1.3	2.3	3.6	3.9	3.1	1.5	2.1	1.1	1.0	-.7	.6
2008	....	-2.4	-5.5	2.5	6.3	7.4	4.2	.3	-2.0	-3.3	-3.7	-2.7	-2.7
2009	....	1.2	-5.7	3.0	6.2	4.9	8.6	1.0	-.1	-.8	-2.1	.5	.3
2010	....	9.9	12.0	-1.3	1.9	1.3	3.0	-3.5	1.8	3.1	3.3	3.5	3.0
2011	....	4.6	3.8	-3.4	-3.5	-3.6	-3.2	-3.3	1.4	1.6	2.6	2.1	1.9
2012	....	2.1	.6	-2.1	-2.6	-4.7	1.2	-1.7	1.9	1.2	2.6	2.9	2.2
2013	....	6.0	3.0	-2.4	-6.1	-6.5	-5.5	.2	2.0	2.2	2.6	1.5	2.1
2014	....	2.9	6.5	.3	-1.1	-3.4	2.7	1.2	3.2	3.4	4.5	4.2	3.5
2015	....	-1.5	3.2	2.3	1.1	-.4	3.4	3.0	1.8	2.5	2.5	1.3	1.6
2016	....	1.1	3.4	1.5	.1	-.8	1.5	2.3	2.2	2.3	2.8	.9	1.5
2017	....	5.5	5.6	.8	1.7	1.9	1.4	.4	2.9	2.9	3.4	2.5	2.6
2018 P	....	.4	3.2	1.5	2.7	4.0	.7	.9	2.2	2.9	2.8	2.3	2.4
2019 P	....	.2	-2.2	3.0	4.3	4.5	4.0	2.2	2.7	1.9	2.2	....	....
2016: I	....	-3.0	.9	3.8	.7	-.4	2.2	5.8	2.8	2.5	3.0	2.1	2.1
II	....	4.0	.8	-.7	-2.7	-5.2	1.0	.5	2.7	1.5	2.9	-1.7	.1
III	....	6.1	4.7	1.7	2.0	3.4	-.1	1.6	2.7	2.1	2.8	2.0	2.1
IV	....	-2.5	7.5	1.1	.6	-1.0	2.8	1.4	.8	3.3	2.4	1.4	1.7
2017: I	....	6.1	4.1	-.2	-1.2	-1.9	-.2	.3	3.0	2.1	3.4	3.8	3.1
II	....	1.6	3.5	1.4	3.3	6.8	-1.6	.3	2.0	2.4	2.5	2.6	2.4
III	....	4.4	1.3	-.1	.1	-1.6	2.6	-.2	2.2	2.8	2.2	.8	2.0
IV	....	10.1	14.0	2.4	4.6	4.5	4.8	1.1	4.2	4.3	5.5	2.7	3.1
2018: I	....	.8	.6	1.9	2.8	.6	6.0	1.4	2.4	2.5	2.4	4.7	3.6
II	....	5.8	.3	2.6	3.9	7.5	-1.0	1.8	4.8	2.8	4.2	.7	2.1
III	....	-6.2	8.6	2.1	2.9	3.0	2.8	1.6	.8	4.9	2.9	3.3	3.1
IV	....	1.5	3.5	-.4	1.1	5.2	-4.5	-1.2	1.0	1.4	1.7	.8	.9
2019: I	....	4.1	-1.5	2.9	2.2	7.7	-5.4	3.3	2.6	2.3	1.6	3.2	3.2
II	....	-5.7	.0	4.8	8.3	3.3	16.1	2.7	3.0	2.6	3.3	.9	1.4
III	....	1.0	1.8	1.7	3.3	2.2	5.0	.7	2.1	2.2	2.3	2.1	2.1
IV P	....	1.4	-8.7	2.7	3.6	4.9	1.6	2.2	3.2	.6	1.4	....	....

[1] Gross domestic product (GDP) less exports of goods and services plus imports of goods and services.
[2] Personal consumption expenditures plus gross private fixed investment.
[3] Gross domestic income is deflated by the implicit price deflator for GDP.

Note: Percent changes based on unrounded GDP quantity indexes.

Source: Department of Commerce (Bureau of Economic Analysis).

Table B-2. Contributions to percent change in real gross domestic product, 1969–2019

[Percentage points, except as noted; annual average to annual average, quarterly data at seasonally adjusted annual rates]

Year or quarter	Gross domestic product (percent change)	Personal consumption expenditures			Gross private domestic investment							
		Total	Goods	Services	Total	Fixed investment						Change in private inventories
						Total	Nonresidential				Residential	
							Total	Structures	Equipment	Intellectual property products		
1969	3.1	2.20	0.92	1.28	0.93	0.93	0.79	0.19	0.51	0.09	0.14	0.00
1970	.2	1.39	.23	1.16	−1.03	−.33	−.10	.01	−.11	.00	−.23	−.70
1971	3.3	2.29	1.23	1.06	1.63	1.08	−.01	−.06	.05	.01	1.08	.56
1972	5.3	3.66	1.90	1.76	1.90	1.85	.97	.12	.75	.11	.87	.06
1973	5.6	2.97	1.52	1.45	1.95	1.47	1.51	.30	1.12	.08	−.04	.48
1974	−.5	−.50	−1.08	.58	−1.24	−.98	.10	−.08	.14	.05	−1.08	−.26
1975	−.2	1.36	.20	1.16	−2.91	−1.68	−1.13	−.42	−.73	.01	−.54	−1.24
1976	5.4	3.41	2.03	1.38	2.91	1.54	.66	.09	.39	.18	.88	1.37
1977	4.6	2.59	1.26	1.33	2.47	2.23	1.26	.15	1.01	.11	.97	.24
1978	5.5	2.68	1.19	1.49	2.22	2.10	1.72	.52	1.08	.12	.38	.12
1979	3.2	1.44	.45	.99	.72	1.11	1.34	.51	.62	.20	−.22	−.40
1980	−.3	−.19	−.72	.53	−2.07	−1.18	.00	.26	−.35	.09	−1.19	−.89
1981	2.5	.85	.33	.52	1.64	.50	.87	.39	.28	.21	−.37	1.13
1982	−1.8	.88	.19	.69	−2.46	−1.16	−.43	−.09	−.47	.12	−.72	−1.31
1983	4.6	3.51	1.69	1.82	1.60	1.32	−.06	−.56	.32	.17	1.38	.28
1984	7.2	3.30	1.91	1.39	4.73	2.83	2.18	.58	1.29	.30	.65	1.90
1985	4.2	3.20	1.38	1.83	−.01	1.02	.91	.31	.39	.21	.11	−1.03
1986	3.5	2.58	1.45	1.13	.03	.34	−.24	−.49	.08	.17	.58	−.31
1987	3.5	2.15	.47	1.67	.53	.11	.01	−.11	.03	.10	.10	.41
1988	4.2	2.65	.96	1.69	.45	.59	.63	.02	.43	.18	−.05	−.13
1989	3.7	1.86	.64	1.21	.72	.55	.71	.07	.35	.29	−.16	.17
1990	1.9	1.28	.16	1.12	−.45	−.25	.14	.05	−.14	.22	−.38	−.21
1991	−.1	.12	−.49	.61	−1.09	−.84	−.48	−.38	−.28	.18	−.35	−.26
1992	3.5	2.36	.76	1.60	1.11	.83	.33	−.18	.34	.17	.49	.28
1993	2.8	2.24	.99	1.26	1.24	1.17	.84	−.01	.73	.12	.32	.07
1994	4.0	2.51	1.26	1.26	1.90	1.29	.91	.05	.75	.11	.38	.61
1995	2.7	1.91	.71	1.20	.55	.99	1.15	.16	.78	.20	−.15	−.44
1996	3.8	2.26	1.06	1.20	1.49	1.48	1.13	.15	.65	.33	.35	.02
1997	4.4	2.45	1.12	1.33	2.01	1.49	1.38	.21	.76	.41	.11	.52
1998	4.5	3.42	1.54	1.88	1.76	1.82	1.44	.16	.91	.37	.38	−.07
1999	4.8	3.42	1.83	1.59	1.62	1.65	1.36	.01	.89	.45	.29	−.03
2000	4.1	3.32	1.23	2.09	1.31	1.34	1.31	.24	.71	.36	.03	−.03
2001	1.0	1.66	.72	.94	−1.11	−.27	−.31	−.04	−.31	.04	.04	−.84
2002	1.7	1.71	.92	.80	−.16	−.64	−.94	−.56	−.35	−.03	.29	.48
2003	2.9	2.13	1.15	.98	.76	.77	.30	−.09	.26	.14	.47	−.02
2004	3.8	2.53	1.21	1.32	1.64	1.23	.67	.00	.49	.18	.57	.41
2005	3.5	2.39	.98	1.41	1.26	1.33	.92	.06	.60	.26	.41	−.07
2006	2.9	2.05	.87	1.19	.60	.50	1.00	.22	.57	.21	−.50	.10
2007	1.9	1.49	.65	.84	−.48	−.24	.89	.42	.25	.23	−1.13	−.25
2008	−.1	−.14	−.71	.56	−1.52	−1.05	.08	.23	−.29	.14	−1.14	−.46
2009	−2.5	−.85	−.70	−.15	−3.52	−2.70	−1.95	−.72	−1.22	−.02	−.74	−.83
2010	2.6	1.20	.62	.57	1.86	.44	.52	−.50	.92	.11	−.08	1.42
2011	1.6	1.29	.49	.80	.94	.99	1.00	.07	.69	.24	.00	−.05
2012	2.2	1.03	.48	.55	1.64	1.47	1.16	.34	.62	.20	.31	.17
2013	1.8	.99	.70	.29	1.11	.87	.54	.04	.28	.22	.34	.23
2014	2.5	1.99	.90	1.10	.95	1.07	.95	.33	.42	.20	.12	−.12
2015	2.9	2.48	1.01	1.46	.85	.58	.25	−.10	.20	.15	.33	.28
2016	1.6	1.85	.77	1.08	−.23	.32	.09	−.16	−.08	.33	.23	−.55
2017	2.4	1.78	.83	.94	.75	.70	.57	.14	.27	.16	.13	.04
2018	2.9	2.05	.86	1.18	.87	.78	.84	.12	.39	.32	−.06	.09
2019 ᵖ	2.3	1.76	.79	.97	.32	.23	.29	−.14	.08	.35	−.06	.09
2016: I	2.0	2.11	.88	1.23	−.26	.43	−.08	−.35	−.24	.52	.50	−.68
II	1.9	1.95	.94	1.01	−.28	.44	.52	.27	−.14	.39	−.07	−.72
III	2.2	1.74	.84	.90	.09	.62	.72	.50	.02	.20	−.10	−.53
IV	2.0	1.70	.41	1.29	1.50	.33	.09	.07	.02	.00	.24	1.18
2017: I	2.3	1.63	.68	.95	.57	1.27	.84	.21	.36	.27	.43	−.70
II	2.2	1.63	1.14	.49	.59	.48	.57	.06	.50	.01	−.09	.11
III	3.2	1.61	.85	.76	1.25	.25	.32	−.24	.36	.21	−.08	1.00
IV	3.5	3.12	1.55	1.57	.80	1.45	1.08	.15	.72	.20	.37	−.64
2018: I	2.5	1.15	.27	.88	1.07	.94	1.15	.35	.39	.41	−.21	.13
II	3.5	2.70	1.13	1.57	−.30	.89	1.04	.33	.20	.51	−.15	−1.20
III	2.9	2.34	.75	1.59	2.27	.13	.29	−.07	.17	.18	−.16	2.14
IV	1.1	.97	.33	.65	.53	.46	.64	−.29	.42	.51	−.18	.07
2019: I	3.1	.78	.32	.46	1.09	.56	.60	.12	.00	.48	−.04	.53
II	2.0	3.03	1.74	1.29	−1.16	−.25	−.14	−.36	.05	.17	−.11	−.91
III	2.1	2.12	1.09	1.02	−.17	−.14	−.31	−.30	−.22	.22	.17	−.03
IV ᵖ	2.1	1.20	.26	.94	−1.08	.01	−.20	−.30	−.17	.27	.21	−1.09

See next page for continuation of table.

[Percentage points, except as noted; annual average to annual average, quarterly data at seasonally adjusted annual rates]

| Year or quarter | Net exports of goods and services | | | | | | | Government consumption expenditures and gross investment | | | | | Final sales of domestic product |
| | Net exports | Exports | | | Imports | | | Total | Federal | | | State and local | |
		Total	Goods	Services	Total	Goods	Services		Total	National defense	Non-defense		
1969	−0.03	0.25	0.20	0.05	−0.28	−0.20	−0.08	0.02	−0.34	−0.45	0.11	0.36	3.12
1970	.33	.54	.43	.11	−.21	−.14	−.07	−.50	−.80	−.83	.03	.30	.89
1971	−.18	.10	.00	.10	−.28	−.32	.04	−.45	−.80	−.97	.17	.35	2.74
1972	−.19	.42	.43	−.01	−.61	−.55	−.06	−.12	−.37	−.60	.22	.25	5.20
1973	.80	1.08	1.05	.02	−.28	−.33	.05	−.07	−.39	−.40	.01	.32	5.16
1974	.73	.56	.49	.08	.17	.17	.00	.47	.06	−.07	.14	.41	−.28
1975	.86	−.05	−.14	.09	.91	.85	.06	.49	.05	−.07	.13	.43	1.03
1976	−1.05	.36	.34	.02	−1.41	−1.31	−.10	.12	.01	−.04	.06	.10	4.01
1977	−.70	.19	.12	.07	−.89	−.82	−.07	.26	.21	.06	.15	.05	4.38
1978	.05	.80	.64	.17	−.76	−.66	−.10	.60	.23	.04	.19	.37	5.42
1979	.64	.80	.69	.11	−.16	−.13	−.02	.36	.20	.15	.05	.16	3.56
1980	1.64	.95	.88	.07	.69	.66	.03	.36	.38	.22	.16	−.02	.63
1981	−.15	.12	−.05	.17	−.26	−.18	−.09	.20	.43	.40	.03	−.23	1.41
1982	−.59	−.71	−.63	−.08	.12	.20	−.08	.37	.35	.47	−.11	.01	−.50
1983	−1.32	−.22	−.21	.00	−1.10	−.98	−.12	.79	.65	.51	.14	.14	4.31
1984	−1.54	.61	.41	.20	−2.16	−1.78	−.38	.74	.33	.38	−.04	.41	5.34
1985	−.39	.24	.20	.05	−.63	−.50	−.13	1.37	.78	.62	.16	.59	5.20
1986	−.29	.53	.27	.25	−.82	−.80	−.02	1.14	.61	.52	.09	.53	3.77
1987	.17	.77	.62	.15	−.60	−.39	−.21	.62	.38	.38	.01	.24	3.05
1988	.81	1.23	.99	.24	−.41	−.35	−.07	.26	−.15	−.04	−.12	.42	4.31
1989	.51	.97	.72	.26	−.46	−.37	−.09	.58	.15	−.02	.18	.43	3.51
1990	.40	.78	.56	.22	−.37	−.25	−.13	.65	.20	.02	.18	.45	2.09
1991	.62	.61	.45	.16	.01	−.04	.05	.25	.01	−.06	.07	.24	.15
1992	−.04	.66	.52	.14	−.70	−.76	.05	.10	−.15	−.31	.16	.25	3.24
1993	−.56	.31	.22	.09	−.87	−.82	−.05	−.17	−.32	−.32	.00	.15	2.68
1994	−.41	.84	.65	.19	−1.25	−1.15	−.10	.02	−.31	−.28	−.02	.32	3.41
1995	.12	1.02	.83	.19	−.90	−.84	−.06	.10	−.21	−.21	.00	.31	3.13
1996	−.15	.86	.68	.18	−1.01	−.91	−.10	.18	−.09	−.08	−.01	.27	3.76
1997	−.31	1.26	1.10	.16	−1.57	−1.40	−.17	.30	−.06	−.13	.07	.36	3.92
1998	−1.14	.26	.17	.08	−1.39	−1.18	−.21	.44	−.06	−.09	.03	.50	4.55
1999	−.87	.52	.31	.20	−1.39	−1.31	−.07	.58	.13	.06	.07	.46	4.78
2000	−.83	.86	.73	.13	−1.69	−1.44	−.25	.33	.02	−.04	.06	.31	4.16
2001	−.22	−.61	−.48	−.12	.39	.40	−.01	.67	.24	.13	.11	.43	1.84
2002	−.64	−.17	−.23	.06	−.47	−.40	−.07	.82	.47	.30	.18	.35	1.26
2003	−.45	.20	.19	.01	−.64	−.64	−.01	.41	.45	.35	.10	−.03	2.88
2004	−.67	.88	.57	.31	−1.55	−1.30	−.24	.30	.31	.26	.05	−.01	3.39
2005	−.29	.69	.52	.17	−.97	−.88	−.09	.15	.15	.11	.04	.00	3.59
2006	−.10	.94	.70	.23	−1.04	−.82	−.21	.30	.17	.07	.10	.13	2.75
2007	.53	.93	.53	.40	−.41	−.28	−.12	.34	.14	.13	.01	.20	2.12
2008	1.04	.66	.48	.18	.38	.49	−.10	.48	.46	.33	.13	.02	.33
2009	1.13	−1.01	−1.00	−.01	2.14	2.08	.06	.70	.47	.29	.18	.23	−1.71
2010	−.49	1.35	1.12	.23	−1.84	−1.74	−.10	.00	.35	.16	.19	−.35	1.14
2011	−.01	.90	.61	.28	−.91	−.82	−.09	−.66	−.23	−.12	−.11	−.44	1.60
2012	.00	.46	.36	.10	−.46	−.38	−.09	−.42	−.16	−.18	.03	−.26	2.08
2013	.22	.48	.30	.18	−.26	−.25	−.01	−.47	−.44	−.34	−.10	−.03	1.61
2014	−.25	.57	.42	.14	−.81	−.75	−.06	−.17	−.19	−.19	.00	.02	2.65
2015	−.77	.06	−.03	.09	−.83	−.73	−.10	.35	−.01	−.09	.08	.35	2.63
2016	−.30	.00	.04	−.05	−.30	−.18	−.12	.32	.03	−.02	.05	.29	2.19
2017	−.28	.41	.30	.11	−.69	−.57	−.12	.12	.05	.03	.02	.07	2.33
2018 *p*	−.29	.37	.34	.03	−.66	−.61	−.05	.30	.19	.13	.07	.11	2.84
2019 *p*	−.16	.00	.01	−.02	−.15	−.04	−.12	.41	.23	.19	.04	.18	2.24
2016: I	−.50	−.38	.05	−.43	−.11	.03	−.15	.67	.05	−.01	.06	.63	2.71
II	.35	.45	.20	.25	−.10	−.11	.01	−.12	−.18	−.21	.03	.06	2.62
III	.05	.71	.54	.17	−.66	−.42	−.24	.31	.13	.13	.00	.18	2.72
IV	−1.36	−.30	−.06	−.24	−1.06	−.92	−.14	.19	.04	−.04	.08	.15	.85
2017: I	.13	.72	.46	.25	−.58	−.48	−.10	−.04	−.08	−.07	.00	.03	2.99
II	−.31	.20	.18	.01	−.51	−.40	−.11	.24	.21	.25	−.04	.03	2.04
III	.35	.54	.18	.36	−.18	−.10	−.08	−.02	.01	−.06	.07	−.02	2.20
IV	−.80	1.19	1.03	.16	−1.99	−1.86	−.12	.42	.30	.17	.13	.12	4.19
2018: I	.00	.10	.11	.00	−.10	−.18	.08	.33	.18	.02	.16	.15	2.42
II	.67	.71	.94	−.23	−.04	−.10	.06	.44	.25	.28	−.03	.19	4.71
III	−2.05	−.78	−.78	.00	−1.27	−1.11	−.16	.36	.19	.11	.07	.17	.78
IV	−.35	.18	.21	−.03	−.53	−.28	−.24	−.07	.07	.20	−.12	−.14	1.02
2019: I	.73	.49	.36	.13	.23	.36	−.13	.50	.14	.29	−.15	.36	2.57
II	−.68	−.69	−.48	−.21	.01	−.02	.02	.82	.53	.13	.40	.29	2.92
III	−.14	.11	.17	−.05	−.26	−.13	−.13	.30	.22	.09	.13	.08	2.13
IV *p*	1.48	.17	−.08	.25	1.32	1.44	−.12	.47	.23	.19	.04	.23	3.17

Source: Department of Commerce (Bureau of Economic Analysis).

[Quarterly data at seasonally adjusted annual rates]

Year or quarter	Gross domestic product	Personal consumption expenditures			Gross private domestic investment							Change in private inventories
		Total	Goods	Services	Total	Fixed investment					Residential	
						Total	Nonresidential					
							Total	Structures	Equipment	Intellectual property products		
					Billions of dollars							
2004	12,213.7	8,212.7	2,902.0	5,310.6	2,281.3	2,217.2	1,467.4	307.7	721.9	437.8	749.8	64.1
2005	13,036.6	8,747.1	3,082.9	5,664.2	2,534.7	2,477.2	1,621.0	353.0	794.9	473.1	856.2	57.5
2006	13,814.6	9,260.3	3,239.7	6,020.7	2,701.0	2,632.0	1,793.8	425.2	862.3	506.3	838.2	69.0
2007	14,451.9	9,706.4	3,367.0	6,339.4	2,673.0	2,639.1	1,948.6	510.3	893.4	544.8	690.5	34.0
2008	14,712.8	9,976.3	3,363.2	6,613.1	2,477.6	2,506.9	1,990.9	571.1	845.4	574.4	516.0	−29.2
2009	14,448.9	9,842.2	3,180.0	6,662.2	1,929.7	2,080.4	1,690.4	455.8	670.3	564.4	390.0	−150.8
2010	14,992.1	10,185.8	3,317.8	6,868.0	2,165.5	2,111.6	1,735.0	379.8	777.0	578.2	376.6	53.9
2011	15,542.6	10,641.1	3,518.1	7,123.0	2,332.6	2,286.3	1,907.5	404.5	881.3	621.7	378.8	46.3
2012	16,197.0	11,006.8	3,637.7	7,369.1	2,621.8	2,550.5	2,118.5	479.4	983.4	655.7	432.0	71.2
2013	16,784.9	11,317.2	3,730.0	7,587.2	2,826.0	2,721.5	2,211.5	492.5	1,027.0	691.9	510.0	104.5
2014	17,527.3	11,822.8	3,863.0	7,959.8	3,044.2	2,960.2	2,400.1	577.6	1,091.9	730.5	560.2	84.0
2015	18,224.8	12,284.3	3,920.3	8,363.9	3,223.1	3,091.2	2,457.4	572.6	1,121.5	763.3	633.8	131.9
2016	18,715.0	12,748.5	3,995.9	8,752.6	3,178.7	3,151.6	2,453.1	545.8	1,093.6	813.8	698.5	27.1
2017	19,519.4	13,312.1	4,165.0	9,147.0	3,370.7	3,340.5	2,584.7	586.8	1,143.7	854.2	755.7	30.2
2018	20,580.2	13,998.7	4,364.8	9,633.9	3,628.3	3,573.6	2,786.9	633.2	1,222.6	931.1	786.7	54.7
2019 P	21,429.0	14,563.9	4,508.6	10,055.2	3,742.8	3,676.1	2,878.7	625.8	1,240.9	1,012.0	797.4	66.8
2016: I	18,424.3	12,523.5	3,933.2	8,590.3	3,149.1	3,102.2	2,415.6	520.5	1,101.4	793.8	686.6	46.9
II	18,637.3	12,688.3	3,988.6	8,699.6	3,152.9	3,133.8	2,441.8	537.1	1,092.7	812.1	692.0	19.1
III	18,806.7	12,822.4	4,017.8	8,804.6	3,166.6	3,169.3	2,471.6	559.6	1,091.2	820.9	697.7	−2.7
IV	18,991.9	12,959.8	4,044.0	8,915.8	3,246.2	3,201.3	2,483.5	566.0	1,088.9	828.6	717.8	44.9
2017: I	19,190.4	13,104.4	4,097.9	9,006.5	3,288.2	3,274.8	2,531.1	580.2	1,108.8	842.1	743.7	13.4
II	19,356.6	13,212.5	4,124.9	9,087.6	3,335.0	3,316.1	2,567.4	589.0	1,132.9	845.5	748.8	18.8
III	19,611.7	13,345.1	4,173.3	9,171.8	3,401.8	3,345.0	2,591.6	583.7	1,149.5	858.4	753.4	56.8
IV	19,918.9	13,586.3	4,264.0	9,322.3	3,457.7	3,426.0	2,648.9	594.4	1,183.6	870.9	777.1	31.7
2018: I	20,163.2	13,728.4	4,298.5	9,429.8	3,542.4	3,500.9	2,717.3	615.9	1,201.8	899.6	783.7	41.5
II	20,510.2	13,939.8	4,363.2	9,576.6	3,561.6	3,571.6	2,782.0	640.0	1,214.3	927.7	789.5	−10.0
III	20,749.8	14,114.6	4,398.0	9,716.6	3,684.0	3,596.7	2,807.7	641.7	1,227.9	938.1	789.0	87.3
IV	20,897.8	14,211.9	4,399.4	9,812.5	3,725.2	3,625.2	2,840.7	635.2	1,246.4	959.1	784.4	100.1
2019: I	21,098.8	14,266.3	4,397.7	9,868.6	3,783.4	3,670.1	2,882.7	645.8	1,249.0	987.9	787.4	113.3
II	21,340.3	14,511.2	4,507.0	10,004.2	3,749.5	3,674.7	2,890.0	633.2	1,252.9	1,003.9	784.7	74.8
III	21,542.5	14,678.2	4,556.7	10,121.5	3,744.6	3,677.6	2,877.2	619.4	1,237.4	1,020.5	800.3	67.0
IV P	21,734.3	14,799.8	4,573.1	10,226.7	3,693.9	3,682.0	2,864.9	604.7	1,224.4	1,035.8	817.1	11.9
					Billions of chained (2012) dollars							
2004	14,406.4	9,729.3	3,250.0	6,479.2	2,502.6	2,440.7	1,594.0	456.3	688.6	459.2	830.9	82.6
2005	14,912.5	10,075.9	3,384.7	6,689.5	2,670.6	2,618.7	1,716.4	466.1	760.0	493.1	885.4	63.7
2006	15,338.3	10,384.5	3,509.7	6,871.7	2,752.4	2,686.8	1,854.2	501.7	832.6	521.5	818.9	87.1
2007	15,626.0	10,615.3	3,607.6	7,003.6	2,684.1	2,653.5	1,982.1	568.6	865.8	554.3	665.8	40.6
2008	15,604.7	10,592.8	3,498.9	7,093.0	2,462.9	2,499.4	1,994.2	605.4	824.4	575.3	504.6	−32.7
2009	15,208.8	10,460.0	3,389.8	7,070.1	1,942.0	2,099.8	1,704.3	492.2	649.7	572.4	395.3	−177.3
2010	15,598.8	10,643.0	3,485.7	7,157.4	2,216.5	2,164.2	1,781.0	412.8	781.2	588.1	383.0	57.3
2011	15,840.7	10,843.8	3,561.8	7,282.1	2,362.1	2,317.8	1,935.4	424.1	886.2	624.8	382.5	46.7
2012	16,197.0	11,006.8	3,637.7	7,369.1	2,621.8	2,550.5	2,118.5	479.4	983.4	655.7	432.0	71.2
2013	16,495.4	11,166.9	3,752.2	7,415.5	2,801.5	2,692.1	2,206.0	485.5	1,029.2	691.4	485.5	108.7
2014	16,912.0	11,497.4	3,905.1	7,594.9	2,959.2	2,869.2	2,365.3	538.8	1,101.1	724.8	504.1	86.3
2015	17,403.8	11,921.2	4,088.6	7,838.5	3,104.3	2,967.0	2,408.2	522.4	1,136.6	750.7	555.3	132.4
2016	17,688.9	12,247.5	4,236.6	8,021.1	3,064.0	3,023.6	2,425.3	496.4	1,122.3	810.0	591.2	23.0
2017	18,108.1	12,566.9	4,403.4	8,182.2	3,198.9	3,149.7	2,531.2	519.5	1,175.6	839.6	611.9	31.7
2018	18,638.2	12,944.6	4,583.3	8,388.1	3,360.5	3,293.4	2,692.3	540.9	1,255.3	901.6	602.9	48.1
2019 P	19,072.5	13,279.6	4,756.6	8,560.8	3,421.2	3,337.1	2,749.8	516.8	1,272.4	971.1	593.5	65.3
2016: I	17,556.8	12,124.2	4,176.2	7,955.8	3,054.7	2,991.0	2,389.8	476.4	1,126.5	792.0	593.0	51.1
II	17,639.4	12,211.3	4,222.4	7,998.9	3,041.6	3,010.9	2,413.6	487.9	1,120.0	809.8	590.1	10.8
III	17,735.1	12,289.1	4,263.8	8,037.2	3,045.5	3,038.9	2,446.8	509.0	1,120.9	819.2	586.2	−14.7
IV	17,824.2	12,365.3	4,284.2	8,092.2	3,114.0	3,053.7	2,451.2	512.1	1,122.0	819.2	595.5	44.8
2017: I	17,925.3	12,438.9	4,318.2	8,133.0	3,140.3	3,111.1	2,490.5	521.1	1,139.3	831.8	612.4	8.7
II	18,021.0	12,512.9	4,375.9	8,154.1	3,167.9	3,133.0	2,517.4	523.7	1,163.8	832.3	608.9	16.6
III	18,163.6	12,586.3	4,419.7	8,186.6	3,225.2	3,144.1	2,532.6	513.3	1,181.4	842.3	605.9	70.2
IV	18,322.5	12,729.7	4,499.8	8,254.9	3,262.1	3,210.7	2,584.2	519.9	1,217.8	852.0	620.4	31.1
2018: I	18,438.3	12,782.9	4,513.9	8,293.5	3,311.8	3,254.0	2,639.5	534.9	1,237.5	872.0	612.1	40.5
II	18,598.1	12,909.2	4,573.5	8,362.9	3,296.6	3,295.4	2,689.9	549.1	1,247.8	896.9	606.3	−28.0
III	18,732.7	13,019.8	4,614.0	8,433.6	3,404.2	3,301.3	2,703.9	546.2	1,256.7	905.9	600.1	87.2
IV	18,783.5	13,066.3	4,631.8	8,462.6	3,429.5	3,323.0	2,735.8	533.4	1,279.2	931.3	593.0	93.0
2019: I	18,927.3	13,103.3	4,649.2	8,483.1	3,481.1	3,349.4	2,765.6	538.6	1,278.9	955.6	591.4	116.0
II	19,021.9	13,250.0	4,746.4	8,541.4	3,424.7	3,337.4	2,758.5	523.0	1,281.5	964.2	587.0	69.4
III	19,121.1	13,353.1	4,808.0	8,587.9	3,416.2	3,330.5	2,742.7	509.6	1,269.3	975.2	593.7	69.4
IV P	19,219.8	13,411.9	4,822.8	8,630.9	3,363.0	3,331.0	2,732.4	496.2	1,259.9	989.3	602.1	6.5

See next page for continuation of table.

[Quarterly data at seasonally adjusted annual rates]

Year or quarter	Net exports	Exports	Imports	Total	Federal Total	National defense	Nondefense	State and local	Final sales of domestic product	Gross domestic purchases [1]	Final sales to private domestic purchasers [2]	Gross domestic income (GDI) [3]	Average of GDP and GDI
	Net exports of goods and services			Government consumption expenditures and gross investment									

Billions of dollars

2004	−619.1	1,177.6	1,796.7	2,338.9	891.7	569.9	321.9	1,447.1	12,149.7	12,832.8	10,429.8	12,235.8	12,224.8
2005	−721.2	1,305.2	2,026.4	2,476.0	947.5	609.4	338.0	1,528.5	12,979.1	13,757.8	11,224.3	13,091.7	13,064.2
2006	−770.9	1,472.6	2,243.5	2,624.2	1,000.7	640.8	359.9	1,623.5	13,745.6	14,585.5	11,892.3	14,022.5	13,918.6
2007	−718.4	1,660.9	2,379.3	2,790.8	1,050.5	679.3	371.2	1,740.3	14,417.9	15,170.3	12,345.5	14,434.2	14,443.0
2008	−723.1	1,837.1	2,560.1	2,982.0	1,150.6	750.3	400.2	1,831.4	14,742.1	15,435.9	12,483.2	14,530.0	14,621.4
2009	−396.5	1,582.0	1,978.4	3,073.5	1,218.2	787.6	430.6	1,855.3	14,599.7	14,845.4	11,922.6	14,256.8	14,352.9
2010	−513.9	1,846.3	2,360.2	3,154.6	1,297.9	828.0	469.9	1,856.7	14,938.1	15,506.0	12,297.4	14,931.0	14,961.5
2011	−579.5	2,103.0	2,682.5	3,148.4	1,298.9	834.0	465.0	1,849.4	15,496.3	16,122.0	12,927.4	15,595.8	15,569.2
2012	−568.6	2,191.3	2,759.9	3,137.0	1,286.5	814.2	472.4	1,850.5	16,125.8	16,765.6	13,557.4	16,438.4	16,317.7
2013	−490.8	2,273.4	2,764.2	3,132.4	1,226.6	764.2	462.4	1,905.8	16,680.3	17,275.6	14,038.7	16,945.2	16,865.0
2014	−507.7	2,371.7	2,879.4	3,168.0	1,215.0	743.4	471.6	1,953.0	17,443.3	18,034.9	14,783.0	17,816.4	17,671.8
2015	−519.8	2,266.8	2,786.6	3,237.3	1,221.5	730.1	491.4	2,015.7	18,092.9	18,744.6	15,375.5	18,479.7	18,352.2
2016	−518.8	2,220.6	2,739.4	3,306.7	1,234.1	728.4	505.7	2,072.6	18,688.0	19,233.6	15,900.1	18,827.0	18,771.0
2017	−575.3	2,356.7	2,932.1	3,412.0	1,269.3	746.2	523.1	2,142.7	19,489.2	20,094.8	16,652.6	19,587.0	19,553.2
2018	−638.2	2,510.3	3,148.5	3,591.5	1,347.3	793.6	553.7	2,244.2	20,525.5	21,218.4	17,572.2	20,569.4	20,574.8
2019 *p*	−632.0	2,503.8	3,135.7	3,754.3	1,423.4	846.6	576.8	2,330.8	21,362.2	22,061.0	18,239.9		
2016: I	−522.2	2,164.9	2,687.1	3,273.8	1,227.5	727.6	500.0	2,046.3	18,377.4	18,946.5	15,625.7	18,673.5	18,548.9
II	−495.3	2,208.1	2,703.4	3,291.4	1,226.2	722.3	503.9	2,065.2	18,618.1	19,132.6	15,822.0	18,718.3	18,677.8
III	−499.7	2,254.4	2,754.1	3,317.5	1,237.5	731.3	506.1	2,080.0	18,809.5	19,306.5	15,991.7	18,880.6	18,843.7
IV	−558.0	2,255.1	2,813.1	3,343.9	1,245.2	732.3	512.9	2,098.7	18,946.9	19,549.8	16,161.0	19,035.5	19,013.7
2017: I	−570.9	2,303.3	2,874.2	3,368.7	1,248.4	732.1	516.3	2,120.3	19,177.0	19,761.4	16,379.2	19,307.0	19,248.7
II	−583.7	2,313.2	2,896.9	3,392.9	1,263.6	746.2	517.4	2,129.3	19,337.8	19,940.4	16,528.6	19,496.9	19,426.8
III	−550.6	2,360.1	2,910.7	3,415.4	1,270.2	746.2	524.0	2,145.2	19,554.9	20,162.3	16,690.0	19,638.4	19,625.0
IV	−596.1	2,450.3	3,046.5	3,471.0	1,295.1	760.4	534.8	2,175.9	19,887.2	20,515.0	17,012.3	19,905.6	19,912.3
2018: I	−629.0	2,476.6	3,105.6	3,521.4	1,318.2	769.9	548.3	2,203.2	20,121.7	20,792.1	17,229.3	20,252.2	20,207.7
II	−568.4	2,543.6	3,112.0	3,577.1	1,340.4	789.5	550.9	2,236.7	20,520.1	21,078.6	17,511.4	20,460.1	20,485.1
III	−671.4	2,510.3	3,181.6	3,622.6	1,358.6	800.6	558.0	2,263.9	20,662.4	21,421.1	17,711.2	20,716.9	20,733.3
IV	−684.1	2,510.5	3,194.7	3,644.8	1,371.8	814.4	557.4	2,273.0	20,797.7	21,582.0	17,837.1	20,848.6	20,873.2
2019: I	−633.8	2,520.3	3,154.1	3,683.1	1,394.7	831.8	562.9	2,288.4	20,985.5	21,732.7	17,936.3	21,056.7	21,077.8
II	−662.7	2,504.0	3,166.7	3,742.3	1,415.2	841.6	573.5	2,327.1	21,265.5	22,002.9	18,185.9	21,237.8	21,289.0
III	−653.0	2,495.1	3,148.2	3,772.8	1,432.2	849.3	583.0	2,340.5	21,475.5	22,195.6	18,355.8	21,440.4	21,491.5
IV *p*	−578.4	2,495.6	3,074.0	3,818.9	1,451.6	863.9	587.7	2,367.3	21,722.4	22,312.7	18,481.8		

Billions of chained (2012) dollars

2004	−841.4	1,431.2	2,272.6	2,992.7	1,077.5	692.7	384.8	1,920.1	14,335.7	15,254.1	12,194.2	14,432.4	14,419.4
2005	−887.8	1,533.2	2,421.0	3,015.5	1,099.1	708.6	390.6	1,920.1	14,852.3	15,804.5	12,775.4	14,975.5	14,944.0
2006	−905.0	1,676.4	2,581.5	3,063.5	1,125.0	719.8	405.3	1,941.6	15,263.0	16,246.7	13,102.6	15,569.1	15,453.7
2007	−823.6	1,822.3	2,646.0	3,118.6	1,147.0	740.3	406.7	1,974.7	15,588.7	16,454.6	13,293.8	15,606.9	15,616.5
2008	−661.6	1,925.4	2,587.1	3,195.6	1,218.8	791.5	427.3	1,978.7	15,639.7	16,270.7	13,108.0	15,410.8	15,507.7
2009	−484.8	1,763.8	2,248.6	3,307.3	1,293.0	836.7	456.3	2,015.6	15,373.0	15,698.9	12,557.6	15,006.6	15,107.7
2010	−565.9	1,977.9	2,543.8	3,307.2	1,346.1	861.3	484.8	1,961.3	15,546.6	16,164.7	12,805.7	15,535.2	15,567.0
2011	−568.1	2,119.0	2,687.1	3,203.3	1,311.1	842.9	468.3	1,892.2	15,796.5	16,408.8	13,161.2	15,894.9	15,867.8
2012	−568.6	2,191.3	2,759.9	3,137.0	1,286.5	814.2	472.4	1,850.5	16,125.8	16,765.6	13,557.4	16,438.4	16,317.7
2013	−532.8	2,269.6	2,802.4	3,061.0	1,215.3	759.6	455.6	1,845.3	16,386.2	17,028.6	13,858.9	16,652.9	16,574.1
2014	−577.2	2,365.3	2,942.5	3,033.4	1,183.8	728.4	455.2	1,848.6	16,822.3	17,487.7	14,366.5	17,191.1	17,051.5
2015	−721.6	2,376.5	3,098.1	3,091.8	1,182.7	713.0	469.3	1,907.5	17,267.1	18,114.2	14,888.0	17,647.3	17,525.6
2016	−783.7	2,376.1	3,159.8	3,147.7	1,187.8	708.7	478.5	1,957.9	17,647.6	18,455.9	15,270.8	17,794.7	17,741.8
2017	−849.8	2,458.8	3,308.5	3,169.6	1,197.0	714.0	482.4	1,970.6	18,058.4	18,931.2	15,716.4	18,170.8	18,139.4
2018	−920.0	2,532.9	3,453.0	3,223.9	1,232.2	737.5	494.2	1,990.0	18,571.3	19,523.2	16,237.8	18,628.4	18,633.3
2019 *p*	−954.2	2,531.9	3,486.1	3,299.4	1,275.7	773.6	501.9	2,022.5	18,988.7	19,994.4	16,616.3		
2016: I	−777.7	2,345.1	3,122.7	3,143.0	1,190.6	713.2	476.8	1,950.5	17,492.6	18,318.9	15,114.9	17,794.3	17,675.6
II	−760.9	2,367.9	3,128.9	3,137.5	1,182.5	703.8	478.0	1,953.0	17,607.5	18,387.3	15,221.9	17,716.2	17,677.8
III	−761.4	2,403.4	3,164.9	3,151.0	1,188.2	709.8	477.8	1,960.8	17,726.7	18,482.5	15,327.6	17,804.7	17,769.9
IV	−834.6	2,388.1	3,222.7	3,159.3	1,189.9	708.1	481.1	1,967.4	17,763.5	18,635.1	15,418.7	17,865.2	17,844.7
2017: I	−831.5	2,423.5	3,255.0	3,157.3	1,186.4	704.7	480.9	1,968.9	17,895.1	18,732.7	15,549.7	18,034.1	17,979.7
II	−850.0	2,432.9	3,282.9	3,168.0	1,195.9	716.4	479.0	1,970.1	17,985.3	18,844.8	15,645.6	18,151.7	18,086.3
III	−833.7	2,459.5	3,293.2	3,167.1	1,196.1	713.4	482.0	1,969.0	18,082.5	18,974.1	15,730.1	18,188.3	18,175.9
IV	−883.8	2,519.2	3,403.0	3,186.1	1,209.8	721.4	487.7	1,974.5	18,270.7	19,173.1	15,940.2	18,310.2	18,316.3
2018: I	−884.2	2,524.0	3,408.2	3,201.1	1,218.1	722.5	494.9	1,981.2	18,380.4	19,290.7	16,036.7	18,519.7	18,479.0
II	−850.5	2,559.9	3,410.4	3,221.4	1,229.9	735.7	493.6	1,989.9	18,595.6	19,422.1	16,204.4	18,552.7	18,575.4
III	−962.4	2,519.3	3,481.8	3,238.0	1,238.7	741.2	497.0	1,997.7	18,630.9	19,656.0	16,320.9	18,703.1	18,717.9
IV	−983.0	2,528.5	3,511.6	3,234.9	1,242.1	750.6	491.3	1,991.4	18,678.3	19,724.2	16,389.2	18,739.3	18,761.4
2019: I	−944.0	2,554.4	3,498.3	3,258.1	1,248.8	764.5	484.5	2,007.9	18,797.5	19,836.1	16,452.7	18,889.5	18,908.4
II	−980.7	2,517.5	3,498.2	3,296.6	1,273.9	770.8	502.9	2,021.4	18,935.2	19,965.4	16,587.1	18,930.5	18,976.2
III	−990.1	2,523.4	3,513.6	3,310.4	1,284.4	775.0	509.1	2,024.9	19,035.7	20,073.7	16,683.1	19,030.5	19,075.8
IV *p*	−902.0	2,532.4	3,434.4	3,332.4	1,295.7	784.3	511.1	2,035.8	19,186.4	20,102.2	16,742.4		

[1] Gross domestic product (GDP) less exports of goods and services plus imports of goods and services.
[2] Personal consumption expenditures plus gross private fixed investment.
[3] For chained dollar measures, gross domestic income is deflated by the implicit price deflator for GDP.

Source: Department of Commerce (Bureau of Economic Analysis).

TABLE B–4. Percentage shares of gross domestic product, 1969–2019

[Percent of nominal GDP]

Year or quarter	Gross domestic product (percent)	Personal consumption expenditures			Gross private domestic investment								
					Total	Fixed investment							Change in private inventories
						Total	Nonresidential					Residential	
		Total	Goods	Services			Total	Total	Structures	Equipment	Intellectual property products		
1969	100.0	59.3	29.9	29.4	17.1	16.2	11.8	3.7	6.4	1.7	4.4	0.9
1970	100.0	60.3	29.7	30.6	15.8	15.7	11.6	3.8	6.2	1.7	4.0	.2
1971	100.0	60.1	29.4	30.7	16.9	16.2	11.2	3.7	5.9	1.6	5.0	.7
1972	100.0	60.1	29.2	30.8	17.8	17.1	11.5	3.7	6.2	1.6	5.7	.7
1973	100.0	59.6	29.2	30.4	18.7	17.6	12.1	3.9	6.7	1.6	5.5	1.1
1974	100.0	60.2	29.2	31.0	17.8	16.9	12.4	4.0	6.8	1.7	4.5	.9
1975	100.0	61.2	29.2	32.0	15.3	15.6	11.7	3.6	6.4	1.7	4.0	−.4
1976	100.0	61.3	29.2	32.1	17.3	16.3	11.7	3.5	6.5	1.7	4.6	.9
1977	100.0	61.2	28.8	32.4	19.1	18.0	12.4	3.6	7.1	1.7	5.5	1.1
1978	100.0	60.5	28.2	32.3	20.3	19.2	13.4	4.0	7.7	1.7	5.9	1.1
1979	100.0	60.3	28.1	32.3	20.5	19.9	14.2	4.5	7.9	1.8	5.6	.7
1980	100.0	61.3	28.0	33.3	18.6	18.8	14.2	4.8	7.6	1.9	4.5	−.2
1981	100.0	60.3	27.1	33.2	19.7	18.8	14.7	5.2	7.5	2.0	4.0	.9
1982	100.0	61.9	26.9	35.0	17.4	17.8	14.5	5.3	7.0	2.2	3.3	−.4
1983	100.0	62.8	26.8	36.0	17.5	17.7	13.3	4.2	6.8	2.2	4.4	−.2
1984	100.0	61.7	26.3	35.4	20.3	18.7	14.0	4.4	7.2	2.4	4.7	1.6
1985	100.0	62.5	26.2	36.3	19.1	18.6	14.0	4.5	7.1	2.4	4.6	.5
1986	100.0	63.0	26.1	36.9	18.5	18.4	13.3	3.9	6.9	2.5	5.1	.1
1987	100.0	63.4	25.9	37.5	18.4	17.8	12.7	3.6	6.6	2.5	5.1	.6
1988	100.0	63.6	25.5	38.1	17.9	17.5	12.6	3.5	6.6	2.5	4.9	.4
1989	100.0	63.4	25.2	38.2	17.7	17.2	12.7	3.4	6.6	2.7	4.5	.5
1990	100.0	63.9	25.0	38.9	16.7	16.4	12.4	3.4	6.2	2.8	4.0	.2
1991	100.0	64.0	24.3	39.7	15.3	15.3	11.8	3.0	5.9	2.9	3.6	.0
1992	100.0	64.4	24.0	40.4	15.5	15.3	11.4	2.6	5.9	2.9	3.9	.3
1993	100.0	64.9	23.9	41.0	16.1	15.8	11.7	2.6	6.2	2.9	4.2	.3
1994	100.0	64.8	24.0	40.8	17.2	16.4	11.9	2.6	6.5	2.8	4.4	.9
1995	100.0	65.0	23.8	41.2	17.2	16.8	12.6	2.7	6.9	3.0	4.2	.4
1996	100.0	65.0	23.8	41.2	17.7	17.4	12.9	2.8	7.0	3.1	4.4	.4
1997	100.0	64.5	23.4	41.2	18.6	17.8	13.4	2.9	7.1	3.4	4.4	.8
1998	100.0	64.9	23.3	41.6	19.2	18.5	13.8	3.0	7.3	3.5	4.6	.7
1999	100.0	65.2	23.7	41.5	19.6	19.0	14.2	3.0	7.4	3.8	4.8	.6
2000	100.0	66.0	23.9	42.0	19.9	19.4	14.6	3.1	7.5	4.0	4.7	.5
2001	100.0	66.8	23.9	42.9	18.3	18.6	13.8	3.2	6.7	3.9	4.8	−.4
2002	100.0	67.1	23.8	43.4	17.7	17.5	12.4	2.6	6.0	3.7	5.1	.2
2003	100.0	67.4	23.8	43.6	17.7	17.6	12.0	2.5	5.9	3.7	5.6	.1
2004	100.0	67.2	23.8	43.5	18.7	18.2	12.0	2.5	5.9	3.6	6.1	.5
2005	100.0	67.1	23.6	43.4	19.4	19.0	12.4	2.7	6.1	3.6	6.6	.4
2006	100.0	67.0	23.5	43.6	19.6	19.1	13.0	3.1	6.2	3.7	6.1	.5
2007	100.0	67.2	23.3	43.9	18.5	18.3	13.5	3.5	6.2	3.8	4.8	.2
2008	100.0	67.8	22.9	44.9	16.8	17.0	13.5	3.9	5.7	3.9	3.5	−.2
2009	100.0	68.1	22.0	46.1	13.4	14.4	11.7	3.2	4.6	3.9	2.7	−1.0
2010	100.0	67.9	22.1	45.8	14.4	14.1	11.6	2.5	5.2	3.9	2.5	.4
2011	100.0	68.5	22.6	45.8	15.0	14.7	12.3	2.6	5.7	4.0	2.4	.3
2012	100.0	68.0	22.5	45.5	16.2	15.7	13.1	3.0	6.1	4.0	2.7	.4
2013	100.0	67.4	22.2	45.2	16.8	16.2	13.2	2.9	6.1	4.1	3.0	.6
2014	100.0	67.5	22.0	45.4	17.4	16.9	13.7	3.3	6.2	4.2	3.2	.5
2015	100.0	67.4	21.5	45.9	17.7	17.0	13.5	3.1	6.2	4.2	3.5	.7
2016	100.0	68.1	21.4	46.8	17.0	16.8	13.1	2.9	5.8	4.3	3.7	.1
2017	100.0	68.2	21.3	46.9	17.3	17.1	13.2	3.0	5.9	4.4	3.9	.2
2018	100.0	68.0	21.2	46.8	17.6	17.4	13.5	3.1	5.9	4.5	3.8	.3
2019 ᵖ	100.0	68.0	21.0	46.9	17.5	17.2	13.4	2.9	5.8	4.7	3.7	.3
2016: I	100.0	68.0	21.3	46.6	17.1	16.8	13.1	2.8	6.0	4.3	3.7	.3
II	100.0	68.1	21.4	46.7	16.9	16.8	13.1	2.9	5.9	4.4	3.7	.1
III	100.0	68.2	21.4	46.8	16.8	16.9	13.1	3.0	5.8	4.4	3.7	.0
IV	100.0	68.2	21.3	46.9	17.1	16.9	13.1	3.0	5.7	4.4	3.8	.2
2017: I	100.0	68.3	21.4	46.9	17.1	17.1	13.2	3.0	5.8	4.4	3.9	.1
II	100.0	68.3	21.3	46.9	17.2	17.1	13.3	3.0	5.9	4.4	3.9	.1
III	100.0	68.0	21.3	46.8	17.3	17.1	13.2	3.0	5.9	4.4	3.8	.3
IV	100.0	68.2	21.4	46.8	17.4	17.2	13.3	3.0	5.9	4.4	3.9	.2
2018: I	100.0	68.1	21.3	46.8	17.6	17.4	13.5	3.1	6.0	4.5	3.9	.2
II	100.0	68.0	21.3	46.7	17.4	17.4	13.6	3.1	5.9	4.5	3.8	.0
III	100.0	68.0	21.2	46.8	17.8	17.3	13.5	3.1	5.9	4.5	3.8	.4
IV	100.0	68.0	21.1	47.0	17.8	17.3	13.6	3.0	6.0	4.6	3.8	.5
2019: I	100.0	67.6	20.8	46.8	17.9	17.4	13.7	3.1	5.9	4.7	3.7	.5
II	100.0	68.0	21.1	46.9	17.6	17.2	13.5	3.0	5.9	4.7	3.7	.4
III	100.0	68.1	21.2	47.0	17.4	17.1	13.4	2.9	5.7	4.7	3.7	.3
IV ᵖ	100.0	68.1	21.0	47.1	17.0	16.9	13.2	2.8	5.6	4.8	3.8	.1

See next page for continuation of table.

Table B–4. Percentage shares of gross domestic product, 1969–2019—*Continued*

[Percent of nominal GDP]

Year or quarter	Net exports of goods and services							Government consumption expenditures and gross investment				
	Net exports	Exports			Imports			Total	Federal			State and local
		Total	Goods	Services	Total	Goods	Services		Total	National defense	Non-defense	
1969	0.1	5.1	3.8	1.3	5.0	3.6	1.3	23.5	12.9	10.0	2.9	10.6
1970	.4	5.6	4.2	1.4	5.2	3.8	1.4	23.5	12.4	9.4	3.0	11.2
1971	.1	5.4	4.0	1.4	5.4	4.0	1.4	23.0	11.5	8.4	3.1	11.4
1972	−.3	5.5	4.1	1.4	5.8	4.5	1.4	22.4	11.1	7.9	3.2	11.3
1973	.3	6.7	5.3	1.4	6.4	5.0	1.4	21.4	10.3	7.2	3.1	11.1
1974	−.1	8.2	6.7	1.5	8.2	6.8	1.5	22.1	10.3	7.1	3.2	11.8
1975	.9	8.2	6.7	1.6	7.3	5.9	1.4	22.6	10.3	7.0	3.3	12.3
1976	−.1	8.0	6.5	1.5	8.1	6.7	1.4	21.6	9.9	6.7	3.2	11.7
1977	−1.1	7.7	6.2	1.5	8.8	7.3	1.4	20.9	9.6	6.5	3.2	11.2
1978	−1.1	7.9	6.4	1.6	9.0	7.5	1.5	20.3	9.3	6.2	3.1	10.9
1979	−.9	8.8	7.1	1.6	9.6	8.1	1.5	20.0	9.2	6.1	3.0	10.8
1980	−.5	9.8	8.1	1.8	10.3	8.7	1.6	20.6	9.6	6.4	3.2	11.0
1981	−.4	9.5	7.6	1.9	9.9	8.4	1.6	20.4	9.8	6.7	3.1	10.6
1982	−.6	8.5	6.7	1.8	9.1	7.5	1.6	21.3	10.4	7.3	3.1	10.9
1983	−1.4	7.6	5.9	1.7	9.0	7.5	1.5	21.1	10.5	7.5	3.0	10.6
1984	−2.5	7.5	5.7	1.8	10.0	8.3	1.7	20.5	10.2	7.4	2.8	10.3
1985	−2.6	7.0	5.2	1.7	9.6	7.9	1.7	21.0	10.4	7.6	2.8	10.5
1986	−2.9	7.0	5.1	2.0	9.9	8.1	1.8	21.3	10.5	7.7	2.8	10.8
1987	−3.0	7.5	5.5	2.0	10.5	8.5	1.9	21.2	10.4	7.7	2.7	10.9
1988	−2.1	8.5	6.3	2.1	10.6	8.6	1.9	20.6	9.8	7.3	2.5	10.8
1989	−1.5	8.9	6.6	2.3	10.5	8.6	1.9	20.4	9.5	6.9	2.5	11.0
1990	−1.3	9.3	6.8	2.5	10.6	8.5	2.0	20.8	9.4	6.8	2.6	11.3
1991	−.5	9.7	7.0	2.7	10.1	8.1	2.0	21.1	9.5	6.7	2.7	11.6
1992	−.5	9.7	7.0	2.7	10.2	8.4	1.9	20.6	9.0	6.2	2.8	11.6
1993	−1.0	9.5	6.8	2.7	10.5	8.6	1.9	19.9	8.5	5.7	2.7	11.4
1994	−1.3	9.9	7.1	2.8	11.2	9.3	1.9	19.2	7.9	5.2	2.6	11.4
1995	−1.2	10.6	7.8	2.9	11.8	9.9	1.9	19.0	7.5	4.9	2.6	11.4
1996	−1.2	10.7	7.8	3.0	11.9	10.0	1.9	18.5	7.2	4.7	2.5	11.3
1997	−1.2	11.1	8.2	3.0	12.3	10.3	2.0	18.0	6.8	4.3	2.5	11.2
1998	−1.8	10.5	7.6	2.9	12.3	10.3	2.0	17.8	6.5	4.1	2.4	11.3
1999	−2.7	10.3	7.4	2.9	13.0	10.9	2.0	17.9	6.3	4.0	2.4	11.5
2000	−3.7	10.7	7.8	2.9	14.4	12.2	2.2	17.8	6.2	3.8	2.4	11.6
2001	−3.5	9.7	7.0	2.7	13.2	11.1	2.1	18.4	6.3	3.9	2.4	12.1
2002	−3.9	9.1	6.5	2.6	13.0	10.9	2.1	19.1	6.8	4.2	2.6	12.3
2003	−4.4	9.0	6.4	2.6	13.4	11.3	2.2	19.3	7.2	4.5	2.7	12.1
2004	−5.1	9.6	6.8	2.8	14.7	12.3	2.4	19.1	7.3	4.7	2.6	11.8
2005	−5.5	10.0	7.1	2.9	15.5	13.2	2.4	19.0	7.3	4.7	2.6	11.7
2006	−5.6	10.7	7.6	3.1	16.2	13.7	2.5	19.0	7.2	4.6	2.6	11.8
2007	−5.0	11.5	8.0	3.5	16.5	13.8	2.6	19.3	7.3	4.7	2.6	12.0
2008	−4.9	12.5	8.8	3.7	17.4	14.6	2.8	20.3	7.8	5.1	2.7	12.4
2009	−2.7	10.9	7.3	3.6	13.7	11.0	2.7	21.3	8.4	5.5	3.0	12.8
2010	−3.4	12.3	8.5	3.8	15.7	13.0	2.8	21.0	8.7	5.5	3.1	12.4
2011	−3.7	13.5	9.4	4.1	17.3	14.4	2.8	20.3	8.4	5.4	3.0	11.9
2012	−3.5	13.5	9.4	4.1	17.0	14.2	2.8	19.4	7.9	5.0	2.9	11.4
2013	−2.9	13.5	9.3	4.3	16.5	13.7	2.8	18.7	7.3	4.6	2.8	11.4
2014	−2.9	13.5	9.2	4.3	16.4	13.6	2.8	18.1	6.9	4.2	2.7	11.1
2015	−2.9	12.4	8.2	4.2	15.3	12.6	2.7	17.8	6.7	4.0	2.7	11.1
2016	−2.8	11.9	7.7	4.1	14.6	11.9	2.8	17.7	6.6	3.9	2.7	11.1
2017	−2.9	12.1	7.9	4.2	15.0	12.2	2.8	17.5	6.5	3.8	2.7	11.0
2018	−3.1	12.2	8.1	4.1	15.3	12.5	2.8	17.5	6.5	3.9	2.7	10.9
2019 *p*	−2.9	11.7	7.7	4.0	14.6	11.8	2.8	17.5	6.6	4.0	2.7	10.9
2016: I	−2.8	11.8	7.6	4.1	14.6	11.8	2.8	17.8	6.7	3.9	2.7	11.1
II	−2.7	11.8	7.7	4.2	14.5	11.8	2.7	17.7	6.6	3.9	2.7	11.1
III	−2.7	12.0	7.8	4.2	14.6	11.9	2.8	17.6	6.6	3.9	2.7	11.1
IV	−2.9	11.9	7.7	4.1	14.8	12.0	2.8	17.6	6.6	3.9	2.7	11.1
2017: I	−3.0	12.0	7.8	4.2	15.0	12.2	2.8	17.6	6.5	3.8	2.7	11.0
II	−3.0	12.0	7.8	4.2	15.0	12.1	2.8	17.5	6.5	3.9	2.7	11.0
III	−2.8	12.0	7.8	4.2	14.8	12.0	2.8	17.4	6.5	3.8	2.7	10.9
IV	−3.0	12.3	8.1	4.2	15.3	12.4	2.8	17.4	6.5	3.8	2.7	10.9
2018: I	−3.1	12.3	8.1	4.2	15.4	12.6	2.8	17.5	6.5	3.8	2.7	10.9
II	−2.8	12.4	8.3	4.1	15.2	12.4	2.8	17.4	6.5	3.8	2.7	10.9
III	−3.2	12.1	8.0	4.1	15.3	12.5	2.8	17.5	6.5	3.9	2.7	10.9
IV	−3.3	12.0	7.9	4.1	15.3	12.4	2.8	17.4	6.6	3.9	2.7	10.9
2019: I	−3.0	11.9	7.9	4.1	14.9	12.1	2.8	17.5	6.6	3.9	2.7	10.8
II	−3.1	11.7	7.7	4.0	14.8	12.0	2.8	17.5	6.6	3.9	2.7	10.9
III	−3.0	11.6	7.6	4.0	14.6	11.8	2.8	17.5	6.6	3.9	2.7	10.9
IV *p*	−2.7	11.5	7.5	4.0	14.1	11.3	2.8	17.6	6.7	4.0	2.7	10.9

Source: Department of Commerce (Bureau of Economic Analysis).

TABLE B–5. Chain-type price indexes for gross domestic product, 1969–2019

[Index numbers, 2012=100, except as noted; quarterly data seasonally adjusted]

Year or quarter	Gross domestic product	Personal consumption expenditures			Gross private domestic investment						
		Total	Goods	Services	Total	Fixed investment					Residential
						Total	Nonresidential				
							Total	Structures	Equipment	Intellectual property products	
1969	20.590	20.015	30.934	15.078	28.402	27.498	34.638	11.114	59.657	36.204	15.518
1970	21.676	20.951	32.114	15.913	29.624	28.699	36.295	11.845	61.891	37.929	16.016
1971	22.776	21.841	33.079	16.781	31.092	30.134	37.997	12.757	63.848	39.318	16.943
1972	23.760	22.586	33.926	17.491	32.388	31.420	39.297	13.674	64.686	40.490	17.975
1973	25.061	23.802	35.949	18.336	34.153	33.169	40.882	14.734	65.780	42.494	19.571
1974	27.309	26.280	40.436	19.890	37.559	36.449	44.857	16.770	70.713	46.461	21.593
1975	29.846	28.470	43.703	21.595	42.059	40.874	50.766	18.773	81.484	50.190	23.590
1976	31.490	30.032	45.413	23.093	44.384	43.232	53.562	19.692	86.486	52.408	25.117
1977	33.445	31.986	47.837	24.841	47.655	46.550	57.111	21.401	91.800	54.709	27.683
1978	35.798	34.211	50.773	26.750	51.517	50.444	60.930	23.468	96.900	57.557	31.082
1979	38.766	37.251	55.574	28.994	56.141	54.977	65.830	26.194	103.167	61.382	34.593
1980	42.278	41.262	61.797	32.009	61.395	60.105	71.641	28.629	112.249	66.123	38.325
1981	46.269	44.958	66.389	35.288	67.123	65.624	78.453	32.566	120.463	71.058	41.425
1982	49.130	47.456	68.198	38.058	70.679	69.311	82.911	35.136	125.415	75.093	43.646
1983	51.051	49.474	69.429	40.396	70.896	69.575	82.774	34.241	125.776	77.898	44.680
1984	52.894	51.343	70.742	42.498	71.661	70.253	83.036	34.540	124.748	80.081	46.003
1985	54.568	53.134	71.877	44.577	72.548	71.277	83.893	35.361	124.748	81.413	47.267
1986	55.673	54.290	71.541	46.408	74.178	73.021	85.365	36.039	127.254	82.047	49.351
1987	57.041	55.964	73.842	47.796	75.723	74.506	86.339	36.618	128.083	83.518	51.486
1988	59.055	58.151	75.788	50.082	77.627	76.586	88.514	38.171	129.854	86.129	53.278
1989	61.370	60.690	78.704	52.443	79.606	78.561	90.572	39.666	132.337	87.240	55.020
1990	63.676	63.355	81.927	54.846	81.270	80.278	92.516	40.948	135.042	88.147	56.288
1991	65.819	65.473	83.930	56.992	82.648	81.683	94.267	41.689	137.330	90.271	57.021
1992	67.321	67.218	84.943	59.018	82.647	81.728	93.960	41.699	137.121	89.373	57.723
1993	68.917	68.892	85.681	61.059	83.627	82.711	94.161	42.922	135.518	89.998	60.074
1994	70.386	70.330	86.552	62.719	84.875	83.983	94.904	44.437	135.277	90.468	62.247
1995	71.864	71.811	87.361	64.471	86.240	85.378	95.849	46.362	133.796	93.134	64.473
1996	73.178	73.346	88.321	66.240	86.191	85.450	95.267	47.540	130.762	93.544	65.856
1997	74.446	74.623	88.219	68.107	86.241	85.599	94.735	49.355	127.156	94.052	67.444
1998	75.267	75.216	86.893	69.549	85.608	85.133	93.248	51.612	121.451	93.595	69.223
1999	76.346	76.338	87.349	70.970	85.690	85.277	92.314	53.198	116.763	95.105	71.816
2000	78.069	78.235	89.082	72.938	86.815	86.486	92.718	55.283	114.224	97.814	75.004
2001	79.822	79.738	89.015	75.171	87.555	87.241	92.346	58.178	110.858	97.684	78.564
2002	81.039	80.789	88.166	77.123	87.841	87.500	91.863	60.603	108.531	96.376	80.510
2003	82.567	82.358	88.054	79.506	88.561	88.265	91.156	62.769	105.725	95.647	84.325
2004	84.778	84.411	89.292	81.965	91.148	90.843	92.055	67.416	104.841	95.335	90.243
2005	87.407	86.812	91.084	84.673	94.839	94.597	94.443	75.733	104.598	95.952	96.706
2006	90.074	89.174	92.306	87.616	98.176	97.958	96.745	84.749	103.560	97.088	102.355
2007	92.498	91.438	93.331	90.516	99.656	99.456	98.310	89.748	103.191	98.284	103.708
2008	94.264	94.180	96.122	93.235	100.474	100.296	99.832	94.335	102.542	99.834	102.249
2009	94.999	94.094	93.812	94.231	99.331	99.076	99.184	92.613	103.169	98.589	98.671
2010	96.109	95.705	95.183	95.957	97.687	97.568	97.416	92.006	99.471	98.306	98.317
2011	98.112	98.131	98.773	97.814	98.704	98.641	98.559	95.362	99.447	99.517	99.049
2012	100.000	100.000	100.000	100.000	100.000	100.000	100.000	100.000	100.000	100.000	100.000
2013	101.773	101.346	99.407	102.316	100.979	101.091	100.251	105.446	99.787	100.881	105.054
2014	103.647	102.830	98.920	104.804	102.922	103.172	101.469	107.198	99.169	100.791	111.118
2015	104.688	103.045	95.885	106.704	103.666	104.187	102.042	109.598	98.672	101.677	114.129
2016	105.770	104.091	94.318	109.120	103.567	104.234	101.146	109.958	97.436	100.464	118.148
2017	107.795	105.929	94.586	111.793	105.378	106.057	102.116	112.952	97.287	101.742	123.510
2018	110.382	108.143	95.232	114.851	107.757	108.501	103.515	117.062	97.396	103.282	130.488
2019 ᵖ	112.358	109.670	94.785	117.458	109.418	110.164	104.694	121.097	97.525	104.211	134.310
2016: I	104.933	103.297	94.181	107.979	103.031	103.720	101.080	109.254	97.771	100.224	115.777
II	105.618	103.910	94.465	108.765	103.419	104.082	101.169	100.089	97.562	100.280	117.271
III	105.987	104.344	94.231	109.553	103.635	104.297	101.017	109.949	97.353	100.204	119.006
IV	106.543	104.812	94.393	110.182	104.184	104.837	101.319	110.542	97.056	101.149	120.540
2017: I	107.040	105.355	94.898	110.745	104.588	105.269	101.633	111.333	97.319	101.245	121.452
II	107.394	105.596	94.264	111.452	105.151	105.852	101.989	112.456	97.338	101.592	122.970
III	108.032	106.033	94.425	112.038	105.787	106.395	102.333	113.703	97.297	101.914	124.348
IV	108.715	106.733	94.759	112.935	105.985	106.714	102.509	114.317	97.194	102.216	125.270
2018: I	109.341	107.401	95.228	113.707	106.862	107.595	102.950	115.133	97.116	103.154	128.031
II	110.209	107.988	95.400	114.520	107.615	108.386	103.428	116.547	97.321	103.433	130.203
III	110.765	108.413	95.319	115.220	108.186	108.951	103.841	117.480	97.710	103.558	131.450
IV	111.212	108.772	94.982	115.958	108.366	109.096	103.839	119.087	97.436	102.984	132.267
2019: I	111.504	108.879	94.590	116.339	108.832	109.577	104.241	119.899	97.669	103.378	133.108
II	112.173	109.522	94.955	117.133	109.382	110.110	104.770	121.074	97.764	104.123	133.655
III	112.679	109.928	94.772	117.865	109.678	110.426	104.911	121.543	97.487	104.638	134.780
IV ᵖ	113.076	110.352	94.822	118.497	109.779	110.543	104.854	121.871	97.182	104.704	135.697

See next page for continuation of table.

[Index numbers, 2012=100, except as noted; quarterly data seasonally adjusted]

| Year or quarter | Exports and imports of goods and services | | Government consumption expenditures and gross investment | | | | | Final sales of domestic product | Personal consumption expenditures excluding food and energy | Gross domestic purchases[1] | Percent change[2] | | | |
| | | | | Federal | | | | | | | | Personal consumption expenditures | | |
	Exports	Imports	Total	Total	National defense	Non-defense	State and local				Gross domestic product	Total	Excluding food and energy	Gross domestic purchases[1]
1969	28.589	18.839	14.892	17.715	17.019	19.154	13.063	20.465	21.136	20.010	4.9	4.5	4.7	4.9
1970	29.711	19.954	16.078	19.109	18.294	20.906	14.117	21.547	22.126	21.087	5.3	4.7	4.7	5.4
1971	30.796	21.179	17.352	20.670	19.817	22.521	15.198	22.642	23.167	22.185	5.1	4.2	4.7	5.2
1972	32.145	22.662	18.662	22.485	21.883	23.579	16.163	23.624	23.912	23.175	4.3	3.4	3.2	4.5
1973	36.382	26.601	19.936	24.051	23.484	25.018	17.246	24.923	24.823	24.499	5.5	5.4	3.8	5.7
1974	44.807	38.058	21.852	25.971	25.404	26.904	19.157	27.154	26.788	26.986	9.0	10.4	7.9	10.2
1975	49.388	41.226	23.870	28.254	27.545	29.484	20.999	29.680	29.026	29.452	9.3	8.3	8.4	9.1
1976	51.009	42.467	25.181	30.012	29.345	31.124	22.024	31.326	30.791	31.071	5.5	5.5	6.1	5.5
1977	53.088	46.209	26.739	31.858	31.268	32.782	23.394	33.284	32.771	33.119	6.2	6.5	6.4	6.6
1978	56.317	49.466	28.507	34.008	33.561	34.612	24.914	35.637	34.943	35.474	7.0	7.0	6.6	7.1
1979	63.101	57.930	30.853	36.566	36.216	36.952	27.114	38.591	37.490	38.585	8.3	8.9	7.3	8.8
1980	69.503	72.166	34.045	40.099	39.919	40.106	30.081	42.084	40.936	42.602	9.1	10.8	9.2	10.4
1981	74.650	76.066	37.424	43.843	43.747	43.643	33.226	46.046	44.523	46.532	9.4	9.0	8.8	9.2
1982	75.006	73.506	39.969	46.943	47.039	46.289	35.401	48.921	47.417	49.214	6.2	5.6	6.5	5.8
1983	75.311	70.751	41.516	48.499	48.778	47.397	36.964	50.836	49.844	50.926	3.9	4.3	5.1	3.5
1984	76.016	70.139	43.317	50.637	51.013	49.279	38.544	52.671	51.911	52.649	3.6	3.8	4.1	3.4
1985	73.753	67.836	44.659	51.712	51.872	50.907	40.113	54.371	54.019	54.214	3.2	3.5	4.1	3.0
1986	72.523	67.834	45.409	51.957	51.894	51.748	41.269	55.492	55.883	55.345	2.0	2.2	3.5	2.1
1987	74.124	71.935	46.635	52.318	52.267	52.076	43.196	56.851	57.683	56.908	2.5	3.1	3.2	2.8
1988	77.920	75.377	48.177	54.025	53.904	53.974	44.640	58.890	60.134	58.921	3.5	3.9	4.2	3.5
1989	79.210	77.024	50.016	55.534	55.365	55.605	46.752	61.205	62.630	61.240	3.9	4.4	4.2	3.9
1990	79.657	79.233	52.113	57.250	57.162	57.093	49.153	63.519	65.168	63.663	3.8	4.4	4.1	4.0
1991	80.545	78.573	54.005	59.309	58.964	59.787	50.953	65.663	67.495	65.662	3.4	3.3	3.6	3.1
1992	80.153	78.636	55.642	60.824	60.678	60.825	52.690	67.169	69.547	67.190	2.3	2.7	3.0	2.3
1993	80.277	78.033	56.953	62.151	61.615	62.994	54.002	68.765	71.436	68.706	2.4	2.5	2.7	2.3
1994	81.210	78.766	58.463	63.861	63.229	64.898	55.394	70.239	73.034	70.147	2.1	2.1	2.2	2.1
1995	83.025	80.924	60.123	65.838	65.027	67.223	56.871	71.722	74.625	71.661	2.1	2.1	2.2	2.2
1996	81.923	79.514	61.355	66.937	66.114	68.344	58.177	73.055	76.040	72.908	1.8	2.1	1.9	1.7
1997	80.479	76.750	62.560	67.972	67.035	69.591	59.471	74.344	77.382	73.983	1.7	1.7	1.8	1.5
1998	78.574	72.618	63.624	68.841	67.871	70.518	60.630	75.200	78.366	74.476	1.1	.8	1.3	.7
1999	77.971	73.019	65.778	70.519	69.559	72.178	63.008	76.296	79.425	75.632	1.4	1.5	1.4	1.6
2000	79.467	76.221	68.601	72.886	71.908	74.578	66.032	78.037	80.804	77.575	2.3	2.5	1.7	2.6
2001	78.836	74.223	70.567	74.236	73.270	75.906	68.281	79.793	82.258	79.039	2.2	1.9	1.8	1.9
2002	78.201	73.242	72.393	76.631	75.714	78.222	69.815	81.004	83.639	80.125	1.5	1.3	1.7	1.4
2003	79.400	75.454	75.028	80.008	79.505	80.895	72.050	82.541	84.837	81.776	1.9	1.9	1.4	2.1
2004	82.284	79.060	78.153	82.760	82.263	83.637	75.369	84.751	86.515	84.126	2.7	2.5	2.0	2.9
2005	85.131	83.703	82.110	86.204	86.011	86.531	79.609	87.388	88.373	87.037	3.1	2.8	2.1	3.5
2006	87.842	86.909	85.661	88.949	89.022	88.799	83.617	90.058	90.392	89.783	3.1	2.7	2.3	3.2
2007	91.139	89.921	69.491	91.589	91.750	91.279	88.133	92.489	92.378	92.206	2.7	2.5	2.2	2.7
2008	95.410	98.960	93.308	94.381	94.801	93.597	92.558	94.259	94.225	94.849	1.9	3.0	2.0	2.9
2009	89.694	87.987	92.931	94.214	94.126	94.364	92.048	94.970	95.315	94.559	.8	-.1	1.2	-.3
2010	93.348	92.783	95.386	96.421	96.128	96.942	94.669	96.086	96.608	95.923	1.2	1.7	1.4	1.4
2011	99.242	99.826	98.285	99.070	98.946	99.289	97.739	98.100	98.139	98.246	2.1	2.5	1.6	2.4
2012	100.000	100.000	100.000	100.000	100.000	100.000	100.000	100.000	100.000	100.000	1.9	1.9	1.9	1.8
2013	100.168	98.636	102.332	100.931	100.609	101.478	103.279	101.795	101.526	101.468	1.8	1.3	1.5	1.5
2014	100.272	97.854	104.435	102.632	102.056	103.593	105.645	103.692	103.122	103.138	1.8	1.5	1.6	1.6
2015	95.385	89.947	104.705	103.282	102.402	104.718	105.677	104.782	104.407	103.453	1.0	.2	1.2	.3
2016	93.455	86.696	105.050	103.900	102.776	105.701	105.854	105.895	106.070	104.185	1.0	1.0	1.6	.7
2017	95.850	88.622	107.647	106.040	104.518	108.435	106.737	107.923	107.795	106.148	1.9	1.8	1.6	1.9
2018	99.104	91.181	111.403	109.336	107.609	112.040	112.772	110.523	109.897	108.647	2.4	2.1	1.9	2.4
2019 p	98.886	89.945	113.787	111.587	109.441	114.931	115.244	112.499	111.670	110.339	1.8	1.4	1.6	1.6
2016: I	92.321	86.050	104.165	103.105	102.013	104.858	104.913	105.061	105.322	103.418	-.2	.2	1.7	-.6
II	93.253	86.407	104.906	103.697	102.631	105.412	105.746	105.743	105.848	104.016	2.6	2.4	2.0	2.3
III	93.803	87.028	105.285	104.147	103.041	105.921	106.062	106.112	106.363	104.405	1.4	1.7	2.0	1.5
IV	94.441	87.298	105.843	104.651	103.419	106.613	106.674	106.666	106.746	104.902	2.1	1.8	1.4	1.9
2017: I	95.054	88.312	106.697	105.230	103.893	107.347	107.694	107.168	107.189	105.474	1.9	2.1	1.7	2.2
II	95.094	88.251	107.102	105.647	104.165	108.032	108.081	107.525	107.540	105.797	1.3	.9	1.3	1.2
III	95.974	88.394	107.843	106.201	104.601	108.710	108.949	108.147	107.934	106.319	2.4	1.7	1.5	2.0
IV	97.277	89.529	108.946	107.063	105.411	109.651	110.200	108.853	108.516	107.001	2.6	2.7	2.2	2.6
2018: I	98.129	91.124	110.007	108.219	106.576	110.795	111.204	109.809	109.131	107.770	2.3	2.5	2.3	2.9
II	99.364	91.250	111.047	108.992	107.317	111.617	112.408	110.354	109.707	108.461	3.2	2.2	2.1	2.6
III	99.640	91.378	111.882	109.685	108.027	112.284	113.332	110.908	110.136	108.978	2.0	1.6	1.6	1.9
IV	99.284	90.972	112.674	110.450	108.517	113.464	114.142	111.351	110.612	109.378	1.6	1.3	1.7	1.5
2019: I	98.663	90.158	113.046	111.691	108.804	116.187	113.973	111.644	110.902	109.591	1.1	.4	1.1	.8
II	99.463	90.521	113.526	111.096	109.207	114.042	115.125	112.311	111.414	110.192	2.4	2.4	1.9	2.2
III	98.876	89.597	113.973	111.517	109.595	114.513	115.589	112.821	111.997	110.585	1.8	1.5	2.1	1.4
IV p	98.544	89.503	114.605	112.043	110.158	114.980	116.290	113.222	112.366	110.990	1.4	1.6	1.3	1.5

[1] Gross domestic product (GDP) less exports of goods and services plus imports of goods and services.
[2] Quarterly percent changes are at annual rates.

Source: Department of Commerce (Bureau of Economic Analysis).

National Income or Expenditure | 371

Table B–6. Gross value added by sector, 1969–2019

[Billions of dollars; quarterly data at seasonally adjusted annual rates]

Year or quarter	Gross domestic product	Business[1] Total	Business[1] Nonfarm[1]	Business[1] Farm	Households and institutions Total	Households and institutions House-holds	Households and institutions Nonprofit institutions serving house-holds[2]	General government[3] Total	General government[3] Federal	General government[3] State and local	Addendum: Gross housing value added
1969	1,017.6	782.7	759.9	22.8	87.0	57.1	30.0	147.9	76.9	70.9	73.0
1970	1,073.3	815.9	792.3	23.7	94.6	61.2	33.4	162.8	82.5	80.3	78.8
1971	1,164.9	882.5	857.2	25.4	104.5	67.2	37.4	177.8	87.5	90.3	86.4
1972	1,279.1	972.5	942.9	29.7	114.0	72.7	41.4	192.6	92.4	100.2	93.9
1973	1,425.4	1,094.0	1,047.2	46.8	124.6	78.5	46.1	206.8	96.4	110.4	101.4
1974	1,545.2	1,182.8	1,138.5	44.2	137.2	85.5	51.7	225.3	102.5	122.8	110.4
1975	1,684.9	1,284.8	1,239.2	45.6	151.6	93.7	58.0	248.4	110.5	138.0	121.3
1976	1,873.4	1,443.3	1,400.2	43.0	164.9	101.7	63.2	265.3	117.3	148.0	130.9
1977	2,081.8	1,616.2	1,572.7	43.5	179.9	110.7	69.2	285.7	125.2	160.6	144.2
1978	2,351.6	1,838.2	1,787.5	50.7	202.1	124.8	77.3	311.3	135.8	175.5	160.2
1979	2,627.3	2,062.8	2,002.7	60.1	226.3	139.5	86.9	338.2	145.4	192.8	177.7
1980	2,857.3	2,225.8	2,174.4	51.4	258.2	158.8	99.3	373.4	159.8	213.5	204.0
1981	3,207.0	2,502.0	2,437.0	65.0	291.6	179.2	112.4	413.5	178.3	235.2	231.6
1982	3,343.8	2,568.6	2,508.2	60.4	323.8	198.2	125.6	451.4	195.7	255.6	258.6
1983	3,634.0	2,801.9	2,757.0	44.9	352.5	213.6	138.9	479.7	207.1	272.6	280.6
1984	4,037.6	3,136.7	3,072.6	64.2	383.8	230.9	152.8	517.1	225.3	291.9	303.1
1985	4,339.0	3,369.6	3,305.9	63.7	411.8	248.2	163.6	557.5	240.0	317.6	333.8
1986	4,579.6	3,539.3	3,479.4	59.9	447.0	268.4	178.6	593.3	250.6	342.7	364.5
1987	4,855.2	3,735.2	3,673.2	62.0	489.5	289.8	199.7	630.4	261.0	369.4	392.1
1988	5,236.4	4,019.3	3,957.9	61.4	539.8	316.4	223.4	677.4	278.5	398.8	424.2
1989	5,641.6	4,326.7	4,252.8	73.9	586.0	341.4	244.6	728.8	292.8	436.1	452.7
1990	5,963.1	4,542.0	4,464.2	77.8	636.3	367.6	268.8	784.9	306.7	478.2	487.0
1991	6,158.1	4,645.0	4,574.7	70.4	677.3	386.6	290.7	835.8	323.5	512.2	515.3
1992	6,520.3	4,920.2	4,840.4	79.9	720.3	407.1	313.2	879.8	329.6	550.2	545.2
1993	6,858.6	5,177.4	5,106.2	71.3	772.8	437.6	335.1	908.3	331.5	576.9	578.4
1994	7,287.2	5,523.7	5,440.1	83.6	824.7	472.7	352.0	938.8	332.6	606.2	619.6
1995	7,639.7	5,795.1	5,726.7	68.4	877.8	506.9	370.9	966.9	333.0	633.9	662.6
1996	8,073.1	6,159.5	6,066.9	92.6	923.2	534.6	388.7	990.3	331.8	658.6	695.0
1997	8,577.6	6,578.8	6,490.8	88.1	975.9	565.7	410.2	1,022.9	333.5	689.3	731.9
1998	9,062.8	6,959.2	6,880.2	79.0	1,040.6	601.6	439.0	1,063.0	336.8	726.2	774.8
1999	9,630.7	7,400.1	7,329.2	70.9	1,112.4	645.2	467.3	1,118.1	345.0	773.1	826.2
2000	10,252.3	7,876.1	7,800.1	76.0	1,191.9	693.5	498.5	1,184.3	360.3	824.0	881.7
2001	10,581.8	8,062.0	7,983.9	78.1	1,267.2	744.7	522.6	1,252.6	370.3	882.3	943.5
2002	10,936.4	8,264.4	8,190.4	74.0	1,343.6	780.7	562.9	1,328.4	397.8	930.6	985.1
2003	11,458.2	8,642.4	8,551.3	91.1	1,411.0	816.6	594.4	1,404.8	434.7	970.1	1,016.4
2004	12,213.7	9,240.6	9,121.2	119.4	1,494.5	868.4	626.1	1,478.7	459.4	1,019.3	1,075.2
2005	13,036.6	9,898.0	9,793.5	104.5	1,583.3	933.4	649.8	1,555.4	488.4	1,067.0	1,151.9
2006	13,814.6	10,509.1	10,412.8	96.3	1,673.6	991.2	682.4	1,631.9	509.9	1,122.1	1,224.2
2007	14,451.9	10,994.6	10,878.9	115.7	1,730.3	1,016.9	713.4	1,726.9	535.7	1,191.2	1,273.4
2008	14,712.8	11,054.9	10,935.4	119.5	1,836.8	1,075.2	761.6	1,821.2	569.1	1,252.1	1,349.5
2009	14,448.9	10,669.9	10,566.8	103.1	1,895.5	1,097.0	798.5	1,883.5	603.0	1,280.5	1,393.8
2010	14,992.1	11,140.5	11,022.8	117.6	1,905.5	1,091.0	814.5	1,946.1	640.0	1,306.1	1,400.2
2011	15,542.6	11,612.9	11,460.7	152.2	1,956.8	1,108.0	848.8	1,972.9	659.8	1,313.1	1,445.7
2012	16,197.0	12,189.5	12,040.5	148.9	2,018.4	1,128.0	890.3	1,989.1	663.7	1,325.5	1,478.5
2013	16,784.9	12,670.5	12,485.9	184.6	2,075.0	1,157.0	918.0	2,039.3	658.4	1,380.9	1,511.2
2014	17,527.3	13,280.5	13,112.4	168.1	2,158.8	1,203.3	955.4	2,088.0	666.8	1,421.1	1,585.1
2015	18,224.8	13,826.3	13,680.3	146.0	2,256.2	1,250.9	1,005.4	2,142.2	674.8	1,467.4	1,685.9
2016	18,715.0	14,180.6	14,051.6	129.0	2,349.0	1,301.8	1,047.2	2,185.4	686.3	1,499.1	1,769.5
2017	19,519.4	14,830.7	14,691.2	139.4	2,445.7	1,363.0	1,082.7	2,243.1	701.7	1,541.4	1,852.2
2018	20,580.2	15,680.8	15,551.2	129.6	2,569.9	1,437.4	1,132.5	2,329.5	729.0	1,600.5	1,942.8
2019 *p*	21,429.0	16,329.9	16,200.4	129.5	2,686.5	1,503.4	1,183.0	2,412.6	754.7	1,657.9	2,030.6
2016: I	18,424.3	13,942.9	13,813.5	129.4	2,315.6	1,282.7	1,032.8	2,165.8	680.3	1,485.5	1,740.9
II	18,637.3	14,120.5	13,987.4	132.8	2,338.0	1,296.4	1,041.5	2,178.8	684.6	1,494.2	1,761.3
III	18,806.7	14,255.5	14,124.8	130.7	2,358.2	1,306.9	1,051.3	2,193.0	688.5	1,504.5	1,777.6
IV	18,991.9	14,403.6	14,280.5	123.1	2,384.3	1,321.2	1,063.0	2,204.0	691.9	1,512.1	1,798.2
2017: I	19,190.4	14,557.5	14,411.1	146.4	2,414.1	1,342.4	1,071.7	2,218.9	695.4	1,523.5	1,823.8
II	19,356.6	14,690.6	14,547.0	143.6	2,434.2	1,355.7	1,078.5	2,231.8	698.0	1,533.8	1,841.7
III	19,611.7	14,910.7	14,776.6	134.1	2,450.5	1,366.3	1,084.3	2,250.4	703.3	1,547.2	1,861.5
IV	19,918.9	15,163.9	15,030.2	133.7	2,483.8	1,387.5	1,096.4	2,271.2	710.1	1,561.1	1,881.8
2018: I	20,163.2	15,345.7	15,212.9	132.8	2,523.8	1,409.2	1,114.6	2,293.6	718.2	1,575.5	1,908.0
II	20,510.2	15,633.5	15,498.2	135.3	2,559.2	1,432.5	1,126.7	2,317.5	725.7	1,591.8	1,935.5
III	20,749.8	15,823.3	15,699.6	123.7	2,582.2	1,446.0	1,136.2	2,344.3	733.4	1,610.9	1,953.6
IV	20,897.8	15,920.7	15,794.2	126.5	2,614.5	1,462.0	1,152.5	2,362.6	738.7	1,624.0	1,974.1
2019: I	21,098.8	16,070.6	15,946.8	123.8	2,648.3	1,480.6	1,167.7	2,379.9	745.3	1,634.6	1,998.5
II	21,340.3	16,271.9	16,143.9	128.0	2,669.7	1,497.5	1,172.2	2,398.7	750.5	1,648.1	2,022.4
III	21,542.5	16,417.6	16,283.3	134.4	2,698.6	1,510.6	1,188.0	2,426.3	758.4	1,668.0	2,041.4
IV *p*	21,734.3	16,559.4	16,427.5	131.9	2,729.3	1,525.0	1,204.3	2,445.6	764.7	1,680.8	2,060.2

[1] Gross domestic business value added equals gross domestic product excluding gross value added of households and institutions and of general government. Nonfarm value added equals gross domestic business value added excluding gross farm value added.
[2] Equals compensation of employees of nonprofit institutions, the rental value of nonresidential fixed assets owned and used by nonprofit institutions serving households, and rental income of persons for tenant-occupied housing owned by nonprofit institutions.
[3] Equals compensation of general government employees plus general government consumption of fixed capital.

Source: Department of Commerce (Bureau of Economic Analysis).

TABLE B–7. Real gross value added by sector, 1969–2019

[Billions of chained (2012) dollars; quarterly data at seasonally adjusted annual rates]

Year or quarter	Gross domestic product	Business[1]			Households and institutions			General government[3]			Addendum: Gross housing value added
		Total	Nonfarm[1]	Farm	Total	Households	Nonprofit institutions serving households[2]	Total	Federal	State and local	
1969	4,942.1	3,272.7	3,232.1	45.1	648.6	379.9	267.1	1,221.2	543.2	643.9	480.4
1970	4,951.3	3,271.3	3,227.9	46.4	660.5	388.7	269.5	1,226.5	525.5	672.7	496.4
1971	5,114.3	3,394.9	3,348.6	48.8	690.6	408.3	279.5	1,228.7	506.6	700.2	520.8
1972	5,383.3	3,616.6	3,574.1	48.8	717.9	425.2	289.6	1,226.9	487.2	724.6	545.5
1973	5,687.2	3,867.8	3,833.7	48.2	741.9	438.8	300.0	1,232.9	473.6	750.1	562.9
1974	5,656.5	3,808.8	3,776.2	47.2	772.2	458.4	310.3	1,257.1	473.8	777.4	590.5
1975	5,644.8	3,772.6	3,714.5	56.1	799.1	471.5	324.2	1,276.0	472.1	801.0	609.4
1976	5,949.0	4,027.5	3,980.8	53.4	809.4	477.7	328.4	1,286.8	473.3	811.7	615.4
1977	6,224.1	4,258.1	4,209.4	56.2	815.8	477.6	335.3	1,300.3	475.2	824.3	624.3
1978	6,568.6	4,529.7	4,490.5	54.1	846.3	500.5	342.1	1,325.1	481.5	843.7	646.7
1979	6,776.6	4,690.6	4,642.4	59.2	869.8	510.8	355.7	1,339.9	482.5	859.1	659.2
1980	6,759.2	4,648.3	4,602.9	57.6	896.0	525.3	367.4	1,359.9	490.3	871.1	682.5
1981	6,930.7	4,783.9	4,707.8	76.0	913.2	531.0	379.3	1,369.5	498.5	871.0	695.9
1982	6,805.8	4,646.5	4,563.8	79.7	940.9	538.3	401.1	1,385.7	507.7	876.9	712.1
1983	7,117.7	4,892.8	4,846.6	55.1	979.7	559.3	419.0	1,397.7	520.6	873.5	739.6
1984	7,632.8	5,326.8	5,256.6	73.5	1,002.2	569.8	431.3	1,418.3	534.1	879.0	753.8
1985	7,951.1	5,575.2	5,488.1	87.1	1,019.6	582.8	435.3	1,461.1	551.1	904.3	785.0
1986	8,226.4	5,777.7	5,695.7	83.3	1,051.5	594.4	456.5	1,500.5	564.4	930.7	806.3
1987	8,511.0	5,985.1	5,902.7	84.1	1,090.9	609.5	481.9	1,537.5	582.2	949.1	825.1
1988	8,866.5	6,241.4	6,171.6	74.8	1,146.9	634.8	513.6	1,580.7	593.4	981.6	852.3
1989	9,192.1	6,480.4	6,398.4	85.0	1,193.5	654.5	541.3	1,619.4	602.4	1,011.9	870.1
1990	9,365.5	6,584.1	6,494.1	91.7	1,231.8	667.2	568.3	1,659.8	612.9	1,042.2	887.5
1991	9,355.4	6,544.0	6,453.2	92.3	1,257.0	677.5	583.9	1,676.7	616.4	1,055.9	905.7
1992	9,684.9	6,821.1	6,715.4	106.6	1,288.8	692.8	600.7	1,683.9	606.3	1,073.9	927.7
1993	9,951.5	7,015.7	6,922.7	94.4	1,355.2	726.4	634.0	1,687.9	596.3	1,088.7	961.0
1994	10,352.4	7,354.0	7,241.3	114.3	1,400.9	763.3	641.4	1,689.5	579.7	1,107.7	1,002.0
1995	10,630.3	7,580.0	7,490.0	91.0	1,442.7	789.7	656.3	1,691.9	561.2	1,129.6	1,037.8
1996	11,031.4	7,931.9	7,827.1	105.3	1,471.4	805.9	669.0	1,695.2	547.8	1,147.1	1,055.7
1997	11,521.9	8,348.3	8,230.6	118.1	1,516.7	828.7	691.7	1,708.1	538.8	1,169.7	1,081.1
1998	12,038.3	8,781.0	8,666.5	114.0	1,567.5	850.2	722.2	1,726.8	533.1	1,194.6	1,106.4
1999	12,610.5	9,277.8	9,159.7	116.8	1,610.7	883.9	730.3	1,742.1	528.9	1,214.4	1,144.2
2000	13,131.0	9,728.6	9,593.7	138.2	1,640.6	923.9	717.8	1,770.3	531.7	1,240.0	1,184.9
2001	13,262.1	9,796.7	9,668.7	128.1	1,676.7	953.7	723.3	1,801.4	533.2	1,269.6	1,218.3
2002	13,493.1	9,968.0	9,835.5	133.5	1,702.5	960.1	743.4	1,835.6	542.6	1,294.4	1,221.4
2003	13,879.1	10,295.0	10,153.1	145.1	1,735.0	984.3	751.3	1,858.5	557.0	1,302.8	1,234.6
2004	14,406.4	10,736.4	10,581.6	159.8	1,803.1	1,024.9	778.7	1,871.5	565.1	1,307.5	1,278.2
2005	14,912.5	11,157.9	10,995.0	168.8	1,867.3	1,078.1	788.9	1,888.4	572.3	1,317.0	1,339.1
2006	15,338.3	11,533.3	11,370.8	165.5	1,898.7	1,107.0	790.9	1,903.9	576.7	1,328.3	1,376.2
2007	15,626.0	11,795.2	11,646.9	144.6	1,896.1	1,096.5	799.2	1,930.9	584.6	1,347.3	1,380.2
2008	15,604.7	11,679.1	11,527.7	148.5	1,953.1	1,131.2	821.4	1,970.9	606.3	1,365.3	1,424.7
2009	15,208.8	11,245.6	11,079.9	170.7	1,956.2	1,122.8	833.1	2,006.7	636.6	1,370.5	1,432.1
2010	15,598.8	11,607.3	11,443.9	165.1	1,975.0	1,126.3	848.6	2,016.3	658.0	1,358.5	1,449.0
2011	15,840.7	11,830.4	11,673.0	157.5	2,003.1	1,129.9	873.1	2,007.2	664.3	1,343.0	1,476.5
2012	16,197.0	12,189.5	12,040.5	148.9	2,018.4	1,128.0	890.3	1,989.1	663.7	1,325.5	1,478.5
2013	16,495.4	12,487.3	12,307.3	179.8	2,032.8	1,135.7	897.1	1,975.7	652.0	1,323.7	1,481.2
2014	16,912.0	12,877.1	12,695.0	181.6	2,064.8	1,158.6	906.3	1,971.9	646.9	1,324.7	1,520.0
2015	17,403.8	13,332.5	13,138.9	194.4	2,099.9	1,173.9	925.9	1,975.9	642.4	1,332.9	1,571.6
2016	17,688.9	13,567.8	13,365.6	205.8	2,132.3	1,189.6	942.7	1,994.0	645.1	1,348.2	1,601.9
2017	18,108.1	13,950.2	13,748.1	202.3	2,160.8	1,208.2	952.6	2,005.5	645.4	1,359.3	1,623.2
2018	18,638.2	14,425.1	14,224.0	196.5	2,203.4	1,236.8	966.6	2,022.2	648.1	1,373.1	1,650.0
2019 [p]	19,072.5	14,816.8	14,608.8	204.6	2,234.6	1,250.4	984.2	2,037.6	653.0	1,383.7	1,666.0
2016: I	17,556.8	13,450.5	13,254.1	197.6	2,124.0	1,186.1	937.8	1,986.8	644.3	1,341.9	1,595.9
II	17,639.4	13,521.4	13,319.0	206.6	2,132.0	1,190.0	942.0	1,990.8	645.0	1,345.2	1,601.7
III	17,735.1	13,606.9	13,399.7	214.1	2,134.9	1,190.1	944.8	1,998.5	645.8	1,352.1	1,603.3
IV	17,824.2	13,692.4	13,489.9	204.8	2,138.4	1,192.2	946.1	1,999.7	645.3	1,353.7	1,606.5
2017: I	17,925.3	13,780.4	13,573.4	211.3	2,150.2	1,202.0	948.1	2,001.4	645.5	1,355.1	1,616.1
II	18,021.0	13,868.8	13,664.9	205.8	2,157.1	1,206.7	950.3	2,002.7	644.6	1,357.3	1,620.8
III	18,163.6	14,004.8	13,805.9	196.8	2,160.9	1,206.9	953.9	2,007.0	645.4	1,360.8	1,625.2
IV	18,322.5	14,146.9	13,948.2	195.3	2,175.0	1,217.1	957.8	2,010.8	646.2	1,363.8	1,630.7
2018: I	18,438.3	14,247.7	14,049.1	194.2	2,187.2	1,226.0	961.2	2,014.3	646.1	1,367.4	1,639.6
II	18,598.1	14,388.3	14,186.0	198.9	2,201.5	1,236.9	964.6	2,020.4	648.4	1,371.1	1,650.1
III	18,732.7	14,509.6	14,308.4	195.9	2,208.8	1,239.7	969.1	2,027.5	650.1	1,376.5	1,652.5
IV	18,783.5	14,554.7	14,352.5	196.9	2,216.0	1,244.6	971.4	2,026.4	647.9	1,377.6	1,657.7
2019: I	18,927.3	14,696.2	14,492.0	199.0	2,225.2	1,247.3	977.9	2,021.6	640.8	1,379.7	1,661.8
II	19,021.9	14,770.3	14,561.2	207.0	2,231.3	1,249.4	981.8	2,036.2	654.5	1,380.8	1,664.7
III	19,121.1	14,856.3	14,644.9	210.2	2,237.5	1,251.0	986.4	2,040.0	657.4	1,385.8	1,667.0
IV [p]	19,219.8	14,944.4	14,737.0	202.3	2,244.4	1,253.7	990.7	2,048.6	659.2	1,388.6	1,670.5

[1] Gross domestic business value added equals gross domestic product excluding gross value added of households and institutions and of general government. Nonfarm value added equals gross domestic business value added excluding gross farm value added.
[2] Equals compensation of employees of nonprofit institutions, the rental value of nonresidential fixed assets owned and used by nonprofit institutions serving households, and rental income of persons for tenant-occupied housing owned by nonprofit institutions.
[3] Equals compensation of general government employees plus general government consumption of fixed capital.

Source: Department of Commerce (Bureau of Economic Analysis).

National Income or Expenditure | 373

TABLE B–8. Gross domestic product (GDP) by industry, value added, in current dollars and as a percentage of GDP, 1997–2018

[Billions of dollars; except as noted]

Year	Gross domestic product	Private industries									
		Total private industries	Agriculture, forestry, fishing, and hunting	Mining	Construction	Manufacturing			Utilities	Wholesale trade	Retail trade
						Total manufacturing	Durable goods	Nondurable goods			
					Value added						
1997	8,577.6	7,432.0	108.6	95.1	339.6	1,382.9	823.8	559.1	171.5	527.5	579.9
1998	9,062.8	7,871.5	99.8	81.7	379.8	1,430.6	850.7	579.9	163.7	563.7	626.9
1999	9,630.7	8,378.3	92.6	84.5	417.6	1,488.9	874.9	614.1	179.9	584.0	652.6
2000	10,252.3	8,929.3	98.3	110.6	461.3	1,550.2	924.8	625.4	180.1	622.6	685.5
2001	10,581.8	9,188.9	99.8	123.9	486.5	1,473.9	833.4	640.5	181.3	613.8	709.5
2002	10,936.4	9,462.0	95.6	112.4	493.6	1,468.5	832.8	635.7	177.6	613.1	732.6
2003	11,458.2	9,905.9	114.0	139.0	525.2	1,524.2	863.2	661.0	184.0	641.5	769.6
2004	12,213.7	10,582.5	142.9	166.5	584.6	1,608.1	905.1	703.0	199.2	697.1	795.6
2005	13,036.6	11,326.4	128.3	225.7	651.8	1,693.4	956.8	736.6	198.1	754.9	840.8
2006	13,814.6	12,022.6	125.1	273.3	697.1	1,793.8	1,004.4	789.4	226.8	811.5	869.9
2007	14,451.9	12,564.8	144.1	314.0	715.3	1,844.7	1,030.6	814.1	231.9	857.8	869.2
2008	14,712.8	12,731.2	147.2	392.2	648.9	1,800.8	999.7	801.1	241.7	884.3	848.7
2009	14,448.9	12,403.9	130.0	275.8	565.6	1,702.1	881.0	821.2	258.2	834.2	827.6
2010	14,992.1	12,884.1	146.3	305.8	525.1	1,797.0	964.3	832.7	278.8	888.9	851.5
2011	15,542.6	13,405.5	180.9	356.3	524.4	1,867.6	1,015.2	852.4	287.5	934.9	871.9
2012	16,197.0	14,037.5	179.6	358.8	553.4	1,927.1	1,061.7	865.3	279.7	997.4	908.4
2013	16,784.9	14,572.3	215.6	386.5	587.6	1,991.9	1,102.0	889.9	286.3	1,040.1	949.5
2014	17,527.3	15,255.9	201.0	416.4	636.9	2,050.2	1,134.1	916.1	298.1	1,088.2	974.5
2015	18,224.8	15,883.9	180.7	259.9	695.6	2,126.5	1,184.0	942.5	299.2	1,142.5	1,024.7
2016	18,715.0	16,326.1	164.3	215.6	745.5	2,101.2	1,190.5	910.6	302.4	1,133.8	1,056.5
2017	19,519.4	17,065.8	174.6	287.3	790.4	2,185.1	1,230.7	954.4	315.1	1,164.6	1,084.3
2018	20,580.2	18,035.6	166.5	346.6	839.1	2,321.2	1,296.4	1,024.8	325.9	1,212.2	1,126.9
	Percent				Industry value added as a percentage of GDP (percent)						
1997	100.0	86.6	1.3	1.1	4.0	16.1	9.6	6.5	2.0	6.2	6.8
1998	100.0	86.9	1.1	.9	4.2	15.8	9.4	6.4	1.8	6.2	6.9
1999	100.0	87.0	1.0	.9	4.3	15.5	9.1	6.4	1.9	6.1	6.8
2000	100.0	87.1	1.0	1.1	4.5	15.1	9.0	6.1	1.8	6.1	6.7
2001	100.0	86.8	.9	1.2	4.6	13.9	7.9	6.1	1.7	5.8	6.7
2002	100.0	86.5	.9	1.0	4.5	13.4	7.6	5.8	1.6	5.6	6.7
2003	100.0	86.5	1.0	1.2	4.6	13.3	7.5	5.8	1.6	5.6	6.7
2004	100.0	86.6	1.2	1.4	4.8	13.2	7.4	5.8	1.6	5.7	6.5
2005	100.0	86.9	1.0	1.7	5.0	13.0	7.3	5.7	1.5	5.8	6.4
2006	100.0	87.0	.9	2.0	5.0	13.0	7.3	5.7	1.6	5.9	6.3
2007	100.0	86.9	1.0	2.2	4.9	12.8	7.1	5.6	1.6	5.9	6.0
2008	100.0	86.5	1.0	2.7	4.4	12.2	6.8	5.4	1.6	6.0	5.8
2009	100.0	85.8	.9	1.9	3.9	11.8	6.1	5.7	1.8	5.8	5.7
2010	100.0	85.9	1.0	2.0	3.5	12.0	6.4	5.6	1.9	5.9	5.7
2011	100.0	86.2	1.2	2.3	3.4	12.0	6.5	5.5	1.8	6.0	5.6
2012	100.0	86.7	1.1	2.2	3.4	11.9	6.6	5.3	1.7	6.2	5.6
2013	100.0	86.8	1.3	2.3	3.5	11.9	6.6	5.3	1.7	6.2	5.7
2014	100.0	87.0	1.1	2.4	3.6	11.7	6.5	5.2	1.7	6.2	5.6
2015	100.0	87.2	1.0	1.4	3.8	11.7	6.5	5.2	1.6	6.3	5.6
2016	100.0	87.2	.9	1.2	4.0	11.2	6.4	4.9	1.6	6.1	5.6
2017	100.0	87.4	.9	1.5	4.0	11.2	6.3	4.9	1.6	6.0	5.6
2018	100.0	87.6	.8	1.7	4.1	11.3	6.3	5.0	1.6	5.9	5.5

[1] Consists of agriculture, forestry, fishing, and hunting; mining; construction; and manufacturing.

[2] Consists of utilities; wholesale trade; retail trade; transportation and warehousing; information; finance, insurance, real estate, rental, and leasing; professional and business services; educational services, health care, and social assistance; arts, entertainment, recreation, accommodation, and food services; and other services, except government.

Note: Data shown in Tables B–8 and B–9 are consistent with the 2019 annual revision of the industry accounts released in July 2019. For details see *Survey of Current Business*, November 2019.

See next page for continuation of table.

[Billions of dollars; except as noted]

Year	Transportation and warehousing	Information	Finance, insurance, real estate, rental, and leasing	Professional and business services	Educational services, health care, and social assistance	Arts, entertainment, recreation, accommodation, and food services	Other services, except government	Government	Private goods-producing industries [1]	Private services-producing industries [2]
					Value added					
1997	257.3	394.1	1,612.4	840.6	590.6	301.8	230.3	1,145.6	1,926.1	5,505.9
1998	280.0	434.6	1,710.1	914.0	615.8	322.1	248.7	1,191.3	1,991.8	5,879.7
1999	290.0	485.0	1,837.1	997.2	653.9	354.1	260.8	1,252.3	2,083.7	6,294.6
2000	307.8	471.3	1,974.7	1,105.1	695.4	386.5	279.7	1,323.0	2,220.4	6,708.9
2001	308.1	502.4	2,128.1	1,155.5	749.9	390.7	265.6	1,392.9	2,184.1	7,004.8
2002	305.7	550.6	2,217.0	1,189.9	807.0	413.5	284.9	1,474.4	2,170.1	7,291.9
2003	321.4	564.9	2,295.9	1,247.4	862.8	432.1	283.8	1,552.3	2,302.4	7,603.5
2004	352.1	620.4	2,389.1	1,341.0	927.3	461.2	297.3	1,631.3	2,502.2	8,080.3
2005	375.8	642.3	2,606.2	1,446.4	970.5	481.2	310.7	1,710.3	2,699.3	8,627.1
2006	410.4	652.0	2,743.9	1,546.6	1,035.5	511.5	325.0	1,792.0	2,889.4	9,133.2
2007	413.9	706.9	2,848.3	1,666.7	1,087.9	533.5	330.5	1,887.1	3,018.1	9,546.7
2008	426.8	743.0	2,762.7	1,777.1	1,184.8	542.7	330.3	1,981.6	2,989.1	9,742.1
2009	404.6	721.9	2,867.7	1,688.7	1,267.5	533.3	326.5	2,045.1	2,673.6	9,730.3
2010	433.0	753.3	2,943.0	1,766.8	1,310.7	555.8	328.0	2,108.0	2,774.3	10,109.8
2011	451.4	759.8	3,045.3	1,856.7	1,354.7	580.9	333.1	2,137.1	2,929.3	10,476.3
2012	472.0	759.0	3,261.0	1,964.7	1,407.4	621.4	348.0	2,159.5	3,018.8	11,018.7
2013	491.1	828.9	3,322.8	2,017.3	1,447.2	651.3	356.3	2,212.5	3,181.6	11,390.8
2014	521.8	842.4	3,548.0	2,118.4	1,491.9	691.4	376.6	2,271.4	3,304.5	11,951.4
2015	564.4	898.0	3,753.5	2,234.9	1,571.9	739.7	392.4	2,340.8	3,262.7	12,621.3
2016	580.8	959.3	3,930.2	2,302.5	1,650.7	781.3	402.1	2,388.9	3,226.6	13,099.5
2017	612.4	997.6	4,088.5	2,427.6	1,708.9	815.4	414.1	2,453.6	3,437.4	13,628.4
2018	658.1	1,067.7	4,301.6	2,579.4	1,792.5	860.6	437.2	2,544.6	3,673.4	14,362.1
				Industry value added as a percentage of GDP (percent)						
1997	3.0	4.6	18.8	9.8	6.9	3.5	2.7	13.4	22.5	64.2
1998	3.1	4.8	18.9	10.1	6.8	3.6	2.7	13.1	22.0	64.9
1999	3.0	5.0	19.1	10.4	6.8	3.7	2.7	13.0	21.6	65.4
2000	3.0	4.6	19.3	10.8	6.8	3.8	2.7	12.9	21.7	65.4
2001	2.9	4.7	20.1	10.9	7.1	3.7	2.5	13.2	20.6	66.2
2002	2.8	5.0	20.3	10.9	7.4	3.8	2.6	13.5	19.8	66.7
2003	2.8	4.9	20.0	10.9	7.5	3.8	2.5	13.5	20.1	66.4
2004	2.9	5.1	19.6	11.0	7.6	3.8	2.4	13.4	20.5	66.2
2005	2.9	4.9	20.0	11.1	7.4	3.7	2.4	13.1	20.7	66.2
2006	3.0	4.7	19.9	11.2	7.5	3.7	2.4	13.0	20.9	66.1
2007	2.9	4.9	19.7	11.5	7.5	3.7	2.3	13.1	20.9	66.1
2008	2.9	5.0	18.8	12.1	8.1	3.7	2.2	13.5	20.3	66.2
2009	2.8	5.0	19.8	11.7	8.8	3.7	2.3	14.2	18.5	67.3
2010	2.9	5.0	19.6	11.8	8.7	3.7	2.2	14.1	18.5	67.4
2011	2.9	4.9	19.6	11.9	8.7	3.7	2.1	13.7	18.8	67.4
2012	2.9	4.7	20.1	12.1	8.7	3.8	2.1	13.3	18.6	68.0
2013	2.9	4.9	19.8	12.0	8.6	3.9	2.1	13.2	19.0	67.9
2014	3.0	4.8	20.2	12.1	8.5	3.9	2.1	13.0	18.9	68.2
2015	3.1	4.9	20.6	12.3	8.6	4.1	2.2	12.8	17.9	69.3
2016	3.1	5.1	21.0	12.3	8.8	4.2	2.1	12.8	17.2	70.0
2017	3.1	5.1	20.9	12.4	8.8	4.2	2.1	12.6	17.6	69.8
2018	3.2	5.2	20.9	12.5	8.7	4.2	2.1	12.4	17.8	69.8

Note (cont'd): Value added is the contribution of each private industry and of government to GDP. Value added is equal to an industry's gross output minus its intermediate inputs. Current-dollar value added is calculated as the sum of distributions by an industry to its labor and capital, which are derived from the components of gross domestic income.

Value added industry data shown in Tables B–8 and B–9 are based on the 2012 North American Industry Classification System (NAICS).

Source: Department of Commerce (Bureau of Economic Analysis).

TABLE B–9. Real gross domestic product by industry, value added, and percent changes, 1997–2018

Year	Gross domestic product	Private industries									
		Total private industries	Agriculture, forestry, fishing, and hunting	Mining	Construction	Manufacturing			Utilities	Wholesale trade	Retail trade
						Total manufacturing	Durable goods	Non-durable goods			
	Chain-type quantity indexes for value added (2012=100)										
1997	71.136	70.417	78.122	73.569	124.924	73.952	54.862	108.774	82.684	68.023	76.897
1998	74.324	73.791	76.225	76.540	130.646	76.995	59.373	106.919	78.993	74.707	84.286
1999	77.857	77.614	78.531	74.233	136.033	81.273	63.518	110.673	92.023	77.183	87.388
2000	81.070	81.097	90.102	65.831	141.541	87.116	70.928	111.745	93.244	81.126	90.310
2001	81.880	81.675	86.959	76.178	138.629	83.415	66.355	110.500	77.009	82.663	93.582
2002	83.306	83.128	90.001	78.193	134.131	84.146	67.757	109.712	79.706	83.546	97.689
2003	85.689	85.527	96.987	69.241	136.316	88.809	72.791	113.126	77.930	88.159	102.703
2004	88.945	89.042	104.744	69.643	141.182	95.078	78.019	120.927	82.678	91.924	104.467
2005	92.070	92.473	109.218	70.809	141.809	97.970	83.413	118.785	78.378	96.071	107.851
2006	94.698	95.475	111.013	81.679	138.846	103.527	89.812	122.532	83.261	98.749	108.686
2007	96.475	97.063	98.327	87.975	134.563	106.948	93.989	124.516	84.935	102.073	105.144
2008	96.343	96.460	100.402	85.158	121.446	104.777	94.526	118.051	89.475	101.967	101.290
2009	93.899	93.523	111.362	97.660	104.296	95.141	80.927	114.724	84.828	89.701	97.020
2010	96.306	95.938	107.954	86.193	98.928	100.289	91.144	112.361	95.043	95.040	99.094
2011	97.800	97.577	103.799	89.398	97.334	100.663	97.290	104.898	98.680	96.794	99.277
2012	100.000	100.000	100.000	100.000	100.000	100.000	100.000	100.000	100.000	100.000	100.000
2013	101.842	101.886	116.603	103.938	102.485	103.068	102.463	103.817	98.916	102.293	103.112
2014	104.415	104.833	117.923	115.332	104.396	104.832	103.973	105.900	95.102	106.201	105.005
2015	107.451	108.266	125.752	125.082	109.250	105.731	105.504	106.004	94.941	110.759	108.513
2016	109.211	110.049	131.765	117.847	112.975	105.187	105.917	104.238	99.769	109.317	112.262
2017	111.799	112.867	129.793	126.275	115.580	107.925	109.486	105.923	101.498	111.297	116.226
2018	115.072	116.441	127.954	130.409	118.118	112.157	114.663	108.991	101.330	113.090	120.332
	Percent change from year earlier										
1997	....	....	....	....	....	....	....	....	....	....	....
1998	4.5	4.8	-2.4	4.0	4.6	4.1	8.2	-1.7	-4.5	9.8	9.6
1999	4.8	5.2	3.0	-3.0	4.1	5.6	7.0	3.5	16.5	3.3	3.7
2000	4.1	4.5	14.7	-11.3	4.0	7.2	11.7	1.0	1.3	5.1	3.3
2001	1.0	.7	-3.5	15.7	-2.1	-4.2	-6.4	-1.1	-17.4	1.9	3.6
2002	1.7	1.8	3.5	2.6	-3.2	.9	2.1	-.7	3.5	1.1	4.4
2003	2.9	2.9	7.8	-11.4	1.6	5.5	7.4	3.1	-2.2	5.5	5.1
2004	3.8	4.1	8.0	.6	3.6	7.1	7.2	6.9	6.1	4.3	1.7
2005	3.5	3.9	4.3	1.7	.4	3.0	6.9	-1.8	-5.2	4.5	3.2
2006	2.9	3.2	1.6	15.4	-2.1	5.7	7.7	3.2	6.2	2.8	.8
2007	1.9	1.7	-11.4	7.7	-3.1	3.3	4.7	1.6	2.0	3.4	-3.3
2008	-.1	-.6	2.1	-3.2	-9.7	-2.0	.6	-5.2	5.3	-.1	-3.7
2009	-2.5	-3.0	10.9	14.7	-14.1	-9.2	-14.4	-2.8	-5.2	-12.0	-4.2
2010	2.6	2.6	-3.1	-11.7	-5.1	5.4	12.6	-2.1	12.0	6.0	2.1
2011	1.6	1.7	-3.8	3.7	-1.6	.4	6.7	-6.6	3.8	1.8	.2
2012	2.2	2.5	-3.7	11.9	2.7	-.7	2.8	-4.7	1.3	3.3	.7
2013	1.8	1.9	16.6	3.9	2.5	3.1	2.5	3.8	-1.1	2.3	3.1
2014	2.5	2.9	1.1	11.0	1.9	1.7	1.5	2.0	-3.9	3.8	1.8
2015	2.9	3.3	6.6	8.5	4.6	.9	1.5	.1	-.2	4.3	3.3
2016	1.6	1.6	4.8	-5.8	3.4	-.5	.4	-1.7	5.1	-1.3	3.5
2017	2.4	2.6	-1.5	7.2	2.3	2.6	3.4	1.6	1.7	1.8	3.5
2018	2.9	3.2	-1.4	3.3	2.2	3.9	4.7	2.9	-.2	1.6	3.5

[1] Consists of agriculture, forestry, fishing, and hunting; mining; construction; and manufacturing.
[2] Consists of utilities; wholesale trade; retail trade; transportation and warehousing; information; finance, insurance, real estate, rental, and leasing; professional and business services; educational services, health care, and social assistance; arts, entertainment, recreation, accommodation, and food services; and other services, except government.

See next page for continuation of table.

Year	Transportation and warehousing	Information	Finance, insurance, real estate, rental, and leasing	Professional and business services	Educational services, health care, and social assistance	Arts, entertainment, recreation, accommodation, and food services	Other services, except government	Government	Private goods-producing industries[1]	Private services-producing industries[2]
	Chain-type quantity indexes for value added (2012=100)									
1997	85.155	45.779	64.494	63.672	65.203	78.811	115.601	87.669	81.548	67.403
1998	89.482	50.548	67.298	66.614	65.487	80.968	120.416	88.689	84.672	70.856
1999	90.225	56.651	71.498	69.758	67.685	85.402	121.187	89.756	88.733	74.618
2000	90.015	55.600	75.255	73.866	70.186	90.569	123.985	91.578	94.034	77.602
2001	83.969	58.897	79.439	75.941	71.869	87.406	111.728	92.511	91.428	79.044
2002	80.939	64.594	80.102	76.841	74.748	89.727	114.785	94.159	91.560	80.849
2003	83.784	66.612	81.058	79.221	77.673	92.055	111.552	95.294	94.958	82.982
2004	90.758	74.307	82.263	81.173	81.384	96.188	113.022	96.155	100.536	85.949
2005	95.120	79.284	87.902	84.782	82.907	96.474	113.811	97.036	102.929	89.658
2006	100.720	82.056	90.292	87.152	86.241	99.144	114.372	97.580	107.432	92.253
2007	99.935	90.123	91.815	90.025	86.891	98.599	111.727	98.528	108.998	93.847
2008	99.042	95.903	88.295	94.309	92.433	96.435	107.629	100.447	104.880	94.207
2009	93.111	93.560	92.578	88.315	95.708	90.853	101.336	100.560	97.869	92.358
2010	97.611	98.866	93.968	91.987	96.712	94.349	99.397	101.063	98.681	95.192
2011	99.380	100.275	95.903	95.662	98.366	97.660	98.508	100.747	98.817	97.237
2012	100.000	100.000	100.000	100.000	100.000	100.000	100.000	100.000	100.000	100.000
2013	101.455	109.095	99.099	101.293	101.289	102.128	99.257	99.297	103.878	101.342
2014	104.591	111.815	102.053	105.908	103.098	105.845	102.117	99.069	106.798	104.296
2015	107.467	122.088	104.674	109.338	107.117	108.505	103.006	99.146	109.744	107.853
2016	109.351	132.685	105.816	111.445	109.914	109.859	102.351	100.180	109.984	110.022
2017	114.358	140.455	107.043	116.260	111.624	112.213	102.446	101.103	112.903	112.815
2018	118.971	152.407	108.318	122.486	115.108	115.151	105.610	101.891	116.520	116.376
	Percent change from year earlier									
1997	....	....	....	....	....	....	....	....	....	....
1998	5.1	10.4	4.3	4.6	0.4	2.7	4.2	1.2	3.8	5.1
1999	.8	12.1	6.2	4.7	3.4	5.5	.6	1.2	4.8	5.3
2000	−.2	−1.9	5.3	5.9	3.7	6.1	2.3	2.0	6.0	4.0
2001	−6.7	5.9	5.6	2.8	2.4	−3.5	−9.9	1.0	−2.8	1.9
2002	−3.6	9.7	.8	1.2	4.0	2.7	2.7	1.8	.1	2.3
2003	3.5	3.1	1.2	3.1	3.9	2.6	−2.8	1.2	3.7	2.6
2004	8.3	11.6	1.5	2.5	4.8	4.5	1.3	.9	5.9	3.6
2005	4.8	6.7	6.9	4.4	1.9	.3	.7	.9	2.4	4.3
2006	5.9	3.5	2.7	2.8	4.0	2.8	.5	.6	4.4	2.9
2007	−.8	9.8	1.7	3.3	.8	−.5	−2.3	1.0	1.5	1.7
2008	−.9	6.4	−3.8	4.8	6.4	−2.2	−3.7	1.9	−3.8	.4
2009	−6.0	−2.4	4.9	−6.4	3.5	−5.8	−5.8	.1	−6.7	−2.0
2010	4.8	5.7	1.5	4.2	1.0	3.8	−1.9	.5	.8	3.1
2011	1.8	1.4	2.1	4.0	1.7	3.5	−.9	−.3	.1	2.1
2012	.6	−.3	4.3	4.5	1.7	2.4	1.5	−.7	1.2	2.8
2013	1.5	9.1	−.9	1.3	1.3	2.1	−.7	−.7	3.9	1.3
2014	3.1	2.5	3.0	4.6	1.8	3.6	2.9	−.2	2.8	2.9
2015	2.7	9.2	2.6	3.2	3.9	2.5	.9	.1	2.8	3.4
2016	1.8	8.7	1.1	1.9	2.6	1.2	−.6	1.0	.2	2.0
2017	4.6	5.9	1.2	4.3	1.6	2.1	.1	.9	2.7	2.5
2018	4.0	8.5	1.2	5.4	3.1	2.6	3.1	.8	3.2	3.2

Note: Data are based on the 2012 North American Industry Classification System (NAICS).
See Note, Table B–8.

Source: Department of Commerce (Bureau of Economic Analysis).

National Income or Expenditure | 377

TABLE B–10. Personal consumption expenditures, 1969–2019

[Billions of dollars; quarterly data at seasonally adjusted annual rates]

Year or quarter	Personal consumption expenditures	Goods						Services					Addendum: Personal consumption expenditures excluding food and energy [2]
		Total	Durable		Nondurable			Total	Household consumption expenditures				
			Total [1]	Motor vehicles and parts	Total [1]	Food and beverages purchased for off-premises consumption	Gasoline and other energy goods		Total [1]	Housing and utilities	Health care	Financial services and insurance	
1969	603.6	304.7	90.5	37.4	214.2	95.4	25.0	299.0	289.5	101.0	42.1	27.7	469.3
1970	646.7	318.8	90.0	34.5	228.8	103.5	26.3	327.9	317.5	109.4	47.7	30.1	501.7
1971	699.9	342.1	102.4	43.2	239.7	107.1	27.6	357.8	346.1	120.0	53.7	33.1	548.5
1972	768.2	373.8	116.4	49.4	257.4	114.5	29.4	394.3	381.5	131.2	59.8	37.1	605.8
1973	849.6	416.6	130.5	54.4	286.1	126.7	34.3	432.9	419.2	143.5	67.2	39.9	668.5
1974	930.2	451.5	130.2	48.2	321.4	143.0	43.8	478.6	463.1	158.6	76.1	44.1	719.7
1975	1,030.5	491.3	142.2	52.6	349.2	156.6	48.0	539.2	522.2	176.5	89.0	51.8	797.3
1976	1,147.7	546.3	168.6	68.2	377.7	167.3	53.0	601.4	582.4	194.7	101.8	56.8	894.7
1977	1,274.0	600.4	192.0	79.8	408.4	179.8	57.8	673.6	653.0	217.8	115.7	65.1	998.6
1978	1,422.3	663.6	213.3	89.2	450.2	196.1	61.5	758.7	735.7	244.3	131.2	76.7	1,122.4
1979	1,585.4	737.9	226.3	90.2	511.6	218.4	80.4	847.5	821.4	273.4	148.8	83.6	1,239.7
1980	1,750.7	799.8	226.4	84.4	573.4	239.2	101.9	950.9	920.8	312.5	171.7	91.7	1,353.1
1981	1,934.0	869.4	243.9	93.0	625.4	255.3	113.4	1,064.6	1,030.4	352.1	201.9	98.5	1,501.5
1982	2,071.3	899.3	253.0	100.0	646.3	267.1	108.4	1,172.0	1,134.0	387.5	225.2	113.7	1,622.9
1983	2,281.6	973.8	295.0	122.9	678.8	277.0	106.5	1,307.8	1,267.1	421.2	253.1	141.0	1,817.2
1984	2,492.3	1,063.7	342.2	147.2	721.5	291.1	108.2	1,428.6	1,383.3	457.5	276.5	150.8	2,008.1
1985	2,712.8	1,137.6	380.4	170.1	757.2	303.0	110.5	1,575.2	1,527.3	500.6	302.2	178.2	2,210.3
1986	2,886.3	1,195.6	421.4	187.5	774.2	316.4	91.2	1,690.7	1,638.0	537.0	330.2	187.7	2,391.3
1987	3,076.3	1,256.3	442.0	188.2	814.3	324.3	96.4	1,820.0	1,764.3	571.6	366.0	189.5	2,566.6
1988	3,330.1	1,337.3	475.1	202.2	862.3	342.8	99.9	1,992.7	1,929.4	614.4	410.1	202.9	2,793.1
1989	3,576.8	1,423.8	494.3	207.8	929.5	365.4	110.4	2,153.0	2,084.9	655.2	451.2	222.3	3,002.1
1990	3,809.0	1,491.3	497.1	205.1	994.2	391.2	124.2	2,317.7	2,241.8	696.5	506.2	230.8	3,194.9
1991	3,943.4	1,497.4	477.2	185.7	1,020.3	403.0	121.1	2,446.0	2,365.9	735.2	555.8	250.1	3,314.4
1992	4,197.6	1,563.5	508.1	204.8	1,055.2	404.5	125.0	2,634.3	2,546.4	771.1	612.8	277.0	3,561.7
1993	4,452.0	1,642.3	551.5	224.7	1,090.8	413.5	126.9	2,809.6	2,719.6	814.9	648.8	314.0	3,796.6
1994	4,721.0	1,746.6	607.2	249.8	1,139.4	432.1	129.2	2,974.4	2,876.6	863.3	680.5	327.9	4,042.5
1995	4,962.6	1,815.5	635.7	255.7	1,179.8	443.7	133.4	3,147.1	3,044.7	913.7	719.9	347.0	4,267.2
1996	5,244.6	1,917.7	676.3	273.5	1,241.4	461.9	144.7	3,326.9	3,216.9	962.4	752.1	372.1	4,513.0
1997	5,536.8	2,006.5	715.5	293.1	1,291.0	474.8	147.7	3,530.3	3,424.7	1,009.8	790.9	408.9	4,787.8
1998	5,877.2	2,108.4	779.3	320.2	1,329.1	487.4	132.4	3,768.8	3,645.0	1,065.5	832.0	446.1	5,132.4
1999	6,279.1	2,287.1	855.6	350.7	1,431.5	515.5	146.5	3,992.0	3,853.8	1,123.1	863.6	486.4	5,491.2
2000	6,762.1	2,453.2	912.6	363.2	1,540.6	540.6	184.5	4,309.0	4,150.9	1,198.6	918.4	543.0	5,899.4
2001	7,065.6	2,525.6	941.5	383.3	1,584.1	564.0	178.0	4,540.0	4,361.0	1,287.5	996.6	525.7	6,174.0
2002	7,342.7	2,598.8	985.4	401.3	1,613.4	575.1	167.9	4,743.9	4,545.5	1,333.6	1,082.9	534.7	6,454.1
2003	7,723.1	2,722.6	1,017.8	401.5	1,704.8	599.6	196.4	5,000.5	4,795.0	1,394.1	1,154.0	560.3	6,766.8
2004	8,212.7	2,902.0	1,080.6	409.3	1,821.4	632.6	232.7	5,310.6	5,104.3	1,469.1	1,238.9	605.5	7,179.2
2005	8,747.1	3,082.9	1,128.6	410.0	1,954.3	668.2	283.8	5,664.2	5,453.9	1,583.6	1,320.5	659.0	7,605.3
2006	9,260.3	3,239.7	1,158.3	394.9	2,081.3	700.3	319.7	6,020.7	5,781.5	1,682.4	1,391.9	695.0	8,039.7
2007	9,706.4	3,367.0	1,188.0	400.6	2,179.0	737.3	345.5	6,339.4	6,090.6	1,758.2	1,478.2	737.2	8,413.4
2008	9,976.3	3,363.2	1,098.8	343.3	2,264.5	769.1	391.1	6,613.1	6,325.8	1,835.4	1,555.3	756.6	8,592.6
2009	9,842.2	3,180.0	1,012.1	318.6	2,167.9	772.9	287.0	6,662.2	6,373.0	1,877.7	1,632.7	711.3	8,567.0
2010	10,185.8	3,317.8	1,049.0	344.5	2,268.9	786.9	336.7	6,868.0	6,573.6	1,903.9	1,699.6	754.4	8,840.8
2011	10,641.1	3,518.1	1,093.5	365.2	2,424.6	819.5	413.8	7,123.0	6,811.1	1,955.9	1,757.1	797.9	9,188.9
2012	11,006.8	3,637.7	1,144.2	396.6	2,493.5	846.2	421.9	7,369.1	7,027.5	1,996.3	1,821.3	820.1	9,531.1
2013	11,317.2	3,730.0	1,189.4	417.5	2,540.6	864.0	418.2	7,587.2	7,234.6	2,055.3	1,858.2	858.4	9,815.1
2014	11,822.8	3,863.0	1,242.1	442.0	2,620.9	896.9	403.3	7,959.8	7,594.2	2,149.9	1,940.5	908.1	10,290.4
2015	12,284.3	3,920.3	1,305.9	474.2	2,614.4	920.1	309.4	8,363.9	7,992.5	2,255.7	2,057.2	956.9	10,829.1
2016	12,748.5	3,995.9	1,352.6	483.6	2,643.3	937.8	275.0	8,752.6	8,355.0	2,355.3	2,160.1	977.5	11,314.7
2017	13,312.1	4,165.0	1,412.6	502.2	2,752.5	967.5	308.0	9,147.0	8,733.3	2,455.0	2,243.4	1,040.4	11,810.6
2018	13,998.7	4,364.8	1,475.6	521.5	2,889.2	1,003.4	349.6	9,633.9	9,190.9	2,567.2	2,352.6	1,111.0	12,404.2
2019 ᵖ	14,563.9	4,508.6	1,527.0	530.7	2,981.6	1,032.4	339.7	10,055.2	9,606.6	2,671.5	2,466.4	1,155.6	12,948.8
2016: I	12,523.5	3,933.2	1,330.0	472.1	2,603.2	929.5	256.4	8,590.3	8,203.6	2,307.2	2,117.2	960.1	11,126.0
II	12,688.3	3,988.6	1,343.3	476.0	2,645.4	938.8	277.1	8,699.6	8,312.6	2,342.5	2,163.9	967.9	11,251.9
III	12,822.4	4,017.8	1,364.9	489.6	2,652.9	939.0	275.6	8,804.6	8,398.6	2,377.7	2,156.5	987.1	11,377.2
IV	12,959.8	4,044.0	1,372.4	496.8	2,671.6	943.9	291.0	8,915.8	8,505.3	2,393.7	2,202.8	995.1	11,503.8
2017: I	13,104.4	4,097.9	1,385.1	492.4	2,712.8	952.3	305.8	9,006.5	8,590.9	2,407.5	2,211.8	1,012.3	11,634.5
II	13,212.5	4,124.9	1,398.7	493.9	2,726.2	960.8	295.0	9,087.6	8,674.1	2,444.8	2,218.9	1,030.4	11,727.6
III	13,345.1	4,173.3	1,415.9	501.6	2,757.4	970.7	304.1	9,171.8	8,759.2	2,465.8	2,253.2	1,044.8	11,844.5
IV	13,586.3	4,264.0	1,450.5	521.1	2,813.4	986.2	327.1	9,322.3	8,908.7	2,501.8	2,289.5	1,074.1	12,035.9
2018: I	13,728.4	4,298.5	1,454.8	512.8	2,843.7	993.0	340.3	9,429.8	9,008.0	2,524.3	2,307.7	1,091.2	12,159.8
II	13,939.8	4,363.2	1,476.7	520.7	2,886.5	1,000.5	352.2	9,576.6	9,140.7	2,558.3	2,341.4	1,102.7	12,343.6
III	14,114.6	4,398.0	1,485.2	524.0	2,912.8	1,008.0	357.9	9,716.6	9,271.7	2,579.0	2,380.3	1,118.4	12,508.1
IV	14,211.9	4,399.4	1,485.6	528.5	2,913.8	1,012.1	348.2	9,812.5	9,343.3	2,607.2	2,381.1	1,131.7	12,605.4
2019: I	14,266.3	4,397.7	1,485.4	513.6	2,912.3	1,015.4	321.8	9,868.6	9,426.9	2,627.7	2,426.2	1,129.4	12,688.6
II	14,511.2	4,507.0	1,524.6	533.1	2,982.4	1,030.1	349.3	10,004.2	9,558.5	2,655.9	2,459.0	1,149.1	12,893.2
III	14,678.2	4,556.7	1,549.7	537.1	3,007.0	1,042.8	338.0	10,121.5	9,670.9	2,688.1	2,476.0	1,167.1	13,052.5
IV ᵖ	14,799.8	4,573.1	1,548.5	539.0	3,024.6	1,041.6	349.8	10,226.7	9,770.3	2,714.3	2,504.3	1,176.6	13,160.7

[1] Includes other items not shown separately.
[2] Food consists of food and beverages purchased for off-premises consumption; food services, which include purchased meals and beverages, are not classified as food.

Source: Department of Commerce (Bureau of Economic Analysis).

[Billions of chained (2012) dollars; quarterly data at seasonally adjusted annual rates]

Year or quarter	Personal consumption expenditures	Goods						Services					Addendum: Personal consumption expenditures excluding food and energy[2]
		Total	Durable		Nondurable			Total	Household consumption expenditures				
			Total[1]	Motor vehicles and parts	Total[1]	Food and beverages purchased for off-premises consumption	Gasoline and other energy goods		Total[1]	Housing and utilities	Health care	Financial services and insurance	
2002	9,088.7	2,947.6	820.2	416.9	2,157.5	744.5	455.2	6,151.1	5,966.4	1,707.6	1,440.7	700.3	7,716.7
2003	9,377.5	3,092.0	879.3	429.2	2,233.6	761.8	455.6	6,289.4	6,087.7	1,730.5	1,479.3	704.3	7,976.2
2004	9,729.3	3,250.0	952.1	441.1	2,306.5	779.5	459.4	6,479.2	6,275.1	1,773.8	1,531.2	728.5	8,298.2
2005	10,075.9	3,384.7	1,004.9	435.1	2,383.4	809.2	457.4	6,689.5	6,487.6	1,846.6	1,581.9	767.9	8,605.9
2006	10,384.5	3,509.7	1,049.3	419.0	2,461.6	834.0	456.3	6,871.7	6,640.7	1,882.5	1,618.2	785.8	8,894.3
2007	10,615.3	3,607.6	1,099.7	427.3	2,503.4	845.2	455.4	7,003.6	6,765.7	1,900.7	1,657.2	808.3	9,107.6
2008	10,592.8	3,498.9	1,036.4	373.1	2,463.9	831.0	437.5	7,093.0	6,815.4	1,921.2	1,697.9	825.0	9,119.2
2009	10,460.0	3,389.8	973.0	346.7	2,423.1	825.3	440.1	7,070.1	6,781.3	1,943.1	1,735.1	809.5	8,988.1
2010	10,643.0	3,485.7	1,027.3	360.0	2,461.3	837.7	437.9	7,157.4	6,859.0	1,966.8	1,761.7	810.5	9,151.3
2011	10,843.8	3,561.8	1,079.7	370.1	2,482.9	839.0	427.8	7,282.1	6,969.3	1,993.0	1,788.7	831.4	9,363.2
2012	11,006.8	3,637.7	1,144.2	396.6	2,493.5	846.2	421.9	7,369.1	7,027.5	1,996.3	1,821.3	820.1	9,531.1
2013	11,166.9	3,752.2	1,214.1	415.3	2,538.5	855.5	429.7	7,415.5	7,069.8	2,006.4	1,832.6	815.2	9,667.6
2014	11,497.4	3,905.1	1,301.6	439.4	2,605.3	871.4	430.0	7,594.9	7,249.6	2,039.9	1,892.8	817.9	9,978.8
2015	11,921.2	4,088.6	1,398.8	471.7	2,693.2	884.0	450.1	7,838.5	7,500.8	2,087.3	1,995.0	836.3	10,372.0
2016	12,247.5	4,236.6	1,484.2	486.3	2,757.5	910.5	452.1	8,021.1	7,671.0	2,118.6	2,070.7	817.8	10,667.2
2017	12,566.9	4,403.4	1,586.4	511.1	2,825.2	940.5	448.2	8,182.2	7,831.4	2,134.9	2,119.4	832.9	10,956.6
2018	12,944.6	4,583.3	1,685.2	533.1	2,909.6	970.4	447.4	8,388.1	8,019.7	2,164.2	2,181.6	841.5	11,287.2
2019 p	13,279.6	4,756.6	1,765.7	541.1	3,005.5	988.6	450.5	8,560.8	8,196.7	2,184.8	2,246.5	855.6	11,595.6
2016: I	12,124.2	4,176.2	1,441.3	471.2	2,738.9	895.8	457.4	7,955.8	7,610.5	2,103.0	2,042.5	822.2	10,564.1
II	12,211.3	4,222.4	1,466.0	477.8	2,760.7	909.1	453.2	7,998.9	7,656.3	2,117.8	2,079.9	813.9	10,630.7
III	12,289.1	4,263.8	1,504.1	493.8	2,765.2	914.6	451.0	8,037.2	7,680.7	2,129.2	2,062.2	817.9	10,697.0
IV	12,365.3	4,284.2	1,525.4	502.4	2,765.2	922.3	446.9	8,092.2	7,736.7	2,124.3	2,098.3	816.9	10,777.2
2017: I	12,438.9	4,318.2	1,538.3	496.8	2,786.4	929.2	444.3	8,133.0	7,777.2	2,118.9	2,102.5	829.9	10,854.6
II	12,512.9	4,375.9	1,567.0	501.9	2,816.1	933.3	451.5	8,154.1	7,803.5	2,134.5	2,101.2	829.4	10,905.7
III	12,586.3	4,419.7	1,596.9	513.2	2,831.3	942.4	448.8	8,186.6	7,838.6	2,136.0	2,127.0	833.4	10,974.2
IV	12,729.7	4,499.8	1,643.5	532.6	2,866.7	957.2	448.0	8,254.9	7,906.2	2,150.0	2,146.9	838.8	11,091.8
2018: I	12,782.9	4,513.9	1,652.8	524.7	2,872.0	962.9	445.7	8,293.5	7,940.3	2,152.2	2,156.2	840.9	11,142.8
II	12,909.2	4,573.5	1,685.1	534.2	2,900.8	967.5	449.2	8,362.9	7,999.1	2,164.5	2,174.7	839.2	11,251.9
III	13,019.8	4,614.0	1,699.8	534.8	2,926.6	973.8	446.3	8,433.6	8,064.3	2,167.7	2,203.2	841.1	11,357.5
IV	13,066.3	4,631.8	1,705.2	538.5	2,938.9	977.2	448.5	8,462.6	8,075.1	2,172.7	2,192.4	844.9	11,396.5
2019: I	13,103.3	4,649.2	1,706.3	524.2	2,954.6	973.1	449.0	8,483.1	8,119.9	2,173.1	2,227.0	850.7	11,441.8
II	13,250.0	4,746.4	1,759.3	544.1	3,001.3	985.8	450.1	8,541.4	8,177.2	2,179.1	2,245.5	852.7	11,572.9
III	13,353.1	4,808.0	1,793.9	547.5	3,030.0	999.0	448.9	8,587.9	8,224.7	2,191.4	2,247.7	857.6	11,654.9
IV p	13,411.9	4,822.8	1,803.2	548.6	3,036.0	996.5	454.1	8,630.9	8,265.2	2,195.5	2,264.8	861.5	11,712.9

[1] Includes other items not shown separately.
[2] Food consists of food and beverages purchased for off-premises consumption; food services, which include purchased meals and beverages, are not classified as food.

Source: Department of Commerce (Bureau of Economic Analysis).

TABLE B–12. Private fixed investment by type, 1969–2019

[Billions of dollars; quarterly data at seasonally adjusted annual rates]

Year or quarter	Private fixed investment	Nonresidential											Residential		
		Total nonresidential	Structures	Equipment						Intellectual property products			Total residential[1]	Structures	
				Total[1]	Information processing equipment			Industrial equipment	Transportation equipment	Total[1]	Software	Research and development[2]		Total[1]	Single family
					Total	Computers and peripheral equipment	Other								
1969	164.4	120.0	37.7	65.2	12.8	2.4	10.4	19.1	18.9	17.2	1.8	11.0	44.4	43.4	19.7
1970	168.0	124.6	40.3	66.4	14.3	2.7	11.6	20.3	16.2	17.9	2.3	11.5	43.4	42.3	17.5
1971	188.6	130.4	42.7	69.1	14.9	2.8	12.2	19.5	18.4	18.7	2.4	11.9	58.2	56.9	25.8
1972	219.0	146.6	47.2	78.9	16.7	3.5	13.2	21.4	21.8	20.6	2.8	12.9	72.4	70.9	32.8
1973	251.0	172.7	55.0	95.1	19.9	3.5	16.3	26.0	26.6	22.7	3.2	14.6	78.3	76.6	35.2
1974	260.5	191.1	61.2	104.3	23.1	3.9	19.2	30.7	26.3	25.5	3.9	16.4	69.5	67.6	29.7
1975	263.5	196.8	61.4	107.6	23.8	3.6	20.2	31.3	25.2	27.8	4.8	17.5	66.7	64.8	29.6
1976	306.1	219.3	65.9	121.2	27.5	4.4	23.1	34.1	30.0	32.2	5.2	19.6	86.8	84.6	43.9
1977	374.3	259.1	74.6	148.7	33.7	5.7	28.0	39.4	39.3	35.8	5.5	21.8	115.2	112.8	62.2
1978	452.6	314.6	93.6	180.6	42.3	7.6	34.8	47.7	47.3	40.4	6.3	24.9	138.0	135.3	72.8
1979	521.7	373.8	117.7	208.1	50.3	10.2	40.2	56.2	53.6	48.1	8.1	29.1	147.8	144.7	72.3
1980	536.4	406.9	136.2	216.4	58.9	12.5	46.4	60.7	48.4	54.4	9.8	34.2	129.5	126.1	52.9
1981	601.4	472.9	167.3	240.9	69.6	17.1	52.5	65.5	50.6	64.8	11.8	39.7	128.5	124.9	52.0
1982	595.9	485.1	177.6	234.9	74.2	18.9	55.3	62.7	46.8	72.7	14.0	44.8	110.8	107.2	41.5
1983	643.3	482.2	154.3	246.5	83.7	23.9	59.8	58.9	53.5	81.3	16.4	49.6	161.1	156.9	72.5
1984	754.7	564.3	177.4	291.9	101.2	31.6	69.6	68.1	64.4	95.0	20.4	56.9	190.4	185.6	86.4
1985	807.8	607.8	194.5	307.9	106.6	33.7	72.9	72.5	69.0	105.3	23.8	63.0	200.1	195.0	87.4
1986	842.6	607.8	176.5	317.7	111.1	33.4	77.7	75.4	70.5	113.5	25.6	66.5	234.8	229.3	104.1
1987	865.0	615.2	174.2	320.9	112.2	35.8	76.4	76.7	68.1	120.1	29.0	69.2	249.8	244.0	117.2
1988	918.5	662.3	182.8	346.8	120.8	38.0	82.8	84.2	72.9	132.7	33.3	76.4	256.2	250.1	120.1
1989	972.0	716.0	193.7	372.2	130.7	43.1	87.6	93.3	67.9	150.1	40.6	84.1	256.0	249.9	120.9
1990	978.9	739.2	202.9	371.9	129.6	38.6	90.9	92.1	70.0	164.4	45.4	91.5	239.7	233.7	112.9
1991	944.7	723.6	183.6	360.8	129.2	37.7	91.5	89.3	71.5	179.1	48.7	101.0	221.2	215.4	99.4
1992	996.7	741.9	172.6	381.7	142.1	44.0	98.1	93.0	74.7	187.7	51.1	105.4	254.7	248.8	122.0
1993	1,086.0	799.2	177.2	425.1	153.3	47.9	105.4	102.2	89.4	196.9	57.2	106.3	286.8	280.7	140.1
1994	1,192.7	868.9	186.8	476.4	167.0	52.4	114.6	113.6	107.7	205.7	60.4	109.2	323.8	317.6	162.3
1995	1,286.3	962.2	207.3	528.1	188.4	66.1	122.3	129.0	116.1	226.8	65.5	121.2	324.1	317.7	153.5
1996	1,401.3	1,043.2	224.6	565.3	204.7	72.8	131.9	136.5	123.2	253.3	74.5	134.5	358.1	351.7	170.8
1997	1,524.7	1,149.1	250.3	610.9	222.8	81.4	141.4	140.4	135.5	288.0	93.8	148.1	375.6	369.3	175.2
1998	1,673.0	1,254.1	276.0	660.0	240.1	87.9	152.2	147.4	147.1	318.1	109.2	160.6	418.8	412.1	199.4
1999	1,826.2	1,364.5	285.7	713.6	259.8	97.2	162.5	149.1	174.4	365.1	136.6	177.5	461.8	454.5	223.8
2000	1,983.9	1,498.4	321.0	766.1	293.8	103.2	190.6	162.9	170.8	411.3	156.8	199.0	485.4	477.7	236.8
2001	1,973.1	1,460.1	333.5	711.5	265.9	87.6	178.4	151.9	154.2	415.0	157.7	202.7	513.1	505.2	249.1
2002	1,910.4	1,352.8	287.0	659.6	236.7	79.7	157.0	141.7	141.6	406.2	152.5	196.1	557.6	549.6	265.9
2003	2,013.0	1,375.9	286.6	670.6	242.7	79.9	162.8	143.4	134.1	418.7	155.0	201.0	637.1	628.8	310.6
2004	2,217.2	1,467.4	307.7	721.9	255.8	84.2	171.6	144.2	159.2	437.8	166.3	207.4	749.8	740.8	377.6
2005	2,477.2	1,621.0	353.0	794.9	267.0	84.2	182.8	162.4	179.6	473.1	178.6	224.7	856.2	846.6	433.5
2006	2,632.0	1,793.8	425.2	862.3	288.5	92.6	195.9	181.6	194.3	506.3	189.5	245.6	838.2	828.1	416.0
2007	2,639.1	1,948.6	510.3	893.4	310.9	95.4	215.5	194.1	188.8	544.8	206.4	268.0	690.5	680.6	305.2
2008	2,506.9	1,990.9	571.1	845.4	306.3	93.9	212.4	194.3	148.7	574.4	223.8	284.2	516.0	506.4	185.8
2009	2,080.4	1,690.4	455.8	670.3	275.6	88.9	186.7	153.7	74.9	564.4	226.0	274.6	390.0	381.2	105.3
2010	2,111.6	1,735.0	379.8	777.0	307.5	99.6	207.9	155.2	135.8	578.2	226.4	282.4	376.6	367.4	112.6
2011	2,286.3	1,907.5	404.5	881.3	313.3	95.6	217.7	191.5	177.8	621.7	249.8	303.4	378.8	369.1	108.2
2012	2,550.5	2,118.5	479.4	983.4	331.2	103.5	227.7	211.2	215.3	655.7	272.1	313.4	432.0	421.5	132.0
2013	2,721.5	2,211.5	492.5	1,027.0	341.7	102.1	239.6	209.3	242.5	691.9	283.7	337.9	510.0	499.0	170.8
2014	2,960.2	2,400.1	572.6	1,091.9	346.0	101.9	244.1	218.8	272.8	730.5	297.5	359.5	560.2	548.8	193.6
2015	3,091.2	2,457.4	572.6	1,121.5	353.8	101.6	252.2	218.5	306.7	763.3	307.1	378.9	633.8	622.1	221.1
2016	3,151.6	2,453.1	545.8	1,093.6	355.4	99.5	255.8	215.1	293.0	813.8	327.6	405.2	698.5	686.4	242.5
2017	3,340.5	2,584.7	586.8	1,143.7	381.0	107.8	273.2	230.7	283.0	854.2	347.9	422.0	755.7	743.3	270.2
2018	3,573.6	2,786.9	633.2	1,222.6	408.6	118.8	289.8	245.9	301.8	931.1	380.0	461.7	786.7	773.7	284.3
2019 p	3,676.1	2,878.7	625.8	1,240.9	411.9	119.9	292.1	252.4	302.4	1,012.0	416.0	502.9	797.4	784.2	272.1
2016: I	3,102.2	2,415.6	520.5	1,101.4	352.9	100.8	252.1	213.2	302.7	793.8	321.4	392.7	686.6	674.5	240.4
II	3,133.8	2,441.8	537.1	1,092.7	353.0	99.6	253.4	215.0	296.3	812.1	325.2	406.4	692.0	679.9	241.2
III	3,169.3	2,471.6	559.6	1,091.2	357.5	98.1	259.4	214.7	289.5	820.9	329.7	409.7	697.7	685.5	238.1
IV	3,201.3	2,483.5	566.0	1,088.9	358.1	99.7	258.4	217.6	283.6	828.6	334.2	411.9	717.8	705.6	250.2
2017: I	3,274.8	2,531.1	580.2	1,108.8	366.1	102.4	263.7	222.3	283.4	842.1	341.1	417.9	743.7	731.3	259.6
II	3,316.1	2,567.4	589.0	1,132.9	377.1	107.7	269.5	229.6	280.1	845.5	345.7	416.1	748.8	736.5	267.7
III	3,345.0	2,591.6	583.7	1,149.5	384.1	111.6	272.5	232.8	280.0	858.4	350.6	423.2	753.4	741.0	273.6
IV	3,426.0	2,648.9	594.4	1,183.6	396.7	109.7	287.1	238.2	288.7	870.9	354.3	430.9	777.1	764.4	279.7
2018: I	3,500.9	2,717.3	615.9	1,201.8	404.4	117.2	287.2	243.1	294.9	899.6	367.9	444.4	783.7	770.9	286.8
II	3,571.6	2,782.0	640.0	1,214.3	405.8	120.1	285.7	242.1	301.5	927.7	377.3	461.6	789.5	776.6	288.2
III	3,596.7	2,807.7	641.7	1,227.9	414.8	120.2	294.6	246.9	299.7	938.1	383.8	464.1	789.0	775.9	285.8
IV	3,625.2	2,840.7	635.2	1,246.4	409.5	117.7	291.8	251.6	311.0	959.1	391.0	476.8	784.4	771.6	276.3
2019: I	3,670.1	2,882.5	645.8	1,249.0	416.0	119.4	296.6	250.8	309.4	987.9	404.1	492.0	787.4	774.3	268.7
II	3,674.7	2,890.0	633.2	1,252.9	419.0	126.1	292.9	252.4	306.0	1,003.9	411.4	499.9	784.7	771.6	266.0
III	3,677.6	2,877.2	619.4	1,237.4	409.2	114.2	295.0	257.3	294.8	1,020.5	421.1	505.8	800.3	787.1	271.3
IV p	3,682.0	2,864.9	604.7	1,224.4	403.6	119.8	283.8	248.9	299.1	1,035.8	427.4	513.7	817.1	803.9	282.4

[1] Includes other items not shown separately.
[2] Research and development investment includes expenditures for software.

Source: Department of Commerce (Bureau of Economic Analysis).

Table B–13. Real private fixed investment by type, 2002–2019

[Billions of chained (2012) dollars; quarterly data at seasonally adjusted annual rates]

Year or quarter	Private fixed investment	Nonresidential											Residential		
		Total nonresidential	Structures	Equipment						Intellectual property products			Total residential²	Structures	
				Total²	Information processing equipment			Industrial equipment	Transportation equipment	Total²	Software	Research and development³		Total²	Single family
					Total	Computers and peripheral equipment¹	Other								
2002	2,183.4	1,472.7	473.5	607.8	133.3	35.9	98.3	181.4	162.4	421.5	125.5	244.1	692.6	685.1	327.1
2003	2,280.6	1,509.4	456.6	634.3	150.4	40.2	111.1	182.2	150.3	437.7	133.5	246.1	755.5	747.7	362.0
2004	2,440.7	1,594.0	456.3	688.6	169.4	45.7	124.7	178.8	171.2	459.2	149.3	248.1	830.9	822.1	405.4
2005	2,618.7	1,716.4	466.1	760.0	187.6	51.8	136.5	194.2	192.1	493.1	163.4	261.6	885.4	876.3	432.8
2006	2,686.8	1,854.2	501.7	832.6	217.0	64.7	152.4	210.6	206.4	521.5	173.5	279.6	818.9	809.5	390.4
2007	2,653.5	1,982.1	568.6	865.8	247.2	73.9	173.3	217.3	197.7	554.3	191.1	296.1	665.8	656.6	283.5
2008	2,499.4	1,994.2	605.4	824.4	260.6	79.7	180.9	208.3	155.0	575.3	206.7	304.8	504.6	495.7	178.1
2009	2,099.8	1,704.3	492.2	649.7	247.5	81.1	166.5	162.7	72.5	572.4	212.9	297.4	395.3	386.9	105.3
2010	2,164.2	1,781.0	412.8	781.2	289.1	94.1	195.1	162.5	141.5	588.1	220.9	298.5	383.0	373.8	114.3
2011	2,317.8	1,935.4	424.1	886.2	303.2	93.9	209.3	194.9	181.8	624.8	245.2	311.0	382.5	372.4	109.1
2012	2,550.5	2,118.5	479.4	983.4	331.2	103.5	227.7	211.2	215.3	655.7	272.1	313.4	432.0	421.5	132.0
2013	2,692.1	2,206.0	485.5	1,029.2	351.8	103.0	248.8	208.4	238.5	691.4	287.2	333.8	485.5	474.1	161.8
2014	2,869.2	2,365.3	538.8	1,101.1	370.2	102.9	267.7	216.5	265.0	724.8	305.3	346.9	504.1	491.8	171.8
2015	2,967.0	2,408.2	522.4	1,136.6	394.6	103.7	291.9	217.0	293.2	750.7	319.8	355.9	555.3	541.9	191.4
2016	3,023.6	2,425.3	496.4	1,122.3	415.5	103.2	314.2	214.6	277.0	810.0	346.0	386.9	591.2	576.7	201.3
2017	3,149.7	2,531.2	519.5	1,175.6	456.3	112.3	346.5	228.2	263.3	839.6	373.8	388.5	611.9	596.6	214.7
2018	3,293.4	2,692.3	540.9	1,255.3	498.5	123.5	377.5	238.5	280.1	901.6	413.5	409.2	602.9	587.5	216.6
2019ᵖ	3,337.1	2,749.8	516.8	1,272.4	517.0	129.2	390.1	241.0	278.8	971.1	456.3	435.5	593.5	578.2	200.7
2016: I	2,991.0	2,389.8	476.4	1,126.5	406.5	104.1	303.9	212.8	287.8	792.0	336.9	378.7	593.0	578.8	204.7
II	3,010.9	2,413.6	487.9	1,120.0	409.1	102.9	307.9	214.6	281.0	809.8	342.7	390.7	590.1	575.7	202.3
III	3,038.9	2,446.8	509.0	1,120.9	420.2	101.7	321.1	213.9	272.8	819.2	349.5	391.9	586.2	571.7	195.8
IV	3,053.7	2,451.2	512.1	1,122.0	426.0	104.3	324.1	217.0	266.3	819.2	354.9	386.2	595.5	580.7	202.2
2017: I	3,111.1	2,490.5	521.1	1,139.3	436.4	106.9	331.9	220.8	263.2	831.8	364.5	389.6	612.4	597.2	208.7
II	3,133.0	2,517.4	523.7	1,163.8	451.2	112.3	341.0	227.3	259.7	832.3	369.3	385.9	608.9	593.8	213.1
III	3,144.1	2,532.6	513.3	1,181.4	460.6	116.3	346.1	230.0	260.4	842.3	378.1	387.5	605.9	590.6	216.5
IV	3,210.7	2,584.2	519.9	1,217.8	477.2	113.8	366.8	234.4	269.9	852.0	383.5	390.9	620.4	604.7	220.6
2018: I	3,254.0	2,639.5	534.9	1,237.5	489.3	121.6	370.0	237.7	275.4	872.0	399.2	395.4	612.1	596.4	222.4
II	3,295.4	2,689.9	549.1	1,247.8	493.9	124.8	371.0	235.2	279.4	896.9	409.2	409.0	606.3	590.9	219.9
III	3,301.3	2,703.9	546.2	1,256.7	506.6	124.9	384.4	238.7	275.9	905.9	417.4	409.6	600.1	584.9	216.6
IV	3,323.0	2,735.8	533.4	1,279.2	504.2	122.7	384.5	242.5	289.6	931.3	428.0	422.7	593.0	578.0	207.6
2019: I	3,349.4	2,765.6	538.6	1,278.9	515.4	125.5	393.1	240.4	286.6	955.6	443.0	432.6	591.4	576.3	199.5
II	3,337.4	2,758.5	523.0	1,281.5	524.1	135.2	390.2	241.4	279.7	964.2	449.3	435.5	587.0	571.9	197.7
III	3,330.5	2,742.7	509.6	1,269.3	515.5	124.0	394.9	245.3	271.5	975.2	460.0	436.2	593.7	578.3	199.8
IVᵖ	3,331.0	2,732.4	496.2	1,259.9	512.8	132.0	382.2	236.8	277.2	989.3	472.8	437.9	602.1	586.3	205.9

[1] Because computers exhibit rapid changes in prices relative to other prices in the economy, the chained-dollar estimates should not be used to measure the component's relative importance or its contribution to the growth rate of more aggregate series. The quantity index for computers can be used to accurately measure the real growth rate of this series. For information on this component, see *Survey of Current Business* Table 5.3.1 (for growth rates), Table 5.3.2 (for contributions), and Table 5.3.3 (for quantity indexes).

[2] Includes other items not shown separately.

[3] Research and development investment includes expenditures for software.

Source: Department of Commerce (Bureau of Economic Analysis).

National Income or Expenditure | 381

TABLE B–14. Foreign transactions in the national income and product accounts, 1969–2019

[Billions of dollars; quarterly data at seasonally adjusted annual rates]

Year or quarter	Current receipts from rest of the world					Current payments to rest of the world									
	Total	Exports of goods and services			Income re-ceipts	Total	Imports of goods and services			Income pay-ments	Current taxes and transfer payments to rest of the world (net)				Balance on current account, NIPA[2]
		Total	Goods[1]	Serv-ices[1]			Total	Goods[1]	Serv-ices[1]		Total	From per-sons (net)	From gov-ern-ment (net)	From busi-ness (net)	
1969	63.7	51.9	38.7	13.2	11.8	62.1	50.5	36.8	13.7	5.7	5.9	1.1	4.5	0.3	1.6
1970	72.5	59.7	45.0	14.7	12.8	68.8	55.8	40.9	14.9	6.4	6.6	1.3	4.9	.4	3.7
1971	77.0	63.0	46.2	16.8	14.0	76.7	62.3	46.6	15.8	6.4	7.9	1.4	6.1	.4	.3
1972	87.1	70.8	52.6	18.3	16.3	91.2	74.2	56.9	17.3	7.7	9.2	1.4	7.4	.5	-4.0
1973	118.8	95.3	75.8	19.5	23.5	109.9	91.2	71.8	19.3	10.9	7.9	1.6	5.6	.7	8.9
1974	156.5	126.7	103.5	23.2	29.8	150.5	127.5	104.5	22.9	14.3	8.7	1.4	6.4	1.0	6.0
1975	166.7	138.7	112.5	26.2	28.0	146.9	122.7	99.0	23.7	15.0	9.1	1.3	7.1	.7	19.8
1976	181.9	149.5	121.5	28.0	32.4	174.8	151.1	124.6	26.5	15.5	8.1	1.4	5.7	1.1	7.1
1977	196.5	159.3	128.4	30.9	37.2	207.5	182.4	152.6	29.8	16.9	8.1	1.4	5.3	1.4	-10.9
1978	233.1	186.9	149.9	37.0	46.3	245.8	212.3	177.4	34.8	24.7	8.8	1.6	5.9	1.4	-12.6
1979	298.5	230.1	187.3	42.9	68.3	299.6	252.7	212.8	39.9	36.4	10.6	1.7	6.8	2.0	-1.2
1980	359.9	280.8	230.4	50.3	79.1	351.4	293.8	248.6	45.3	44.9	12.6	2.0	8.3	2.4	8.5
1981	397.3	305.2	245.2	60.0	92.0	393.9	317.8	267.8	49.9	59.1	17.0	5.6	8.3	3.2	3.4
1982	384.2	283.2	222.6	60.7	101.0	387.5	303.2	250.5	52.6	64.5	19.8	6.7	9.7	3.4	-3.3
1983	378.9	277.0	214.0	62.9	101.9	413.9	328.6	272.7	56.0	64.8	20.5	7.0	10.1	3.4	-35.1
1984	424.2	302.4	231.3	71.1	121.9	514.3	405.1	336.3	68.8	85.6	23.6	7.9	12.2	3.5	-90.1
1985	415.9	303.2	227.5	75.7	112.7	530.2	417.2	343.3	73.9	87.3	25.7	8.3	14.4	2.9	-114.3
1986	432.3	321.0	231.4	89.6	111.3	575.0	452.9	370.0	82.9	94.4	27.8	9.1	15.4	3.2	-142.7
1987	487.2	363.9	265.6	98.4	123.3	641.3	508.7	414.8	93.9	105.8	26.8	10.0	13.4	3.4	-154.1
1988	596.7	444.6	332.1	112.5	152.1	712.4	554.0	452.1	101.9	129.5	29.0	10.8	13.7	4.5	-115.7
1989	682.0	504.3	374.8	129.5	177.7	774.3	591.0	484.8	106.2	152.9	30.4	11.6	14.2	4.6	-92.4
1990	740.7	551.9	403.3	148.6	188.8	815.6	629.7	508.1	121.7	154.2	31.7	12.2	14.7	4.8	-74.9
1991	763.3	594.9	430.1	164.8	168.4	755.4	623.5	500.7	122.8	136.8	-4.9	14.1	-24.0	5.0	7.9
1992	785.1	633.1	455.3	177.7	152.1	830.7	667.8	544.9	122.9	121.0	41.9	14.5	22.0	5.4	-45.6
1993	810.4	654.8	467.7	187.1	155.6	889.8	720.0	592.8	127.2	124.4	45.4	17.1	22.9	5.4	-79.4
1994	905.5	720.9	518.4	202.6	184.5	1,021.1	813.4	676.8	136.6	161.6	46.1	18.9	21.1	6.0	-115.6
1995	1,042.6	812.8	592.4	220.4	229.8	1,148.5	902.6	757.4	145.1	201.9	44.1	20.3	15.6	8.2	-105.9
1996	1,114.0	867.6	628.8	238.8	246.4	1,229.0	964.0	807.4	156.5	215.5	49.5	22.6	20.0	6.9	-115.0
1997	1,233.9	953.8	699.9	253.9	280.1	1,364.0	1,055.8	885.7	170.1	256.8	51.4	25.7	16.7	9.1	-130.1
1998	1,239.8	953.0	692.6	260.4	286.8	1,445.1	1,115.7	930.8	184.9	269.4	60.0	29.7	17.4	13.0	-205.3
1999	1,350.9	992.8	711.7	281.1	320.2	1,629.3	1,248.6	1,051.2	197.4	294.7	86.0	58.4	27.3	.3	-278.4
2000	1,518.0	1,096.3	795.9	300.3	380.6	1,914.4	1,471.3	1,250.1	221.2	345.6	97.6	61.9	31.0	4.7	-396.4
2001	1,394.1	1,024.6	741.2	283.4	324.1	1,777.0	1,392.6	1,173.8	218.8	275.3	109.1	71.7	27.7	9.7	-383.0
2002	1,370.4	998.7	709.0	289.7	314.8	1,813.6	1,424.1	1,194.4	229.8	269.6	119.9	82.1	33.0	4.8	-443.2
2003	1,456.1	1,036.2	737.1	299.1	353.8	1,969.4	1,539.3	1,291.3	248.0	295.4	134.6	89.4	38.7	6.5	-513.2
2004	1,689.3	1,177.6	830.0	347.7	446.9	2,314.5	1,796.7	1,507.3	289.4	368.8	149.0	85.4	41.4	22.2	-625.2
2005	1,941.5	1,305.2	921.9	383.3	566.0	2,678.8	2,026.4	1,715.5	311.0	488.1	164.3	90.6	52.1	21.7	-737.3
2006	2,259.9	1,472.6	1,044.9	427.7	712.0	3,061.7	2,243.5	1,895.7	347.8	661.5	156.7	95.0	47.4	14.2	-801.9
2007	2,603.0	1,660.9	1,161.3	499.6	866.6	3,313.7	2,379.3	1,999.7	379.6	757.6	176.9	105.5	55.6	15.7	-710.8
2008	2,775.8	1,837.1	1,292.5	544.5	848.8	3,458.9	2,560.1	2,144.3	415.9	694.2	204.6	129.5	60.5	14.6	-683.2
2009	2,321.5	1,582.0	1,058.4	523.6	647.8	2,693.6	1,978.4	1,585.4	393.1	505.8	209.3	133.2	68.7	7.4	-372.1
2010	2,657.2	1,846.3	1,272.4	573.8	715.2	3,093.9	2,360.2	1,944.8	415.4	519.5	214.2	141.9	70.0	2.4	-436.7
2011	2,996.3	2,103.0	1,462.3	640.7	789.2	3,461.8	2,682.5	2,240.5	441.9	552.8	226.6	157.8	74.6	-5.9	-465.6
2012	3,104.3	2,191.3	1,521.6	669.7	799.7	3,552.4	2,759.9	2,301.4	458.5	567.4	225.2	151.8	73.2	.2	-448.1
2013	3,228.0	2,273.4	1,559.2	714.2	823.4	3,596.5	2,764.2	2,296.4	467.8	592.7	239.6	167.7	72.7	-.8	-368.5
2014	3,371.1	2,371.7	1,615.0	756.7	853.5	3,746.7	2,879.4	2,391.6	487.8	612.5	254.8	177.6	72.3	4.9	-375.6
2015	3,240.3	2,266.8	1,494.6	772.2	837.7	3,664.4	2,786.6	2,288.1	498.6	613.1	264.7	181.2	73.1	10.4	-424.1
2016	3,224.6	2,220.6	1,444.0	776.6	861.7	3,665.9	2,739.4	2,221.1	518.3	643.5	283.0	187.5	75.6	19.9	-441.4
2017	3,478.6	2,356.7	1,538.4	818.4	957.9	3,945.2	2,932.1	2,379.8	552.3	714.6	298.5	205.2	74.4	18.9	-466.6
2018	3,771.8	2,510.3	1,661.3	848.9	1,106.2	4,281.3	3,148.5	2,570.6	577.9	838.3	294.5	200.6	81.4	12.5	-509.5
2019 p		2,503.8	1,643.8	859.9			3,135.7	2,529.6	605.8		311.8	199.4	80.2	32.3	
2016: I	3,129.1	2,164.9	1,405.1	759.8	826.4	3,594.8	2,687.1	2,177.4	509.6	624.9	282.8	183.9	82.0	16.9	-465.7
II	3,210.9	2,208.1	1,433.6	774.4	861.8	3,623.7	2,703.4	2,192.2	511.2	648.0	272.2	185.3	70.4	16.6	-412.8
III	3,256.7	2,254.4	1,466.7	787.7	860.1	3,693.0	2,754.1	2,231.7	522.4	655.3	283.6	188.1	76.4	19.1	-436.4
IV	3,301.6	2,255.1	1,470.7	784.5	898.4	3,752.2	2,813.1	2,283.0	530.1	645.7	293.3	192.6	73.8	26.9	-450.6
2017: I	3,376.0	2,303.3	1,503.0	800.3	898.4	3,826.4	2,874.2	2,337.5	536.7	665.2	287.0	197.7	74.5	14.8	-450.4
II	3,388.7	2,313.2	1,508.7	804.5	924.9	3,904.6	2,896.9	2,349.6	547.4	708.4	299.2	202.4	71.0	25.9	-515.8
III	3,521.0	2,360.1	1,535.4	824.7	982.1	3,944.9	2,910.7	2,353.3	557.4	725.9	308.3	216.9	70.0	21.4	-423.9
IV	3,628.6	2,450.3	1,606.4	844.0	1,026.2	4,104.9	3,046.5	2,478.8	567.6	758.9	299.6	203.9	81.9	13.7	-476.2
2018: I	3,694.9	2,476.6	1,626.4	850.2	1,070.5	4,172.8	3,105.6	2,536.5	569.1	789.5	277.7	202.4	72.5	2.9	-477.9
II	3,810.0	2,543.6	1,697.6	846.0	1,111.4	4,254.3	3,112.0	2,542.7	569.3	845.8	296.6	201.3	87.9	7.4	-444.3
III	3,786.0	2,510.3	1,661.3	849.0	1,116.0	4,316.1	3,181.6	2,602.0	579.6	843.6	290.8	199.6	78.9	12.3	-530.1
IV	3,796.6	2,510.5	1,659.9	850.6	1,127.0	4,382.1	3,194.7	2,601.2	593.4	874.4	313.0	199.2	86.2	27.6	-585.5
2019: I	3,817.2	2,520.3	1,661.8	858.5	1,149.0	4,363.8	3,154.1	2,554.3	599.8	891.2	318.5	199.5	85.2	33.8	-546.6
II	3,827.8	2,504.0	1,646.1	858.0	1,177.2	4,341.9	3,166.7	2,566.1	600.6	876.2	299.0	198.7	73.2	27.1	-514.1
III	3,806.1	2,495.1	1,638.0	857.1	1,160.4	4,313.0	3,148.2	2,540.9	607.2	851.4	313.5	199.1	78.3	36.1	-506.9
IV p		2,495.6	1,629.5	866.1			3,074.0	2,458.4	615.5		316.3	200.1	84.1	32.0	

[1] Certain goods, primarily military equipment purchased and sold by the Federal Government, are included in services. Beginning with 1986, repairs and alterations of equipment were reclassified from goods to services.
[2] National income and product accounts (NIPA).

Source: Department of Commerce (Bureau of Economic Analysis).

TABLE B–15. Real exports and imports of goods and services, 2002–2019

[Billions of chained (2012) dollars; quarterly data at seasonally adjusted annual rates]

Year or quarter	Exports of goods and services						Imports of goods and services					
	Total	Goods[1]				Services[1]	Total	Goods[1]				Services[1]
		Total	Durable goods	Non-durable goods	Non-agricultural goods			Total	Durable goods	Non-durable goods	Non-petroleum goods	
2002	1,277.1	900.6	524.7	388.8	797.3	376.5	1,944.4	1,634.0	785.6	896.4	1,207.4	309.4
2003	1,305.0	927.1	542.4	396.4	821.8	377.8	2,040.1	1,729.0	831.2	948.7	1,276.4	310.5
2004	1,431.2	1,008.3	604.0	410.3	904.9	422.8	2,272.6	1,926.8	951.0	1,012.5	1,430.8	345.2
2005	1,533.2	1,085.4	663.4	423.3	975.8	447.6	2,421.0	2,062.3	1,036.9	1,053.0	1,543.4	358.6
2006	1,676.4	1,193.0	739.4	451.5	1,073.6	483.3	2,581.5	2,190.9	1,135.6	1,069.5	1,664.8	390.2
2007	1,822.3	1,276.1	796.6	475.7	1,148.3	546.0	2,646.0	2,236.0	1,168.3	1,078.9	1,714.6	409.2
2008	1,925.4	1,350.4	835.0	512.7	1,215.0	574.7	2,587.1	2,160.8	1,130.6	1,040.7	1,657.1	425.2
2009	1,763.8	1,190.3	694.5	499.9	1,060.0	572.9	2,248.6	1,830.1	902.3	948.3	1,375.9	415.9
2010	1,977.9	1,368.7	818.1	551.7	1,223.8	609.2	2,543.8	2,112.7	1,115.6	1,001.5	1,636.1	430.8
2011	2,119.0	1,465.3	893.7	571.6	1,321.6	653.8	2,687.1	2,242.5	1,227.0	1,016.2	1,769.8	444.6
2012	2,191.3	1,521.6	937.7	583.9	1,376.4	669.7	2,759.9	2,301.4	1,326.4	975.0	1,867.1	458.5
2013	2,269.6	1,570.0	960.1	609.9	1,422.9	699.5	2,802.4	2,341.9	1,385.9	956.1	1,932.5	460.6
2014	2,365.3	1,642.7	1,001.3	641.5	1,484.2	722.7	2,942.5	2,472.2	1,508.8	963.8	2,076.6	471.0
2015	2,376.5	1,637.0	979.3	659.7	1,475.7	738.4	3,098.1	2,612.5	1,608.0	1,004.1	2,207.1	487.4
2016	2,376.1	1,646.1	968.7	682.9	1,477.0	730.4	3,159.8	2,650.6	1,631.2	1,019.0	2,231.8	508.9
2017	2,458.8	1,710.0	999.1	718.2	1,537.7	750.3	3,308.5	2,777.1	1,749.6	1,020.5	2,348.3	531.3
2018	2,532.9	1,782.8	1,033.6	758.1	1,609.3	755.4	3,453.0	2,916.1	1,849.5	1,058.2	2,489.7	539.9
2019 p	2,531.9	1,785.6	1,008.0	790.7	1,608.8	752.1	3,486.1	2,923.0	1,851.1	1,063.8	2,514.4	562.1
2016: I	2,345.1	1,624.3	958.8	670.3	1,467.8	721.1	3,122.7	2,620.5	1,604.7	1,017.4	2,207.7	502.0
II	2,367.9	1,635.2	964.9	675.1	1,478.9	732.1	3,128.9	2,627.4	1,610.2	1,018.4	2,213.9	501.6
III	2,403.4	1,664.0	971.7	699.7	1,477.0	739.5	3,164.9	2,651.2	1,638.6	1,010.7	2,229.7	512.6
IV	2,388.1	1,660.7	979.2	686.6	1,484.2	728.8	3,222.7	2,703.1	1,671.2	1,029.6	2,275.8	519.2
2017: I	2,423.5	1,684.7	978.5	714.5	1,510.4	740.1	3,255.0	2,730.4	1,698.2	1,028.2	2,293.6	524.1
II	2,432.9	1,694.0	985.2	717.0	1,521.0	740.7	3,282.9	2,753.2	1,734.5	1,011.6	2,325.9	529.3
III	2,459.5	1,703.1	1,006.0	702.3	1,530.3	756.6	3,293.2	2,759.2	1,748.0	1,002.9	2,338.9	533.0
IV	2,519.2	1,758.1	1,026.6	739.1	1,589.3	763.7	3,403.0	2,865.8	1,817.8	1,039.1	2,434.7	538.9
2018: I	2,524.0	1,763.3	1,042.6	726.7	1,597.0	763.6	3,408.2	2,875.7	1,821.9	1,045.3	2,453.5	535.0
II	2,559.9	1,814.1	1,041.9	782.4	1,626.9	753.2	3,410.4	2,881.2	1,817.5	1,055.9	2,452.3	532.4
III	2,519.3	1,771.2	1,020.7	760.2	1,592.5	753.0	3,481.8	2,945.4	1,871.0	1,065.9	2,509.2	540.3
IV	2,528.5	1,782.5	1,029.0	763.1	1,620.8	751.7	3,511.6	2,962.0	1,887.5	1,065.8	2,543.9	552.0
2019: I	2,554.4	1,802.6	1,037.2	775.6	1,630.5	757.8	3,498.3	2,940.7	1,874.5	1,057.5	2,530.9	558.1
II	2,517.5	1,775.3	1,001.3	787.1	1,590.6	748.0	3,498.2	2,941.7	1,858.6	1,075.2	2,527.5	557.2
III	2,523.4	1,784.7	999.5	799.6	1,601.4	745.5	3,513.6	2,949.6	1,866.1	1,075.4	2,540.3	563.7
IV p	2,532.4	1,779.8	994.1	800.5	1,612.7	757.2	3,434.4	2,859.8	1,805.2	1,047.0	2,459.0	569.6

[1] Certain goods, primarily military equipment purchased and sold by the Federal Government, are included in services. Repairs and alterations of equipment are also included in services.

Source: Department of Commerce (Bureau of Economic Analysis).

TABLE B–16. Sources of personal income, 1969–2019

[Billions of dollars; quarterly data at seasonally adjusted annual rates]

Year or quarter	Personal income	Compensation of employees							Proprietors' income with inventory valuation and capital consumption adjustments			Rental income of persons with capital consumption adjustment
		Total	Wages and salaries			Supplements to wages and salaries			Total	Farm	Nonfarm	
			Total	Private industries	Government	Total	Employer contributions for employee pension and insurance funds	Employer contributions for government social insurance				
1969	800.3	584.5	518.3	412.7	105.6	66.1	43.4	22.8	77.0	12.8	64.2	20.3
1970	865.0	623.3	551.6	434.3	117.2	71.8	47.9	23.8	77.8	12.9	64.9	20.7
1971	932.8	665.0	584.5	457.8	126.8	80.4	54.0	26.4	83.9	13.4	70.5	21.8
1972	1,024.5	731.3	638.8	500.9	137.9	92.5	61.4	31.2	95.1	17.0	78.1	22.7
1973	1,140.8	812.7	708.8	560.0	148.8	103.9	64.1	39.8	112.5	29.1	83.4	23.1
1974	1,251.8	887.7	772.3	611.8	160.5	115.4	70.7	44.7	112.2	23.5	88.7	23.2
1975	1,369.4	947.2	814.8	638.6	176.2	132.4	85.7	46.7	118.2	22.0	96.2	22.3
1976	1,502.6	1,048.3	899.7	710.8	188.9	148.6	94.2	54.4	131.0	17.2	113.8	20.3
1977	1,659.2	1,165.8	994.2	791.6	202.6	171.7	110.6	61.1	144.5	16.0	128.5	15.9
1978	1,863.7	1,316.8	1,120.6	900.6	220.0	196.2	124.7	71.5	166.0	19.9	146.1	16.5
1979	2,082.7	1,477.2	1,253.3	1,016.2	237.1	223.9	141.3	82.6	179.4	22.2	157.3	16.1
1980	2,323.6	1,622.2	1,373.4	1,112.0	261.5	248.8	159.9	88.9	171.6	11.7	159.9	19.0
1981	2,605.1	1,792.5	1,511.4	1,225.5	285.8	281.2	177.5	103.6	179.7	19.0	160.7	23.8
1982	2,791.6	1,893.0	1,587.5	1,280.0	307.5	305.5	195.7	109.8	171.2	13.3	157.9	23.8
1983	2,981.1	2,012.5	1,677.5	1,352.7	324.8	335.0	215.1	119.9	186.3	6.2	180.1	24.4
1984	3,292.7	2,215.9	1,844.9	1,496.8	348.1	371.0	231.9	139.0	228.2	20.9	207.3	24.7
1985	3,524.9	2,387.3	1,982.6	1,608.7	373.9	404.8	257.0	147.7	241.1	21.0	220.1	26.2
1986	3,733.1	2,542.1	2,102.3	1,705.1	397.2	439.7	281.9	157.9	256.5	22.8	233.7	18.3
1987	3,961.6	2,722.4	2,256.3	1,833.2	423.1	466.1	299.9	166.3	286.5	28.9	257.6	16.6
1988	4,283.4	2,948.0	2,439.8	1,987.7	452.0	508.2	323.6	184.6	325.5	26.8	298.7	22.5
1989	4,625.6	3,139.6	2,583.1	2,101.9	481.1	556.6	362.9	193.7	341.1	33.0	308.1	21.5
1990	4,913.8	3,340.4	2,741.2	2,222.2	519.0	599.2	392.7	206.5	353.2	32.2	321.0	28.2
1991	5,084.9	3,450.5	2,814.5	2,265.7	548.8	636.0	420.9	215.1	354.2	26.8	327.4	38.6
1992	5,420.9	3,668.2	2,965.5	2,393.5	572.0	702.7	474.3	228.4	400.2	34.8	365.4	60.6
1993	5,657.9	3,817.3	3,079.3	2,490.3	589.0	737.9	498.3	239.7	428.0	31.4	396.6	90.1
1994	5,947.1	4,006.2	3,236.6	2,627.1	609.5	769.6	515.5	254.1	456.6	34.7	422.0	113.7
1995	6,291.4	4,198.1	3,418.0	2,789.0	629.0	780.1	515.9	264.1	481.2	22.0	459.2	124.9
1996	6,678.5	4,416.9	3,616.5	2,968.4	648.1	800.5	525.7	274.8	543.8	37.3	506.4	142.5
1997	7,092.5	4,708.8	3,876.8	3,205.0	671.9	832.0	542.4	289.6	584.0	32.4	551.6	147.1
1998	7,606.7	5,071.1	4,181.6	3,480.3	701.3	889.5	582.3	307.2	640.2	28.5	611.7	165.2
1999	8,001.9	5,402.8	4,458.0	3,724.2	733.8	944.8	621.4	323.3	696.4	28.1	668.3	178.5
2000	8,652.6	5,848.1	4,825.9	4,046.1	779.8	1,022.2	677.0	345.2	753.9	31.5	722.4	183.5
2001	9,005.6	6,039.1	4,954.4	4,132.4	822.0	1,084.7	726.7	358.0	831.0	32.1	798.9	202.4
2002	9,159.0	6,135.6	4,996.3	4,123.4	872.9	1,139.3	773.2	366.0	869.8	19.9	849.8	211.1
2003	9,487.5	6,354.1	5,138.7	4,224.8	914.0	1,215.3	832.8	382.5	896.9	36.5	860.4	231.5
2004	10,035.1	6,720.1	5,421.6	4,469.2	952.3	1,298.5	889.7	408.8	962.0	51.5	910.5	248.9
2005	10,598.2	7,066.6	5,691.9	4,700.6	991.3	1,374.7	946.7	428.1	978.0	46.8	931.2	232.0
2006	11,381.7	7,479.9	6,057.0	5,022.4	1,034.5	1,422.9	975.6	447.3	1,049.6	33.1	1,016.6	202.3
2007	12,007.8	7,878.9	6,396.8	5,308.2	1,088.5	1,482.1	1,020.4	461.7	994.0	40.3	953.8	184.4
2008	12,442.2	8,057.0	6,534.2	5,390.4	1,143.9	1,522.7	1,051.3	471.4	960.9	40.2	920.7	256.7
2009	12,059.1	7,758.5	6,248.6	5,073.4	1,175.2	1,509.9	1,051.8	458.1	938.5	28.1	910.5	327.3
2010	12,551.6	7,924.9	6,372.1	5,180.9	1,191.2	1,552.9	1,083.9	469.0	1,108.7	39.0	1,069.7	394.2
2011	13,326.8	8,225.9	6,625.9	5,431.1	1,194.9	1,600.0	1,107.3	492.7	1,229.3	64.9	1,164.4	478.6
2012	14,010.1	8,566.7	6,927.5	5,729.2	1,198.3	1,639.2	1,125.9	513.3	1,347.3	60.9	1,286.4	518.0
2013	14,181.1	8,834.2	7,113.2	5,905.2	1,208.0	1,721.0	1,194.7	526.3	1,403.6	88.3	1,315.3	557.0
2014	14,991.7	9,249.1	7,475.2	6,238.3	1,236.9	1,773.9	1,227.5	546.4	1,447.7	69.8	1,377.9	604.6
2015	15,717.8	9,698.2	7,856.7	6,581.0	1,275.6	1,841.5	1,272.3	569.2	1,422.2	56.0	1,366.2	648.1
2016	16,121.2	9,960.3	8,083.5	6,775.5	1,308.0	1,876.8	1,295.6	581.2	1,423.7	35.6	1,388.1	681.4
2017	16,878.8	10,411.6	8,462.1	7,114.1	1,348.0	1,949.5	1,343.9	605.7	1,518.2	38.1	1,480.1	718.8
2018 p	17,819.2	10,928.5	8,888.5	7,485.9	1,402.6	2,040.0	1,417.2	622.8	1,588.8	27.2	1,561.6	756.8
2019 p	18,624.2	11,447.9	9,323.0	7,871.2	1,451.8	2,124.8	1,473.2	651.6	1,656.2	31.1	1,625.1	778.1
2016: I	15,937.6	9,843.5	7,982.8	6,688.5	1,294.2	1,860.7	1,286.5	574.2	1,415.2	36.5	1,378.7	669.9
II	16,029.0	9,900.1	8,032.1	6,729.6	1,302.5	1,868.0	1,290.5	577.5	1,410.2	38.3	1,371.9	680.2
III	16,175.5	9,993.2	8,112.2	6,798.1	1,314.1	1,881.1	1,298.0	583.1	1,429.5	36.5	1,393.0	683.6
IV	16,342.6	10,104.5	8,206.9	6,885.7	1,321.2	1,897.5	1,307.5	590.0	1,440.0	31.2	1,408.9	692.1
2017: I	16,604.1	10,227.6	8,310.6	6,979.2	1,331.4	1,917.0	1,320.4	596.6	1,494.8	44.5	1,450.3	707.4
II	16,749.6	10,334.2	8,397.7	7,057.4	1,340.3	1,936.5	1,334.3	602.2	1,512.2	42.1	1,470.1	709.9
III	16,930.4	10,456.7	8,497.9	7,144.9	1,353.0	1,958.8	1,350.8	607.9	1,523.1	34.1	1,489.0	722.0
IV	17,231.2	10,628.0	8,642.0	7,274.9	1,367.2	1,985.9	1,370.0	615.9	1,542.9	31.8	1,511.1	736.0
2018: I	17,540.3	10,786.0	8,776.7	7,396.3	1,380.4	2,009.4	1,391.8	617.6	1,567.5	28.1	1,539.4	743.8
II	17,725.0	10,876.1	8,845.0	7,450.9	1,394.1	2,031.1	1,410.9	620.2	1,573.3	27.5	1,545.8	754.0
III	17,928.5	10,994.3	8,942.2	7,529.6	1,412.6	2,052.0	1,426.6	625.4	1,590.0	17.4	1,572.6	765.2
IV	18,082.8	11,057.4	8,990.0	7,566.8	1,423.3	2,067.4	1,439.3	628.1	1,624.4	35.9	1,588.4	764.1
2019: I	18,355.4	11,306.6	9,211.5	7,779.5	1,432.0	2,095.1	1,450.3	644.8	1,621.2	24.8	1,596.3	767.0
II	18,555.9	11,386.9	9,273.6	7,830.9	1,442.7	2,113.3	1,464.7	648.6	1,632.9	19.2	1,613.7	777.2
III	18,718.4	11,489.0	9,354.0	7,893.8	1,460.2	2,135.1	1,481.6	653.5	1,683.4	41.8	1,641.5	779.7
IV p	18,867.1	11,608.9	9,453.1	7,980.6	1,472.4	2,155.9	1,496.4	659.5	1,687.6	38.6	1,649.0	788.3

See next page for continuation of table.

[Billions of dollars; quarterly data at seasonally adjusted annual rates]

Year or quarter	Personal income receipts on assets			Personal current transfer receipts								Less: Contributions for government social insurance, domestic
					Government social benefits to persons						Other current transfer receipts, from business (net)	
	Total	Personal interest income	Personal dividend income	Total	Total[1]	Social security[2]	Medicare[3]	Medicaid	Unemployment insurance	Other		
1969	100.3	76.1	24.2	62.3	59.0	26.4	6.7	4.6	2.3	12.4	3.3	44.1
1970	114.9	90.6	24.3	74.7	71.7	31.4	7.3	5.5	4.2	16.0	2.9	46.4
1971	125.1	100.1	25.0	88.1	85.4	36.6	8.0	6.7	6.2	19.4	2.7	51.2
1972	136.6	109.8	26.8	97.9	94.8	40.9	8.8	8.2	6.0	21.4	3.1	59.2
1973	155.4	125.5	29.9	112.6	108.6	50.7	10.2	9.6	4.6	23.3	3.9	75.5
1974	180.6	147.4	33.2	133.3	128.6	57.6	12.7	11.2	7.0	28.4	4.7	85.2
1975	201.0	168.0	32.9	170.0	163.1	65.9	15.6	13.9	18.1	35.7	6.8	89.3
1976	220.0	181.0	39.0	184.3	177.6	74.5	18.8	15.5	16.4	38.7	6.7	101.3
1977	251.6	206.9	44.7	194.6	189.5	83.2	22.1	16.7	13.1	40.9	5.1	113.1
1978	285.8	235.1	50.7	209.9	203.4	91.4	25.5	18.6	9.4	44.9	6.5	131.3
1979	327.1	269.7	57.4	235.6	227.3	102.6	29.9	21.1	9.7	49.9	8.2	152.7
1980	396.9	332.9	64.0	280.1	271.5	118.6	36.2	23.9	16.1	62.1	8.6	166.2
1981	485.8	412.2	73.6	319.0	307.8	138.6	43.5	27.7	15.9	66.3	11.2	195.7
1982	557.0	479.5	77.6	355.5	343.1	153.7	50.9	30.2	25.2	66.8	12.4	208.9
1983	599.5	516.3	83.3	384.3	370.5	164.4	57.8	33.9	26.4	71.5	13.8	226.0
1984	680.8	590.1	90.6	400.6	380.9	173.0	64.7	36.6	16.0	74.3	19.7	257.5
1985	726.3	628.9	97.4	425.4	403.1	183.3	69.7	39.7	15.9	78.0	22.3	281.4
1986	768.2	662.1	106.0	451.6	428.6	193.6	75.3	43.6	16.5	83.0	22.9	303.4
1987	791.1	679.0	112.2	468.1	447.9	201.0	81.6	47.8	14.6	86.4	20.2	323.1
1988	851.4	721.7	129.7	497.5	476.9	213.9	86.3	53.0	13.3	93.6	20.6	361.5
1989	964.3	806.5	157.8	544.2	521.1	227.4	98.2	60.8	14.4	103.1	23.2	385.2
1990	1,005.3	836.5	168.8	596.9	574.7	244.1	107.6	73.1	18.2	113.9	22.2	410.1
1991	1,003.7	823.5	180.2	668.1	650.5	264.2	117.5	96.9	26.8	127.0	17.6	430.2
1992	998.8	809.8	189.1	748.0	731.8	281.8	132.6	116.2	39.6	142.9	16.3	455.0
1993	1,007.0	802.3	204.7	793.0	778.9	297.9	146.8	130.1	34.8	150.0	14.1	477.4
1994	1,049.8	814.6	235.2	829.0	815.7	312.2	164.4	139.4	23.9	156.1	13.3	508.2
1995	1,136.6	878.6	258.0	883.5	864.7	327.7	181.2	149.6	21.7	164.0	18.7	532.8
1996	1,201.2	899.0	302.2	929.2	906.3	342.0	194.9	158.2	22.3	167.6	22.9	555.1
1997	1,285.0	947.1	337.9	954.9	935.4	356.6	206.9	163.1	20.1	166.4	19.4	587.2
1998	1,370.9	1,015.5	355.4	983.9	957.9	369.2	205.6	170.2	19.7	170.0	26.0	624.7
1999	1,359.3	1,012.7	346.6	1,026.2	992.2	379.9	208.7	184.6	20.5	174.4	34.0	661.3
2000	1,485.7	1,102.2	383.5	1,087.3	1,044.9	401.4	219.1	199.5	20.7	179.1	42.4	705.8
2001	1,473.7	1,104.3	369.3	1,192.6	1,145.8	425.1	242.6	227.3	31.9	192.4	46.8	733.2
2002	1,408.9	1,010.1	398.8	1,285.2	1,251.0	446.9	259.7	250.0	53.5	211.3	34.2	751.5
2003	1,437.2	1,005.0	432.1	1,347.3	1,321.0	463.5	276.7	264.5	53.2	231.2	26.3	779.3
2004	1,512.1	950.4	561.7	1,421.2	1,404.5	485.5	304.4	289.8	36.4	254.3	16.8	829.2
2005	1,678.2	1,100.4	577.8	1,516.7	1,490.9	512.7	332.1	304.4	31.8	273.5	25.8	873.3
2006	1,958.6	1,235.8	722.8	1,613.8	1,593.0	544.1	399.1	299.1	30.4	281.5	20.8	922.5
2007	2,183.8	1,368.6	815.3	1,728.1	1,697.3	575.7	428.2	324.2	32.7	294.9	30.8	961.4
2008	2,200.9	1,396.3	804.6	1,955.1	1,919.3	605.5	461.6	338.3	51.1	417.7	35.8	988.4
2009	1,852.2	1,299.3	553.0	2,146.7	2,107.7	664.5	493.0	369.6	131.2	398.0	39.0	964.3
2010	1,782.3	1,238.5	543.9	2,325.2	2,281.4	690.2	513.4	396.9	138.9	484.2	43.7	983.7
2011	1,950.9	1,269.4	681.5	2,358.7	2,310.1	713.3	535.6	406.0	107.2	484.8	48.5	916.7
2012	2,165.6	1,330.5	835.1	2,363.0	2,322.6	762.1	554.7	417.5	83.6	434.4	40.4	950.5
2013	2,066.3	1,273.0	793.3	2,424.3	2,385.9	799.0	572.8	440.0	62.5	432.5	38.4	1,104.3
2014	2,302.2	1,349.0	953.2	2,541.5	2,498.6	834.6	600.0	490.9	35.5	453.5	42.9	1,153.6
2015	2,470.8	1,437.9	1,032.9	2,683.3	2,633.0	871.8	633.5	535.9	32.1	467.1	50.3	1,204.7
2016	2,521.4	1,457.4	1,064.0	2,774.2	2,714.6	896.5	660.2	562.7	31.7	467.6	59.7	1,239.9
2017	2,681.6	1,551.6	1,130.0	2,848.1	2,800.1	926.1	689.3	577.4	29.8	473.5	48.1	1,299.6
2018	2,930.1	1,702.7	1,227.5	2,971.5	2,918.3	972.4	730.9	597.7	27.1	480.3	53.2	1,356.5
2019 *p*	2,992.7	1,720.5	1,272.2	3,172.2	3,117.6	1,034.7	800.5	632.1	26.1	504.8	54.6	1,422.8
2016: I	2,490.6	1,447.1	1,043.5	2,743.7	2,684.2	885.8	650.5	550.2	32.3	471.3	59.5	1,225.3
II	2,505.3	1,449.1	1,056.2	2,765.5	2,704.2	892.9	656.7	558.6	31.9	469.3	61.3	1,232.4
III	2,529.4	1,457.9	1,071.5	2,783.7	2,723.2	899.1	663.3	566.5	31.6	466.4	60.6	1,244.0
IV	2,560.2	1,475.6	1,084.7	2,803.8	2,746.6	908.2	670.3	575.6	30.8	463.4	57.2	1,258.0
2017: I	2,630.7	1,545.4	1,085.3	2,823.6	2,772.4	916.2	677.6	573.2	30.7	474.1	51.2	1,280.0
II	2,657.1	1,523.5	1,133.5	2,828.2	2,780.6	921.7	685.2	569.0	29.6	471.6	47.6	1,292.0
III	2,671.3	1,528.9	1,142.4	2,861.9	2,815.7	928.7	693.1	583.7	29.6	475.1	46.2	1,304.6
IV	2,767.4	1,608.6	1,158.8	2,878.8	2,831.5	937.7	701.3	584.0	29.2	473.1	47.3	1,321.8
2018: I	2,851.6	1,669.6	1,182.0	2,935.4	2,884.8	960.5	710.2	589.8	28.8	486.7	50.6	1,344.0
II	2,909.3	1,694.6	1,214.7	2,963.1	2,910.1	968.0	721.9	600.4	27.2	483.5	53.0	1,350.9
III	2,957.7	1,719.3	1,238.4	2,983.8	2,929.4	976.0	736.7	602.9	26.6	477.4	54.4	1,362.4
IV	3,002.0	1,727.2	1,274.8	3,003.7	2,949.0	985.1	754.6	597.6	26.0	473.8	54.7	1,368.7
2019: I	2,955.1	1,699.3	1,255.8	3,113.1	3,058.7	1,022.9	774.9	610.3	26.9	507.3	54.4	1,407.6
II	3,016.5	1,750.5	1,266.0	3,158.6	3,104.2	1,030.5	793.6	631.4	25.9	504.4	54.4	1,416.3
III	2,997.7	1,716.8	1,280.9	3,195.8	3,141.2	1,037.7	809.9	644.2	25.8	503.5	54.6	1,427.1
IV *p*	3,001.4	1,715.3	1,286.1	3,221.2	3,166.2	1,047.6	823.8	642.5	26.0	504.0	54.9	1,440.3

[1] Includes Veterans' benefits, not shown seperately.
[2] Includes old-age, survivors, and disability insurance benefits that are distributed from the federal old-age and survivors insurance trust fund and the disability insurance trust fund.
[3] Includes hospital and supplementary medical insurance benefits that are distributed from the federal hospital insurance trust fund and the supplementary medical insurance trust fund.

Source: Department of Commerce (Bureau of Economic Analysis).

[Billions of dollars, except as noted; quarterly data at seasonally adjusted annual rates]

Year or quarter	Personal income	Less: Personal current taxes	Equals: Disposable personal income	Less: Personal outlays				Equals: Personal saving	Percent of disposable personal income [2]		
				Total	Personal consumption expenditures	Personal interest payments [1]	Personal current transfer payments		Personal outlays		Personal saving
									Total	Personal consumption expenditures	
1969	800.3	104.5	695.8	619.8	603.6	13.9	2.2	76.1	89.1	86.7	10.9
1970	865.0	103.1	762.0	664.4	646.7	15.1	2.6	97.6	87.2	84.9	12.8
1971	932.8	101.7	831.1	719.2	699.9	16.4	2.8	111.9	86.5	84.2	13.5
1972	1,024.5	123.6	900.8	789.3	768.2	18.0	3.2	111.5	87.6	85.3	12.4
1973	1,140.8	132.4	1,008.4	872.6	849.6	19.6	3.4	135.8	86.5	84.3	13.5
1974	1,251.8	151.0	1,100.8	954.5	930.2	20.9	3.4	146.3	86.7	84.5	13.3
1975	1,369.4	147.6	1,221.8	1,057.8	1,030.5	23.4	3.8	164.0	86.6	84.3	13.4
1976	1,502.6	172.7	1,330.0	1,175.6	1,147.7	23.5	4.4	154.4	88.4	86.3	11.6
1977	1,659.2	197.9	1,461.4	1,305.4	1,274.0	26.6	4.8	155.9	89.3	87.2	10.7
1978	1,863.7	229.6	1,634.1	1,459.0	1,422.3	31.3	5.4	175.1	89.3	87.0	10.7
1979	2,082.7	268.9	1,813.8	1,627.0	1,585.4	35.5	6.0	186.8	89.7	87.4	10.3
1980	2,323.6	299.5	2,024.1	1,800.1	1,750.7	42.5	6.9	224.1	88.9	86.5	11.1
1981	2,605.1	345.8	2,259.3	1,993.9	1,934.0	48.4	11.5	265.5	88.3	85.6	11.8
1982	2,791.6	354.7	2,436.9	2,143.5	2,071.3	58.5	13.8	293.3	88.0	85.0	12.0
1983	2,981.1	352.9	2,628.2	2,364.2	2,281.6	67.4	15.1	264.0	90.0	86.8	10.0
1984	3,292.7	377.9	2,914.8	2,584.5	2,492.3	75.0	17.1	330.3	88.7	85.5	11.3
1985	3,524.9	417.8	3,107.1	2,822.1	2,712.8	90.6	18.8	284.9	90.8	87.3	9.2
1986	3,733.1	437.8	3,295.3	3,004.7	2,886.3	97.3	21.1	290.6	91.2	87.6	8.8
1987	3,961.6	489.6	3,472.0	3,196.6	3,076.3	97.1	23.2	275.4	92.1	88.6	7.9
1988	4,283.4	505.9	3,777.5	3,457.0	3,330.0	101.3	25.6	320.5	91.5	88.2	8.5
1989	4,625.6	567.7	4,057.8	3,717.9	3,576.8	113.1	28.0	340.0	91.6	88.1	8.4
1990	4,913.8	594.7	4,319.1	3,958.0	3,809.0	118.4	30.6	361.1	91.6	88.2	8.4
1991	5,084.9	588.9	4,496.0	4,100.0	3,943.4	119.9	36.7	396.0	91.2	87.7	8.8
1992	5,420.9	612.8	4,808.1	4,354.2	4,197.6	116.1	40.5	453.9	90.6	87.3	9.4
1993	5,657.9	648.8	5,009.2	4,611.5	4,452.0	113.9	45.6	397.7	92.1	88.9	7.9
1994	5,947.1	693.1	5,254.0	4,890.6	4,721.0	119.9	49.8	363.4	93.1	89.9	6.9
1995	6,291.4	748.4	5,543.0	5,155.9	4,962.6	140.4	52.9	387.1	93.0	89.5	7.0
1996	6,678.5	837.1	5,841.4	5,459.2	5,244.6	157.0	57.6	382.3	93.5	89.8	6.5
1997	7,092.5	931.8	6,160.7	5,770.4	5,536.8	169.7	63.9	390.3	93.7	89.9	6.3
1998	7,606.7	1,032.4	6,574.2	6,127.7	5,877.2	180.9	69.5	446.5	93.2	89.4	6.8
1999	8,001.9	1,111.9	6,890.0	6,540.6	6,279.1	187.5	74.1	349.4	94.9	91.1	5.1
2000	8,652.6	1,236.3	7,416.3	7,058.0	6,762.1	214.8	81.0	358.3	95.2	91.2	4.8
2001	9,005.6	1,239.0	7,766.6	7,374.9	7,065.6	220.0	89.3	391.6	95.0	91.0	5.0
2002	9,159.0	1,052.2	8,106.8	7,633.1	7,342.7	195.7	94.7	473.7	94.2	90.6	5.8
2003	9,487.5	1,003.5	8,484.0	8,012.5	7,723.1	190.9	98.5	471.5	94.4	91.0	5.6
2004	10,035.1	1,048.7	8,986.4	8,522.6	8,212.7	202.2	107.7	463.8	94.8	91.4	5.2
2005	10,598.2	1,212.4	9,385.8	9,089.1	8,747.1	230.5	111.5	296.7	96.8	93.2	3.2
2006	11,381.7	1,356.8	10,024.9	9,639.3	9,260.3	258.4	120.5	385.6	96.2	92.4	3.8
2007	12,007.8	1,492.2	10,515.6	10,123.9	9,706.4	284.6	132.9	391.6	96.3	92.3	3.7
2008	12,442.2	1,507.2	10,935.0	10,390.1	9,976.3	268.8	144.9	544.9	95.0	91.2	5.0
2009	12,059.1	1,152.0	10,907.1	10,240.6	9,842.2	254.0	144.3	666.5	93.9	90.2	6.1
2010	12,551.6	1,237.3	11,314.3	10,573.5	10,185.8	242.8	144.8	740.9	93.5	90.0	6.5
2011	13,326.8	1,453.2	11,873.6	11,023.7	10,641.1	232.1	150.6	849.8	92.8	89.6	7.2
2012	14,010.1	1,508.9	12,501.2	11,393.6	11,006.8	232.4	154.4	1,107.6	91.1	88.0	8.9
2013	14,181.1	1,675.8	12,505.3	11,703.9	11,317.2	229.5	157.2	801.4	93.6	90.5	6.4
2014	14,991.7	1,784.0	13,207.7	12,237.0	11,822.8	243.8	170.4	970.8	92.7	89.5	7.3
2015	15,717.8	1,937.8	13,780.0	12,731.2	12,284.3	264.1	182.8	1,048.8	92.4	89.1	7.6
2016	16,121.2	1,956.1	14,165.1	13,206.3	12,748.5	273.7	184.1	958.8	93.2	90.0	6.8
2017	16,878.8	2,045.8	14,833.0	13,802.1	13,312.1	299.3	190.7	1,030.9	93.0	89.7	7.0
2018	17,819.2	2,077.6	15,741.5	14,531.1	13,998.7	336.7	195.8	1,210.4	92.3	88.9	7.7
2019 ᵖ	18,624.2	2,186.2	16,438.1	15,126.6	14,563.9	361.7	201.0	1,311.5	92.0	88.6	8.0
2016: I	15,937.6	1,922.0	14,015.6	12,977.5	12,523.5	267.4	186.6	1,038.1	92.6	89.4	7.4
II	16,029.0	1,945.3	14,083.7	13,138.6	12,688.3	271.1	179.3	945.1	93.3	90.1	6.7
III	16,175.5	1,969.6	14,205.9	13,280.4	12,822.4	275.5	182.5	925.5	93.5	90.3	6.5
IV	16,342.6	1,987.4	14,355.2	13,428.6	12,959.8	281.0	187.9	926.5	93.5	90.3	6.5
2017: I	16,604.1	2,001.5	14,602.6	13,576.8	13,104.4	286.5	185.9	1,025.8	93.0	89.7	7.0
II	16,749.6	2,016.0	14,733.5	13,699.7	13,212.5	294.8	192.4	1,033.9	93.0	89.7	7.0
III	16,930.4	2,049.8	14,880.6	13,841.8	13,345.1	305.8	191.0	1,038.8	93.0	89.7	7.0
IV	17,231.2	2,115.8	15,115.4	14,090.2	13,586.3	310.3	193.7	1,025.2	93.2	89.9	6.8
2018: I	17,540.3	2,074.9	15,465.4	14,245.2	13,728.4	322.3	194.5	1,220.2	92.1	88.8	7.9
II	17,725.0	2,071.7	15,653.3	14,465.9	13,939.8	329.6	196.4	1,187.4	92.4	89.1	7.6
III	17,928.5	2,086.5	15,842.0	14,655.6	14,114.6	341.5	199.6	1,186.4	92.5	89.1	7.5
IV	18,082.8	2,077.4	16,005.4	14,757.8	14,211.9	353.4	192.5	1,247.6	92.2	88.8	7.8
2019: I	18,355.4	2,156.9	16,198.5	14,823.0	14,266.3	359.1	197.7	1,375.5	91.5	88.1	8.5
II	18,555.9	2,200.1	16,355.7	15,073.1	14,511.2	363.0	198.9	1,282.6	92.2	88.7	7.8
III	18,718.4	2,183.2	16,535.3	15,237.2	14,678.2	359.1	200.0	1,298.0	92.1	88.8	7.8
IV ᵖ	18,867.1	2,204.4	16,662.7	15,372.9	14,799.8	365.8	207.3	1,289.8	92.3	88.8	7.7

[1] Consists of nonmortgage interest paid by households.
[2] Percents based on data in millions of dollars.

Source: Department of Commerce (Bureau of Economic Analysis).

Table B-18. Total and per capita disposable personal income and personal consumption expenditures, and per capita gross domestic product, in current and real dollars, 1969–2019

[Quarterly data at seasonally adjusted annual rates, except as noted]

| Year or quarter | Disposable personal income | | | | Personal consumption expenditures | | | | Gross domestic product per capita (dollars) | | Population (thousands)[1] |
| | Total (billions of dollars) | | Per capita (dollars) | | Total (billions of dollars) | | Per capita (dollars) | | | | |
	Current dollars	Chained (2012) dollars	Current dollars	Chained (2012) dollars	Current dollars	Chained (2012) dollars	Current dollars	Chained (2012) dollars	Current dollars	Chained (2012) dollars	
1969	695.8	3,476.5	3,432	17,148	603.6	3,015.9	2,977	14,876	5,019	24,377	202,736
1970	762.0	3,637.0	3,715	17,734	646.7	3,086.9	3,153	15,051	5,233	24,142	205,089
1971	831.1	3,805.2	4,002	18,321	699.9	3,204.8	3,370	15,430	5,609	24,625	207,692
1972	900.8	3,988.4	4,291	18,999	768.2	3,401.0	3,659	16,201	6,093	25,644	209,924
1973	1,008.4	4,236.5	4,758	19,989	849.6	3,569.4	4,009	16,841	6,725	26,834	211,939
1974	1,100.8	4,188.7	5,146	19,583	930.2	3,539.5	4,349	16,547	7,224	26,445	213,898
1975	1,221.8	4,291.4	5,657	19,869	1,030.5	3,619.7	4,771	16,759	7,801	26,136	215,981
1976	1,330.0	4,428.5	6,098	20,306	1,147.7	3,821.5	5,262	17,523	8,590	27,278	218,086
1977	1,461.4	4,568.8	6,634	20,740	1,274.0	3,983.0	5,783	18,081	9,450	28,254	220,289
1978	1,634.1	4,776.4	7,340	21,455	1,422.3	4,157.3	6,388	18,674	10,563	29,505	222,629
1979	1,813.8	4,869.1	8,057	21,630	1,585.4	4,256.1	7,043	18,907	11,672	30,104	225,106
1980	2,024.1	4,905.6	8,888	21,542	1,750.7	4,242.8	7,688	18,631	12,547	29,681	227,726
1981	2,259.3	5,025.4	9,823	21,849	1,934.0	4,301.6	8,408	18,702	13,943	30,132	230,008
1982	2,436.9	5,135.0	10,494	22,113	2,071.3	4,364.6	8,919	18,795	14,399	29,308	232,218
1983	2,628.2	5,312.2	11,216	22,669	2,281.6	4,611.7	9,737	19,680	15,508	30,374	234,333
1984	2,914.8	5,677.1	12,330	24,016	2,492.3	4,854.3	10,543	20,535	17,080	32,289	236,394
1985	3,107.1	5,847.6	13,027	24,518	2,712.8	5,105.6	11,374	21,407	18,192	33,337	238,506
1986	3,295.3	6,069.8	13,691	25,219	2,886.3	5,316.4	11,992	22,089	19,028	34,179	240,683
1987	3,472.0	6,204.1	14,297	25,548	3,076.3	5,496.9	12,668	22,636	19,993	35,047	242,843
1988	3,777.5	6,496.0	15,414	26,508	3,330.0	5,726.5	13,589	23,368	21,368	36,181	245,061
1989	4,057.8	6,686.2	16,403	27,027	3,576.8	5,893.5	14,458	23,823	22,805	37,157	247,387
1990	4,319.1	6,817.4	17,264	27,250	3,809.0	6,012.2	15,225	24,031	23,835	37,435	250,181
1991	4,496.0	6,867.0	17,734	27,086	3,943.4	6,023.0	15,554	23,757	24,290	36,900	253,530
1992	4,808.1	7,152.9	18,714	27,841	4,197.6	6,244.7	16,338	24,306	25,379	37,696	256,922
1993	5,009.2	7,271.1	19,245	27,935	4,452.0	6,462.2	17,104	24,828	26,350	38,234	260,282
1994	5,254.0	7,470.6	19,943	28,356	4,721.0	6,712.6	17,919	25,479	27,660	39,295	263,455
1995	5,543.0	7,718.9	20,792	28,954	4,962.6	6,910.7	18,615	25,923	28,658	39,875	266,588
1996	5,841.4	7,964.2	21,658	29,528	5,244.6	7,150.5	19,445	26,511	29,932	40,900	269,714
1997	6,160.7	8,255.8	22,570	30,246	5,536.8	7,419.7	20,284	27,183	31,424	42,211	272,958
1998	6,574.2	8,740.4	23,806	31,651	5,877.2	7,813.8	21,283	28,295	32,818	43,593	276,154
1999	6,890.0	9,025.6	24,666	32,312	6,279.1	8,225.4	22,479	29,447	34,478	45,146	279,328
2000	7,416.3	9,479.5	26,262	33,568	6,762.1	8,643.4	23,945	30,607	36,305	46,498	282,398
2001	7,766.6	9,740.1	27,230	34,149	7,065.6	8,861.1	24,772	31,067	37,100	46,497	285,225
2002	8,106.8	10,034.5	28,153	34,848	7,342.7	9,088.7	25,499	31,563	37,980	46,858	287,955
2003	8,484.0	10,301.4	29,192	35,446	7,723.1	9,377.5	26,574	32,267	39,426	47,756	290,626
2004	8,986.4	10,645.9	30,643	36,302	8,212.7	9,729.3	28,004	33,176	41,648	49,125	293,262
2005	9,385.8	10,811.6	31,710	36,527	8,747.1	10,075.9	29,552	34,041	44,044	50,381	295,993
2006	10,024.9	11,241.9	33,549	37,621	9,260.3	10,384.5	30,990	34,752	46,231	51,330	298,818
2007	10,515.6	11,500.3	34,855	38,119	9,706.4	10,615.3	32,173	35,186	47,902	51,794	301,696
2008	10,935.0	11,610.8	35,906	38,125	9,976.3	10,592.8	32,758	34,783	48,311	51,240	304,543
2009	10,907.1	11,591.7	35,500	37,728	9,842.2	10,460.0	32,034	34,045	47,028	49,501	307,240
2010	11,314.3	11,822.1	36,524	38,164	10,185.6	10,643.0	32,881	34,357	48,397	50,355	309,774
2011	11,873.6	12,099.8	38,055	38,780	10,641.1	10,843.8	34,105	34,755	49,814	50,770	312,010
2012	12,501.2	12,501.2	39,786	39,786	11,006.8	11,006.8	35,030	35,030	51,548	51,548	314,212
2013	12,505.3	12,339.1	39,529	39,004	11,317.2	11,166.9	35,774	35,298	53,057	52,142	316,357
2014	13,207.7	12,844.3	41,451	40,311	11,822.8	11,497.4	37,105	36,084	55,008	53,077	318,631
2015	13,780.0	13,372.7	42,939	41,670	12,284.3	11,921.2	38,279	37,147	56,790	54,231	320,918
2016	14,165.1	13,608.4	43,829	42,107	12,748.5	12,247.5	39,446	37,896	57,908	54,733	323,186
2017	14,833.0	14,002.8	45,609	43,056	13,312.1	12,566.9	40,932	38,641	60,019	55,679	325,220
2018	15,741.5	14,556.2	48,147	44,521	13,998.7	12,944.6	42,816	39,592	62,946	57,006	326,949
2019 p	16,438.1	14,988.5	50,036	45,623	14,563.9	13,279.6	44,331	40,422	65,227	58,055	328,527
2016: I	14,015.6	13,568.7	43,479	42,093	12,523.5	12,124.2	38,850	37,611	57,155	54,464	322,354
II	14,083.7	13,554.3	43,620	41,980	12,688.3	12,211.3	39,298	37,821	57,724	54,633	322,871
III	14,205.9	13,615.0	43,917	42,090	12,822.4	12,289.1	39,640	37,991	58,140	54,827	323,473
IV	14,355.2	13,696.7	44,299	42,267	12,959.8	12,365.3	39,993	38,159	58,608	55,005	324,048
2017: I	14,602.6	13,860.9	45,001	42,715	13,104.4	12,438.9	40,384	38,333	59,139	55,240	324,496
II	14,733.5	13,953.4	45,341	42,940	13,212.5	12,512.9	40,660	38,507	59,568	55,458	324,948
III	14,880.6	14,034.5	45,720	43,120	13,345.1	12,586.3	41,002	38,670	60,256	55,806	325,475
IV	15,115.4	14,162.4	46,372	43,448	13,586.3	12,729.7	41,680	39,053	61,108	56,210	325,963
2018: I	15,465.4	14,400.3	47,393	44,129	13,728.4	12,782.9	42,070	39,172	61,789	56,503	326,325
II	15,653.3	14,495.9	47,913	44,370	13,939.8	12,909.2	42,668	39,514	62,779	56,927	326,703
III	15,842.0	14,613.3	48,422	44,666	14,114.6	13,019.8	43,142	39,796	63,423	57,257	327,167
IV	16,005.4	14,715.2	48,856	44,918	14,211.9	13,066.3	43,382	39,885	63,790	57,336	327,602
2019: I	16,198.5	14,878.1	49,397	45,371	14,266.3	13,103.3	43,505	39,958	64,341	57,719	327,923
II	16,355.7	14,934.3	49,824	45,494	14,511.2	13,250.0	44,205	40,363	65,008	57,946	328,270
III	16,535.3	15,042.5	50,300	45,760	14,678.2	13,353.1	44,651	40,620	65,533	58,167	328,730
IV p	16,662.7	15,100.1	50,618	45,871	14,799.8	13,411.9	44,959	40,743	66,024	58,386	329,186

[1] Population of the United States including Armed Forces overseas. Annual data are averages of quarterly data. Quarterly data are averages for the period.

Source: Department of Commerce (Bureau of Economic Analysis and Bureau of the Census).

TABLE B–19. Gross saving and investment, 1969–2019

[Billions of dollars, except as noted; quarterly data at seasonally adjusted annual rates]

Year or quarter	Total gross saving	Gross saving									
		Net saving							Consumption of fixed capital		
		Total net saving	Net private saving			Net government saving			Total	Private	Government
			Total	Personal saving	Undistributed corporate profits [1]	Total	Federal	State and local			
1969	233.1	108.2	110.3	76.1	34.2	−2.0	−5.1	3.1	124.9	89.4	35.5
1970	228.2	91.4	124.8	97.6	27.2	−33.4	−34.8	1.4	136.8	98.3	38.6
1971	246.1	97.2	149.4	111.9	37.5	−52.2	−50.9	−1.3	148.9	107.6	41.3
1972	277.6	116.6	159.6	111.5	48.0	−42.9	−49.0	6.1	161.0	117.5	43.5
1973	335.3	156.6	189.3	135.8	53.5	−32.7	−38.3	5.6	178.7	131.5	47.2
1974	349.2	142.3	186.0	146.3	39.7	−43.7	−41.3	−2.3	206.9	153.2	53.7
1975	348.1	109.6	218.3	164.0	54.3	−108.7	−97.9	−10.7	238.5	178.8	59.7
1976	399.3	139.1	224.4	154.4	70.0	−85.3	−80.9	−4.4	260.2	196.5	63.7
1977	459.4	169.6	242.5	155.9	86.6	−72.9	−73.4	.5	289.8	221.1	68.7
1978	548.0	220.8	278.0	175.1	102.9	−57.2	−62.0	4.9	327.2	252.1	75.1
1979	613.5	239.6	288.2	186.8	101.4	−48.6	−47.4	−1.2	373.9	290.7	83.1
1980	630.1	201.7	296.4	224.1	72.3	−94.7	−88.8	−5.9	428.4	335.0	93.5
1981	743.9	256.6	354.9	265.5	89.4	−98.2	−88.1	−10.2	487.2	381.9	105.3
1982	725.8	188.9	379.0	293.3	85.6	−190.1	−167.4	−22.8	537.0	420.4	116.6
1983	716.7	154.1	379.7	264.0	115.7	−225.6	−207.2	−18.4	562.6	438.8	123.8
1984	881.6	283.2	479.9	330.3	149.5	−196.7	−196.5	−.2	598.4	463.5	134.9
1985	881.0	240.8	442.5	284.9	157.5	−201.7	−199.2	−2.4	640.1	496.4	143.7
1986	864.5	179.2	399.1	290.6	108.5	−219.9	−215.9	−4.0	685.3	531.6	153.7
1987	948.9	218.5	398.6	275.4	123.2	−180.1	−165.7	−14.4	730.4	566.3	164.1
1988	1,076.6	292.1	463.4	320.5	142.9	−171.3	−160.0	−11.3	784.5	607.9	176.6
1989	1,109.8	271.5	450.2	340.0	110.3	−178.7	−159.4	−19.3	838.3	649.6	188.6
1990	1,113.4	224.8	464.4	361.1	103.2	−239.5	−203.3	−36.2	888.5	688.4	200.1
1991	1,153.4	221.0	529.5	396.0	133.5	−308.5	−248.4	−60.1	932.4	721.5	210.9
1992	1,147.6	187.4	592.8	453.9	139.0	−405.5	−334.5	−71.0	960.2	742.9	217.4
1993	1,163.4	159.9	545.9	397.7	148.2	−386.0	−313.5	−72.5	1,003.5	778.2	225.3
1994	1,295.1	239.5	559.0	363.4	195.7	−319.6	−255.6	−63.9	1,055.6	822.5	233.1
1995	1,426.3	303.9	616.5	387.1	229.4	−312.5	−242.1	−70.4	1,122.4	880.7	241.7
1996	1,578.9	403.6	636.8	382.3	254.5	−233.2	−179.4	−53.8	1,175.3	929.1	246.2
1997	1,780.5	541.2	675.1	390.3	284.9	−133.9	−92.0	−42.0	1,239.3	987.8	251.6
1998	1,930.6	620.8	649.5	446.5	203.0	−28.7	1.4	−30.1	1,309.7	1,052.2	257.6
1999	2,010.3	611.4	583.4	349.4	234.1	28.0	66.9	−38.9	1,398.9	1,132.2	266.7
2000	2,127.3	616.1	501.2	358.3	142.9	114.8	155.5	−40.6	1,511.2	1,231.5	279.7
2001	2,076.9	477.4	582.4	391.6	190.8	−105.0	14.0	−119.0	1,599.5	1,311.7	287.8
2002	2,003.6	345.6	799.9	473.7	326.2	−454.4	−271.5	−182.9	1,658.0	1,361.8	296.2
2003	1,991.7	272.6	858.0	471.5	386.5	−585.4	−404.1	−181.3	1,719.1	1,411.9	307.1
2004	2,164.3	342.5	892.4	463.8	428.6	−549.9	−400.9	−149.0	1,821.8	1,497.1	324.7
2005	2,365.8	394.8	803.5	296.7	506.8	−408.7	−305.9	−102.8	1,971.0	1,622.6	348.4
2006	2,657.9	533.8	846.4	385.6	460.8	−312.6	−227.6	−85.0	2,124.1	1,751.8	372.3
2007	2,536.6	283.8	679.2	391.6	287.6	−395.4	−266.1	−129.3	2,252.8	1,852.5	400.3
2008	2,241.2	−117.7	734.3	544.9	189.4	−852.0	−631.1	−220.9	2,358.8	1,931.8	427.0
2009	2,008.3	−363.2	1,227.1	666.5	560.6	−1,590.3	−1,248.9	−341.3	2,371.5	1,928.7	442.8
2010	2,312.2	−78.7	1,553.9	740.9	813.0	−1,632.6	−1,325.1	−307.5	2,390.9	1,933.8	457.2
2011	2,556.9	82.4	1,599.4	849.8	749.6	−1,517.1	−1,242.0	−275.1	2,474.5	1,997.3	477.2
2012	3,036.0	460.0	1,821.5	1,107.6	713.9	−1,361.4	−1,078.6	−282.8	2,576.0	2,082.4	493.6
2013	3,218.2	537.0	1,440.3	801.4	638.9	−903.3	−637.9	−265.4	2,681.2	2,176.6	504.6
2014	3,560.3	745.3	1,587.6	970.8	616.8	−842.3	−604.3	−238.0	2,815.0	2,298.5	516.6
2015	3,674.9	758.4	1,548.8	1,048.8	500.0	−790.4	−570.1	−220.3	2,916.5	2,393.7	522.8
2016	3,484.5	493.0	1,416.8	958.8	458.0	−923.8	−677.0	−246.8	2,991.6	2,463.2	528.4
2017	3,626.5	505.0	1,477.8	1,030.9	446.9	−972.8	−724.7	−248.1	3,121.4	2,578.2	543.2
2018	3,795.2	503.8	1,752.7	1,210.4	542.3	−1,248.9	−1,009.8	−239.2	3,291.4	2,725.8	565.7
2019 p					1,311.5				3,462.6	2,875.8	586.9
2016: I	3,570.1	620.3	1,518.2	1,038.1	480.1	−897.9	−644.5	−253.4	2,949.8	2,426.6	523.2
II	3,454.7	474.9	1,402.7	945.1	457.6	−927.8	−674.8	−253.0	2,979.8	2,452.4	527.4
III	3,435.5	433.2	1,363.5	925.5	438.0	−930.3	−687.2	−243.0	3,002.3	2,472.7	529.5
IV	3,477.9	443.5	1,382.7	926.5	456.2	−939.3	−701.6	−237.6	3,034.4	2,501.1	533.3
2017: I	3,600.7	535.8	1,478.9	1,025.8	453.1	−943.1	−685.0	−258.1	3,064.9	2,527.9	537.0
II	3,613.8	512.1	1,481.0	1,033.9	447.1	−968.9	−699.2	−269.7	3,101.7	2,561.0	540.7
III	3,658.6	517.1	1,479.8	1,038.8	441.0	−962.7	−707.1	−255.6	3,141.4	2,596.1	545.4
IV	3,632.8	455.1	1,471.6	1,025.2	446.5	−1,016.6	−807.6	−208.9	3,177.7	2,628.0	549.8
2018: I	3,826.2	605.9	1,798.6	1,220.2	578.4	−1,192.6	−976.3	−216.3	3,220.2	2,664.1	556.1
II	3,753.8	482.2	1,729.3	1,187.4	541.9	−1,247.1	−1,013.8	−233.3	3,271.6	2,708.0	563.7
III	3,814.9	499.1	1,730.6	1,186.4	544.2	−1,231.5	−981.3	−250.1	3,315.8	2,746.8	569.1
IV	3,785.9	427.8	1,752.2	1,247.6	504.6	−1,324.5	−1,067.6	−256.8	3,358.1	2,784.2	573.9
2019: I	3,909.8	507.6	1,842.3	1,375.5	466.8	−1,334.7	−1,122.9	−211.7	3,402.2	2,822.6	579.5
II	3,866.8	420.3	1,793.3	1,282.6	510.7	−1,373.0	−1,188.0	−185.0	3,446.5	2,861.9	584.6
III	3,874.1	388.2	1,827.1	1,298.0	529.1	−1,438.9	−1,211.5	−227.4	3,485.9	2,896.1	589.8
IV p					1,289.8				3,516.0	2,922.6	593.5

[1] With inventory valuation and capital consumption adjustments.

See next page for continuation of table.

[Billions of dollars, except as noted; quarterly data at seasonally adjusted annual rates]

Year or quarter	Gross domestic investment, capital account transactions, and net lending, NIPA[2]						Statistical discrepancy	Addenda:						
	Gross domestic investment				Capital account transactions (net)[3]	Net lending or net borrowing (−)[1] NIPA[2,4]		Gross private saving	Gross government saving			Net domestic investment	Gross saving as a percent of gross national income	Net saving as a percent of gross national income
	Total	Total	Gross private domestic investment	Gross government investment					Total	Federal	State and local			
1969	234.7	233.1	173.6	59.5	0.0	1.6	1.6	199.7	33.4	20.7	12.8	108.2	22.8	10.6
1970	233.6	229.8	170.0	59.8	.0	3.7	5.3	223.0	5.2	−7.2	12.4	93.0	21.2	8.5
1971	255.6	255.3	196.8	58.5	.0	.3	9.5	257.0	−10.9	−21.8	10.9	106.4	21.2	8.4
1972	284.8	288.8	228.1	60.7	.0	−4.1	7.2	277.1	.6	−18.8	19.4	127.8	21.7	9.1
1973	341.4	332.6	266.9	65.6	.0	8.8	6.1	320.8	14.5	−6.0	20.4	153.9	23.4	10.9
1974	356.6	350.7	274.5	76.2	.0	5.9	7.4	339.1	10.1	−6.0	16.0	143.8	22.5	9.2
1975	361.5	341.7	257.3	84.4	.1	19.8	13.3	397.1	−48.9	−59.2	10.3	103.1	20.7	6.5
1976	420.0	412.9	323.2	89.6	.1	7.0	20.7	420.9	−21.6	−39.2	17.6	152.6	21.4	7.4
1977	478.9	489.8	396.6	93.2	.1	−11.0	19.4	463.6	−4.2	−28.2	24.0	199.9	22.1	8.1
1978	571.3	583.9	478.4	105.6	.1	−12.7	23.3	530.1	17.9	−12.4	30.3	256.7	23.3	9.4
1979	658.6	659.8	539.7	120.1	.1	−1.3	45.1	579.0	34.6	7.2	27.3	285.9	23.5	9.2
1980	674.6	666.0	530.1	135.9	.1	8.4	44.4	631.4	−1.2	−28.4	27.1	237.6	22.1	7.1
1981	781.9	778.6	631.2	147.3	.1	3.3	38.1	736.8	7.1	−20.6	27.6	291.3	23.2	8.0
1982	734.7	738.0	581.0	156.9	.1	−3.4	8.8	799.4	−73.5	−92.0	18.4	201.0	21.5	5.6
1983	773.6	808.7	637.5	171.2	.1	−35.2	57.0	818.5	−101.8	−126.1	24.3	246.1	19.8	4.3
1984	923.2	1,013.3	820.1	193.2	.1	−90.2	41.6	943.4	−61.8	−105.9	44.1	414.9	21.9	7.0
1985	935.2	1,049.5	829.7	219.9	.1	−114.5	54.3	938.9	−57.9	−102.3	44.4	409.4	20.4	5.6
1986	944.6	1,087.2	849.1	238.1	.1	−142.8	80.1	930.7	−66.2	−112.4	46.2	401.9	19.1	4.0
1987	992.7	1,146.8	892.2	254.6	.1	−154.2	43.8	964.9	−16.0	−55.6	39.6	416.4	19.7	4.5
1988	1,079.6	1,195.4	937.0	258.4	.1	−115.9	3.0	1,071.3	5.3	−41.0	46.4	410.9	20.5	5.6
1989	1,177.8	1,270.1	999.7	270.4	.3	−92.7	68.0	1,099.9	9.9	−32.5	42.4	431.9	19.8	4.9
1990	1,208.9	1,283.8	993.4	290.4	7.4	−82.3	95.5	1,152.8	−39.4	−69.8	30.4	395.3	18.9	3.8
1991	1,246.3	1,238.4	944.3	294.1	5.3	2.6	93.0	1,250.9	−97.6	−108.3	10.8	306.0	18.9	3.6
1992	1,263.6	1,309.1	1,013.0	296.1	−1.3	−44.3	115.9	1,335.7	−188.1	−191.2	3.1	348.9	17.8	2.9
1993	1,319.3	1,398.7	1,106.8	291.9	.9	−80.2	156.0	1,324.1	−160.7	−166.5	5.8	395.2	17.3	2.4
1994	1,435.1	1,550.7	1,256.5	294.2	1.3	−116.9	140.0	1,381.6	−86.4	−105.3	18.8	495.0	18.1	3.3
1995	1,519.3	1,625.2	1,317.5	307.7	.4	−106.3	93.0	1,497.2	−70.9	−88.6	17.7	502.8	18.8	4.0
1996	1,637.0	1,752.0	1,432.1	320.0	.2	−115.2	58.1	1,565.9	13.0	−25.7	38.7	576.7	19.6	5.0
1997	1,792.1	1,922.2	1,595.6	326.6	.5	−130.6	11.6	1,662.9	117.6	62.3	55.3	682.9	20.7	6.3
1998	1,875.3	2,080.7	1,736.7	344.0	.2	−205.6	−55.2	1,701.7	228.9	156.8	72.1	770.9	21.1	6.8
1999	1,977.2	2,255.5	1,887.1	368.5	4.5	−282.8	−33.2	1,715.6	294.7	225.0	69.7	856.6	20.7	6.3
2000	2,030.8	2,427.3	2,038.4	388.9	.3	−396.8	−96.5	1,732.7	394.6	318.6	76.0	916.0	20.5	5.9
2001	1,963.8	2,346.7	1,934.8	411.9	−12.9	−370.0	−113.1	1,894.1	182.8	178.5	4.4	747.2	19.3	4.4
2002	1,930.9	2,374.1	1,930.4	443.7	.5	−443.7	−72.7	2,161.7	−158.2	−104.7	−53.5	716.1	18.1	3.1
2003	1,978.1	2,491.3	2,027.1	464.2	2.1	−515.3	−13.7	2,270.0	−278.2	−231.8	−46.4	772.2	17.3	2.4
2004	2,142.2	2,767.5	2,281.3	486.2	−2.8	−622.4	−22.1	2,389.5	−225.2	−220.4	−4.8	945.6	17.6	2.8
2005	2,310.7	3,048.0	2,534.7	513.3	−12.9	−724.5	−55.1	2,426.1	−60.3	−115.4	55.1	1,077.0	18.0	3.0
2006	2,450.0	3,251.8	2,701.0	550.9	2.1	−803.9	−207.9	2,598.2	59.7	−26.3	86.0	1,127.7	18.9	3.8
2007	2,554.3	3,265.0	2,673.0	592.0	−.1	−710.7	17.7	2,531.7	4.9	−53.3	58.2	1,012.2	17.4	2.0
2008	2,424.0	3,107.2	2,477.6	629.6	−5.4	−677.8	182.9	2,666.2	−425.0	−405.3	−19.7	748.4	15.3	−.8
2009	2,200.5	2,572.6	1,929.7	642.9	.6	−372.7	192.2	3,155.8	−1,147.5	−1,015.3	−132.2	201.1	13.9	−2.5
2010	2,373.3	2,810.0	2,165.5	644.5	.7	−437.4	61.0	3,487.6	−1,175.4	−1,081.3	−94.1	419.1	15.3	−.5
2011	2,503.6	2,969.2	2,332.6	636.6	1.6	−467.2	−53.2	3,596.8	−1,039.9	−987.0	−52.9	494.7	16.1	.5
2012	2,794.7	3,242.8	2,621.8	621.0	−6.5	−441.6	−241.3	3,903.8	−867.8	−817.0	−50.8	666.8	18.2	2.8
2013	3,057.9	3,426.4	2,826.0	600.4	.8	−369.4	−160.3	3,616.9	−398.7	−372.0	−26.6	745.2	18.7	3.1
2014	3,271.1	3,646.7	3,044.2	602.6	.4	−376.0	−289.2	3,886.1	−325.8	−334.1	8.3	831.7	19.7	4.1
2015	3,420.0	3,844.1	3,223.1	621.0	.4	−424.5	−254.9	3,942.5	−267.6	−298.7	31.1	927.6	19.6	4.1
2016	3,372.6	3,813.9	3,178.7	635.2	.5	−441.9	−112.0	3,880.0	−395.5	−405.3	9.8	822.4	18.3	2.6
2017	3,558.9	4,025.5	3,370.7	654.8	9.5	−476.0	−67.6	4,056.0	−429.6	−447.6	18.0	904.0	18.3	2.5
2018	3,806.0	4,315.5	3,628.3	687.2	−2.8	−506.7	10.8	4,478.4	−683.2	−723.6	40.4	1,024.0	18.2	2.4
2019 *p*	....	4,478.2	3,742.8	735.3	....	....	....	....	....	....	....	1,015.5	....	....
2016: I	3,320.9	3,786.6	3,149.1	637.5	.6	−466.3	−249.2	3,944.8	−374.7	−374.6	−.2	836.8	18.9	3.3
II	3,373.6	3,786.4	3,152.9	633.5	.4	−413.2	−81.1	3,855.1	−400.4	−403.7	3.3	806.6	18.2	2.5
III	3,361.6	3,798.0	3,166.6	631.4	.8	−437.1	−73.9	3,836.2	−400.7	−415.1	14.4	795.7	18.0	2.3
IV	3,434.2	3,884.8	3,246.2	638.6	.4	−451.0	−43.7	3,883.8	−406.0	−427.7	21.7	850.4	18.0	2.3
2017: I	3,484.1	3,934.5	3,288.2	646.2	.6	−451.0	−116.6	4,006.8	−406.1	−410.1	4.0	869.6	18.4	2.7
II	3,473.5	3,989.3	3,335.0	654.4	.8	−516.6	−140.3	4,041.9	−428.1	−423.1	−5.0	887.7	18.3	2.6
III	3,631.9	4,055.8	3,401.8	653.9	35.8	−459.7	−26.7	4,075.9	−417.3	−429.4	12.1	914.3	18.4	2.6
IV	3,646.1	4,122.4	3,457.7	664.6	.6	−476.8	13.3	4,099.6	−466.8	−527.9	61.1	944.6	18.0	2.3
2018: I	3,737.1	4,215.0	3,542.4	672.6	.4	−478.4	−89.1	4,462.7	−636.6	−693.6	57.1	994.8	18.6	3.0
II	3,804.0	4,248.3	3,561.6	686.7	.4	−444.8	50.1	4,437.3	−683.4	−728.6	45.2	976.7	18.1	2.3
III	3,847.8	4,377.9	3,684.0	693.9	−1.7	−528.4	32.9	4,477.4	−662.4	−693.8	31.3	1,062.1	18.2	2.4
IV	3,835.1	4,420.6	3,725.2	695.4	−10.5	−575.1	49.2	4,536.4	−750.6	−778.6	28.1	1,062.5	17.9	2.0
2019: I	3,951.9	4,498.5	3,783.4	715.1	.5	−547.0	42.1	4,664.9	−755.1	−831.1	76.0	1,096.3	18.3	2.4
II	3,969.3	4,483.4	3,749.5	733.9	.4	−514.5	102.5	4,655.2	−788.4	−895.4	107.0	1,036.9	18.0	2.0
III	3,976.2	4,483.1	3,744.6	738.5	.5	−507.4	102.1	4,723.2	−849.1	−916.4	67.4	997.3	17.8	1.8
IV *p*	....	4,447.8	3,693.9	753.9	....	....	....	....	....	....	....	931.8	....	....

[2] National income and product accounts (NIPA).
[3] Consists of capital transfers and the acquisition and disposal of nonproduced nonfinancial assets.
[4] Prior to 1982, equals the balance on current account, NIPA.

Source: Department of Commerce (Bureau of Economic Analysis).

National Income or Expenditure | 389

TABLE B-20. Median money income (in 2018 dollars) and poverty status of families and people, by race, 2011-2018

Race, Hispanic origin, and year	Families [1]						People below poverty level [2]		Median money income (in 2018 dollars) of people 15 years old and over with income [3]			
	Number (millions)	Median money income (in 2018 dollars) [3]	Below poverty level [2]				Number (millions)	Percent	Males		Females	
			Total		Female householder, no husband present				All people	Year-round full-time workers	All people	Year-round full-time workers
			Number (millions)	Percent	Number (millions)	Percent						
TOTAL (all races) [4]												
2011	80.5	$68,224	9.5	11.8	4.9	31.2	46.2	15.0	$36,908	$56,299	$23,611	$43,285
2012	80.9	68,198	9.5	11.8	4.8	30.9	46.5	15.0	37,149	55,534	23,580	43,849
2013 [5]	81.2	68,902	9.1	11.2	4.6	30.6	45.3	14.5	38,036	55,004	23,822	43,833
2013 [6]	82.3	70,690	9.6	11.7	5.2	32.2	46.3	14.8	38,470	55,516	23,890	43,943
2014	81.7	70,745	9.5	11.6	4.8	30.6	46.7	14.8	38,543	54,632	23,613	43,315
2015	82.2	74,932	8.6	10.4	4.4	28.2	43.1	13.5	39,363	55,377	25,193	44,255
2016	82.9	76,081	8.1	9.8	4.1	26.6	40.6	12.7	40,673	55,954	26,047	45,204
2017	83.1	77,789	7.8	9.3	4.0	25.7	39.7	12.3	41,381	57,195	26,107	45,461
2017 [7]	83.5	77,991	7.8	9.3	4.0	26.2	39.6	12.3	41,380	56,855	26,528	46,948
2018	83.5	78,646	7.5	9.0	3.7	24.9	38.1	11.8	41,615	57,219	27,079	46,528
WHITE, non-Hispanic [8]												
2011	54.2	78,132	4.0	7.3	1.8	23.4	19.2	9.8	42,684	62,394	24,869	46,293
2012	54.0	78,319	3.8	7.1	1.7	23.4	18.9	9.7	42,460	61,630	25,094	46,207
2013 [5]	53.8	78,413	3.7	6.9	1.6	22.6	18.8	9.6	43,320	60,956	25,675	46,194
2013 [6]	54.7	80,581	4.0	7.3	1.9	25.8	19.6	10.0	44,113	63,568	25,625	46,511
2014	53.8	81,390	3.9	7.3	1.7	23.7	19.7	10.1	43,607	62,336	25,487	46,967
2015	53.8	85,351	3.5	6.4	1.6	21.7	17.8	9.1	44,735	64,389	27,164	48,431
2016	54.1	85,878	3.4	6.3	1.6	21.1	17.3	8.8	45,414	64,037	27,725	49,505
2017	53.9	87,945	3.2	6.0	1.4	19.8	17.0	8.7	46,953	63,944	27,777	50,152
2017 [7]	54.2	89,085	3.2	5.9	1.4	20.2	16.6	8.5	47,318	63,839	28,489	51,790
2018	54.2	89,448	3.2	5.8	1.4	19.7	15.7	8.1	47,817	65,282	29,468	50,694
BLACK [8]												
2011	9.7	45,310	2.3	24.2	1.7	39.0	10.9	27.6	26,266	44,909	22,104	39,263
2012	9.8	44,395	2.3	23.7	1.6	37.8	10.9	27.2	27,308	43,801	21,937	38,465
2013 [5]	9.9	44,903	2.3	22.8	1.6	38.5	11.0	27.2	26,836	44,867	21,642	38,286
2013 [6]	9.9	45,229	2.2	22.4	1.7	36.7	10.2	25.2	27,122	43,618	22,747	37,167
2014	9.9	45,815	2.3	22.9	1.6	37.2	10.8	26.2	28,209	43,708	22,260	37,386
2015	9.8	48,523	2.1	21.1	1.5	33.9	10.0	24.1	29,046	44,174	22,908	39,319
2016	10.0	51,656	1.9	19.0	1.3	31.6	9.2	22.0	31,013	43,963	23,895	39,080
2017	10.0	51,830	1.8	18.2	1.3	30.8	9.0	21.2	30,846	44,743	24,215	38,393
2017 [7]	10.0	51,884	1.9	18.9	1.4	31.9	9.2	21.7	30,092	43,640	24,510	39,257
2018	9.8	53,105	1.7	17.7	1.2	29.4	8.9	20.8	31,122	45,621	25,462	40,304
ASIAN [8]												
2011	4.2	81,676	.4	9.7	.1	19.1	2.0	12.3	40,655	62,757	24,660	46,644
2012	4.1	85,316	.4	9.4	.1	19.2	1.9	11.7	44,077	65,228	25,568	50,666
2013 [5]	4.4	82,492	.4	8.7	.1	14.9	1.8	10.5	43,354	64,989	26,820	48,949
2013 [6]	4.4	89,392	.4	10.2	.1	25.7	2.3	13.1	46,200	65,998	27,903	50,185
2014	4.5	87,839	.4	8.9	.1	18.9	2.1	12.0	43,426	63,455	26,958	51,334
2015	4.7	96,289	.4	8.0	.1	16.2	2.1	11.4	46,323	67,244	28,121	53,031
2016	4.7	97,837	.3	7.2	.1	19.4	1.9	10.1	48,752	70,081	28,013	53,409
2017	4.9	95,046	.4	7.8	.1	15.5	2.0	10.0	50,033	72,127	28,949	53,030
2017 [7]	4.9	97,015	.4	7.4	.1	16.3	1.9	9.7	50,385	71,882	28,275	53,751
2018	5.1	101,244	.4	7.6	.1	19.6	2.0	10.1	51,788	71,239	31,187	57,158
HISPANIC (any race) [8]												
2011	11.6	44,825	2.7	22.9	1.3	41.2	13.2	25.3	26,553	35,904	18,830	33,681
2012	12.0	44,665	2.8	23.5	1.3	40.7	13.6	25.6	26,946	35,628	18,326	32,332
2013 [5]	12.1	45,638	2.6	21.6	1.3	40.4	12.7	23.5	27,436	35,575	19,178	33,254
2013 [6]	12.4	44,202	2.9	23.1	1.4	40.5	13.4	24.7	26,130	34,946	18,303	33,654
2014	12.5	47,899	2.7	21.5	1.3	37.9	13.1	23.6	28,322	37,282	18,670	32,732
2015	12.8	50,163	2.5	19.6	1.2	35.5	12.1	21.4	29,794	38,128	20,037	33,553
2016	13.0	53,477	2.3	17.3	1.1	32.7	11.1	19.4	31,928	39,955	20,830	33,524
2017	13.2	54,921	2.2	16.3	1.1	32.7	10.8	18.3	31,439	40,874	20,807	33,230
2017 [7]	13.3	54,901	2.2	16.4	1.1	33.4	10.8	18.3	31,235	39,486	21,011	33,652
2018	13.3	55,093	2.1	15.5	1.0	30.8	10.5	17.6	31,417	40,360	21,687	35,169

[1] The term "family" refers to a group of two or more persons related by birth, marriage, or adoption and residing together. Every family must include a reference person.

[2] Poverty thresholds are updated each year to reflect changes in the consumer price index for all urban consumers (CPI-U).

[3] Adjusted by consumer price index research series (CPI-U-RS).

[4] Data for American Indians and Alaska natives, native Hawaiians and other Pacific Islanders, and those reporting two or more races are included in the total but not shown separately.

[5] The 2014 Current Population Survey (CPS) Annual Social and Economic Supplement (ASEC) included redesigned income questions, which were implemented to a subsample of the 98,000 addresses using a probability split panel design. These 2013 data are based on the 2014 ASEC sample of 68,000 addresses that received income questions similar to those used in the 2013 ASEC and are consistent with data in earlier years.

[6] These 2013 data are based on the 2014 ASEC sample of 30,000 addresses that received redesigned income questions and are consistent with data in later years.

[7] Reflects implementation of an updated processing system.

[8] The CPS allows respondents to choose more than one race. Data shown are for "white alone, non-Hispanic," "black alone," and "Asian alone" race categories. ("Black" is also "black or African American.") Family race and Hispanic origin are based on the reference person.

Note: For details see *Income and Poverty in the United States* in publication Series P–60 on the CPS ASEC.

Source: Department of Commerce (Bureau of the Census).

TABLE B–21. Real farm income, 1954–2019

[Billions of chained (2019) dollars]

Year	Income of farm operators from farming [1]							
	Gross farm income						Production expenses	Net farm income
		Value of agricultural sector production				Direct Federal Government payments		
	Total	Total	Crops [2,3]	Animals and animal products [3]	Farm-related income [4]			
1954	263.5	261.5	111.2	136.3	14.0	2.0	168.1	95.4
1955	254.4	252.7	108.3	130.2	14.2	1.7	168.5	85.9
1956	249.6	245.5	106.1	125.6	13.8	4.1	166.9	82.7
1957	247.0	239.8	97.0	128.9	13.9	7.2	168.3	78.7
1958	270.3	262.8	104.1	144.2	14.4	7.6	178.9	91.4
1959	259.5	254.8	101.1	138.2	15.5	4.7	186.1	73.4
1960	260.7	256.0	105.9	134.3	15.8	4.7	185.0	75.7
1961	271.1	261.1	105.8	139.0	16.3	10.0	191.1	79.9
1962	279.7	268.1	110.0	141.5	16.6	11.5	200.0	79.7
1963	283.2	272.1	117.1	137.7	17.3	11.1	206.3	76.9
1964	272.1	258.1	108.5	131.7	17.9	14.0	204.6	67.5
1965	294.0	278.4	120.2	140.2	18.1	15.6	212.5	81.5
1966	310.1	289.9	112.5	158.9	18.5	20.1	224.3	85.8
1967	301.6	283.3	114.7	149.2	19.3	18.4	228.0	73.7
1968	296.9	277.1	108.4	149.5	19.2	19.8	226.3	70.6
1969	307.9	287.2	107.5	160.1	19.7	20.7	229.9	78.0
1970	305.0	285.7	106.4	159.5	19.8	19.3	230.5	74.5
1971	306.6	291.0	115.6	155.3	20.2	15.5	232.5	74.1
1972	336.5	317.8	122.8	174.6	20.5	18.7	244.5	92.0
1973	443.6	431.9	193.1	216.9	22.0	11.7	289.5	154.1
1974	404.4	402.2	202.3	176.2	23.7	2.2	292.1	112.2
1975	378.7	375.7	189.8	161.9	23.9	3.0	282.6	96.1
1976	367.4	364.7	172.6	166.4	25.7	2.6	295.3	72.0
1977	365.5	359.4	171.9	159.0	28.5	6.1	298.7	66.8
1978	403.3	393.8	177.8	184.8	31.2	9.5	324.2	79.1
1979	437.0	433.0	193.3	206.4	33.3	4.0	357.5	79.5
1980	396.9	393.5	171.1	187.0	35.4	3.4	354.0	42.9
1981	404.0	399.4	191.7	171.0	36.6	4.7	338.8	65.3
1982	375.5	367.6	164.3	161.3	42.0	8.0	321.0	54.5
1983	338.8	318.3	125.2	154.2	38.9	20.5	307.4	31.4
1984	357.0	339.1	165.2	153.1	20.8	17.9	301.8	55.2
1985	331.8	315.9	151.7	142.1	22.1	15.9	273.1	58.7
1986	315.2	291.4	127.8	142.8	20.7	23.9	252.4	62.8
1987	331.9	298.9	127.1	149.3	22.5	33.0	257.0	74.9
1988	338.6	311.1	131.8	149.7	29.6	27.6	263.2	75.4
1989	350.9	331.0	149.3	152.9	28.9	19.9	265.8	85.1
1990	349.2	332.7	146.9	158.9	26.9	16.4	267.5	81.7
1991	328.0	313.9	138.6	149.0	26.3	14.0	259.3	68.7
1992	334.9	319.5	148.7	145.5	25.4	15.3	251.1	83.8
1993	334.4	312.5	134.8	150.0	27.7	21.9	258.2	76.2
1994	345.1	332.5	160.5	143.3	28.8	12.6	261.2	83.9
1995	329.8	318.4	150.0	137.3	31.1	11.4	267.6	62.2
1996	362.2	350.9	177.7	141.4	31.8	11.3	271.7	90.5
1997	359.4	348.1	169.9	145.4	32.8	11.3	281.9	77.5
1998	347.3	328.9	152.5	140.6	35.7	18.5	277.0	70.4
1999	345.9	314.2	136.6	140.2	37.5	31.7	275.7	70.2
2000	347.9	314.5	136.7	142.6	35.2	33.4	275.0	73.0
2001	351.9	320.3	133.8	149.8	36.7	31.6	274.6	77.3
2002	319.8	302.6	135.8	129.6	37.2	17.2	265.5	54.3
2003	352.2	329.7	147.8	142.9	39.0	22.5	269.2	83.0
2004	391.0	373.8	165.9	164.8	43.1	17.2	275.0	115.9
2005	383.9	352.5	147.1	162.7	42.8	31.4	282.6	101.3
2006	362.1	342.4	148.1	148.9	45.4	19.7	290.4	71.7
2007	412.6	398.2	183.6	168.2	46.4	14.5	327.5	85.1
2008	434.7	420.1	207.2	166.2	46.6	14.6	341.6	93.0
2009	398.3	383.9	194.8	141.5	47.5	14.4	324.6	73.6
2010	417.0	402.5	196.6	164.0	41.8	14.5	326.8	90.2
2011	481.7	469.7	228.4	187.6	53.8	11.9	351.5	130.1
2012	505.6	493.6	239.3	190.1	64.2	12.0	397.2	108.4
2013	534.6	522.5	258.2	200.0	64.3	12.2	398.0	136.6
2014	524.1	513.5	223.7	232.4	57.3	10.6	424.1	100.0
2015	473.3	461.7	197.9	208.4	55.3	11.6	385.7	87.6
2016	438.1	424.3	201.2	175.8	47.3	13.8	372.0	66.1
2017	443.6	431.6	196.0	184.5	51.2	12.0	365.3	78.3
2018	435.6	421.7	192.2	180.8	48.7	13.9	350.1	85.5
2019 [p]	437.1	414.7	183.2	177.5	54.0	22.4	344.6	92.5

[1] The GDP chain-type price index is used to convert the current-dollar statistics to 2019=100 equivalents.
[2] Crop receipts include proceeds received from commodities placed under Commodity Credit Corporation loans.
[3] The value of production equates to the sum of cash receipts, home consumption, and the value of the change in inventories.
[4] Includes income from forest products sold, the gross imputed rental value of farm dwellings, machine hire and custom work, and other sources of farm income such as commodity insurance indemnities.

Note: Data for 2019 are forecasts.

Source: Department of Agriculture (Economic Research Service).

National Income or Expenditure | 391

Labor Market Indicators

TABLE B–22. Civilian labor force, 1929–2019

[Monthly data seasonally adjusted, except as noted]

Year or month	Civilian noninstitu- tional popula- tion [1]	Civilian labor force					Not in labor force	Civilian labor force participa- tion rate [2]	Civilian employ- ment/ population ratio [3]	Unemploy- ment rate, civilian workers [4]
		Total	Employment			Unemploy- ment				
			Total	Agricultural	Non- agricultural					
		Thousands of persons 14 years of age and over								Percent
1929		49,180	47,630	10,450	37,180	1,550				3.2
1930		49,820	45,480	10,340	35,140	4,340				8.7
1931		50,420	42,400	10,290	32,110	8,020				15.9
1932		51,000	38,940	10,170	28,770	12,060				23.6
1933		51,590	38,760	10,090	28,670	12,830				24.9
1934		52,230	40,890	9,900	30,990	11,340				21.7
1935		52,870	42,260	10,110	32,150	10,610				20.1
1936		53,440	44,410	10,000	34,410	9,030				16.9
1937		54,000	46,300	9,820	36,480	7,700				14.3
1938		54,610	44,220	9,690	34,530	10,390				19.0
1939		55,230	45,750	9,610	36,140	9,480				17.2
1940	99,840	55,640	47,520	9,540	37,980	8,120	44,200	55.7	47.6	14.6
1941	99,900	55,910	50,350	9,100	41,250	5,560	43,990	56.0	50.4	9.9
1942	98,640	56,410	53,750	9,250	44,500	2,660	42,230	57.2	54.5	4.7
1943	94,640	55,540	54,470	9,080	45,390	1,070	39,100	58.7	57.6	1.9
1944	93,220	54,630	53,960	8,950	45,010	670	38,590	58.6	57.9	1.2
1945	94,090	53,860	52,820	8,580	44,240	1,040	40,230	57.2	56.1	1.9
1946	103,070	57,520	55,250	8,320	46,930	2,270	45,550	55.8	53.6	3.9
1947	106,018	60,168	57,812	8,256	49,557	2,356	45,850	56.8	54.5	3.9
		Thousands of persons 16 years of age and over								
1947	101,827	59,350	57,038	7,890	49,148	2,311	42,477	58.3	56.0	3.9
1948	103,068	60,621	58,343	7,629	50,714	2,276	42,447	58.8	56.6	3.8
1949	103,994	61,286	57,651	7,658	49,993	3,637	42,708	58.9	55.4	5.9
1950	104,995	62,208	58,918	7,160	51,758	3,288	42,787	59.2	56.1	5.3
1951	104,621	62,017	59,961	6,726	53,235	2,055	42,604	59.2	57.3	3.3
1952	105,231	62,138	60,250	6,500	53,749	1,883	43,093	59.0	57.3	3.0
1953	107,056	63,015	61,179	6,260	54,919	1,834	44,041	58.9	57.1	2.9
1954	108,321	63,643	60,109	6,205	53,904	3,532	44,678	58.8	55.5	5.5
1955	109,683	65,023	62,170	6,450	55,722	2,852	44,660	59.3	56.7	4.4
1956	110,954	66,552	63,799	6,283	57,514	2,750	44,402	60.0	57.5	4.1
1957	112,265	66,929	64,071	5,947	58,123	2,859	45,336	59.6	57.1	4.3
1958	113,727	67,639	63,036	5,586	57,450	4,602	46,088	59.5	55.4	6.8
1959	115,329	68,369	64,630	5,565	59,065	3,740	46,960	59.3	56.0	5.5
1960	117,245	69,628	65,778	5,458	60,318	3,852	47,617	59.4	56.1	5.5
1961	118,771	70,459	65,746	5,200	60,546	4,714	48,312	59.3	55.4	6.7
1962	120,153	70,614	66,702	4,944	61,759	3,911	49,539	58.8	55.5	5.5
1963	122,416	71,833	67,762	4,687	63,076	4,070	50,583	58.7	55.4	5.7
1964	124,485	73,091	69,305	4,523	64,782	3,786	51,394	58.7	55.7	5.2
1965	126,513	74,455	71,088	4,361	66,726	3,366	52,058	58.9	56.2	4.5
1966	128,058	75,770	72,895	3,979	68,915	2,875	52,288	59.2	56.9	3.8
1967	129,874	77,347	74,372	3,844	70,527	2,975	52,527	59.6	57.3	3.8
1968	132,028	78,737	75,920	3,817	72,103	2,817	53,291	59.6	57.5	3.6
1969	134,335	80,734	77,902	3,606	74,296	2,832	53,602	60.1	58.0	3.5
1970	137,085	82,771	78,678	3,463	75,215	4,093	54,315	60.4	57.4	4.9
1971	140,216	84,382	79,367	3,394	75,972	5,016	55,834	60.2	56.6	5.9
1972	144,126	87,034	82,153	3,484	78,669	4,882	57,091	60.4	57.0	5.6
1973	147,096	89,429	85,064	3,470	81,594	4,365	57,667	60.8	57.8	4.9
1974	150,120	91,949	86,794	3,515	83,279	5,156	58,171	61.3	57.8	5.6
1975	153,153	93,775	85,846	3,408	82,438	7,929	59,377	61.2	56.1	8.5
1976	156,150	96,158	88,752	3,331	85,421	7,406	59,991	61.6	56.8	7.7
1977	159,033	99,009	92,017	3,283	88,734	6,991	60,025	62.3	57.9	7.1
1978	161,910	102,251	96,048	3,387	92,661	6,202	59,659	63.2	59.3	6.1
1979	164,863	104,962	98,824	3,347	95,477	6,137	59,900	63.7	59.9	5.8
1980	167,745	106,940	99,303	3,364	95,938	7,637	60,806	63.8	59.2	7.1
1981	170,130	108,670	100,397	3,368	97,030	8,273	61,460	63.9	59.0	7.6
1982	172,271	110,204	99,526	3,401	96,125	10,678	62,067	64.0	57.8	9.7
1983	174,215	111,550	100,834	3,383	97,450	10,717	62,665	64.0	57.9	9.6
1984	176,383	113,544	105,005	3,321	101,685	8,539	62,839	64.4	59.5	7.5
1985	178,206	115,461	107,150	3,179	103,971	8,312	62,744	64.8	60.1	7.2
1986	180,587	117,834	109,597	3,163	106,434	8,237	62,752	65.3	60.7	7.0
1987	182,753	119,865	112,440	3,208	109,232	7,425	62,888	65.6	61.5	6.2
1988	184,613	121,669	114,968	3,169	111,800	6,701	62,944	65.9	62.3	5.5
1989	186,393	123,869	117,342	3,199	114,142	6,528	62,523	66.5	63.0	5.3

[1] Not seasonally adjusted.
[2] Civilian labor force as percent of civilian noninstitutional population.
[3] Civilian employment as percent of civilian noninstitutional population.
[4] Unemployed as percent of civilian labor force.

See next page for continuation of table.

[Monthly data seasonally adjusted, except as noted]

Year or month	Civilian noninstitutional population [1]	Civilian labor force					Not in labor force	Civilian labor force participation rate [2]	Civilian employment/population ratio [3]	Unemployment rate, civilian workers [4]
		Total	Employment			Unemployment				
			Total	Agricultural	Nonagricultural					
	Thousands of persons 16 years of age and over							Percent		
1990	189,164	125,840	118,793	3,223	115,570	7,047	63,324	66.5	62.8	5.6
1991	190,925	126,346	117,718	3,269	114,449	8,628	64,578	66.2	61.7	6.8
1992	192,805	128,105	118,492	3,247	115,245	9,613	64,700	66.4	61.5	7.5
1993	194,838	129,200	120,259	3,115	117,144	8,940	65,638	66.3	61.7	6.9
1994	196,814	131,056	123,060	3,409	119,651	7,996	65,758	66.6	62.5	6.1
1995	198,584	132,304	124,900	3,440	121,460	7,404	66,280	66.6	62.9	5.6
1996	200,591	133,943	126,708	3,443	123,264	7,236	66,647	66.8	63.2	5.4
1997	203,133	136,297	129,558	3,399	126,159	6,739	66,837	67.1	63.8	4.9
1998	205,220	137,673	131,463	3,378	128,085	6,210	67,547	67.1	64.1	4.5
1999	207,753	139,368	133,488	3,281	130,207	5,880	68,385	67.1	64.3	4.2
2000 [5]	212,577	142,583	136,891	2,464	134,427	5,692	69,994	67.1	64.4	4.0
2001	215,092	143,734	136,933	2,299	134,635	6,801	71,359	66.8	63.7	4.7
2002	217,570	144,863	136,485	2,311	134,174	8,378	72,707	66.6	62.7	5.8
2003	221,168	146,510	137,736	2,275	135,461	8,774	74,658	66.2	62.3	6.0
2004	223,357	147,401	139,252	2,232	137,020	8,149	75,956	66.0	62.3	5.5
2005	226,082	149,320	141,730	2,197	139,532	7,591	76,762	66.0	62.7	5.1
2006	228,815	151,428	144,427	2,206	142,221	7,001	77,387	66.2	63.1	4.6
2007	231,867	153,124	146,047	2,095	143,952	7,078	78,743	66.0	63.0	4.6
2008	233,788	154,287	145,362	2,168	143,194	8,924	79,501	66.0	62.2	5.8
2009	235,801	154,142	139,877	2,103	137,775	14,265	81,659	65.4	59.3	9.3
2010	237,830	153,889	139,064	2,206	136,858	14,825	83,941	64.7	58.5	9.6
2011	239,618	153,617	139,869	2,254	137,615	13,747	86,001	64.1	58.4	8.9
2012	243,284	154,975	142,469	2,186	140,283	12,506	88,310	63.7	58.6	8.1
2013	245,679	155,389	143,929	2,130	141,799	11,460	90,290	63.2	58.6	7.4
2014	247,947	155,922	146,305	2,237	144,068	9,617	92,025	62.9	59.0	6.2
2015	250,801	157,130	148,834	2,422	146,411	8,296	93,671	62.7	59.3	5.3
2016	253,538	159,187	151,436	2,460	148,976	7,751	94,351	62.8	59.7	4.9
2017	255,079	160,320	153,337	2,454	150,883	6,982	94,759	62.9	60.1	4.4
2018	257,791	162,075	155,761	2,425	153,336	6,314	95,716	62.9	60.4	3.9
2019	259,175	163,539	157,538	2,425	155,113	6,001	95,636	63.1	60.8	3.7
2017: Jan	254,082	159,647	152,129	2,388	149,719	7,518	94,435	62.8	59.9	4.7
Feb	254,246	159,767	152,368	2,423	149,904	7,399	94,479	62.8	59.9	4.6
Mar	254,414	160,066	152,978	2,506	150,282	7,088	94,348	62.9	60.1	4.4
Apr	254,588	160,309	153,224	2,696	150,503	7,085	94,279	63.0	60.2	4.4
May	254,767	160,060	153,001	2,502	150,548	7,059	94,707	62.8	60.1	4.4
June	254,957	160,232	153,299	2,491	150,881	6,933	94,725	62.8	60.1	4.3
July	255,151	160,339	153,471	2,338	151,126	6,867	94,812	62.8	60.1	4.3
Aug	255,357	160,690	153,593	2,406	151,295	7,097	94,667	62.9	60.1	4.4
Sept	255,562	161,212	154,371	2,293	152,085	6,841	94,350	63.1	60.4	4.2
Oct	255,766	160,378	153,779	2,480	151,287	6,599	95,388	62.7	60.1	4.1
Nov	255,949	160,510	153,813	2,455	151,448	6,697	95,439	62.7	60.1	4.2
Dec	256,109	160,538	153,977	2,491	151,420	6,561	95,571	62.7	60.1	4.1
2018: Jan	256,780	161,068	154,486	2,443	152,053	6,582	95,712	62.7	60.2	4.1
Feb	256,934	161,783	155,142	2,430	152,659	6,641	95,151	63.0	60.4	4.1
Mar	257,097	161,684	155,191	2,340	152,714	6,493	95,414	62.9	60.4	4.0
Apr	257,272	161,742	155,324	2,330	153,007	6,418	95,529	62.9	60.4	4.0
May	257,454	161,874	155,665	2,353	153,353	6,209	95,579	62.9	60.5	3.8
June	257,642	162,269	155,750	2,398	153,383	6,519	95,373	63.0	60.5	4.0
July	257,843	162,173	155,993	2,483	153,519	6,180	95,670	62.9	60.5	3.8
Aug	258,066	161,768	155,601	2,377	153,329	6,167	96,297	62.7	60.3	3.8
Sept	258,290	162,078	156,032	2,487	153,528	6,045	96,212	62.8	60.4	3.7
Oct	258,514	162,605	156,482	2,407	153,989	6,123	95,909	62.9	60.5	3.8
Nov	258,708	162,662	156,628	2,549	154,102	6,034	96,045	62.9	60.5	3.7
Dec	258,888	163,111	156,825	2,491	154,286	6,286	95,777	63.0	60.6	3.9
2019: Jan	258,239	163,142	156,627	2,546	154,112	6,516	95,097	63.2	60.7	4.0
Feb	258,392	163,047	156,866	2,488	154,354	6,181	95,345	63.1	60.7	3.8
Mar	258,537	162,935	156,741	2,336	154,346	6,194	95,602	63.0	60.6	3.8
Apr	258,693	162,546	156,696	2,389	154,369	5,850	96,147	62.8	60.6	3.6
May	258,861	162,782	156,844	2,423	154,486	5,938	96,079	62.9	60.6	3.6
June	259,037	163,133	157,148	2,330	154,835	5,985	95,905	63.0	60.7	3.7
July	259,225	163,373	157,346	2,400	155,035	6,027	95,852	63.0	60.7	3.7
Aug	259,432	163,894	157,895	2,414	155,546	5,999	95,538	63.2	60.9	3.7
Sept	259,638	164,051	158,298	2,416	155,816	5,753	95,587	63.2	61.0	3.5
Oct	259,845	164,401	158,544	2,473	155,970	5,857	95,444	63.3	61.0	3.6
Nov	260,020	164,347	158,536	2,356	156,167	5,811	95,673	63.2	61.0	3.5
Dec	260,181	164,556	158,803	2,533	156,241	5,753	95,625	63.2	61.0	3.5

[5] Beginning in 2000, data for agricultural employment are for agricultural and related industries; data for this series and for nonagricultural employment are not strictly comparable with data for earlier years. Because of independent seasonal adjustment for these two series, monthly data will not add to total civilian employment.

Note: Labor force data in Tables B–22 through B–28 are based on household interviews and usually relate to the calendar week that includes the 12th of the month. Historical comparability is affected by revisions to population controls, changes in occupational and industry classification, and other changes to the survey. In recent years, updated population controls have been introduced annually with the release of January data, so data are not strictly comparable with earlier periods. Particularly notable changes were introduced for data in the years 1953, 1960, 1962, 1972, 1973, 1978, 1980, 1990, 1994, 1997, 1998, 2000, 2003, 2008 and 2012. For definitions of terms, area samples used, historical comparability of the data, comparability with other series, etc., see *Employment and Earnings* or concepts and methodology of the CPS at http://www.bls.gov/cps/documentation.htm#concepts.

Source: Department of Labor (Bureau of Labor Statistics).

[Thousands of persons 16 years of age and over, except as noted; monthly data seasonally adjusted]

Year or month	All civilian workers	Men 20 years and over	Women 20 years and over	Both sexes 16–19	White Total	White Men 20 years and over	White Women 20 years and over	Black or African American Total	Black Men 20 years and over	Black Women 20 years and over	Asian Total	Hispanic or Latino ethnicity[1] Total	Hispanic Men 20 years and over	Hispanic Women 20 years and over
1975	85,846	48,018	30,726	7,104	76,411	43,192	26,731	7,894	3,998	3,388	....	3,663	2,117	1,224
1976	88,752	49,190	32,226	7,336	78,853	44,171	27,958	8,227	4,120	3,599	....	3,720	2,109	1,288
1977	92,017	50,555	33,775	7,688	81,700	45,326	29,306	8,540	4,273	3,758	....	4,079	2,335	1,370
1978	96,048	52,143	35,836	8,070	84,936	46,594	30,975	9,102	4,483	4,047	....	4,527	2,568	1,537
1979	98,824	53,308	37,434	8,083	87,259	47,546	32,357	9,359	4,606	4,174	....	4,785	2,701	1,638
1980	99,303	53,101	38,492	7,710	87,715	47,419	33,275	9,313	4,498	4,267	....	5,527	3,142	1,886
1981	100,397	53,582	39,590	7,225	88,709	47,846	34,275	9,355	4,520	4,329	....	5,813	3,325	2,029
1982	99,526	52,891	40,086	6,549	87,903	47,209	34,710	9,189	4,414	4,347	....	5,805	3,354	2,040
1983	100,834	53,487	41,004	6,342	88,893	47,618	35,476	9,375	4,531	4,428	....	6,072	3,523	2,127
1984	105,005	55,769	42,793	6,444	92,120	49,461	36,823	10,119	4,871	4,773	....	6,651	3,825	2,357
1985	107,150	56,562	44,154	6,434	93,736	50,061	37,907	10,501	4,992	4,977	....	6,888	3,994	2,456
1986	109,597	57,569	45,556	6,472	95,660	50,818	39,050	10,814	5,150	5,128	....	7,219	4,174	2,615
1987	112,440	58,726	47,074	6,640	97,789	51,649	40,242	11,309	5,357	5,365	....	7,790	4,444	2,872
1988	114,968	59,781	48,383	6,805	99,812	52,466	41,316	11,658	5,509	5,548	....	8,250	4,680	3,047
1989	117,342	60,837	49,745	6,759	101,584	53,292	42,346	11,953	5,602	5,727	....	8,573	4,853	3,172
1990	118,793	61,678	50,535	6,581	102,261	53,685	42,796	12,175	5,692	5,884	....	9,845	5,609	3,567
1991	117,718	61,178	50,634	5,906	101,182	53,103	42,862	12,074	5,706	5,874	....	9,828	5,623	3,603
1992	118,492	61,496	51,328	5,669	101,669	53,357	43,327	12,151	5,681	5,978	....	10,027	5,757	3,693
1993	120,259	62,355	52,099	5,805	103,045	54,021	43,910	12,382	5,793	6,095	....	10,361	5,992	3,800
1994	123,060	63,294	53,606	6,161	105,190	54,676	45,116	12,835	5,964	6,320	....	10,788	6,189	3,989
1995	124,900	64,085	54,396	6,419	106,490	55,254	45,643	13,279	6,137	6,556	....	11,127	6,367	4,116
1996	126,708	64,897	55,311	6,500	107,808	55,977	46,164	13,542	6,167	6,762	....	11,642	6,655	4,341
1997	129,558	66,284	56,613	6,661	109,856	56,986	47,063	13,969	6,325	7,013	....	12,726	7,307	4,705
1998	131,463	67,135	57,278	7,051	110,931	57,500	47,342	14,556	6,530	7,290	....	13,291	7,570	4,928
1999	133,488	67,761	58,555	7,172	112,235	57,934	48,098	15,056	6,702	7,663	....	13,720	7,576	5,290
2000	136,891	69,634	60,067	7,189	114,424	59,119	49,145	15,156	6,741	7,703	6,043	15,735	8,859	5,903
2001	136,933	69,776	60,417	6,740	114,430	59,245	49,369	15,006	6,627	7,741	6,180	16,190	9,100	6,121
2002	136,485	69,734	60,420	6,332	114,013	59,124	49,448	14,872	6,652	7,610	6,215	16,590	9,341	6,367
2003	137,736	70,415	61,402	5,919	114,235	59,348	49,823	14,739	6,586	7,636	5,756	17,372	10,063	6,541
2004	139,252	71,572	61,773	5,907	115,239	60,159	50,040	14,909	6,681	7,707	5,994	17,930	10,385	6,752
2005	141,730	73,050	62,702	5,978	116,949	61,255	50,589	15,313	6,901	7,876	6,244	18,632	10,872	6,913
2006	144,427	74,431	63,834	6,162	118,833	62,259	51,359	15,765	7,079	8,068	6,522	19,613	11,391	7,321
2007	146,047	75,337	64,799	5,911	119,792	62,806	51,996	16,051	7,245	8,240	6,839	20,382	11,827	7,662
2008	145,362	74,750	65,039	5,573	119,126	62,304	52,124	15,953	7,151	8,260	6,917	20,346	11,769	7,707
2009	139,877	71,341	63,699	4,837	114,996	59,626	51,231	15,025	6,628	7,956	6,635	19,647	11,256	7,649
2010	139,064	71,230	63,456	4,378	114,168	59,438	50,997	15,010	6,680	7,944	6,705	19,906	11,438	7,788
2011	139,869	72,182	63,360	4,327	114,690	60,118	50,881	15,051	6,765	7,906	6,867	20,269	11,685	7,918
2012	142,469	73,403	64,640	4,426	114,769	60,193	50,911	15,856	7,104	8,313	7,705	21,878	12,212	8,858
2013	143,929	74,176	65,295	4,458	115,379	60,511	51,198	16,151	7,304	8,408	8,136	22,514	12,638	9,056
2014	146,305	75,471	66,287	4,548	116,788	61,289	51,798	16,732	7,613	8,663	8,325	23,492	13,202	9,431
2015	148,834	76,776	67,323	4,734	117,944	61,959	52,161	17,472	7,938	9,032	8,706	24,400	13,624	9,853
2016	151,436	78,084	68,387	4,965	119,313	62,575	52,771	17,982	8,228	9,219	9,213	25,249	14,055	10,217
2017	153,337	78,919	69,344	5,074	120,176	63,009	53,179	18,587	8,500	9,514	9,448	25,938	14,355	10,543
2018	155,761	80,211	70,424	5,126	121,461	63,719	53,682	19,091	8,745	9,751	9,832	27,012	14,873	11,045
2019	157,538	80,917	71,470	5,150	122,441	64,070	54,304	19,381	8,883	9,910	10,179	27,805	15,204	11,516
2018: Jan	154,486	79,723	69,628	5,135	120,915	63,498	53,286	18,673	8,579	9,528	9,600	26,446	14,668	10,736
Feb	155,142	80,138	69,807	5,198	121,175	63,631	53,399	19,123	8,897	9,641	9,607	26,698	14,741	10,840
Mar	155,191	80,092	69,979	5,120	121,140	63,706	53,355	19,094	8,759	9,724	9,782	26,555	14,703	10,714
Apr	155,324	80,140	70,066	5,118	121,298	63,761	53,451	18,921	8,672	9,716	9,778	26,906	14,909	10,885
May	155,665	80,275	70,270	5,119	121,455	63,748	53,617	19,106	8,788	9,757	9,738	26,857	14,840	10,948
June	155,750	80,084	70,528	5,137	121,444	63,699	53,712	19,084	8,589	9,850	9,802	27,110	14,971	11,098
July	155,993	80,208	70,671	5,114	121,582	63,703	53,837	19,145	8,740	9,803	9,846	27,260	15,036	11,145
Aug	155,601	80,160	70,553	4,888	121,136	63,529	53,658	19,110	8,828	9,776	9,947	26,915	14,846	11,010
Sept	156,032	80,259	70,657	5,116	121,417	63,637	53,731	19,236	8,791	9,857	9,934	27,063	14,818	11,165
Oct	156,482	80,400	70,858	5,224	121,826	63,782	53,976	19,288	8,806	9,839	9,939	27,194	14,831	11,226
Nov	156,628	80,567	70,892	5,169	121,941	63,922	53,988	19,223	8,768	9,797	10,040	27,476	15,027	11,301
Dec	156,825	80,496	71,123	5,205	122,209	64,015	54,144	19,082	8,712	9,727	9,951	27,652	15,083	11,469
2019: Jan	156,627	80,474	71,004	5,149	121,812	63,869	53,895	19,211	8,714	9,833	9,991	27,558	15,068	11,386
Feb	156,866	80,677	71,169	5,019	122,119	64,067	54,114	19,140	8,744	9,819	10,046	27,499	15,127	11,328
Mar	156,741	80,570	71,056	5,115	122,111	63,937	54,102	19,093	8,765	9,776	10,082	27,562	15,192	11,324
Apr	156,696	80,609	71,136	4,951	121,964	63,915	54,120	19,235	8,823	9,860	9,969	27,364	15,034	11,337
May	156,844	80,761	71,038	5,044	121,970	64,041	53,930	19,302	8,840	9,947	10,057	27,507	15,185	11,341
June	157,148	80,780	71,209	5,159	122,199	64,015	54,054	19,216	8,773	9,858	10,302	27,621	15,099	11,396
July	157,346	80,975	71,120	5,250	122,213	64,007	54,060	19,502	8,956	9,893	10,163	27,610	15,028	11,493
Aug	157,895	81,046	71,665	5,184	122,566	64,099	54,379	19,485	8,937	9,944	10,227	27,876	15,191	11,609
Sept	158,298	81,146	71,990	5,162	122,955	64,224	54,709	19,550	8,976	9,987	10,262	28,156	15,320	11,723
Oct	158,544	81,196	72,130	5,218	123,028	64,173	54,755	19,571	9,003	9,984	10,409	28,279	15,310	11,834
Nov	158,536	81,377	71,881	5,278	123,077	64,247	54,666	19,557	9,019	9,929	10,429	28,339	15,498	11,675
Dec	158,803	81,390	72,200	5,213	123,175	64,238	54,827	19,712	9,034	10,094	10,214	28,286	15,393	11,736

[1] Beginning in 2003, persons who selected this race group only. Persons whose ethnicity is identified as Hispanic or Latino may be of any race. Prior to 2003, persons who selected more than one race were included in the group they identified as the main race. Data for "black or African American" were for "black" prior to 2003. See Employment and Earnings or concepts and methodology of the Current Population Survey (CPS) at http://www.bls.gov/cps/documentation.htm#concepts for details.

Note: Detail will not sum to total because data for all race groups are not shown here.
See footnote 5 and Note, Table B–22.

Source: Department of Labor (Bureau of Labor Statistics).

TABLE B–24. Unemployment by sex, age, and demographic characteristic, 1975–2019

[Thousands of persons 16 years of age and over, except as noted; monthly data seasonally adjusted]

| Year or month | All civilian workers | By sex and age | | | By race or ethnicity [1] | | | | | | | | | |
| | | Men 20 years and over | Women 20 years and over | Both sexes 16–19 | White | | | Black or African American | | | Asian | Hispanic or Latino ethnicity | | |
					Total	Men 20 years and over	Women 20 years and over	Total	Men 20 years and over	Women 20 years and over	Total	Total	Men 20 years and over	Women 20 years and over
1975	7,929	3,476	2,684	1,767	6,421	2,841	2,166	1,369	571	469	....	508	225	160
1976	7,406	3,098	2,588	1,719	5,914	2,504	2,045	1,334	528	477	....	485	217	166
1977	6,991	2,794	2,535	1,663	5,441	2,211	1,946	1,393	512	528	....	456	195	153
1978	6,202	2,328	2,292	1,583	4,698	1,797	1,713	1,330	462	510	....	452	175	168
1979	6,137	2,308	2,276	1,555	4,664	1,773	1,699	1,319	473	513	....	434	168	160
1980	7,637	3,353	2,615	1,669	5,884	2,629	1,964	1,553	636	574	....	620	284	190
1981	8,273	3,615	2,895	1,763	6,343	2,825	2,143	1,731	703	671	....	678	321	212
1982	10,678	5,089	3,613	1,977	8,241	3,991	2,715	2,142	954	793	....	929	461	293
1983	10,717	5,257	3,632	1,829	8,128	4,098	2,643	2,272	1,002	878	....	961	491	302
1984	8,539	3,932	3,107	1,499	6,372	2,992	2,264	1,914	815	747	....	800	393	258
1985	8,312	3,715	3,129	1,468	6,191	2,834	2,283	1,864	757	750	....	811	401	269
1986	8,237	3,751	3,032	1,454	6,140	2,857	2,213	1,840	765	728	....	857	438	278
1987	7,425	3,369	2,709	1,347	5,501	2,584	1,922	1,684	666	706	....	751	374	241
1988	6,701	2,987	2,487	1,226	4,944	2,268	1,766	1,547	617	642	....	732	351	234
1989	6,528	2,867	2,467	1,194	4,770	2,149	1,758	1,544	619	625	....	750	342	276
1990	7,047	3,239	2,596	1,212	5,186	2,431	1,852	1,565	664	633	....	876	425	289
1991	8,628	4,195	3,074	1,359	6,560	3,284	2,248	1,723	745	698	....	1,092	575	339
1992	9,613	4,717	3,469	1,427	7,169	3,620	2,512	2,011	886	800	....	1,311	675	418
1993	8,940	4,287	3,288	1,365	6,655	3,263	2,400	1,844	801	729	....	1,248	629	418
1994	7,996	3,627	3,049	1,320	5,892	2,735	2,157	1,666	682	685	....	1,187	558	431
1995	7,404	3,239	2,819	1,346	5,459	2,465	2,042	1,538	593	620	....	1,140	530	404
1996	7,236	3,146	2,783	1,306	5,300	2,363	1,998	1,592	639	643	....	1,132	495	438
1997	6,739	2,882	2,585	1,271	4,836	2,140	1,784	1,560	585	673	....	1,069	471	401
1998	6,210	2,580	2,424	1,205	4,484	1,920	1,688	1,426	524	622	....	1,026	436	376
1999	5,880	2,433	2,285	1,162	4,273	1,813	1,616	1,309	480	561	....	945	374	376
2000	5,692	2,376	2,235	1,081	4,121	1,731	1,595	1,241	499	512	227	954	388	371
2001	6,801	3,040	2,599	1,162	4,969	2,275	1,849	1,416	573	582	288	1,138	495	436
2002	8,378	3,896	3,228	1,253	6,137	2,943	2,269	1,693	695	738	389	1,353	636	496
2003	8,774	4,209	3,314	1,251	6,311	3,125	2,276	1,787	760	772	366	1,441	693	555
2004	8,149	3,791	3,150	1,208	5,847	2,785	2,172	1,729	733	755	277	1,342	635	504
2005	7,591	3,392	3,013	1,186	5,350	2,450	2,054	1,700	699	734	259	1,191	536	464
2006	7,001	3,131	2,751	1,119	5,002	2,281	1,927	1,549	640	656	205	1,081	497	414
2007	7,078	3,259	2,718	1,101	5,143	2,408	1,930	1,445	622	588	229	1,220	576	446
2008	8,924	4,297	3,342	1,285	6,509	3,179	2,384	1,788	811	732	285	1,678	860	567
2009	14,265	7,555	5,157	1,552	10,648	5,746	3,745	2,606	1,286	1,032	522	2,706	1,474	911
2010	14,825	7,763	5,534	1,527	10,916	5,828	3,960	2,852	1,396	1,165	543	2,843	1,519	1,001
2011	13,747	6,898	5,450	1,400	9,889	5,046	3,818	2,831	1,360	1,204	518	2,629	1,345	984
2012	12,506	5,984	5,125	1,397	8,915	4,347	3,564	2,544	1,152	1,119	483	2,514	1,195	995
2013	11,460	5,568	4,565	1,327	8,033	3,994	3,102	2,429	1,082	1,069	448	2,257	1,090	855
2014	9,617	4,585	3,926	1,106	6,540	3,141	2,623	2,141	973	943	436	1,878	864	764
2015	8,296	3,959	3,371	966	5,662	2,751	2,249	1,846	835	811	347	1,726	820	686
2016	7,751	3,675	3,151	925	5,345	2,594	2,100	1,655	737	724	349	1,548	720	627
2017	6,982	3,287	2,868	827	4,765	2,248	1,923	1,501	663	657	333	1,401	632	585
2018	6,314	2,976	2,578	759	4,354	2,094	1,743	1,322	582	573	304	1,323	591	547
2019	6,001	2,819	2,435	746	4,159	1,967	1,664	1,251	571	527	280	1,248	553	497
2018: Jan	6,582	3,159	2,608	815	4,380	2,195	1,616	1,503	671	654	299	1,380	653	516
Feb	6,641	3,072	2,720	849	4,657	2,255	1,819	1,367	538	624	291	1,375	598	596
Mar	6,493	3,043	2,657	793	4,478	2,174	1,806	1,389	566	611	309	1,401	665	551
Apr	6,418	3,101	2,565	752	4,486	2,211	1,763	1,298	578	527	286	1,363	628	545
May	6,209	2,992	2,468	750	4,429	2,124	1,771	1,195	592	478	217	1,380	600	590
June	6,519	3,111	2,669	739	4,412	2,148	1,794	1,331	603	565	329	1,291	593	560
July	6,180	2,795	2,621	764	4,186	1,914	1,771	1,357	574	630	311	1,264	494	555
Aug	6,167	2,880	2,572	715	4,239	1,998	1,740	1,293	554	608	305	1,318	574	582
Sept	6,045	2,868	2,435	742	4,109	1,999	1,590	1,276	563	565	359	1,299	604	503
Oct	6,123	2,880	2,518	725	4,182	1,983	1,718	1,299	605	502	321	1,249	594	502
Nov	6,034	2,774	2,530	729	4,277	1,983	1,783	1,244	563	520	284	1,297	539	548
Dec	6,286	2,987	2,550	750	4,337	2,066	1,750	1,340	592	582	335	1,268	552	512
2019: Jan	6,516	3,112	2,639	765	4,448	2,165	1,755	1,404	660	569	318	1,400	628	569
Feb	6,181	2,911	2,497	773	4,157	1,970	1,668	1,417	667	544	320	1,248	561	465
Mar	6,194	2,995	2,451	747	4,286	2,083	1,676	1,344	630	542	318	1,357	641	517
Apr	5,850	2,812	2,304	734	3,947	1,900	1,538	1,352	628	556	225	1,198	581	433
May	5,938	2,808	2,401	730	4,121	1,938	1,670	1,265	579	533	260	1,197	543	480
June	5,985	2,788	2,447	751	4,120	1,928	1,704	1,223	548	546	225	1,252	564	503
July	6,027	2,796	2,465	767	4,185	1,980	1,666	1,220	543	537	290	1,305	625	450
Aug	5,999	2,806	2,451	742	4,286	1,965	1,773	1,119	550	456	299	1,213	528	510
Sept	5,753	2,695	2,323	735	4,063	1,886	1,639	1,135	512	491	259	1,137	473	468
Oct	5,857	2,715	2,411	730	4,094	1,941	1,644	1,133	482	511	305	1,203	531	485
Nov	5,811	2,679	2,411	721	4,115	1,957	1,633	1,148	485	516	276	1,236	485	521
Dec	5,753	2,618	2,383	752	4,022	1,839	1,602	1,238	557	530	264	1,231	483	558

[1] See footnote 1 and Note, Table B–23.

Note: See footnote 5 and Note, Table B–22.

Source: Department of Labor (Bureau of Labor Statistics).

[Percent [1]; monthly data seasonally adjusted]

Year or month	All civilian workers	Men 20 years and over	Men 20–24 years	Men 25–54 years	Men 55 years and over	Women 20 years and over	Women 20–24 years	Women 25–54 years	Women 55 years and over	Both sexes 16–19 years	White	Black or African American	Asian	Hispanic or Latino ethnicity
1975	61.2	80.3	84.5	94.4	49.4	46.0	64.1	55.1	23.1	54.0	61.5	58.8	....	60.8
1976	61.6	79.8	85.2	94.2	47.8	47.0	65.0	56.8	23.0	54.5	61.8	59.0	....	60.8
1977	62.3	79.7	85.6	94.2	47.4	48.1	66.5	58.5	22.9	56.0	62.5	59.8	....	61.6
1978	63.2	79.8	85.9	94.3	47.2	49.6	68.3	60.6	23.1	57.8	63.3	61.5	....	62.9
1979	63.7	79.8	86.4	94.4	46.6	50.6	69.0	62.3	23.2	57.9	63.9	61.4	....	63.6
1980	63.8	79.4	85.9	94.2	45.6	51.3	68.9	64.0	22.8	56.7	64.1	61.0	....	64.0
1981	63.9	79.0	85.5	94.1	44.5	52.1	69.6	65.3	22.7	55.4	64.3	60.8	....	64.1
1982	64.0	78.7	84.9	94.0	43.8	52.7	69.8	66.3	22.7	54.1	64.3	61.0	....	63.6
1983	64.0	78.5	84.8	93.8	43.0	53.1	69.9	67.1	22.4	53.5	64.3	61.5	....	63.8
1984	64.4	78.3	85.0	93.9	41.8	53.7	70.4	68.2	22.2	53.9	64.6	62.2	....	64.9
1985	64.8	78.1	85.0	93.9	41.0	54.7	71.8	69.6	22.0	54.5	65.0	62.9	....	64.6
1986	65.3	78.1	85.8	93.8	40.4	55.5	72.4	70.8	22.1	54.7	65.5	63.3	....	65.4
1987	65.6	78.0	85.2	93.7	40.4	56.2	73.0	71.9	22.0	54.7	65.8	63.8	....	66.4
1988	65.9	77.9	85.0	93.6	39.9	56.8	72.7	72.7	22.3	55.3	66.2	63.8	....	67.4
1989	66.5	78.1	85.3	93.7	39.6	57.7	72.4	73.6	23.0	55.9	66.7	64.2	....	67.6
1990	66.5	78.2	84.4	93.4	39.4	58.0	71.3	74.0	22.9	53.7	66.9	64.0	....	67.4
1991	66.2	77.7	83.5	93.1	38.5	57.9	70.1	74.1	22.6	51.6	66.6	63.3	....	66.5
1992	66.4	77.7	83.3	93.0	38.4	58.5	70.9	74.6	22.8	51.3	66.8	63.9	....	66.8
1993	66.3	77.3	83.2	92.6	37.7	58.5	70.9	74.6	22.8	51.5	66.8	63.2	....	66.2
1994	66.6	76.8	83.1	91.7	37.8	59.3	71.0	75.3	24.0	52.7	67.1	63.4	....	66.1
1995	66.6	76.7	83.1	91.6	37.9	59.4	70.3	75.6	23.9	53.5	67.1	63.7	....	65.8
1996	66.8	76.8	82.5	91.8	38.3	59.9	71.3	76.1	23.9	52.3	67.2	64.1	....	66.5
1997	67.1	77.0	82.5	91.8	38.9	60.5	72.7	76.7	24.6	51.6	67.5	64.7	....	67.9
1998	67.1	76.8	82.0	91.8	39.1	60.4	73.0	76.5	25.0	52.8	67.3	65.6	....	67.9
1999	67.1	76.7	81.9	91.7	39.6	60.7	73.2	76.8	25.6	52.0	67.3	65.8	....	67.7
2000	67.1	76.7	82.6	91.6	40.1	60.6	73.1	76.7	26.1	52.0	67.3	65.8	67.2	69.7
2001	66.8	76.5	81.6	91.3	40.9	60.6	72.7	76.4	27.0	49.6	67.0	65.3	67.2	69.5
2002	66.6	76.3	80.7	91.0	42.0	60.5	72.1	75.9	28.5	47.4	66.8	64.8	67.2	69.1
2003	66.2	75.9	80.0	90.6	42.6	60.6	70.8	75.6	30.0	44.5	66.5	64.3	66.4	68.3
2004	66.0	75.8	79.6	90.5	43.2	60.3	70.5	75.3	30.5	43.9	66.3	63.8	65.9	68.6
2005	66.0	75.8	79.1	90.5	44.2	60.4	70.1	75.3	31.4	43.7	66.3	64.2	66.1	68.0
2006	66.2	75.9	79.6	90.6	44.9	60.5	69.5	75.5	32.3	43.7	66.5	64.1	66.2	68.7
2007	66.0	75.9	78.7	90.9	45.2	60.6	70.1	75.4	33.2	41.3	66.4	63.7	66.5	68.8
2008	66.0	75.7	78.7	90.5	46.0	60.9	70.0	75.8	33.9	40.2	66.3	63.7	67.0	68.5
2009	65.4	74.8	76.2	89.7	46.3	60.8	69.6	75.6	34.7	37.5	65.8	62.4	66.0	68.0
2010	64.7	74.1	74.5	89.3	46.4	60.3	68.3	75.2	35.1	34.9	65.1	62.2	64.7	67.5
2011	64.1	73.4	74.7	88.7	46.3	59.8	67.8	74.7	35.1	34.1	64.5	61.4	64.6	66.5
2012	63.7	73.0	74.5	88.7	46.8	59.3	67.4	74.5	35.1	34.3	64.0	61.5	63.9	66.4
2013	63.2	72.5	73.9	88.4	46.5	58.8	67.5	73.9	35.1	34.5	63.5	61.2	64.6	66.0
2014	62.9	71.9	73.9	88.2	45.9	58.5	67.7	73.9	34.9	34.0	63.1	61.2	63.6	66.1
2015	62.7	71.7	73.0	88.3	45.9	58.2	68.3	73.7	34.7	34.3	62.8	61.5	62.8	65.9
2016	62.8	71.7	73.0	88.5	46.2	58.3	68.0	74.3	34.7	35.2	62.9	61.6	63.2	65.8
2017	62.9	71.6	74.1	88.6	46.1	58.5	68.5	75.0	34.7	35.2	62.8	62.3	63.6	66.1
2018	62.9	71.6	73.2	89.0	46.2	58.5	69.0	75.3	34.7	35.1	62.8	62.3	63.5	66.3
2019	63.1	71.6	74.0	89.1	46.3	58.9	70.4	76.0	35.0	35.3	63.0	62.5	64.0	66.8
2018: Jan	62.7	71.7	74.7	89.0	45.8	58.1	68.8	74.8	34.1	35.5	62.7	61.9	62.9	65.9
Feb	63.0	71.9	74.8	89.3	46.1	58.3	68.5	75.2	34.5	36.0	63.0	62.8	62.8	66.3
Mar	62.9	71.8	75.5	89.1	46.0	58.3	69.0	75.1	34.6	35.2	62.8	62.8	63.1	65.9
Apr	62.9	71.8	73.8	89.2	46.1	58.3	68.8	74.9	34.7	35.0	62.9	61.9	63.2	66.5
May	62.9	71.8	73.1	89.1	46.4	58.3	68.8	74.9	34.8	35.0	62.9	62.1	62.7	66.3
June	63.0	71.6	73.3	89.0	46.2	58.7	69.1	75.5	34.9	35.1	62.9	62.4	63.6	66.5
July	62.9	71.4	72.4	88.8	46.2	58.7	70.2	75.6	34.8	35.1	62.8	62.6	63.8	66.7
Aug	62.7	71.4	71.0	88.7	46.2	58.5	68.8	75.4	34.9	33.4	62.6	62.2	63.7	65.9
Sept	62.8	71.4	72.8	88.7	46.1	58.4	69.0	75.2	34.9	34.9	62.6	62.4	64.3	66.0
Oct	62.9	71.5	72.1	89.0	46.1	58.6	68.6	75.7	34.8	35.5	62.8	62.6	64.0	66.1
Nov	62.9	71.4	72.4	89.0	46.2	58.6	68.9	75.5	34.9	35.2	62.9	62.2	64.1	66.7
Dec	63.0	71.5	72.5	89.0	46.3	58.8	69.3	75.7	35.1	35.5	63.0	62.0	63.7	66.9
2019: Jan	63.2	71.8	73.6	89.4	46.4	58.9	69.3	75.9	35.0	35.4	63.0	62.7	64.3	67.3
Feb	63.1	71.7	73.4	89.4	46.4	58.8	70.1	75.8	35.2	34.7	63.0	62.5	64.6	66.7
Mar	63.0	71.7	74.2	89.5	46.0	58.7	69.9	75.7	35.0	35.1	63.0	62.1	64.0	66.9
Apr	62.8	71.5	74.1	89.1	45.9	58.6	70.2	75.5	34.9	34.1	62.8	62.5	62.6	66.0
May	62.9	71.6	75.5	88.8	46.2	58.6	70.7	75.6	34.5	34.6	62.8	62.4	63.1	66.2
June	63.0	71.5	74.5	88.7	46.3	58.7	70.2	75.9	34.7	35.4	62.9	61.9	63.6	66.4
July	63.0	71.6	74.2	88.9	46.7	58.6	70.7	75.4	35.1	36.1	62.9	62.7	63.7	66.4
Aug	63.2	71.6	73.2	89.0	46.5	59.0	70.5	76.3	35.0	35.5	63.1	62.3	64.1	66.7
Sept	63.2	71.6	73.9	89.1	46.3	59.1	71.0	76.3	35.1	35.3	63.2	62.5	64.2	67.0
Oct	63.3	71.6	74.1	89.1	46.3	59.2	71.4	76.6	35.1	35.6	63.2	62.5	65.3	67.3
Nov	63.2	71.6	73.4	89.3	46.5	59.0	70.0	76.5	35.0	35.9	63.2	62.3	64.7	67.4
Dec	63.2	71.5	73.3	89.2	46.4	59.2	70.3	76.8	35.0	35.7	63.2	63.1	63.6	67.1

[1] Civilian labor force as percent of civilian noninstitutional population in group specified.
[2] See footnote 1, Table B–23.

Note: Data relate to persons 16 years of age and over, except as noted.
See footnote 5 and Note, Table B–22.

Source: Department of Labor (Bureau of Labor Statistics).

TABLE B–26. Civilian employment/population ratio, 1975–2019

[Percent [1]; monthly data seasonally adjusted]

Year or month	All civilian workers	Men 20 years and over	Men 20–24 years	Men 25–54 years	Men 55 years and over	Women 20 years and over	Women 20–24 years	Women 25–54 years	Women 55 years and over	Both sexes 16–19 years	White	Black or African American	Asian	Hispanic or Latino ethnicity
1975	56.1	74.8	72.4	89.0	47.0	42.3	56.0	51.0	21.9	43.3	56.7	50.1	....	53.4
1976	56.8	75.1	74.9	89.5	45.7	43.5	57.3	52.9	21.9	44.2	57.5	50.8	....	53.8
1977	57.9	75.6	76.3	90.1	45.5	44.8	59.0	54.8	21.9	46.1	58.6	51.4	....	55.4
1978	59.3	76.4	78.0	91.0	45.7	46.6	61.4	57.3	22.3	48.3	60.0	53.6	....	57.2
1979	59.9	76.5	78.9	91.1	45.2	47.7	62.4	59.0	22.5	48.5	60.6	53.8	....	58.3
1980	59.2	74.6	75.1	89.4	44.1	48.1	61.8	60.1	22.1	46.6	60.0	52.3	....	57.6
1981	59.0	74.0	74.2	89.0	42.9	48.6	61.8	61.2	21.9	44.6	60.0	51.3	....	57.4
1982	57.8	71.8	71.0	86.5	41.6	48.4	60.6	61.2	21.6	41.5	58.8	49.4	....	54.9
1983	57.9	71.4	71.3	86.1	40.6	48.8	60.9	62.0	21.4	41.5	58.9	49.5	....	55.1
1984	59.5	73.2	74.9	88.4	39.8	50.1	62.7	63.9	21.3	43.7	60.5	52.3	....	57.9
1985	60.1	73.3	75.3	88.7	39.3	51.0	64.1	65.3	21.1	44.4	61.0	53.4	....	57.8
1986	60.7	73.3	76.3	88.5	38.8	52.0	64.9	66.6	21.3	44.6	61.5	54.1	....	58.5
1987	61.5	73.8	76.8	89.0	38.6	53.1	66.1	68.2	21.3	45.5	62.3	55.6	....	60.5
1988	62.3	74.2	77.5	89.5	38.6	54.0	66.6	69.3	21.7	46.8	63.1	56.3	....	61.9
1989	63.0	74.5	77.8	89.9	38.3	54.9	66.4	70.4	22.4	47.5	63.8	56.9	....	62.2
1990	62.8	74.3	76.7	89.1	38.0	55.2	65.2	70.6	22.2	45.3	63.7	56.7	....	61.9
1991	61.7	72.7	73.8	87.5	36.8	54.6	63.2	70.1	21.9	42.0	62.6	55.4	....	59.8
1992	61.5	72.1	73.1	86.8	36.4	55.0	63.0	70.1	21.8	41.0	62.4	54.9	....	59.1
1993	61.7	72.3	73.8	87.0	35.9	55.6	64.0	70.4	22.0	41.7	62.7	55.0	....	59.1
1994	62.5	72.6	74.6	87.2	36.2	56.2	64.5	71.5	23.1	43.4	63.5	56.1	....	59.5
1995	62.9	73.0	75.4	87.6	36.5	56.5	64.0	72.2	23.0	44.2	63.8	57.1	....	59.7
1996	63.2	73.2	74.7	87.9	37.0	57.0	64.9	72.8	23.1	43.5	64.1	57.4	....	60.6
1997	63.8	73.7	75.2	88.4	37.7	57.8	66.8	73.5	23.8	43.4	64.6	58.2	....	62.6
1998	64.1	73.9	75.4	88.8	38.0	58.0	67.3	73.6	24.4	45.1	64.7	59.7	....	63.1
1999	64.3	74.0	75.6	89.0	38.5	58.5	68.0	74.1	24.9	44.7	64.8	60.6	....	63.4
2000	64.4	74.2	76.6	89.0	39.1	58.4	67.9	74.2	25.5	45.2	64.9	60.9	64.8	65.7
2001	63.7	73.3	74.2	87.9	39.6	58.1	67.3	73.4	26.3	42.3	64.2	59.7	64.2	64.9
2002	62.7	72.3	72.5	86.6	40.3	57.5	65.6	72.3	27.5	39.6	63.4	58.1	63.2	63.9
2003	62.3	71.7	71.5	85.9	40.7	57.5	64.2	72.0	28.9	36.8	63.0	57.4	62.4	63.1
2004	62.3	71.9	71.6	86.3	41.5	57.4	64.3	71.8	29.4	36.4	63.1	57.2	63.0	63.8
2005	62.7	72.4	71.5	86.9	42.7	57.6	64.5	72.0	30.4	36.5	63.4	57.7	63.4	64.0
2006	63.1	72.9	72.7	87.3	43.5	58.0	64.2	72.5	31.4	36.9	63.8	58.4	64.2	65.2
2007	63.0	72.8	71.7	87.5	43.7	58.2	65.0	72.5	32.2	34.8	63.6	58.4	64.3	64.9
2008	62.2	71.6	69.7	86.0	44.2	57.9	63.8	72.3	32.7	32.6	62.8	57.3	64.3	63.3
2009	59.3	67.6	63.3	81.5	43.0	56.2	61.1	70.2	32.6	28.4	60.2	53.2	61.2	59.7
2010	58.5	66.8	61.3	81.0	42.8	55.5	59.4	69.3	32.9	25.9	59.4	52.3	59.9	59.0
2011	58.4	67.0	63.0	81.4	43.1	55.0	58.7	69.0	32.9	25.8	59.4	51.7	60.0	58.9
2012	58.6	67.5	63.8	82.5	43.8	55.0	59.2	69.2	33.1	26.1	59.4	53.0	60.1	59.5
2013	58.6	67.4	63.5	82.8	43.8	54.9	59.8	69.3	33.3	26.6	59.4	53.2	61.2	60.0
2014	59.0	67.8	64.9	83.6	43.9	55.2	60.9	70.0	33.4	27.3	59.7	54.3	60.4	61.2
2015	59.3	68.1	65.1	84.4	44.1	55.4	62.5	70.3	33.5	28.5	59.9	55.7	60.4	61.6
2016	59.7	68.5	66.2	85.0	44.4	55.7	63.0	71.1	33.5	29.7	60.2	56.4	60.9	62.0
2017	60.1	68.8	67.9	85.4	44.6	56.1	64.2	72.1	33.6	30.3	60.4	57.6	61.5	62.7
2018	60.4	69.0	67.6	86.2	44.7	56.4	64.7	72.8	33.7	30.6	60.7	58.3	61.6	63.2
2019	60.8	69.2	68.3	86.4	45.1	56.9	66.4	73.7	34.0	30.9	61.0	58.7	62.3	63.9
2018: Jan	60.2	68.9	68.8	85.9	44.3	56.0	64.5	72.2	33.3	30.6	60.5	57.3	61.0	62.6
Feb	60.4	69.2	69.1	86.4	44.5	56.1	64.4	72.4	33.4	31.0	60.6	58.6	61.0	63.1
Mar	60.4	69.1	69.9	86.1	44.5	56.2	64.9	72.5	33.4	30.5	60.6	58.5	61.2	62.6
Apr	60.4	69.1	68.1	86.2	44.6	56.2	64.8	72.3	33.7	30.5	60.7	57.9	61.4	63.3
May	60.5	69.2	67.5	86.3	45.0	56.2	64.5	72.5	33.9	30.5	60.7	58.4	61.3	63.1
June	60.5	69.0	67.2	86.1	44.7	56.5	64.5	72.9	33.9	30.7	60.7	58.3	61.5	63.5
July	60.5	69.0	67.0	86.2	44.8	56.6	65.8	73.0	33.7	30.5	60.7	58.4	61.8	63.7
Aug	60.3	68.9	65.7	86.0	44.8	56.5	64.6	72.9	33.8	29.2	60.5	58.2	61.8	62.8
Sept	60.4	68.9	67.3	86.0	44.8	56.5	64.6	72.9	33.9	30.5	60.6	58.6	62.0	63.0
Oct	60.5	69.0	66.8	86.2	44.9	56.6	64.3	73.4	33.8	31.2	60.7	58.6	62.0	63.2
Nov	60.5	69.1	67.0	86.3	44.9	56.6	64.9	73.1	33.9	30.8	60.8	58.4	62.4	63.7
Dec	60.6	69.0	66.8	86.1	44.9	56.7	64.8	73.3	34.1	31.1	60.9	57.9	61.7	64.0
2019: Jan	60.7	69.1	67.5	86.4	44.9	56.8	64.8	73.4	34.0	30.8	60.8	58.4	62.3	64.0
Feb	60.7	69.2	67.9	86.5	45.1	56.9	65.3	73.4	34.3	30.1	60.9	58.2	62.6	63.8
Mar	60.6	69.1	67.7	86.7	44.7	56.7	66.0	73.2	34.1	30.6	60.9	58.0	62.1	63.8
Apr	60.6	69.1	68.4	86.4	44.7	56.8	66.4	73.3	33.9	29.7	60.8	58.4	61.2	63.2
May	60.6	69.2	69.2	86.2	45.0	56.6	66.7	73.3	33.4	30.2	60.8	58.5	61.5	63.4
June	60.7	69.1	69.0	86.1	45.1	56.7	66.6	73.6	33.6	30.9	60.9	58.2	62.2	63.6
July	60.7	69.2	68.6	86.2	45.5	56.6	66.6	73.0	34.1	31.5	60.8	59.0	62.0	63.4
Aug	60.9	69.2	67.4	86.3	45.4	57.0	66.1	74.0	34.0	31.1	61.0	58.9	62.2	63.9
Sept	61.0	69.3	68.5	86.4	45.2	57.2	67.2	74.0	34.2	30.9	61.2	59.0	62.6	64.4
Oct	61.0	69.3	68.5	86.5	45.2	57.3	68.0	74.2	34.1	31.3	61.2	59.0	63.5	64.5
Nov	61.0	69.4	68.1	86.7	45.3	57.0	66.1	74.1	34.1	31.6	61.2	58.8	63.0	64.6
Dec	61.0	69.3	68.0	86.6	45.4	57.3	66.5	74.4	34.1	31.2	61.2	59.3	62.0	64.3

[1] Civilian employment as percent of civilian noninstitutional population in group specified.
[2] See footnote 1, Table B–23.

Note: Data relate to persons 16 years of age and over, except as noted.
See footnote 5 and Note, Table B–22.

Source: Department of Labor (Bureau of Labor Statistics).

[Percent [1]; monthly data seasonally adjusted]

Year or month	All civilian workers	By sex and age			By race or ethnicity [2]				U-6 measure of labor under-utiliza-tion [3]	By educational attainment (25 years & over)			
		Men 20 years and over	Women 20 years and over	Both sexes 16–19	White	Black or African American	Asian	His-panic or Latino ethnic-ity		Less than a high school diploma	High school gradu-ates, no college	Some college or as-sociate degree	Bach-elor's degree and higher [4]
1975	8.5	6.8	8.0	19.9	7.8	14.8	....	12.2	....	....	....	....	....
1976	7.7	5.9	7.4	19.0	7.0	14.0	....	11.5	....	....	....	....	....
1977	7.1	5.2	7.0	17.8	6.2	14.0	....	10.1	....	....	....	....	....
1978	6.1	4.3	6.0	16.4	5.2	12.8	....	9.1	....	....	....	....	....
1979	5.8	4.2	5.7	16.1	5.1	12.3	....	8.3	....	....	....	....	....
1980	7.1	5.9	6.4	17.8	6.3	14.3	....	10.1	....	....	....	....	....
1981	7.6	6.3	6.8	19.6	6.7	15.6	....	10.4	....	....	....	....	....
1982	9.7	8.8	8.3	23.2	8.6	18.9	....	13.8	....	....	....	....	....
1983	9.6	8.9	8.1	22.4	8.4	19.5	....	13.7	....	....	....	....	....
1984	7.5	6.6	6.8	18.9	6.5	15.9	....	10.7	....	....	....	....	....
1985	7.2	6.2	6.6	18.6	6.2	15.1	....	10.5	....	....	....	....	....
1986	7.0	6.1	6.2	18.3	6.0	14.5	....	10.6	....	....	....	....	....
1987	6.2	5.4	5.4	16.9	5.3	13.0	....	8.8	....	....	....	....	....
1988	5.5	4.8	4.9	15.3	4.7	11.7	....	8.2	....	....	....	....	....
1989	5.3	4.5	4.7	15.0	4.5	11.4	....	8.0	....	....	....	....	....
1990	5.6	5.0	4.9	15.5	4.8	11.4	....	8.2	....	....	....	....	....
1991	6.8	6.4	5.7	18.7	6.1	12.5	....	10.0	....	....	....	....	....
1992	7.5	7.1	6.3	20.1	6.6	14.2	....	11.6	....	11.5	6.8	5.6	3.2
1993	6.9	6.4	5.9	19.0	6.1	13.0	....	10.8	....	10.8	6.3	5.2	2.9
1994	6.1	5.4	5.4	17.6	5.3	11.5	....	9.9	10.9	9.8	5.4	4.5	2.6
1995	5.6	4.8	4.9	17.3	4.9	10.4	....	9.3	10.1	9.0	4.8	4.0	2.4
1996	5.4	4.6	4.8	16.7	4.7	10.5	....	8.9	9.7	8.7	4.7	3.7	2.2
1997	4.9	4.2	4.4	16.0	4.2	10.0	....	7.7	8.9	8.1	4.3	3.3	2.0
1998	4.5	3.7	4.1	14.6	3.9	8.9	....	7.2	8.0	7.1	4.0	3.0	1.8
1999	4.2	3.5	3.8	13.9	3.7	8.0	....	6.4	7.4	6.7	3.5	2.8	1.8
2000	4.0	3.3	3.6	13.1	3.5	7.6	3.6	5.7	7.0	6.3	3.4	2.7	1.7
2001	4.7	4.2	4.1	14.7	4.2	8.6	4.5	6.6	8.1	7.2	4.2	3.3	2.3
2002	5.8	5.3	5.1	16.5	5.1	10.2	5.9	7.5	9.6	8.4	5.3	4.5	2.9
2003	6.0	5.6	5.1	17.5	5.2	10.8	6.0	7.7	10.1	8.8	5.5	4.8	3.1
2004	5.5	5.0	4.9	17.0	4.8	10.4	4.4	7.0	9.6	8.5	5.0	4.2	2.7
2005	5.1	4.4	4.6	16.6	4.4	10.0	4.0	6.0	8.9	7.6	4.7	3.9	2.3
2006	4.6	4.0	4.1	15.4	4.0	8.9	3.0	5.2	8.2	6.8	4.3	3.6	2.0
2007	4.6	4.1	4.0	15.7	4.1	8.3	3.2	5.6	8.3	7.1	4.4	3.6	2.0
2008	5.8	5.4	4.9	18.7	5.2	10.1	4.0	7.6	10.5	9.0	5.7	4.6	2.6
2009	9.3	9.6	7.5	24.3	8.5	14.8	7.3	12.1	16.2	14.6	9.7	8.0	4.6
2010	9.6	9.8	8.0	25.9	8.7	16.0	7.5	12.5	16.7	14.9	10.3	8.4	4.7
2011	8.9	8.7	7.9	24.4	7.9	15.8	7.0	11.5	15.9	14.1	9.4	8.0	4.3
2012	8.1	7.5	7.3	24.0	7.2	13.8	5.9	10.3	14.7	12.4	8.3	7.1	4.0
2013	7.4	7.0	6.5	22.9	6.5	13.1	5.2	9.1	13.8	11.0	7.5	6.4	3.7
2014	6.2	5.7	5.6	19.6	5.3	11.3	5.0	7.4	12.0	9.0	6.0	5.4	3.2
2015	5.3	4.9	4.8	16.9	4.6	9.6	3.8	6.6	10.4	8.0	5.4	4.5	2.6
2016	4.9	4.5	4.4	15.7	4.3	8.4	3.6	5.8	9.6	7.4	5.2	4.1	2.5
2017	4.4	4.0	4.0	14.0	3.8	7.5	3.4	5.1	8.5	6.5	4.6	3.8	2.3
2018	3.9	3.6	3.5	12.9	3.5	6.5	3.0	4.7	7.7	5.6	4.1	3.3	2.1
2019	3.7	3.4	3.3	12.7	3.3	6.1	2.7	4.3	7.2	5.4	3.7	3.0	2.1
2018: Jan	4.1	3.8	3.6	13.7	3.5	7.5	3.0	5.0	8.1	5.4	4.4	3.4	2.1
Feb	4.1	3.7	3.8	14.0	3.7	6.7	2.9	4.9	8.2	5.7	4.4	3.5	2.2
Mar	4.0	3.7	3.7	13.4	3.6	6.8	3.1	5.0	7.9	5.5	4.3	3.5	2.2
Apr	4.0	3.7	3.5	12.8	3.6	6.4	2.8	4.8	7.8	5.8	4.3	3.4	2.1
May	3.8	3.6	3.4	12.8	3.5	5.9	2.2	4.9	7.7	5.5	3.9	3.3	2.0
June	4.0	3.7	3.6	12.6	3.5	6.5	3.2	4.5	7.8	5.5	4.1	3.3	2.3
July	3.8	3.4	3.6	13.0	3.3	6.6	3.1	4.4	7.5	5.2	4.1	3.2	2.2
Aug	3.8	3.5	3.5	12.8	3.4	6.3	3.0	4.7	7.3	5.7	3.9	3.5	2.0
Sept	3.7	3.4	3.3	12.7	3.3	6.2	3.5	4.6	7.5	5.7	3.8	3.2	2.0
Oct	3.8	3.5	3.4	12.2	3.3	6.3	3.1	4.4	7.4	5.9	4.0	3.1	2.0
Nov	3.7	3.3	3.4	12.4	3.4	6.1	2.8	4.5	7.6	5.6	3.5	3.1	2.2
Dec	3.9	3.6	3.5	12.6	3.4	6.6	3.3	4.4	7.6	5.8	3.8	3.3	2.2
2019: Jan	4.0	3.7	3.6	12.9	3.5	6.8	3.1	4.8	8.0	5.7	3.7	3.4	2.4
Feb	3.8	3.5	3.4	13.3	3.3	6.9	3.1	4.3	7.2	5.3	3.7	3.1	2.2
Mar	3.8	3.6	3.3	12.7	3.4	6.6	3.1	4.7	7.3	5.8	3.7	3.4	2.0
Apr	3.6	3.4	3.1	12.9	3.1	6.6	2.2	4.2	7.3	5.3	3.4	3.1	2.1
May	3.6	3.4	3.3	12.6	3.3	6.2	2.5	4.2	7.1	5.4	3.6	2.8	2.1
June	3.7	3.3	3.3	12.7	3.3	6.0	2.1	4.3	7.2	5.3	3.9	3.0	2.1
July	3.7	3.3	3.3	12.7	3.3	5.9	2.8	4.5	7.0	5.2	3.6	3.2	2.1
Aug	3.7	3.3	3.3	12.5	3.4	5.4	2.8	4.2	7.2	5.4	3.6	3.0	2.1
Sept	3.5	3.2	3.1	12.5	3.2	5.5	2.5	3.9	6.9	4.8	3.6	2.9	2.0
Oct	3.6	3.2	3.2	12.3	3.2	5.5	2.8	4.1	6.9	5.5	3.7	2.8	2.1
Nov	3.5	3.2	3.2	12.0	3.2	5.6	2.6	4.2	6.9	5.3	3.7	2.9	2.0
Dec	3.5	3.1	3.2	12.6	3.2	5.9	2.5	4.2	6.7	5.2	3.7	2.7	1.9

[1] Unemployed as percent of civilian labor force in group specified.
[2] See footnote 1, Table B–23.
[3] Total unemployed, plus all persons marginally attached to the labor force, plus total employed part time for economic reasons, as a percent of the civilian labor force plus all persons marginally attached to the labor force.
[4] Includes persons with bachelor's, master's, professional, and doctoral degrees.

Note: Data relate to persons 16 years of age and over, except as noted.
See Note, Table B–22.

Source: Department of Labor (Bureau of Labor Statistics).

Table B–28. Unemployment by duration and reason, 1975–2019

[Thousands of persons, except as noted; monthly data seasonally adjusted [1]]

Year or month	Un-employ-ment	Duration of unemployment						Reason for unemployment					
		Less than 5 weeks	5–14 weeks	15–26 weeks	27 weeks and over	Average (mean) duration (weeks) [2]	Median duration (weeks)	Job losers [3]			Job leavers	Re-entrants	New entrants
								Total	On layoff	Other			
1975	7,929	2,940	2,484	1,303	1,203	14.2	8.4	4,386	1,671	2,714	827	1,892	823
1976	7,406	2,844	2,196	1,018	1,348	15.8	8.2	3,679	1,050	2,628	903	1,928	895
1977	6,991	2,919	2,132	913	1,028	14.3	7.0	3,166	865	2,300	909	1,963	953
1978	6,202	2,865	1,923	766	648	11.9	5.9	2,585	712	1,873	874	1,857	885
1979	6,137	2,950	1,946	706	535	10.8	5.4	2,635	851	1,784	880	1,806	817
1980	7,637	3,295	2,470	1,052	820	11.9	6.5	3,947	1,488	2,459	891	1,927	872
1981	8,273	3,449	2,539	1,122	1,162	13.7	6.9	4,267	1,430	2,837	923	2,102	981
1982	10,678	3,883	3,311	1,708	1,776	15.6	8.7	6,268	2,127	4,141	840	2,384	1,185
1983	10,717	3,570	2,937	1,652	2,559	20.0	10.1	6,258	1,780	4,478	830	2,412	1,216
1984	8,539	3,350	2,451	1,104	1,634	18.2	7.9	4,421	1,171	3,250	823	2,184	1,110
1985	8,312	3,498	2,509	1,025	1,280	15.6	6.8	4,139	1,157	2,982	877	2,256	1,039
1986	8,237	3,448	2,557	1,045	1,187	15.0	6.9	4,033	1,090	2,943	1,015	2,160	1,029
1987	7,425	3,246	2,196	943	1,040	14.5	6.5	3,566	943	2,623	965	1,974	920
1988	6,701	3,084	2,007	801	809	13.5	5.9	3,092	851	2,241	983	1,809	816
1989	6,528	3,174	1,978	730	646	11.9	4.8	2,983	850	2,133	1,024	1,843	677
1990	7,047	3,265	2,257	822	703	12.0	5.3	3,387	1,028	2,359	1,041	1,930	688
1991	8,628	3,480	2,791	1,246	1,111	13.7	6.8	4,694	1,292	3,402	1,004	2,139	792
1992	9,613	3,376	2,830	1,453	1,954	17.7	8.7	5,389	1,260	4,129	1,002	2,285	937
1993	8,940	3,262	2,584	1,297	1,798	18.0	8.3	4,848	1,115	3,733	976	2,198	919
1994	7,996	2,728	2,408	1,237	1,623	18.8	9.2	3,815	977	2,838	791	2,786	604
1995	7,404	2,700	2,342	1,085	1,278	16.6	8.3	3,476	1,030	2,446	824	2,525	579
1996	7,236	2,633	2,287	1,053	1,262	16.7	8.3	3,370	1,021	2,349	774	2,512	580
1997	6,739	2,538	2,138	995	1,067	15.8	8.0	3,037	931	2,106	795	2,338	569
1998	6,210	2,622	1,950	763	875	14.5	6.7	2,822	866	1,957	734	2,132	520
1999	5,880	2,568	1,832	755	725	13.4	6.4	2,622	848	1,774	783	2,005	469
2000	5,692	2,558	1,815	669	649	12.6	5.9	2,517	852	1,664	780	1,961	434
2001	6,801	2,853	2,196	951	801	13.1	6.8	3,476	1,067	2,409	835	2,031	459
2002	8,378	2,893	2,580	1,369	1,535	16.6	9.1	4,607	1,124	3,483	866	2,368	536
2003	8,774	2,785	2,612	1,442	1,936	19.2	10.1	4,838	1,121	3,717	818	2,477	641
2004	8,149	2,696	2,382	1,293	1,779	19.6	9.8	4,197	998	3,199	858	2,408	686
2005	7,591	2,667	2,304	1,130	1,490	18.4	8.9	3,667	933	2,734	872	2,386	666
2006	7,001	2,614	2,121	1,031	1,235	16.8	8.3	3,321	921	2,400	827	2,237	616
2007	7,078	2,542	2,232	1,061	1,243	16.8	8.5	3,515	976	2,539	793	2,142	627
2008	8,924	2,932	2,804	1,427	1,761	17.9	9.4	4,789	1,176	3,614	896	2,472	766
2009	14,265	3,165	3,828	2,775	4,496	24.4	15.1	9,160	1,630	7,530	882	3,187	1,035
2010	14,825	2,771	3,267	2,371	6,415	33.0	21.4	9,250	1,431	7,819	889	3,466	1,220
2011	13,747	2,677	2,993	2,061	6,016	39.3	21.4	8,106	1,230	6,876	956	3,401	1,284
2012	12,506	2,644	2,866	1,859	5,136	39.4	19.3	6,877	1,183	5,694	967	3,345	1,316
2013	11,460	2,584	2,759	1,807	4,310	36.5	17.0	6,073	1,136	4,937	932	3,207	1,247
2014	9,617	2,471	2,432	1,497	3,218	33.7	14.0	4,878	1,007	3,871	824	2,829	1,086
2015	8,296	2,399	2,302	1,267	2,328	29.2	11.6	4,063	974	3,089	819	2,535	879
2016	7,751	2,362	2,226	1,158	2,005	27.5	10.6	3,740	966	2,774	858	2,330	823
2017	6,982	2,270	2,008	1,017	1,687	25.0	10.0	3,434	956	2,479	778	2,079	690
2018	6,314	2,170	1,876	917	1,350	22.7	9.3	2,990	852	2,138	794	1,928	602
2019	6,001	2,086	1,789	860	1,266	21.6	9.1	2,786	823	1,963	814	1,810	591
2018: Jan	6,582	2,255	1,913	955	1,437	24.2	9.6	3,199	889	2,309	725	1,953	634
Feb	6,641	2,412	1,907	918	1,410	23.1	9.2	3,244	885	2,359	778	1,958	691
Mar	6,493	2,257	1,987	889	1,333	24.1	9.0	3,091	850	2,241	867	1,934	599
Apr	6,418	2,139	1,957	1,026	1,316	22.9	9.9	2,999	884	2,115	812	1,984	622
May	6,209	2,021	1,943	993	1,193	21.1	9.4	2,865	771	2,094	841	1,883	571
June	6,519	2,222	1,867	865	1,457	21.2	8.6	3,081	917	2,164	795	2,073	585
July	6,180	2,093	1,810	967	1,417	23.2	10.0	2,978	858	2,119	829	1,802	591
Aug	6,167	2,189	1,755	933	1,321	22.6	9.3	2,843	844	1,999	875	1,856	591
Sept	6,045	2,088	1,747	859	1,372	23.5	9.1	2,864	857	2,007	742	1,907	582
Oct	6,123	2,098	1,832	847	1,363	22.3	9.4	2,876	825	2,050	732	1,925	597
Nov	6,034	2,133	1,820	860	1,263	22.0	8.8	2,849	835	2,014	709	1,897	585
Dec	6,286	2,117	2,007	899	1,311	22.0	9.4	2,892	768	2,123	827	1,968	600
2019: Jan	6,516	2,319	1,999	898	1,259	20.6	9.0	3,060	940	2,120	816	1,944	607
Feb	6,181	2,169	1,809	928	1,279	22.0	9.4	2,863	828	2,036	841	1,902	619
Mar	6,194	2,116	1,812	936	1,305	22.2	9.5	2,826	866	1,959	780	2,002	605
Apr	5,850	1,906	1,835	860	1,227	22.8	9.3	2,660	722	1,938	728	1,899	535
May	5,938	2,158	1,572	822	1,298	24.1	9.1	2,674	865	1,810	809	1,850	602
June	5,985	1,949	1,832	776	1,413	22.1	9.4	2,744	805	1,939	889	1,850	537
July	6,027	2,222	1,795	909	1,170	19.7	9.0	2,796	828	1,968	832	1,794	597
Aug	5,999	2,218	1,746	831	1,251	22.1	9.0	2,864	812	2,052	784	1,785	577
Sept	5,753	1,869	1,778	806	1,318	21.7	9.4	2,575	729	1,846	840	1,669	673
Oct	5,857	1,978	1,747	884	1,259	21.6	9.2	2,691	772	1,919	846	1,698	622
Nov	5,811	2,026	1,753	865	1,219	20.2	9.2	2,804	768	2,036	776	1,663	581
Dec	5,753	2,065	1,730	812	1,186	20.8	9.0	2,686	807	1,880	829	1,655	551

[1] Because of independent seasonal adjustment of the various series, detail will not sum to totals.
[2] Beginning with 2011, includes unemployment durations of up to 5 years; prior data are for up to 2 years.
[3] Beginning with 1994, job losers and persons who completed temporary jobs.

Note: Data relate to persons 16 years of age and over.
See Note, Table B–22.

Source: Department of Labor (Bureau of Labor Statistics).

Table B–29. Employees on nonagricultural payrolls, by major industry, 1975–2019

[Thousands of jobs; monthly data seasonally adjusted]

Year or month	Total non-agricultural employment	Private industries									
		Total private	Goods-producing industries						Private service-providing industries		
			Total	Mining and logging	Construction	Manufacturing			Total	Trade, transportation, and utilities [1]	
						Total	Durable goods	Non-durable goods		Total	Retail trade
1975	77,069	62,250	21,318	802	3,608	16,909	10,266	6,643	40,932	15,583	8,604
1976	79,502	64,501	22,025	832	3,662	17,531	10,640	6,891	42,476	16,105	8,970
1977	82,593	67,334	22,972	865	3,940	18,167	11,132	7,035	44,362	16,741	9,363
1978	86,826	71,014	24,156	902	4,322	18,932	11,770	7,162	46,858	17,633	9,882
1979	89,933	73,865	24,997	1,008	4,562	19,426	12,220	7,206	48,869	18,276	10,185
1980	90,533	74,158	24,263	1,077	4,454	18,733	11,679	7,054	49,895	18,387	10,249
1981	91,297	75,117	24,118	1,180	4,304	18,634	11,611	7,023	50,999	18,577	10,369
1982	89,689	73,706	22,550	1,163	4,024	17,363	10,610	6,753	51,156	18,430	10,377
1983	90,295	74,284	22,110	997	4,065	17,048	10,326	6,722	52,174	18,642	10,640
1984	94,548	78,389	23,435	1,014	4,501	17,920	11,050	6,870	54,954	19,624	11,227
1985	97,532	81,000	23,585	974	4,793	17,819	11,034	6,784	57,415	20,350	11,738
1986	99,500	82,661	23,318	829	4,937	17,552	10,795	6,757	59,343	20,765	12,082
1987	102,116	84,960	23,470	771	5,090	17,609	10,767	6,842	61,490	21,271	12,422
1988	105,378	87,838	23,909	770	5,233	17,906	10,969	6,938	63,929	21,942	12,812
1989	108,051	90,124	24,045	750	5,309	17,985	11,004	6,981	66,079	22,477	13,112
1990	109,527	91,112	23,723	765	5,263	17,695	10,737	6,958	67,389	22,634	13,186
1991	108,427	89,881	22,588	739	4,780	17,068	10,220	6,848	67,293	22,249	12,900
1992	108,802	90,015	22,095	689	4,608	16,799	9,946	6,853	67,921	22,094	12,831
1993	110,935	91,946	22,219	666	4,779	16,774	9,901	6,872	69,727	22,347	13,024
1994	114,399	95,124	22,774	659	5,095	17,020	10,132	6,889	72,350	23,096	13,494
1995	117,407	97,975	23,156	641	5,274	17,241	10,373	6,868	74,819	23,800	13,900
1996	119,836	100,297	23,409	637	5,536	17,237	10,486	6,751	76,888	24,205	14,146
1997	122,951	103,287	23,886	654	5,813	17,419	10,705	6,714	79,401	24,665	14,393
1998	126,157	106,248	24,354	645	6,149	17,560	10,911	6,649	81,894	25,150	14,613
1999	129,240	108,933	24,465	598	6,545	17,322	10,831	6,491	84,468	25,734	14,974
2000	132,024	111,235	24,649	599	6,787	17,263	10,877	6,386	86,585	26,187	15,284
2001	132,087	110,969	23,873	606	6,826	16,441	10,336	6,105	87,096	25,945	15,242
2002	130,649	109,136	22,557	583	6,716	15,259	9,485	5,774	86,579	25,458	15,029
2003	130,347	108,764	21,816	572	6,735	14,509	8,964	5,546	86,948	25,245	14,922
2004	131,787	110,166	21,882	591	6,976	14,315	8,925	5,390	88,284	25,487	15,063
2005	134,051	112,247	22,190	628	7,336	14,227	8,956	5,271	90,057	25,910	15,285
2006	136,453	114,479	22,530	684	7,691	14,155	8,981	5,174	91,949	26,223	15,359
2007	137,999	115,781	22,233	724	7,630	13,879	8,808	5,071	93,548	26,573	15,526
2008	137,241	114,732	21,335	767	7,162	13,406	8,463	4,943	93,398	26,236	15,289
2009	131,313	108,758	18,558	694	6,016	11,847	7,284	4,564	90,201	24,850	14,528
2010	130,362	107,871	17,751	705	5,518	11,528	7,064	4,464	90,121	24,581	14,446
2011	131,932	109,845	18,047	788	5,533	11,726	7,273	4,453	91,798	25,008	14,674
2012	134,175	112,255	18,420	848	5,646	11,927	7,470	4,457	93,835	25,416	14,847
2013	136,381	114,529	18,738	863	5,856	12,020	7,548	4,472	95,791	25,801	15,085
2014	138,958	117,076	19,226	891	6,151	12,185	7,674	4,512	97,850	26,321	15,363
2015	141,843	119,814	19,610	813	6,461	12,336	7,765	4,571	100,204	26,824	15,611
2016	144,352	122,128	19,750	668	6,728	12,354	7,714	4,640	102,379	27,195	15,832
2017	146,624	124,275	20,084	676	6,969	12,439	7,741	4,699	104,191	27,409	15,846
2018	149,074	126,625	20,710	732	7,289	12,689	7,945	4,743	105,916	27,659	15,833
2019 ᵖ	151,404	128,828	21,085	751	7,493	12,841	8,058	4,783	107,743	27,839	15,795
2018: Jan	147,767	125,393	20,386	699	7,126	12,561	7,838	4,723	105,007	27,502	15,809
Feb	148,097	125,697	20,497	706	7,199	12,592	7,865	4,727	105,200	27,560	15,833
Mar	148,279	125,870	20,527	714	7,201	12,612	7,886	4,726	105,343	27,591	15,834
Apr	148,475	126,054	20,587	723	7,230	12,634	7,903	4,731	105,467	27,589	15,838
May	148,745	126,318	20,650	728	7,267	12,655	7,917	4,738	105,668	27,630	15,856
June	149,007	126,554	20,706	735	7,284	12,687	7,944	4,743	105,848	27,622	15,822
July	149,185	126,727	20,744	734	7,303	12,707	7,961	4,746	105,983	27,643	15,824
Aug	149,467	126,973	20,794	742	7,337	12,715	7,973	4,742	106,179	27,693	15,830
Sept	149,575	127,081	20,832	745	7,354	12,733	7,987	4,746	106,249	27,692	15,804
Oct	149,852	127,366	20,892	751	7,379	12,762	8,006	4,756	106,474	27,715	15,794
Nov	150,048	127,566	20,921	748	7,384	12,789	8,022	4,767	106,645	27,783	15,827
Dec	150,275	127,790	20,961	752	7,400	12,809	8,036	4,773	106,829	27,788	15,821
2019: Jan	150,587	128,087	21,041	759	7,456	12,826	8,055	4,771	107,046	27,836	15,830
Feb	150,643	128,133	21,022	755	7,433	12,834	8,060	4,774	107,111	27,827	15,817
Mar	150,796	128,286	21,035	756	7,448	12,831	8,054	4,777	107,251	27,810	15,802
Apr	151,012	128,481	21,072	756	7,482	12,834	8,055	4,779	107,409	27,809	15,787
May	151,074	128,562	21,077	758	7,483	12,836	8,058	4,778	107,485	27,807	15,775
June	151,252	128,723	21,104	756	7,502	12,846	8,067	4,779	107,619	27,815	15,763
July	151,418	128,845	21,100	751	7,499	12,850	8,069	4,781	107,745	27,817	15,761
Aug	151,637	129,008	21,104	746	7,506	12,852	8,067	4,785	107,904	27,809	15,760
Sept	151,830	129,191	21,115	746	7,515	12,854	8,066	4,788	108,076	27,834	15,772
Oct	151,982	129,355	21,086	748	7,529	12,809	8,015	4,794	108,269	27,877	15,802
Nov ᵖ	152,238	129,598	21,138	740	7,531	12,867	8,063	4,804	108,460	27,873	15,788
Dec ᵖ	152,383	129,737	21,137	731	7,551	12,855	8,056	4,799	108,600	27,913	15,830

[1] Includes wholesale trade, transportation and warehousing, and utilities, not shown separately.

Note: Data in Tables B–29 and B–30 are based on reports from employing establishments and relate to full- and part-time wage and salary workers in nonagricultural establishments who received pay for any part of the pay period that includes the 12th of the month. Not comparable with labor force data (Tables B–22 through B–28), which include proprietors, self-employed persons, unpaid family workers, and private household workers; which count persons as

See next page for continuation of table.

Year or month	Private industries—Continued						Government			
	Private service-providing industries—Continued									
	Information	Financial activities	Professional and business services	Education and health services	Leisure and hospitality	Other services	Total	Federal	State	Local
1975	2,061	4,047	6,056	5,497	5,544	2,144	14,820	2,882	3,179	8,758
1976	2,111	4,155	6,310	5,756	5,794	2,244	15,001	2,863	3,273	8,865
1977	2,185	4,348	6,611	6,052	6,065	2,359	15,258	2,859	3,377	9,023
1978	2,287	4,599	6,997	6,427	6,411	2,505	15,812	2,893	3,474	9,446
1979	2,375	4,843	7,339	6,768	6,631	2,637	16,068	2,894	3,541	9,633
1980	2,361	5,025	7,571	7,077	6,721	2,755	16,375	3,000	3,610	9,765
1981	2,382	5,163	7,809	7,364	6,840	2,865	16,180	2,922	3,640	9,619
1982	2,317	5,209	7,875	7,526	6,874	2,924	15,982	2,884	3,640	9,458
1983	2,253	5,334	8,065	7,781	7,078	3,021	16,011	2,915	3,662	9,434
1984	2,398	5,553	8,493	8,211	7,489	3,186	16,159	2,943	3,734	9,482
1985	2,437	5,815	8,900	8,679	7,869	3,366	16,533	3,014	3,832	9,687
1986	2,445	6,128	9,241	9,086	8,156	3,523	16,838	3,044	3,893	9,901
1987	2,507	6,385	9,639	9,543	8,446	3,699	17,156	3,089	3,967	10,100
1988	2,585	6,500	10,121	10,096	8,778	3,907	17,540	3,124	4,076	10,339
1989	2,622	6,562	10,588	10,652	9,062	4,116	17,927	3,136	4,182	10,609
1990	2,688	6,614	10,881	11,024	9,288	4,261	18,415	3,196	4,305	10,914
1991	2,677	6,561	10,746	11,556	9,256	4,249	18,545	3,110	4,355	11,081
1992	2,641	6,559	11,001	11,948	9,437	4,240	18,787	3,111	4,408	11,267
1993	2,668	6,742	11,527	12,362	9,732	4,350	18,989	3,063	4,488	11,438
1994	2,738	6,910	12,207	12,872	10,100	4,428	19,275	3,018	4,576	11,682
1995	2,843	6,866	12,878	13,360	10,501	4,572	19,432	2,949	4,635	11,849
1996	2,940	7,018	13,497	13,761	10,777	4,690	19,539	2,877	4,606	12,056
1997	3,084	7,255	14,371	14,185	11,018	4,825	19,664	2,806	4,582	12,276
1998	3,218	7,565	15,183	14,570	11,232	4,976	19,909	2,772	4,612	12,525
1999	3,419	7,753	15,994	14,939	11,543	5,087	20,307	2,769	4,709	12,829
2000	3,630	7,783	16,704	15,252	11,862	5,168	20,790	2,865	4,786	13,139
2001	3,629	7,900	16,514	15,814	12,036	5,258	21,118	2,764	4,905	13,449
2002	3,395	7,956	16,016	16,398	11,986	5,372	21,513	2,766	5,029	13,718
2003	3,188	8,078	16,029	16,835	12,173	5,401	21,583	2,761	5,002	13,820
2004	3,118	8,105	16,440	17,230	12,493	5,409	21,621	2,730	4,982	13,909
2005	3,061	8,197	17,003	17,676	12,816	5,395	21,804	2,732	5,032	14,041
2006	3,038	8,367	17,619	18,154	13,110	5,438	21,974	2,732	5,075	14,167
2007	3,032	8,348	17,998	18,676	13,427	5,494	22,218	2,734	5,122	14,362
2008	2,984	8,206	17,792	19,228	13,436	5,515	22,509	2,762	5,177	14,571
2009	2,804	7,838	16,634	19,630	13,077	5,367	22,555	2,832	5,169	14,554
2010	2,707	7,695	16,783	19,975	13,049	5,331	22,490	2,977	5,137	14,376
2011	2,674	7,697	17,389	20,318	13,353	5,360	22,086	2,859	5,078	14,150
2012	2,676	7,784	17,992	20,769	13,768	5,430	21,920	2,820	5,055	14,045
2013	2,706	7,886	18,575	21,086	14,254	5,483	21,853	2,769	5,046	14,037
2014	2,726	7,977	19,124	21,439	14,696	5,567	21,882	2,733	5,050	14,098
2015	2,750	8,123	19,695	22,029	15,160	5,622	22,029	2,757	5,077	14,195
2016	2,794	8,287	20,114	22,639	15,660	5,691	22,224	2,795	5,110	14,319
2017	2,814	8,451	20,508	23,188	16,051	5,770	22,350	2,805	5,165	14,379
2018	2,828	8,569	20,999	23,667	16,348	5,845	22,449	2,796	5,176	14,477
2019 ᵖ	2,824	8,676	21,462	24,270	16,741	5,932	22,576	2,820	5,184	14,573
2018: Jan	2,812	8,502	20,730	23,445	16,208	5,808	22,374	2,795	5,147	14,432
Feb	2,812	8,528	20,774	23,481	16,233	5,812	22,400	2,792	5,155	14,453
Mar	2,824	8,537	20,816	23,518	16,244	5,813	22,409	2,792	5,160	14,457
Apr	2,829	8,541	20,878	23,542	16,262	5,826	22,421	2,793	5,169	14,459
May	2,831	8,556	20,929	23,581	16,300	5,841	22,427	2,793	5,168	14,466
June	2,831	8,567	20,980	23,646	16,343	5,859	22,453	2,795	5,178	14,480
July	2,832	8,572	21,017	23,694	16,378	5,847	22,458	2,796	5,179	14,483
Aug	2,826	8,583	21,075	23,754	16,395	5,853	22,494	2,796	5,190	14,508
Sept	2,822	8,597	21,128	23,779	16,371	5,860	22,494	2,797	5,204	14,493
Oct	2,832	8,611	21,183	23,816	16,450	5,867	22,486	2,798	5,197	14,491
Nov	2,829	8,614	21,217	23,845	16,489	5,868	22,482	2,804	5,180	14,498
Dec	2,827	8,615	21,254	23,912	16,554	5,879	22,485	2,798	5,183	14,504
2019: Jan	2,815	8,621	21,259	23,980	16,647	5,888	22,500	2,797	5,184	14,519
Feb	2,808	8,626	21,313	23,999	16,646	5,892	22,510	2,804	5,186	14,520
Mar	2,812	8,637	21,332	24,071	16,678	5,911	22,510	2,803	5,184	14,523
Apr	2,806	8,651	21,387	24,142	16,687	5,927	22,531	2,810	5,176	14,545
May	2,815	8,656	21,408	24,176	16,699	5,924	22,512	2,815	5,159	14,538
June	2,828	8,659	21,451	24,224	16,703	5,939	22,529	2,817	5,165	14,547
July	2,826	8,678	21,488	24,300	16,690	5,946	22,573	2,817	5,182	14,574
Aug	2,822	8,695	21,526	24,363	16,738	5,951	22,629	2,844	5,191	14,594
Sept	2,828	8,701	21,553	24,420	16,794	5,946	22,639	2,846	5,190	14,603
Oct	2,828	8,717	21,588	24,451	16,864	5,944	22,627	2,828	5,191	14,608
Nov ᵖ	2,836	8,731	21,641	24,523	16,902	5,954	22,640	2,826	5,193	14,621
Dec ᵖ	2,839	8,737	21,651	24,559	16,942	5,959	22,646	2,826	5,185	14,635

Note (cont'd): employed when they are not at work because of industrial disputes, bad weather, etc., even if they are not paid for the time off; which are based on a sample of the working-age population; and which count persons only once—as employed, unemployed, or not in the labor force. In the data shown here, persons who work at more than one job are counted each time they appear on a payroll.

Establishment data for employment, hours, and earnings are classified based on the 2017 North American Industry Classification System (NAICS). For further description and details see *Employment and Earnings*.

Source: Department of Labor (Bureau of Labor Statistics).

TABLE B–30. Hours and earnings in private nonagricultural industries, 1975–2019

[Monthly data seasonally adjusted]

Year or month	All employees							Production and nonsupervisory employees [1]						
	Average weekly hours	Average hourly earnings		Average weekly earnings				Average weekly hours	Average hourly earnings		Average weekly earnings			
				Level		Percent change from year earlier					Level		Percent change from year earlier	
		Current dollars	1982–84 dollars [2]	Current dollars	1982–84 dollars [2]	Current dollars	1982–84 dollars [2]		Current dollars	1982–84 dollars [3]	Current dollars	1982–84 dollars [3]	Current dollars	1982–84 dollars [3]
1975	....	....	....	....	....	....	....	36.0	$4.74	$8.76	$170.45	$315.06	5.4	–3.4
1976	....	....	....	....	....	....	....	36.0	5.06	8.85	182.36	318.81	7.0	1.2
1977	....	....	....	....	....	....	....	35.9	5.44	8.93	195.34	320.76	7.1	.6
1978	....	....	....	....	....	....	....	35.8	5.88	8.96	210.17	320.38	7.6	–.1
1979	....	....	....	....	....	....	....	35.6	6.34	8.67	225.46	308.43	7.3	–3.7
1980	....	....	....	....	....	....	....	35.2	6.84	8.25	240.83	290.51	6.8	–5.8
1981	....	....	....	....	....	....	....	35.2	7.43	8.13	261.29	285.88	8.5	–1.6
1982	....	....	....	....	....	....	....	34.7	7.86	8.11	272.98	281.71	4.5	–1.5
1983	....	....	....	....	....	....	....	34.9	8.20	8.22	286.34	286.91	4.9	1.8
1984	....	....	....	....	....	....	....	35.1	8.49	8.22	298.08	288.56	4.1	.6
1985	....	....	....	....	....	....	....	34.9	8.73	8.17	304.37	284.72	2.1	–1.3
1986	....	....	....	....	....	....	....	34.7	8.92	8.21	309.69	285.17	1.7	.2
1987	....	....	....	....	....	....	....	34.7	9.14	8.12	317.33	282.07	2.5	–1.1
1988	....	....	....	....	....	....	....	34.6	9.44	8.07	326.50	279.06	2.9	–1.1
1989	....	....	....	....	....	....	....	34.5	9.81	8.00	338.42	276.04	3.7	–1.1
1990	....	....	....	....	....	....	....	34.3	10.20	7.91	349.63	271.03	3.3	–1.8
1991	....	....	....	....	....	....	....	34.1	10.51	7.83	358.46	266.91	2.5	–1.5
1992	....	....	....	....	....	....	....	34.2	10.77	7.79	368.20	266.43	2.7	–.2
1993	....	....	....	....	....	....	....	34.3	11.05	7.78	378.89	266.64	2.9	.1
1994	....	....	....	....	....	....	....	34.5	11.34	7.79	391.17	268.66	3.2	.8
1995	....	....	....	....	....	....	....	34.3	11.65	7.78	400.04	267.05	2.3	–.6
1996	....	....	....	....	....	....	....	34.3	12.04	7.81	413.25	268.17	3.3	.4
1997	....	....	....	....	....	....	....	34.5	12.51	7.94	431.86	274.02	4.5	2.2
1998	....	....	....	....	....	....	....	34.5	13.01	8.15	448.59	280.90	3.9	2.5
1999	....	....	....	....	....	....	....	34.3	13.49	8.27	463.15	283.79	3.2	1.0
2000	....	....	....	....	....	....	....	34.3	14.02	8.30	480.99	284.78	3.9	.3
2001	....	....	....	....	....	....	....	33.9	14.54	8.38	493.61	284.50	2.6	–.1
2002	....	....	....	....	....	....	....	33.9	14.96	8.50	506.54	287.97	2.6	1.2
2003	....	....	....	....	....	....	....	33.7	15.37	8.55	517.76	287.96	2.2	.0
2004	....	....	....	....	....	....	....	33.7	15.68	8.50	528.84	286.63	2.1	–.5
2005	....	....	....	....	....	....	....	33.8	16.12	8.44	544.02	284.83	2.9	–.6
2006	....	....	....	....	....	....	....	33.9	16.75	8.50	567.09	287.72	4.2	1.0
2007	34.4	$20.92	$10.09	$719.85	$347.18	....	....	33.8	17.42	8.59	589.18	290.57	3.9	1.0
2008	34.3	21.56	10.01	739.02	343.25	2.7	–1.1	33.6	18.06	8.56	607.42	287.80	3.1	–1.0
2009	33.8	22.17	10.33	749.98	349.58	1.5	1.8	33.1	18.61	8.68	615.96	293.83	1.4	2.1
2010	34.1	22.56	10.35	769.63	352.95	2.6	1.0	33.4	19.05	8.90	636.19	297.33	3.3	1.2
2011	34.3	23.03	10.24	790.85	351.58	2.8	–.4	33.6	19.44	8.77	652.89	294.66	2.6	–.9
2012	34.5	23.49	10.23	809.57	352.61	2.4	.3	33.7	19.74	8.73	665.65	294.24	2.0	–.1
2013	34.4	23.96	10.29	825.02	354.15	1.9	.4	33.7	20.13	8.78	677.70	295.52	1.8	.4
2014	34.5	24.47	10.34	844.91	356.90	2.4	.8	33.7	20.61	8.85	694.85	298.51	2.5	1.0
2015	34.5	25.02	10.56	864.21	364.62	2.3	2.2	33.7	21.03	9.07	708.90	305.81	2.0	2.4
2016	34.4	25.64	10.68	881.20	367.16	2.0	.7	33.6	21.54	9.20	723.31	309.01	2.0	1.0
2017	34.4	26.33	10.74	906.30	369.74	2.8	.7	33.7	22.06	9.23	742.62	310.65	2.7	.5
2018	34.5	27.11	10.80	936.06	372.77	3.3	.8	33.8	22.71	9.26	767.08	312.91	3.3	.7
2019 p	34.4	27.95	10.93	961.42	376.06	2.7	.9	33.6	23.48	9.42	789.35	316.73	2.9	1.2
2018: Jan	34.4	26.71	10.73	918.82	369.18	2.8	.7	33.6	22.36	9.20	751.30	309.16	2.5	.3
Feb	34.5	26.75	10.73	922.88	370.09	3.2	.9	33.8	22.40	9.20	757.12	310.89	3.1	.7
Mar	34.5	26.84	10.76	925.98	371.14	3.4	1.0	33.7	22.49	9.23	757.91	311.19	3.4	.9
Apr	34.5	26.90	10.76	928.05	371.29	3.1	.7	33.8	22.55	9.24	762.19	312.38	3.1	.5
May	34.5	26.99	10.77	931.16	371.50	3.2	.5	33.8	22.62	9.24	764.56	312.45	3.5	.6
June	34.5	27.05	10.77	933.23	371.61	3.2	.4	33.8	22.67	9.24	766.25	312.44	3.2	.1
July	34.5	27.11	10.78	935.30	371.75	3.1	.2	33.8	22.71	9.24	767.60	312.45	3.2	.0
Aug	34.5	27.23	10.81	939.44	372.97	3.5	.8	33.8	22.80	9.27	770.64	313.24	3.7	.8
Sept	34.5	27.30	10.83	941.85	373.74	3.6	1.3	33.7	22.86	9.29	770.38	313.13	3.3	1.0
Oct	34.5	27.35	10.82	943.58	373.26	3.6	1.1	33.7	22.90	9.27	771.73	312.56	3.2	.6
Nov	34.4	27.43	10.85	943.59	373.31	3.0	.8	33.7	22.99	9.32	774.76	314.08	3.4	1.2
Dec	34.5	27.53	10.89	949.79	375.82	3.3	1.4	33.7	23.09	9.37	778.13	315.86	3.2	1.4
2019: Jan	34.5	27.56	10.91	950.82	376.30	3.5	1.9	33.8	23.11	9.39	781.12	317.33	4.0	2.6
Feb	34.4	27.66	10.93	951.50	375.92	3.1	1.6	33.6	23.17	9.39	778.51	315.56	2.8	1.5
Mar	34.5	27.71	10.90	956.00	376.16	3.2	1.4	33.7	23.25	9.38	783.53	316.12	3.4	1.6
Apr	34.4	27.75	10.88	954.60	374.41	2.9	.8	33.6	23.30	9.37	782.88	314.76	2.7	.8
May	34.4	27.82	10.90	957.01	375.07	2.8	1.0	33.6	23.38	9.40	785.57	315.74	2.7	1.1
June	34.4	27.91	10.93	960.10	376.06	2.9	1.2	33.6	23.43	9.42	787.25	316.39	2.7	1.3
July	34.3	27.99	10.93	960.06	374.79	2.6	.8	33.5	23.51	9.41	787.59	315.35	2.6	.9
Aug	34.4	28.11	10.97	966.98	377.28	2.9	1.2	33.6	23.60	9.45	792.96	317.42	2.9	1.3
Sept	34.4	28.12	10.97	967.33	377.34	2.7	1.0	33.6	23.67	9.48	795.31	318.45	3.2	1.7
Oct	34.3	28.20	10.96	967.26	375.97	2.5	.7	33.5	23.73	9.46	794.96	316.99	3.0	1.4
Nov p	34.3	28.29	10.97	970.35	376.20	2.8	.8	33.5	23.77	9.46	796.30	316.76	2.8	.9
Dec p	34.3	28.32	10.96	971.38	375.77	2.3	.0	33.5	23.79	9.44	796.97	316.17	2.4	.1

[1] Production employees in goods-producing industries and nonsupervisory employees in service-providing industries. These groups account for four-fifths of the total employment on private nonfarm payrolls.

[2] Current dollars divided by the consumer price index for all urban consumers (CPI-U) on a 1982–84=100 base.

[3] Current dollars divided by the consumer price index for urban wage earners and clerical workers (CPI-W) on a 1982–84=100 base.

Note: See Note, Table B–29.

Source: Department of Labor (Bureau of Labor Statistics).

Table B–31. Employment cost index, private industry, 2002–2019

Year and month	Total private			Goods-producing			Service-providing[1]			Manufacturing		
	Total compensation	Wages and salaries	Benefits[2]	Total compensation	Wages and salaries	Benefits[2]	Total compensation	Wages and salaries	Benefits[2]	Total compensation	Wages and salaries	Benefits[2]
	Indexes on NAICS basis, December 2005=100; not seasonally adjusted											
December:												
2002	90.0	92.2	84.7	89.0	92.6	82.3	90.4	92.1	85.8	88.7	92.8	81.3
2003	93.6	95.1	90.2	92.6	94.9	88.2	94.0	95.2	91.0	92.4	95.1	87.3
2004	97.2	97.6	96.2	96.9	97.2	96.3	97.3	97.7	96.1	96.9	97.4	96.0
2005	100.0	100.0	100.0	100.0	100.0	100.0	100.0	100.0	100.0	100.0	100.0	100.0
2006	103.2	103.2	103.1	102.5	102.9	101.7	103.4	103.3	103.7	101.8	102.3	100.8
2007	106.3	106.6	105.6	105.0	106.0	103.2	106.7	106.8	106.6	103.8	104.9	101.7
2008	108.9	109.4	107.7	107.5	109.0	104.7	109.4	109.6	108.9	105.9	107.7	102.5
2009	110.2	110.8	108.7	108.6	110.0	105.8	110.8	111.1	109.9	107.0	108.9	103.6
2010	112.5	112.8	111.9	111.1	111.6	110.1	113.0	113.1	112.6	110.0	110.7	108.8
2011	115.0	114.6	115.9	113.8	113.5	114.4	115.3	114.9	116.4	113.1	112.7	113.9
2012	117.1	116.6	118.2	115.6	115.4	116.0	117.6	117.0	119.1	114.9	114.8	115.0
2013	119.4	119.0	120.5	117.7	117.6	118.0	120.0	119.4	121.5	117.0	117.2	116.6
2014	122.2	121.6	123.5	120.3	120.1	120.7	122.8	122.1	124.6	119.8	119.8	119.8
2015	124.5	124.2	125.1	123.2	123.2	123.1	124.9	124.5	125.9	122.8	123.0	122.5
2016	127.2	127.1	127.3	125.8	126.2	124.9	127.7	127.4	128.3	125.5	126.2	124.3
2017	130.5	130.6	130.2	128.9	129.3	128.0	131.0	131.0	131.2	128.9	129.3	128.0
2018	134.4	134.7	133.6	131.9	133.0	129.6	135.2	135.2	135.1	131.6	132.9	129.1
2019	138.0	138.7	136.2	135.8	137.5	132.5	138.7	139.1	137.6	135.3	137.1	131.9
2019: Mar	135.6	135.9	134.7	133.1	134.2	130.8	136.3	136.4	136.1	132.9	134.2	130.5
June	136.4	136.9	135.3	134.1	135.3	131.6	137.1	137.3	136.7	133.8	135.2	131.1
Sept	137.4	138.0	135.8	135.1	136.5	132.3	138.1	138.4	137.2	134.5	136.1	131.7
Dec	138.0	138.7	136.2	135.8	137.5	132.5	138.7	139.1	137.6	135.3	137.1	131.9
	Indexes on NAICS basis, December 2005=100; seasonally adjusted											
2018: Mar	131.9	132.0	131.5	129.9	130.4	129.0	132.5	132.4	132.6	129.9	130.4	129.1
June	132.7	132.8	132.7	130.8	131.3	129.7	133.4	133.2	133.9	130.7	131.2	129.7
Sept	133.7	133.9	133.2	131.2	132.2	129.2	134.5	134.4	134.7	130.9	132.0	128.8
Dec	134.6	134.9	133.9	131.9	133.1	129.6	135.4	135.4	135.5	131.7	133.0	129.2
2019: Mar	135.5	135.9	134.6	133.1	134.2	130.8	136.2	136.4	136.0	132.9	134.2	130.4
June	136.2	136.7	135.1	134.0	135.2	131.6	137.0	137.2	136.5	133.7	135.1	131.1
Sept	137.3	137.9	135.8	135.1	136.5	132.2	138.0	138.3	137.2	134.5	136.1	131.6
Dec	138.2	138.9	136.5	135.9	137.6	132.5	138.9	139.3	138.0	135.4	137.3	131.9
	Percent change from 12 months earlier, not seasonally adjusted											
December:												
2002	3.1	2.6	4.2	3.5	2.9	4.8	3.0	2.6	4.1	3.7	2.9	5.3
2003	4.0	3.1	6.5	4.0	2.5	7.2	4.0	3.4	6.1	4.2	2.5	7.4
2004	3.8	2.6	6.7	4.6	2.4	9.2	3.5	2.6	5.6	4.9	2.4	10.0
2005	2.9	2.5	4.0	3.2	2.9	3.8	2.8	2.4	4.1	3.2	2.7	4.2
2006	3.2	3.2	3.1	2.5	2.9	1.7	3.4	3.3	3.7	1.8	2.3	.8
2007	3.0	3.3	2.4	2.4	3.0	1.5	3.2	3.4	2.8	2.0	2.5	.9
2008	2.4	2.6	2.0	2.4	2.8	1.5	2.5	2.6	2.2	2.0	2.7	.8
2009	1.2	1.3	.9	1.0	.9	1.1	1.3	1.4	.9	1.0	1.1	1.1
2010	2.1	1.8	2.9	2.3	1.5	4.1	2.0	1.8	2.5	2.8	1.7	5.0
2011	2.2	1.6	3.6	2.4	1.7	3.9	2.0	1.6	3.4	2.8	1.8	4.7
2012	1.8	1.7	2.0	1.6	1.7	1.4	2.0	1.8	2.3	1.6	1.9	1.0
2013	2.0	2.1	1.9	1.8	1.9	1.7	2.0	2.1	2.0	1.8	2.1	1.4
2014	2.3	2.2	2.5	2.2	2.1	2.3	2.3	2.3	2.6	2.4	2.2	2.7
2015	1.9	2.1	1.3	2.4	2.6	2.0	1.7	2.0	1.0	2.5	2.7	2.3
2016	2.2	2.3	1.8	2.1	2.4	1.5	2.2	2.3	1.9	2.2	2.6	1.5
2017	2.6	2.8	2.3	2.5	2.5	2.5	2.6	2.8	2.3	2.7	2.5	3.0
2018	3.0	3.1	2.6	2.3	2.9	1.3	3.2	3.2	3.0	2.1	2.8	.9
2019	2.7	3.0	1.9	3.0	3.4	2.2	2.6	2.9	1.9	2.8	3.2	2.2
2019: Mar	2.8	3.0	2.4	2.5	2.9	1.4	2.8	2.9	2.6	2.2	2.9	1.1
June	2.6	3.0	1.8	2.4	3.0	1.4	2.7	3.0	1.9	2.3	3.0	1.0
Sept	2.7	3.0	2.0	3.0	3.3	2.3	2.6	2.9	1.9	2.8	3.1	2.2
Dec	2.7	3.0	1.9	3.0	3.4	2.2	2.6	2.9	1.9	2.8	3.2	2.2
	Percent change from 3 months earlier, seasonally adjusted											
2018: Mar	0.9	0.9	0.8	0.7	0.7	0.8	0.9	0.9	0.8	0.7	0.7	0.8
June	.6	.6	.9	.7	.7	.5	.7	.6	1.0	.6	.6	.5
Sept	.8	.8	.4	.3	.7	–.4	.8	.9	.6	.2	.6	–.7
Dec	.7	.7	.5	.5	.7	.3	.7	.7	.6	.6	.8	.3
2019: Mar	.7	.7	.5	.9	.8	.9	.6	.7	.4	.9	.9	.9
June	.5	.6	.4	.7	.7	.6	.6	.6	.4	.6	.7	.5
Sept	.8	.9	.5	.8	1.0	.5	.7	.8	.5	.6	.7	.4
Dec	.7	.7	.5	.6	.8	.2	.7	.7	.6	.7	.9	.2

[1] On Standard Industrial Classification (SIC) basis, data are for service-producing industries.
[2] Employer costs for employee benefits.

Note: Changes effective with the release of March 2006 data (in April 2006) include changing industry classification to NAICS from SIC and rebasing data to December 2005=100. Historical SIC data are available through December 2005.
Data exclude farm and household workers.

Source: Department of Labor (Bureau of Labor Statistics).

[Index numbers, 2012=100; quarterly data seasonally adjusted]

Year or quarter	Labor productivity (output per hour) Business sector	Labor productivity (output per hour) Nonfarm business sector	Output[1] Business sector	Output[1] Nonfarm business sector	Hours of all persons[2] Business sector	Hours of all persons[2] Nonfarm business sector	Compensation per hour[3] Business sector	Compensation per hour[3] Nonfarm business sector	Real compensation per hour[4] Business sector	Real compensation per hour[4] Nonfarm business sector	Unit labor costs Business sector	Unit labor costs Nonfarm business sector	Implicit price deflator[5] Business sector	Implicit price deflator[5] Nonfarm business sector
1970	42.2	43.5	26.8	26.8	63.6	61.7	12.1	12.2	65.2	65.9	28.6	28.0	24.9	24.5
1971	43.9	45.2	27.9	27.8	63.4	61.5	12.8	12.9	66.2	67.0	29.1	28.6	26.0	25.6
1972	45.4	46.8	29.7	29.7	65.3	63.5	13.6	13.8	68.2	69.1	30.0	29.5	26.9	26.4
1973	46.8	48.2	31.7	31.8	67.9	66.1	14.7	14.8	69.3	70.0	31.4	30.8	28.3	27.3
1974	46.0	47.4	31.2	31.4	68.0	66.1	16.0	16.2	68.2	69.0	34.9	34.2	31.1	30.2
1975	47.6	48.7	31.0	30.9	65.0	63.3	17.8	17.9	69.2	69.9	37.3	36.8	34.1	33.4
1976	49.2	50.4	33.0	33.1	67.2	65.6	19.2	19.3	70.7	71.2	39.0	38.4	35.8	35.2
1977	50.1	51.3	34.9	35.0	69.8	68.2	20.7	20.9	71.7	72.4	41.4	40.8	38.0	37.4
1978	50.7	52.0	37.2	37.3	73.3	71.7	22.5	22.7	72.6	73.4	44.3	43.7	40.6	39.8
1979	50.7	51.9	38.5	38.6	75.8	74.3	24.6	24.9	72.7	73.5	48.6	47.9	44.0	43.1
1980	50.7	51.9	38.1	38.2	75.2	73.7	27.3	27.6	72.4	72.4	53.8	53.1	47.9	47.2
1981	51.8	52.7	39.2	39.1	75.7	74.3	29.9	30.2	72.4	73.3	57.6	57.4	52.3	51.8
1982	51.6	52.2	38.1	37.9	73.9	72.5	32.1	32.4	73.4	74.2	62.2	62.1	55.3	55.0
1983	53.3	54.4	40.1	40.3	75.3	74.0	33.5	33.9	73.5	74.3	62.8	62.3	57.3	56.9
1984	54.8	55.6	43.7	43.7	79.7	78.5	35.0	35.3	73.7	74.4	63.8	63.6	58.9	58.5
1985	56.1	56.6	45.7	45.6	81.5	80.6	36.8	37.1	74.9	75.5	65.5	65.5	60.4	60.2
1986	57.7	58.3	47.4	47.3	82.2	81.2	38.8	39.2	77.8	78.5	67.4	67.3	61.3	61.1
1987	58.0	58.6	49.1	49.0	84.6	83.7	40.3	40.7	78.0	78.7	69.5	69.4	62.4	62.2
1988	58.9	59.5	51.2	51.3	87.0	86.1	42.4	42.8	79.3	79.9	72.1	71.8	64.4	64.1
1989	59.6	60.1	53.2	53.1	89.3	88.4	43.7	44.0	78.3	78.8	73.4	73.2	66.8	66.5
1990	60.8	61.1	54.0	53.9	88.9	88.3	46.5	46.7	79.3	79.6	76.5	76.3	69.0	68.7
1991	61.7	62.1	53.7	53.6	87.0	86.3	48.6	48.9	80.0	80.4	78.8	78.7	71.0	70.9
1992	64.6	64.9	56.0	55.8	86.6	85.9	51.6	51.9	82.9	83.4	79.9	80.0	72.1	72.1
1993	64.7	65.0	57.6	57.5	89.0	88.5	52.4	52.6	82.0	82.3	81.0	80.9	73.8	73.8
1994	65.0	65.4	60.3	60.1	92.8	91.9	52.8	53.1	80.9	81.4	81.1	81.1	75.1	75.1
1995	65.5	66.1	62.2	62.2	94.9	94.0	54.0	54.4	80.9	81.5	82.5	82.2	76.5	76.5
1996	67.1	67.5	65.1	65.0	97.0	96.2	56.0	56.3	81.7	82.1	83.4	83.3	77.7	77.5
1997	68.6	68.8	68.5	68.4	99.9	99.3	58.2	58.5	83.2	83.5	84.9	84.9	78.8	78.9
1998	70.7	71.0	72.0	72.0	101.9	101.4	61.7	61.9	86.9	87.2	87.2	87.2	79.3	79.4
1999	73.5	73.7	76.1	76.1	103.5	103.3	64.6	64.7	89.2	89.3	87.9	87.9	79.8	80.0
2000	76.1	76.1	79.8	79.7	104.9	104.7	69.1	69.3	92.3	92.4	90.9	91.0	81.0	81.3
2001	78.2	78.2	80.4	80.3	102.8	102.7	72.3	72.3	93.8	93.8	92.5	92.4	82.3	82.6
2002	81.5	81.6	81.8	81.7	100.3	100.1	73.9	74.0	94.4	94.5	90.7	90.7	82.9	83.3
2003	84.7	84.7	84.5	84.3	99.7	99.6	76.7	76.7	95.8	95.8	90.5	90.6	83.9	84.2
2004	87.3	87.1	88.1	87.9	100.9	100.9	80.3	80.2	97.6	97.6	92.0	92.1	86.1	86.2
2005	89.2	89.0	91.5	91.3	102.6	102.6	83.2	83.1	97.9	97.8	93.2	93.4	88.7	89.1
2006	90.3	90.0	94.6	94.4	104.8	104.9	86.4	86.3	98.4	98.4	95.7	95.9	91.1	91.6
2007	91.7	91.6	96.8	96.7	105.5	105.6	90.3	90.1	100.0	99.8	98.4	98.4	93.2	93.4
2008	92.7	92.6	95.8	95.7	103.3	103.4	92.8	92.7	99.0	98.9	100.0	100.1	94.7	94.9
2009	96.1	95.9	92.3	92.0	96.0	96.0	93.6	93.5	100.2	100.2	97.4	97.5	94.9	95.4
2010	99.3	99.2	95.2	95.0	95.9	95.8	95.3	95.3	100.4	100.4	95.9	96.1	96.0	96.3
2011	99.2	99.2	97.1	96.9	97.8	97.8	97.3	97.4	99.4	99.5	98.1	98.2	98.2	98.2
2012	100.0	100.0	100.0	100.0	100.0	100.0	100.0	100.0	100.0	100.0	100.0	100.0	100.0	100.0
2013	100.9	100.5	102.4	102.2	101.5	101.7	101.5	101.3	100.0	99.8	100.6	100.8	101.5	101.5
2014	101.6	101.4	105.6	105.4	103.9	104.0	104.1	104.1	100.9	100.9	102.5	102.7	103.1	103.3
2015	102.9	102.7	109.4	109.1	106.3	106.2	107.1	107.3	103.6	103.8	104.1	104.5	103.7	104.1
2016	103.2	103.0	111.3	111.0	107.9	107.8	108.3	108.5	103.4	103.6	105.0	105.4	104.5	105.1
2017	104.6	104.4	114.4	114.2	109.4	109.4	112.1	112.3	104.8	105.0	107.2	107.6	106.3	106.9
2018	106.0	105.7	118.3	118.1	111.7	111.8	115.7	115.8	105.6	105.7	109.2	109.5	108.7	109.3
2016: I	102.7	102.6	110.3	110.1	107.4	107.3	107.5	107.7	103.6	103.8	104.6	105.0	103.7	104.2
II	102.8	102.7	110.9	110.6	107.9	107.7	107.7	108.0	103.1	103.4	104.7	105.2	104.4	105.0
III	103.3	103.1	111.6	111.3	108.1	107.9	108.3	108.6	103.2	103.4	104.9	105.3	104.8	105.4
IV	103.9	103.6	112.3	112.0	108.1	108.2	109.7	109.7	103.8	103.9	105.6	106.0	105.2	105.9
2017: I	104.0	103.8	113.1	112.7	108.7	108.6	110.7	110.9	104.0	104.2	106.4	106.8	105.6	106.2
II	104.2	103.9	113.8	113.5	109.2	109.2	111.2	111.4	104.5	104.6	106.8	107.2	105.9	106.5
III	105.0	104.7	114.9	114.7	109.4	109.5	112.6	112.7	105.2	105.2	107.2	107.6	106.5	107.0
IV	105.1	104.9	116.1	115.8	110.5	110.4	113.8	114.1	105.5	105.7	108.3	108.7	107.2	107.8
2018: I	105.4	105.2	116.9	116.7	110.9	110.9	115.1	115.2	105.9	106.0	109.2	109.6	107.7	108.3
II	106.0	105.7	118.0	117.8	111.3	111.5	115.4	115.3	105.5	105.5	108.8	109.1	108.7	109.3
III	106.3	106.0	119.0	118.8	112.0	112.1	116.1	116.1	105.7	105.7	109.3	109.6	109.1	109.7
IV	106.3	106.0	119.4	119.2	112.4	112.4	116.2	116.4	105.4	105.5	109.4	109.8	109.4	110.0
2019: I	107.2	106.9	120.6	120.4	112.5	112.6	118.9	119.0	107.6	107.6	110.9	111.3	109.4	110.0
II	107.9	107.6	121.2	120.9	112.3	112.4	119.7	119.7	107.6	107.5	110.9	111.3	110.2	110.9
III	107.9	107.5	121.9	121.6	113.0	113.1	120.4	120.4	107.7	107.7	111.6	112.0	110.5	111.2

[1] Output refers to real gross domestic product in the sector.
[2] Hours at work of all persons engaged in sector, including hours of employees, proprietors, and unpaid family workers. Estimates based primarily on establishment data.
[3] Wages and salaries of employees plus employers' contributions for social insurance and private benefit plans. Also includes an estimate of wages, salaries, and supplemental payments for the self-employed.
[4] Hourly compensation divided by consumer price series. The trend for 1978-2018 is based on the consumer price index research series (CPI-U-RS). The change for prior years and recent quarters is based on the consumer price index for all urban consumers (CPI-U).
[5] Current dollar output divided by the output index.

Source: Department of Labor (Bureau of Labor Statistics).

TABLE B–33. Changes in productivity and related data, business and nonfarm business sectors, 1970–2019

[Percent change from preceding period; quarterly data at seasonally adjusted annual rates]

Year or quarter	Output per hour of all persons		Output [1]		Hours of all persons [2]		Compensation per hour [3]		Real compensation per hour [4]		Unit labor costs		Implicit price deflator [5]	
	Business sector	Nonfarm business sector	Business sector	Nonfarm business sector	Business sector	Nonfarm business sector	Business sector	Nonfarm business sector	Business sector	Nonfarm business sector	Business sector	Nonfarm business sector	Business sector	Nonfarm business sector
1970	2.0	1.5	0.0	−0.1	−2.0	−1.6	7.5	7.0	1.7	1.2	5.4	5.4	4.3	4.4
1971	4.1	3.9	3.8	3.7	−.3	−.2	6.0	6.1	1.6	1.7	1.9	2.1	4.2	4.3
1972	3.4	3.5	6.5	6.7	3.0	3.1	6.3	6.5	3.0	3.2	2.9	2.9	3.4	3.1
1973	3.0	3.1	6.9	7.3	3.8	4.1	7.9	7.6	1.6	1.3	4.8	4.4	5.2	3.5
1974	−1.7	−1.6	−1.5	−1.5	.2	.1	9.3	9.5	−1.5	−1.4	11.2	11.3	9.8	10.4
1975	3.5	2.8	−1.0	−1.6	−4.3	−4.3	10.7	10.5	1.4	1.3	6.9	7.6	9.7	10.7
1976	3.3	3.5	6.8	7.2	3.3	3.6	8.0	7.8	2.1	1.9	4.5	4.1	5.2	5.4
1977	1.8	1.7	5.7	5.7	3.8	3.9	8.0	8.2	1.4	1.6	6.1	6.4	5.9	6.2
1978	1.2	1.4	6.4	6.7	5.1	5.2	8.4	8.6	1.3	1.5	7.1	7.1	6.9	6.5
1979	.1	−.2	3.6	3.4	3.4	3.6	9.7	9.5	.2	.0	9.5	9.8	8.4	8.4
1980	.0	.0	−.9	−.9	−.9	−.8	10.7	10.8	−.4	−.4	10.8	10.8	8.9	9.5
1981	2.2	1.5	2.9	2.3	.8	.8	9.4	9.6	.0	.2	7.1	8.0	9.2	9.6
1982	−.5	−.8	−2.9	−3.1	−2.4	−2.3	7.5	7.4	1.4	1.2	8.0	8.2	5.7	6.2
1983	3.4	4.1	5.3	6.2	1.8	2.0	4.4	4.5	.1	.2	1.0	.4	3.6	3.5
1984	2.9	2.2	8.9	8.5	5.9	6.1	4.4	4.3	.2	.1	1.5	2.0	2.8	2.8
1985	2.3	1.8	4.7	4.4	2.3	2.6	5.1	4.9	1.6	1.4	2.7	3.1	2.6	3.1
1986	2.8	3.0	3.6	3.8	.8	.8	5.7	5.8	3.8	4.0	2.8	2.7	1.4	1.4
1987	.6	.6	3.6	3.6	3.0	3.0	3.8	3.8	.3	.3	3.2	3.2	1.9	1.9
1988	1.5	1.6	4.3	4.6	2.7	2.9	5.3	5.1	1.6	1.5	3.7	3.4	3.2	3.1
1989	1.2	.9	3.8	3.7	2.6	2.7	3.0	2.9	−1.3	−1.4	1.8	2.0	3.7	3.6
1990	2.0	1.7	1.6	1.5	−.4	−.2	6.3	6.0	1.3	1.0	4.2	4.2	3.3	3.4
1991	1.6	1.6	−.6	−.6	−2.2	−2.2	4.6	4.8	1.0	1.1	3.0	3.1	2.9	3.1
1992	4.7	4.5	4.2	4.1	−.4	−.4	6.1	6.2	3.6	3.6	1.4	1.7	1.6	1.7
1993	.1	.1	2.9	3.1	2.8	3.0	1.5	1.2	−1.0	−1.3	1.4	1.1	2.3	2.3
1994	.6	.7	4.8	4.6	4.2	3.9	.7	1.0	−1.3	−1.1	.1	.3	1.8	1.9
1995	.7	1.1	3.1	3.4	2.3	2.3	2.4	2.5	.0	.1	1.7	1.4	1.8	1.8
1996	2.5	2.1	4.6	4.5	2.1	2.3	3.6	3.5	.9	.8	1.1	1.3	1.6	1.4
1997	2.2	1.9	5.2	5.2	3.0	3.2	4.0	3.9	1.8	1.7	1.8	1.9	1.5	1.7
1998	3.1	3.1	5.2	5.3	2.0	2.2	5.9	5.8	4.5	4.4	2.7	2.6	.6	.7
1999	4.0	3.8	5.7	5.7	1.6	1.8	4.8	4.6	2.7	2.5	.8	.8	.6	.8
2000	3.4	3.3	4.9	4.7	1.4	1.4	6.9	7.0	3.4	3.5	3.4	3.6	1.5	1.6
2001	2.8	2.7	.7	.8	−2.0	−1.9	4.6	4.4	1.7	1.5	1.7	1.6	1.6	1.6
2002	4.3	4.3	1.7	1.7	−2.4	−2.5	2.2	2.3	.6	.7	−1.9	−1.9	.7	.8
2003	4.0	3.8	3.3	3.2	−.6	−.6	3.8	3.7	1.5	1.4	−.2	−.1	1.3	1.1
2004	3.0	2.9	4.3	4.2	1.2	1.3	4.7	4.5	1.9	1.8	1.6	1.6	2.5	2.3
2005	2.2	2.2	3.9	3.9	1.7	1.7	3.6	3.7	.2	.3	1.4	1.4	3.1	3.3
2006	1.1	1.1	3.4	3.4	2.2	2.3	3.9	3.8	.6	.6	2.7	2.7	2.7	2.8
2007	1.6	1.7	2.3	2.4	.6	.7	4.5	4.3	1.6	1.5	2.8	2.6	2.3	2.0
2008	1.1	1.1	−1.0	−1.0	−2.1	−2.1	2.8	2.9	−1.0	−.9	1.6	1.7	1.5	1.6
2009	3.6	3.6	−3.7	−3.9	−7.1	−7.2	.9	.9	1.2	1.3	−2.7	−2.5	.2	.5
2010	3.3	3.4	3.2	3.3	−.1	−.1	1.8	1.9	.2	.2	−1.5	−1.5	1.2	1.0
2011	−.1	.0	1.9	2.0	2.0	2.0	2.1	2.2	−1.0	−.9	2.2	2.2	2.3	1.9
2012	.8	.9	3.0	3.1	2.3	2.3	2.8	2.7	.6	.5	2.0	1.8	1.9	1.9
2013	.9	.5	2.4	2.2	1.5	1.7	1.5	1.3	.0	−.2	.6	.8	1.5	1.5
2014	.7	.9	3.1	3.2	2.4	2.3	2.6	2.8	.9	1.1	1.9	1.9	1.6	1.8
2015	1.2	1.3	3.5	3.5	2.3	2.1	2.9	3.1	2.7	2.9	1.6	1.7	.6	.8
2016	.3	.3	1.8	1.7	1.5	1.4	1.1	1.1	−.2	−.2	.8	.8	.8	1.0
2017	1.3	1.3	2.8	2.9	1.5	1.5	3.5	3.5	1.3	1.3	2.1	2.1	1.7	1.6
2018	1.3	1.3	3.4	3.5	2.0	2.1	3.2	3.1	.8	.7	1.9	1.8	2.3	2.3
2016: I	1.0	1.2	2.3	2.3	1.3	1.1	.3	.4	.4	.5	−.7	−.8	−.9	−.5
II	.4	.6	2.1	2.0	1.7	1.4	.8	1.2	−2.0	−1.6	.4	.6	3.0	3.1
III	1.8	1.4	2.6	2.4	.8	1.0	2.3	2.0	.4	.1	.6	.6	1.3	1.5
IV	2.4	1.8	2.5	2.7	.2	.9	5.2	4.4	2.5	1.7	2.8	2.5	1.6	1.7
2017: I	.6	1.0	2.6	2.5	2.0	1.5	3.5	4.2	.7	1.4	2.9	3.1	1.7	1.2
II	.4	.5	2.6	2.7	2.2	2.2	2.1	2.1	1.7	1.7	1.7	1.6	1.1	1.1
III	3.4	3.0	4.0	4.2	.5	1.2	5.0	4.4	2.8	2.2	1.5	1.4	2.1	2.2
IV	.1	.9	4.1	4.2	4.0	3.3	4.4	5.2	1.2	2.0	4.3	4.3	2.7	2.7
2018: I	1.3	.9	2.9	2.9	1.6	2.0	4.7	4.1	1.4	.9	3.4	3.2	2.0	2.0
II	2.4	1.8	4.0	4.0	1.5	2.1	.7	.3	−1.4	−1.9	−1.7	−1.6	3.6	3.6
III	.8	1.2	3.4	3.5	2.6	2.2	2.6	2.9	.6	.9	1.7	1.6	1.5	1.7
IV	.0	.1	1.2	1.2	1.3	1.1	.5	.7	−1.0	−.8	.5	.6	1.2	1.2
2019: I	3.6	3.5	3.9	3.9	.3	.4	9.5	9.4	8.5	8.4	5.7	5.7	−.1	.0
II	2.8	2.5	2.0	1.9	−.7	−.5	2.8	2.5	−.1	−.4	†.1	.1	3.0	3.1
III	−.2	−.2	2.4	2.3	2.6	2.5	2.3	2.3	.5	.5	2.5	2.5	1.2	1.1

[1] Output refers to real gross domestic product in the sector.
[2] Hours at work of all persons engaged in the sector. See footnote 2, Table B–32.
[3] Wages and salaries of employees plus employers' contributions for social insurance and private benefit plans. Also includes an estimate of wages, salaries, and supplemental payments for the self-employed.
[4] Hourly compensation divided by a consumer price index. See footnote 4, Table B–32.
[5] Current dollar output divided by the output index.

Note: Percent changes are calculated using index numbers to three decimal places and may differ slightly from percent changes based on indexes in Table B–32, which are rounded to one decimal place.

Source: Department of Labor (Bureau of Labor Statistics).

Production and Business Activity

TABLE B–34. Industrial production indexes, major industry divisions, 1975–2019

[2012=100, except as noted; monthly data seasonally adjusted]

Year or month	Total industrial production [1]		Manufacturing					Mining	Utilities
	Index, 2012=100	Percent change from year earlier [2]	Total [1]	Percent change from year earlier [2]	Durable	Nondurable	Other (non-NAICS) [1]		
1975	42.2	−8.9	39.2	−10.6	24.8	62.6	117.4	89.1	50.5
1976	45.5	7.9	42.7	9.0	27.1	68.3	121.1	89.7	52.9
1977	48.9	7.6	46.4	8.6	29.8	73.0	132.7	91.8	55.1
1978	51.6	5.5	49.2	6.1	32.1	75.6	137.3	94.6	56.5
1979	53.2	3.0	50.7	3.1	33.7	76.1	140.2	97.5	57.7
1980	51.8	−2.6	48.9	−3.6	32.2	73.7	145.0	99.3	58.1
1981	52.5	1.3	49.4	1.0	32.5	74.4	148.4	101.8	58.9
1982	49.8	−5.2	46.7	−5.5	29.7	73.3	150.2	96.8	57.0
1983	51.1	2.7	49.0	4.8	31.2	76.7	154.5	91.7	57.4
1984	55.7	8.9	53.7	9.8	35.6	80.2	161.6	97.6	60.8
1985	56.4	1.2	54.6	1.6	36.4	80.7	168.0	95.7	62.3
1986	56.9	1.0	55.8	2.2	37.0	83.0	171.4	88.8	62.9
1987	59.9	5.2	59.0	5.7	39.2	87.4	181.2	89.6	65.9
1988	63.0	5.2	62.1	5.3	42.1	90.4	180.4	91.9	69.9
1989	63.6	.9	62.6	.8	42.6	90.9	177.9	91.0	72.1
1990	64.2	1.0	63.1	.8	42.7	92.4	175.8	92.2	73.5
1991	63.2	−1.5	61.9	−1.9	41.4	92.1	168.6	90.3	75.3
1992	65.1	2.9	64.2	3.7	43.6	94.5	165.1	88.6	75.3
1993	67.2	3.3	66.5	3.6	46.1	95.9	166.3	88.4	77.9
1994	70.8	5.3	70.4	5.9	50.0	99.2	164.9	90.0	79.5
1995	74.0	4.6	74.0	5.1	54.1	100.9	164.8	89.9	82.3
1996	77.4	4.5	77.6	4.9	59.1	101.2	163.3	91.5	84.6
1997	83.0	7.2	84.2	8.4	66.1	105.0	177.1	93.2	84.5
1998	87.8	5.8	89.8	6.7	73.0	106.7	187.6	91.5	86.8
1999	91.7	4.4	94.3	5.1	79.3	107.3	193.0	86.9	89.5
2000	95.2	3.9	98.2	4.1	85.0	107.8	192.5	88.8	92.0
2001	92.3	−3.1	94.6	−3.7	81.6	104.7	180.0	89.0	91.7
2002	92.6	.4	95.1	.5	82.0	106.0	173.9	84.9	94.4
2003	93.8	1.3	96.4	1.3	84.2	106.2	169.0	85.1	96.0
2004	96.4	2.7	99.4	3.1	88.2	107.8	169.7	85.0	97.4
2005	99.6	3.3	103.4	4.1	93.4	110.5	169.2	84.0	99.5
2006	101.8	2.3	106.1	2.6	97.8	111.2	167.2	86.1	99.2
2007	104.4	2.5	109.0	2.8	102.7	112.5	157.7	86.8	102.3
2008	100.8	−3.5	103.8	−4.8	99.2	105.8	143.9	88.0	101.9
2009	89.2	−11.5	89.5	−13.8	80.6	97.7	120.4	83.1	99.0
2010	94.1	5.5	94.7	5.8	89.2	99.8	111.3	87.2	102.8
2011	97.1	3.1	97.5	2.9	94.7	99.9	106.1	92.6	102.4
2012	100.0	3.0	100.0	2.6	100.0	100.0	100.0	100.0	100.0
2013	102.0	2.0	100.9	.9	102.1	100.0	95.0	106.3	102.2
2014	105.2	3.1	102.0	1.1	105.1	99.3	93.8	117.8	103.5
2015	104.1	−1.0	101.5	−.5	103.9	99.6	90.4	113.9	102.7
2016	102.1	−2.0	100.7	−.8	101.7	100.4	88.0	102.6	102.3
2017	104.4	2.3	102.7	2.0	104.0	102.3	87.5	110.1	101.5
2018	108.6	3.9	105.0	2.3	107.5	104.3	78.9	123.8	105.9
2019 [p]	109.4	.8	104.8	−.2	108.2	103.4	73.7	132.7	104.5
2018: Jan	106.3	3.1	103.3	1.3	105.1	102.9	83.1	114.7	108.3
Feb	106.6	3.9	104.4	2.4	106.3	103.9	84.0	117.3	100.6
Mar	107.3	3.8	104.5	2.7	106.6	103.7	82.9	118.7	104.5
Apr	108.2	3.8	104.9	2.0	107.1	104.3	81.3	119.9	108.7
May	107.4	2.8	104.1	1.4	105.7	104.1	79.3	120.8	105.4
June	108.2	3.4	104.8	2.0	107.1	104.4	76.7	123.3	104.6
July	108.7	3.9	105.2	2.6	107.2	105.1	76.5	124.4	104.6
Aug	109.5	5.3	105.7	3.3	108.4	104.9	76.7	127.1	106.0
Sept	109.7	5.4	105.7	3.5	108.7	104.5	77.0	128.5	105.6
Oct	109.9	4.1	105.6	2.0	108.9	104.2	77.5	128.6	108.3
Nov	110.5	4.1	105.8	2.0	109.2	104.3	77.0	129.7	111.2
Dec	110.6	3.8	106.4	2.6	110.0	104.8	75.6	132.5	103.6
2019: Jan	110.1	3.6	105.8	2.4	108.9	104.7	75.7	132.1	104.4
Feb	109.6	2.7	105.3	.8	108.5	104.0	76.3	130.3	105.0
Mar	109.7	2.3	105.2	.7	108.5	103.9	75.2	130.1	106.8
Apr	109.0	.7	104.3	−.6	107.6	103.0	74.7	133.4	103.3
May	109.2	1.7	104.4	.3	108.0	102.9	73.5	133.1	105.2
June	109.3	1.0	105.0	.2	108.4	103.6	73.8	133.6	100.9
July	109.1	.4	104.6	−.6	108.4	102.8	73.0	130.7	105.3
Aug	110.0	.4	105.3	−.3	109.1	103.7	72.6	133.8	104.6
Sept [p]	109.4	−.2	104.5	−1.1	107.8	103.2	72.7	133.6	106.1
Oct [p]	108.9	−1.0	103.8	−1.7	106.6	103.0	73.1	132.9	106.5
Nov [p]	109.8	−.7	104.8	−.9	108.9	102.9	72.2	132.6	107.6
Dec [p]	109.4	−1.0	105.0	−1.3	108.6	103.5	72.1	134.4	101.6

[1] Total industry and total manufacturing series include manufacturing as defined in the North American Industry Classification System (NAICS) plus those industries—logging and newspaper, periodical, book, and directory publishing—that have traditionally been considered to be manufacturing and included in the industrial sector.
[2] Percent changes based on unrounded indexes.

Note: Data based on NAICS; see footnote 1.

Source: Board of Governors of the Federal Reserve System.

TABLE B–35. Capacity utilization rates, 1975–2019

[Percent [1]; monthly data seasonally adjusted]

Year or month	Total industry [2]	Manufacturing				Mining	Utilities	Stage-of-process		
		Total [2]	Durable goods	Nondurable goods	Other (non-NAICS) [2]			Crude	Primary and semi-finished	Finished
1975	75.8	73.7	71.8	76.1	77.3	89.5	85.2	84.0	75.2	73.7
1976	79.8	78.4	76.5	81.2	77.6	89.6	85.7	87.0	80.2	76.9
1977	83.4	82.5	81.1	84.4	83.2	89.5	86.9	89.1	84.6	79.9
1978	85.1	84.4	83.8	85.3	85.1	89.7	87.2	88.7	86.3	82.3
1979	85.0	84.0	84.0	83.9	85.6	91.2	87.2	90.0	85.9	81.7
1980	80.8	78.7	77.5	79.7	86.8	91.3	85.5	89.4	78.8	79.4
1981	79.5	76.9	75.1	78.8	87.5	90.9	84.4	89.3	77.1	77.5
1982	73.6	70.9	66.4	76.4	87.4	84.1	80.0	82.3	70.4	73.1
1983	74.9	73.5	68.8	79.4	88.0	79.8	79.3	79.9	74.5	73.0
1984	80.4	79.4	76.9	82.1	89.5	85.8	81.9	85.8	81.2	77.2
1985	79.2	78.1	75.8	80.5	90.4	84.4	81.7	83.8	79.8	76.6
1986	78.6	78.4	75.4	81.8	88.8	77.6	80.9	79.2	79.7	77.1
1987	81.1	80.9	77.6	84.7	90.5	80.3	83.5	82.8	82.8	78.7
1988	84.2	83.9	81.9	86.2	88.6	84.1	86.8	86.3	85.8	81.6
1989	83.7	83.2	81.7	84.9	85.4	85.1	86.8	86.8	84.6	81.6
1990	82.4	81.5	79.3	84.2	83.7	86.9	86.6	87.9	82.6	80.5
1991	79.9	78.6	75.4	82.3	80.8	85.4	87.8	85.5	80.0	78.2
1992	80.6	79.6	77.1	82.7	80.1	85.2	86.4	85.9	81.5	78.2
1993	81.5	80.5	78.6	82.7	81.4	85.8	88.2	85.8	83.3	78.4
1994	83.5	82.8	81.5	84.6	81.5	86.8	88.3	87.8	86.3	79.2
1995	83.9	83.1	82.1	84.5	82.2	87.6	89.3	89.0	86.4	79.7
1996	83.4	82.1	81.6	83.1	80.6	90.5	90.7	89.1	85.6	79.3
1997	84.1	83.0	82.3	83.8	85.6	91.8	90.1	90.4	86.0	80.3
1998	82.8	81.6	80.7	82.2	86.8	89.3	92.6	87.1	84.2	80.3
1999	81.8	80.5	80.2	80.1	87.2	86.2	94.2	86.1	84.3	78.0
2000	81.5	79.7	79.7	78.9	87.5	90.5	94.3	88.5	84.0	76.9
2001	76.2	73.8	71.6	75.7	82.9	89.8	90.1	85.5	77.4	72.6
2002	74.9	73.0	70.1	75.9	81.6	86.0	87.6	83.2	77.4	70.5
2003	76.0	74.0	71.1	76.8	81.5	87.8	85.7	85.0	78.2	71.3
2004	78.2	76.5	74.2	78.7	82.4	88.2	84.5	86.5	80.2	73.4
2005	80.1	78.5	76.7	80.3	81.9	88.5	85.1	86.7	81.9	75.7
2006	80.6	78.8	77.9	79.8	79.8	90.1	83.7	88.1	81.5	76.4
2007	80.8	78.9	78.8	79.3	76.3	89.4	85.9	88.7	81.2	77.1
2008	77.8	74.7	74.9	74.1	77.3	90.0	84.2	87.5	77.0	73.9
2009	68.5	65.5	61.4	69.8	69.6	80.3	80.6	77.9	65.8	68.1
2010	73.5	70.7	68.8	73.3	66.2	83.9	83.0	83.2	71.8	71.2
2011	76.1	73.5	72.6	75.2	65.4	85.9	81.5	84.5	74.4	73.7
2012	76.9	74.5	75.1	75.0	63.1	87.3	78.4	85.5	74.7	74.8
2013	77.2	74.4	74.9	74.9	62.2	87.2	79.9	86.0	75.5	73.8
2014	78.6	75.2	76.2	75.1	63.7	90.5	80.8	88.4	76.7	74.6
2015	76.9	75.3	75.3	76.3	63.8	84.2	79.9	82.7	76.3	75.1
2016	75.0	74.2	73.1	76.2	64.2	77.6	78.8	78.4	75.2	73.6
2017	76.5	75.1	74.2	76.8	66.3	84.3	77.0	83.7	75.7	74.2
2018	78.7	76.6	76.1	78.0	62.3	90.2	79.3	88.8	77.5	75.4
2019 [p]	77.8	75.6	75.6	76.5	59.5	90.4	76.7	88.5	75.8	74.7
2018: Jan	77.6	75.5	74.7	77.2	64.5	86.6	81.7	85.2	77.2	74.6
Feb	77.8	76.3	75.6	77.9	65.4	88.1	75.8	86.3	76.6	75.3
Mar	78.2	76.3	75.7	77.8	64.8	88.6	78.6	87.2	77.3	75.0
Apr	78.8	76.6	76.0	78.2	63.8	89.0	81.7	87.5	78.2	75.4
May	78.1	76.0	75.0	78.0	62.3	89.0	79.2	87.9	77.2	74.5
June	78.6	76.5	75.9	78.2	60.5	90.2	78.5	89.1	77.1	75.2
July	78.8	76.7	75.9	78.7	60.5	90.4	78.3	89.5	77.2	75.5
Aug	79.3	77.0	76.7	78.4	60.8	91.8	79.2	90.6	77.6	75.8
Sept	79.3	76.9	76.8	78.1	61.2	92.1	78.7	90.7	77.4	75.8
Oct	79.3	76.8	76.9	77.8	61.8	91.6	80.6	90.2	77.9	75.6
Nov	79.6	76.9	77.0	77.8	61.6	91.8	82.6	90.4	78.5	75.5
Dec	79.5	77.3	77.5	78.1	60.6	93.3	76.8	91.5	77.4	76.0
2019: Jan	79.0	76.7	76.6	77.9	60.8	92.4	77.3	90.6	77.2	75.4
Feb	78.5	76.3	76.2	77.4	61.4	90.7	77.6	89.1	76.7	75.3
Mar	78.4	76.2	76.1	77.2	60.5	90.1	78.7	88.2	76.7	75.5
Apr	77.8	75.4	75.4	76.4	60.2	91.9	75.9	89.6	75.7	74.5
May	77.8	75.4	75.5	76.2	59.3	91.3	77.2	89.1	76.0	74.4
June	77.7	75.7	75.7	76.7	59.6	91.3	73.9	88.7	75.2	75.2
July	77.4	75.3	75.6	76.0	59.0	88.9	76.9	86.8	75.6	74.8
Aug	77.9	75.8	76.0	76.6	58.7	90.7	76.3	88.7	76.0	74.9
Sept [p]	77.4	75.1	75.0	76.1	58.8	90.2	77.2	88.4	75.9	74.1
Oct [p]	76.9	74.5	74.0	75.9	59.2	89.4	77.4	87.9	75.1	73.5
Nov [p]	77.4	75.1	75.5	75.7	58.5	88.8	78.0	87.4	75.4	74.7
Dec [p]	77.0	75.2	75.2	76.1	58.4	89.6	73.5	87.8	74.6	74.5

[1] Output as percent of capacity.
[2] See footnote 1 and Note, Table B–34.

Source: Board of Governors of the Federal Reserve System.

TABLE B–36. New private housing units started, authorized, and completed and houses sold, 1975–2019

[Thousands; monthly data at seasonally adjusted annual rates]

Year or month	New housing units started				New housing units authorized [1]				New housing units completed	New houses sold
	Total	1 unit	2 to 4 units [2]	5 units or more	Total	1 unit	2 to 4 units	5 units or more		
1975	1,160.4	892.2	64.0	204.3	939.2	675.5	63.8	199.8	1,317.2	549
1976	1,537.5	1,162.4	85.8	289.2	1,296.2	893.6	93.1	309.5	1,377.2	646
1977	1,987.1	1,450.9	121.7	414.4	1,690.0	1,126.1	121.3	442.7	1,657.1	819
1978	2,020.3	1,433.3	125.1	462.0	1,800.5	1,182.6	130.6	487.3	1,867.5	817
1979	1,745.1	1,194.1	122.0	429.0	1,551.8	981.5	125.4	444.8	1,870.8	709
1980	1,292.2	852.2	109.5	330.5	1,190.6	710.4	114.5	365.7	1,501.6	545
1981	1,084.2	705.4	91.2	287.7	985.5	564.3	101.8	319.4	1,265.7	436
1982	1,062.2	662.6	80.1	319.6	1,000.5	546.4	88.3	365.8	1,005.5	412
1983	1,703.0	1,067.6	113.5	522.0	1,605.2	901.5	133.7	570.1	1,390.3	623
1984	1,749.5	1,084.2	121.4	543.9	1,681.8	922.4	142.6	616.8	1,652.2	639
1985	1,741.8	1,072.4	93.5	576.0	1,733.3	956.6	120.1	656.6	1,703.3	688
1986	1,805.4	1,179.4	84.0	542.0	1,769.4	1,077.6	108.4	583.5	1,756.4	750
1987	1,620.5	1,146.4	65.1	408.7	1,534.8	1,024.4	89.3	421.1	1,668.8	671
1988	1,488.1	1,081.3	58.7	348.0	1,455.6	993.8	75.7	386.1	1,529.8	676
1989	1,376.1	1,003.3	55.3	317.6	1,338.4	931.7	66.9	339.8	1,422.8	650
1990	1,192.7	894.8	37.6	260.4	1,110.8	793.9	54.3	262.6	1,308.0	534
1991	1,013.9	840.4	35.6	137.9	948.8	753.5	43.1	152.1	1,090.8	509
1992	1,199.7	1,029.9	30.9	139.0	1,094.9	910.7	45.8	138.4	1,157.5	610
1993	1,287.6	1,125.7	29.4	132.6	1,199.1	986.5	52.4	160.2	1,192.7	666
1994	1,457.0	1,198.4	35.2	223.5	1,371.6	1,068.5	62.2	241.0	1,346.9	670
1995	1,354.1	1,076.2	33.8	244.1	1,332.5	997.3	63.8	271.5	1,312.6	667
1996	1,476.8	1,160.9	45.3	270.8	1,425.6	1,069.5	65.8	290.3	1,412.9	757
1997	1,474.0	1,133.7	44.5	295.8	1,441.1	1,062.4	68.4	310.3	1,400.5	804
1998	1,616.9	1,271.4	42.6	302.9	1,612.3	1,187.6	69.2	355.5	1,474.2	886
1999	1,640.9	1,302.4	31.9	306.6	1,663.5	1,246.7	65.8	351.1	1,604.9	880
2000	1,568.7	1,230.9	38.7	299.1	1,592.3	1,198.1	64.9	329.3	1,573.7	877
2001	1,602.7	1,273.3	36.6	292.8	1,636.7	1,235.6	66.0	335.2	1,570.8	908
2002	1,704.9	1,358.6	38.5	307.9	1,747.7	1,332.6	73.7	341.4	1,648.4	973
2003	1,847.7	1,499.0	33.5	315.2	1,889.2	1,460.9	82.5	345.8	1,678.7	1,086
2004	1,955.8	1,610.5	42.3	303.0	2,070.1	1,613.4	90.4	366.2	1,841.9	1,203
2005	2,068.3	1,715.8	41.1	311.4	2,155.3	1,682.0	84.0	389.3	1,931.4	1,283
2006	1,800.9	1,465.4	42.7	292.8	1,838.9	1,378.2	76.6	384.1	1,979.4	1,051
2007	1,355.0	1,046.0	31.7	277.3	1,398.4	979.9	59.6	359.0	1,502.8	776
2008	905.5	622.0	17.5	266.0	905.4	575.6	34.4	295.4	1,119.7	485
2009	554.0	445.1	11.6	97.3	583.0	441.1	20.7	121.1	794.4	375
2010	586.9	471.2	11.4	104.3	604.6	447.3	22.0	135.3	651.7	323
2011	608.8	430.6	10.9	167.3	624.1	418.5	21.6	184.0	584.9	306
2012	780.6	535.3	11.4	233.9	829.7	518.7	25.9	285.1	649.2	368
2013	924.9	617.6	13.6	293.7	990.8	620.8	29.0	341.1	764.4	429
2014	1,003.3	647.9	13.7	341.7	1,052.1	640.3	29.9	382.0	883.8	437
2015	1,111.8	714.5	11.5	385.8	1,182.6	696.0	32.1	454.5	968.2	501
2016	1,173.8	781.5	11.5	380.8	1,206.6	750.8	34.8	421.1	1,059.7	561
2017	1,203.0	848.9	11.4	342.7	1,282.0	820.0	37.2	424.8	1,152.9	613
2018	1,249.9	875.8	13.9	360.3	1,328.8	855.3	39.7	433.8	1,184.9	617
2019 [p]	1,289.8	888.2	13.2	388.4	1,370.3	854.2	41.7	474.4	1,250.6	681
2018: Jan	1,335	883	....	439	1,366	870	45	451	1,215	628
Feb	1,295	906	....	371	1,323	886	46	391	1,290	644
Mar	1,332	889	....	429	1,377	851	40	486	1,220	654
Apr	1,267	892	....	354	1,364	863	41	460	1,244	629
May	1,332	937	....	383	1,301	843	34	424	1,248	650
June	1,180	854	....	316	1,292	853	36	403	1,205	618
July	1,184	860	....	318	1,303	873	28	402	1,176	609
Aug	1,279	889	....	373	1,249	827	35	387	1,232	604
Sept	1,236	880	....	347	1,270	854	40	376	1,150	607
Oct	1,211	865	....	327	1,265	847	36	382	1,117	557
Nov	1,202	804	....	387	1,322	848	39	435	1,107	615
Dec	1,142	814	....	307	1,326	829	37	460	1,068	564
2019: Jan	1,291	966	....	308	1,316	821	45	450	1,261	644
Feb	1,149	792	....	352	1,287	814	36	437	1,332	669
Mar	1,199	833	....	361	1,288	813	36	439	1,348	693
Apr	1,270	862	....	385	1,290	786	45	459	1,330	656
May	1,264	814	....	438	1,299	810	35	454	1,228	598
June	1,233	864	....	358	1,232	823	46	363	1,170	729
July	1,204	871	....	322	1,317	829	45	443	1,245	660
Aug	1,375	909	....	451	1,425	875	42	508	1,253	708
Sept	1,266	902	....	353	1,391	881	34	476	1,129	725
Oct	1,340	914	....	414	1,461	911	48	502	1,276	705
Nov [p]	1,375	949	....	406	1,474	921	38	515	1,215	697
Dec [p]	1,608	1,055	....	536	1,420	928	39	453	1,277	694

[1] Authorized by issuance of local building permits in permit-issuing places: 20,100 places beginning with 2014; 19,300 for 2004–2013; 19,000 for 1994–2003; 17,000 for 1984–93; 16,000 for 1978–83; and 14,000 for 1975–77.
[2] Monthly data do not meet publication standards because tests for identifiable and stable seasonality do not meet reliability standards.

Note: One-unit estimates prior to 1999, for new housing units started and completed and for new houses sold, include an upward adjustment of 3.3 percent to account for structures in permit-issuing areas that did not have permit authorization.

Source: Department of Commerce (Bureau of the Census).

[Amounts in millions of dollars; monthly data seasonally adjusted]

Year or month	Total manufacturing and trade			Manufacturing			Merchant wholesalers [1]			Retail trade			Retail and food services sales
	Sales [2]	Inventories [3]	Ratio [4]	Sales [2]	Inventories [3]	Ratio [4]	Sales [2]	Inventories [3]	Ratio [4]	Sales [2,5]	Inventories [3]	Ratio [4]	
SIC: [6]													
1979	297,701	452,640	1.52	143,936	242,157	1.68	79,051	99,679	1.26	74,713	110,804	1.48	
1980	327,233	508,924	1.56	154,391	265,215	1.72	93,099	122,631	1.32	79,743	121,078	1.52	
1981	355,822	545,786	1.53	168,129	283,413	1.69	101,180	129,654	1.28	86,514	132,719	1.53	
1982	347,625	573,908	1.67	163,351	311,852	1.95	95,211	127,428	1.36	89,062	134,628	1.49	
1983	369,286	590,287	1.56	172,547	312,379	1.78	99,225	130,075	1.28	97,514	147,833	1.44	
1984	410,124	649,780	1.53	190,682	339,516	1.73	112,199	142,452	1.23	107,243	167,812	1.49	
1985	422,583	664,039	1.56	194,538	334,749	1.73	113,459	147,409	1.28	114,586	181,881	1.52	
1986	430,419	662,738	1.55	194,657	322,654	1.68	114,960	153,574	1.32	120,803	186,510	1.56	
1987	457,735	709,848	1.50	206,326	338,109	1.59	122,968	163,903	1.29	128,442	207,836	1.55	
1988	497,157	767,222	1.49	224,619	369,374	1.57	134,521	178,801	1.30	138,017	219,047	1.54	
1989	527,039	815,455	1.52	236,698	391,212	1.63	143,760	187,009	1.28	146,581	237,234	1.58	
1990	545,909	840,594	1.52	242,686	405,073	1.65	149,506	195,833	1.29	153,718	239,688	1.56	
1991	542,815	834,609	1.53	239,847	390,950	1.65	148,306	200,448	1.33	154,661	243,211	1.54	
1992	567,176	842,809	1.48	250,394	382,510	1.54	154,150	208,302	1.32	162,632	251,997	1.52	
NAICS: [6]													
1992	540,199	835,800	1.53	242,002	378,609	1.57	147,261	196,914	1.31	150,936	260,277	1.67	167,842
1993	567,195	863,125	1.50	251,708	379,806	1.50	154,018	204,842	1.30	161,469	278,477	1.68	179,425
1994	609,854	926,395	1.46	269,843	399,934	1.44	164,575	221,978	1.29	175,436	304,483	1.66	194,186
1995	654,689	985,385	1.48	289,973	424,802	1.44	179,915	238,392	1.29	184,801	322,191	1.72	204,219
1996	686,923	1,004,646	1.45	299,766	430,366	1.44	190,362	241,058	1.27	196,796	333,222	1.67	216,983
1997	723,443	1,045,495	1.42	319,558	443,227	1.37	198,154	258,454	1.26	205,731	343,814	1.64	227,178
1998	742,391	1,077,183	1.44	324,984	448,373	1.39	202,260	272,297	1.32	215,147	356,513	1.62	237,746
1999	786,178	1,137,260	1.40	335,991	463,004	1.35	216,597	290,182	1.30	233,591	384,074	1.59	257,249
2000	833,868	1,195,894	1.41	350,715	480,748	1.35	234,546	309,191	1.29	248,606	405,955	1.59	273,961
2001	818,160	1,118,552	1.42	330,875	427,353	1.38	232,096	297,536	1.32	255,189	393,663	1.58	281,576
2002	823,234	1,139,523	1.36	326,227	423,028	1.29	236,294	301,310	1.26	260,713	415,185	1.55	288,256
2003	854,700	1,147,795	1.34	334,616	408,302	1.25	248,190	308,274	1.22	271,894	431,219	1.56	301,038
2004	926,002	1,241,744	1.30	359,081	441,222	1.19	277,501	340,128	1.17	289,421	460,394	1.56	320,550
2005	1,005,821	1,314,317	1.27	395,173	474,639	1.17	303,208	367,978	1.17	307,440	471,700	1.51	340,479
2006	1,069,032	1,408,812	1.28	417,963	523,476	1.20	328,438	398,924	1.17	322,631	486,412	1.49	357,863
2007	1,128,176	1,487,636	1.28	443,288	562,714	1.22	351,956	424,344	1.17	332,932	500,578	1.49	369,978
2008	1,160,722	1,466,023	1.31	455,750	543,317	1.26	377,030	445,529	1.20	327,943	477,177	1.52	365,965
2009	988,802	1,332,351	1.38	368,648	505,452	1.39	319,115	397,699	1.29	301,039	429,200	1.47	338,706
2010	1,088,890	1,451,079	1.27	409,273	554,328	1.28	361,447	442,154	1.15	318,171	454,597	1.39	357,081
2011	1,206,660	1,565,659	1.26	457,658	606,839	1.29	407,090	488,061	1.15	341,913	470,759	1.35	383,192
2012	1,267,248	1,654,225	1.28	474,727	624,905	1.30	434,002	524,005	1.17	358,519	505,315	1.38	402,199
2013	1,303,229	1,718,818	1.29	484,145	630,267	1.29	447,546	545,175	1.19	371,538	543,376	1.41	416,814
2014	1,340,932	1,778,197	1.31	490,630	640,437	1.31	463,682	577,344	1.22	386,620	560,416	1.43	434,638
2015	1,294,787	1,808,388	1.39	459,918	635,783	1.39	441,036	585,167	1.33	393,833	587,438	1.46	445,791
2016	1,286,246	1,838,515	1.42	446,225	631,247	1.41	435,707	596,302	1.35	404,315	610,966	1.49	459,110
2017	1,350,809	1,900,128	1.38	467,076	659,418	1.37	463,158	615,722	1.30	420,575	624,988	1.47	478,384
2018	1,434,984	1,996,625	1.36	499,964	682,655	1.35	494,747	660,492	1.29	440,273	653,478	1.45	501,758
2019 [p]	....	....	....	....	....	....	....	675,596	....	455,632	661,219	1.45	519,796
2018: Jan	1,405,006	1,910,650	1.36	489,058	661,954	1.35	481,495	621,149	1.29	434,453	627,547	1.44	494,208
Feb	1,411,196	1,920,723	1.36	490,494	664,577	1.35	485,732	625,490	1.29	434,970	630,656	1.45	495,028
Mar	1,415,738	1,921,801	1.36	493,240	664,676	1.35	488,298	627,707	1.29	434,200	629,418	1.45	494,681
Apr	1,419,942	1,926,701	1.36	493,337	667,705	1.35	489,732	627,672	1.28	436,873	631,324	1.45	496,763
May	1,440,273	1,934,054	1.34	497,081	669,775	1.35	501,595	629,910	1.26	441,597	634,369	1.44	502,987
June	1,441,800	1,934,716	1.34	501,313	669,588	1.34	499,388	630,558	1.26	441,099	634,570	1.44	503,283
July	1,444,499	1,948,232	1.35	501,740	676,291	1.35	499,489	634,281	1.27	443,270	637,660	1.44	506,047
Aug	1,448,482	1,959,161	1.35	504,405	676,016	1.34	502,373	640,883	1.28	441,704	642,262	1.45	504,897
Sept	1,451,908	1,968,204	1.36	507,438	680,293	1.34	501,656	645,486	1.29	442,814	642,425	1.45	504,604
Oct	1,457,287	1,981,503	1.36	507,985	682,510	1.34	501,166	650,679	1.30	448,136	648,314	1.45	510,412
Nov	1,451,741	1,982,144	1.37	506,252	682,391	1.35	496,733	653,384	1.32	448,756	646,369	1.44	510,826
Dec	1,435,551	1,996,625	1.39	505,209	682,655	1.35	491,945	660,492	1.34	438,397	653,478	1.49	500,455
2019: Jan	1,443,911	2,010,849	1.39	504,075	686,221	1.36	494,587	660,494	1.35	445,249	657,134	1.48	507,222
Feb	1,444,010	2,018,638	1.40	505,803	688,334	1.36	496,126	670,217	1.35	442,081	660,087	1.49	504,441
Mar	1,462,677	2,018,737	1.38	506,780	691,141	1.36	505,145	670,076	1.33	450,752	657,520	1.46	513,608
Apr	1,459,042	2,029,828	1.39	503,881	692,729	1.37	502,929	675,713	1.34	452,232	661,386	1.46	515,545
May	1,458,214	2,035,784	1.40	504,257	694,247	1.38	499,822	678,352	1.36	454,135	663,185	1.46	518,131
June	1,458,631	2,035,201	1.40	504,952	695,281	1.38	498,133	677,905	1.36	455,546	662,015	1.45	520,055
July	1,461,641	2,041,782	1.40	503,617	696,204	1.38	499,050	679,131	1.36	458,974	666,447	1.45	523,922
Aug	1,462,583	2,040,517	1.40	502,177	695,671	1.39	498,513	679,474	1.36	461,893	665,372	1.44	526,862
Sept	1,457,140	2,039,070	1.40	500,121	697,912	1.40	497,828	664,897	1.36	459,191	666,261	1.45	524,651
Oct	1,454,942	2,041,178	1.40	500,488	699,024	1.40	493,407	675,386	1.37	461,047	666,768	1.45	526,420
Nov [p]	1,465,240	2,038,234	1.39	501,706	701,083	1.40	500,651	675,997	1.35	462,883	661,154	1.43	527,841
Dec [p]	....	....	....	....	....	....	....	675,596	....	464,516	661,219	1.42	529,606

[1] Excludes manufacturers' sales branches and offices.
[2] Annual data are averages of monthly not seasonally adjusted figures.
[3] Seasonally adjusted, end of period. Inventories beginning with January 1982 for manufacturing and December 1980 for wholesale and retail trade are not comparable with earlier periods.
[4] Inventory/sales ratio. Monthly inventories are inventories at the end of the month to sales for the month. Annual data beginning with 1982 are the average of monthly ratios for the year. Annual data for 1979–81 are the ratio of December inventories to monthly average sales for the year.
[5] Food services included on Standard Industrial Classification (SIC) basis and excluded on North American Industry Classification System (NAICS) basis. See last column for retail and food services sales.
[6] Effective in 2001, data classified based on NAICS. Data on NAICS basis available beginning with 1992. Earlier data based on SIC. Data on both NAICS and SIC basis include semiconductors.

Source: Department of Commerce (Bureau of the Census).

Prices

TABLE B–38. Changes in consumer price indexes, 1977–2019

[For all urban consumers; percent change]

Year or month	All items	All items less food and energy Total[1]	Shelter[2]	Medical care[3]	Apparel	New vehicles	Food Total[1]	At home	Away from home	Energy[4] Total[1,3]	Gasoline	C-CPI-U[5]
						December to December, NSA						
1977	6.7	6.5	8.8	8.9	4.3	7.2	8.1	7.9	7.9	7.2	4.8	
1978	9.0	8.5	11.4	8.8	3.1	6.2	11.8	12.5	10.4	7.9	8.6	
1979	13.3	11.3	17.5	10.1	5.5	7.4	10.2	9.7	11.4	37.5	52.1	
1980	12.5	12.2	15.0	9.9	6.8	7.4	10.2	10.5	9.6	18.0	18.9	
1981	8.9	9.5	9.9	12.5	3.5	6.8	4.3	2.9	7.1	11.9	9.4	
1982	3.8	4.5	2.4	11.0	1.6	1.4	3.1	2.3	5.1	1.3	−6.7	
1983	3.8	4.8	4.7	6.4	2.9	3.3	2.7	1.8	4.1	−.5	−1.6	
1984	3.9	4.7	5.2	6.1	2.0	2.5	3.8	3.6	4.2	.2	−2.5	
1985	3.8	4.3	6.0	6.8	2.8	3.6	2.6	2.0	3.8	1.8	3.0	
1986	1.1	3.8	4.6	7.7	.9	5.6	3.8	3.7	4.3	−19.7	−30.7	
1987	4.4	4.2	4.8	5.8	4.8	1.8	3.5	3.5	3.7	8.2	18.6	
1988	4.4	4.7	4.5	6.9	4.7	2.2	5.2	5.6	4.4	.5	−1.8	
1989	4.6	4.4	4.9	8.5	1.0	2.4	5.6	6.2	4.6	5.1	6.5	
1990	6.1	5.2	5.2	9.6	5.1	2.0	5.3	5.8	4.5	18.1	36.8	
1991	3.1	4.4	3.9	7.9	3.4	3.2	1.9	1.3	2.9	−7.4	−16.2	
1992	2.9	3.3	2.9	6.6	1.4	2.3	1.5	1.5	1.4	2.0	2.0	
1993	2.7	3.2	3.0	5.4	.9	3.3	2.9	3.5	1.9	−1.4	−5.9	
1994	2.7	2.6	3.0	4.9	−1.6	3.3	2.9	3.5	1.9	2.2	6.4	
1995	2.5	3.0	3.5	3.9	.1	1.9	2.1	2.0	2.2	−1.3	−4.2	
1996	3.3	2.6	2.9	3.0	−.2	1.8	4.3	4.9	3.1	8.6	12.4	
1997	1.7	2.2	3.4	2.8	1.0	−.9	1.5	1.0	2.6	−3.4	−6.1	
1998	1.6	2.4	3.3	3.4	−.7	.0	2.3	2.1	2.5	−8.8	−15.4	
1999	2.7	1.9	2.5	3.7	−.5	−.3	1.9	1.7	2.3	13.4	30.1	
2000	3.4	2.6	3.4	4.2	−1.8	.0	2.8	2.9	2.4	14.2	13.9	2.6
2001	1.6	2.7	4.2	4.7	−3.2	−.1	2.8	2.6	3.0	−13.0	−24.9	1.3
2002	2.4	1.9	3.1	5.0	−1.8	−2.0	1.5	.8	2.3	10.7	24.8	2.0
2003	1.9	1.1	2.2	3.7	−2.1	−1.8	3.6	4.5	2.3	6.9	6.8	1.7
2004	3.3	2.2	2.7	4.2	−.2	.6	2.7	2.4	3.0	16.6	26.1	3.2
2005	3.4	2.2	2.6	4.3	−1.1	−.4	2.3	1.7	3.2	17.1	16.1	2.9
2006	2.5	2.6	4.2	3.6	.9	−.9	2.1	1.4	3.2	2.9	6.4	2.3
2007	4.1	2.4	3.1	5.2	−.3	−.3	4.9	5.6	4.0	17.4	29.6	3.7
2008	.1	1.8	1.9	2.6	−1.0	−3.2	5.9	6.6	5.0	−21.3	−43.1	.2
2009	2.7	1.8	.3	3.4	1.9	4.9	−.5	−2.4	1.9	18.2	53.5	2.5
2010	1.5	.8	.4	3.3	−1.1	−.2	1.5	1.7	1.3	7.7	13.8	1.3
2011	3.0	2.2	1.9	3.5	4.6	3.2	4.7	6.0	2.9	6.6	9.9	2.9
2012	1.7	1.9	2.2	3.2	1.8	1.6	1.8	1.3	2.5	.5	1.7	1.5
2013	1.5	1.7	2.5	2.0	.6	.4	1.1	.4	2.1	.5	−1.0	1.3
2014	.8	1.6	2.9	3.0	−2.0	.5	3.4	3.7	3.0	−10.6	−21.0	.5
2015	.7	2.1	3.2	2.6	−.9	.2	.8	−.4	2.6	−12.6	−19.7	.4
2016	2.1	2.2	3.6	4.1	−.1	.3	−.2	−2.0	2.3	5.4	9.1	1.8
2017	2.1	1.8	3.2	1.8	−1.6	−.5	1.6	.9	2.5	6.9	10.7	1.7
2018	1.9	2.2	3.2	2.0	−.1	−.3	1.6	.6	2.8	−.3	−2.1	1.5
2019	2.3	2.3	3.2	4.6	−1.2	.1	1.8	.7	3.1	3.4	7.9	2.1
						Change from year earlier, NSA						
2018: Jan	2.1	1.8	3.2	2.0	−0.7	−1.2	1.7	1.0	2.5	5.5	8.5	1.6
Feb	2.2	1.8	3.1	1.8	.4	−1.5	1.4	.5	2.6	7.7	12.6	1.7
Mar	2.4	2.1	3.3	2.0	.3	−1.2	1.3	.4	2.5	7.0	11.1	1.9
Apr	2.5	2.1	3.4	2.2	.8	−1.6	1.4	.5	2.5	7.9	13.4	2.1
May	2.8	2.2	3.5	2.4	1.4	−1.1	1.2	.1	2.7	11.7	21.8	2.3
June	2.9	2.3	3.4	2.5	.6	−.5	1.4	.4	2.8	12.0	24.3	2.4
July	2.9	2.4	3.5	1.9	.3	.2	1.4	.4	2.8	12.1	25.4	2.6
Aug	2.7	2.2	3.4	1.5	−1.4	.3	1.4	.5	2.6	10.2	20.3	2.3
Sept	2.3	2.2	3.3	1.7	−.6	.5	1.4	.4	2.6	4.8	9.1	1.9
Oct	2.5	2.1	3.2	1.7	−.4	.5	1.2	.1	2.5	8.9	16.1	2.1
Nov	2.2	2.2	3.2	2.0	−.4	.3	1.4	.4	2.6	3.1	5.0	1.8
Dec	1.9	2.2	3.2	2.0	−.1	−.3	1.6	.6	2.8	−.3	−2.1	1.5
2019: Jan	1.6	2.2	3.2	1.9	.1	.0	1.6	.6	2.8	−4.8	−10.1	1.2
Feb	1.5	2.1	3.4	1.7	−.8	.3	2.0	1.2	2.9	−5.0	−9.1	1.3
Mar	1.9	2.0	3.4	1.7	−2.2	.7	2.1	1.4	3.0	−.4	−.7	1.6
Apr	2.0	2.1	3.4	1.9	−3.0	1.2	1.8	.7	3.1	1.7	3.1	1.7
May	1.8	2.0	3.3	2.1	−3.1	.9	2.0	1.2	2.9	−.5	−.2	1.6
June	1.6	2.1	3.5	2.0	−1.3	.6	1.9	.9	3.1	−3.4	−5.4	1.4
July	1.8	2.2	3.5	2.6	−.5	.3	1.8	.6	3.2	−2.0	−3.3	1.6
Aug	1.7	2.4	3.4	3.5	1.0	.2	1.7	.5	3.2	−4.4	−7.1	1.6
Sept	1.7	2.4	3.5	3.5	−.3	.1	1.8	.6	3.2	−4.8	−8.2	1.6
Oct	1.8	2.3	3.3	4.3	−2.3	.1	2.1	1.0	3.3	−4.2	−7.3	1.6
Nov	2.1	2.3	3.3	4.2	−1.6	−.1	2.0	1.0	3.2	−.6	−1.2	1.9
Dec	2.3	2.3	3.2	4.6	−1.2	.1	1.8	.7	3.1	3.4	7.9	2.1

[1] Includes other items not shown separately.
[2] Data beginning with 1983 incorporate a rental equivalence measure for homeowners' costs.
[3] Commodities and services.
[4] Household energy--electricity, utility (piped) gas service, fuel oil, etc.--and motor fuel.
[5] Chained consumer price index (C-CPI-U) introduced in 2002. Reflects the effect of substitution that consumers make across item categories in response to changes in relative prices. Data for 2019 are subject to revision.

Source: Department of Labor (Bureau of Labor Statistics).

[Chain-type price index numbers, 2012=100; monthly data seasonally adjusted]

Year or month	Personal consumption expenditures (PCE)						Percent change from year earlier					
	Total	Goods	Services	Food¹	Energy goods and services²	PCE less food and energy	Total	Goods	Services	Food¹	Energy goods and services²	PCE less food and energy
1972	22.586	33.926	17.491	22.371	10.716	23.912	3.4	2.6	4.2	4.8	2.6	3.2
1973	23.802	35.949	18.336	25.202	11.640	24.823	5.4	6.0	4.8	12.7	8.6	3.8
1974	26.280	40.436	19.890	29.034	15.176	26.788	10.4	12.5	8.5	15.2	30.4	7.9
1975	28.470	43.703	21.595	31.217	16.672	29.026	8.3	8.1	8.6	7.5	9.9	8.4
1976	30.032	45.413	23.093	31.798	17.791	30.791	5.5	3.9	6.9	1.9	6.7	6.1
1977	31.986	47.837	24.841	33.671	19.294	32.771	6.5	5.3	7.6	5.9	8.4	6.4
1978	34.211	50.773	26.750	36.892	20.380	34.943	7.0	6.1	7.7	9.6	5.6	6.6
1979	37.251	55.574	28.994	40.516	25.414	37.490	8.9	9.5	8.4	9.8	24.7	7.3
1980	41.262	61.797	32.009	43.922	33.203	40.936	10.8	11.2	10.4	8.4	30.6	9.2
1981	44.958	66.389	35.288	47.051	37.668	44.523	9.0	7.4	10.2	7.1	13.4	8.8
1982	47.456	68.198	38.058	48.289	38.326	47.417	5.6	2.7	7.8	2.6	1.7	6.5
1983	49.474	69.429	40.396	48.844	38.684	49.844	4.3	1.8	6.1	1.1	.9	5.1
1984	51.343	70.742	42.498	50.312	39.172	51.911	3.8	1.9	5.2	3.0	1.3	4.1
1985	53.134	71.877	44.577	50.859	39.585	54.019	3.5	1.6	4.9	1.1	1.1	4.1
1986	54.290	71.541	46.408	52.056	34.685	55.883	2.2	−.5	4.1	2.4	−12.4	3.5
1987	55.964	73.842	47.796	53.699	35.069	57.683	3.1	3.2	3.0	3.2	1.1	3.2
1988	58.151	75.788	50.082	56.300	35.337	60.134	3.9	2.6	4.8	3.0	.8	4.2
1989	60.690	78.704	52.443	58.216	37.425	62.630	4.4	3.8	4.7	5.3	5.9	4.2
1990	63.355	81.927	54.846	61.060	40.589	65.168	4.4	4.1	4.6	4.9	8.5	4.1
1991	65.473	83.930	56.992	62.977	40.769	67.495	3.3	2.4	3.9	3.1	.4	3.6
1992	67.218	84.943	59.018	63.461	40.959	69.547	2.7	1.2	3.6	.8	.5	3.0
1993	68.892	85.681	61.059	64.348	41.331	71.436	2.5	.9	3.5	1.4	.9	2.7
1994	70.330	86.552	62.719	65.426	41.493	73.034	2.1	1.0	2.7	1.7	.4	2.2
1995	71.811	87.361	64.471	66.844	41.819	74.625	2.1	.9	2.8	2.2	.8	2.2
1996	73.346	88.321	66.240	68.883	43.777	76.040	2.1	1.1	2.7	3.1	4.7	1.9
1997	74.623	88.219	68.107	70.195	44.236	77.382	1.7	−.1	2.8	1.9	1.0	1.8
1998	75.216	86.893	69.549	71.077	40.502	78.366	.8	−1.5	2.1	1.3	−8.4	1.3
1999	76.338	87.349	70.970	72.241	42.143	79.425	1.5	.5	2.0	1.6	4.1	1.4
2000	78.235	89.082	72.938	73.933	49.843	80.804	2.5	2.0	2.8	2.3	18.3	1.7
2001	79.738	89.015	75.171	76.089	51.088	82.258	1.9	−.1	3.1	2.9	2.5	1.8
2002	80.789	88.166	77.123	77.239	48.110	83.639	1.3	−1.0	2.6	1.5	−5.8	1.7
2003	82.358	88.054	79.506	78.701	54.190	84.837	1.9	−.1	3.1	1.9	12.6	1.4
2004	84.411	89.292	81.965	81.157	60.339	86.515	2.5	1.4	3.1	3.1	11.3	2.0
2005	86.812	91.084	84.673	82.575	70.752	88.373	2.8	2.0	3.3	1.7	17.3	2.1
2006	89.174	92.306	87.616	83.963	78.812	90.392	2.7	1.3	3.5	1.7	11.4	2.3
2007	91.438	93.331	90.516	87.239	83.557	92.378	2.5	1.1	3.3	3.9	6.0	2.2
2008	94.180	96.122	93.235	92.552	95.464	94.225	3.0	3.0	3.0	6.1	14.3	2.0
2009	94.094	93.812	94.231	93.651	77.393	95.315	−.1	−2.4	1.1	1.2	−18.9	1.2
2010	95.705	95.183	95.957	93.931	85.120	96.608	1.7	1.5	1.8	.3	10.0	1.4
2011	98.131	98.773	97.814	97.682	98.601	98.139	2.5	3.8	1.9	4.0	15.8	1.6
2012	100.000	100.000	100.000	100.000	100.000	100.000	1.9	1.2	2.2	2.4	1.4	1.9
2013	101.346	99.407	102.316	100.989	99.109	101.526	1.3	−.6	2.3	1.0	−.9	1.5
2014	102.830	98.920	104.804	102.925	98.279	103.122	1.5	−.5	2.4	1.9	−.8	1.6
2015	103.045	95.885	106.704	104.084	80.632	104.407	.2	−3.1	1.8	1.1	−18.0	1.2
2016	104.091	94.318	109.120	103.004	74.776	106.070	1.0	−1.6	2.3	−1.0	−7.3	1.6
2017	105.929	94.586	111.793	102.866	81.269	107.795	1.8	.3	2.4	−.1	8.7	1.6
2018ᵖ	108.143	95.232	114.851	103.407	87.809	109.897	2.1	.7	2.7	.5	8.0	1.9
2019ᵖ	109.670	94.785	117.458	104.433	85.956	111.670	1.4	−.5	2.3	1.0	−2.1	1.6
2018: Jan	107.223	95.316	113.386	103.106	86.869	108.923	1.8	.2	2.5	.8	5.8	1.7
Feb	107.423	95.287	113.711	103.046	87.329	109.131	1.9	.4	2.6	.6	8.2	1.7
Mar	107.555	95.081	114.026	103.231	86.076	109.341	2.1	.4	2.9	.4	7.6	2.0
Apr	107.765	95.288	114.237	103.511	86.899	109.509	2.1	.8	2.7	.5	8.2	2.0
May	108.017	95.439	114.542	103.316	88.215	109.735	2.3	1.4	2.8	.3	12.4	2.1
June	108.182	95.473	114.779	103.420	88.855	109.878	2.4	1.5	2.8	.5	13.5	2.0
July	108.353	95.518	115.018	103.545	88.844	110.064	2.5	1.5	2.9	.5	14.1	2.1
Aug	108.390	95.285	115.202	103.467	89.280	110.086	2.3	1.0	2.8	.5	11.4	2.0
Sept	108.496	95.154	115.438	103.518	88.375	110.257	2.0	.3	2.8	.5	5.0	2.0
Oct	108.710	95.360	115.656	103.396	90.136	110.409	2.0	.7	2.6	.3	9.1	1.9
Nov	108.776	95.018	115.945	103.590	87.647	110.616	1.9	.3	2.7	.6	3.0	2.0
Dec	108.830	94.570	116.274	103.737	85.181	110.812	1.8	−.3	2.7	.7	−.3	2.0
2019: Jan	108.739	94.511	116.165	103.902	82.477	110.852	1.4	−.8	2.5	.8	−5.1	1.8
Feb	108.835	94.500	116.320	104.428	82.866	110.894	1.3	−.8	2.3	1.3	−5.1	1.6
Mar	109.064	94.760	116.532	104.687	85.845	110.960	1.4	−.3	2.2	1.4	−.3	1.5
Apr	109.403	94.949	116.951	104.326	88.365	111.232	1.5	−.4	2.4	.8	1.7	1.6
May	109.511	95.013	117.084	104.615	87.851	111.362	1.4	−.4	2.2	1.3	−.4	1.5
June	109.653	94.903	117.364	104.545	85.811	111.648	1.4	−.6	2.3	1.1	−3.4	1.6
July	109.909	95.048	117.682	104.482	87.008	111.878	1.4	−.5	2.3	.9	−2.1	1.6
Aug	109.938	94.795	117.869	104.299	85.291	112.027	1.4	−.5	2.3	.8	−4.5	1.8
Sept	109.935	94.474	118.043	104.344	84.156	112.085	1.3	−.7	2.3	.8	−4.8	1.7
Octᵖ	110.179	94.745	118.270	104.507	86.369	112.221	1.4	−.6	2.3	1.1	−4.2	1.6
Novᵖ	110.294	94.747	118.447	104.548	87.060	112.309	1.4	−.3	2.2	.9	−.7	1.5
Decᵖ	110.585	94.972	118.773	104.519	88.375	112.567	1.6	.4	2.1	.8	3.7	1.6

¹ Food consists of food and beverages purchased for off-premises consumption; food services, which include purchased meals and beverages, are not classified as food.
² Consists of gasoline and other energy goods and of electricity and gas services.

Source: Department of Commerce (Bureau of Economic Analysis).

Money Stock, Credit, and Finance

TABLE B–40. Money stock and debt measures, 1980–2019

[Averages of daily figures, except debt end-of-period basis; billions of dollars, seasonally adjusted]

Year and month	M1 — Sum of currency, demand deposits, travelers checks, and other checkable deposits	M2 — M1 plus savings deposits, retail MMMF balances, and small time deposits [1]	Debt — Debt of domestic nonfinancial sectors [2]	Percent change — From year or 6 months earlier [3] M1	M2	From previous period [4] Debt
December:						
1980	408.5	1,599.8	4,051.5	7.0	8.6	9.6
1981	436.7	1,755.5	4,464.7	6.9	9.7	10.2
1982	474.8	1,905.9	4,900.3	8.7	8.6	10.2
1983	521.4	2,123.5	5,497.7	9.8	11.4	12.1
1984	551.6	2,306.4	6,308.4	5.8	8.6	14.8
1985	619.8	2,492.1	7,341.7	12.4	8.1	16.1
1986	724.7	2,728.0	8,216.7	16.9	9.5	12.0
1987	750.2	2,826.4	8,936.1	3.5	3.6	9.0
1988	786.7	2,988.2	9,753.9	4.9	5.7	9.2
1989	792.9	3,152.5	10,501.9	.8	5.5	7.5
1990	824.7	3,271.8	11,218.1	4.0	3.8	6.6
1991	897.0	3,372.2	11,746.7	8.8	3.1	4.7
1992	1,024.9	3,424.1	12,298.0	14.3	1.6	4.7
1993	1,129.6	3,474.5	13,021.3	10.2	1.5	5.8
1994	1,150.7	3,486.4	13,701.7	1.9	.3	5.2
1995	1,127.5	3,629.5	14,386.1	−2.0	4.1	4.9
1996	1,081.3	3,810.4	15,135.9	−4.1	5.0	5.2
1997	1,072.3	4,022.8	15,974.5	−.8	5.6	5.6
1998	1,095.0	4,365.0	17,054.4	2.1	8.5	6.8
1999	1,122.2	4,627.4	18,227.3	2.5	6.0	6.7
2000	1,088.6	4,913.7	19,111.2	−3.0	6.2	4.8
2001	1,183.2	5,421.6	20,186.7	8.7	10.3	5.7
2002	1,220.2	5,759.7	21,536.9	3.1	6.2	6.7
2003	1,306.2	6,054.2	23,234.6	7.0	5.1	7.7
2004	1,376.0	6,405.0	26,144.5	5.3	5.8	9.2
2005	1,374.3	6,668.0	28,425.4	−.1	4.1	8.8
2006	1,366.6	7,057.5	30,866.6	−.6	5.8	8.5
2007	1,373.4	7,458.0	33,361.5	.5	5.7	8.2
2008	1,601.7	8,181.0	35,141.2	16.6	9.7	5.8
2009	1,692.8	8,483.4	36,116.9	5.7	3.7	3.7
2010	1,836.7	8,789.3	37,493.0	8.5	3.6	4.4
2011	2,164.2	9,651.1	38,700.4	17.8	9.8	3.6
2012	2,461.2	10,445.7	40,387.6	13.7	8.2	4.8
2013	2,664.5	11,015.0	41,795.2	8.3	5.5	3.7
2014	2,940.3	11,668.0	43,472.1	10.4	5.9	4.1
2015	3,093.8	12,330.1	45,218.1	5.2	5.7	4.4
2016	3,339.8	13,198.9	47,197.7	8.0	7.0	4.5
2017	3,607.3	13,835.6	49,290.4	8.0	4.8	4.2
2018	3,746.5	14,351.7	51,876.2	3.9	3.7	4.6
2019 ᴾ	3,978.3	15,318.3	....	6.2	6.7	....
2018: Jan	3,649.5	13,858.3		5.5	3.5	
Feb	3,619.7	13,892.8		1.9	3.2	
Mar	3,661.9	13,952.6	50,109.5	4.9	3.4	6.7
Apr	3,662.4	13,989.1		3.2	3.2	
May	3,658.1	14,054.9		1.7	3.8	
June	3,657.6	14,120.0	50,920.3	2.8	4.1	4.0
July	3,677.1	14,153.0		1.5	4.3	
Aug	3,686.4	14,197.0		3.7	4.4	
Sept	3,703.9	14,228.5	51,448.2	2.3	4.0	4.1
Oct	3,719.1	14,235.4		3.1	3.5	
Nov	3,698.1	14,245.4		2.2	2.7	
Dec	3,746.5	14,351.7	51,876.2	4.9	3.3	3.4
2019: Jan	3,740.5	14,434.6		3.4	4.0	
Feb	3,759.7	14,464.4		4.0	3.8	
Mar	3,730.0	14,511.8	52,649.9	1.4	4.0	6.0
Apr	3,781.0	14,558.3		3.3	4.5	
May	3,792.5	14,653.2		5.1	5.7	
June	3,832.9	14,780.7	53,060.4	4.6	6.0	3.2
July	3,858.2	14,860.8		6.3	5.9	
Aug	3,853.4	14,933.7		5.0	6.5	
Sept	3,903.3	15,024.9	53,895.6	9.3	7.1	6.3
Oct	3,923.3	15,154.6		7.5	8.2	
Nov	3,948.2	15,259.1		8.2	8.3	
Dec ᴾ	3,978.3	15,318.3		7.6	7.3	

[1] Money market mutual fund (MMMF). Savings deposits include money market deposit accounts.
[2] Consists of outstanding debt securities and loans of the U.S. Government, State and local governments, and private nonfinancial sectors. Quarterly data shown in last month of quarter. End-of-year data are for fourth quarter.
[3] Annual changes are from December to December; monthly changes are from six months earlier at an annual rate.
[4] Debt growth of domestic nonfinancial sectors is the seasonally adjusted borrowing flow divided by the seasonally adjusted level of debt outstanding in the previous period. Annual changes are from fourth quarter to fourth quarter; quarterly changes are from previous quarter at an annual rate.

Note: For further information on the composition of M1 and M2, see the H.6 release.
For further information on the debt of domestic nonfinancial sectors and the derivation of debt growth, see the Z.1 release.

Source: Board of Governors of the Federal Reserve System.

TABLE B–41. Consumer credit outstanding, 1970–2019

[Amount outstanding (end of month); millions of dollars, seasonally adjusted]

Year and month	Total consumer credit [1]	Revolving	Nonrevolving [2]
December:			
1970	131,551.55	4,961.46	126,590.09
1971	146,930.18	8,245.33	138,684.84
1972	166,189.10	9,379.24	156,809.86
1973	190,086.31	11,342.22	178,744.09
1974	198,917.84	13,241.26	185,676.58
1975	204,002.00	14,495.27	189,506.73
1976	225,721.59	16,489.05	209,232.54
1977	260,562.70	37,414.82	223,147.88
1978	306,100.39	45,690.95	260,409.43
1979	348,589.11	53,596.43	294,992.67
1980	351,920.05	54,970.05	296,950.00
1981	371,301.44	60,928.00	310,373.44
1982	389,848.74	66,348.30	323,500.44
1983	437,068.86	79,027.25	358,041.61
1984	517,278.98	100,385.63	416,893.35
1985	599,711.23	124,465.80	475,245.43
1986	654,750.24	141,068.15	513,682.08
1987	686,318.77	160,853.91	525,464.86
1988 [3]	731,917.76	184,593.12	547,324.64
1989	794,612.18	211,229.83	583,382.34
1990	808,230.57	238,642.62	569,587.95
1991	798,028.97	263,768.55	534,260.42
1992	806,118.69	278,449.67	527,669.02
1993	865,650.58	309,908.02	555,742.56
1994	997,301.74	365,569.56	631,732.19
1995	1,140,744.36	443,920.09	696,824.27
1996	1,253,437.09	507,516.57	745,920.52
1997	1,324,757.33	540,005.56	784,751.77
1998	1,420,996.44	581,414.78	839,581.66
1999	1,531,105.96	610,696.47	920,409.49
2000	1,716,969.72	682,646.37	1,034,323.35
2001	1,867,852.87	714,840.73	1,153,012.14
2002	1,972,112.21	750,947.45	1,221,164.76
2003	2,077,360.69	768,258.31	1,309,102.38
2004	2,192,246.17	799,552.18	1,392,693.99
2005	2,290,928.13	829,518.36	1,461,409.78
2006	2,456,715.70	923,876.78	1,532,838.92
2007	2,609,476.53	1,001,625.30	1,607,851.24
2008	2,643,788.96	1,003,997.04	1,639,791.92
2009	2,555,016.64	916,076.63	1,638,940.01
2010	2,646,811.26	839,102.67	1,807,708.59
2011	2,756,560.85	840,353.23	1,916,207.63
2012	2,913,573.02	840,363.84	2,073,209.18
2013	3,091,413.78	854,663.80	2,236,749.97
2014	3,312,505.08	888,017.64	2,424,487.44
2015	3,410,996.57	906,744.37	2,504,252.20
2016	3,644,143.62	967,960.66	2,676,182.96
2017	3,828,250.27	1,022,134.80	2,806,115.47
2018	4,009,717.68	1,053,479.02	2,956,238.65
2018: Jan	3,840,176.17	1,024,054.87	2,816,121.30
Feb	3,852,003.88	1,024,708.23	2,827,295.65
Mar	3,862,271.47	1,023,932.68	2,838,338.79
Apr	3,864,949.99	1,016,775.15	2,848,174.84
May	3,886,398.36	1,025,130.91	2,861,267.45
June	3,895,227.04	1,024,156.53	2,871,070.51
July	3,920,294.63	1,034,058.42	2,886,236.22
Aug	3,941,733.06	1,039,029.18	2,902,703.88
Sept	3,956,036.79	1,040,481.75	2,915,555.05
Oct	3,975,943.48	1,049,193.85	2,926,749.63
Nov	3,997,751.70	1,056,201.47	2,941,550.23
Dec	4,009,717.68	1,053,479.02	2,956,238.65
2019: Jan	4,026,836.02	1,056,679.40	2,970,156.62
Feb	4,042,533.60	1,060,280.73	2,982,252.86
Mar	4,052,519.03	1,057,464.98	2,995,054.05
Apr	4,069,111.45	1,064,251.54	3,004,859.91
May	4,086,179.75	1,071,936.03	3,014,243.72
June	4,094,633.74	1,071,171.24	3,023,462.51
July	4,117,566.83	1,081,526.26	3,036,040.58
Aug	4,135,608.55	1,080,636.56	3,054,971.99
Sept	4,144,551.33	1,080,825.99	3,063,725.34
Oct	4,163,527.69	1,088,739.32	3,074,788.37
Nov [p]	4,176,041.03	1,086,304.05	3,089,736.98

[1] Covers most short- and intermediate-term credit extended to individuals. Credit secured by real estate is excluded.
[2] Includes automobile loans and all other loans not included in revolving credit, such as loans for mobile homes, education, boats, trailers, or vacations. These loans may be secured or unsecured. Beginning with 1977, includes student loans extended by the Federal Government and by SLM Holding Corporation.
[3] Data newly available in January 1989 result in breaks in these series between December 1988 and subsequent months.

Source: Board of Governors of the Federal Reserve System.

Table B–42. Bond yields and interest rates, 1949–2019

[Percent per annum]

Year	U.S. Treasury securities — Bills (at auction)[1] 3-month	6-month	Constant maturities[2] 3-year	10-year	30-year	Corporate bonds (Moody's) Aaa[3]	Baa	High-grade municipal bonds (Standard & Poor's)	New-home mortgage yields[4]	Prime rate charged by banks[5]	Discount window (Federal Reserve Bank of New York)[5,6] Primary credit	Adjustment credit	Federal funds rate[7]
1949	1.102	....	....	....	....	2.66	3.42	2.21	....	2.00	....	1.50	....
1950	1.218	....	....	....	....	2.62	3.24	1.98	....	2.07	....	1.59	....
1951	1.552	....	....	....	....	2.86	3.41	2.00	....	2.56	....	1.75	....
1952	1.766	....	....	....	....	2.96	3.52	2.19	....	3.00	....	1.75	....
1953	1.931	....	2.47	2.85	....	3.20	3.74	2.72	....	3.17	....	1.99	....
1954	.953	....	1.63	2.40	....	2.90	3.51	2.37	....	3.05	....	1.60	....
1955	1.753	....	2.47	2.82	....	3.06	3.53	2.53	....	3.16	....	1.89	1.79
1956	2.658	....	3.19	3.18	....	3.36	3.88	2.93	....	3.77	....	2.77	2.73
1957	3.267	....	3.98	3.65	....	3.89	4.71	3.60	....	4.20	....	3.12	3.11
1958	1.839	....	2.84	3.32	....	3.79	4.73	3.56	....	3.83	....	2.15	1.57
1959	3.405	3.832	4.46	4.33	....	4.38	5.05	3.95	....	4.48	....	3.36	3.31
1960	2.93	3.25	3.98	4.12	....	4.41	5.19	3.73	....	4.82	....	3.53	3.21
1961	2.38	2.61	3.54	3.88	....	4.35	5.08	3.46	....	4.50	....	3.00	1.95
1962	2.78	2.91	3.47	3.95	....	4.33	5.02	3.18	....	4.50	....	3.00	2.71
1963	3.16	3.25	3.67	4.00	....	4.26	4.86	3.23	5.89	4.50	....	3.23	3.18
1964	3.56	3.69	4.03	4.19	....	4.40	4.83	3.22	5.83	4.50	....	3.55	3.50
1965	3.95	4.05	4.22	4.28	....	4.49	4.87	3.27	5.81	4.54	....	4.04	4.07
1966	4.88	5.08	5.23	4.93	....	5.13	5.67	3.82	6.25	5.63	....	4.50	5.11
1967	4.32	4.63	5.03	5.07	....	5.51	6.23	3.98	6.46	5.63	....	4.19	4.22
1968	5.34	5.47	5.68	5.64	....	6.18	6.94	4.51	6.97	6.31	....	5.17	5.66
1969	6.68	6.85	7.02	6.67	....	7.03	7.81	5.81	7.81	7.96	....	5.87	8.21
1970	6.43	6.53	7.29	7.35	....	8.04	9.11	6.51	8.45	7.91	....	5.95	7.17
1971	4.35	4.51	5.66	6.16	....	7.39	8.56	5.70	7.74	5.73	....	4.88	4.67
1972	4.07	4.47	5.72	6.21	....	7.21	8.16	5.27	7.60	5.25	....	4.50	4.44
1973	7.04	7.18	6.96	6.85	....	7.44	8.24	5.18	7.96	8.03	....	6.45	8.74
1974	7.89	7.93	7.84	7.56	....	8.57	9.50	6.09	8.92	10.81	....	7.83	10.51
1975	5.84	6.12	7.50	7.99	....	8.83	10.61	6.89	9.00	7.86	....	6.25	5.82
1976	4.99	5.27	6.77	7.61	....	8.43	9.75	6.49	9.00	6.84	....	5.50	5.05
1977	5.27	5.52	6.68	7.42	7.75	8.02	8.97	5.56	9.02	6.83	....	5.46	5.54
1978	7.22	7.58	8.29	8.41	8.49	8.73	9.49	5.90	9.56	9.06	....	7.46	7.94
1979	10.05	10.02	9.70	9.43	9.28	9.63	10.69	6.39	10.78	12.67	....	10.29	11.20
1980	11.51	11.37	11.51	11.43	11.27	11.94	13.67	8.51	12.66	15.26	....	11.77	13.35
1981	14.03	13.78	14.46	13.92	13.45	14.17	16.04	11.23	14.70	18.87	....	13.42	16.39
1982	10.69	11.08	12.93	13.01	12.76	13.79	16.11	11.57	15.14	14.85	....	11.01	12.24
1983	8.63	8.75	10.45	11.10	11.18	12.04	13.55	9.47	12.57	10.79	....	8.50	9.09
1984	9.53	9.77	11.92	12.46	12.41	12.71	14.19	10.15	12.38	12.04	....	8.80	10.23
1985	7.47	7.64	9.64	10.62	10.79	11.37	12.72	9.18	11.55	9.93	....	7.69	8.10
1986	5.98	6.03	7.06	7.67	7.78	9.02	10.39	7.38	10.17	8.33	....	6.32	6.80
1987	5.82	6.05	7.68	8.39	8.59	9.38	10.58	7.73	9.31	8.21	....	5.66	6.66
1988	6.69	6.92	8.26	8.85	8.96	9.71	10.83	7.76	9.19	9.32	....	6.20	7.57
1989	8.12	8.04	8.55	8.49	8.45	9.26	10.18	7.24	10.13	10.87	....	6.93	9.21
1990	7.51	7.47	8.26	8.55	8.61	9.32	10.36	7.25	10.05	10.01	....	6.98	8.10
1991	5.42	5.49	6.82	7.86	8.14	8.77	9.80	6.89	9.32	8.46	....	5.45	5.69
1992	3.45	3.57	5.30	7.01	7.67	8.14	8.98	6.41	8.24	6.25	....	3.25	3.52
1993	3.02	3.14	4.44	5.87	6.59	7.22	7.93	5.63	7.20	6.00	....	3.00	3.02
1994	4.29	4.66	6.27	7.09	7.37	7.96	8.62	6.19	7.49	7.15	....	3.60	4.21
1995	5.51	5.59	6.25	6.57	6.88	7.59	8.20	5.95	7.87	8.83	....	5.21	5.83
1996	5.02	5.09	5.99	6.44	6.71	7.37	8.05	5.75	7.80	8.27	....	5.02	5.30
1997	5.07	5.18	6.10	6.35	6.61	7.26	7.86	5.55	7.71	8.44	....	5.00	5.46
1998	4.81	4.85	5.14	5.26	5.58	6.53	7.22	5.12	7.07	8.35	....	4.92	5.35
1999	4.66	4.76	5.49	5.65	5.87	7.04	7.87	5.43	7.04	8.00	....	4.62	4.97
2000	5.85	5.92	6.22	6.03	5.94	7.62	8.36	5.77	7.52	9.23	....	5.73	6.24
2001	3.44	3.39	4.09	5.02	5.49	7.08	7.95	5.19	7.00	6.91	....	3.40	3.88
2002	1.62	1.69	3.10	4.61	5.43	6.49	7.80	5.05	6.43	4.67	....	1.17	1.67
2003	1.01	1.06	2.10	4.01	....	5.67	6.77	4.73	5.80	4.12	2.12	....	1.13
2004	1.38	1.57	2.78	4.27	....	5.63	6.39	4.63	5.77	4.34	2.34	....	1.35
2005	3.16	3.40	3.93	4.29	....	5.24	6.06	4.29	5.94	6.19	4.19	....	3.22
2006	4.73	4.80	4.77	4.80	4.91	5.59	6.48	4.42	6.63	7.96	5.96	....	4.97
2007	4.41	4.48	4.35	4.63	4.84	5.56	6.48	4.42	6.41	8.05	5.86	....	5.02
2008	1.48	1.71	2.24	3.66	4.28	5.63	7.45	4.80	6.05	5.09	2.39	....	1.92
2009	.16	.29	1.43	3.26	4.08	5.31	7.30	4.64	5.14	3.25	.50	....	.16
2010	.14	.20	1.11	3.22	4.25	4.94	6.04	4.16	4.80	3.25	.72	....	.18
2011	.06	.10	.75	2.78	3.91	4.64	5.66	4.29	4.56	3.25	.75	....	.10
2012	.09	.13	.38	1.80	2.92	3.67	4.94	3.14	3.69	3.25	.75	....	.14
2013	.06	.09	.54	2.35	3.45	4.24	5.10	3.96	4.00	3.25	.75	....	.11
2014	.03	.06	.90	2.54	3.34	4.16	4.85	3.78	4.22	3.25	.75	....	.09
2015	.06	.17	1.02	2.14	2.84	3.89	5.00	3.48	4.01	3.26	.76	....	.13
2016	.33	.46	1.00	1.84	2.59	3.67	4.72	3.07	3.76	3.51	1.01	....	.39
2017	.94	1.05	1.58	2.33	2.89	3.74	4.44	3.36	3.97	4.10	1.60	....	1.00
2018	1.94	2.10	2.63	2.91	3.11	3.93	4.80	3.53	4.53	4.91	2.41	....	1.83
2019	2.08	2.07	1.94	2.14	2.58	3.39	4.38	3.38	....	5.28	2.78	....	2.16

[1] High bill rate at auction, issue date within period, bank-discount basis. On or after October 28, 1998, data are stop yields from uniform-price auctions. Before that date, they are weighted average yields from multiple-price auctions.

See next page for continuation of table.

[Percent per annum]

Year and month	U.S. Treasury securities					Corporate bonds (Moody's)		High-grade municipal bonds (Standard & Poor's)	New-home mortgage yields[4]	Prime rate charged by banks[5]	Discount window (Federal Reserve Bank of New York)[5,6]		Federal funds rate[7]
	Bills (at auction)[1]		Constant maturities[2]								Primary credit	Adjustment credit	
	3-month	6-month	3-year	10-year	30-year	Aaa[3]	Baa			High-low	High-low	High-low	
2015: Jan	0.03	0.10	0.90	1.88	2.46	3.46	4.45	3.16	4.05	3.25–3.25	0.75–0.75	....	0.11
Feb	.02	.07	.99	1.98	2.57	3.61	4.51	3.26	3.91	3.25–3.25	0.75–0.75	....	.11
Mar	.02	.11	1.02	2.04	2.63	3.64	4.54	3.29	3.93	3.25–3.25	0.75–0.75	....	.11
Apr	.03	.10	.87	1.94	2.59	3.52	4.48	3.40	3.92	3.25–3.25	0.75–0.75	....	.12
May	.02	.08	.98	2.20	2.96	3.98	4.89	3.77	3.89	3.25–3.25	0.75–0.75	....	.12
June	.01	.08	1.07	2.36	3.11	4.19	5.13	3.76	3.98	3.25–3.25	0.75–0.75	....	.13
July	.03	.12	1.03	2.32	3.07	4.15	5.20	3.73	4.10	3.25–3.25	0.75–0.75	....	.13
Aug	.09	.21	1.03	2.17	2.86	4.04	5.19	3.57	4.12	3.25–3.25	0.75–0.75	....	.14
Sept	.06	.23	1.01	2.17	2.95	4.07	5.34	3.56	4.09	3.25–3.25	0.75–0.75	....	.14
Oct	.01	.10	.93	2.07	2.89	3.95	5.34	3.48	4.02	3.25–3.25	0.75–0.75	....	.12
Nov	.13	.33	1.20	2.26	3.03	4.06	5.46	3.50	4.00	3.25–3.25	0.75–0.75	....	.12
Dec	.26	.52	1.28	2.24	2.97	3.97	5.46	3.23	4.03	3.50–3.25	1.00–0.75	....	.24
2016: Jan	.25	.44	1.14	2.09	2.86	4.00	5.45	3.01	4.04	3.50–3.50	1.00–1.00	....	.34
Feb	.32	.44	.90	1.78	2.62	3.96	5.34	3.21	4.01	3.50–3.50	1.00–1.00	....	.38
Mar	.32	.48	1.04	1.89	2.68	3.82	5.13	3.28	3.92	3.50–3.50	1.00–1.00	....	.36
Apr	.23	.37	.92	1.81	2.62	3.62	4.79	3.04	3.86	3.50–3.50	1.00–1.00	....	.37
May	.27	.41	.97	1.81	2.63	3.65	4.68	2.95	3.82	3.50–3.50	1.00–1.00	....	.37
June	.29	.41	.86	1.64	2.45	3.50	4.53	2.84	3.81	3.50–3.50	1.00–1.00	....	.38
July	.31	.40	.79	1.50	2.23	3.28	4.22	2.57	3.74	3.50–3.50	1.00–1.00	....	.39
Aug	.30	.43	.85	1.56	2.26	3.32	4.24	2.77	3.68	3.50–3.50	1.00–1.00	....	.40
Sept	.32	.48	.90	1.63	2.35	3.41	4.31	2.86	3.58	3.50–3.50	1.00–1.00	....	.40
Oct	.34	.48	.99	1.76	2.50	3.51	4.38	3.13	3.57	3.50–3.50	1.00–1.00	....	.40
Nov	.44	.57	1.22	2.14	2.86	3.86	4.71	3.36	3.63	3.50–3.50	1.00–1.00	....	.41
Dec	.52	.64	1.49	2.49	3.11	4.06	4.83	3.81	3.74	3.75–3.50	1.25–1.00	....	.54
2017: Jan	.52	.61	1.48	2.43	3.02	3.92	4.66	3.68	4.06	3.75–3.75	1.25–1.25	....	.65
Feb	.53	.64	1.47	2.42	3.03	3.95	4.64	3.74	4.21	3.75–3.75	1.25–1.25	....	.66
Mar	.72	.84	1.59	2.48	3.08	4.01	4.68	3.78	4.16	4.00–3.75	1.50–1.25	....	.79
Apr	.81	.94	1.44	2.30	2.94	3.87	4.57	3.54	4.10	4.00–4.00	1.50–1.50	....	.90
May	.89	1.02	1.48	2.30	2.96	3.85	4.55	3.47	4.04	4.00–4.00	1.50–1.50	....	.91
June	.99	1.09	1.49	2.19	2.80	3.68	4.37	3.06	4.00	4.25–4.00	1.75–1.50	....	1.04
July	1.08	1.12	1.54	2.32	2.88	3.70	4.39	3.03	3.88	4.25–4.25	1.75–1.75	....	1.15
Aug	1.03	1.12	1.48	2.21	2.80	3.63	4.31	3.23	3.97	4.25–4.25	1.75–1.75	....	1.16
Sept	1.04	1.15	1.51	2.20	2.78	3.63	4.30	3.27	3.89	4.25–4.25	1.75–1.75	....	1.15
Oct	1.08	1.22	1.68	2.36	2.88	3.60	4.32	3.31	3.76	4.25–4.25	1.75–1.75	....	1.15
Nov	1.23	1.35	1.81	2.35	2.80	3.57	4.27	3.03	3.81	4.25–4.25	1.75–1.75	....	1.16
Dec	1.35	1.48	1.96	2.40	2.77	3.51	4.22	3.21	3.90	4.50–4.25	2.00–1.75	....	1.30
2018: Jan	1.43	1.59	2.15	2.58	2.88	3.55	4.26	3.29	3.94	4.50–4.50	2.00–2.00	....	1.41
Feb	1.53	1.72	2.36	2.86	3.13	3.82	4.51	3.54	4.15	4.50–4.50	2.00–2.00	....	1.42
Mar	1.70	1.87	2.42	2.84	3.09	3.87	4.64	3.58	4.33	4.75–4.50	2.25–2.00	....	1.51
Apr	1.76	1.93	2.52	2.87	3.07	3.85	4.67	3.55	4.52	4.75–4.75	2.25–2.25	....	1.69
May	1.87	2.03	2.66	2.98	3.13	4.00	4.83	3.38	4.55	4.75–4.75	2.25–2.25	....	1.70
June	1.91	2.08	2.65	2.91	3.05	3.96	4.83	3.15	4.58	5.00–4.75	2.50–2.25	....	1.82
July	1.96	2.12	2.70	2.89	3.01	3.87	4.79	3.45	4.62	5.00–5.00	2.50–2.50	....	1.91
Aug	2.03	2.18	2.71	2.89	3.04	3.88	4.77	3.58	4.57	5.00–5.00	2.50–2.50	....	1.91
Sept	2.13	2.28	2.84	3.00	3.15	3.98	4.88	3.63	4.64	5.25–5.00	2.75–2.50	....	1.95
Oct	2.24	2.39	2.94	3.15	3.34	4.14	5.07	3.88	4.67	5.25–5.25	2.75–2.75	....	2.19
Nov	2.34	2.46	2.91	3.12	3.36	4.22	5.22	3.64	4.77	5.25–5.25	2.75–2.75	....	2.20
Dec	2.38	2.49	2.67	2.83	3.10	4.02	5.13	3.69	4.84	5.50–5.25	3.00–2.75	....	2.27
2019: Jan	2.41	2.47	2.52	2.71	3.04	3.93	5.12	3.61	4.76	5.50–5.50	3.00–3.00	....	2.40
Feb	2.40	2.45	2.48	2.68	3.02	3.79	4.95	3.57	4.60	5.50–5.50	3.00–3.00	....	2.40
Mar	2.41	2.45	2.37	2.57	2.98	3.77	4.84	3.43	4.51	5.50–5.50	3.00–3.00	....	2.41
Apr	2.38	2.39	2.31	2.53	2.94	3.69	4.70	3.27	4.34	5.50–5.50	3.00–3.00	....	2.42
May	2.35	2.36	2.16	2.40	2.82	3.67	4.63	3.11	....	5.50–5.50	3.00–3.00	....	2.39
June	2.20	2.14	1.78	2.07	2.57	3.42	4.46	2.87	....	5.50–5.50	3.00–3.00	....	2.38
July	2.13	2.03	1.80	2.06	2.57	3.29	4.28	3.32	....	5.50–5.50	3.00–3.00	....	2.40
Aug	1.97	1.91	1.51	1.63	2.12	2.98	3.87	3.61	....	5.50–5.25	3.00–2.75	....	2.13
Sept	1.93	1.85	1.59	1.70	2.16	3.03	3.91	3.57	....	5.25–5.00	2.75–2.50	....	2.04
Oct	1.68	1.66	1.53	1.71	2.19	3.01	3.93	3.67	....	5.00–4.75	2.50–2.25	....	1.83
Nov	1.55	1.55	1.61	1.81	2.28	3.06	3.94	3.26	....	4.75–4.75	2.25–2.25	....	1.55
Dec	1.54	1.55	1.63	1.86	2.30	3.01	3.88	3.26	....	4.75–4.75	2.25–2.25	....	1.55

[2] Yields on the more actively traded issues adjusted to constant maturities by the Department of the Treasury. The 30-year Treasury constant maturity series was discontinued on February 18, 2002, and reintroduced on February 9, 2006.
[3] Beginning with December 7, 2001, data for corporate Aaa series are industrial bonds only.
[4] Effective rate (in the primary market) on conventional mortgages, reflecting fees and charges as well as contract rate and assuming, on the average, repayment at end of 10 years. Rates beginning with January 1973 not strictly comparable with prior rates.
[5] For monthly data, high and low for the period.
[6] Primary credit replaced adjustment credit as the Federal Reserve's principal discount window lending program effective January 9, 2003.
[7] Beginning March 1, 2016, the daily effective federal funds rate is a volume-weighted median of transaction-level data collected from depository institutions in the Report of Selected Money Market Rates (FR 2420). Between July 21, 1975 and February 29, 2016, the daily effective rate was a volume-weighted mean of rates on brokered trades. Prior to that, the daily effective rate was the rate considered most representative of the day's transactions, usually the one at which most transactions occurred.

Sources: Department of the Treasury, Board of Governors of the Federal Reserve System, Federal Housing Finance Agency, Moody's Investors Service, Bloomberg, and Standard & Poor's.

[Billions of dollars]

End of year or quarter	All properties	Farm properties	Nonfarm properties Total	1- to 4-family houses	Multi-family properties	Commercial properties	Government underwritten Total[1]	Government underwritten 1- to 4-family houses Total	FHA-insured	VA-guaranteed	Conventional[2] Total	Conventional 1- to 4-family houses
1960	227.1	17.4	209.7	137.8	28.0	43.9	62.3	56.4	26.7	29.7	147.4	81.4
1961	248.6	18.7	229.9	149.5	31.5	48.9	65.6	59.1	29.5	29.6	164.3	90.4
1962	271.8	20.3	251.6	163.1	34.6	53.8	69.4	62.2	32.3	29.9	182.2	100.9
1963	297.6	22.4	275.1	179.0	37.5	58.7	73.4	65.9	35.0	30.9	201.7	113.1
1964	324.2	25.3	298.9	195.7	41.6	61.7	77.2	69.2	38.3	30.9	221.7	126.4
1965	349.5	28.2	321.3	212.0	44.2	65.2	81.2	73.1	42.0	31.1	240.2	138.9
1966	373.7	30.3	343.4	225.3	46.9	71.2	84.1	76.1	44.8	31.3	259.3	149.3
1967	396.9	32.9	363.9	238.0	50.0	75.9	88.2	79.9	47.4	32.5	275.7	158.1
1968	424.5	36.0	388.5	254.2	53.0	81.3	93.4	84.4	50.6	33.8	295.1	169.8
1969	450.5	38.4	412.1	269.0	56.5	86.6	100.2	90.2	54.5	35.7	311.9	178.9
1970	498.5	40.8	457.6	292.2	68.1	97.3	109.2	97.3	59.9	37.3	348.4	195.0
1971	544.5	43.9	500.6	318.4	76.6	105.6	120.7	105.2	65.7	39.5	379.9	213.2
1972	618.2	47.7	570.5	357.4	89.7	123.5	131.1	113.0	68.2	44.7	439.4	244.4
1973	694.2	53.4	640.7	399.8	99.0	141.9	135.0	116.2	66.2	50.0	505.7	283.6
1974	766.2	62.5	703.7	441.2	105.7	156.7	140.2	121.3	65.1	56.2	563.5	319.9
1975	830.2	68.9	761.3	483.0	105.5	172.8	147.0	127.7	66.1	61.6	614.3	355.2
1976	917.5	76.7	840.8	544.8	110.1	185.9	154.0	133.5	66.5	67.0	686.8	411.2
1977	1,049.7	88.3	961.4	638.5	118.0	204.9	161.7	141.6	68.0	73.6	799.7	496.9
1978	1,206.8	100.3	1,106.4	751.4	128.7	226.3	176.4	153.4	71.4	82.0	930.0	598.0
1979	1,381.0	120.5	1,260.5	870.2	139.4	250.8	199.3	172.9	81.0	92.0	1,061.4	697.3
1980	1,528.2	132.7	1,395.5	977.3	146.4	271.8	225.1	195.2	93.6	101.6	1,170.4	782.2
1981	1,654.6	146.7	1,507.9	1,052.6	146.4	308.9	238.9	207.6	101.3	106.2	1,269.0	845.1
1982	1,741.4	150.9	1,590.4	1,097.2	152.4	340.9	248.9	217.9	108.0	109.9	1,341.6	879.3
1983	1,942.4	153.9	1,788.5	1,217.8	171.9	398.8	279.8	248.8	127.4	121.4	1,508.7	968.9
1984	2,178.3	150.1	2,028.1	1,350.7	197.2	480.2	294.8	265.9	136.7	129.1	1,733.3	1,084.9
1985	2,439.9	125.3	2,314.6	1,548.9	213.9	551.8	328.3	288.8	153.0	135.8	1,986.3	1,260.1
1986	2,676.3	101.3	2,574.9	1,730.1	241.8	603.0	370.5	328.6	185.5	143.1	2,204.4	1,401.5
1987	2,968.8	89.9	2,878.9	1,928.5	258.4	692.1	431.4	387.9	235.5	152.4	2,447.5	1,540.6
1988	3,283.8	82.3	3,201.5	2,162.8	274.5	764.2	459.7	414.2	258.8	155.4	2,741.8	1,748.6
1989	3,534.5	79.2	3,455.3	2,369.6	287.0	798.7	486.8	440.1	282.8	157.3	2,968.4	1,929.5
1990	3,790.0	77.6	3,712.5	2,606.8	287.4	818.3	517.9	470.9	310.9	160.0	3,194.5	2,135.9
1991	3,941.7	77.7	3,864.0	2,774.7	284.1	805.2	537.2	493.3	330.6	162.7	3,326.8	2,281.4
1992	4,052.4	78.6	3,973.8	2,942.1	270.9	760.8	533.3	489.8	326.0	163.8	3,440.5	2,452.3
1993	4,183.7	79.8	4,103.9	3,101.0	267.7	735.2	513.4	469.5	303.2	166.2	3,590.4	2,631.5
1994	4,348.1	81.6	4,266.5	3,278.2	268.2	720.1	559.3	514.2	336.8	177.3	3,707.2	2,764.0
1995	4,520.7	71.7	4,449.0	3,445.7	273.9	729.4	584.3	537.1	352.3	184.7	3,864.7	2,908.6
1996	4,801.2	74.4	4,726.8	3,681.9	286.1	758.8	620.3	571.2	379.2	192.0	4,106.5	3,110.8
1997	5,114.0	78.5	5,035.5	3,916.5	298.0	821.0	656.7	605.7	405.7	200.0	4,378.9	3,310.8
1998	5,603.2	83.1	5,520.1	4,275.8	334.5	909.8	674.0	623.8	417.9	205.9	4,846.1	3,652.0
1999	6,209.5	87.2	6,122.3	4,701.2	375.2	1,046.0	731.5	678.8	462.3	216.5	5,390.9	4,022.4
2000	6,766.6	84.7	6,681.9	5,125.0	404.5	1,152.4	773.1	719.9	499.9	220.1	5,908.8	4,405.0
2001	7,450.0	88.5	7,361.5	5,678.0	446.1	1,237.4	772.7	718.5	497.4	221.2	6,588.8	4,959.5
2002	8,358.7	95.4	8,263.3	6,434.4	486.3	1,342.5	759.3	704.0	486.2	217.7	7,504.0	5,730.4
2003	9,366.8	83.2	9,283.6	7,261.4	560.5	1,461.7	709.2	653.3	438.7	214.6	8,574.4	6,608.1
2004	10,648.6	95.7	10,552.9	8,293.1	610.1	1,649.7	660.2	604.1	398.1	206.0	9,892.7	7,689.0
2005	12,116.7	104.8	12,011.9	9,449.6	675.2	1,887.0	606.6	550.4	348.4	202.0	11,405.3	8,899.2
2006	13,529.5	108.0	13,421.4	10,531.8	718.4	2,171.2	600.2	543.5	336.9	206.6	12,821.3	9,988.4
2007	14,613.1	112.7	14,500.4	11,253.2	811.4	2,435.8	609.2	552.6	342.6	210.0	13,891.3	10,700.6
2008	14,693.6	134.7	14,558.9	11,152.0	853.9	2,553.1	807.2	750.7	534.0	216.7	13,751.7	10,401.3
2009	14,449.3	146.0	14,303.3	10,962.3	864.0	2,477.0	1,005.0	944.3	752.6	191.7	13,298.3	10,018.1
2010	13,896.3	154.1	13,742.2	10,524.6	864.0	2,353.6	1,227.6	1,156.1	934.4	221.7	12,514.5	9,368.5
2011	13,571.8	167.2	13,404.6	10,282.8	864.6	2,257.2	1,368.6	1,291.3	1,036.0	255.3	12,036.0	8,991.6
2012	13,335.8	173.4	13,162.4	10,049.7	892.8	2,219.8	1,544.8	1,459.7	1,165.4	294.2	11,617.5	8,590.1
2013	13,344.0	185.2	13,158.8	9,959.2	940.7	2,258.9	3,927.2	3,832.6	3,480.8	351.8	9,231.6	6,126.6
2014	13,489.8	196.8	13,293.0	9,938.3	1,010.5	2,344.2	4,130.9	4,028.1	3,615.3	412.8	9,162.1	5,910.2
2015	13,880.1	208.8	13,671.9	10,076.3	1,118.5	2,477.1	4,432.7	4,326.7	3,851.3	475.4	9,239.2	5,749.5
2016	14,332.4	226.0	14,106.4	10,277.5	1,236.6	2,592.3	4,764.8	4,654.9	4,106.9	548.1	9,341.6	5,622.5
2017	14,888.7	236.2	14,652.5	10,580.3	1,357.5	2,714.7	5,079.1	4,958.2	4,344.3	613.9	9,573.4	5,622.2
2018	15,424.0	245.7	15,178.3	10,866.8	1,473.8	2,837.7	5,380.0	5,246.5	4,562.3	684.2	9,798.3	5,620.2
2018: I	14,979.0	238.5	14,740.5	10,619.7	1,378.0	2,742.8	5,148.7	5,024.1	4,393.2	630.9	9,591.8	5,595.6
II	15,144.9	240.9	14,904.0	10,704.7	1,405.4	2,793.9	5,219.0	5,090.9	4,444.8	646.1	9,685.0	5,613.8
III	15,290.1	243.3	15,046.8	10,803.2	1,440.6	2,803.0	5,292.3	5,162.2	4,498.6	663.7	9,754.5	5,640.9
IV	15,424.0	245.7	15,178.3	10,866.8	1,473.8	2,837.7	5,380.0	5,246.5	4,562.3	684.2	9,798.3	5,620.2
2019: I	15,512.6	248.5	15,264.1	10,896.3	1,497.6	2,870.3	5,416.7	5,281.4	4,588.7	692.7	9,847.5	5,614.9
II	15,653.7	251.3	15,402.4	10,983.4	1,523.5	2,895.6	5,479.8	5,343.7	4,643.4	700.3	9,922.6	5,639.7
III p	15,841.1	254.1	15,587.0	11,074.9	1,565.1	2,947.1	5,563.7	5,425.5	4,713.2	712.3	10,023.3	5,649.3

[1] Includes Federal Housing Administration (FHA)–insured multi-family properties, not shown separately.
[2] Derived figures. Total includes multi-family and commercial properties with conventional mortgages, not shown separately.

Source: Board of Governors of the Federal Reserve System, based on data from various Government and private organizations.

End of year or quarter	Total	Major financial institutions			Other holders		
		Total	Depository Institutions [1,2]	Life insurance companies	Federal and related agencies [3]	Mortgage pools or trusts [4]	Individuals and others
1960	227.1	156.4	114.6	41.8	11.3	0.2	59.2
1961	248.6	171.1	126.9	44.2	11.9	.3	65.3
1962	271.8	190.5	143.6	46.9	12.2	.4	68.7
1963	297.6	214.6	164.1	50.5	11.3	.5	71.2
1964	324.2	238.8	183.6	55.2	11.6	.6	73.2
1965	349.5	262.4	202.4	60.0	12.7	.9	73.6
1966	373.7	279.5	214.8	64.6	16.2	1.3	76.7
1967	396.9	296.4	228.9	67.5	19.0	2.0	79.5
1968	424.5	317.3	247.3	70.0	22.6	2.5	82.2
1969	450.5	336.6	264.6	72.0	27.9	3.2	82.8
1970	498.5	352.9	278.5	74.4	33.6	4.8	107.3
1971	544.5	389.2	313.7	75.5	36.8	9.5	109.0
1972	618.2	443.8	366.8	76.9	40.1	14.4	119.9
1973	694.2	500.7	419.4	81.4	46.6	18.0	128.8
1974	766.2	539.3	453.1	86.2	68.2	23.8	134.9
1975	830.2	576.1	486.9	89.2	80.2	34.1	139.9
1976	917.5	640.7	549.1	91.6	82.4	49.8	144.7
1977	1,049.7	735.3	638.4	96.8	87.6	70.3	156.5
1978	1,206.8	837.5	731.3	106.2	103.4	88.6	177.3
1979	1,381.0	928.6	810.2	118.4	123.7	118.7	210.0
1980	1,528.2	988.0	857.0	131.1	142.6	145.9	251.6
1981	1,654.6	1,034.1	896.4	137.7	160.8	168.0	291.7
1982	1,741.4	1,019.6	877.6	142.0	177.3	224.4	320.1
1983	1,942.4	1,108.4	957.4	151.0	188.3	297.3	348.4
1984	2,178.3	1,248.2	1,091.5	156.7	202.3	350.7	377.1
1985	2,439.9	1,368.7	1,196.9	171.8	213.7	438.6	419.0
1986	2,676.3	1,483.3	1,289.5	193.8	202.1	549.5	441.3
1987	2,968.8	1,631.5	1,419.1	212.4	188.5	700.8	447.9
1988	3,283.8	1,797.8	1,564.9	232.9	192.5	785.7	507.8
1989	3,534.5	1,897.4	1,643.2	254.2	197.8	922.2	517.1
1990	3,790.0	1,918.8	1,651.0	267.9	239.0	1,085.9	546.3
1991	3,941.7	1,846.2	1,586.7	259.5	266.0	1,269.6	560.0
1992	4,052.4	1,770.5	1,528.5	242.0	286.1	1,440.0	555.9
1993	4,183.7	1,770.1	1,546.3	223.9	326.1	1,561.1	526.4
1994	4,348.1	1,824.7	1,608.9	215.8	315.6	1,696.9	511.0
1995	4,520.7	1,900.1	1,687.0	213.1	307.9	1,812.0	500.6
1996	4,801.2	1,982.2	1,773.7	208.5	294.4	1,989.1	535.6
1997	5,114.0	2,084.2	1,877.1	207.0	285.2	2,166.5	578.2
1998	5,603.2	2,194.7	1,981.0	213.8	291.9	2,487.1	629.5
1999	6,209.5	2,394.5	2,163.5	231.0	319.8	2,832.3	663.0
2000	6,766.6	2,619.2	2,383.0	236.2	339.9	3,097.5	710.0
2001	7,450.0	2,791.0	2,547.9	243.1	372.0	3,532.4	754.7
2002	8,358.7	3,089.4	2,839.3	250.1	432.3	3,978.4	858.5
2003	9,366.8	3,387.5	3,126.4	261.2	694.1	4,330.3	954.9
2004	10,648.6	3,926.5	3,653.0	273.5	703.2	4,834.5	1,184.4
2005	12,116.7	4,396.5	4,110.8	285.7	665.4	5,711.8	1,343.1
2006	13,529.5	4,784.0	4,479.8	304.1	687.5	6,631.4	1,426.6
2007	14,613.1	5,065.5	4,738.4	327.1	725.5	7,436.3	1,385.9
2008	14,693.6	5,045.8	4,702.0	343.8	801.2	7,594.4	1,252.3
2009	14,449.3	4,779.4	4,452.0	327.4	816.1	7,651.3	1,202.5
2010	13,896.3	4,585.2	4,266.1	319.2	5,127.5	3,109.6	1,073.9
2011	13,571.8	4,450.3	4,115.7	334.6	5,033.9	3,035.6	1,052.0
2012	13,335.8	4,438.2	4,091.3	346.9	4,935.0	2,948.4	1,014.2
2013	13,344.0	4,412.3	4,046.1	366.3	4,993.2	2,774.1	1,164.4
2014	13,489.8	4,546.7	4,158.5	388.2	4,987.7	2,742.6	1,212.9
2015	13,880.7	4,804.2	4,373.6	430.7	5,036.6	2,791.6	1,248.3
2016	14,332.4	5,096.7	4,631.2	465.5	5,146.9	2,827.2	1,261.7
2017	14,888.7	5,308.0	4,801.3	506.7	5,314.9	2,972.7	1,293.0
2018	15,424.0	5,487.9	4,919.8	568.1	5,458.3	3,144.9	1,332.9
2018: I	14,979.0	5,345.6	4,824.8	520.8	5,338.4	3,002.3	1,292.7
II	15,144.9	5,404.5	4,868.1	536.4	5,369.8	3,067.4	1,303.3
III	15,290.1	5,450.0	4,897.1	552.9	5,415.4	3,105.4	1,319.3
IV	15,424.0	5,487.9	4,919.8	568.1	5,458.3	3,144.9	1,332.9
2019: I	15,512.6	5,516.9	4,936.6	580.3	5,481.6	3,161.8	1,352.3
II	15,653.7	5,589.3	5,001.0	588.3	5,511.4	3,182.0	1,371.0
III p	15,841.1	5,646.5	5,044.1	602.4	5,584.9	3,219.1	1,390.6

[1] Includes savings banks and savings and loan associations. Data reported by Federal Savings and Loan Insurance Corporation–insured institutions include loans in process for 1987 and exclude loans in process beginning with 1988.
[2] Includes loans held by nondeposit trust companies but not loans held by bank trust departments.
[3] Includes Government National Mortgage Association (GNMA or Ginnie Mae), Federal Housing Administration, Veterans Administration, Farmers Home Administration (FmHA), Federal Deposit Insurance Corporation, Resolution Trust Corporation (through 1995), and in earlier years Reconstruction Finance Corporation, Homeowners Loan Corporation, Federal Farm Mortgage Corporation, and Public Housing Administration. Also includes U.S.-sponsored agencies such as Federal National Mortgage Association (FNMA or Fannie Mae), Federal Land Banks, Federal Home Loan Mortgage Corporation (FHLMC or Freddie Mac), Federal Agricultural Mortgage Corporation (Farmer Mac, beginning 1994), Federal Home Loan Banks (beginning 1997), and mortgage pass-through securities issued or guaranteed by GNMA, FHLMC, FNMA, FmHA, or Farmer Mac. Other U.S. agencies (amounts small or current separate data not readily available) included with "individuals and others."
[4] Includes private mortgage pools.

Source: Board of Governors of the Federal Reserve System, based on data from various Government and private organizations.

Government Finance

Table B-45. Federal receipts, outlays, surplus or deficit, and debt, fiscal years 1955–2021
[Billions of dollars; fiscal years]

Fiscal year or period	Total			On-budget			Off-budget			Federal debt (end of period)		Addendum: Gross domestic product
	Receipts	Outlays	Surplus or deficit (−)	Receipts	Outlays	Surplus or deficit (−)	Receipts	Outlays	Surplus or deficit (−)	Gross Federal	Held by the public	
1955	65.5	68.4	−3.0	60.4	64.5	−4.1	5.1	4.0	1.1	274.4	226.6	406.3
1956	74.6	70.6	3.9	68.2	65.7	2.5	6.4	5.0	1.5	272.7	222.2	438.2
1957	80.0	76.6	3.4	73.2	70.6	2.6	6.8	6.0	.8	272.3	219.3	463.4
1958	79.6	82.4	−2.8	71.6	74.9	−3.3	8.0	7.5	.5	279.7	226.3	473.5
1959	79.2	92.1	−12.8	71.0	83.1	−12.1	8.3	9.0	−.7	287.5	234.7	504.6
1960	92.5	92.2	.3	81.9	81.3	.5	10.6	10.9	−.2	290.5	236.8	534.3
1961	94.4	97.7	−3.3	82.3	86.0	−3.8	12.1	11.7	.4	292.6	238.4	546.6
1962	99.7	106.8	−7.1	87.4	93.3	−5.9	12.3	13.5	−1.3	302.9	248.0	585.7
1963	106.6	111.3	−4.8	92.4	96.4	−4.0	14.2	15.0	−.8	310.3	254.0	618.2
1964	112.6	118.5	−5.9	96.2	102.8	−6.5	16.4	15.7	.6	316.1	256.8	661.7
1965	116.8	118.2	−1.4	100.1	101.7	−1.6	16.7	16.5	.2	322.3	260.8	709.3
1966	130.8	134.5	−3.7	111.7	114.8	−3.1	19.1	19.7	−.6	328.5	263.7	780.5
1967	148.8	157.5	−8.6	124.4	137.0	−12.6	24.4	20.4	4.0	340.4	266.6	836.5
1968	153.0	178.1	−25.2	128.1	155.8	−27.7	24.9	22.3	2.6	368.7	289.5	897.6
1969	186.9	183.6	3.2	157.9	158.4	−.5	29.0	25.2	3.7	365.8	278.1	980.3
1970	192.8	195.6	−2.8	159.3	168.0	−8.7	33.5	27.6	5.9	380.9	283.2	1,046.7
1971	187.1	210.2	−23.0	151.3	177.3	−26.1	35.8	32.8	3.0	408.2	303.0	1,116.6
1972	207.3	230.7	−23.4	167.4	193.5	−26.1	39.9	37.2	2.7	435.9	322.4	1,216.2
1973	230.8	245.7	−14.9	184.7	200.0	−15.2	46.1	45.7	.3	466.3	340.9	1,352.7
1974	263.2	269.4	−6.1	209.3	216.5	−7.2	53.9	52.9	1.1	483.9	343.7	1,482.8
1975	279.1	332.3	−53.2	216.6	270.8	−54.1	62.5	61.6	.9	541.9	394.7	1,606.9
1976	298.1	371.8	−73.7	231.7	301.1	−69.4	66.4	70.7	−4.3	629.0	477.4	1,786.1
Transition quarter	81.2	96.0	−14.7	63.2	77.3	−14.1	18.0	18.7	−.7	643.6	495.5	471.6
1977	355.6	409.2	−53.7	278.7	328.7	−49.9	76.8	80.5	−3.7	706.4	549.1	2,024.3
1978	399.6	458.7	−59.2	314.2	369.6	−55.4	85.4	89.2	−3.8	776.6	607.1	2,273.4
1979	463.3	504.0	−40.7	365.3	404.9	−39.6	98.0	99.1	−1.1	829.5	640.3	2,565.6
1980	517.1	590.9	−73.8	403.9	477.0	−73.1	113.2	113.9	−.7	909.0	711.9	2,791.9
1981	599.3	678.2	−79.0	469.1	543.0	−73.9	130.2	135.3	−5.1	994.8	789.4	3,133.2
1982	617.8	745.7	−128.0	474.3	594.9	−120.6	143.5	150.9	−7.4	1,137.3	924.6	3,313.4
1983	600.6	808.4	−207.8	453.2	660.9	−207.7	147.3	147.4	−.1	1,371.7	1,137.3	3,536.0
1984	666.4	851.8	−185.4	500.4	685.6	−185.3	166.1	166.2	−.1	1,564.6	1,307.0	3,949.2
1985	734.0	946.3	−212.3	547.9	769.4	−221.5	186.2	176.9	9.2	1,817.4	1,507.3	4,265.1
1986	769.2	990.4	−221.2	568.9	806.8	−237.9	200.2	183.5	16.7	2,120.5	1,740.6	4,526.2
1987	854.3	1,004.0	−149.7	640.9	809.2	−168.4	213.4	194.8	18.6	2,346.0	1,889.8	4,767.6
1988	909.2	1,064.4	−155.2	667.7	860.0	−192.3	241.5	204.4	37.1	2,601.1	2,051.6	5,138.6
1989	991.1	1,143.7	−152.6	727.4	932.8	−205.4	263.7	210.9	52.8	2,867.8	2,190.7	5,554.7
1990	1,032.0	1,253.0	−221.0	750.3	1,027.9	−277.6	281.7	225.1	56.6	3,206.3	2,411.6	5,898.8
1991	1,055.0	1,324.2	−269.2	761.1	1,082.5	−321.4	293.9	241.7	52.2	3,598.2	2,689.0	6,093.2
1992	1,091.2	1,381.5	−290.3	788.8	1,129.2	−340.4	302.4	252.3	50.1	4,001.8	2,999.7	6,416.2
1993	1,154.3	1,409.4	−255.1	842.4	1,142.8	−300.4	311.9	266.6	45.3	4,351.0	3,248.4	6,775.3
1994	1,258.6	1,461.8	−203.2	923.5	1,182.4	−258.8	335.0	279.4	55.7	4,643.3	3,433.1	7,176.8
1995	1,351.8	1,515.7	−164.0	1,000.7	1,227.1	−226.4	351.1	288.7	62.4	4,920.6	3,604.4	7,560.4
1996	1,453.1	1,560.5	−107.4	1,085.6	1,259.6	−174.0	367.5	300.9	66.6	5,181.5	3,734.1	7,951.3
1997	1,579.2	1,601.1	−21.9	1,187.2	1,290.5	−103.2	392.0	310.6	81.4	5,369.2	3,772.3	8,451.0
1998	1,721.7	1,652.5	69.3	1,305.9	1,335.9	−29.9	415.8	316.6	99.2	5,478.2	3,721.1	8,930.8
1999	1,827.5	1,701.8	125.6	1,383.0	1,381.1	1.9	444.5	320.8	123.7	5,605.5	3,632.4	9,479.4
2000	2,025.2	1,789.0	236.2	1,544.6	1,458.2	86.4	480.6	330.8	149.8	5,628.7	3,409.8	10,117.4
2001	1,991.1	1,862.8	128.2	1,483.6	1,516.0	−32.4	507.5	346.8	160.7	5,769.9	3,319.6	10,526.5
2002	1,853.1	2,010.9	−157.8	1,337.8	1,655.2	−317.4	515.3	355.7	159.7	6,198.4	3,540.4	10,833.6
2003	1,782.3	2,159.9	−377.6	1,258.5	1,796.9	−538.4	523.8	363.0	160.8	6,760.0	3,913.4	11,283.8
2004	1,880.1	2,292.8	−412.7	1,345.4	1,913.3	−568.0	534.7	379.5	155.2	7,354.7	4,295.5	12,025.4
2005	2,153.6	2,472.0	−318.3	1,576.1	2,069.7	−493.6	577.5	402.2	175.3	7,905.3	4,592.2	12,834.2
2006	2,406.9	2,655.1	−248.2	1,798.5	2,233.0	−434.5	608.4	422.1	186.3	8,451.4	4,829.0	13,638.4
2007	2,568.0	2,728.7	−160.7	1,932.9	2,275.0	−342.2	635.1	453.6	181.5	8,950.7	5,035.1	14,290.8
2008	2,524.0	2,982.5	−458.6	1,865.9	2,507.8	−641.8	658.0	474.8	183.3	9,986.1	5,803.1	14,743.3
2009	2,105.0	3,517.7	−1,412.7	1,451.0	3,000.7	−1,549.7	654.0	517.0	137.0	11,875.9	7,544.7	14,431.8
2010	2,162.7	3,457.1	−1,294.4	1,531.0	2,902.4	−1,371.4	631.7	554.7	77.0	13,528.8	9,018.9	14,838.8
2011	2,303.5	3,603.1	−1,299.6	1,737.7	3,104.5	−1,366.8	565.8	498.6	67.2	14,764.2	10,128.2	15,403.7
2012	2,450.0	3,526.6	−1,076.6	1,880.5	3,019.0	−1,138.5	569.5	507.6	61.9	16,050.9	11,281.1	16,056.4
2013	2,775.1	3,454.9	−679.8	2,101.8	2,821.1	−719.2	673.3	633.8	39.5	16,719.4	11,982.7	16,603.8
2014	3,021.5	3,506.3	−484.8	2,285.9	2,800.2	−514.3	735.6	706.1	29.5	17,794.5	12,779.9	17,335.6
2015	3,249.9	3,691.9	−442.0	2,479.5	2,948.8	−469.3	770.4	743.1	27.3	18,120.1	13,116.7	18,099.6
2016	3,268.0	3,852.6	−584.7	2,457.8	3,077.9	−620.2	810.2	774.7	35.5	19,539.5	14,167.6	18,554.8
2017	3,316.2	3,981.6	−665.4	2,465.6	3,180.4	−714.9	850.6	801.2	49.4	20,205.7	14,665.4	19,287.6
2018	3,329.9	4,109.0	−779.1	2,475.2	3,260.5	−785.3	854.7	848.6	6.2	21,462.3	15,749.6	20,335.5
2019	3,464.2	4,448.3	−984.2	2,549.9	3,541.7	−991.8	914.3	906.6	7.7	22,669.5	16,800.7	21,215.7
2020 (estimates)	3,706.3	4,789.7	−1,083.4	2,739.3	3,829.6	−1,090.7	967.1	959.8	7.3	23,900.2	17,881.2	22,210.9
2021 (estimates)	3,863.3	4,829.4	−966.1	2,852.3	3,811.1	−958.9	1,011.0	1,018.2	−7.2	25,077.4	18,912.1	23,353.1

Note: Fiscal years through 1976 were on a July 1–June 30 basis; beginning with October 1976 (fiscal year 1977), the fiscal year is on an October 1–September 30 basis. The transition quarter is the three-month period from July 1, 1976 through September 30, 1976.

See *Budget of the United States Government, Fiscal Year 2021,* for additional information.

Sources: Department of Commerce (Bureau of Economic Analysis), Department of the Treasury, and Office of Management and Budget.

Federal receipts, outlays, surplus or deficit, and debt, as percent of gross domestic product, fiscal years 1949–2021

[Percent; fiscal years]

Fiscal year or period	Receipts	Outlays		Surplus or deficit (−)	Federal debt (end of period)	
		Total	National defense		Gross Federal	Held by public
1949	14.3	14.0	4.8	0.2	91.4	77.5
1950	14.2	15.3	4.9	−1.1	92.2	78.6
1951	15.8	13.9	7.2	1.9	78.1	65.5
1952	18.5	19.0	12.9	−.4	72.6	60.1
1953	18.2	19.9	13.8	−1.7	69.6	57.2
1954	18.0	18.3	12.7	−.3	70.0	58.0
1955	16.1	16.8	10.5	−.7	67.5	55.8
1956	17.0	16.1	9.7	.9	62.2	50.7
1957	17.3	16.5	9.8	.7	58.8	47.3
1958	16.8	17.4	9.9	−.6	59.1	47.8
1959	15.7	18.3	9.7	−2.5	57.0	46.5
1960	17.3	17.3	9.0	.1	54.4	44.3
1961	17.3	17.9	9.1	−.6	53.5	43.6
1962	17.0	18.2	8.9	−1.2	51.7	42.3
1963	17.2	18.0	8.6	−.8	50.2	41.1
1964	17.0	17.9	8.3	−.9	47.8	38.8
1965	16.5	16.7	7.1	−.2	45.4	36.8
1966	16.8	17.2	7.4	−.5	42.1	33.8
1967	17.8	18.8	8.5	−1.0	40.7	31.9
1968	17.0	19.8	9.1	−2.8	41.1	32.3
1969	19.1	18.7	8.4	.3	37.3	28.4
1970	18.4	18.7	7.8	−.3	36.4	27.1
1971	16.8	18.8	7.1	−2.1	36.6	27.1
1972	17.0	19.0	6.5	−1.9	35.8	26.5
1973	17.1	18.2	5.7	−1.1	34.5	25.2
1974	17.8	18.2	5.4	−.4	32.6	23.2
1975	17.4	20.7	5.4	−3.3	33.7	24.6
1976	16.7	20.8	5.0	−4.1	35.2	26.7
Transition quarter	17.2	20.3	4.7	−3.1	34.1	26.3
1977	17.6	20.2	4.8	−2.7	34.9	27.1
1978	17.6	20.2	4.6	−2.6	34.2	26.7
1979	18.1	19.6	4.5	−1.6	32.3	25.0
1980	18.5	21.2	4.8	−2.6	32.6	25.5
1981	19.1	21.6	5.0	−2.5	31.8	25.2
1982	18.6	22.5	5.6	−3.9	34.3	27.9
1983	17.0	22.9	5.9	−5.9	38.8	32.2
1984	16.9	21.6	5.8	−4.7	39.6	33.1
1985	17.2	22.2	5.9	−5.0	42.6	35.3
1986	17.0	21.9	6.0	−4.9	46.8	38.5
1987	17.9	21.1	5.9	−3.1	49.2	39.6
1988	17.7	20.7	5.7	−3.0	50.6	39.9
1989	17.8	20.6	5.5	−2.7	51.6	39.4
1990	17.5	21.2	5.1	−3.7	54.4	40.9
1991	17.3	21.7	4.5	−4.4	59.1	44.1
1992	17.0	21.5	4.6	−4.5	62.4	46.8
1993	17.0	20.8	4.3	−3.8	64.2	47.9
1994	17.5	20.4	3.9	−2.8	64.7	47.8
1995	17.9	20.0	3.6	−2.2	65.1	47.7
1996	18.3	19.6	3.3	−1.4	65.2	47.0
1997	18.7	18.9	3.2	−.3	63.5	44.6
1998	19.3	18.5	3.0	.8	61.3	41.7
1999	19.3	18.0	2.9	1.3	59.1	38.3
2000	20.0	17.7	2.9	2.3	55.6	33.7
2001	18.9	17.7	2.9	1.2	54.8	31.5
2002	17.1	18.6	3.2	−1.5	57.2	32.7
2003	15.8	19.1	3.6	−3.3	59.9	34.7
2004	15.6	19.1	3.8	−3.4	61.2	35.7
2005	16.8	19.3	3.9	−2.5	61.6	35.8
2006	17.6	19.5	3.8	−1.8	62.0	35.4
2007	18.0	19.1	3.9	−1.1	62.6	35.2
2008	17.1	20.2	4.2	−3.1	67.7	39.4
2009	14.6	24.4	4.6	−9.8	82.3	52.3
2010	14.6	23.3	4.7	−8.7	91.2	60.8
2011	15.0	23.4	4.6	−8.4	95.8	65.8
2012	15.3	22.0	4.2	−6.7	100.0	70.3
2013	16.7	20.8	3.8	−4.1	100.7	72.2
2014	17.4	20.2	3.5	−2.8	102.6	73.7
2015	18.0	20.4	3.3	−2.4	100.1	72.5
2016	17.6	20.8	3.2	−3.2	105.3	76.4
2017	17.2	20.6	3.1	−3.5	104.8	76.0
2018	16.4	20.2	3.1	−3.8	105.5	77.4
2019	16.3	21.0	3.2	−4.6	106.9	79.2
2020 (estimates)	16.7	21.6	3.3	−4.9	107.6	80.5
2021 (estimates)	16.5	20.7	3.3	−4.1	107.4	81.0

Note: See Note, Table B–45.

Sources: Department of the Treasury and Office of Management and Budget.

TABLE B–47. Federal receipts and outlays, by major category, and surplus or deficit, fiscal years 1955–2021

[Billions of dollars; fiscal years]

Fiscal year or period	Receipts (on-budget and off-budget)					Outlays (on-budget and off-budget)										Surplus or deficit (−) (on-budget and off-budget)
	Total	Individual income taxes	Corporation income taxes	Social insurance and retirement receipts	Other	Total	National defense		International affairs	Health	Medicare	Income security	Social security	Net interest	Other	
							Total	Department of Defense, military								
1955	65.5	28.7	17.9	7.9	11.0	68.4	42.7		2.2	0.3		5.1	4.4	4.9	8.9	−3.0
1956	74.6	32.2	20.9	9.3	12.2	70.6	42.5		2.4	.4		4.7	5.5	5.1	10.1	3.9
1957	80.0	35.6	21.2	10.0	13.2	76.6	45.4		3.1	.5		5.4	6.7	5.4	10.1	3.4
1958	79.6	34.7	20.1	11.2	13.6	82.4	46.8		3.4	.5		7.5	8.2	5.6	10.3	−2.8
1959	79.2	36.7	17.3	11.7	13.5	92.1	49.0		3.1	.7		8.2	9.7	5.8	15.5	−12.8
1960	92.5	40.7	21.5	14.7	15.6	92.2	48.1		3.0	.8		7.4	11.6	6.9	14.4	.3
1961	94.4	41.3	21.0	16.4	15.7	97.7	49.6		3.2	.9		9.7	12.5	6.7	15.2	−3.3
1962	99.7	45.6	20.5	17.0	16.5	106.8	52.3	50.1	5.6	1.2		9.2	14.4	6.9	17.2	−7.1
1963	106.6	47.6	21.6	19.8	17.6	111.3	53.4	51.1	5.3	1.5		9.3	15.8	7.7	18.3	−4.8
1964	112.6	48.7	23.5	22.0	18.5	118.5	54.8	52.6	4.9	1.8		9.7	16.6	8.2	22.6	−5.9
1965	116.8	48.8	25.5	22.2	20.3	118.2	50.6	48.8	5.3	1.8		9.5	17.5	8.6	25.0	−1.4
1966	130.8	55.4	30.1	25.5	19.8	134.5	58.1	56.6	5.6	2.5	0.1	9.7	20.7	9.4	28.5	−3.7
1967	148.8	61.5	34.0	32.6	20.7	157.5	71.4	70.1	5.6	3.4	2.7	10.3	21.7	10.3	32.1	−8.6
1968	153.0	68.7	28.7	33.9	21.7	178.1	81.9	80.4	5.3	4.4	4.6	11.8	23.9	11.1	35.1	−25.2
1969	186.9	87.2	36.7	39.0	23.9	183.6	82.5	80.8	4.6	5.2	5.7	13.1	27.3	12.7	32.6	3.2
1970	192.8	90.4	32.8	44.4	25.2	195.6	81.7	80.1	4.3	5.9	6.2	15.6	30.3	14.4	37.2	−2.8
1971	187.1	86.2	26.8	47.3	26.8	210.2	78.9	77.5	4.2	6.8	6.6	22.9	35.9	14.8	40.0	−23.0
1972	207.3	94.7	32.2	52.6	27.8	230.7	79.2	77.6	4.8	8.7	7.5	27.6	40.2	15.5	47.3	−23.4
1973	230.8	103.2	36.2	63.1	28.3	245.7	76.7	75.0	4.1	9.4	8.1	28.3	49.1	17.3	52.8	−14.9
1974	263.2	119.0	38.6	75.1	30.6	269.4	79.3	77.9	5.7	10.7	9.6	33.7	55.9	21.4	52.9	−6.1
1975	279.1	122.4	40.6	84.5	31.5	332.3	86.5	84.9	7.1	12.9	12.9	50.2	64.7	23.2	74.9	−53.2
1976	298.1	131.6	41.4	90.8	34.3	371.8	89.6	87.9	6.4	15.7	15.8	60.8	73.9	26.7	82.8	−73.7
Transition quarter	81.2	38.8	8.5	25.2	8.8	96.0	22.3	21.8	2.5	3.9	4.3	15.0	19.8	6.9	21.4	−14.7
1977	355.6	157.6	54.9	106.5	36.6	409.2	97.2	95.1	6.4	17.3	19.3	61.0	85.1	29.9	93.0	−53.7
1978	399.6	181.0	60.0	121.0	37.7	458.7	104.5	102.3	7.5	18.5	22.8	61.5	93.9	35.5	114.7	−59.2
1979	463.3	217.8	65.7	138.9	40.8	504.0	116.3	113.6	7.5	20.5	26.5	66.4	104.1	42.6	120.2	−40.7
1980	517.1	244.1	64.6	157.8	50.6	590.9	134.0	130.9	12.7	23.2	32.1	86.5	118.5	52.5	131.3	−73.8
1981	599.3	285.9	61.1	182.7	69.5	678.2	157.5	153.9	13.1	26.9	39.1	100.3	139.6	68.8	133.0	−79.0
1982	617.8	297.7	49.2	201.5	69.3	745.7	185.3	180.7	12.3	27.4	46.6	108.1	156.0	85.0	125.0	−128.0
1983	600.6	288.9	37.0	209.0	65.6	808.4	209.9	204.4	11.8	28.6	52.6	123.0	170.7	89.8	121.8	−207.8
1984	666.4	298.4	56.9	239.4	71.8	851.8	227.4	220.9	15.9	30.4	57.5	113.4	178.2	111.1	117.9	−185.4
1985	734.0	334.5	61.3	265.2	73.0	946.3	252.7	245.1	16.2	33.5	65.8	129.0	186.6	129.5	131.0	−212.3
1986	769.2	349.0	63.1	283.9	73.2	990.4	273.4	265.4	14.1	35.9	70.2	120.7	198.8	136.0	141.3	−221.2
1987	854.3	392.6	83.9	303.3	74.5	1,004.0	282.0	273.9	11.6	40.0	75.1	124.1	207.4	138.6	125.2	−149.7
1988	909.2	401.2	94.5	334.3	79.2	1,064.4	290.4	281.9	10.5	44.5	78.9	130.4	219.3	151.8	138.7	−155.2
1989	991.1	445.7	103.3	359.4	82.7	1,143.7	303.6	294.8	9.6	48.4	85.0	137.6	232.5	169.0	158.2	−152.6
1990	1,032.0	466.9	93.5	380.0	91.5	1,253.0	299.3	289.7	13.8	57.7	98.1	148.8	248.6	184.3	202.4	−221.0
1991	1,055.0	467.8	98.1	396.0	93.1	1,324.2	273.3	262.3	15.8	71.1	104.5	172.6	269.0	194.4	223.4	−269.2
1992	1,091.2	476.0	100.3	413.7	101.3	1,381.5	298.3	286.8	16.1	89.4	119.0	199.7	287.6	199.3	172.1	−290.3
1993	1,154.3	509.7	117.5	428.3	98.8	1,409.4	291.1	278.5	17.2	99.3	130.6	210.1	304.6	198.7	157.8	−255.1
1994	1,258.6	543.1	140.4	461.5	113.7	1,461.8	281.6	268.6	17.1	107.1	144.7	217.2	319.6	202.9	171.5	−203.2
1995	1,351.8	590.2	157.0	484.5	120.1	1,515.7	272.1	259.4	16.4	115.4	159.5	223.8	335.8	232.1	160.3	−164.0
1996	1,453.1	656.4	171.8	509.4	115.4	1,560.5	265.7	253.1	13.5	119.3	174.2	229.7	349.7	241.1	167.3	−107.4
1997	1,579.2	737.5	182.3	539.4	120.1	1,601.1	270.5	258.3	15.2	123.8	190.0	235.0	365.3	244.0	157.4	−21.9
1998	1,721.7	828.6	188.7	571.8	132.6	1,652.5	268.2	255.8	13.1	131.4	192.8	237.7	379.2	241.1	189.0	69.3
1999	1,827.5	879.5	184.7	611.8	151.5	1,701.8	274.8	261.2	15.2	141.0	190.4	242.4	390.0	229.8	218.1	125.6
2000	2,025.2	1,004.5	207.3	652.9	160.6	1,789.0	294.4	281.0	17.2	154.5	197.1	253.7	409.4	222.9	239.7	236.2
2001	1,991.1	994.3	151.1	694.0	151.7	1,862.8	304.7	290.2	16.5	172.2	217.4	269.7	433.0	206.2	243.2	128.2
2002	1,853.1	858.3	148.0	700.8	146.0	2,010.9	348.5	331.8	22.3	196.5	230.9	312.7	456.0	170.9	273.2	−157.8
2003	1,782.3	793.7	131.8	713.0	143.9	2,159.9	404.7	387.1	21.2	219.6	249.4	334.6	474.7	153.1	302.6	−377.6
2004	1,880.1	809.0	189.4	733.4	148.4	2,292.8	455.8	436.4	26.9	240.1	269.4	333.0	495.5	160.2	341.7	−412.7
2005	2,153.6	927.2	278.3	794.1	154.0	2,472.0	495.3	474.1	34.6	250.6	298.6	345.8	523.3	184.0	339.8	−318.3
2006	2,406.9	1,043.9	353.9	837.8	171.2	2,655.1	521.8	499.3	29.5	252.8	329.9	352.4	548.5	226.6	349.5	−248.2
2007	2,568.0	1,163.5	370.2	869.6	164.7	2,728.7	551.3	528.5	28.5	266.4	375.4	365.9	586.2	237.1	317.9	−160.7
2008	2,524.0	1,145.7	304.3	900.2	173.7	2,982.5	616.1	594.6	28.9	280.6	390.8	431.2	617.0	252.8	365.2	−458.6
2009	2,105.0	915.3	138.2	890.9	160.5	3,517.7	661.0	636.7	37.5	334.4	430.1	533.1	683.0	186.9	651.7	−1,412.7
2010	2,162.7	898.5	191.4	864.8	207.9	3,457.1	693.5	666.7	45.2	369.1	451.6	622.1	706.7	196.2	372.6	−1,294.4
2011	2,303.5	1,091.5	181.1	818.8	212.1	3,603.1	705.6	678.1	45.7	372.5	485.7	597.3	730.8	230.0	435.7	−1,299.6
2012	2,450.0	1,132.2	242.3	845.3	230.2	3,526.6	677.9	650.9	36.8	346.8	471.8	541.2	773.3	220.4	458.4	−1,076.6
2013	2,775.1	1,316.4	273.5	947.8	237.4	3,454.9	633.4	607.8	46.5	358.3	497.8	536.4	813.6	220.9	348.0	−679.8
2014	3,021.5	1,394.6	320.7	1,023.5	282.7	3,506.3	603.5	577.9	46.9	409.5	511.7	513.6	850.5	229.0	341.7	−484.8
2015	3,249.9	1,540.8	343.8	1,065.3	300.0	3,691.9	589.7	562.5	52.0	482.3	546.2	508.8	887.8	223.2	402.0	−442.0
2016	3,268.0	1,546.1	299.6	1,115.1	307.3	3,852.6	593.4	565.4	45.3	511.3	594.5	514.1	916.1	240.0	437.9	−584.7
2017	3,316.2	1,587.1	297.0	1,161.9	270.1	3,981.6	598.7	568.9	46.3	533.2	597.3	503.4	944.9	262.6	495.3	−665.4
2018	3,329.9	1,683.5	204.7	1,170.7	270.9	4,109.0	631.1	600.7	49.0	551.2	588.7	495.3	987.8	325.0	480.9	−779.1
2019	3,464.2	1,717.9	230.2	1,243.4	272.7	4,448.3	686.0	654.0	52.7	584.8	651.0	514.8	1,044.4	375.2	539.4	−984.2
2020 (estimates)	3,706.5	1,812.0	263.6	1,312.0	318.6	4,789.7	724.5	689.6	58.3	640.9	699.3	529.3	1,097.2	376.2	664.1	−1,083.4
2021 (estimates)	3,863.3	1,931.7	284.1	1,373.6	273.9	4,829.4	767.1	729.3	60.7	648.6	728.5	523.8	1,156.2	378.2	566.3	−966.1

Note: See Note, Table B–45.

Sources: Department of the Treasury and Office of Management and Budget.

TABLE B–48. Federal receipts, outlays, surplus or deficit, and debt, fiscal years 2016–2021

[Millions of dollars; fiscal years]

Description	Actual				Estimates	
	2016	2017	2018	2019	2020	2021
RECEIPTS, OUTLAYS, AND SURPLUS OR DEFICIT						
Total:						
Receipts	3,267,965	3,316,184	3,329,907	3,464,161	3,706,327	3,863,293
Outlays	3,852,616	3,981,630	4,109,044	4,448,316	4,789,746	4,829,359
Surplus or deficit (−)	−584,651	−665,446	−779,137	−984,155	−1,083,419	−966,066
On-budget:						
Receipts	2,457,785	2,465,566	2,475,160	2,549,858	2,739,254	2,852,257
Outlays	3,077,943	3,180,429	3,260,472	3,541,699	3,829,949	3,811,118
Surplus or deficit (−)	−620,158	−714,863	−785,312	−991,841	−1,090,695	−958,861
Off-budget:						
Receipts	810,180	850,618	854,747	914,303	967,073	1,011,036
Outlays	774,673	801,201	848,572	906,617	959,797	1,018,241
Surplus or deficit (−)	35,507	49,417	6,175	7,686	7,276	−7,205
OUTSTANDING DEBT, END OF PERIOD						
Gross Federal debt	19,539,450	20,205,704	21,462,277	22,669,466	23,900,244	25,077,416
Held by Federal Government accounts	5,371,826	5,540,265	5,712,710	5,868,720	6,019,063	6,165,331
Held by the public	14,167,624	14,665,439	15,749,567	16,800,746	17,881,181	18,912,085
Federal Reserve System	2,463,456	2,465,418	2,313,209	2,113,329	....	....
Other	11,704,168	12,200,021	13,436,358	14,687,417	....	....
RECEIPTS BY SOURCE						
Total: On-budget and off-budget	3,267,965	3,316,184	3,329,907	3,464,161	3,706,327	3,863,293
Individual income taxes	1,546,075	1,587,120	1,683,538	1,717,857	1,812,040	1,931,678
Corporation income taxes	299,571	297,048	204,733	230,245	263,642	284,093
Social insurance and retirement receipts	1,115,065	1,161,897	1,170,701	1,243,372	1,312,026	1,373,594
On-budget	304,885	311,279	315,954	329,069	344,953	362,558
Off-budget	810,180	850,618	854,747	914,303	967,073	1,011,036
Excise taxes	95,026	83,823	94,986	99,452	94,593	87,206
Estate and gift taxes	21,354	22,768	22,983	16,672	20,389	21,641
Customs duties and fees	34,838	34,574	41,299	70,784	92,304	53,811
Miscellaneous receipts	156,036	128,954	111,667	85,779	111,333	111,270
Deposits of earnings by Federal Reserve System	115,672	81,287	70,750	52,793	72,681	70,814
All other	40,364	47,667	40,917	32,986	38,652	40,456
OUTLAYS BY FUNCTION						
Total: On-budget and off-budget	3,852,616	3,981,630	4,109,044	4,448,316	4,789,746	4,829,359
National defense	593,372	598,722	631,130	686,003	724,480	767,104
International affairs	45,306	46,309	48,996	52,739	58,320	60,684
General science, space, and technology	30,174	30,394	31,534	32,410	35,032	37,548
Energy	3,721	3,856	2,169	5,041	4,596	4,910
Natural resources and environment	39,082	37,896	39,140	37,844	42,817	43,908
Agriculture	18,344	18,872	21,789	38,257	38,332	27,522
Commerce and housing credit	−34,077	−26,685	−9,470	−25,715	684	691
On-budget	−32,716	−24,412	−8,005	−24,612	624	−99
Off-budget	−1,361	−2,273	−1,465	−1,103	60	790
Transportation	92,566	93,552	92,785	97,116	101,560	104,300
Community and regional development	20,140	24,907	42,159	26,876	30,306	33,796
Education, training, employment, and social services	109,709	143,953	95,503	136,752	195,526	111,993
Health	511,325	533,152	551,219	584,816	640,878	648,564
Medicare	594,536	597,307	588,706	650,996	699,281	728,497
Income security	514,098	503,443	495,289	514,787	529,335	523,791
Social security	916,067	944,878	987,791	1,044,409	1,097,184	1,156,204
On-budget	32,522	37,393	35,752	36,130	39,284	43,205
Off-budget	883,545	907,485	952,039	1,008,279	1,057,900	1,112,999
Veterans benefits and services	174,557	176,584	178,895	199,843	215,077	235,757
Administration of justice	55,768	57,944	60,418	65,740	79,570	75,803
General government	23,146	23,821	23,885	23,436	29,465	28,867
Net interest	240,033	262,551	324,975	375,158	376,171	378,189
On-budget	330,608	349,063	408,784	457,662	455,199	453,856
Off-budget	−90,575	−86,512	−83,809	−82,504	−79,028	−75,667
Allowances	....	....	....	....	364	358
Undistributed offsetting receipts	−95,251	−89,826	−97,869	−98,192	−109,232	−139,127
On-budget	−78,315	−72,327	−79,676	−80,137	−90,097	−119,246
Off-budget	−16,936	−17,499	−18,193	−18,055	−19,135	−19,881

Note: See Note, Table B–45

Sources: Department of the Treasury and Office of Management and Budget.

TABLE B–49. Federal and State and local government current receipts and expenditures, national income and product accounts (NIPA) basis, 1969–2019

[Billions of dollars; quarterly data at seasonally adjusted annual rates]

Year or quarter	Total government			Federal Government			State and local government			Addendum: Grants-in-aid to State and local governments
	Current receipts	Current expenditures	Net government saving (NIPA)	Current receipts	Current expenditures	Net Federal Government saving (NIPA)	Current receipts	Current expenditures	Net State and local government saving (NIPA)	
1969	282.7	284.7	−2.0	191.8	197.0	−5.1	104.5	101.4	3.1	13.7
1970	285.8	319.2	−33.4	185.1	219.9	−34.8	119.1	117.6	1.4	18.3
1971	302.3	354.5	−52.2	190.7	241.6	−50.9	133.7	135.0	−1.3	22.1
1972	345.6	388.5	−42.9	219.0	268.0	−49.0	157.1	151.0	6.1	30.5
1973	388.8	421.5	−32.7	249.2	287.6	−38.3	173.0	167.4	5.6	33.5
1974	430.2	473.9	−43.7	278.5	319.8	−41.3	186.6	189.0	−2.3	34.9
1975	441.2	549.9	−108.7	276.8	374.8	−97.9	208.0	218.7	−10.7	43.6
1976	505.7	591.0	−85.3	322.6	403.5	−80.9	232.2	236.6	−4.4	49.1
1977	567.4	640.3	−72.9	363.9	437.3	−73.4	258.3	257.8	.5	54.8
1978	646.1	703.3	−57.2	423.8	485.9	−62.0	285.8	280.9	4.9	63.5
1979	729.3	777.9	−48.6	487.0	534.4	−47.4	306.3	307.5	−1.2	64.0
1980	799.9	894.6	−94.7	533.7	622.5	−88.8	335.9	341.8	−5.9	69.7
1981	919.1	1,017.4	−98.2	621.1	709.1	−88.1	367.5	377.6	−10.2	69.4
1982	940.9	1,131.0	−190.1	618.7	786.0	−167.4	388.5	411.3	−22.8	66.3
1983	1,002.1	1,227.7	−225.6	644.8	851.9	−207.2	425.3	443.7	−18.4	67.9
1984	1,115.0	1,311.7	−196.7	711.2	907.7	−196.5	476.1	476.3	−.2	72.3
1985	1,217.0	1,418.7	−201.7	775.7	975.0	−199.2	517.5	519.9	−2.4	76.2
1986	1,292.9	1,512.8	−219.9	817.9	1,033.8	−215.9	557.4	561.3	−4.0	82.4
1987	1,406.6	1,586.7	−180.1	899.5	1,065.2	−165.7	585.5	599.9	−14.4	78.4
1988	1,507.1	1,678.3	−171.3	962.4	1,122.4	−160.0	630.4	641.7	−11.3	85.7
1989	1,632.0	1,810.7	−178.7	1,042.5	1,201.8	−159.4	681.4	700.7	−19.3	91.8
1990	1,713.3	1,952.9	−239.5	1,087.6	1,290.9	−203.3	730.1	766.3	−36.2	104.4
1991	1,763.7	2,072.2	−308.5	1,107.8	1,356.2	−248.4	779.9	840.0	−60.1	124.0
1992	1,848.7	2,254.2	−405.5	1,154.4	1,488.9	−334.5	836.1	907.0	−71.0	141.7
1993	1,953.3	2,339.3	−386.0	1,231.0	1,544.6	−313.5	878.0	950.4	−72.5	155.7
1994	2,097.6	2,417.2	−319.6	1,329.3	1,585.0	−255.6	935.1	999.1	−63.9	166.8
1995	2,223.9	2,536.5	−312.5	1,417.4	1,659.5	−242.1	981.0	1,051.4	−70.4	174.5
1996	2,388.6	2,621.8	−233.2	1,536.3	1,715.7	−179.4	1,033.7	1,087.5	−53.8	181.5
1997	2,565.9	2,699.9	−133.9	1,667.4	1,759.4	−92.0	1,086.7	1,128.7	−42.0	188.1
1998	2,738.6	2,767.4	−28.7	1,789.8	1,788.4	1.4	1,149.6	1,179.7	−30.1	200.8
1999	2,910.1	2,882.2	28.0	1,906.6	1,839.7	66.9	1,222.7	1,261.6	−38.9	219.2
2000	3,139.4	3,024.6	114.8	2,068.4	1,912.9	155.5	1,304.1	1,344.8	−40.6	233.1
2001	3,124.4	3,229.4	−105.0	2,032.2	2,018.2	14.0	1,353.4	1,472.4	−119.0	261.3
2002	2,968.3	3,422.6	−454.4	1,870.8	2,142.3	−271.5	1,386.2	1,569.1	−182.9	288.7
2003	3,045.9	3,631.3	−585.4	1,895.6	2,299.7	−404.1	1,472.0	1,653.3	−181.3	321.7
2004	3,275.7	3,825.6	−549.9	2,027.7	2,428.6	−400.9	1,580.3	1,729.3	−149.0	332.3
2005	3,679.3	4,088.1	−408.7	2,304.4	2,610.3	−305.9	1,718.5	1,821.3	−102.8	343.5
2006	4,013.4	4,326.1	−312.6	2,538.3	2,765.9	−227.6	1,816.2	1,901.2	−85.0	341.0
2007	4,210.8	4,606.2	−395.4	2,667.8	2,933.9	−266.1	1,902.1	2,031.4	−129.3	359.1
2008	4,125.0	4,977.0	−852.0	2,580.7	3,211.8	−631.1	1,915.5	2,136.4	−220.9	371.2
2009	3,696.6	5,286.8	−1,590.3	2,239.5	3,488.4	−1,248.9	1,915.2	2,256.6	−341.3	458.1
2010	3,933.2	5,565.7	−1,632.6	2,444.0	3,769.1	−1,325.1	1,994.4	2,301.8	−307.5	505.2
2011	4,130.6	5,647.7	−1,517.1	2,572.8	3,814.7	−1,242.0	2,030.4	2,305.4	−275.1	472.5
2012	4,312.2	5,673.6	−1,361.4	2,700.3	3,779.0	−1,078.6	2,056.3	2,339.1	−282.8	444.4
2013	4,834.5	5,737.8	−903.3	3,139.0	3,776.9	−637.9	2,145.6	2,411.0	−265.4	450.1
2014	5,054.4	5,896.7	−842.3	3,292.0	3,896.3	−604.3	2,257.4	2,495.4	−238.0	495.0
2015	5,288.2	6,078.5	−790.4	3,446.0	4,016.0	−570.1	2,375.3	2,595.7	−220.3	533.2
2016	5,335.4	6,259.2	−923.8	3,460.3	4,137.4	−677.0	2,431.9	2,678.7	−246.8	556.9
2017	5,481.7	6,454.5	−972.8	3,526.4	4,251.1	−724.7	2,515.1	2,763.2	−248.1	559.8
2018 ᵖ	5,537.7	6,786.6	−1,248.9	3,497.7	4,507.4	−1,009.8	2,623.0	2,862.1	−239.2	582.9
2019 ᵖ	....	7,139.3	....	....	4,797.9	....	....	2,950.9	....	609.5
2016: I	5,282.4	6,180.3	−897.9	3,439.4	4,083.9	−644.5	2,380.7	2,634.1	−253.4	537.7
II	5,300.7	6,228.5	−927.8	3,440.1	4,114.9	−674.8	2,413.8	2,666.9	−253.0	553.2
III	5,360.4	6,290.6	−930.3	3,472.7	4,159.9	−687.2	2,451.9	2,694.9	−243.0	564.2
IV	5,398.1	6,337.3	−939.3	3,489.1	4,190.8	−701.6	2,481.3	2,718.9	−237.6	572.4
2017: I	5,452.6	6,395.7	−943.1	3,532.2	4,217.2	−685.0	2,478.7	2,736.8	−258.1	558.3
II	5,421.9	6,390.8	−968.9	3,496.2	4,195.4	−699.2	2,471.3	2,740.9	−269.7	545.5
III	5,492.4	6,455.1	−962.7	3,535.8	4,242.9	−707.1	2,520.8	2,776.4	−255.6	564.3
IV	5,560.1	6,576.6	−1,016.6	3,541.5	4,349.1	−807.6	2,589.8	2,798.7	−208.9	571.2
2018: I	5,475.2	6,667.9	−1,192.6	3,446.9	4,423.2	−976.3	2,607.3	2,823.6	−216.3	578.9
II	5,509.2	6,756.2	−1,247.1	3,469.3	4,483.1	−1,013.8	2,622.4	2,855.8	−233.3	582.6
III	5,589.7	6,821.1	−1,231.5	3,545.4	4,526.8	−981.3	2,629.9	2,880.1	−250.1	585.7
IV	5,576.6	6,901.0	−1,324.5	3,529.0	4,596.6	−1,067.6	2,632.2	2,889.1	−256.8	584.6
2019: I	5,663.9	6,998.5	−1,334.7	3,576.7	4,699.6	−1,122.9	2,687.7	2,899.4	−211.7	600.5
II	5,750.0	7,123.0	−1,373.0	3,606.3	4,794.2	−1,188.0	2,757.8	2,942.9	−185.0	614.1
III	5,751.8	7,190.7	−1,438.9	3,622.0	4,833.5	−1,211.5	2,744.1	2,971.5	−227.4	614.3
IV ᵖ	....	7,245.1	....	....	4,864.4	....	....	2,989.8	....	609.2

Note: Federal grants-in-aid to State and local governments are reflected in Federal current expenditures and State and local current receipts. Total government current receipts and expenditures have been adjusted to eliminate this duplication.

Source: Department of Commerce (Bureau of Economic Analysis).

TABLE B–50. State and local government revenues and expenditures, fiscal years 1956–2017

[Millions of dollars]

Fiscal year [1]	General revenues by source [2]							General expenditures by function [2]				
	Total	Property taxes	Sales and gross receipts taxes	Individual income taxes	Corporation net income taxes	Revenue from Federal Government	All other [3]	Total [4]	Education	Highways	Public welfare [4]	All other [4, 5]
1956	34,670	11,749	8,691	1,538	890	3,335	8,467	36,715	13,224	6,953	3,139	13,399
1957	38,164	12,864	9,467	1,754	984	3,843	9,252	40,375	14,134	7,816	3,485	14,940
1958	41,219	14,047	9,829	1,759	1,018	4,865	9,701	44,851	15,919	8,567	3,818	16,547
1959	45,306	14,983	10,437	1,994	1,001	6,377	10,514	48,887	17,283	9,592	4,136	17,876
1960	50,505	16,405	11,849	2,463	1,180	6,974	11,634	51,876	18,719	9,428	4,404	19,325
1961	54,037	18,002	12,463	2,613	1,266	7,131	12,562	56,201	20,574	9,844	4,720	21,063
1962	58,252	19,054	13,494	3,037	1,308	7,871	13,488	60,206	22,216	10,357	5,084	22,549
1963	62,891	20,089	14,456	3,269	1,505	8,722	14,850	64,815	23,776	11,135	5,481	24,423
1963–64	68,443	21,241	15,762	3,791	1,695	10,002	15,952	69,302	26,286	11,664	5,766	25,586
1964–65	74,000	22,583	17,118	4,090	1,929	11,029	17,251	74,678	28,563	12,221	6,315	27,579
1965–66	83,036	24,670	19,085	4,760	2,038	13,214	19,269	82,843	33,287	12,770	6,757	30,029
1966–67	91,197	26,047	20,530	5,825	2,227	15,370	21,198	93,350	37,919	13,932	8,218	33,281
1967–68	101,264	27,747	22,911	7,308	2,518	17,181	23,599	102,411	41,158	14,481	9,857	36,915
1968–69	114,550	30,673	26,519	8,908	3,180	19,153	26,117	116,728	47,238	15,417	12,110	41,963
1969–70	130,756	34,054	30,322	10,812	3,738	21,857	29,973	131,332	52,718	16,427	14,679	47,508
1970–71	144,927	37,852	33,233	11,900	3,424	26,146	32,372	150,674	59,413	18,095	18,226	54,940
1971–72	167,535	42,877	37,518	15,227	4,416	31,342	36,156	168,549	65,813	19,021	21,117	62,598
1972–73	190,222	45,283	42,047	17,994	5,425	39,264	40,210	181,357	69,713	18,615	23,582	69,447
1973–74	207,670	47,705	46,098	19,491	6,015	41,820	46,542	199,222	75,833	19,946	25,085	78,358
1974–75	228,171	51,491	49,815	21,454	6,642	47,034	51,735	230,722	87,858	22,528	28,156	92,180
1975–76	256,176	57,001	54,547	24,575	7,273	55,589	57,191	256,731	97,216	23,907	32,604	103,004
1976–77	285,157	62,527	60,641	29,246	9,174	62,444	61,125	274,215	102,780	23,058	35,906	112,472
1977–78	315,960	66,422	67,596	33,176	10,738	69,592	68,435	296,984	110,758	24,609	39,140	122,478
1978–79	343,236	64,944	74,247	36,932	12,128	75,164	79,822	327,517	119,448	28,440	41,898	137,731
1979–80	382,322	68,499	79,927	42,080	13,321	83,029	95,467	369,086	133,211	33,311	47,288	155,276
1980–81	423,404	74,969	85,971	46,426	14,143	90,294	111,599	407,449	145,784	34,603	54,105	172,957
1981–82	457,654	82,067	93,613	50,738	15,028	87,282	128,925	436,733	154,282	34,520	57,996	189,935
1982–83	486,753	89,105	100,247	55,129	14,258	90,007	138,008	466,516	163,876	36,655	60,906	205,080
1983–84	542,730	96,457	114,097	64,871	16,798	96,935	153,571	505,008	176,108	39,419	66,414	223,068
1984–85	598,121	103,757	126,376	70,361	19,152	106,158	172,317	553,899	192,686	44,989	71,479	244,745
1985–86	641,486	111,709	135,005	74,365	19,994	113,099	187,314	605,623	210,819	49,368	75,868	269,568
1986–87	686,660	121,203	144,091	83,935	22,425	114,857	200,350	657,134	226,619	52,355	82,650	295,510
1987–88	726,762	132,212	156,452	88,350	23,663	117,602	208,482	704,921	242,683	55,621	89,090	317,527
1988–89	786,129	142,400	166,336	97,806	25,926	125,824	227,838	762,360	263,898	58,105	97,879	342,479
1989–90	849,502	155,613	177,885	105,640	23,566	136,802	249,996	834,818	288,148	61,057	110,518	375,094
1990–91	902,207	167,999	185,570	109,341	22,242	154,099	262,955	908,108	309,302	64,937	130,402	403,467
1991–92	979,137	180,337	197,731	115,638	23,880	179,174	282,376	981,253	324,652	67,351	158,723	430,526
1992–93	1,041,643	189,744	209,649	123,235	26,417	198,663	293,935	1,030,434	342,287	68,370	170,705	449,072
1993–94	1,100,490	197,141	223,628	128,810	28,320	215,492	307,099	1,077,665	353,287	72,067	183,394	468,916
1994–95	1,169,505	203,451	237,268	137,931	31,406	228,771	330,677	1,149,863	378,273	77,109	196,703	497,779
1995–96	1,222,821	209,440	248,993	146,844	32,009	234,891	350,645	1,193,276	398,859	79,092	197,354	517,971
1996–97	1,289,237	218,877	261,418	159,042	33,820	244,847	371,233	1,249,984	418,416	82,062	203,779	545,727
1997–98	1,365,762	230,150	274,883	175,630	34,412	255,048	395,639	1,318,042	450,365	87,214	208,120	572,343
1998–99	1,434,029	239,672	290,993	189,309	33,922	270,628	409,505	1,402,369	483,259	93,018	218,957	607,134
1999–2000	1,541,322	249,178	309,290	211,661	36,059	291,950	443,186	1,506,797	521,612	101,336	237,336	646,512
2000–01	1,647,161	263,689	320,217	226,334	35,296	324,033	477,592	1,626,063	563,572	107,235	261,622	693,634
2001–02	1,684,879	279,191	324,123	202,832	28,152	360,546	490,035	1,736,866	594,694	115,295	285,464	741,413
2002–03	1,763,212	296,683	337,787	199,407	31,369	389,264	508,702	1,821,917	621,335	117,696	310,783	772,102
2003–04	1,887,397	317,941	361,027	215,215	33,716	423,112	536,386	1,908,543	655,182	117,215	340,523	795,622
2004–05	2,026,034	335,779	384,266	242,273	43,256	438,558	581,902	2,012,110	688,314	126,350	365,295	832,151
2005–06	2,197,475	364,559	417,735	268,667	53,081	452,975	640,458	2,123,663	728,917	136,502	373,846	884,398
2006–07	2,330,611	388,905	440,470	290,278	60,955	464,914	685,089	2,264,035	774,170	145,011	389,259	955,595
2007–08	2,421,977	409,540	449,945	304,902	57,231	477,441	722,919	2,406,183	826,061	153,831	408,920	1,017,372
2008–09	2,429,672	434,818	434,128	270,942	46,280	537,949	705,555	2,500,796	851,689	154,338	437,184	1,057,586
2009–10	2,510,846	443,947	435,571	261,510	44,108	623,801	701,909	2,542,231	867,059	155,912	460,230	1,065,971
2010–11	2,618,037	445,771	463,979	285,293	48,422	647,606	726,966	2,583,805	862,271	153,895	494,682	1,072,957
2011–12	2,595,822	445,857	478,148	307,921	48,885	584,669	730,341	2,593,404	867,839	160,370	487,942	1,077,253
2012–13	2,682,661	453,214	503,486	338,617	52,898	583,545	750,901	2,626,497	879,159	157,627	518,485	1,073,526
2013–14	2,763,644	465,317	522,013	341,357	54,611	602,851	777,496	2,714,357	905,213	161,954	546,735	1,100,455
2014–15	2,915,426	484,351	544,973	367,917	57,235	657,567	803,384	2,842,867	935,754	167,769	617,768	1,121,576
2015–16	3,008,262	503,262	558,871	376,297	54,259	690,209	825,363	2,948,039	972,906	174,990	640,860	1,159,284
2016–17	3,112,651	525,897	574,253	383,980	52,806	707,710	868,005	3,075,404	1,011,708	181,162	676,258	1,206,276

[1] Fiscal years not the same for all governments. See Note.
[2] Excludes revenues or expenditures of publicly owned utilities and liquor stores and of insurance-trust activities. Intergovernmental receipts and payments between State and local governments are also excluded.
[3] Includes motor vehicle license taxes, other taxes, and charges and miscellaneous revenues.
[4] Includes intergovernmental payments to the Federal Government.
[5] Includes expenditures for libraries, hospitals, health, employment security administration, veterans' services, air transportation, sea and inland port facilities, parking facilities, police protection, fire protection, correction, protective inspection and regulation, sewerage, natural resources, parks and recreation, housing and community development, solid waste management, financial administration, judicial and legal, general public buildings, other government administration, interest on general debt, and other general expenditures, not elsewhere classified.

Note: Except for States listed, data for fiscal years listed from 1963–64 to 2016–17 are the aggregation of data for government fiscal years that ended in the 12-month period from July 1 to June 30 of those years; Texas used August and Alabama and Michigan used September as end dates. Data for 1963 and earlier years include data for government fiscal years ending during that particular calendar year.

Source: Department of Commerce (Bureau of the Census).

Table B–51. U.S. Treasury securities outstanding by kind of obligation, 1980–2019
[Billions of dollars]

End of fiscal year or month	Total Treasury securities outstanding [1]	Marketable							Nonmarketable				
		Total [2]	Treasury bills	Treasury notes	Treasury bonds	Treasury inflation-protected securities			Total	U.S. savings securities [3]	Foreign series [4]	Government account series	Other [5]
						Total	Notes	Bonds					
1980	906.8	594.5	199.8	310.9	83.8	....	....	....	312.3	73.0	25.2	189.8	24.2
1981	996.8	683.2	223.4	363.6	96.2	....	....	....	313.6	68.3	20.5	201.1	23.7
1982	1,141.2	824.4	277.9	442.9	103.6	....	....	....	316.8	67.6	14.6	210.5	24.1
1983	1,376.3	1,024.0	340.7	557.5	125.7	....	....	....	352.3	70.6	11.5	234.7	35.6
1984	1,560.4	1,176.6	356.8	661.7	158.1	....	....	....	383.8	73.7	8.8	259.5	41.8
1985	1,822.3	1,360.2	384.2	776.4	199.5	....	....	....	462.1	78.2	6.6	313.9	63.3
1986	2,124.9	1,564.3	410.7	896.9	241.7	....	....	....	560.5	87.8	4.1	365.9	102.8
1987	2,349.4	1,676.0	378.3	1,005.1	277.6	....	....	....	673.4	98.5	4.4	440.7	129.8
1988	2,601.4	1,802.9	398.5	1,089.6	299.9	....	....	....	798.5	107.8	6.3	536.5	148.0
1989	2,837.9	1,892.8	406.6	1,133.2	338.0	....	....	....	945.2	115.7	6.8	663.7	159.0
1990	3,212.7	2,092.8	482.5	1,218.1	377.2	....	....	....	1,119.9	123.9	36.0	779.4	180.6
1991	3,664.5	2,390.7	564.6	1,387.1	423.4	....	....	....	1,273.9	135.4	41.6	908.4	188.5
1992	4,063.8	2,677.5	634.3	1,566.3	461.8	....	....	....	1,386.3	150.3	37.0	1,011.0	188.0
1993	4,410.7	2,904.9	658.4	1,734.2	497.4	....	....	....	1,505.8	169.1	42.5	1,114.3	179.9
1994	4,691.7	3,091.6	697.3	1,867.5	511.8	....	....	....	1,600.1	178.6	42.0	1,211.7	167.8
1995	4,953.0	3,260.4	742.5	1,980.3	522.6	....	....	....	1,692.6	183.5	41.0	1,324.3	143.8
1996	5,220.8	3,418.4	761.2	2,098.7	543.5	....	....	....	1,802.4	184.1	37.5	1,454.7	126.1
1997	5,407.6	3,439.6	701.9	2,122.2	576.2	24.4	24.4	....	1,968.0	182.7	34.9	1,608.5	141.9
1998	5,518.7	3,331.0	637.6	2,009.1	610.4	58.8	41.9	17.0	2,187.6	180.8	35.1	1,777.3	194.4
1999	5,647.3	3,233.0	653.2	1,828.8	643.7	92.4	67.6	24.8	2,414.3	180.0	31.0	2,005.2	198.1
2000	5,622.1	2,992.8	616.2	1,611.3	635.3	115.0	81.6	33.4	2,629.4	177.7	25.4	2,242.9	183.3
2001 [1]	5,807.5	2,930.7	734.9	1,433.0	613.0	134.9	95.1	39.7	2,876.7	186.5	18.3	2,492.1	179.9
2002	6,228.2	3,136.7	868.3	1,521.6	593.0	138.9	93.7	45.1	3,091.5	193.3	12.5	2,707.3	178.4
2003	6,783.2	3,460.7	918.2	1,799.5	576.9	166.1	120.0	46.1	3,322.5	201.6	11.0	2,912.2	197.7
2004	7,379.1	3,846.1	961.5	2,109.6	552.0	223.0	164.5	58.5	3,533.0	204.2	5.9	3,130.0	192.9
2005	7,932.7	4,084.9	914.3	2,328.8	520.7	307.1	229.1	78.0	3,847.8	203.6	3.1	3,380.6	260.5
2006	8,507.0	4,303.0	911.5	2,447.2	534.7	395.6	293.9	101.7	4,203.9	203.7	3.0	3,722.7	274.5
2007	9,007.7	4,448.1	958.1	2,458.0	561.1	456.9	335.7	121.2	4,559.5	197.1	3.0	4,026.8	332.6
2008	10,024.7	5,236.0	1,489.8	2,624.8	582.9	524.5	380.2	144.3	4,788.7	194.3	3.0	4,297.7	293.8
2009	11,909.8	7,009.7	1,992.5	3,773.8	679.8	551.7	396.2	155.5	4,900.1	192.5	4.9	4,454.3	248.4
2010	13,561.6	8,498.3	1,788.5	5,255.9	849.9	593.8	421.1	172.7	5,063.3	188.7	4.2	4,645.3	225.1
2011	14,790.3	9,624.5	1,477.5	6,412.5	1,020.4	705.7	509.4	196.3	5,165.8	185.1	3.0	4,793.9	183.8
2012	16,066.2	10,749.7	1,616.0	7,120.7	1,198.2	807.7	584.7	223.0	5,316.5	183.8	3.0	4,939.3	190.4
2013	16,738.2	11,596.2	1,530.0	7,758.0	1,366.2	936.4	685.5	250.8	5,142.0	180.0	3.0	4,803.1	156.0
2014	17,824.1	12,294.2	1,411.0	8,167.8	1,534.1	1,044.7	765.2	279.5	5,529.9	176.7	3.0	5,212.5	137.7
2015	18,150.6	12,853.8	1,358.0	8,372.7	1,688.3	1,135.4	832.1	303.3	5,296.9	172.8	.3	5,013.5	110.3
2016	19,573.4	13,660.6	1,647.0	8,631.0	1,825.5	1,210.0	881.6	328.3	5,912.8	167.5	.3	5,604.1	141.0
2017	20,244.9	14,199.8	1,801.9	8,805.5	1,951.7	1,286.5	933.3	353.2	6,045.1	161.7	.3	5,771.1	112.0
2018	21,516.1	15,278.0	2,239.9	9,154.4	2,127.8	1,376.4	993.4	383.0	6,238.0	156.8	.3	5,977.6	103.4
2019	22,719.4	16,347.3	2,377.0	9,762.8	2,319.1	1,455.7	1,044.9	410.8	6,372.1	152.3	.3	6,133.7	85.8
2018: Jan	20,493.7	14,514.5	1,966.9	8,889.2	2,004.9	1,323.1	961.9	361.2	5,979.2	159.9	.3	5,700.7	118.4
Feb	20,855.7	14,677.9	2,078.0	8,899.6	2,024.0	1,331.0	961.3	369.7	6,177.7	159.4	.3	5,902.8	115.2
Mar	21,089.9	14,945.0	2,289.0	8,924.6	2,037.0	1,349.0	977.4	371.6	6,144.9	159.0	.3	5,869.3	116.3
Apr	21,068.2	14,849.9	2,169.0	8,974.2	2,050.0	1,319.4	946.1	373.3	6,218.3	158.6	.3	5,945.6	113.9
May	21,145.2	14,939.4	2,184.0	9,002.2	2,064.4	1,335.6	961.4	374.2	6,205.8	158.2	.3	5,932.1	115.3
June	21,195.3	14,982.6	2,158.0	9,032.2	2,078.4	1,345.9	965.2	380.7	6,212.8	157.8	.3	5,943.9	110.8
July	21,313.1	15,085.3	2,205.9	9,094.9	2,092.4	1,347.8	965.5	382.3	6,227.8	157.5	.3	5,962.2	107.8
Aug	21,458.8	15,301.8	2,340.9	9,120.4	2,112.8	1,365.2	982.3	383.0	6,157.0	157.0	.3	5,895.9	103.8
Sept	21,516.1	15,278.0	2,239.9	9,154.4	2,127.8	1,376.4	993.4	383.0	6,238.0	156.8	.3	5,977.6	103.4
Oct	21,702.4	15,357.9	2,258.0	9,218.2	2,142.8	1,382.3	994.0	388.3	6,344.5	156.4	.3	6,084.1	103.7
Nov	21,850.1	15,560.1	2,389.1	9,240.4	2,158.5	1,395.9	1,007.1	388.8	6,290.0	156.2	.3	6,032.9	100.7
Dec	21,974.1	15,618.3	2,340.0	9,297.0	2,174.5	1,412.6	1,023.2	389.4	6,355.8	155.7	.3	6,101.9	97.9
2019: Jan	21,982.4	15,619.8	2,299.1	9,355.8	2,190.5	1,403.8	1,015.6	388.2	6,362.6	155.2	.3	6,114.0	93.1
Feb	22,115.5	15,769.7	2,396.0	9,376.3	2,201.0	1,407.7	1,012.4	395.3	6,345.8	154.9	.3	6,097.9	92.8
Mar	22,028.0	15,939.0	2,480.0	9,414.3	2,217.0	1,421.1	1,025.1	396.0	6,089.0	154.5	.3	5,840.6	93.7
Apr	22,027.7	15,880.9	2,384.0	9,491.4	2,233.0	1,390.3	992.6	397.7	6,146.8	154.1	.3	5,902.6	89.8
May	22,026.4	15,941.3	2,353.9	9,516.4	2,258.5	1,410.3	1,010.4	399.9	6,085.2	153.7	.3	5,846.6	84.6
June	22,023.5	15,931.2	2,250.9	9,554.4	2,274.5	1,432.7	1,030.8	401.9	6,092.4	153.4	.3	5,859.0	79.7
July	22,022.4	15,968.1	2,205.9	9,642.2	2,290.6	1,432.5	1,029.6	402.9	6,054.2	153.0	.3	5,825.5	75.5
Aug	22,460.5	16,146.3	2,331.9	9,656.4	2,303.1	1,440.0	1,029.9	410.1	6,314.2	152.6	.3	6,084.6	76.7
Sept	22,719.4	16,347.3	2,377.0	9,762.8	2,319.1	1,455.7	1,044.9	410.8	6,372.1	152.3	.3	6,133.7	85.8
Oct	23,008.4	16,514.1	2,456.1	9,834.9	2,335.1	1,474.4	1,063.6	410.8	6,494.3	152.0	.3	6,251.8	90.1
Nov	23,076.2	16,627.8	2,515.1	9,830.4	2,363.1	1,487.6	1,076.5	411.1	6,448.5	151.8	.3	6,200.0	96.4
Dec	23,201.4	16,682.1	2,416.9	9,929.2	2,379.1	1,507.4	1,095.3	412.0	6,519.2	151.3	.3	6,262.4	105.3

[1] Data beginning with January 2001 are interest-bearing and non-interest-bearing securities; prior data are interest-bearing securities only.
[2] Data from 1986 to 2002 and 2005 forward include Federal Financing Bank securities, not shown separately. Beginning with data for January 2014, includes Floating Rate Notes, not shown separately.
[3] Through 1996, series is U.S. savings bonds. Beginning 1997, includes U.S. retirement plan bonds, U.S. individual retirement bonds, and U.S. savings notes previously included in "other" nonmarketable securities.
[4] Nonmarketable certificates of indebtedness, notes, bonds, and bills in the Treasury foreign series of dollar-denominated and foreign-currency-denominated issues.
[5] Includes depository bonds; retirement plan bonds through 1996; Rural Electrification Administration bonds; State and local bonds; special issues held only by U.S. Government agencies and trust funds and the Federal home loan banks; for the period July 2003 through February 2004, depositary compensation securities; and for the period August 2008 through April 2016, Hope bonds for the HOPE For Homeowners Program.

Note: The fiscal year is on an October 1–September 30 basis.

Source: Department of the Treasury.

Table B–52. Estimated ownership of U.S. Treasury securities, 2006–2019

[Billions of dollars]

End of month	Total public debt [1]	Federal Reserve and Intra-governmental holdings [2]	Held by private investors			Pension funds		Insurance companies	Mutual funds [6]	State and local governments	Foreign and international [7]	Other investors [8]
			Total privately held	Depository institutions [3]	U.S. savings bonds [4]	Private [5]	State and local governments					
2006: Mar	8,371.2	4,257.2	4,114.0	113.0	206.0	116.8	152.9	200.3	254.2	515.7	2,082.1	473.0
June	8,420.0	4,389.2	4,030.8	119.5	205.2	117.7	149.6	196.1	243.4	531.6	1,977.8	490.1
Sept	8,507.0	4,432.8	4,074.2	113.6	203.7	125.8	149.3	196.8	234.2	542.3	2,025.3	483.2
Dec	8,680.2	4,558.1	4,122.1	114.8	202.4	139.8	153.4	197.9	248.2	570.5	2,103.1	392.0
2007: Mar	8,849.7	4,576.6	4,273.1	119.8	200.3	139.7	156.3	185.4	263.2	608.3	2,194.8	405.2
June	8,867.7	4,715.1	4,152.6	110.4	198.6	139.9	162.3	168.9	257.6	637.8	2,192.0	285.1
Sept	9,007.7	4,738.0	4,269.7	119.7	197.1	140.5	153.2	155.1	292.7	643.1	2,235.3	332.9
Dec	9,229.2	4,833.5	4,395.7	129.8	196.5	141.0	144.2	141.9	343.5	647.8	2,353.2	297.8
2008: Mar	9,437.6	4,694.7	4,742.9	125.0	195.4	143.7	135.4	152.1	466.7	646.4	2,506.3	371.9
June	9,492.0	4,685.8	4,806.2	112.7	195.0	145.0	135.5	159.4	440.3	635.1	2,587.4	395.9
Sept	10,024.7	4,692.7	5,332.0	130.0	194.3	147.0	136.7	163.4	631.4	614.0	2,802.4	512.9
Dec	10,699.8	4,806.4	5,893.4	105.0	194.1	147.4	129.9	171.4	758.2	601.4	3,077.2	708.9
2009: Mar	11,126.9	4,785.2	6,341.7	125.7	194.0	155.4	137.0	191.0	721.1	588.2	3,265.7	963.7
June	11,545.3	5,026.8	6,518.5	140.8	193.6	164.1	144.6	200.0	711.8	588.5	3,460.8	914.2
Sept	11,909.8	5,127.1	6,782.7	198.2	192.5	167.2	145.6	210.2	668.5	583.6	3,570.6	1,046.3
Dec	12,311.3	5,276.9	7,034.4	202.5	191.3	175.6	151.4	222.0	668.8	585.6	3,685.1	1,152.1
2010: Mar	12,773.1	5,259.8	7,513.3	269.3	190.2	183.0	153.6	225.7	678.5	585.0	3,877.9	1,350.1
June	13,201.8	5,345.1	7,856.7	266.1	189.6	190.8	150.1	231.8	676.8	584.4	4,070.0	1,497.1
Sept	13,561.6	5,350.5	8,211.1	322.8	188.7	198.2	145.2	240.6	671.0	586.0	4,324.2	1,534.4
Dec	14,025.2	5,656.2	8,368.9	319.3	187.9	206.8	153.7	248.4	721.7	595.7	4,435.6	1,499.9
2011: Mar	14,270.0	5,958.9	8,311.1	321.0	186.7	215.8	157.9	253.5	749.4	585.3	4,481.4	1,360.1
June	14,343.1	6,220.4	8,122.7	279.4	186.0	251.8	158.0	254.8	753.7	572.2	4,690.6	976.1
Sept	14,790.3	6,328.0	8,462.4	293.8	185.1	373.6	155.7	259.6	788.7	557.9	4,912.1	935.8
Dec	15,222.8	6,439.6	8,783.3	279.7	185.2	391.9	160.7	297.3	927.9	562.2	5,006.9	971.4
2012: Mar	15,582.3	6,397.2	9,185.1	317.0	184.8	406.6	169.4	298.1	1,015.4	567.4	5,145.1	1,081.2
June	15,855.5	6,475.8	9,379.7	303.2	184.7	427.4	171.2	293.6	997.8	585.4	5,310.9	1,105.4
Sept	16,066.2	6,446.8	9,619.4	338.2	183.8	453.9	181.7	292.6	1,080.7	596.9	5,476.1	1,015.4
Dec	16,432.7	6,523.7	9,909.1	347.7	182.5	468.0	183.6	292.7	1,031.8	599.6	5,573.8	1,229.4
2013: Mar	16,771.6	6,656.8	10,114.8	338.9	181.7	463.4	193.4	284.3	1,066.7	615.6	5,725.0	1,245.7
June	16,738.2	6,773.3	9,964.9	300.2	180.9	444.5	187.7	276.2	1,000.1	612.6	5,595.0	1,367.8
Sept	16,738.2	6,834.2	9,904.0	293.2	180.0	347.8	187.5	273.2	986.1	624.3	5,652.8	1,359.1
Dec	17,352.0	7,205.3	10,146.6	321.1	179.2	464.9	181.3	271.2	983.3	633.6	5,792.6	1,319.5
2014: Mar	17,601.2	7,301.5	10,299.7	368.4	178.3	474.3	184.3	276.8	1,060.4	632.0	5,948.3	1,177.0
June	17,632.6	7,461.0	10,171.6	409.5	177.6	482.6	198.3	287.7	986.2	638.8	6,018.7	972.1
Sept	17,824.1	7,490.8	10,333.2	471.1	176.7	490.7	198.7	298.1	1,075.8	628.7	6,069.2	924.1
Dec	18,141.4	7,578.9	10,562.6	516.8	175.9	507.1	199.2	307.0	1,121.8	654.5	6,157.7	922.4
2015: Mar	18,152.1	7,521.3	10,630.8	518.1	174.9	447.8	176.7	305.1	1,170.4	674.2	6,172.6	990.9
June	18,152.0	7,536.5	10,615.5	518.5	173.9	373.8	185.7	304.3	1,139.8	655.0	6,163.1	1,101.3
Sept	18,150.6	7,488.7	10,661.9	519.1	172.8	305.3	171.0	306.6	1,195.1	646.4	6,105.9	1,239.7
Dec	18,922.2	7,711.2	11,211.0	547.4	171.6	504.7	174.5	306.7	1,318.3	680.4	6,146.2	1,361.1
2016: Mar	19,264.9	7,801.4	11,463.6	562.9	170.3	524.4	170.4	315.5	1,404.1	692.6	6,284.4	1,339.0
June	19,381.6	7,911.2	11,470.4	580.6	169.0	537.9	185.0	329.8	1,434.2	710.0	6,279.1	1,244.8
Sept	19,573.4	7,863.5	11,709.9	627.6	167.5	545.6	203.8	341.2	1,600.4	734.0	6,155.9	1,333.9
Dec	19,976.9	8,005.6	11,971.3	663.9	165.8	538.0	218.8	330.2	1,705.4	744.2	6,006.3	1,598.8
2017: Mar	19,846.4	7,941.1	11,905.3	658.6	164.2	444.2	239.5	338.4	1,669.1	751.1	6,075.3	1,564.9
June	19,844.6	7,943.4	11,901.1	621.9	162.8	425.9	262.8	348.4	1,608.5	736.4	6,151.9	1,582.5
Sept	20,244.9	8,036.9	12,208.0	611.8	161.7	570.8	266.5	359.7	1,697.8	716.0	6,301.9	1,521.9
Dec	20,492.7	8,132.1	12,360.6	638.3	160.4	432.0	289.4	372.6	1,797.5	732.3	6,211.3	1,726.9
2018: Mar	21,089.9	8,086.6	13,003.3	639.7	159.0	597.7	300.1	361.8	1,977.1	712.9	6,223.4	2,031.6
June	21,195.3	8,106.9	13,088.5	665.3	157.8	622.5	307.3	225.9	1,843.4	727.3	6,225.0	2,314.0
Sept	21,516.1	8,068.1	13,447.9	683.9	156.8	644.0	304.7	226.1	1,898.2	722.2	6,225.9	2,586.3
Dec	21,974.1	8,095.0	13,879.1	771.5	155.7	670.9	372.8	203.7	2,023.3	693.0	6,271.1	2,717.0
2019: Mar	22,028.0	7,999.1	14,028.9	771.3	154.5	478.2	405.1	201.1	2,058.3	691.8	6,474.9	2,793.6
June	22,023.5	7,945.2	14,078.4	810.0	153.4	506.0	414.7	202.1	1,929.9	674.5	6,640.5	2,747.3
Sept	22,719.4	8,023.6	14,695.8	909.9	152.3	727.5	424.5	208.2	2,173.5	676.7	6,779.1	2,644.1
Dec	23,201.4	8,359.9	14,841.5	....	151.3	....	....	....	....	....	....	....

[1] Face value.
[2] Federal Reserve holdings exclude Treasury securities held under repurchase agreements.
[3] Includes U.S. chartered depository institutions, foreign banking offices in U.S., banks in U.S. affiliated areas, credit unions, and bank holding companies.
[4] Current accrual value includes myRA.
[5] Includes Treasury securities held by the Federal Employees Retirement System Thrift Savings Plan "G Fund."
[6] Includes money market mutual funds, mutual funds, and closed-end investment companies.
[7] Includes nonmarketable foreign series, Treasury securities, and Treasury deposit funds. Excludes Treasury securities held under repurchase agreements in custody accounts at the Federal Reserve Bank of New York. Estimates reflect benchmarks to this series at differing intervals; for further detail, see *Treasury Bulletin* and http://www.treasury.gov/resource-center/data-chart-center/tic/pages/index.aspx.
[8] Includes individuals, Government-sponsored enterprises, brokers and dealers, bank personal trusts and estates, corporate and noncorporate businesses, and other investors.

Source: Department of the Treasury.

Corporate Profits and Finance

Table B-53. Corporate profits with inventory valuation and capital consumption adjustments, 1969–2019

[Billions of dollars; quarterly data at seasonally adjusted annual rates]

Year or quarter	Corporate profits with inventory valuation and capital consumption adjustments	Taxes on corporate income	Corporate profits after tax with inventory valuation and capital consumption adjustments		
			Total	Net dividends	Undistributed profits with inventory valuation and capital consumption adjustments
1969	98.4	37.0	61.5	27.3	34.2
1970	86.2	31.3	55.0	27.8	27.2
1971	100.6	34.8	65.8	28.4	37.5
1972	117.2	39.1	78.1	30.1	48.0
1973	133.4	45.6	87.8	34.2	53.5
1974	125.7	47.2	78.5	38.8	39.7
1975	138.9	46.3	92.6	38.3	54.3
1976	174.3	59.4	114.9	44.9	70.0
1977	205.8	68.5	137.3	50.7	86.6
1978	238.6	77.9	160.7	57.8	102.9
1979	249.0	80.7	168.2	66.8	101.4
1980	223.6	75.5	148.1	75.8	72.3
1981	247.5	70.3	177.2	87.8	89.4
1982	229.9	51.3	178.6	92.9	85.6
1983	279.8	66.4	213.3	97.7	115.7
1984	337.9	81.5	256.4	106.9	149.5
1985	354.5	81.6	272.9	115.3	157.5
1986	324.4	91.9	232.5	124.0	108.5
1987	366.0	112.7	253.3	130.1	123.2
1988	414.5	124.3	290.2	147.3	142.9
1989	414.3	124.4	289.9	179.6	110.3
1990	417.7	121.8	295.9	192.7	103.2
1991	452.6	117.8	334.8	201.3	133.5
1992	477.2	131.9	345.3	206.3	139.0
1993	524.6	155.0	369.5	221.3	148.2
1994	624.8	172.7	452.1	256.4	195.7
1995	706.2	194.4	511.8	282.3	229.4
1996	789.5	211.4	578.1	323.6	254.5
1997	869.7	224.8	645.0	360.1	284.9
1998	808.5	221.8	586.6	383.6	203.0
1999	834.9	227.4	607.5	373.5	234.1
2000	786.6	233.4	553.2	410.2	142.9
2001	758.7	170.1	588.6	397.9	190.8
2002	911.7	160.6	751.1	424.9	326.2
2003	1,056.3	213.7	842.5	456.0	386.5
2004	1,289.3	278.5	1,010.8	582.2	428.6
2005	1,488.6	379.8	1,108.8	602.0	506.8
2006	1,646.3	430.4	1,215.8	755.1	460.8
2007	1,533.2	392.1	1,141.1	853.5	287.6
2008	1,285.8	256.1	1,029.7	840.3	189.4
2009	1,386.8	204.2	1,182.6	622.1	560.6
2010	1,728.7	272.5	1,456.2	643.2	813.0
2011	1,809.8	281.1	1,528.7	779.1	749.6
2012	1,997.4	334.9	1,662.5	948.7	713.9
2013	2,010.7	362.8	1,647.9	1,009.0	638.9
2014	2,120.2	407.3	1,712.9	1,096.1	616.8
2015	2,061.5	396.6	1,664.9	1,164.9	500.0
2016	2,011.5	377.6	1,633.9	1,175.9	458.0
2017	2,005.9	319.4	1,686.5	1,239.6	446.9
2018	2,074.6	219.8	1,854.9	1,312.6	542.3
2019 ᵖ	....	....	....	1,340.7	....
2016: I	2,022.2	373.3	1,649.0	1,168.9	480.1
II	1,998.1	373.8	1,624.3	1,166.7	457.6
III	2,013.0	391.7	1,621.3	1,183.3	438.0
IV	2,012.6	371.5	1,641.0	1,184.8	456.2
2017: I	1,995.4	322.8	1,672.5	1,219.5	453.1
II	2,008.0	314.1	1,693.9	1,246.8	447.1
III	2,019.0	335.3	1,683.7	1,242.7	441.0
IV	2,001.4	305.4	1,696.0	1,249.5	446.5
2018: I	2,052.3	207.6	1,844.7	1,266.3	578.4
II	2,056.4	222.6	1,833.8	1,291.9	541.9
III	2,104.2	230.3	1,873.9	1,329.7	544.2
IV	2,085.6	218.5	1,867.1	1,362.5	504.6
2019: I	2,006.9	215.4	1,791.4	1,324.6	466.8
II	2,082.7	225.2	1,857.5	1,346.9	510.7
III	2,078.0	209.3	1,868.7	1,339.6	529.1
IV ᵖ	....	....	....	1,351.6	....

Source: Department of Commerce (Bureau of Economic Analysis).

TABLE B–54. Corporate profits by industry, 1969–2019

[Billions of dollars; quarterly data at seasonally adjusted annual rates]

Year or quarter	Total	Corporate profits with inventory valuation adjustment and without capital consumption adjustment												Rest of the world
		Domestic industries												
		Total	Financial			Nonfinancial								
			Total	Federal Reserve banks	Other	Total	Manufacturing	Transportation [1]	Utilities	Wholesale trade	Retail trade	Information	Other	
SIC: [2]														
1969	90.8	84.2	13.6	3.1	10.6	70.6	41.6	11.1	....	4.9	6.4	....	6.5	6.6
1970	79.7	72.6	15.5	3.5	12.0	57.1	32.0	8.8	....	4.6	6.1	....	5.8	7.1
1971	94.7	86.8	17.9	3.3	14.6	68.9	40.0	9.6	....	5.4	7.3	....	6.7	7.9
1972	109.3	99.7	19.5	3.3	16.1	80.3	47.6	10.4	....	7.2	7.5	....	7.6	9.5
1973	126.6	111.7	21.1	4.5	16.6	90.6	55.0	10.2	....	8.8	7.0	....	9.6	14.9
1974	123.3	105.8	20.8	5.7	15.1	85.1	51.0	9.1	....	12.2	2.8	....	10.0	17.5
1975	144.2	129.6	20.4	5.6	14.8	109.2	63.0	11.7	....	14.3	8.4	....	11.8	14.6
1976	182.1	165.6	25.6	5.9	19.7	140.0	82.5	17.5	....	13.7	10.9	....	15.3	16.5
1977	212.8	193.7	32.6	6.1	26.5	161.1	91.5	21.2	....	16.4	12.8	....	19.2	19.1
1978	246.7	223.8	40.8	7.6	33.1	183.1	105.8	25.5	....	16.7	13.1	....	22.0	22.9
1979	261.0	226.4	41.8	9.4	32.3	184.6	107.1	21.6	....	20.0	10.7	....	25.2	34.6
1980	240.6	205.2	35.2	11.8	23.5	169.9	97.6	22.2	....	18.5	7.0	....	24.6	35.5
1981	252.0	222.3	30.3	14.4	15.9	192.0	112.5	25.1	....	23.7	10.7	....	20.1	29.7
1982	224.6	192.2	27.2	15.2	12.0	165.0	89.6	28.1	....	20.7	14.3	....	12.3	32.6
1983	256.4	221.4	36.2	14.6	21.6	185.2	97.3	34.3	....	21.9	19.3	....	12.3	35.1
1984	294.3	257.7	34.7	16.4	18.3	223.0	114.2	44.7	....	30.4	21.5	....	12.1	36.6
1985	289.7	251.6	46.5	16.3	30.2	205.1	107.1	39.1	....	24.6	22.8	....	11.4	38.1
1986	273.3	233.8	56.4	15.5	40.8	177.4	75.6	39.3	....	24.4	23.4	....	14.7	39.5
1987	314.6	266.5	60.3	16.2	44.1	206.2	101.8	42.0	....	18.9	23.3	....	20.3	48.0
1988	366.2	309.2	66.9	18.1	48.8	242.3	132.8	46.8	....	20.4	19.8	....	22.5	57.0
1989	373.1	305.9	78.3	20.6	57.6	227.6	122.3	41.9	....	22.0	20.9	....	20.5	67.1
1990	391.2	315.1	89.6	21.8	67.8	225.5	120.9	43.5	....	19.4	20.3	....	21.3	76.1
1991	434.2	357.8	120.4	20.7	99.7	237.3	109.3	54.5	....	22.3	26.9	....	24.3	76.5
1992	459.7	386.6	132.4	18.3	114.1	254.2	109.8	57.7	....	25.3	28.1	....	33.4	73.1
1993	501.9	425.0	119.9	16.7	103.2	305.1	122.9	70.1	....	26.5	39.7	....	45.8	76.9
1994	589.3	511.3	125.9	18.5	107.4	385.4	162.6	83.9	....	31.4	46.3	....	61.2	78.0
1995	667.0	574.0	140.3	22.9	117.3	433.7	199.8	89.0	....	28.0	43.9	....	73.1	92.9
1996	741.8	639.8	147.9	22.5	125.3	492.0	220.4	91.2	....	39.9	52.0	....	88.5	102.0
1997	811.0	703.4	162.2	24.3	137.9	541.2	248.5	81.0	....	48.1	63.4	....	100.3	107.6
1998	743.8	641.1	138.9	25.6	113.3	502.1	220.4	72.6	....	50.6	72.3	....	86.3	102.8
1999	761.9	640.2	154.6	26.7	127.9	485.6	219.4	49.3	....	46.8	72.5	....	97.6	121.7
2000	729.8	584.1	149.7	31.2	118.5	434.4	205.9	33.8	....	50.4	68.9	....	75.4	145.7
NAICS: [2]														
1998	743.8	641.1	138.9	25.6	113.3	502.1	193.5	12.8	33.3	57.3	62.5	33.1	109.7	102.8
1999	761.9	640.2	154.6	26.7	127.9	485.6	184.5	7.2	34.4	55.6	59.5	20.8	123.5	121.7
2000	729.8	584.1	149.7	31.2	118.5	434.4	175.6	9.5	24.3	59.5	51.3	−11.9	126.1	145.7
2001	697.1	528.3	195.0	28.9	166.1	333.3	75.1	−.7	22.5	51.1	71.3	−26.4	140.2	168.8
2002	797.4	640.6	265.3	23.5	241.9	375.3	78.3	−6.5	10.5	53.5	83.3	5.0	151.2	156.8
2003	955.7	796.7	302.8	20.0	282.7	494.0	123.9	4.4	13.2	56.6	87.9	28.1	179.9	158.9
2004	1,217.5	1,022.4	346.0	20.0	326.0	676.3	186.2	12.0	21.1	72.7	94.0	61.6	228.8	195.1
2005	1,629.2	1,403.4	409.5	26.5	383.0	993.9	279.7	28.4	32.4	96.0	123.3	100.7	333.5	225.7
2006	1,812.2	1,572.5	413.1	33.8	379.3	1,159.4	352.9	40.8	55.2	105.0	133.6	115.2	356.8	239.7
2007	1,708.3	1,370.5	300.2	36.0	264.2	1,070.3	321.1	23.3	49.6	102.8	119.4	120.5	333.6	337.8
2008	1,344.5	954.3	94.6	35.1	59.5	859.7	240.0	29.3	30.4	92.7	82.2	98.8	286.3	390.2
2009	1,470.1	1,121.3	362.7	47.3	315.3	758.7	164.7	21.7	23.4	88.9	107.9	87.0	265.1	348.8
2010	1,786.4	1,400.6	405.8	71.6	334.3	994.8	281.8	44.6	30.6	99.3	115.9	102.3	320.4	385.8
2011	1,750.2	1,337.7	378.4	76.0	302.4	959.3	296.0	30.6	10.2	97.2	115.1	95.7	314.5	412.6
2012	2,144.7	1,739.3	482.4	71.7	410.6	1,256.9	403.0	54.4	13.8	137.9	155.7	112.0	380.1	405.4
2013	2,165.9	1,767.1	430.7	79.7	351.1	1,336.3	446.9	45.2	28.3	146.4	153.3	137.6	378.6	398.8
2014	2,266.6	1,861.7	483.1	103.5	379.6	1,378.6	458.7	55.7	32.8	150.6	157.3	126.6	397.0	404.9
2015	2,190.0	1,787.5	448.1	100.7	347.4	1,339.4	424.8	61.0	20.1	152.0	169.3	135.6	376.5	402.5
2016	2,116.5	1,704.6	456.8	92.0	364.8	1,247.8	332.2	63.9	9.4	126.6	170.5	157.4	387.8	411.9
2017	2,084.1	1,630.0	413.5	78.3	335.2	1,216.5	315.5	58.2	11.6	124.2	156.9	141.0	409.1	454.1
2018	2,011.9	1,510.3	405.0	63.6	341.4	1,105.3	283.7	45.0	−4.0	108.9	133.1	121.7	416.9	501.7
2017: I	2,128.9	1,692.3	409.8	89.3	320.5	1,282.5	306.5	63.2	13.5	132.7	174.5	158.0	434.3	436.6
II	2,151.4	1,728.1	417.0	80.2	336.8	1,311.1	337.1	67.5	14.2	140.0	168.1	145.6	438.6	423.3
III	2,171.5	1,703.8	440.9	71.9	369.0	1,262.9	348.8	59.4	11.7	127.8	161.9	151.2	402.0	467.6
IV	1,884.5	1,395.8	386.3	71.8	314.5	1,009.5	269.6	42.8	6.8	96.4	123.2	109.2	361.5	488.7
2018: I	1,979.9	1,472.1	413.3	70.0	343.3	1,058.8	246.0	42.9	1.7	109.3	137.7	123.9	397.2	507.7
II	1,991.5	1,496.5	418.4	65.6	352.8	1,078.2	287.0	39.9	−1.6	92.3	128.8	127.3	410.4	495.0
III	2,045.0	1,533.4	397.4	61.9	335.5	1,136.1	298.9	43.5	−5.4	110.9	141.8	124.3	422.1	511.6
IV	2,031.3	1,539.1	390.8	56.8	334.0	1,148.2	303.0	53.6	−10.7	122.9	130.0	111.4	438.1	492.3
2019: I	1,999.9	1,500.4	419.0	50.6	368.4	1,081.4	260.1	41.1	−4.2	116.1	151.2	108.6	408.5	499.6
II	2,080.5	1,542.3	424.6	55.6	368.8	1,120.0	265.5	38.1	−1.4	120.6	161.5	111.6	424.0	538.2
III	2,073.9	1,530.1	417.7	50.6	367.2	1,112.4	274.8	43.4	−2.0	120.7	164.3	78.0	433.3	543.7

[1] Data on Standard Industrial Classification (SIC) basis include transportation and public utilities. Those on North American Industry Classification System (NAICS) basis include transporation and warehousing. Utilities classified separately in NAICS (as shown beginning 1998).

[2] SIC-based industry data use the 1987 SIC for data beginning in 1987 and the 1972 SIC for prior data. NAICS-based data use 2002 NAICS.

Note: Industry data on SIC basis and NAICS basis are not necessarily the same and are not strictly comparable.

Source: Department of Commerce (Bureau of Economic Analysis).

TABLE B–55. Historical stock prices and yields, 1949–2003

End of year	Common stock prices (end of period) [1]									Common stock yields (Standard & Poor's) (percent) [5]	
	New York Stock Exchange (NYSE) indexes [2]						Dow Jones industrial average [2]	Standard & Poor's composite index (1941–43=10) [2]	Nasdaq composite index (Feb. 5, 1971=100) [2]	Dividend-price ratio [6]	Earnings-price ratio [7]
	Composite (Dec. 31, 2002= 5,000) [3]	December 31, 1965=50									
		Composite	Industrial	Transportation	Utility [4]	Finance					
1949	....	....	....	....	....	....	200.52	16.76	....	6.59	15.48
1950	....	....	....	....	....	....	235.42	20.41	....	6.57	13.99
1951	....	....	....	....	....	....	269.23	23.77	....	6.13	11.82
1952	....	....	....	....	....	....	291.90	26.57	....	5.80	9.47
1953	....	13.60	....	....	....	....	280.90	24.81	....	5.80	10.26
1954	....	19.40	....	....	....	....	404.39	35.98	....	4.95	8.57
1955	....	23.71	....	....	....	....	488.40	45.48	....	4.08	7.95
1956	....	24.35	....	....	....	....	499.47	46.67	....	4.09	7.55
1957	....	21.11	....	....	....	....	435.69	39.99	....	4.35	7.89
1958	....	28.85	....	....	....	....	583.65	55.21	....	3.97	6.23
1959	....	32.15	....	....	....	....	679.36	59.89	....	3.23	5.78
1960	....	30.94	....	....	....	....	615.89	58.11	....	3.47	5.90
1961	....	38.93	....	....	....	....	731.14	71.55	....	2.98	4.62
1962	....	33.81	....	....	....	....	652.10	63.10	....	3.37	5.82
1963	....	39.92	....	....	....	....	762.95	75.02	....	3.17	5.50
1964	....	45.65	....	....	....	....	874.13	84.75	....	3.01	5.32
1965	528.69	50.00	....	....	....	....	969.26	92.43	....	3.00	5.59
1966	462.28	43.72	43.13	47.56	90.38	44.91	785.69	80.33	....	3.40	6.63
1967	569.18	53.83	56.59	49.66	86.76	53.80	905.11	96.47	....	3.20	5.73
1968	622.79	58.90	61.69	56.27	91.64	76.48	943.75	103.86	....	3.07	5.67
1969	544.86	51.53	54.74	37.85	77.54	67.87	800.36	92.06	....	3.24	6.08
1970	531.12	50.23	52.91	35.70	81.64	64.34	838.92	92.15	....	3.83	6.45
1971	596.68	56.43	60.53	49.56	78.78	73.83	890.20	102.09	114.12	3.14	5.41
1972	681.79	64.48	70.33	47.69	84.34	83.34	1,020.02	118.05	133.73	2.84	5.50
1973	547.93	51.82	56.60	37.53	68.66	64.51	850.86	97.55	92.19	3.06	7.12
1974	382.03	36.13	39.15	26.36	53.30	39.84	616.24	68.56	59.82	4.47	11.59
1975	503.73	47.64	52.73	32.98	66.94	45.20	852.41	90.19	77.62	4.31	9.15
1976	612.01	57.88	63.36	42.57	82.54	59.23	1,004.65	107.46	97.88	3.77	8.90
1977	555.12	52.50	56.43	40.50	81.08	53.85	831.17	95.10	105.05	4.62	10.79
1978	566.96	53.62	58.87	41.58	75.38	55.01	805.01	96.11	117.98	5.28	12.03
1979	655.04	61.95	70.24	50.64	73.80	63.45	838.74	107.94	151.14	5.47	13.46
1980	823.27	77.86	91.52	76.19	76.90	70.83	963.99	135.76	202.34	5.26	12.66
1981	751.90	71.11	80.89	66.85	80.10	73.68	875.00	122.55	195.84	5.20	11.96
1982	856.79	81.03	93.02	73.63	86.94	85.00	1,046.54	140.64	232.41	5.81	11.60
1983	1,006.41	95.18	111.35	98.09	92.48	94.32	1,258.64	164.93	278.60	4.40	8.03
1984	1,013.91	96.38	110.58	90.61	103.14	97.63	1,211.57	167.24	247.35	4.64	10.02
1985	1,285.66	121.59	139.27	113.97	126.38	131.29	1,546.67	211.28	324.93	4.25	8.12
1986	1,465.31	138.59	160.11	117.65	147.54	140.05	1,895.95	242.17	348.83	3.49	6.09
1987	1,461.61	138.23	167.04	118.57	134.62	114.57	1,938.83	247.08	330.47	3.08	5.48
1988	1,652.25	156.26	189.42	146.60	149.38	128.19	2,168.57	277.72	381.38	3.64	8.01
1989	2,062.30	195.04	232.76	178.33	204.00	156.15	2,753.20	353.40	454.82	3.45	7.42
1990	1,908.45	180.49	223.60	141.49	182.60	122.06	2,633.66	330.22	373.84	3.61	6.47
1991	2,426.04	229.44	285.82	201.87	204.26	172.68	3,168.83	417.09	586.34	3.24	4.79
1992	2,539.92	240.21	294.39	214.72	209.66	200.83	3,301.11	435.71	676.95	2.99	4.22
1993	2,739.44	259.08	315.26	270.48	229.92	216.82	3,754.09	466.45	776.80	2.78	4.46
1994	2,653.37	250.94	318.10	222.46	198.41	195.80	3,834.44	459.27	751.96	2.82	5.83
1995	3,484.15	329.51	413.29	301.96	252.90	274.25	5,117.12	615.93	1,052.13	2.56	6.09
1996	4,148.07	392.30	494.38	352.30	259.91	351.17	6,448.27	740.74	1,291.03	2.19	5.24
1997	5,405.19	511.19	630.38	466.25	335.19	495.96	7,908.25	970.43	1,570.35	1.77	4.57
1998	6,299.94	595.81	743.65	482.38	445.94	521.42	9,181.43	1,229.23	2,192.69	1.49	3.46
1999	6,876.10	650.30	828.21	466.70	511.15	516.61	11,497.12	1,469.25	4,069.31	1.25	3.17
2000	6,945.57	656.87	803.29	462.76	440.54	646.95	10,786.85	1,320.28	2,470.52	1.15	3.63
2001	6,236.39	589.80	735.71	438.81	329.84	593.69	10,021.50	1,148.08	1,950.40	1.32	2.95
2002	5,000.00	472.87	583.95	395.81	233.08	510.46	8,341.63	879.82	1,335.51	1.61	2.92
2003 [3]	6,440.30	572.56	735.50	519.58	265.58	655.12	10,453.92	1,111.92	2,003.37	1.77	3.84

[1] End of period.

[2] Includes stocks as follows: for NYSE, all stocks listed; for Dow Jones industrial average, 30 stocks; for Standard & Poor's (S&P) composite index, 500 stocks; and for Nasdaq composite index, over 5,000.

[3] The NYSE relaunched the composite index on January 9, 2003, incorporating new definitions, methodology, and base value. (The composite index based on December 31, 1965=50 was discontinued.) Subset indexes on financial, energy, and health care were released by the NYSE on January 8, 2004 (see Table B–56). NYSE indexes shown in this table for industrials, utilities, transportation, and finance were discontinued.

[4] Effective April 1993, the NYSE doubled the value of the utility index to facilitate trading of options and futures on the index. Indexes prior to 1993 reflect the doubling.

[5] Based on 500 stocks in the S&P composite index.

[6] Aggregate cash dividends (based on latest known annual rate) divided by aggregate market value based on Wednesday closing prices. Monthly data are averages of weekly figures; annual data are averages of monthly figures.

[7] Quarterly data are ratio of earnings (after taxes) for four quarters ending with particular quarter-to-price index for last day of that quarter. Annual data are averages of quarterly ratios.

Sources: New York Stock Exchange, Dow Jones & Co., Inc., Standard & Poor's, and Nasdaq Stock Market.

TABLE B–56. Common stock prices and yields, 2000–2019

End of year or month	Common stock prices (end of period) [1]							Common stock yields (Standard & Poor's) (percent) [4]	
	New York Stock Exchange (NYSE) indexes (December 31, 2002=5,000) [2,3]				Dow Jones industrial average [2]	Standard & Poor's composite index (1941–43=10) [2]	Nasdaq composite index (Feb. 5, 1971=100) [2]	Dividend-price ratio [5]	Earnings-price ratio [6]
	Composite	Financial	Energy	Health care					
2000	6,945.57	....	....	....	10,786.85	1,320.28	2,470.52	1.15	3.63
2001	6,236.39	....	....	....	10,021.50	1,148.08	1,950.40	1.32	2.95
2002	5,000.00	5,000.00	5,000.00	5,000.00	8,341.63	879.82	1,335.51	1.61	2.92
2003	6,440.30	6,676.42	6,321.05	5,925.97	10,453.92	1,111.92	2,003.37	1.77	3.84
2004	7,250.06	7,493.92	7,934.49	6,119.07	10,783.01	1,211.92	2,175.44	1.72	4.89
2005	7,753.95	7,996.94	10,109.61	6,458.20	10,717.50	1,248.29	2,205.32	1.83	5.36
2006	9,139.02	9,552.22	11,967.88	6,958.64	12,463.15	1,418.30	2,415.29	1.87	5.78
2007	9,740.32	8,300.68	15,283.81	7,170.42	13,264.82	1,468.36	2,652.28	1.86	5.29
2008	5,757.05	3,848.42	9,434.01	5,340.73	8,776.39	903.25	1,577.03	2.37	3.54
2009	7,184.96	4,721.02	11,415.03	6,427.27	10,428.05	1,115.10	2,269.15	2.40	1.86
2010	7,964.02	4,958.62	12,520.29	6,501.53	11,577.51	1,257.64	2,652.87	1.98	6.04
2011	7,477.03	4,062.88	12,409.61	7,045.61	12,217.56	1,257.60	2,605.15	2.05	6.77
2012	8,443.51	5,114.54	12,606.06	7,904.06	13,104.14	1,426.19	3,019.51	2.24	6.20
2013	10,400.33	6,353.68	14,557.54	10,245.31	16,576.66	1,848.36	4,176.59	2.14	5.57
2014	10,839.24	6,707.16	12,533.54	11,967.04	17,823.07	2,058.90	4,736.05	2.04	5.25
2015	10,143.42	6,305.68	9,343.81	12,385.19	17,425.03	2,043.94	5,007.41	2.10	4.59
2016	11,056.89	6,961.56	11,503.76	11,907.20	19,762.60	2,238.83	5,383.12	2.19	4.17
2017	12,808.84	8,235.89	11,470.58	14,220.58	24,719.22	2,673.61	6,903.39	1.97	4.22
2018	11,374.39	6,969.48	9,341.44	15,158.38	23,327.46	2,506.85	6,635.28	1.90	4.66
2019	13,913.03	8,700.11	10,037.30	18,070.10	28,538.44	3,230.78	8,972.60	1.93	....
2017: Jan	11,222.95	7,064.02	11,202.98	12,061.43	19,864.09	2,278.87	5,614.79	2.08	
Feb	11,512.39	7,320.48	10,854.83	12,761.57	20,812.24	2,363.64	5,825.44	2.04	
Mar	11,492.85	7,216.68	10,834.06	12,728.55	20,663.22	2,362.72	5,911.74	2.02	4.24
Apr	11,536.08	7,208.13	10,521.74	13,000.70	20,940.51	2,384.20	6,047.61	2.03	
May	11,598.03	7,159.54	10,235.99	13,318.92	21,008.65	2,411.80	6,198.52	2.02	
June	11,761.70	7,468.28	10,083.36	13,732.80	21,349.63	2,423.41	6,140.42	2.01	4.29
July	11,967.67	7,652.38	10,416.42	13,636.10	21,891.12	2,470.30	6,348.12	1.99	
Aug	11,875.69	7,527.52	9,978.32	13,727.98	21,948.10	2,471.65	6,428.66	2.00	
Sept	12,209.16	7,780.56	10,911.61	13,959.19	22,405.09	2,519.36	6,495.96	1.99	4.25
Oct	12,341.01	7,921.32	10,889.68	13,971.09	23,377.24	2,575.26	6,727.67	1.94	
Nov	12,627.80	8,108.70	10,994.32	14,331.40	24,272.35	2,647.58	6,873.97	1.93	
Dec	12,808.84	8,235.89	11,470.58	14,220.58	24,719.22	2,673.61	6,903.39	1.89	4.11
2018: Jan	13,367.96	8,637.58	11,843.94	15,051.71	26,149.39	2,823.81	7,411.48	1.82	
Feb	12,652.55	8,246.24	10,625.83	14,357.41	25,029.20	2,713.83	7,273.01	1.89	
Mar	12,452.06	8,029.25	10,863.28	14,040.86	24,103.11	2,640.87	7,063.45	1.90	4.37
Apr	12,515.36	7,995.25	11,878.26	14,198.80	24,163.15	2,648.05	7,066.27	1.95	
May	12,527.14	7,877.77	12,056.61	14,292.95	24,415.84	2,705.27	7,442.12	1.92	
June	12,504.25	7,781.67	12,131.49	14,464.62	24,271.41	2,718.37	7,510.30	1.90	4.51
July	12,963.28	8,097.12	12,282.46	15,409.93	25,415.19	2,816.29	7,671.79	1.85	
Aug	13,016.89	8,109.69	11,837.21	15,887.99	25,964.82	2,901.52	8,109.54	1.82	
Sept	13,082.52	7,979.54	12,169.73	16,299.34	26,458.31	2,913.98	8,046.35	1.81	4.47
Oct	12,208.06	7,543.04	10,915.63	15,506.53	25,115.76	2,711.74	7,305.90	1.89	
Nov	12,457.55	7,713.77	10,478.32	16,505.42	25,538.46	2,760.17	7,330.54	1.95	
Dec	11,374.39	6,969.48	9,341.44	15,158.38	23,327.46	2,506.85	6,635.28	2.10	5.28
2019: Jan	12,299.03	7,613.43	10,351.36	15,655.94	24,999.67	2,704.10	7,281.74	2.07	
Feb	12,644.81	7,770.10	10,560.79	15,932.89	25,916.00	2,784.49	7,532.53	1.98	
Mar	12,696.88	7,685.02	10,679.94	16,182.85	25,928.68	2,834.40	7,729.32	1.96	4.74
Apr	13,060.65	8,138.15	10,699.48	15,706.22	26,592.91	2,945.83	8,095.39	1.90	
May	12,264.49	7,663.98	9,679.30	15,380.82	24,815.04	2,752.06	7,453.15	1.95	
June	13,049.71	8,064.09	10,334.74	16,347.65	26,599.96	2,941.76	8,006.24	1.94	4.60
July	13,066.60	8,130.16	9,973.03	16,209.28	26,864.27	2,980.38	8,175.42	1.88	
Aug	12,736.88	7,824.31	9,138.41	16,119.87	26,403.28	2,926.46	7,962.88	1.96	
Sept	13,004.74	8,115.96	9,564.95	15,990.79	26,916.83	2,976.74	7,999.34	1.92	4.46
Oct	13,171.81	8,293.63	9,423.40	16,716.08	27,046.23	3,037.56	8,292.36	1.93	
Nov	13,545.21	8,516.89	9,445.81	17,407.66	28,051.41	3,140.98	8,665.47	1.87	
Dec	13,913.03	8,700.11	10,037.30	18,070.10	28,538.44	3,230.78	8,972.60	1.84	

[1] End of year or month.
[2] Includes stocks as follows: for NYSE, all stocks listed (in 2018, over 2,700); for Dow Jones industrial average, 30 stocks; for Standard & Poor's (S&P) composite index, 500 stocks; and for Nasdaq composite index, in 2018, over 3,000.
[3] The NYSE relaunched the composite index on January 9, 2003, incorporating new definitions, methodology, and base value. Subset indexes on financial, energy, and health care were released by the NYSE on January 8, 2004.
[4] Based on 500 stocks in the S&P composite index.
[5] Aggregate cash dividends (based on latest known annual rate) divided by aggregate market value based on Wednesday closing prices. Monthly data are averages of weekly figures, annual data are averages of monthly figures.
[6] Quarterly data are ratio of earnings (after taxes) for four quarters ending with particular quarter-to-price index for last day of that quarter. Annual data are averages of quarterly ratios.

Sources: New York Stock Exchange, Dow Jones & Co., Inc., Standard & Poor's, and Nasdaq Stock Market.

Corporate Profits and Finance | 429

International Statistics

Table B–57. U.S. international transactions, 1969–2019

[Millions of dollars; quarterly data seasonally adjusted]

| Year or quarter | Current Account[1] | | | | | | | | | | | | | Current account balance as a percentage of GDP |
| | Goods[2] | | | Services | | | Balance on goods and services | Primary income receipts and payments | | | Balance on secondary income[3] | Balance on current account | |
	Exports	Imports	Balance on goods	Exports	Imports	Balance on services		Receipts	Payments	Balance on primary income			
1969	36,414	35,807	607	12,806	13,323	−517	90	10,913	4,869	6,044	−5,735	399	0.0
1970	42,469	39,866	2,603	14,171	14,519	−348	2,255	11,748	5,514	6,234	−6,156	2,331	.2
1971	43,319	45,579	−2,260	16,358	15,401	959	−1,301	12,706	5,436	7,270	−7,402	−1,433	−.1
1972	49,381	55,797	−6,416	17,842	16,867	973	−5,443	14,764	6,572	8,192	−8,544	−5,796	−.5
1973	71,410	70,499	911	19,832	18,843	989	1,900	21,809	9,656	12,153	−6,914	7,140	.5
1974	98,306	103,811	−5,505	22,591	21,378	1,212	−4,293	27,587	12,084	15,503	−9,248	1,961	.1
1975	107,088	98,185	8,903	25,497	21,996	3,500	12,403	25,351	12,565	12,786	−7,076	18,117	1.1
1976	114,745	124,228	−9,483	27,971	24,570	3,402	−6,082	29,374	13,312	16,062	−5,686	4,296	.2
1977	120,816	151,907	−31,091	31,486	27,640	3,845	−27,247	32,355	14,218	18,137	−5,227	−14,336	−.7
1978	142,075	176,002	−33,927	36,353	32,189	4,164	−29,763	42,087	21,680	20,407	−5,788	−15,143	−.6
1979	184,439	212,007	−27,568	39,693	36,689	3,003	−24,566	63,835	32,961	30,874	−6,593	−285	.0
1980	224,250	249,750	−25,500	47,585	41,492	6,093	−19,407	72,605	42,533	30,072	−8,349	2,331	.1
1981	237,044	265,067	−28,023	57,355	45,503	11,851	−16,172	86,529	53,626	32,903	−11,702	5,029	.2
1982	211,157	247,642	−36,485	64,078	51,750	12,330	−24,156	96,522	61,359	35,163	−16,545	−5,537	−.2
1983	201,799	268,901	−67,102	64,307	54,973	9,335	−57,767	96,031	59,643	36,388	−17,311	−38,691	−1.1
1984	219,926	332,418	−112,492	71,168	67,748	3,418	−109,074	115,639	80,574	35,065	−20,334	−94,344	−2.3
1985	215,915	338,088	−122,173	73,156	72,863	294	−121,879	105,046	79,324	25,722	−21,999	−118,155	−2.7
1986	223,344	368,425	−145,081	86,690	80,147	6,543	−138,539	102,798	87,304	15,494	−24,131	−147,176	−3.2
1987	250,208	409,765	−159,557	98,661	90,788	7,874	−151,683	113,603	99,309	14,294	−23,265	−160,655	−3.3
1988	320,230	447,189	−126,959	110,920	98,525	12,394	−114,566	141,666	122,981	18,685	−25,274	−121,153	−2.3
1989	359,916	477,665	−117,749	127,087	102,480	24,607	−93,142	166,384	146,560	19,824	−26,169	−99,487	−1.8
1990	387,401	498,438	−111,037	147,833	117,660	30,173	−80,865	176,894	148,345	28,549	−26,654	−78,969	−1.3
1991	414,083	491,020	−76,937	164,260	118,459	45,802	−31,136	155,327	131,198	24,129	9,904	2,897	.0
1992	439,631	536,528	−96,897	177,251	119,566	57,685	−39,212	139,082	114,845	24,237	−36,635	−51,613	−.8
1993	456,943	589,394	−132,451	185,920	123,780	62,141	−70,311	141,606	116,287	25,319	−39,811	−84,805	−1.2
1994	502,859	668,690	−165,831	200,395	133,057	67,338	−98,493	169,447	152,302	17,145	−40,265	−121,612	−1.7
1995	575,204	749,374	−174,170	219,183	141,397	77,786	−96,384	213,661	192,771	20,890	−38,074	−113,567	−1.5
1996	612,113	803,113	−191,000	239,489	152,554	86,935	−104,065	229,530	207,212	22,318	−43,017	−124,764	−1.5
1997	678,366	876,794	−198,428	256,087	165,932	90,155	−108,273	261,357	248,750	12,607	−45,062	−140,726	−1.6
1998	670,416	918,637	−248,221	262,758	180,677	82,081	−166,140	266,244	261,978	4,266	−53,187	−215,062	−2.4
1999	698,524	1,035,592	−337,068	271,343	192,893	78,450	−258,617	299,114	287,981	11,134	−40,881	−288,365	−3.0
2000	784,940	1,231,722	−446,783	290,381	216,115	74,266	−372,517	356,706	338,637	18,069	−49,003	−403,450	−3.9
2001	731,331	1,153,701	−422,370	274,323	213,465	60,858	−361,511	296,977	269,447	27,530	−55,708	−389,689	−3.7
2002	698,036	1,173,281	−475,245	280,670	224,379	56,290	−418,955	286,525	263,860	22,665	−54,507	−450,797	−4.1
2003	730,446	1,272,089	−541,643	289,972	242,219	47,754	−493,890	324,374	289,657	34,716	−59,571	−518,744	−4.5
2004	823,584	1,488,349	−664,766	337,966	283,083	54,882	−609,883	416,085	362,179	53,906	−75,614	−631,591	−5.2
2005	913,016	1,695,820	−782,804	373,006	304,448	68,558	−714,245	534,215	480,311	53,898	−84,887	−745,234	−5.7
2006	1,040,905	1,878,194	−837,289	416,738	341,165	75,573	−761,716	680,830	653,928	26,902	−71,149	−805,964	−5.8
2007	1,165,151	1,986,347	−821,196	488,396	372,575	115,821	−705,375	834,983	749,977	85,005	−90,665	−711,035	−4.9
2008	1,308,795	2,141,287	−832,492	532,817	409,052	123,765	−708,726	815,567	685,918	129,649	−102,312	−681,389	−4.6
2009	1,070,331	1,580,025	−509,694	512,722	386,801	125,920	−383,774	613,249	498,089	115,160	−103,907	−372,521	−2.6
2010	1,290,273	1,938,950	−648,651	562,759	409,313	153,446	−495,225	680,169	511,948	168,221	−104,261	−431,265	−2.9
2011	1,498,887	2,239,886	−740,999	627,061	435,761	191,300	−549,699	755,937	544,853	211,084	−107,047	−445,662	−2.9
2012	1,562,630	2,303,749	−741,119	655,724	452,013	203,711	−537,408	767,972	560,497	207,475	−96,900	−426,832	−2.6
2013	1,593,708	2,294,247	−700,539	700,491	461,087	239,404	−461,135	792,819	586,842	205,977	−93,643	−348,801	−2.1
2014	1,635,563	2,385,480	−749,917	741,094	480,761	260,333	−489,584	824,543	606,152	218,391	−94,000	−365,199	−2.1
2015	1,511,381	2,273,249	−761,868	755,310	491,966	263,343	−498,525	810,073	606,464	203,608	−112,848	−407,764	−2.2
2016	1,457,393	2,207,195	−749,801	758,446	511,627	246,819	−502,982	835,509	636,855	198,654	−124,022	−428,349	−2.3
2017	1,553,589	2,358,789	−805,200	798,957	543,880	255,077	−550,123	933,307	707,508	225,799	−115,322	−439,646	−2.3
2018	1,674,330	2,561,667	−887,338	826,980	567,322	259,659	−627,679	1,084,183	830,198	253,985	−117,284	−490,978	−2.4
2016: I	353,872	539,242	−185,370	185,531	125,795	59,736	−125,634	199,956	154,582	45,374	−32,175	−112,435	−2.4
II	360,934	547,002	−186,068	189,091	126,173	62,918	−123,150	208,855	160,359	48,496	−28,662	−103,316	−2.2
III	370,377	555,893	−185,515	192,341	128,916	63,425	−122,090	208,521	162,155	46,367	−31,069	−106,792	−2.3
IV	372,210	565,058	−192,848	191,483	130,743	60,740	−132,108	218,177	159,759	58,418	−32,116	−105,806	−2.2
2017: I	381,680	578,875	−197,195	195,426	132,281	63,145	−134,050	218,217	164,608	53,609	−23,854	−104,295	−2.2
II	381,677	582,901	−201,224	196,368	134,821	61,547	−139,677	224,980	175,374	49,606	−32,804	−122,874	−2.5
III	387,127	582,711	−195,584	201,350	137,188	64,162	−131,422	239,396	179,703	59,693	−27,979	−99,708	−2.0
IV	403,106	614,303	−211,197	205,812	139,589	66,223	−144,974	250,714	187,823	62,890	−30,686	−112,769	−2.3
2018: I	410,732	631,449	−220,716	207,387	139,778	67,608	−153,108	261,844	195,472	66,372	−27,264	−114,001	−2.3
II	427,088	633,485	−206,396	206,103	139,707	66,396	−140,001	272,285	209,456	62,829	−30,139	−107,311	−2.1
III	419,545	647,447	−227,902	206,694	142,216	64,478	−163,424	273,570	208,846	64,724	−27,039	−125,739	−2.4
IV	416,964	649,288	−232,323	206,797	145,620	61,177	−171,146	276,483	216,424	60,059	−32,841	−143,927	−2.8
2019: I	419,100	635,844	−216,744	207,870	147,599	60,271	−156,473	278,138	221,275	56,864	−36,585	−136,194	−2.6
II	414,694	637,911	−223,218	212,259	148,150	64,109	−159,108	286,142	219,517	66,625	−32,726	−125,210	−2.3
III ᴾ	413,812	633,370	−219,558	211,983	149,784	62,199	−157,358	282,007	213,288	68,719	−35,454	−124,094	−2.3

[1] Current and capital account statistics in the international transactions accounts differ slightly from statistics in the National Income and Product Accounts (NIPAs) because of adjustments made to convert the international statistics to national accounting concepts. A reconciliation can be found in NIPA table 4.3B.

[2] Adjusted from Census data to align with concepts and definitions used to prepare the international and national economic accounts. The adjustments are necessary to supplement coverage of Census data, to eliminate duplication of transactions recorded elsewhere in the international accounts, to value transactions according to a standard definition, and for earlier years, to record transactions in the appropriate period.

See next page for continuation of table.

TABLE B–57. U.S. international transactions, 1969–2019—*Continued*

[Millions of dollars; quarterly data seasonally adjusted]

Year or quarter	Balance on capital account [1]	Net U.S. acquisition of financial assets excluding financial derivatives [net increase in assets / financial outflow (+)]					Net U.S. incurrence of liabilities excluding financial derivatives [net increase in liabilities / financial inflow (+)]				Financial derivatives other than reserves, net transactions	Net lending (+) or net borrowing (−) from financial account transactions [5]	Statistical discrepancy
		Total	Direct investment assets	Portfolio investment assets	Other investment assets	Reserve assets [4]	Total	Direct investment liabilities	Portfolio investment liabilities	Other investment liabilities			
1969		11,584	5,960	1,549	2,896	1,179	12,702	1,263	719	10,720		−1,118	−1,517
1970		9,336	7,590	1,076	3,151	−2,481	7,226	1,464	11,710	−5,948		2,110	−219
1971		12,474	7,618	1,113	6,092	−2,349	23,687	368	28,835	−5,516		−11,213	−9,779
1972		14,497	7,747	619	6,127	4	22,171	948	13,123	8,100		−7,674	−1,879
1973		22,874	11,353	672	11,007	−158	18,388	2,800	4,790	10,798		4,486	−2,654
1974		34,745	9,052	1,853	22,373	1,467	35,228	4,761	5,500	24,967		−483	−2,444
1975		39,703	14,244	6,247	18,363	849	16,870	2,603	12,761	1,506		22,833	4,717
1976		51,269	11,949	8,885	27,877	2,558	37,840	4,347	16,165	17,328		13,429	9,134
1977		34,785	11,891	5,459	17,060	375	52,770	3,728	37,615	11,427		−17,985	−3,651
1978		61,130	16,057	3,626	42,179	−732	66,275	7,896	30,083	28,296		−5,145	9,997
1979		66,053	25,223	12,430	27,267	1,133	40,693	11,876	−13,502	42,319		25,360	25,647
1980		86,968	19,222	6,042	53,550	8,154	62,036	16,918	23,825	21,293		24,932	22,614
1981		114,147	9,624	15,650	83,697	5,176	85,684	25,196	17,509	42,979		28,463	23,433
1982		142,722	19,397	12,395	105,965	4,965	109,897	27,475	19,695	62,727		32,825	38,362
1983		74,690	20,844	2,063	50,588	1,195	95,715	18,688	18,382	58,645		−21,025	17,666
1984		50,740	26,770	3,498	17,340	3,132	126,413	34,832	38,695	52,886		−75,673	18,673
1985		47,064	21,241	3,008	18,957	3,858	146,544	22,057	68,004	56,483		−99,480	18,617
1986		107,252	19,524	8,984	79,057	−313	223,854	30,946	104,497	88,411		−116,602	30,570
1987		84,058	39,795	7,903	45,508	−9,148	251,863	63,232	79,631	109,000		−167,805	−7,149
1988		105,747	21,701	4,589	75,544	3,913	244,008	56,910	86,786	100,312		−138,261	−17,108
1989	−207	182,908	50,973	31,166	75,476	25,293	230,302	75,801	74,852	79,649		−47,394	52,299
1990	−7,221	103,985	59,934	30,557	11,336	2,158	162,109	71,247	25,767	65,095		−58,124	28,066
1991	−5,129	75,753	49,253	32,053	210	−5,763	119,586	34,535	72,562	12,489		−43,833	−41,601
1992	1,449	84,899	58,755	50,684	−20,639	−3,901	178,842	30,315	92,199	56,328		−93,943	−43,776
1993	−714	199,399	82,799	137,917	−22,696	1,379	278,607	50,211	174,387	54,009		−79,208	6,313
1994	−1,112	188,758	89,988	54,088	50,028	−5,346	312,995	55,942	131,849	125,204		−124,237	−1,514
1995	−221	363,555	110,041	143,506	100,266	9,742	446,393	69,067	254,431	122,895		−82,838	30,951
1996	−8	424,548	103,024	160,179	168,013	−6,668	559,027	97,644	392,107	69,276		−134,479	−9,706
1997	−256	502,024	121,352	121,036	258,626	1,010	720,999	122,150	311,105	287,744		−218,975	−77,995
1998	−7	385,936	174,751	132,186	72,216	6,783	452,901	211,152	225,878	15,871		−66,965	148,106
1999	−4,176	526,612	247,484	141,007	146,868	−8,747	765,215	312,449	278,697	174,069		−238,603	53,938
2000	−1	587,682	186,371	159,713	241,308	290	1,066,074	349,124	441,966	274,984		−478,392	−74,941
2001	13,198	386,308	146,041	106,919	128,437	4,911	788,345	172,496	431,492	184,357		−402,037	−25,546
2002	−141	319,170	178,984	79,532	56,973	3,681	821,844	111,056	504,155	206,634		−502,673	−51,735
2003	−1,821	371,074	195,218	133,059	44,313	−1,524	911,660	117,107	550,163	244,390		−540,586	−20,021
2004	3,049	1,058,654	374,006	191,956	495,498	−2,806	1,600,881	213,642	867,340	519,899		−542,226	86,316
2005	13,116	562,983	52,591	267,290	257,196	−14,094	1,277,056	142,345	832,037	302,673		−714,073	18,045
2006	−1,788	1,324,607	283,800	493,366	549,814	−2,373	2,120,480	298,464	1,126,735	695,280	−29,710	−825,583	−17,832
2007	384	1,563,459	523,889	380,807	658,641	122	2,190,087	346,615	1,156,612	686,860	−6,222	−632,850	77,801
2008	6,010	−317,607	343,584	−284,269	−381,770	4,848	462,408	341,091	523,683	−402,367	32,947	−747,069	−71,690
2009	−140	131,074	312,597	375,883	−609,662	52,256	325,644	161,082	357,352	−192,789	−44,816	−239,386	133,275
2010	−157	958,703	349,829	199,620	407,420	1,835	1,391,042	264,039	820,434	306,569	−14,076	−446,415	−14,992
2011	−1,186	492,530	436,615	85,365	−45,327	15,877	983,522	263,499	311,626	408,397	−35,006	−525,998	−79,150
2012	6,904	176,764	377,239	248,760	−453,695	4,460	632,034	250,343	747,017	−365,327	7,064	−448,205	−28,277
2013	−412	649,587	392,796	481,298	−221,408	−3,099	1,052,068	288,131	511,987	251,949	2,222	−400,259	−51,046
2014	−45	866,523	387,528	582,676	−100,099	−3,583	1,109,443	251,857	697,607	159,979	−54,335	−297,255	67,989
2015	−42	202,208	307,058	160,410	−258,968	−6,292	501,121	509,087	213,910	−221,876	−27,035	−325,948	81,859
2016	−152	353,036	318,317	36,283	−3,654	2,090	742,905	494,438	231,349	17,118	7,827	−382,042	46,460
2017	18,950	1,167,447	384,574	569,376	215,187	−1,690	1,549,024	354,651	792,523	401,851	23,998	−357,579	63,117
2018	3,235	310,827	−78,457	334,033	50,262	4,989	735,583	258,392	315,676	161,515	−20,721	−445,477	42,266
2016: I	−58	37,576	76,065	−66,569	29,271	−1,191	152,584	158,754	−52,832	46,662	10,782	−104,226	8,268
II	0	350,640	104,359	146,347	99,744	189	368,264	186,587	4,783	176,894	608	−17,016	86,300
III	−94	42,410	98,034	−33,551	−23,715	1,642	243,457	130,738	217,768	−105,049	3,437	−197,610	−90,724
IV	0	−77,590	39,858	−9,944	−108,954	1,450	−21,400	18,359	61,630	−101,389	−7,000	−63,190	42,616
2017: I	−58	366,412	135,715	141,588	89,350	−241	428,036	111,483	160,111	156,442	−5,609	−67,234	37,119
II	−96	293,237	51,002	154,279	87,805	150	454,247	98,070	259,536	96,641	9,306	−151,704	−28,734
III	19,144	372,237	104,782	175,975	91,541	−61	507,154	106,739	294,395	106,021	18,600	−116,317	−35,754
IV	−40	135,562	93,075	91,534	−53,508	−1,539	159,587	38,358	78,481	42,748	1,701	−22,324	90,486
2018: I	−2	325,143	−46,718	290,488	81,379	−7	447,658	62,143	301,127	84,388	29,139	−93,376	20,626
II	−5	−243,468	−110,279	−17,660	−118,596	3,068	−126,092	16,603	−12,609	−130,087	−15,723	−133,098	−25,783
III	521	81,893	52,845	83,415	−54,189	−177	127,770	22,526	12,274	−11,430	−22,175	−57,381	67,837
IV	2,721	147,259	25,696	−22,210	141,668	2,105	286,247	52,720	14,884	218,644	−22,632	−161,621	−20,414
2019: I	0	110,967	7,878	−41,876	144,757	208	126,280	110,079	−42,822	59,023	−21,421	−36,734	99,461
II	0	142,153	111,272	26,706	1,815	2,359	345,993	93,251	181,016	71,626	−9,642	−213,382	−88,173
III *p*	−10	123,516	33,320	18,461	69,852	1,882	164,922	37,642	86,479	40,801	−6,456	−47,862	76,242

[3] Includes U.S. government and private transfers, such as U.S. government grants and pensions, fines and penalties, withholding taxes, personal transfers, insurance-related transfers, and other current transfers.
[4] Consists of monetary gold, special drawing rights (SDRs), the U.S. reserve position in the International Monetary Fund (IMF), and other reserve assets, including foreign currencies.
[5] Net lending means that U.S. residents are net suppliers of funds to foreign residents, and net borrowing means the opposite.

Source: Department of Commerce (Bureau of Economic Analysis).

[Billions of dollars; monthly data seasonally adjusted]

Year or month	Goods: Exports (f.a.s. value)[1,2]							Goods: Imports (customs value)[6]							Services (BOP basis)	
	Total, BOP basis[3,4]	Census basis (by end-use category)						Total, BOP basis[4]	Census basis (by end-use category)						Exports[4]	Imports[4]
		Total, Census basis[3,5]	Foods, feeds, and beverages	Industrial supplies and materials	Capital goods except automotive	Automotive vehicles, parts, and engines	Consumer goods (nonfood) except automotive		Total, Census basis[5]	Foods, feeds, and beverages	Industrial supplies and materials	Capital goods except automotive	Automotive vehicles, parts, and engines	Consumer goods (nonfood) except automotive		
1991	414.1	421.7	35.7	109.7	166.7	40.0	45.9	491.0	488.5	26.5	131.6	120.7	85.7	108.0	164.3	118.5
1992	439.6	448.2	40.3	109.1	175.9	47.0	51.4	536.5	532.7	27.6	138.6	134.3	91.8	122.7	177.3	119.6
1993	456.9	465.1	40.6	111.8	181.7	52.4	54.7	589.4	580.7	27.9	145.6	152.4	102.4	134.0	185.9	123.8
1994	502.9	512.6	42.0	121.4	205.0	57.8	60.0	668.7	663.3	31.0	162.1	184.4	118.3	146.3	200.4	133.1
1995	575.2	584.7	50.5	146.2	233.0	61.8	64.4	749.4	743.5	33.2	181.8	221.4	123.8	159.9	219.2	141.4
1996	612.1	625.1	55.5	147.7	253.0	65.0	70.1	803.1	795.3	35.7	204.5	228.1	128.9	172.0	239.5	152.6
1997	678.4	689.2	51.5	158.2	294.5	74.0	77.4	876.8	869.7	39.7	213.8	253.3	139.8	193.8	256.1	165.9
1998	670.4	682.1	46.4	148.3	299.4	72.4	80.3	918.6	911.9	41.2	200.1	269.5	148.7	217.0	262.8	180.7
1999	698.5	695.8	46.0	147.5	310.8	75.3	80.9	1,035.6	1,024.6	43.6	221.4	295.7	179.0	241.9	271.3	192.9
2000	784.9	781.9	47.9	172.6	356.9	80.4	89.4	1,231.7	1,218.0	46.0	299.0	347.0	195.9	281.8	290.4	216.1
2001	731.3	729.1	49.4	160.1	321.7	75.4	88.3	1,153.7	1,141.0	46.6	273.9	298.0	189.8	284.3	274.3	213.5
2002	698.0	693.1	49.6	156.8	290.4	78.9	84.4	1,173.3	1,161.4	49.7	267.7	283.3	203.7	307.8	280.7	224.4
2003	730.4	724.8	55.0	173.0	293.7	80.6	89.9	1,272.1	1,257.1	55.8	313.8	295.9	210.1	333.9	290.0	242.2
2004	823.6	814.9	56.6	203.9	327.5	89.2	103.2	1,488.3	1,469.7	62.1	412.8	343.6	228.2	372.9	338.0	283.1
2005	913.0	901.1	59.0	233.0	358.4	98.4	115.3	1,695.8	1,673.5	68.1	523.8	379.3	239.4	407.2	373.0	304.4
2006	1,040.9	1,026.0	66.0	276.0	404.0	107.3	129.1	1,878.2	1,853.9	74.9	602.0	418.3	256.6	442.6	416.7	341.2
2007	1,165.2	1,148.2	84.3	316.4	433.0	121.3	146.0	1,986.3	1,957.0	81.7	634.7	444.5	256.7	474.6	488.4	372.6
2008	1,308.8	1,287.4	108.3	388.0	457.7	121.5	161.3	2,141.3	2,103.6	89.0	779.5	453.7	231.2	481.6	532.8	409.1
2009	1,070.3	1,056.0	93.9	296.5	391.2	81.7	149.5	1,580.0	1,559.6	81.6	462.4	370.5	157.7	427.3	512.7	386.8
2010	1,290.3	1,278.5	107.7	391.7	447.5	112.0	165.2	1,939.0	1,913.9	91.7	603.1	449.4	225.1	483.2	562.8	409.3
2011	1,498.9	1,482.5	126.2	501.1	494.0	133.0	175.3	2,239.9	2,208.0	107.5	755.8	510.8	254.6	514.1	627.1	435.8
2012	1,562.6	1,545.8	133.0	501.2	527.2	146.2	181.7	2,303.7	2,276.3	110.3	730.6	548.7	297.8	516.9	655.7	452.0
2013	1,593.7	1,578.5	136.2	508.2	534.4	152.7	188.8	2,294.2	2,268.0	115.1	681.5	555.7	308.8	531.7	700.5	461.1
2014	1,635.6	1,621.9	143.7	505.8	551.5	158.9	199.0	2,385.5	2,356.4	125.9	667.0	594.1	328.6	557.1	741.1	480.8
2015	1,511.4	1,503.3	127.7	427.0	539.5	151.9	197.7	2,273.2	2,248.8	127.8	486.0	602.5	349.2	594.2	755.3	492.0
2016	1,457.4	1,451.5	130.5	397.3	519.7	150.4	193.7	2,207.2	2,186.8	130.0	443.3	589.7	349.9	583.1	758.4	511.6
2017	1,553.6	1,546.5	132.7	464.7	533.2	157.9	197.7	2,358.8	2,339.9	137.8	507.1	639.9	358.3	601.5	799.0	543.9
2018	1,674.3	1,666.0	133.2	541.7	562.9	158.8	206.0	2,561.7	2,540.8	147.4	575.6	692.6	372.2	646.8	827.0	567.3
2019 [p]		1,651.0	134.7	530.8	548.2	161.6	206.9		2,498.5	150.6	521.1	677.9	376.6	654.6		
2018: Jan	133.6	132.9	10.4	41.1	45.3	13.5	17.7	208.5	206.8	11.9	47.0	55.7	30.5	53.5	69.0	46.2
Feb	136.4	135.6	10.6	43.1	46.1	14.3	16.6	212.2	210.7	12.4	47.1	57.3	30.9	55.0	69.2	47.2
Mar	140.7	140.1	11.1	45.0	47.6	14.0	17.1	210.7	209.2	12.3	47.2	56.7	30.8	54.2	69.2	46.4
Apr	140.4	139.6	11.5	45.8	46.2	13.9	17.2	210.7	209.0	12.3	47.9	57.3	30.2	52.3	68.5	46.4
May	144.6	143.8	13.1	45.4	48.1	13.6	17.7	211.2	209.4	12.4	48.0	58.6	30.0	51.9	68.8	46.5
June	142.2	141.5	12.7	46.6	47.3	12.9	16.5	211.6	210.0	12.2	48.6	57.4	30.4	53.0	68.8	46.8
July	139.9	139.2	12.0	46.9	46.3	13.0	16.1	214.1	212.3	12.4	49.1	58.0	30.9	52.9	68.8	47.1
Aug	138.9	138.2	11.3	44.6	46.6	12.8	17.5	215.4	213.4	12.3	49.4	57.7	31.6	53.3	68.9	47.3
Sept	140.7	140.1	10.5	46.7	47.3	13.0	17.6	218.0	216.3	12.2	49.2	59.7	31.3	54.7	69.0	47.8
Oct	141.3	140.6	10.0	47.3	47.2	12.8	17.8	218.6	216.7	12.3	49.1	57.1	31.8	56.5	68.9	48.3
Nov	139.1	138.5	10.1	45.3	48.1	12.6	17.1	213.2	211.4	12.2	46.4	57.6	32.0	53.7	68.9	48.4
Dec	136.6	136.0	9.9	44.0	46.9	12.5	17.1	217.5	215.8	12.6	46.7	59.6	32.0	55.8	69.1	49.0
2019: Jan	138.1	137.6	11.0	43.8	46.3	13.5	17.6	211.1	209.5	12.3	43.9	57.1	31.8	55.6	68.9	49.0
Feb	139.7	139.0	10.6	43.1	48.3	13.9	17.7	210.7	208.9	11.9	42.7	57.1	31.7	56.1	69.3	49.1
Mar	141.3	140.6	11.1	44.7	47.4	13.9	17.9	214.1	212.4	13.0	45.2	57.4	31.9	55.4	69.6	49.4
Apr	136.8	136.1	11.2	44.6	44.7	13.2	17.3	208.7	207.0	12.8	44.6	55.6	30.9	54.3	70.1	49.2
May	140.8	140.2	12.0	44.4	46.0	13.8	18.1	216.9	215.0	12.8	46.3	57.2	33.2	55.6	71.1	49.4
June	137.0	136.4	12.0	44.6	44.9	13.3	16.2	212.3	210.6	12.7	43.1	56.9	32.6	54.7	71.1	49.6
July	138.3	137.7	11.8	42.8	45.7	13.9	17.7	211.9	210.1	12.8	44.0	55.4	32.7	55.3	70.6	49.7
Aug	138.7	138.1	12.3	44.3	44.3	14.3	16.9	212.9	211.1	12.6	42.5	57.3	32.0	57.2	70.6	49.9
Sept	136.8	136.2	10.8	44.0	45.1	13.3	17.4	208.5	206.8	12.8	41.9	56.2	30.9	54.7	70.7	50.1
Oct	136.2	135.6	10.5	44.6	44.7	13.0	16.6	204.0	202.2	12.4	41.4	56.6	29.0	52.3	71.1	50.2
Nov [p]	137.2	136.6	10.7	44.4	45.3	13.4	17.1	201.1	199.6	12.2	40.8	55.4	30.1	51.3	71.5	50.7
Dec [p]		137.0	10.7	45.6	45.5	12.3	16.5		205.3	12.3	44.6	55.7	29.8	51.9		

[1] Department of Defense shipments of grant-aid military supplies and equipment under the Military Assistance Program are excluded from total exports through 1985 and included beginning 1986.

[2] F.a.s. (free alongside ship) value basis at U.S. port of exportation for exports.

[3] Beginning with data for 1989, exports have been adjusted for undocumented exports to Canada and are included in the appropriate end-use categories. For prior years, only total exports include this adjustment.

[4] Beginning with data for 1999, exports of goods under the U.S. Foreign Military Sales program and fuel purchases by foreign air and ocean carriers in U.S. ports are included in goods exports (BOP basis) and excluded from services exports. Beginning with data for 1999, imports of petroleum abroad by U.S. military agencies and fuel purchases by U.S. air and ocean carriers in foreign ports are included in goods imports (BOP basis) and excluded from services imports.

[5] Total includes "other" exports or imports, not shown separately.

[6] Total arrivals of imported goods other than in-transit shipments.

[7] Total includes revisions not reflected in detail.

[8] Total exports are on a revised statistical month basis; end-use categories are on a statistical month basis.

Note: Goods on a Census basis are adjusted to a BOP basis by the Bureau of Economic Analysis, in line with concepts and definitions used to prepare international and national accounts. The adjustments are necessary to supplement coverage of Census data, to eliminate duplication of transactions recorded elsewhere in international accounts, to value transactions according to a standard definition, and for earlier years, to record transactions in the appropriate period.

Data include international trade of the U.S. Virgin Islands, Puerto Rico, and U.S. Foreign Trade Zones.

Source: Department of Commerce (Bureau of the Census and Bureau of Economic Analysis).

Table B-59. U.S. international trade in goods and services by area and country, 2000–2018

[Millions of dollars]

Item	2000	2005	2010	2013	2014	2015	2016	2017	2018
EXPORTS									
Total, all countries	1,075,321	1,286,022	1,853,038	2,294,199	2,376,657	2,266,691	2,215,839	2,352,546	2,501,310
Europe	296,284	365,200	503,816	580,234	606,544	598,616	602,614	633,490	683,863
Euro area [1]	173,446	214,355	288,604	327,600	347,609	346,115	351,094	366,889	393,763
France	30,759	35,504	44,114	50,672	50,989	49,990	51,176	53,343	57,892
Germany	45,253	55,247	73,378	74,644	77,907	80,134	81,383	86,473	92,447
Italy	16,761	18,727	22,845	25,483	26,212	25,453	25,661	27,833	32,880
United Kingdom	73,139	83,183	102,648	108,030	119,074	124,309	122,267	126,576	140,762
Canada	203,861	245,134	303,409	364,968	374,850	336,261	321,678	341,307	364,515
Latin America and Other Western Hemisphere ..	225,116	256,066	409,201	561,468	585,359	549,554	514,647	549,604	587,419
Brazil	21,858	21,230	53,753	70,900	71,102	59,360	53,766	64,079	67,599
Mexico	127,076	142,977	188,371	256,342	271,635	268,211	261,933	276,563	299,803
Venezuela	8,810	9,068	15,784	20,568	18,045	14,904	11,372	8,782	10,705
Asia and Pacific	299,103	341,564	523,131	634,902	652,735	636,150	640,186	692,573	724,116
China	21,464	50,572	115,559	160,375	169,008	165,526	170,395	186,289	177,969
India	6,472	13,232	29,667	35,231	36,950	40,060	42,243	49,330	58,767
Japan	101,247	94,356	104,731	112,201	114,828	108,417	108,823	114,285	121,155
Korea, Republic of	34,744	38,000	55,533	64,491	66,653	65,327	64,635	73,157	79,919
Singapore	24,400	26,482	39,459	42,025	41,687	42,653	44,576	50,503	54,126
Taiwan	30,403	29,232	36,717	38,317	40,084	38,714	38,175	36,205	41,302
Middle East	28,241	48,427	70,094	100,176	101,881	101,723	97,956	96,314	97,106
Africa	17,178	23,003	40,400	49,212	52,404	41,760	36,179	36,796	41,761
Memorandum: Members of OPEC [2]	29,407	49,194	78,985	117,063	115,626	107,493	106,184	92,093	93,896
IMPORTS									
Total, all countries	1,447,837	2,000,268	2,348,263	2,755,334	2,866,241	2,765,215	2,718,822	2,902,669	3,128,989
Europe	359,670	493,933	559,596	660,838	702,465	703,264	701,380	743,385	811,274
Euro area [1]	217,211	303,692	336,152	407,245	438,198	444,052	442,525	467,913	510,098
France	40,829	47,269	54,637	61,610	64,433	64,666	63,541	67,351	71,313
Germany	74,855	109,551	111,902	147,834	157,554	157,162	148,519	153,362	159,819
Italy	31,888	40,719	38,349	49,464	53,333	55,207	56,825	62,484	68,335
United Kingdom	71,400	85,508	93,860	102,811	108,172	112,216	107,468	110,930	122,133
Canada	251,750	316,798	309,173	369,111	385,992	332,095	314,230	338,493	360,876
Latin America and Other Western Hemisphere ..	249,543	352,076	453,253	538,026	550,327	519,837	508,575	537,084	581,572
Brazil	15,384	26,389	29,343	34,809	37,851	34,663	32,230	34,917	35,858
Mexico	148,258	188,192	246,770	303,988	322,950	326,244	323,955	343,970	378,382
Venezuela	19,291	34,512	33,445	32,781	31,019	16,470	11,743	13,046	13,799
Asia and Pacific	507,225	680,901	836,903	1,004,303	1,061,705	1,094,871	1,082,270	1,156,962	1,234,643
China	103,433	251,556	376,735	455,524	483,677	499,058	479,263	523,492	558,772
India	12,612	23,648	44,394	62,368	67,957	69,561	72,294	76,844	84,046
Japan	164,213	160,965	147,518	171,479	168,511	163,659	165,348	171,496	179,137
Korea, Republic of	46,203	51,128	59,096	73,605	81,412	83,579	81,340	82,669	87,341
Singapore	21,360	18,799	22,733	23,539	22,657	25,058	25,016	27,023	35,809
Taiwan	44,784	41,661	41,881	45,194	48,346	48,661	46,946	50,518	54,056
Middle East	44,296	81,553	95,077	124,016	121,193	81,005	75,381	83,142	92,014
Africa	31,390	69,921	93,190	58,784	43,297	33,893	35,544	43,344	46,898
Memorandum: Members of OPEC [2]	71,068	139,431	164,837	163,732	143,029	76,913	89,518	82,996	92,643
BALANCE (excess of exports +)									
Total, all countries	−372,517	−714,246	−495,225	−461,135	−489,584	−498,525	−502,982	−550,123	−627,679
Europe	−63,386	−128,733	−55,779	−80,604	−95,923	−104,649	−98,766	−109,895	−127,411
Euro area [1]	−43,765	−89,336	−47,548	−79,646	−90,588	−97,938	−91,431	−101,025	−116,335
France	−10,070	−11,765	−10,524	−10,938	−13,444	−14,676	−12,365	−14,009	−13,421
Germany	−29,603	−54,304	−38,524	−73,190	−79,647	−77,029	−67,135	−66,889	−67,372
Italy	−15,127	−21,991	−15,504	−23,980	−27,121	−29,755	−31,164	−34,651	−35,454
United Kingdom	1,739	−2,324	8,786	5,219	10,902	12,093	14,798	15,646	18,629
Canada	−47,889	−71,663	−5,764	−4,144	−11,142	4,165	7,448	2,814	3,639
Latin America and Other Western Hemisphere ..	−24,437	−96,010	−44,052	23,442	35,032	29,718	6,072	12,520	5,847
Brazil	6,474	−5,158	24,410	36,091	33,251	24,697	21,535	29,162	31,741
Mexico	−21,182	−45,215	−58,399	−47,646	−51,317	−58,033	−62,022	−67,407	−78,580
Venezuela	−10,481	−25,443	−17,662	−12,212	−12,974	−1,566	−371	−4,263	−3,094
Asia and Pacific	−208,122	−339,337	−313,772	−369,401	−408,969	−458,722	−442,084	−464,389	−510,526
China	−81,969	−200,984	−261,176	−295,149	−314,669	−333,534	−308,868	−337,204	−380,804
India	−6,140	−10,416	−14,728	−27,136	−31,007	−29,501	−30,052	−27,514	−25,280
Japan	−62,967	−66,609	−42,787	−59,277	−53,683	−55,242	−56,526	−57,211	−57,981
Korea, Republic of	−11,459	−13,128	−3,564	−9,114	−14,759	−18,252	−16,705	−9,512	−7,421
Singapore	3,041	7,683	16,726	18,486	19,029	17,595	19,561	23,481	18,316
Taiwan	−14,381	−12,428	−5,163	−6,878	−8,264	−9,947	−8,771	−14,313	−12,754
Middle East	−16,054	−33,126	−24,983	−23,840	−19,312	20,718	22,575	13,172	5,092
Africa	−14,212	−46,917	−52,790	−9,571	9,107	7,867	637	−6,549	−5,137
Memorandum: Members of OPEC [2]	−41,660	−90,237	−85,853	−46,669	−27,403	30,580	16,666	9,098	1,254

[1] Euro area consists of Austria, Belgium, Finland, France, Germany, Ireland, Italy, Luxembourg, Netherlands, Portugal, Spain and Greece (beginning in 2001), Slovenia (2007), Cyprus and Malta (2008), Slovakia (2009), Estonia (2011), Latvia (2014), and Lithuania (2015).

[2] Organization of Petroleum Exporting Countries, consisting of Iran, Iraq, Kuwait, Saudi Arabia, Venezuela and Qatar (beginning in 1961, ending in 2018), Indonesia (1962 to 2008; 2016), Libya (1962), United Arab Emirates (1967), Algeria (1969), Nigeria (1971), Ecuador (1973 to 1992, rejoined 2007), Gabon (1975 to 1994, rejoined 2016), Angola (2007), Equatorial Guinea (2017), and Congo (2018).

Note: Data are on a balance of payments basis. For further details, and additional data by country, see *Survey of Current Business*, February 2020.

Source: Department of Commerce (Bureau of Economic Analysis).

TABLE B–60. Foreign exchange rates, 2000–2019

[Foreign currency units per U.S. dollar, except as noted; certified noon buying rates in New York]

Period	Australia (dollar)[1]	Brazil (real)	Canada (dollar)	China, P.R. (yuan)	EMU Members (euro)[1,2]	India (rupee)	Japan (yen)	Mexico (peso)	South Korea (won)	Sweden (krona)	Switzerland (franc)	United Kingdom (pound)[1]
March 1973	1.4129	....	0.9967	2.2401	....	7.55	261.90	0.013	398.85	4.4294	3.2171	2.4724
2000	.5815	1.8301	1.4855	8.2784	0.9232	45.00	107.80	9.459	1,130.90	9.1735	1.6904	1.5156
2001	.5169	2.3527	1.5487	8.2770	.8952	47.22	121.57	9.337	1,292.01	10.3425	1.6891	1.4396
2002	.5437	2.9213	1.5704	8.2771	.9454	48.63	125.22	9.663	1,250.31	9.7233	1.5567	1.5025
2003	.6524	3.0750	1.4008	8.2772	1.1321	46.59	115.94	10.793	1,192.08	8.0787	1.3450	1.6347
2004	.7365	2.9262	1.3017	8.2768	1.2438	45.26	108.15	11.290	1,145.24	7.3480	1.2428	1.8330
2005	.7627	2.4352	1.2115	8.1936	1.2449	44.00	110.11	10.894	1,023.75	7.4710	1.2459	1.8204
2006	.7535	2.1738	1.1340	7.9723	1.2563	45.19	116.31	10.906	954.32	7.3718	1.2532	1.8434
2007	.8391	1.9461	1.0734	7.6058	1.3711	41.18	117.76	10.928	928.97	6.7550	1.1999	2.0020
2008	.8537	1.8326	1.0660	6.9477	1.4726	43.39	103.39	11.143	1,098.71	6.5846	1.0816	1.8545
2009	.7927	1.9976	1.1412	6.8307	1.3935	48.33	93.68	13.498	1,274.63	7.6539	1.0860	1.5661
2010	.9200	1.7600	1.0298	6.7696	1.3261	45.65	87.78	12.624	1,155.74	7.2053	1.0432	1.5452
2011	1.0332	1.6723	.9887	6.4630	1.3931	46.58	79.70	12.427	1,106.94	6.4878	.8862	1.6043
2012	1.0359	1.9535	.9995	6.3093	1.2859	53.37	79.82	13.154	1,126.16	6.7721	.9377	1.5853
2013	.9683	2.1570	1.0300	6.1478	1.3281	58.51	97.60	12.758	1,094.67	6.5124	.9269	1.5642
2014	.9034	2.3512	1.1043	6.1620	1.3297	61.00	105.74	13.302	1,052.29	6.8576	.9147	1.6484
2015	.7522	3.3360	1.2791	6.2827	1.1096	64.11	121.05	15.874	1,130.96	8.4350	.9628	1.5284
2016	.7445	3.4839	1.3243	6.6400	1.1072	67.16	108.66	18.667	1,159.34	8.5541	.9848	1.3555
2017	.7671	3.1910	1.2984	6.7569	1.1301	65.07	112.10	18.884	1,129.04	8.5430	.9842	1.2890
2018	.7481	3.6513	1.2957	6.6090	1.1817	68.37	110.40	19.218	1,099.29	8.6945	.9784	1.3363
2019	.6952	3.9440	1.3269	6.9081	1.1194	70.38	109.02	19.247	1,165.80	9.4604	.9937	1.2768
2018: I	.7859	3.2474	1.2656	6.3535	1.2289	64.38	108.27	18.717	1,071.10	8.1182	.9484	1.3920
II	.7568	3.6043	1.2907	6.3772	1.1922	67.00	109.14	19.412	1,079.64	8.6733	.9854	1.3612
III	.7315	3.9492	1.3070	6.8053	1.1629	70.11	111.50	18.945	1,120.84	8.9482	.9843	1.3030
IV	.7174	3.8061	1.3201	6.9143	1.1414	72.13	112.77	19.816	1,126.77	9.0460	.9957	1.2870
2019: I	.7122	3.7696	1.3297	6.7447	1.1354	70.42	110.19	19.204	1,124.80	9.1783	.9971	1.3031
II	.7003	3.9167	1.3378	6.8195	1.1237	69.53	109.95	19.111	1,166.07	9.4439	1.0028	1.2859
III	.6857	3.9688	1.3205	7.0150	1.1120	70.39	107.33	19.421	1,193.90	9.5878	.9856	1.2329
IV	.6837	4.1124	1.3197	7.0448	1.1075	71.21	108.68	19.248	1,175.54	9.6143	.9894	1.2880

Trade-weighted value of the U.S. dollar

Period	Nominal Broad index (January 2006=100)[3]	Nominal Advanced foreign economies index (January 2006=100)[4]	Nominal Emerging market economies index (January 2006=100)[5]	Real[6] Broad index (January 2006=100)[3]	Real[6] Advanced foreign economies index (January 2006=100)[4]	Real[6] Emerging market economies index (January 2006=100)[5]
2000	....	....	....	....	....	....
2001	....	....	....	....	....	....
2002	....	....	....	....	....	....
2003	....	....	....	....	....	....
2004	....	....	....	....	....	....
2005	....	....	....	....	....	....
2006	98.6064	97.6875	99.8131	98.9400	98.3178	99.7559
2007	93.8253	92.0825	96.1230	94.2864	93.6310	95.1418
2008	90.8968	88.4455	94.1511	90.9823	90.8429	91.2038
2009	96.7688	92.8046	102.0228	95.3317	94.7051	96.1083
2010	93.0664	90.1032	97.1794	90.7755	92.0125	89.5939
2011	88.7923	84.8159	94.0346	86.2803	87.3150	85.2816
2012	91.6492	87.9861	96.5675	88.4827	90.8406	86.1745
2013	92.7655	90.6103	96.0743	88.7776	93.8355	83.9809
2014	95.5919	93.3976	98.9816	90.7995	97.0047	85.0032
2015	108.1589	108.1256	109.5474	101.2535	111.8241	91.7997
2016	113.0548	109.3062	118.1998	105.4690	113.9833	97.6132
2017	112.7924	108.8922	118.0915	104.9133	114.1346	96.4974
2018	112.0078	106.4267	119.0263	104.0532	112.1989	96.5013
2019	115.7187	110.1296	122.7855	107.0718	116.6341	98.3594
2018: I	107.9943	102.9077	114.4516	100.4784	108.3307	93.1966
II	110.6202	105.5102	117.1304	102.9872	111.3074	95.3048
III	113.6569	107.8400	120.9399	105.4751	113.6422	97.8925
IV	115.7082	109.3899	123.5388	107.2721	115.5153	99.6111
2019: I	114.4908	109.3956	121.0275	106.0597	115.4795	97.4702
II	115.3739	110.2733	121.9276	106.8149	116.6027	97.9273
III	116.4899	110.4769	124.0091	107.7767	117.0769	99.2648
IV	116.4469	110.3215	124.0809	107.6360	117.3772	98.7751

[1] U.S. dollars per foreign currency unit.
[2] European Economic and Monetary Union (EMU) members consists of Austria, Belgium, Finland, France, Germany, Ireland, Italy, Luxembourg, Netherlands, Portugal, Spain and Greece (beginning in 2001), Slovenia (2007), Cyprus and Malta (2008), Slovakia (2009), Estonia (2011), Latvia (2014), and Lithuania (2015).
[3] Weighted average of the foreign exchange value of the U.S. dollar against the currencies of a broad group of major U.S. trading partners.
[4] Subset of the broad index. Consists of currencies of the Euro area, Australia, Canada, Japan, Sweden, Switzerland, and the United Kingdom.
[5] Subset of the broad index currencies that are emerging market economies. For details, see *Revisions to the Federal Reserve Dollar Indexes*, January 2019.
[6] Adjusted for changes in consumer price indexes for the United States and other countries.

Source: Board of Governors of the Federal Reserve System.

TABLE B-61. Growth rates in real gross domestic product by area and country, 2001-2020

[Percent change]

Area and country	2001-2010 annual average	2011	2012	2013	2014	2015	2016	2017	2018	2019[1]	2020[1]
World	3.9	4.3	3.5	3.5	3.6	3.5	3.4	3.8	3.6	2.9	3.3
Advanced economies	1.7	1.7	1.2	1.4	2.1	2.3	1.7	2.5	2.2	1.7	1.6
Of which:											
United States	1.7	1.6	2.2	1.8	2.5	2.9	1.6	2.4	2.9	2.3	2.0
Euro area[2]	1.2	1.6	−.9	−.3	1.4	2.1	1.9	2.5	1.9	1.2	1.3
Germany	0.9	3.9	.4	.4	2.2	1.7	2.2	2.5	1.5	.5	1.1
France	1.3	2.2	.3	.6	1.0	1.1	1.1	2.3	1.7	1.3	1.3
Italy	0.3	.6	−2.8	−1.7	.1	.9	1.1	1.7	.8	.2	.5
Spain	2.2	−1.0	−2.9	−1.7	1.4	3.6	3.2	3.0	2.4	2.0	1.6
Japan	0.6	−.1	1.5	2.0	.4	1.2	.6	1.9	.3	1.0	.7
United Kingdom	1.6	1.6	1.4	2.0	2.9	2.3	1.8	1.8	1.3	1.3	1.4
Canada	1.9	3.1	1.8	2.3	2.9	.7	1.1	3.0	1.9	1.5	1.8
Other advanced economies	3.5	3.4	2.2	2.5	2.9	2.3	2.4	2.9	2.6	1.5	1.9
Emerging market and developing economies	6.2	6.4	5.4	5.1	4.7	4.3	4.6	4.8	4.5	3.7	4.4
Regional groups:											
Emerging and Developing Asia	8.5	7.9	7.0	6.9	6.8	6.8	6.7	6.6	6.4	5.6	5.8
China	10.5	9.5	7.9	7.8	7.3	6.9	6.7	6.8	6.6	6.1	6.0
India[3]	7.5	6.6	5.5	6.4	7.4	8.0	8.2	7.2	6.8	4.8	5.8
ASEAN-5[4]	5.2	4.7	6.2	5.1	4.6	4.9	5.0	5.3	5.2	4.7	4.8
Emerging and Developing Europe	4.4	5.8	3.0	3.1	1.9	.8	1.8	3.9	3.1	1.8	2.6
Russia	4.8	5.1	3.7	1.8	.7	−2.3	.3	1.6	2.3	1.1	1.9
Latin America and the Caribbean	3.2	4.6	2.9	2.9	1.3	.3	−.6	1.2	1.1	.1	1.6
Brazil	3.7	4.0	1.9	3.0	.5	−3.6	−3.3	1.1	1.3	1.2	2.2
Mexico	1.5	3.7	3.6	1.4	2.8	3.3	2.9	2.1	2.1	.0	1.0
Middle East and Central Asia	5.3	4.6	4.9	3.0	3.1	2.6	5.0	2.3	1.9	.8	2.8
Saudi Arabia	3.4	10.0	5.4	2.7	3.7	4.1	1.7	−.7	2.4	.2	1.9
Sub-Saharan Africa	5.9	5.3	4.7	5.2	5.1	3.1	1.4	3.0	3.2	3.3	3.5
Nigeria	8.9	4.9	4.3	5.4	6.3	2.7	−1.6	.8	1.9	2.3	2.5
South Africa	3.5	3.3	2.2	2.5	1.8	1.2	.4	1.4	.8	.4	.8

[1] All figures are forecasts as published by the International Monetary Fund. For the United States, advance estimates by the Department of Commerce show that real GDP rose 2.3 percent in 2019.

[2] Euro area consists of Austria, Belgium, Finland, France, Germany, Ireland, Italy, Luxembourg, Netherlands, Portugal, Spain and Greece (beginning in 2001), Slovenia (2007), Cyprus and Malta (2008), Slovakia (2009), Estonia (2011), Latvia (2014), and Lithuania (2015).

[3] Data and forecasts are presented on a fiscal year basis and output growth is based on GDP at market prices.

[4] Consists of Indonesia, Malaysia, Philippines, Thailand, and Vietnam.

Note: For details on data shown in this table, see *World Economic Outlook*, October 2019, and *World Economic Outlook Update*, January 2020, published by the International Monetary Fund.

Sources: International Monetary Fund and Department of Commerce (Bureau of Economic Analysis).